# 1,000,000 Books

are available to read at

## www.ForgottenBooks.com

Read online
Download PDF
Purchase in print

ISBN 978-0-332-61787-9
PIBN 11247075

# 1 MONTH OF
# FREE
# READING

## at
## www.ForgottenBooks.com

By purchasing this book you are eligible for one month membership to ForgottenBooks.com, giving you unlimited access to our entire collection of over 1,000,000 titles via our web site and mobile apps.

To claim your free month visit:
www.forgottenbooks.com/free1247075

# INDEX.

[CLERK'S NOTE.—Errors or doubtful matters appearing in the original certified record are printed literally in italic. When possible, an omission from the text is indicated by printing in italic the two words between which the omission seems to occur. Cancelled matter in the original certified record is printed and cancelled herein accordingly.]

Index.           Page

Index.                    Page

## Index.                                    Page

vs. *The United States of America.*

Index. Page

Index.        Page

Index. Page

Index.                         Page

Index.                         Page

Index.                    Page

## Index.                              Page

Index. Page

Index.  Page

Index.    Page

Index. Page

Index.                    Page

Index.                     Page

Index.                    Page

Index. Page

Index. Page

Index.                                    Page

Index.                Page

Index.                    Page

Index. Page

## Index.                    Page

Index.                    Page

Index. Page

Index.                                    Page

Index.                    Page

Index. Page

Index.                           Page
Testimony on Behalf of Defendants—Continued:

Index.                    Page

Index. Page

*In the United States Circuit Court of Appeals, for the Ninth Circuit.*

WILLIAM F. KETTENBACH, GEORGE H. KESTER and WILLIAM DWYER,

Plaintiffs in Error,

vs.

THE UNITED STATES OF AMERICA,

Defendant in Error.

**Order Enlarging Time to File Record Thereof and to Docket Cause.**

For good cause shown, it is hereby ordered that the time to file the record and docket the above-entitled cause in this Court be, and the same is hereby, enlarged and extended from the 13th day of January, 1908, to and including the first day of February, 1908.

Dated January 9th, 1908.

FRANK S. DIETRICH,

Judge.

[Endorsed]: No. 1605. In the U. S. Circuit Court of Appeals for the Ninth Circuit. William F. Kettenbach, George H. Kester and William Dwyer, Plaintiffs in Error, vs. The United States of America, Defendants in Error. Order Extending Time. Filed Jan. 13, 1908. F. D. Monckton, Clerk. Refiled May 8, 1908. F. D. Monckton, Clerk.

*In the Circuit Court of Appeals for the Ninth Circuit.*

WILLIAM F. KETTENBACH, GEORGE H.
KESTER and WILLIAM DWYER,

Plaintiffs in Error,

vs.

THE UNITED STATES,

Defendant in Error.

**Stipulation and Order Enlarging Time to File Record Thereof and to Docket Cause.**

Come now the plaintiffs in error by their counsel, and the defendant in error by N. M. Ruick, Esq., United States Attorney, for the District of Idaho, and stipulate and agree as follows:

That owing to the adverse decision of the United States Supreme Court, recently made in the case of Williamson vs. The United States, and in order to determine the application of the principles there laid down of the above-entitled cause now pending in this court, and also to the cases of Clarence W. Robnett vs. The United States, and to the case of William Dwyer vs. The United States, both of which are now pending in this Court:

That the said plaintiffs in error in each of the above cases do have until the first day of April, 1908, in which to file the transcript of the proceedings in each of the said causes.

GEO. W. TANNAHILL, and
FORNEY & MOORE,
Attorneys for Plaintiffs in Error.
N. M. RUICK,
United States Attorney for Defendants Error.

The foregoing stipulation is approved; and the plaintiff in error in each case is hereby given until April 1st, 1908, in which to file a transcript of the proceedings in each of the said causes.

WM. B. GILBERT,
Circuit Judge.

[Endorsed]: 1605. In the Circuit Court of Appeals for the Ninth Circuit. Wm. F. Kettenbach et al. v. United States. Clarence W. Robnett v. United States. William Dwyer v. United States. Stipulation and Order Extending Time to File Transcripts until April 1, 1908. Filed Jan. 27, 1908. F. D. Monckton, Clerk. Re-filed May 8, 1908. F. D. Monckton, Clerk.

---

*United States Circuit Court of Appeals for the Ninth Circuit.*

WILLIAM F. KETTENBACH, GEORGE H. KESTER and WILLIAM DWYER,
Plaintiffs in Error,

vs.

THE UNITED STATES OF AMERICA,
Defendant in Error.

**Order Enlarging Time to File Record Thereof and to Docket Cause.**

Good cause appearing therefor, it is ordered that the time within which the original certified Transcript of Record in the above-entitled cause may be filed and the cause docketed in this court be, and hereby is, extended to and including May 1, 1908.

WM. W. MOORE,
United States Circuit Judge.

[Endorsed]: No. 1605. United States Circuit Court of Appeals for the Ninth Circuit. Order Enlarging Time to File Record Thereof and to Docket Cause. Filed Mar. 26, 1908. F. D. Monckton. Clerk. Re-filed May 8, 1908. F. D. Monckton. Clerk.

---

### Names and Addresses of Attorneys in Record.

FORNEY & MOORE, Moscow, Idaho,
GEO. W. TANNAHILL, Lewiston, Idaho,
Attorneys for Plaintiff in Error.
N. M. RUICK, U. S. District Attorney, Boise, Idaho,
Attorney for Defendant in Error.

---

*In the District Court of the United States within and for the Northern Division of the District of Idaho.*

THE UNITED STATES OF AMERICA

vs.

WILLIAM F. KETTENBACH, GEORGE H. KESTER and WILLIAM DWYER.

### Indictment.

Conspiracy to Defraud the United States, Violation Sec. 5440, R. S. U. S.

The Grand Jurors of the United States of America, being first duly empanelled and sworn within and for the District of Idaho, Northern Division, in the name and by the authority of the United States of America, upon their oaths do find and present:

That heretofore, to wit, on the 26th day of October, 1904, at the city of Lewiston in the county of Nez Perce, in the State and District of Idaho, and within the jurisdiction of this court, William F. Kettenbach, George H. Kester and William Dwyer, and each of them, and other persons to the Grand Jury unknown, did commit the crime of conspiracy to defraud the United States, committed as follows:

That heretofore, to wit, on the 26th day of October, 1904, at the place aforesaid, William F. Kettenbach, George H. Kester and William Dwyer, and other persons to the Grand Jury unknown, did falsely, unlawfully and wickedly conspire, combine, confederate and agree together among themselves to defraud the United States of the title and possession of large tracts of land situated in the county of Shoshone and State and District of Idaho, and of great value, of which the following land is a part, viz: North half of the Northeast quarter and the Southwest quarter of the Northeast quarter, of Section Twenty-nine, Township 39 North, of Range Five East of Boise Meridian, in the State and District of Idaho, by means of false, fraudulent, untrue and illegal entries of said lands under the laws of the United States, the said lands being then and there public lands of the United States, open to entry and sale under said laws of the United States at the local land office of the United States at said city of Lewiston in said State and District of Idaho. That accord-

ing to and in pursuance of said conspiracy, combination, confederation and agreement among themselves
had as aforesaid, and to effect the object of said conspiracy, the said William F. Kettenbach, George H.
Kester and William Dwyer did on the 26th day of
October, 1904, at the city of Lewiston in the State
and District of Idaho, and within the jurisdiction of
this Court fraudulently, unlawfully and corruptly
persuade and induce one Edward M. Lewis of said
District, then and there being, to take his corporal
oath and be then and there sworn before one J. B.
West, who was then and there the duly appointed,
qualified and acting Register of the United States
Land Office at said city of Lewiston, in said Lewiston Land District, and who was then and there an
officer and person having due and competent authority to administer said oath, and who did then and
there administer said oath to the said Edward M.
Lewis; that a certain written affidavit and statement
by him, the said Edward M. Lewis, then and there
made, sworn to and subscribed, was true, which said
written affidavit and statement then and there subscribed and sworn to by him, the said Edward M.
Lewis, at the request and by the procurement of
them the said William F. Kettenbach, George H.
Kester, and William Dwyer, as aforesaid, was then
and there in a case in which a law of the United
States authorized an oath to be administered and that
said written affidavit and statement was then and
there required of him, the said Edward M. Lewis, by
law, and the rules and regulations of the Interior Department and the General Land Office of the United

States, which said written affidavit and statement was then and there that certain written application to the Register of the United States Land Office at said city of Lewiston duly made and filed by him, the said Edward M. Lewis, in the United States Land Office at said city of Lewiston on the 26th day of October, 1904, whereby he, the said Edward M. Lewis, duly applied to the said Register of the said United States Land Office at said city of Lewiston, to enter and purchase under that certain Act of Congress approved June 3, 1878, entitled: "An Act for the sale of timber lands in the States of California, Oregon, Nevada and in Washington Territory," as amended by that certain Act of Congress approved August 4, 1892, entitled: "An Act to authorize the entry of lands chiefly valuable for building stone under the placer mining laws," the land hereinbefore described, to wit, the North half of the Northeast quarter, and the Southwest quarter of the Northeast quarter of Section Twenty-nine, Township 39 North, of Range Five, East of Boise Meridian, situate within the district of lands subject to entry and sale under the public land laws of the United States at the said United States Land Office at Lewiston, Idaho, and which said written affidavit and statement sworn to as aforesaid, he, the said Edward M. Lewis, and the said William F. Kettenbach, George H. Kester and William Dwyer, and each of them, did then and there know to be false, fraudulent and untrue. That the said William F. Kettenbach, George H. Kester and William Dwyer, did then and there, to wit, on the said 26th day of October, 1904, at said city of Lewiston aforesaid, State and District aforesaid, wilfully and corruptly knowing that said written affidavit and statement so made and subscribed by him, the said Edward M. Lewis, as aforesaid, was knowingly, wilfully and corruptly false, did then and there fraudulently, unlawfully and corruptly incite and procure the said Edward M. Lewis, who, being so sworn as aforesaid, to knowingly, corruptly and falsely and contrary to his said oath taken as aforesaid to depose, state, swear and subscribe, among other things, to certain material matters and statements then and there contained in said written affidavit and statement in substance and effect as follows, to wit:

That I, (the said Edward M. Lewis, meaning,) do not apply to purchase the land above described (the land hereinbefore described, meaning) on speculation, but in good faith to appropriate it to my (the said Edward M. Lewis, meaning) own exclusive use and benefit, and that I (the said Edward M. Lewis, meaning) have not directly or indirectly, made any agreement or contract, in any way or manner, with any person or persons whomsoever, by which the title which I (the said Edward M. Lewis, meaning) may acquire from the Government of the United States may inure in whole or in part to the benefit of any person except myself (the said Edward M. Lewis, meaning).

Whereas, in truth and in fact, as he, the said Edward M. Lewis, and they, the said William F. Kettenbach, George H. Kester and William Dwyer, and each of them, then and there well knew, he the said Edward M. Lewis, did not then and there apply to enter and purchase the land hereinbefore described, and as described in said affidavit and statement in good faith and for the purpose of appropriating the said land to the exclusive use and benefit of him, the said Edward M. Lewis, but in truth and in fact for the use and benefit of the said William F. Kettenbach, George H. Kester and William Dwyer, and other person and persons, whose name or names are to the Grand Jurors unknown.

And whereas, in truth and in fact, as he, the said Edward M. Lewis, and they, the said William F. Kettenbach, George H. Kester, and William Dwyer, and each of them, then and there well knew, he the said Edward M. Lewis, in making and filing said affidavit and statement and in making said application, filing and entry, was then and there acting as the agent of and in collusion with the said William F. Kettenbach, George H. Kester and William Dwyer, and with the intent then and there had and entertained by him, the said Edward M. Lewis, of giving to the said William F. Kettenbach, George H. Kester and William Dwyer, the benefit of said lands and the timber situate thereon; and that the said Edward M. Lewis did then and there apply to enter and purchase said lands for the purpose of speculation and not in good faith for the exclusive use and benefit of him, the said Edward M. Lewis, as in said written affidavit and statement alleged, and that the said Edward M. Lewis, prior to the making and filing of

said affidavit and statement, being said application
to enter and purchase said lands as aforesaid, did
enter into a contract and agreement with the said
William F. Kettenbach, George H. Kester and William Dwyer, whereby he, the said Edward M. Lewis,
had agreed that the title which he, the said Edward
M. Lewis, might acquire from the Government of the
United States to said lands as aforesaid, should inure
to the benefit of the said William F. Kettenbach,
George H. Kester and William Dwyer.

That thereafter, on the 20th day of January, 1905,
at said city of Lewiston, according to and in pursuance of said conspiracy, combination, confederacy
and agreement among themselves had as aforesaid,
and to effect the object of said conspiracy, the said
William F. Kettenbach, George H. Kester and William Dwyer did then and there fraudulently, wilfully
and corruptly persuade and induce the said Edward
M. Lewis to take an oath before J. B. West, Register
of the United States Land Office at Lewiston, as
aforesaid, and to then and there subscribe his name
and make an oath to a certain written affidavit, testimony and statement in support of that certain
written application to the Register of the United
States Land Office at said city of Lewiston theretofore, to wit, on the 26th day of October, 1904, duly
made and filed by him, the said Edward M. Lewis, in
the said United States Land Office at said city of
Lewiston, whereby he, the said Edward M.
Lewis, duly applied to the Register of the said
United States Land Office at said city of Lewiston to enter and purchase under that certain

Act of Congress as aforesaid, the land described as
aforesaid; that said written affidavit, testimony and
statement was then and there required of him, the
said Edward M. Lewis, by law, and the rules and regulations of the Interior Department and the General
Land Office of the United States, in support of said
written application made and filed by said Edward
M. Lewis on the 26th day of October, 1904, as aforesaid, to enter and purchase the said North half of the
Northeast quarter, and the Southwest quarter of the
Northeast quarter, of Section Twenty-nine, Township 39 North, of Range Five, East of Boise Meridian.

That in said written affidavit, testimony and statement so made as aforesaid, on the 20th day of January, 1905, he, the said Edward M. Lewis, did then and
there allege, declare, testify and swear, among other
things, in substance and effect as follows: That he,
the said Edward M. Lewis, had not, since making his,
the said Edward M. Lewis's application, made on
the 26th day of October, 1904, sold or transferred his,
the said Edward M. Lewis's, claim to the land heretofore described, and that he, the said Edward M.
Lewis, had not, directly or indirectly, made any
agreement or contract in any way or manner with any
person whomsoever, by which the title which he, the
said Edward M. Lewis, might acquire from the government of the United States, might inure, in whole
or in part, to the benefit of any person except the said
Edward M. Lewis, and that he, the said Edward M.
Lewis, made the entry for said land in good faith and

for the appropriation of said land exclusively for the use and benefit of the said Edward M. Lewis, and not for the use and benefit of any other person than him, the said Edward M. Lewis, and that no other person than he, the said Edward M. Lewis, nor any firm, corporation, or association, had any interest in said entry, he the said Edward M. Lewis, was then and there making or in the said land or in the timber on said land. The said written affidavit, testimony and statement, he, the said Edward M. Lewis, on the 20th day of January, 1905, at said city of Lewiston, then and there subscribed and swore to before J. B. West, the Register of the United States Land Office at said city of Lewiston, who was then and there an officer and person competent to administer said oath, and who did then and there duly administer said oath to the said Edward M. Lewis, and that said written affidavit, testimony and statement was then and there made and given in a case in which the laws of the United States authorized an oath to be administered, and which said written affidavit, testimony and statement was duly filed by him, the said Edward M. Lewis, in the said United States Land Office at said city of Lewiston on the 20th day of January, 1905.

That said written affidavit, testimony and statement was then and there false, fraudulent and untrue, and the said Edward M. Lewis, and the said William F. Kettenbach, George H. Kester and William Dwyer, and each of them, then and there well knew it to be false and untrue in this: That he, the said Edward M. Lewis, in making and filing said written affidavit, testimony and statement and in

making said filing and entry was then and there acting as the agent of and in collusion with the said
William F. Kettenbach, George H. Kester and William Dwyer, with the intent then and there had and
entertained by him, the said Edward M. Lewis, of
giving to the said William F. Kettenbach, George H.
Kester and William Dwyer the benefit of said lands
and the timber situate thereon, which said lands are
hereinbefore described, and that the said Edward M.
Lewis, did then and there apply to enter and purchase said lands for the purpose of speculation and
not in good faith for the exclusive use and benefit of
him, the said Edward M. Lewis, as in said written
affidavit, testimony and statement alleged, and that
the said Edward M. Lewis, prior to the making and
filing of said application to enter and purchase the
said lands as aforesaid, had entered into a contract
and agreement with the said William F. Kettenbach,
George H. Kester and William Dwyer, whereby he,
the said Edward M. Lewis, had agreed that the title
which he might acquire from the Gevernment of the
United States to the said land heretofore described
should inure to the benefit of the said William F.
Kettenbach, George H. Kester and William Dwyer.

That thereafter, on the 20th day of January, 1905,
at said city of Lewiston, according to and in pursuance of said conspiracy, combination, confederacy
and agreement among themselves had as aforesaid,
and to effect the object of said conspiracy, the said
William F. Kettenbach, George H. Kester and William Dwyer did pay and cause to be paid to the Receiver of the Land Office of the United States at

Lewiston, Idaho, the sum of Three Hundred Dollars as and for the minimum Government price under said entry for the purchase of the said North half of the Northeast quarter and the Southwest quarter of the Northeast quarter, of Section Tweny-nine, Township 39 North, of Range Five, East of Boise Meridian.

That thereafter and on the said 20th day of January, 1905, at said city of Lewiston, according to and in pursuance of said conspiracy, combination, confederation and agreement among themselves, had as aforesaid, and to effect the object of said conspiracy, the said William F. Kettenbach, George H. Kester and William Dwyer, did persuade and induce J. B. West, the Register of the United States Land Office at Lewiston, Idaho, to issue and deliver a certificate of purchase and Register's Receipt No. 5016, in the name of said Edward M. Lewis for the purchase of the said North half of the Northeast quarter and the Southwest quarter of the Northeast quarter, of Section Twenty-nine, Township 39 North, of Range Five East, of Boise Meridian, and did then and there persuade and induce the said J. B. West, as Register as aforesaid, to certify that on presentation of said certificate to the Commissioner of the General Land Office, the said Edward M. Lewis would be entitled to receive a patent for the above-described land.

Which is against the peace and dignity of the United States and contrary to the form, force and effect of the statute in such cases made and provided.

## SECOND COUNT.

And the Grand Jurors aforesaid, being summoned, empaneled and sworn, as aforesaid, in the name and by the authority of the United States, aforesaid, upon their oaths, as aforesaid, do further find and present:

·That heretofore, to wit, on the 29th day of August, 1904, at the city of Lewiston, in the county of Nez Perce, in the State and District of Idaho, and within the jurisdiction of this court, William F. Kettenbach, George H. Kester and William Dwyer, and each of them, and other persons to the Grand Jury unknown, did commit the crime of conspiracy to defraud the United States, committed as follows:

That heretofore, to wit, on the 29th day of August, 1904, at the place aforesaid, William F. Kettenbach, George H. Kester and William Dwyer, and other persons to the Grand Jury unknown, did falsely, unlawfully and wickedly conspire, combine, confederate and agree together among themselves to defraud the United States of the title and possession of large tracts of land situated in the county of Shoshone and State and District of Idaho, and of great value, of which the following described land is a part, viz.: Northwest quarter of Section Twenty, Township 38 North, of Range Five, East, of Boise Meridian, in the State and District of Idaho, by means of false, fraudulent, untrue and illegal entries of said lands under the laws of the United States, the said lands being then and there public lands of the United States open to entry and sale under said laws of the United States at the local land office of the United States at

said city of Lewiston in said State and District of
Idaho. That according to and in pursuance of said
conspiracy, combination, confederation and agreement among themselves had as aforesaid, and to effect
the object of said conspiracy, the said William F.
Kettenbach, George H. Kester and William Dwyer
did on the 29th day of August, 1904, at the city of
Lewiston, in the State and District of Idaho, and
within the jurisdiction of this court, fraudulently,
unlawfully, and corruptly persuade and induce one
Hiram F. Lewis of said District, then and there being, to take his corporal oath and be then and there
sworn before one J. B. West, who was then and there
the duly appointed, qualified and acting Register of
the United States Land Office, at said City of Lewiston, in said Lewiston Land District, and who was
then and there an officer and person having due and
competent authority to administer said oath and who
did then and there administer said oath to the said
Hiram F. Lewis; that a certain written affidavit and
statement by him, the said Hiram F. Lewis, then
and there made, sworn to and subscribed, was true,
which said written affidavit and statement then and
there subscribed and sworn to by him, the said Hiram
F. Lewis, at the request and by the procurement of
them, the said William F. Kettenbach, George H.
Kester and William Dwyer, as aforesaid, was then
and there in a case in which a law of the United
States authorized an oath to be administered and that
said written affidavit and statement was then and
there required of him, the said Hiram F. Lewis, by
law, and the rules and regulations of the Interior

Department and the General Land Office of the United States, which said written affidavit and statement was then and there that certain written application to the Register of the United States Land Office at said city of Lewiston duly made and filed by him, the said Hiram F. Lewis, in the United States Land Office at said City of Lewiston on the 29th day of August, 1904, whereby he, the said Hiram F. Lewis, duly applied to the said Register of the said United States Land Office at said City of Lewiston, to enter and purchase under that certain Act of Congress approved June 3, 1878, entitled: "An Act for the sale of timber lands in the States of California, Oregon, Nevada and in Washington Territory," as amended by that certain Act of Congress approved August 4, 1892, entitled: "An Act to authorize the entry of lands chiefly valuable for building stone under the placer mining laws," the land hereinbefore described, to wit, the Northwest quarter of Section Twenty, Township 38 North, of Range Five East, of Boise Meridian, situate within the District of lands subject to entry and sale under the public land laws of the United States at the said United States Land Office at Lewiston, Idaho, and which said written affidavit and statement sworn to as aforesaid, he, the said Hiram F. Lewis, and the said William F. Kettenbach, George H. Kester and William Dwyer, and each of them, did then and there know to be false, fraudulent and untrue. That the said William F. Kettenbach, George H. Kester and William Dwyer did then and there, to wit, on the said 29th day of August, 1904, at said city of Lewiston aforesaid,

State and District aforesaid, willfully and corruptly knowing that said written affidavit and statement so made and subscribed by him, the said Hiram F. Lewis, as aforesaid, was knowingly, willfully and corruptly false, did then and there fraudulently, unlawfully and corruptly incite and procure the said Hiram F. Lewis, who, being so sworn as aforesaid, to knowingly, corruptly and falsely and contrary to his said oath taken as aforesaid, to depose, state, swear and subscribe, among other things, to certain material matters and statements then and there contained in said written affidavit and statement in substance and effect as follows, to wit:

That I (the said Hiram F. Lewis, meaning) do not apply to purchase the land above described (the land hereinbefore described, meaning) on speculation, but in good faith to appropriate it to my (the said Hiram F. Lewis, meaning) own exclusive use and benefit, and that I (the said Hiram F. Lewis, meaning) have not directly or indirectly, made any agreement or contract, in any way or manner, with any person or persons whomsoever, by which the title which I (the said Hiram F. Lewis, meaning) may acquire from the Government of the United States may inure in whole or in part to the benefit of any person except myself (the said Hiram F. Lewis, meaning).

Whereas, in truth and in fact, as he, the said Hiram F. Lewis, and they, the said William F. Kettenbach, George H. Kester and William Dwyer, and each of them, then and there well knew, he, the said Hiram F. Lewis, did not then and there apply to enter and purchase the land hereinbefore described, and as described in said affidavit and statement in good faith and for the purpose of appropriating the said land to the exclusive use and benefit of him, the said Hiram F. Lewis, but in truth and in fact for the use and benefit of the said William F. Kettenbach, George H. Kester and William Dwyer, and other person and persons, whose name or names are to the Grand Jurors unknown.

And whereas, in truth and in fact, as he, the said Hiram F. Lewis, and they, the said William F. Kettenbach, George M. Kester, and William Dwyer, and each of them, then and there well knew, he, the said Hiram F. Lewis, in making and filing said affidavit and statement and in making said application, filing and entry, was then and there acting as the agent of and in collusion with the said William F. Kettenbach, George H. Kester and William Dwyer, and with the intent then and there had and entertained by him, the said Hiram F. Lewis, of giving to the said William F. Kettenbach, George H. Kester and William Dwyer, the benefit of said lands and the timber situate thereon; and that the said Hiram F. Lewis, did then and there apply to enter and purchase said lands for the purpose of speculation and not in good faith for the exclusive use and benefit of him, the said Hiram F. Lewis, as in said written affidavit and statement alleged, and that the said Hiram F. Lewis, prior to the making and filing of said affidavit and statement, being said application to enter and purchase said lands as aforesaid, did enter into a contract and agreement with the said William F. Kettenbach,

George H. Kester and William Dwyer, whereby he, the said Hiram F. Lewis, had agreed that the title which he, the said Hiram F. Lewis, might acquire from the Government of the United States to said lands as aforesaid, should inure to the benefit of the said William F. Kettenbach, George H. Kester and William Dwyer.

That thereafter, on the 8th day of March, 1905, at said city of Lewiston, according to and in pursuance of said conspiracy, combination, confederacy and agreement among themselves had as aforesaid, and to effect the object of said conspiracy, the said William F. Kettenbach, George H. Kester and William Dwyer did then and there fraudulently, willfully and corruptly persuade and induce the said Hiram F. Lewis to take an oath before J. B. West, Register of the United States Land Office at Lewiston, as aforesaid, and to then and there subscribe his name and make an oath to a certain written affidavit, testimony and statement in support of that certain written application to the Register of the United States Land Office at said city of Lewiston theretofore, to wit, on the 29th day of August, 1904, duly made and filed by him, the said Hiram F. Lewis, in the said United States Land Office at said city of Lewiston, whereby he, the said Hiram F. Lewis, duly applied to the Register of the said United States Land Office at said city of Lewiston to enter and purchase under that certain Act of Congress as aforesaid, the land described as aforesaid; that said written affidavit, testimony and statement was then and there required of him, the said Hiram F. Lewis, by law, and the rules and regulations of the Interior Department and the General Land Office of the United States, in support of said written application made and filed by said Hiram F. Lewis on the 29th day of August, 1904, as aforesaid, to enter and purchase the said Northwest quarter of Section Twenty, Township 38 North, of Range Five East, of Boise Meridian.

That in said writen affidavit, testimony and statement so made as aforesaid, on the 8th day of March, 1905, he, the said Hiram F. Lewis, did then and there allege, declare, testify and swear, among other things, in substance and effect, as follows: That he, the said Hiram F. Lewis, had not, since making his, the said Hiram F. Lewis's, application, made on the 29th day of August, 1904, sold or transferred his, the said Hiram F. Lewis's, claim to the land heretofore described, and that he, the said Hiram F. Lewis, had not directly or indirectly, made any agreement or contract in any way or manner with any person whomsoever, by which the title which he, the said Hiram F. Lewis, might acquire from the Government of the United States, might inure, in whole or in part, to the benefit of any person except the said Hiram F. Lewis, and that he, the said Hiram F. Lewis, made the entry for said land in good faith and for the appropriation of said land exclusively for the use and benefit of the said Hiram F. Lewis, and not for the use and benefit of any other person than him, the said Hiram F. Lewis, and that no other person than he, the said Hiram F. Lewis, nor any firm, corporation or association, had any interest in said entry, he, the said Hiram F. Lewis, was then and there making or in the said land or in the timber on said land. The said written affidavit, testimony and statement he, the said Hiram F. Lewis, on the 8th day of March, 1905, at said city of Lewiston, then and there subscribed and swore to before J. B. West, the Register of the United States Land Office at said city of Lewiston, who was then and there an officer and person competent to administer said oath, and who did then and there duly administer said oath to the said Hiram F. Lewis, and that said written affidavit, testimony and statement was then and there made and given in a case in which the laws of the United States authorize an oath to be administered, and which said written affidavit, testimony and statement was duly filed by him, the said Hiram F. Lewis, in the said United States land office at said city of Lewiston on the 8th day of March, 1905.

That said written affidavit, testimony and statement was then and there false, fraudulent and untrue, and the said Hiram F. Lewis, and the said William v. Kettenbach, George H. Kester and William Dwyer, and each of them, then and there well knew it to be false and untrue in this: That he, the said Hiram F. Lewis, in making and filing said written affidavit, testimony and statement and in making said filing and entry was then and there acting as the agent of and in collusion with the said William F. Kettenbach, George H. Kester, and William Dwyer, with the intent then and there had and entertained by him, the said Hiram F. Lewis, of giving to the said William F. Kettenbach, George H. Kester and William Dwyer the benefit of said lands and the

timber situate thereon, which said lands are hereinbefore described, and that the said Hiram F. Lewis
did then and there apply to enter and purchase said
lands for the purpose of speculation, and not in good
faith for the exclusive use and benefit of him, the
said Hiram F. Lewis, as in said written affidavit, testimony and statement alleged, and that the said
Hiram F. Lewis, prior to the making and filing of
said application to enter and purchase the said lands
as aforesaid, had entered into a contract and agreement with the said William F. Kettenbach, George
H. Kester and William Dwyer, whereby he, the said
Hiram F. Lewis, had agreed that the title which
he might acquire from the Government of the United
States to the said land heretofore described, should
inure to the benefit of the said William F. Kettenbach, George H. Kester and William Dwyer.

That thereafter, on the 8th day of March, 1905, at
said city of Lewiston, according to and in pursuance
of said conspiracy, combination, confederacy and
agreement among themselves, had as aforesaid, and
to effect the object of said conspiracy, the said William F. Kettenbach, George H. Kester and William
Dwyer, did pay and cause to be paid to the Receiver
of the Land Office of the United States, at Lewiston,
Idaho, the sum of Four Hundred Dollars as and for
the minimum Government price under said entry for
the purchase of the said Northwest quarter of Section
Twenty, Township 38 North, of Range Five East, of
Boise Meridian.

That thereafter, and on the said 8th day of March,
1905, at said city of Lewiston, according to and in

pursuance of said conspiracy, combination, confederacy and agreement among themselves, had as aforesaid, and to effect the object of said enterprise, the said William F. Kettenbach, George H. Kester and William Dwyer, did persuade and induce J. B. West, the Register of the United States Land Office at Lewiston, Idaho, to issue and deliver a certificate of purchase and Register's Receipt No. 5046, in the name of said Hiram F. Lewis for the purchase of the said Northwest quarter of Section Twenty, Township 38 North, of Range Five East, of Boise Meridian, and did then and there persuade and induce the said J. B. West, as Register as aforesaid, to certify that on presentation of said certificate to the Commissioner of the General Land Office, the said Hiram F. Lewis would be entitled to receive a patent for the above-described land.

Which is against the peace and dignity of the United States and contrary to the form, force and effect of the statute in such cases made and provided.

## THIRD COUNT.

And the Grand Jurors aforesaid, being summoned, empaneled and sworn, as aforesaid, in the name and by the authority of the United States, aforesaid, upon their oaths, as aforesaid, do further find and present:

That heretofore, to wit, on the 23d day of August, 1904, at the city of Lewiston, in the county of Nez Perce, in the State and District of Idaho, and within the jurisdiction of this Court, William F. Kettenbach, George H. Kester and William Dwyer, and each of them, and other persons to the Grand Jury unknown, did commit the crime of conspiracy to defraud the United States, committed as follows

That heretofore, to wit, on the 23d day of August, 1904, at the place aforesaid, William F. Kettenbach, George H. Kester and William Dwyer, and other persons to the Grand Jury unknown, did falsely, unlawfully and wickedly conspire, combine, confederate and agree together among themselves to defraud the United States of the title and possession of large tracts of land situated in the county of Shoshone and State and District of Idaho, and of great value, of which the following described land is a part, viz.: North half of the Northeast quarter, and the North half of the Northwest quarter of Section Fifteen, Township 38 North, of Range Six East, of Boise Meridian, in the State and District of Idaho, by means of false, fraudulent, untrue and illegal entries of said lands under the laws of the United States, the said lands being then and there public lands of the United States open to entry and sale under said laws of the United States at the local land office of the United States at said city of Lewiston in said State and District of Idaho. That according to and in pursuance of said conspiracy, combination, confederation and agreement among themselves, had as aforesaid, and to effect the object of said conspiracy, the said William F. Kettenbach, George H. Kester and William Dwyer did on the 23d day of August, 1904, at the city of Lewiston in the State and District of Idaho and within the jurisdiction of this court, fraudulently, unlawfully and corruptly persuade and induce one Charles Carey of said district,

then and there being, to take his corporal oath and
be then and there sworn before one J. B. West, who
was then and there the duly appointed, qualified and
acting Register of the United States Land Office at
said city of Lewiston, in said Lewiston Land District,
and who was then and there an officer and person
having due and competent authority to administer
said oath and who did then and there administer
said oath to the said Charles Carey; that a certain
written affidavit and statement by him, the said
Charles Carey, then and there made, sworn to and
subscribed, was true, which said written affidavit and
statement then and there subscribed and sworn to by
him, the said Charles Carey, at the request and by
the procurement of them, the said William F. Kettenbach, George H. Kester and William Dwyer, as aforesaid, was then and there in a case in which a law of the
United States authorized an oath to be administered
and that said written affidavit and statement was
then and there required of him, the said Charles
Carey, by law, and the rules and regulations of the
Interior Department and the General Land Office
of the United States, which said written affidavit
and statement was then and there that certain written application to the Register of the United States
land office at said city of Lewiston duly made and
filed by him, the said Charles Carey, in the United
States Land Office at said city of Lewiston on the
23d day of August, 1905, whereby he, the said Charles
Carey, duly applied to the said Register of the said
United States Land Office at said city of Lewiston,
to enter and purchase under that certain Act of Con-

gress approved June 3, 1878, entitled: "An Act for the sale of timber lands in the States of California, Oregon, Nevada and in Washington Territory," as amended by that certain Act of Congress approved August 4, 1892, entitled: "An Act to authorize the entry of lands chiefly valuable for building stone under the placer mining laws,'" the land hereinbefore described, to wit, the North half of the Northeast quarter and the North half of the Northwest quarter, Section Fifteen, Township 38 North, of Range Six East, of Boise Meridian, situate within the district of lands subject to entry and sale under the public land laws of the United States at the said United States Land Office at Lewiston, Idaho, and which said written affidavit and statement sworn to, as aforesaid, he, the said Charles Carey, and the said William F. Kettenbach, George H. Kester and William Dwyer, and each of them, did then and there know to be false, fraudulent and untrue. That the said William F. Kettenbach, George H. Kester and William Dwyer did then and there, to wit, on the said 23d day of August, 1904, at said city of Lewiston, aforesaid, State and District aforesaid, willfully and corruptly knowing that said written affidavit and statement so made and subscribed by him, the said Charles Carey, as aforesaid, was knowingly, willfully and corruptly false, did then and there fraudulently, willfully and corruptly incite and procure the said Charles Carey, who being so sworn as aforesaid, to knowingly, corruptly and falsely and contrary to his said oath taken as aforesaid, to depose, state, swear and subscribe, among other things, to certain material matters and statements then and there contained in said written affidavit and statement in substance and effect as follows, to wit:

That I (the said Charles Carey, meaning) do not apply to purchase the land above described (the land hereinbefore described meaning) on speculation, but in good faith to appropriate it to my (the said Charles Carey, meaning) own exclusive use and benefit and that I (the said Charles Carey, meaning) have not directly or indirectly, made any agreement or contract, in any way or manner, with any person or persons whomsoever, by which the title which I (the said Charles Carey, meaning) may acquire from the Government of the United States may inure in whole or in part to the benefit of any person except myself (the said Charles Carey, meaning).

Whereas, in truth and in fact, as he, the said Charles Carey, and they, the said William Kettenbach, George H. Kester and William Dwyer, and each of them, then and there well knew, he, the said Charles Carey, did not then and there apply to enter and purchase the land hereinbefore described, and as described in said affidavit and statement in good faith and for the purpose of appropriating the said land to the exclusive use and benefit of him, the said Charles Carey, but in truth and in fact for the use and benefit of the said William F. Kettenbach, George H. Kester and William Dwyer, and other

person or persons, whose name or names are to the
Grand Jury unknown.

And whereas, in truth and in fact, as he, the said
Charles Carey, and they, the said William F. Kettenbach, George H. Kester and William Dwyer, and
each of them, then and there well knew, he, the said
Charles Carey, in making and filing said affidavit
and statement and in making said application, filing
and entry, was then and there acting as the agent of
and in collusion with the said William F. Kettenbach, George H. Kester and William Dwyer, and
with the intent then and there had and entertained
by him, the said Charles Carey, of giving to the said
William F. Kettenbach, George H. Kester and William Dwyer, the benefit of said lands and the timber
situate thereon; and that the said Charles Carey, did
then and there apply to enter and purchase said
lands for the purpose of speculation and not in good
faith for the exclusion use and benefit of him the
said Charles Carey, as in said written affidavit and
statement alleged, and that the said Charles Carey,
prior to the making and filing of said affidavit and
statement, being said application to enter and purchase said lands as aforesaid, did enter into a contract and agreement with the said William F. Kettenbach, George H. Kester and William Dwyer,
whereby he, the said Charles Carey, had agreed that
the title which he, the said Charles Carey, might
acquire from the Government of the United States
to said lands as aforesaid, should inure to the benefit

of the said William F. Kettenbach, George H. Kester and William Dwyer.

That thereafter, on the 18th day of November, 1904, at said city of Lewiston, according to and in pursuance of said conspiracy, combination, confederacy and agreement among themselves had as aforesaid, and to affect the object of said conspiracy, the said William F. Kettenbach, George H. Kester and William Dwyer, did then and there fraudulently, wilfully and corruptly persuade and induce the said Charles Carey to take an oath before J. B. West, Register of the United States Land Office at Lewiston, as aforesaid, and to then and there subscribe his name and make an oath to a certain written affidavit, testimony and statement in support of that certain written application to the Register of the United States land office at said city of Lewiston, theretofore, to wit, on the 23d day of August, 1904, duly made and filed by him, the said Charles Carey, in the said United States Land Office at said city of Lewiston, whereby, he, the said Charles Carey, duly applied to the Register of the said United States Land Office at said city of Lewiston to enter and purchase under that certain Act of Congress as aforesaid, the land described as aforesaid; that said written affidavit, testimony and statement was then and there required of him, the said Charles Carey, by law, and the rules and regulations of the Interior Department and the General Land Office of the United States, in support of said written application made and filed by said Charles Carey on the 23d day of August, 1904, as aforesaid, to enter and purchase the said

North half of the Northeast quarter and the North half of the Northwest quarter of Section Fifteen, Township 38 North, of Range Six East, of Boise Meridian.

That in said written affidavit, testimony and statement so made as aforesaid, on the 18th day of November, 1904, he, the said Charles Carey, did then and there allege, declare, testify and swear, among other things, in substance and effect as follows: That he, the said Charles Carey, had not, since making his, the said Charles Carey's, application, made on the 23d day of August, 1904, sold or transferred his, the said Charles Carey's, claim to the land heretofore described, and that he, the said Charles Carey, had not directly or indirectly, made any agreement or contract in any way or manner with any person whomsoever, by which the title which he, the said Charles Carey, might acquire from the Government of the United States, might inure, in whole or in part, to the benefit of any person except the said Charles Carey, and that he, the said Charles Carey, made the entry for said land in good faith and for the appropriation of said land exclusively for the use and benefit of the said Charles Carey, and not for the use and benefit of any other person than him, the said Charles Carey, and that no other person than he, the said Charles Carey, nor any firm, corporation or association, had any interest in said entry, he. the said Charles Carey, was then and there making, or in the said land, or in the timber on said land. The said written affidavit, testimony and statement, he, the said Charles Carey, on the 18th day of November, 1904, at the said city of Lewiston, then and there subscribed and swore to before J. B. West, the Register of the United States Land Office at said city of Lewiston, who was then and there an officer and person competent to administer said oath, and who did then and there duly administer said oath to the said Charles Carey, and that said written affidavit, testimony and statement was then and there made and given in a case in which the laws of the United States authorize an oath to be administered, and which said written affidavit, testimony and statement was duly filed by him, the said Charles Carey, in the said United States Land Office at said city of Lewiston, on the 18th day of November, 1904.

That said written affidavit, testimony and statement was then and there false, fraudulent and untrue, and the said Charles Carey, and the said William F. Kettenbach, George H. Kester, and William Dwyer, and each of them, then and there well knew. it to be false and untrue in this: That he, the said Charles Carey, in making and filing said written affidavit, testimony and statement and in making said filing and entry was then and there acting as the agent of and in collusion with the said William F. Kettenbach, George H. Kester and William Dwyer, with the intent then and there had and entertained by him, the said Charles Carey, of giving to the said William F. Kettenbach, George H. Kester and William Dwyer, the benefit of said lands and the timber situate thereon, which said lands are hereinbefore described, and that the said Charles Carey did then and there apply to enter and purchase said lands for the purpose of speculation and not in good faith for the exclusive use and benefit of him, the said Charles Carey, as in said written affidavit, testimony and statement alleged, and that the said Charles Carey, prior to the making and filing of said application to enter and purchase the said lands as aforesaid, had entered into a contract and agreement with the said William F. Kettenbach, George H. Kester and William Dwyer, whereby he, the said Charles Carey, had agreed that the title which he might acquire from the Government of the United States to the said land heretofore described should inure to the benefit of the said William F. Kettenbach, George H. Kester and William Dwyer.

That thereafter, on the 18th day of November, 1904, at said city of Lewiston, according to and in pursuance of said conspiracy, combination, confedcracy, and agreement among themselves had as aforesaid, and to effect the object of said conspiracy, the said William F. Kettenbach, George H. Kester and William Dwyer, did pay and cause to be paid to the Receiver of the Land Office of the United States at Lewiston, Idaho, the sum of four hundred dollars as and for the minimum Government price under said entry for the purchase of the said North half of the Northeast quarter and the North half of the Northwest quarter of Section Fifteen, Township 38 North, of Range Six East, of Boise Meridian.

That thereafter and on the said 18th day of November, 1904, at said city of Lewiston, according to and in pursuance of said conspiracy, confederacy and agreement among themselves, had as aforesaid, and to effect the object of said conspiracy, the said William F. Kettenbach, George H. Kester and William Dwyer did persuade and induce J. B. West, the Register of the United States Land Office at Lewiston, Idaho, to issue and deliver a certificate of purchase and Register's receipt No. 4943, in the name of said Charles Carey for the purchase of the said North half of the Northeast quarter and the North half of the Northwest quarter of Section Fifteen, Township 38 North, of Range Six East, of Boise Meridian, and did then and there persuade and induce the said J. B. West, as Register as aforesaid, to certify that on presentation of said certificate to the Commissioner of the General Land Office, the said Charles Carey, would be entitled to receive a patent for the above-described land.

Which is against the peace and dignity of the United States and contrary to the form, force and effect of the statute in such cases made and provided.

### FOURTH COUNT.

And the Grand Jurors aforesaid, being summoned, empaneled and sworn, as aforesaid, in the name and by the authority of the United States, aforesaid, upon their oaths, as aforesaid, do further find and present:

That heretofore, to wit, on the 25th day of April, 1904, at the city of Lewiston, in the county of Nez

Perce, in the State and District of Idaho, and within the jurisdiction of this Court, William F. Kettenbach, George H. Kester and William Dwyer, and each of them, and other persons to the Grand Jury unknown, did commit the crime of conspiracy to defraud the United States, committed as follows:

That heretofore, to wit, on the 25th day of April, 1904, at the place aforesaid, William F. Kettenbach, George H. Kester and William Dwyer, and other persons to the Grand Jury unknown, did falsely, unlawfully and wickedly conspire, confederate and agree together among themselves to defraud the United States of the title and possession of large tracts of land situated in the county of Shoshone and State and District of Idaho, and of great value, of which the following-described land is a part, viz.: Lots 3 and 4, and the Northeast quarter of the Southwest quarter and the Northwest quarter of the Southeast quarter of Section nineteen, Township 39 North, of Range Five East, of Boise Meridian, in the State and District of Idaho, by means of false, fraudulent, untrue and illegal entries of said lands under the laws of the United States, the said lands being then and there public lands of the United States open to entry and sale under said laws of the United States at the local land office of the United States at said city of Lewiston in said State and District of Idaho. That, according to and in pursuance of said conspiracy, combination, confederation and agreement among themselves had as aforesaid, and to effect the object of said conspiracy, the said William F.

Kettenbach, George H. Kester and William Dwyer, did, on the 25th day of April, 1904, at the city of Lewiston, in the State and District of Idaho, and within the jurisdiction of this Court, fraudulently, unlawfully and corruptly persuade and induce one Guy L. Wilson, of said district, then and there being, to take his corporal oath and be then and there sworn before one J. B. West, who was then and there the duly appointed, qualified and acting Register of the United States Land Office at said city of Lewiston, in said Lewiston Land District, and who was then and there an officer and person having due and competent authority to administer said oath, and who did then and there administer said oath to the said Guy L. Wilson; that a certain written affidavit and statement by him, the said Guy L. Wilson, then and there made, sworn to and subscribed, was true, which said written affidavit and statement then and there subscribed and sworn to by him, the said Guy L. Wilson, at the request and by the procurement of them, the said William F. Kettenbach, George H. Kester and William Dwyer, as aforesaid, was then and there in a case in which a law of the United States authorized an oath to be administered, and that said written affidavit and statement was then and there required of him, the said Guy L. Wilson, by a law, and the rules and regulations of the Interior department and the General Land Office of the United States, which said written affidavit and statement was then and there that certain written application to the Register of the United States Land Office at said city of Lewiston, duly made and filed by him, the said Guy L. Wilson, in the United States Land Office at said city of Lewiston, on *on* the 25th day of April, 1904, whereby he, the said Guy L. Wilson, duly applied to the said Register of the said United States Land Office at said city of Lewiston, to enter and purchase under that certain Act of Congress approved June 3, 1878, entitled: "An act for the sale of Timber Lands in the States of California, Oregon, Nevada and in Washington Territory," as amended by that certain act of Congress approved August 4, 1892, entitled: "An Act to authorize the Entry of Lands chiefly valuable for Building Stone under the Placer Mining Laws," the land hereinbefore described, to wit, Lots 3 and 4 and the Northeast quarter of the Southwest quarter, and the Northwest quarter of the Southeast quarter of Section Nineteen, Township 39 North, of Range Five East. of Boise Meridian, situate within the district of lands subject to entry and sale under the public land laws of the United States at the said United States Land Office at Lewiston, Idaho, and which said written affidavit and statement, sworn to as aforesaid, he, the said Guy L. Wilson, and the said William F. Kettenbach, George H. Kester and William Dwyer, and each of them, did then and there know to be false, fraudulent and untrue. That the said William F. Kettenbach, George H. Kester and William Dwyer did then and there, to wit, on the said 25th day of April, 1904, at said city of Lewiston aforesaid, State and District aforesaid, willfully and corruptly, knowing that said written affidavit and state-

ment so made and subscribed by him, the said Guy
L. Wilson, as aforesaid, was knowingly, willfully
and corruptly false, did then and there fraudulently,
unlawfully and corruptly incite and procure the said
Guy L. Wilson, who, being so sworn as aforesaid,
to knowingly, corruptly and falsely and contrary to
his said oath, taken as aforesaid, to depose, state,
swear and subscribe, among other things, to certain
material matters and statements then and there contained in said written affidavit and statement in substance and effect as follows, to wit:

That I (the said Guy L. Wilson, meaning) do not
apply to purchase the land above described (the land
hereinbefore described, meaning) on speculation,
but in good faith to appropriate it to my (the said
Guy L. Wilson, meaning) own exclusive use and benefit, and that I (the said Guy L. Wilson, meaning)
have not, directly or indirectly, made any agreement
or contract, in any manner or form, with any person
or persons whomsoever, by which the title which I
(said Guy L. Wilson, meaning) may acquire from
the Government of the United States may inure in
whole or in part to the benefit of any person except
myself (the said Guy L. Wilson, meaning).

Whereas, in truth and in fact, as he, the said Guy
L. Wilson, and they, the said William F. Kettenbach,
George H. Kester and William Dwyer, and each of
them, then and there well knew, he, the said Guy L.
Wilson, did not then and there apply to enter and
purchase the land hereinbefore described and as described in said affidavit and statement in good faith
and for the purpose of appropriating the said land

to the exclusive use and benefit of him, the said Guy L. Wilson, but in truth and in fact for the use and benefit of the said William F. Kettenbach, George H. Kester and William Dwyer, and other person and persons, whose name or names are to the Grand Jurors unknown.

And whereas, in truth and in fact, as he, the said Guy L. Wilson, and they, the said William F. Kettenbach, George H. Kester and William Dwyer, and each of them, then and there well knew, he, the said Guy L. Wilson, in making and filing said affidavit and statement and in making said application, filing and entry, was then and there acting as the agent of and in collusion with the said William F. Kettenbach, George H. Kester and William Dwyer, and with the intent then and there had and entertained by him, the said Guy L. Wilson, of giving to the said William F. Kettenbach, George H. Kester and William Dwyer, the benefit of said lands and the timber situate thereon; and that the said Guy L. Wilson did then and there apply to enter and purchase said lands for the pur ose of speculation, and not in good faith for the exclusive use and benefit of him, the said Guy L. Wilson, as in said written affidavit and statement alleged, and that the said Guy L. Wilson, prior to the making and filing of said affidavit and statement, being said application to enter and purchase said lands as aforesaid, did enter into a contract and agreement with the said William F. Kettenbach, George H. Kester and William Dwyer, whereby he, the said Guy L. Wilson, had agreed that the title

which he, the said Guy L. Wilson, might acquire
from the Government of the United States to said
lands, as aforesaid, should inure to the benefit of the
said William F. Kettenbach, George H. Kester and
William Dwyer.

That, thereafter, on the 13th day of July, 1904, at
said city of Lewiston, according to and in pursuance
of said conspiracy, combination, confederacy and
agreement among themselves had as aforesaid, and
to effect the object of said conspiracy, the said William F. Kettenbach, George H. Kester and William
Dwyer, did then and there, fraudulently, willfully
and corruptly persuade and induce the said Guy L.
Wilson, to take an oath before J. B. West, Register
of the United States Land Office at Lewiston, as
aforesaid, and to then and there subscribe his name
and make an oath to a certain written affidavit, testimony and statement in support of that certain written application to the Register of the United States
Land Office at said city of Lewiston theretofore, to
wit, on the 25th day of April, 1904, duly made and
filed by him, the said Guy L. Wilson, in the said
United States Land Office, at said city of Lewiston,
whereby he, the said Guy L. Wilson, duly applied to
the Register of the said United States Land Office
at said city of Lewiston, to enter and purchase under that certain Act of Congress as aforesaid, the
land described as aforesaid; that said written affidavit, testimony and statement was then and there required of him, the said Guy L. Wilson, by law, and
the rules and regulations of the Interior Department

and the General Land Office of the United States, in support of said written application made and filed by said Guy L. Wilson, upon the 25th day of April, 1904, as aforesaid, to enter and purchase the said Lots 3 and 4 and the Northeast quarter of the Southwest quarter, and the Northwest quarter of the Southeast quarter, of Section Nineteen, Township 39 North, of Range Five East, of Boise Meridian.

That in said written affidavit, testimony and statement, so made as aforesaid, on the 13th day of July, 1904, he, the said Guy L. Wilson, did then and there allege, declare, testify and swear, among other things, in substance and effect as follows: That he, the said Guy L. Wilson, had not, since making his, the said Guy L. Wilson's, application, made on the 25th day of April, 1904, sold or transferred his, the said Guy L. Wilson's, claim to the land heretofore described, and that he, the said Guy L. Wilson, had not, directly or indirectly, made any. agreement or contract in any way or manner with any person whomsoever, by which the title which he, the said Guy L. Wilson, might acquire from the Government of the United States might inure, in whole or in part, to the benefit of any person except the said Guy L. Wilson, and that he, the said Guy L. Wilson, made the entry for said land in good faith and for the appropriation of said land exclusively for the use and benefit of the said Guy L. Wilson, and not for the use and benefit of any other person than him, the said Guy L. Wilson, and that no other person than he, the said Guy L. Wilson, nor any firm, corporation or association, had any interest in said entry, he, the said Guy L. Wilson, was then and there making or in the said land or in the timber on said land. The said written affidavit, testimony and statement, he the said Guy L. Wilson, on the 13th day of July, 1904, at said city of Lewiston, then and there subscribed and swore to before J. B. West, the Register of the United States Land Office at said City of Lewiston, who was then and there an officer and person competent to administer said oath, and who did then and there duly administer said oath to the said Guy L. Wilson, and that said written affidavit, testimony and statement was then and there made and given in a case in which the laws of the United States authorize an oath to be administered, and which said written affidavit, testimony and statement was duly filed by him, the said Guy L. Wilson, in the said United States Land Office at said city of Lewiston on the 13th day of July, 1904.

That said written affidavit, testimony and statement was then and there false, fraudulent and untrue and the said Guy L. Wilson, and the said William F. Kettenbach, George H. Kester and William Dwyer, and each of them, then and there well knew it to be false and untrue in this: That he, the said Guy L. Wilson, in making and filing said written affidavit, testimony and statement and in making said filing and entry was then and there acting as the agent of and in collusion with the said William F. Kettenbach, George H. Kester and William Dwyer, with the intent then and there had and entertained by him, the said Guy L. Wilson, of giving to the said

William F. Kettenbach, George H. Kester and William Dwyer, the benefit of said lands and the timber situate thereon, which said lands are hereinbefore described, and that the said Guy L. Wilson did then and there apply to enter and purchase said lands for the purpose of speculation and not in good faith for the exclusive use and benefit of him, the said Guy L. wilson, as in said written affidavit, testimony and statement alleged, and that the said Guy L. Wilson, prior to the making and filing of said application to enter and purchase the said lands as aforesaid, had entered into a contract and agreement with the said William F. Kettenbach, George H. Kester and William Dwyer, whereby he, the said Guy L. Wilson, had agreed that the title which he might acquire from the Government of the United States to the said land, heretofore described, should inure to the benefit of the said William F. Kettenbach, George H. Kester and William Dwyer.

That thereafter, on the 13th day of July, 1904, at said city of Lewiston, according to and in pursuance of said conspiracy, combination, confederacy and agreement among themselves had as aforesaid, and to effect the object of said conspiracy, the said William F. Kettenbach, George H. Kester and William Dwyer, did pay and cause to be paid to the Receiver of the United States Land Office, at Lewiston, Idaho, the sum of three hundred ninety-five and 12/100 dollars as and for the minimum Government price under said entry for the purchase of the said Lots 3 and 4 and the Northeast quarter of the Southwest quarter, and the Northwest quarter of the Southeast quarter, Section nineteen, Township 39 North, of Range five East, of Boise Meridian.

That thereafter and on the said 13th day of July, 1904, at said city of Lewiston, according to and in pursuance of said conspiracy, combination, confedcracy and agreement among themselves, had as aforesaid, and to effect the object of said conspiracy, the said William F. Kettenbach, George H. Kester and William Dwyer, did persuade and induce J. B. West, the Register of the United States Land Office at Lewiston, Idaho, to issue and deliver a certificate of purchase and the Register's Receipt No. 4770, in the name of said Guy L. Wilson, for the purchase of the said Lots 3 and 4 and the Northeast quarter of the Southwest quarter and the Northwest quarter of the Southeast quarter of Section nineteen, Township 39 North, of Range Five East, of Boise Meridian, and did then and there persuade and induce the said J. B. West, as Register as aforesaid, to certify that on presentation of said certificate to the Commission of the General Land Office the said Guy L. Wilson would be entitled to receive a patent for the above-described land.

Which is against the peace and dignity of the United States and contrary to the form, force and effect of the statute in such cases made and provided.

### FIFTH COUNT.

And the Grand Jurors aforesaid, being summoned, empaneled and sworn, as aforesaid, in the name and by the authority of the United States, aforesaid, upon their oaths as aforesaid, do further find and present:

That heretofore, to wit, on the 25th day of April, 1904, at the city of Lewiston, in the County of Nez Perce, in the State and District of Idaho, and within the jurisdiction of this Court, William F. Kettenbach, George H. Kester and William Dwyer, and each of them, and other persons to the Grand Jury unknown, did commit the crime of conspiracy to defraud the United States, committed as follows:

That heretofore, to wit, on the 25th day of April, 1904, at the place aforesaid, William F. Kettenbach, George H. Kester and William Dwyer, and other persons to the Grand Jury unknown, did falsely, unlawfully and wickedly conspire, combine, confederate and agree together among themselves to defraud the United States of the title and possession of large tracts of land, situated in the county of Shoshone and State and District of Idaho, and of great value, of which the following land is a part, viz.: Lots 3 and 4, and the East half of the Southwest quarter, of Section nineteen, Township 38 North, of Range six East, of Boise Meridian, in the State and District of Idaho, by means of false, fraudulent, untrue and illegal entries of said lands, under the laws of the United States, the said lands, being then and there public lands of the United States open to entry and sale under said laws of the United States at the local land office of the United States at said city of Lewiston in said State and District of Idaho. That according to and in pursuance of said conspiracy, combination, confederation and agreement among themselves had as aforesaid, and to effect the object of said conspiracy, the said William F. Kettenbach,

George H. Kester and William Dwyer, did on the
25th day of April, 1904, at the city of Lewiston in
the State and District of Idaho and within the jurisdiction of this Court, fraudulently, unlawfully and
corruptly persuade and induce one Frances A. Justice of said district, then and there being, to take her
corporal oath and be then and there sworn before
one J. B. West, who was then and there the duly appointed, qualified and acting Register of the United
States Land Office at said city of Lewiston, in said
Lewiston Land District, and who was then and there
an officer and person having due and competent authority to administer said oath, and who did then
and there administer said oath to the said Frances
A. Justice; that a certain written affidavit and statement by her, the said Frances A. Justice, then and
there made, sworn to and subscribed, was true, which
said written affidavit and statement then and there
subscribed and sworn to by her, the said Frances A.
Justice, at the request and by the procurement of
them, the said William F. Kettenbach, George H.
Kester and William Dwyer, as aforesaid, was then
and there in a case in which a law of the United
States authorized an oath to be administered and
that said written affidavit and statement was then
and there required of her, the said Frances A. Justice, by law, and the rules and regulations of the Interior Department and the General Land Office of
the United States, which said written affidavit and
statement was then and there that certain written
application to the Register of the United States
Land Office at said city of Lewiston, duly made and

filed by her, the said Frances A. Justice, in the
United States Land Office, at said city of Lewiston
on the 25th day of April, 1904, whereby she, the said
Frances A. Justice, duly applied to the said Register of the said United States Land Office at said city
of Lewiston, to enter and purchase under that certain Act of Congress approved June 3, 1878, entitled:
"An Act for the Sale of Timber Lands in the States
of California, Oregon, Nevada and in Washington
Territory," as amended by that certain Act of Congress approved August 4, 1892, entitled: "An Act to
Authorize the entry of lands chiefly valuable for
Building Stone under the Placer Mining Laws," the
land hereinbefore described, to wit, Lots 3 and 4,
and the East half of the Southwest quarter of Section
nineteen, Township 38 North, of Range six East, of
Boise Meridian, situate within the District of Lands
subject to entry and sale under the public land laws
of the United States at the said United States Land
Office at Lewiston, and which said written affidavit
and statement, sworn to as aforesaid, she, the said
Frances A. Justice, and the said William F. Kettenbach, George H. Kester and William Dwyer, and
each of them, did then and there know to be false,
fraudulent and untrue. That the said William F.
Kettenbach, George H. Kester, and William Dwyer
did then and there, to wit, on the said 25th day of
April, 1904, at said city of Lewiston, aforesaid, state
and district aforesaid, willfully and corruptly, knowing that said written affidavit and statement so made
and subscribed by her, the said Frances A. Justice,
as aforesaid, was knowingly, willfully and corruptly

false, did then and there fraudulently, unlawfully and corruptly incite and procure the said Frances A. Justice, who being so sworn as aforesaid, to knowingly, corruptly and falsely and contrary to her said oath taken as aforesaid, to depose, state, swear, and subscribe, among other things, to certain material matters and statements then and there contained in said written affidavit and statement in substance and effect as follows, to wit:

That I (the said Frances A. Justice, meaning) do not apply to purchase the land above described (the land hereinbefore described meaning) on speculation, but in good faith to appropriate it to my (the said Frances A. Justice, meaning) own exclusive use and benefit, and that I (the said Frances A. Justice, meaning) have not directly or indirectly made any agreement or contract, in any way or manner, with any person or persons whomsoever, by which the title which I (the said Frances A. Justice, meaning) may acquire from the Government of the United States may inure in whole or in part to the benefit of any person except myself (the said Frances A. Justice, meaning).

Whereas, in truth and in fact, as she, the said Frances A. Justice, and they, the said William F. Kettenbach, George H. Kester, and William Dwyer, and each of them, then and there well knew, she, the said Frances A. Justice, did not then and there apply to enter and purchase the land hereinbefore described, and as described in said affidavit and statement in good faith and for the purpose and appropriating the said land to the exclusive use and benefit of her, the said Frances A. Jus'ice, l*ut in *ruth and in fact for the use and be.*efit *.f th* said William F. Kettenbach, George H. Kes* *r a*d William Dwyer, and other person and *erso* *, wl*se name or names are to the Grand Jurors unk *own

And whereas, in truth and in fact, a* she, the said Frances A. Justice, and they, the said William F. Kettenbach, George H. Kester and William Dwyer, and each of them, then and there well knew, she, the said Frances A. Justice, in making and filing said affidavit and statement and in making said application, filing and entry, was then and there acting as the agent of and in collusion with the said William F. Kettenbach, George H. Kester and William Dwyer, and with the intent then and there had and entertained by her, the said Frances A. Justice, of giving to the said William F. Kettenbach, George H. Kester and William Dwyer, the benefit of said lands and the timber situate thereon; and that the said Frances A. Justice did then and there apply to enter and purchase said lands for the purpose of speculation and not in good faith for the exclusive use and benefit of her, the said Frances A. Justice, as in said written affidavit and statement alleged, and that the said Frances A. Justice, prior to the making and filing of said affidavit and statement, being said application to enter and purchase said lands as aforesaid, did enter into a contract and agreement with the said William F. Kettenbach, George H. Kester and William Dwyer, whereby she, the said Frances A. Justice, had agreed that the title which she, the said Frances A. Justice, might acquire from the Government of the United States to said lands as aforesaid should inure to the benefit of the said William F. Kettenbach, George H. Kester and William Dwyer.

That thereafter, on the 13th day of July, 1904, at said city of Lewiston, according to and in pursuance of said conspiray, combination, confederacy and agreement among themselves had as aforesaid, and to effect the object of said conspiracy, the said William F. Kettenbach, George H. Kester and William Dwyer, did then and there fraudulently, willfully and corruptly persuade and induce the said Frances A. Justice to take an oath before J. B. West, Register of the United States Land Office, at Lewiston, as aforesaid, and to then and there subscribe her name and make an oath to a certain written affidavit, testimony and statement in support of that certain written application to the Register of the United States Land Office at said city of Lewiston, theretofore, to wit, on the 25th day of April, 1904, duly made and filed by her, the said Frances A. Justice, in the said United States Land Office at said city, of Lewiston, whereby she, the said Frances A. Justice, duly applied to the Register of the said United States Land Office at said city of Lewiston to enter and purchase under that certain act of Congress as aforesaid the land described as aforesaid; that said written affidavit, testimony and statement was then and there required of her, the said Frances A. Justice, by law, and the rules and regulations of the Interior Department and the General Land Office of the United States, in support of said written application made and filed by said Frances A. Justice on the 25th day of April, 1904, as aforesaid, to enter and purchase the said Lots 3 and 4, and the East half of the Southwest quarter, of Section nineteen, Township 38, North of Range six, East of Boise Meridian.

That in said written affidavit, testimony and statement so made as aforesaid, on the 13th day of July, 1904, she, the said Frances A. Justice, did then and there allege, declare, testify and swear, among other things, in substance and effect as follows: That she, the said Frances A. Justice, has not, since making her, the said Frances A. Justice's, application, made on the 25th day of April, 1904, sold or transferred her, the said Frances A. Justice's, claim to the land heretofore described, and that she, the said Frances A. Justice, had not directly or indirectly made any agreement or contract in any way or manner with any person whomsoever, by which the title which she, the said Frances A. Justice, might acquire from the Government of the United States might inure, in whole or in part, to the benefit of any person except the said Frances A. Justice, and that she, the said Frances A. Justice, made the entry for said land in good faith and for the appropriation of said land exclusively for the use and benefit of the said Frances A. Justice and not for the use and benefit of any other person than her, the said Frances A. Justice, and that no other person than she, the said Frances A. Justice, nor any firm, corporation or association, has any interest in said entry, she, the said Frances A. Justice, was then and there making or in the said land or in the timber on said land. The said written affidavit, testimony and statement, she, the said Frances A. Justice, on the 13th day of July, 1904, at said city of Lewiston, then and there subscribed and sworn to before J. B. West, the Register of the United States Land Office at said city of Lewiston, who was then and there an officer and person competent to administer said oath, and who did then and there duly administer said oath to the said Frances A. Justice, and that said written affidavit, testimony and statement was then and there made and given in a case in which the laws of the United States authorize an oath to be administered, and which said written affidavit, testimony and statement was duly filed by her, the said Frances A. Justice, in the said United States Land Office at said city of Lewiston on the 13th day of July, 1904.

That said written affidavit, testimony and statement was then and there false, fraudulent and untrue, and the said Frances A. Justice, and the said William F. Kettenbach, George H. Kester and William Dwyer, and each of them, then and there well knew it to be false and untrue in this: that she, the said Frances A. Justice, in making and filing said written affidavit, testimony and statement, and in making said filing and entry was then and there acting as the agent of and in collusion with the said William F. Kettenbach, George H. Kester and William Dwyer, with the intent then and there had and entertained by her, the said Frances A. Justice, of giving to the said William F. Kettenbach, George H. Kester and William Dwyer, the benefit of said lands and the timber situate thereon, which said lands are hereinbefore described, and that the said Frances A. Justice did then and there apply to enter and purchase said lands for the purpose of speculation and not in good faith for the exclusive use and benefit of her, the said Frances A. Justice, as in said written affidavit, testimony and statement alleged, and that the said Frances A. Justice, prior to the making and filing of said application to enter and purchase the said lands as aforesaid, had entered into a contract with the said William F. Kettenbach, George H. Kester and William Dwyer, whereby she, the said Frances A. Justice, had agreed that the title which she, the said Frances A. Justice, might acquire from the government of the United States to the said lands heretofore described, should inure to the benefit of the said William F. Kettenbach, George H. Kester and William Dwyer.

That thereafter, on the 13th day of July, 1904, at said city of Lewiston, according to and in pursuance of said conspiracy, combination, confederacy and agreement among themselves, had as aforesaid, and to effect the object of said conspiracy, the said William F. Kettenbach, George H. Kester and William Dwyer, did pay and cause to be paid to the Receiver of the Land Office of the United States at Lewiston, Idaho, the sum of three hundred ninety-four and 50/100 dollars as and for the minimum Government price under said entry for the purchase of the said Lots 3 and 4 and the East half of the Southwest quarter of Section nineteen, Township 38 North, of Range six East, of Boise Meridian.

That thereafter, and on the said 13th day of July, 1904, at said city of Lewiston, according to and in pursuance of said conspiracy, combination, confedcracy and agreement among themselves, had as aforesaid, and to effect the object of said conspiracy the said William F. Kettenbach, George H. Kester and William Dwyer did persuade and induce J. B. West, the Register of the United States Land Office at Lewiston, Idaho, to issue and deliver a certificate of purchase and Register's Receipt No. 4771, in the name of Frances A. Justice for the purchase of the said Lots 3 and 4, and the East half of the Southwest quarter, of Section nineteen, Township 38 North, of Range six East, of Boise Meridian, and did then and there persuade and induce the said J. B. West, as Register as aforesaid, to certify that on presentation *on* said certificate to the commissioner of the General Land Office, the said Frances A. Justice would be entitled to receive a patent for the above-described land.

Which is against the peace and dignity of the United States and contrary to the form, force and effect of the statute in such cases made and provided.

N. M. RUICK,

United States District Attorney, District of Idaho.

JOHN CRENSHAW,

Foreman of the United States Grand Jury.

NAMES OF THE WITNESSES EXAMINED BEFORE THE GRAND JURY IN THE ABOVE CASE.

| | |
|---|---|
| Edward M. Lewis, | S. P. Fitzgerald, |
| Guy L. Wilson, | Charles Carey, |
| W. H. Helkenberg, | John P. Roos, |
| Hiram F. Lewis, | Fred Denison. |
| Wynn W. Pefley, | |

[Endorsed]: No. 615. United States District Court, Northern Division, District of Idaho. The United States vs. William F. Kettenbach, George H. Kester and William Dwyer. Indictment for Conspiracy to Defraud. Violation Sec. 5440, R. S. U. S. A True Bill. John Crenshaw, Foreman Grand Jury. Filed Nov. 6, 1905. A. L. Richardson, Clerk. N. M. Ruick, U. S. Attorney.

---

*In the United States District Court, for the Northern Division, District of Idaho.*

THE UNITED STATES OF AMERICA

vs.

WILLIAM F. KETTENBACH, GEORGE H. KESTER, and WILLIAM DWYER.

**Motion for Order Requiring Bill of Particulars, etc.**

Now come the defendants herein, prior to the trial of this cause and prior to the setting of the same for trial, and move the above-entitled court for an order requiring and directing the United States District Attorney for the State of Idaho, the prosecutor herein, to give and furnish the defendants with a particular description of all overt acts, and each of them, the time and place where they are alleged to have been committed or made, with whom, if anyone, and especially the names and places of residences of the persons designated in the indictment, and each and every count thereof where the same are designated, as "and other persons to the Grand jury unknown"; and also, the names of the persons and the circumstances of each and every overt act connected with such persons, and the particular descriptions of each and every entry and the description of the land therein, upon which the Government expects to rely for the purpose of proving motive, intent or system to commit the crime of conspiracy or to defraud the United States in any way or manner.

These defendants further demand a bill of particulars of the overt act upon which the prosecution will rely for a conviction, or for the purpose of connecting the defendants and each thereof with the alleged conspiracy, and whether the same were done in person or by or through some agent or agency existing between the defendants herein, or each thereof, with any one of the defendants or any other person not designated or described in the indictment.

These defendants and each and all thereof further demand and move the above-entitled court, upon the trial of this cause, that the Government be restricted to the items, acts and circumstances specified, set out and particularized in such bill of particulars to be so furnished.

This motion is made and based upon the following grounds:

·First: That the indictment heretofore returned and filed herein is general in its terms charging conspiracy to defraud the United States in violation of Section 5440, R. S. U. S., and that on the 26th day of October, 1904, the defendants, and each thereof, did unlawfully conspire, combine, confederate and agree together with Edward M. Lewis, Hiram F. Lewis, Charles Carey, Guy L. Wilson and Frances A. Justice, and divers other persons whose names are to the Grand Jurors unknown, in each and every particular act and count set out and pleaded in the indictment herein.

And upon the further ground that it is alleged in said indictment that the defendants did conspire, confederate and agree together, among themselves and others to the Grand Jurors unknown, to defraud the United States. That said indictment is insufficient to appraise the defendants of the nature of the offense charged against them and the overt acts alleged to have been committed by these defendants, and each or either thereof, upon which the Government expects to rely for the purpose of connecting these defendants and each thereof with the various acts charged and alleged in the indictment.

Second: That in this class of cases the Government is not confined to any particular date, except that the proof must show the offense was committed within three years proceding the indictment, and might be permitted to introduce evidence of specific overt acts committed with other persons not mentioned or described in the indictment, and the acquiring of additional lands not set out or described in the indictment, for the purpose of showing the intent, motive or system of the defendants to acquire such lands in violation of the laws of the United States and the intent to defraud, although these defendants do not admit that such showing could be made in the case at bar.

Third: That the said indictment is insufficient to apprise these defendants of the nature of the offenses charged against them, and especially as to whether or not the Government expects to rely upon the proof of agency existing between the defendants therein, or either thereof, and any other person or persons not mentioned, designated or described in the indictment.

That the indictment is also insufficient to apprise these defendants of the names or personnel of the persons described in the indictment as "and other persons to the Grand Jurors unknown."

This motion is made and based upon the indictment heretofore returned and filed herein and each and all of the charges set out and described therein, and the files and records in the above-entitled court, and such other documentary evidence as the defendants may see fit to read and use upon the trial of this cause.

Dated this 16th day of May, A .D. 1907.

FORNEY & MOORE,

Attorneys for Defendants, Residing at Moscow, Idaho.

GEORGE W. TANNAHILL,

Attorney for Defendants, Residing at Lewiston, Idaho.

[Endorsed]: Filed May 16, 1907. A. L. Richardson, Clerk.

*In the United States District Court, for the Northern Division, District of Idaho.*

## No. 615.

## THE UNITED STATES OF AMERICA

vs.

## WILLIAM F. KETTENBACH, GEORGE H. KESTER, and WILLIAM DWYER.

**Affidavit in Support of Motion for Bill of Particulars.**

State of Idaho,
County of Latah,—ss.

William F. Kettenbach, George H. Kester and William Dwyer, being first duly sworn, each for himself upon oath says:

That they are the defendants above named and named in the indictment heretofore returned and filed herein, charged with conspiracy to defraud the United States in violation of section 5440, R. S. U. S., filed November 6, 1905. That the charges named in said indictment are general in their nature, charging the violation of certain statutes of the United States, and said indictment is insufficient to apprise the defendants of the nature of the charges they will be required to meet, or the specific overt acts upon which the Government will rely for the purpose of connecting these defendants and each thereof with the charges set out and pleaded in the indictments on file herein. That affiants and these defendants cannot safely go to trial without the furnishing of a bill of particulars for the purpose of apprising these defendants of the nature of the charges and to enable them to bring their witnesses to meet any such charges.

WILLIAM F. KETTENBACH.

GEORGE H. KESTER.

WILLIAM DWYER.

Subscribed and sworn to before me this 16th day of May, A. D. 1907.

[Seal]               S. R. H. McGOWAN,

Notary Public in and for Latah County, State of
    Idaho.

[Endorsed]: No. 615. In the United States District Court, for the Northern Division, District of Idaho. The United States of America vs. William F. Kettenbach, et al. Conspiracy to Defraud in Violation of Sec. 5440, R. S. U. S. Motion for Order Requiring Bill of Particulars, and Affidavit in Support Thereof. Filed May 16, 1907. A. L. Richardson, Clerk.

---

*In the District Court of the United States Within and for the Northern Division of the District of Idaho.*

THE UNITED STATES OF AMERICA

vs.

WILLIAM F. KETTENBACH, GEORGE H. KESTER, and WILLIAM DWYER.

## Notice of Intention of Plaintiff to Move for Trial.

To Messrs. Forney & Moore and G. W. Tannahill,
Esq., Attorneys for the above-named Defendants.

You are hereby notified that the United States elects to proceed to trial in Case No. 615, entitled as above, and pursuant to the order or suggestion of the Court this day made will move said cause for trial and will proceed in the matter of impanelling a jury in said cause at the convening of court at 2 o'clock P. M., to-morrow the 17th inst.

Dated May 16, 1907.

N. M. RUICK,
United States Attorney, District of Idaho.

Service of the foregoing notice and receipt of a copy thereof admitted this 16th day of May, 1907, at 4:15 o'clock P. M.

FORNEY & MOORE and
G. W. TANNAHILL,
Attorneys for Defendants.

[Endorsed]: No. 615. In the District Court of the United States, for the Northern Division of Idaho. United States vs. Wm. F. Kettenbach, et al. Notice of Intention to Move for Trial. Filed May 17, 1907. A. L. Richardson, Clerk. N. M. Ruick, U. S. Attorney.

*In the District Court of the United States Within and for the Northern Division of the District of Idaho.*

## No. 615.

## THE UNITED STATES OF AMERICA

vs.

## WILLIAM F. KETTENBACH, GEORGE H. KESTER, and WILLIAM DWYER.

### Notice of Alleged Co-Conspirators, etc.

To the Above-named Defendants and to Messrs. Forney & Moore, and G. W. Tannahill, Esq., Their Attorneys.

Pursuant to your request for a list of other persons who might be co-conspirators with the defendants named in the above-entitled cause, you will please take notice that the following are such possible or probable co-conspirators, now known to the Government, and said persons are considered such co-conspirators by the Government.

| | |
|---|---|
| J. B. West. | Fred Emory. |
| I. N. Smith. | Clarence W. Robnett. |
| Jackson O'Keefe. | Melvern C. Scott. |
| W. B. Benton. | Edwin F. Bliss. |
| E. L. Knight. | H. J. Steffey. |
| C. W. Colby. | |

In furnishing the above list, however, the United States does not assume the responsibility of establishing upon the trial that the persons above named were, or either of them was, co-conspirators, or a co-conspirator, with the defendants named in the indictment herein.

Further, this list does not include and is not intended to include the names of the entrymen procured and used in furtherance of the conspiracy charged in said indictment.

Dated May 17, 1907.

N. M. RUICK,

U. S. Attorney, Dist. of Idaho.

Service of the foregoing notice accepted this 17th day of May, 1907, at 10 o'clock A. M.

FORNEY & MOORE,

GEO. W. TANNAHILL,

Attorneys for Defendants.

[Endorsed]: No. 615. In the District Court of the United States for the District of Idaho, Northern Division. United States of America vs. William F. Kettenbach, et al. Notice—List of Co-conspirators. Filed May 17th. 1907. A. L. Richardson, Clerk. N. M. Ruick, U. S. Attorney, Attorney for Plaintiff.

---

*In the District Court of the United States Within and for the District of Idaho, Northern Division.*

THE UNITED STATES

vs.

WILLIAM DWYER, W. F. KETTENBACH, and GEORGE H. KESTER,

Defendants.

## Instructions Requested by Defendants.

The defendants and each of them request the Court to charge the jury as follows:

Gentlemen of the jury, you are instructed as matter of law, that there is no evidence upon which you can find a verdict of guilty upon the first count in this indictment, and you will therefore return a verdict of not guilty.

Refused.        Exception.

Gentlemen of the jury, you are instructed that there is no evidence, as matter of law, upon which you can find a verdict of guilty upon the second count in this indictment, and you will therefore return a verdict of not guilty.

Refused.        Exception.

Gentlemen of the jury, you are instructed, as matter of law, that there is no evidence upon which you can find a verdict of guilty upon the third count in this indictment, and you will therefore return a verdict of not guilty.

Refused.        Exception.

Gentlemen of the jury, you are instructed, as matter of law, that there is no evidence upon which to return a verdict of guilty as to the fourth count in this indictment and you will therefore return a verdict as to this count.

Refused.        Exception.

Gentlemen of the jury, you the instructed that there is no evidence upon which to return a verdict of guilty as to the fifth count in this indictment, and you will therefore return a verdict of not guilty, as to the fifth count in this indictment.

Refused.  Exception.

Gentlemen of the jury, you are instructed to return a verdict of not guilty as to the defendant William F. Kettenbach.

Refused.  Exception.

Gentlemen of the jury, you are instructed to return a verdict of not guilty as to the defendant George H. Kester.

Refused.  Exception.

Gentlemen of the jury, you are instructed to return a verdict of not guilty as to the defendant William Dwyer.

Refused.  Exception.

Gentlemen of the jury, you are instructed that the evidence, documents and statement of facts and conditions surrounding the entries of Hiram F. Lewis and Edwin M. Lewis, set forth in the indictment as the first and second counts therein, are all insufficient to show the commission of any crime charged in the indictment, as to said entries, and in the consideration of this case you will therefore disregard the testimony of Hiram F. Lewis and Edwin M. Lewis, and consider as to the guilt or innocence of the said defendants without regard to the testimony concerning the entries of either Hiram F. Lewis or Edwin M. Lewis.

Refused.  Exception.

The jury are instructed that you will exclude from your considerations all the testimony and documentary evidence pertaining to the witnesses George

Ray Robinson, Bertsel H. Ferris, Joel H. Benton, Mary J. Harris, Jeanette Harris, Ethel Harris, R. O. Waldman, P. O. Waldman, and Lewis Dreckman, and all their testimony relating to conversations and dealings had with Clarence W. Robnett, and that you will arrive at your verdict in this case, and make up your minds as to the guilt or innocence of the defendants on the offense charged in this indictment, without regard to the evidence of the witnesses last named, to wit, without regard to the testimony of George Ray Robinson, Bertsel H. Ferris, Joel H. Benton, Mary J. Harris, Jeanette Harris, Ethel Harris, R. O. Waldman, P. O. Waldman and Lewis Dreckman, or any or either of them.

Refused.      Exception.

The jury are further instructed that you will exclude from your considerations, all the testimony of the witnesses C. W. Taylor and E. J. Taylor, and all of the documents relating to their respective entries, and all of the conversations and dealings *with* either or both of said witnesses claim to have had with Jackson O'Keefe, and make up your verdict as to the guilt or the innocence of these defendants of the crime charged in this indictment, without regard to the evidence of either C. W. Taylor and E. J. Taylor.

Refused.      Exception.

Gentlemen of the jury, you are instructed as matter of law, that there is no evidence in this case upon which to base a verdict of guilty and you will therefore return a verdict of not guilty.

Refused.      Exception.

All the following requests are refused except as given in substance.

DIETRICH,

Judge.

The jury are instructed that the defendant William Dwyer, in this case, had a perfect right under the law, to locate and assist in locating parties desiring stone and timber claims, upon the public lands of the United States subject to entry under such acts, and he had a perfect right, under the law, to charge such a sum for his services as the parties desiring to file were willing to pay, and he had a further right to secure money for the parties in the way of a loan, to assist them in making their final proof, and he could either make this loan direct or he could do so through other parties, and either he or they could charge such commission as the parties were willing to pay, and in the doing of all these things, none of the defendants would violate any law of the United States, or be an offender thereunder.

Exception.

You are further instructed that it is a legitimate business for one to undertake, either for hire or not, to locate persons upon stone and timber lands, and that is, he may search out a claim, take upon it a would-be locator, point out to him the lines of the claim, assist him in learning the character of the lands, assist him in filing his papers, and discuss with him the matters and things necessary to be proven in his final proof, and may familiarize the entryman with the requirements of the timber and stone law, and with all requirements to comply with the same in order to obtain title to such lands, and to do any and all similar acts to aid and assist such entryman in acquiring title to the said lands; and it is entirely legitimate for any person to loan money to persons desiring to enter lands under the timber and stone acts, for the purpose of defraying the expenses incident to the entry, and to pay for the land and to agree with the entryman that the loan should be secured by a mortgage on the land after entry, and in doing all these things no law of the United States would be violated.

## Exception.

Evidence has been introduced in relation to entries of lands under the Timber and Stone Acts, other than the entries made by the parties named in the indictment and of the alleged and pretended connection of the defendants with such entries. Such evidence was admitted solely for the purpose of aiding the jury to infer intent or to establish a prior design or system which included the doing of the wrongful and unlawful acts charged in this indictment, to wit (the subornation of perjury), and to enable the jury to reach a just conclusion as to the particular charges made against the defendants. But before such other entries are to be considered by the jury, you must be convinced beyond all reasonable doubt and to a moral certainty that in respect to such other entries, the defendants, or two of them, had also unlawfully and fraudulently conspired together to get such other entrymen to commit perjury in their applications to purchase such lands and in the making of the prior agreement to sell said lands to the defendants or some of them. I instruct you that it is immaterial to what extent the defendants may have been guilty of wrong in other entries than the ones named in this indictment, or however well their criminality in relation to other entries is established, if it is established, yet you cannot find the defendants or any of them guilty in this case, for the crime of which they stand accused, unless you find to a moral certainty, and beyond all reasonable doubt, that two or all of the defendants in this indictment, knowingly, and fraudulently conspired and agreed together, to defraud the United States, by procuring Guy L. Wilson, Frances A. Justice or Charles H. Carey to commit perjury in their acquisition of timber and stone lands.

On the other hand, I instruct you that although you may believe from the testimony, beyond all reasonable doubt, that Frances A. Justice and Guy L. Wilson and Charles H. Carey, committed perjury in their applications to enter the lands sought to be obtained by them, yet that of itself would not warrant a verdict of guilty in this case; you would be required to go further and find that two or more of the defendants in this indictment, knowingly and designedly, procure such entrymen to commit perjury, in furtherance of the conspiracy to defraud the United States, as heretofore explained to you. Unless you are satisfied of this fact beyond all reasonable doubt and to a moral certainty, then you must acquit the defendants.

You are further instructed that when the acts of a person and the conduct of a person are such that they may be equally well explained and understood on a theory that the same were done in furtherance of a lawful purpose of intent, or of a criminal intent, it is the duty of the jury to assume them to have been done and prompted by the lawful intent rather than the unlawful intent or purpose, and that the party whose act is in question, acted from innocent motives, and if you find that the evidence in this case, of the acts, and conduct of the defendants is reasonably explained from a standpoint of innocence, then it is your duty to acquit the defendants, and you should render a verdict of not guilty.

Gentlemen of the Jury: The defendants in this case are charged with a crime of conspiracy to defraud the United States; they have been charged with such crime by an indictment found and presented by a Grand Jury within the District of Idaho. I instruct you that an indictment is simply a formal accusation made by the Grand Jury charging the persons named therein as defendants, with the crime therein set out, these cases with the crime to *fraud* the United States. You are instructed, as a matter of law, that this indictment is no evidence against the defendants or any or either of them, and that you will not take into consideration as an evidence of guilt the fact that an indictment has been returned against these defendants or any or either of them, but I instruct you that none of the defendants in this case is to be prejudicted by the fact that such indictments have been returned and that the guilt or innocence of the defendants is to be tried by this jury without regard to the fact that the defendants or any of them had been indicted. The law is that the defendant is presumed to be innocent of all crime, and especially of the crime charged in the indictment until his guilt is proven by competent evidence beyond a reasonable doubt.

The rule necessarily includes another rule that when the act of a man is such that two conclusions may be drawn therefrom, one of innocence and one of guilt, the jury is bound to presume the defendant innocent, and any act which is consistent with innocence or with guilt is to be taken by you as consistent with innocence, and you are not to construe any such act as consistent with guilt. The presumption of innocence in such a case precludes you from construing a doubtful act to any evidence of guilt whatever.

And upon this point, the same rule applies as to a criminal intent. If any acts have been proven before you in this case which will support a theory of innocence and a theory of guilt, I instruct you that, as a matter of law, you are to be controlled by the presumption that the defendants are innocent, because the presumption of innocence attaches to every man whether charged with crime or not, and is to be taken as so much evidence in his favor, and any act which will support a theory of innocence as well as a theory of guilt is to be taken by you as supporting the theory of innocence and not of guilt, because before a defendant can be convicted of a crime his guilt of the offence charged *sd* well as an intent to commit such an offence must be established by competent evidence and beyond a reasonable doubt.

Courts have tried in numerous ways to aid juries to determine what is a reasonable doubt, and with that sence in view you are instructed that a reasonable doubt is a doubt which arises upon a consideration of all the testimony which will cause any juror to pause before deciding a defendant guilty, as upon a consideration of all the testimony a doubt as to whether the testimony has proven the defendant guilty, or a doubt as to the innocence of the defendants or any of them, or a doubt arising from the evidence as to the criminal intent of the defendants or any of them, must be decided in favor of the defendants, and it is your duty to acquit the defendants or such of the defendants as to which you have a doubt.

This is one of the reasons why an act which is as consistent with innocence as it is with guilt must be resolved in favor of innocence.

Exception.

## INSTRUCTION AS TO ACCOMPLICES.

The *defendant* request the Court to give the following charge:

Gentlemen of the Jury: In the commission of crimes the law recognizes two classes of criminals: First, Principals, or those who commit the crime itself, and second, Accomplices, or those who aid in the commission of the crime. Any person who cooperates or aids or assists in the commission of a crime, is an accomplice.

Under their own testimony in this cause, Guy L. Wilson, Frances A. Justice and Charles H. Carey,

is each an accomplice in the crime which claims to
have aided in commiting; if you believe from the
evidence introduced that the crime charged was committed—which fact you must find beyond a reasonable doubt—than these people named are accomplices. As to the witnesses Hiram F. Lewis and E.
M. Lewis, I instruct you that their evidence does not
show or tend to show that any crime was committed.
*You therefore* disregard their testimony entirely in
this case. As to witnesses Lambdin and Cornell, I
instruct you that even if their testimony be true, and
you should find beyond a reasonable doubt that their
statement of an alleged commission of an offense is
true, such witnesses are accomplices in the commission of the wrong to which they testify, if there was
any wrong.

Your knowledge of human nature is sufficient to
inform you that the most natural thing for a person
who has committed a wrong to do is to try to lay the
blame for the wrong, as well as the wrong itself, on
some one else. From this human experience, the law
has devolved the following positive rule, which is
embodies in our law (Sec. 7871, R. S. Idaho):

"A conviction cannot be had on the testimony of
an accomplice unless he is corroborated by other evidence which in itself and without the aid of the testimony of the accomplice tends to connect the defendant with the commission of the offense; and the
corroboration is not sufficient if it merely shows the
commission of the offense or the circumstances
thereof."

I instruct you, as a matter of law, that the documentary evidence, consisting of deeds, notes, and final proofs or application papers, or all of said documents together, is not of itself sufficient or any corroboration of the testimony of the witnesses for the United States. An accomplice must be corroborated by testimony, other than his own or the testimony of other accomplices. One accomplice cannot corroborate another. To illustrate, I instruct you that the testimony of Guy L. Wilson, of itself, or taken with the documents which he claims relate to his transaction, is not sufficient to show either the crime, or the connection of the defendants therewith; the statement as to him applies to all the witnesses for the State, who are in like position. This being true, the testimony of Frances A. Justice, does not corroborate that of Guy L. Wilson or of any other accomplice. As stated before, the testimony of one accomplice cannot corroborate that of another. The policy of the law, and the plain provisions of the law require that the corroboration shall come from some independent source. If, therefore, you find that the testimony of the witnesses for the Government, who admit to having taken up timber and stone claims and having sold them, but who state that wrong was done by them, is unsupported by independent evidence which of itself tends to prove the crime of conspiracy and to connect the defendant with the commission of the offense, then you must acquit the defendants. This corroboration is not sufficient if it merely shows the commission of the offense, or the circumstances thereof; it must go further and show not only the commission of the offense charged, but the participation of the defendants or some of them therein.

A question which arises in all this class of cases relates to the right of an entryman under the timber and stone law, to dispose of his lands. I instruct you, as matter of law, that the statute does not restrict the right or the power of an entryman to sell or mortgage his lands, after final proof. A person acquiring lands under the timber and stone laws has a perfect right to sell the lands, immediately after the making of final proof, even though final certificate has not issued. Likewise an entryman under these laws has a perfect right to sell the lands so acquired, immediately after the issuance of the final receipt or certificate. The statute in this respect does not require the entryman to hold the lands so acquired any length of time whatever; all that the statute denounces is a prior agreement—the acting for another in the purchase. If at the time of the making of final proof, or the time when title passes from the Government to the entryman, no one save the purchaser has any claim upon the land itself, or any contract or agreement for it, the act is satisfied. The defendants had a *perfect to* go or send into that vicinity and make known generally or to individuals a willingness to buy timber lands, at a price in excess of that which it would cost to obtain it from the Government, and any person knowing of that offer might rightfully go to the Land Office and make application to purchase the timber tract from the Government, with a view of selling the same to the defendants or to any or either of them, and in this there would be no violation of the law.

Another question which arises in this case is the right of the defendants to loan money to applicants. I instruct you that any of the defendants had a perfeet right to loan money to applicants for lands under the Timber and Stone Acts, and to have an agreement with such entrymen that after the title was acquired from the Government, such entryman would mortgage the lands thus acquired to any of the defendants so loaning the money, and in doing this there would be no statute of the United States violated. The entryman has a right to borrow enough money to pay the entry cost of the entry including the location fee and the publication fee and the costs of his trip to examine the lands, and to secure such sum with a mortgage on the lands, after title is acquired, and in so doing there is no violation of the laws of the United States.

The jury are instructed that there is no law of the United States preventing an entryman from agreeing with any person at any time that, when he has proved upon his land, if he desires to sell, he will give that person the first chance to buy it, and that such an understanding of itself is not in violation of law. The very fact that the entryman may have said that, after he should prove up he would sell if he could obtain a satisfactory price, or that he would give another the first chance to purchase, should he conclude to sell, or the mere fact that a party may have said to the entryman, when he proved up, he would give him a stated sum, such statements alone would not constitute an agreement.

The jury are instructed that in this case it is charged that the purpose of the defendants was to defraud the Government by means of false, freigned, fraudulent, untrue, illegal, and fictitious entries of land under the timber and stone laws of the United States, and that they cannot convict these defendants upon this charge in any case where the entry was not false, freigned, fraudulent, untrue, illegal, or fictitions.

The jury are instructed that the defendants, or any of them, had a perfect right to advance money to entrymen to pay filing fees, and to agree that, in the event the entrymen desired to sell after he had proved up and the defendant then desired to buy, such advances should be credited on the sale, or if no such arrangement was thereafter made, the money would be refunded, and that such an agreement would not, in and by itself, be a violation of any law of the United States.

## INSTRUCTIONS AS TO CIRCUMSTANTIAL EVIDENCE.

The defendants request the Court to charge the jury as follows:

Gentlemen of the Jury: The crime of conspiracy, like any other crime, may be proved by the circumstantial evidence thereof. The guilt of a defendant may also be established by like evidence. But as to circumstantial evidence, I instruct you that before you can find such evidence that a crime has been committed—or if you find that crime as charged has been committed, then before you are justified in finding the defendants or any or either of them guilty thereof, the circumstances proven must be such that no reasonable theory of innocence can be based on it; that is to say, in order to convict on circumstantial evidence, the circumstances themselves must be proven; you are not permitted to infer them, but there must be positive proof of the circumstances themselves. After the circumstances are proven, it must follow from such proven circumstances that the defendant is guilty beyond a reasonable doubt. If the circumstances do not point to guilt and to guilt alone, that is to say, if the circumstances are explainable on the theory of innocence, or, in other words, if the circumstances proven are consistent with innocence, then I instruct you that such circumstantial evidence is not sufficient to show guilt on the part of any of the defendants.

## INSTRUCTIONS AS TO ACCOMPLICE—THE PRINCIPAL OFFENDER.

The defendants jointly and severally request the Court to instruct the jury as follows:

Gentlemen of the Jury: In this case, it is sought to prove the conspiracy, by the testimony of entrymen, each of whom testifies that he committed perjury in his application to purchase lands. Without the proof of the perjury itself, there could be no crime of conspiracy to defraud by subornation of perjury. The overt acts charged here is the fact that it is claimed the witnesses for the Government committed perjury in their applications, and one of the defendants at least, in committing an overt act under the conspiracy, suborned these witnesses, or some of them, to commit perjury, in furtherance of the common design charged, to defraud the United States.

I instruct you, as matter of law, that under these circumstances the party committing the perjury is the principal offender. If, then, you believe that Guy L. Wilson, or Frances E. Justice, or Charles H. Carey, or either of them, committed perjury in their preliminary applications or their application to purchase under the timber and stone laws, *that* I instruct you that you must disregard the evidence of such witness as convinces you that he did commit perjury, because he thereby admits that he is the principal offender. As to such witnesses as did not commit perjury in their applications, I instruct you there is no evidence of any crime.

You will therefore bring in a verdict for the defendants and each of them.

## INSTRUCTIONS AS TO CORPUS DELICTI.

Gentlemen of the Jury: Before a conviction can be had in a criminal case, the prosecution must prove two things:

First. The prosecution must prove to a moral certainty and beyond a reasonable doubt that the crime of conspiracy to defraud the United States has been committed.

Second. The prosecution must prove to a moral certainty and beyond all *reasonable* the fact that two or more of these defendants committed this crime.

In this cause it is charged that the defendants conspired to defraud the United States out of large tracts of timber lands, by procuring entrymen to commit perjury in their original applications to purchase these lands.

Before you can find that the crime of conspiracy has been committed in this case, you must find from the evidence and beyond all reasonable doubt:

First. That the defendants, or two of them, agreed together to acquire the public lands of the United States, by means of false entries by individuals, and that they agreed together to procure entrymen to commit perjury in their original applications to enter lands. This fact must be proven to your satisfaction, to a moral certainty and beyond all reasonable doubt. If this fact that the defendants agreed to procure entrymen to commit perjury is not proven beyond all reasonable doubt, to a moral certainty, then it is your duty to acquit the defendants.

Second. You must thereafter find that the defendants did, in the furtherance of such purpose, actually procure the persons named in this defendant, to wit, Guy L. Wilson, or Frances A. Justice, or Charles H. Carey, to commit perjury in their applications to purchase lands. If one of the defedants only did this, then you must acquit the other two, as the crime of conspiracy requires two persons or more to commit it. One person cannot be guilty of the crime of conspiracy, as it requires two or more persons to commit this crime.

You are instructed that the defendants had a right to procure Guy L. Wilson, or Frances A. Justice, or Charles H. Carey, or any other person, to take a timber and stone claim, with the view of buying it from them; the only question as to the wrongfulness of the entry is, was there a prior definite agreement that either of said persons or all of them should sell this claim to the defendants; and did the defendants and each of them know of such agreement, or operate under a common understanding that they would wrongfully procure persons to commit perjury in entering lands which they thereafter were intending to buy. Unless all these things are proven to your satisfaction, to a moral certainty and beyond all reasonable doubt, it is your duty to acquit the defendants.

[Endorsed]: No. 615. United States, Plaintiff, vs. Wm. Dwyer, Wm. F. Kettenbach, and George H. Kester, Defendants. Requests of the Defendants to Charge. Filed June 15, 1907. A. L. Richardson, Clerk.

———

*In the United States District Court, Northern Division, District of Idaho.*

THE UNITED STATES OF AMERICA

vs.

WILLIAM F. KETTENBACH et al.

**Instructions by the Court to the Jury.**

Gentlemen of the Jury: Before finally committing to you the determination of the issues which have engaged our attention now for more than three weeks, it is my duty to explain to you certain principles of law, which should guide you in weighing, and applying to the charges made in the indictment, the evidence which is before you. If I remember correctly, some of you, when you were being interrogated as to your qualifications to sit as jurors, stated that you had never before performed jury duty, and I therefore deem it not improper at the outset, to say some things, which to others of you, more familiar with legal procedure, may seem commonplace, if not wholly unnecessary.

The plaintiff in this case is the United States of America; the defendants are William F. Kettenbach, George H. Kester and William Dwyer—these three alone. Other persons have, during the trial, been referred to as being connected with these three defendants, but such other persons are not now on trial.

Before you were called upon to serve as trial jurors, a grand jury had, on November 6, 1905, presented to this Court what is called an indictment, which, immediately after you were sworn, was read to you and to which, as you were informed, the three defendants each pleaded not guilty. This indictment, you must bear in mind, is in itself no proof of the guilt of the defendants; it is a mere formal accusation made by the Government against the defendants, charging them with the commission of an offense. The Government thus advises the defendants, in advance of their trial, of the issues they must meet, in order that they may prepare their defense. Hence, the defendants are not to be prejudiced, nor are you in any measure to be influenced, by the mere fact that the defendants have been indicted.

Under the procedure provided by law the defendants (after they have pleaded not guilty, that is, denied the charges made in the indictment) are put upon trial before a jury, called a trial jury, whose duty it is to determine whether these charges are true or false. Such a jury you are in this case.

Having been sworn, you were first advised by the Government, through its representative, the District Attorney, somewhat in detail what the Government expected to prove; and of the nature of the proof. This statement, like the indictment, is not to be considered as evidence; it was made merely for the purpose of enabling you the better to understand the testimony which followed, and it is, therefore, now no longer of any value to you. The same may be said of the statement by counsel for the defendants, made before the defendants' proof was offered. You have heard all the evidence, and when you find your verdict, it should be upon the evidence, and that alone.

After the evidence was closed, counsel for the Government and counsel for the defendants made their arguments to you. Under the law these arguments have a legitimate place in the trial of a cause, and are often of great assistance to a jury in analyzing and giving proper wieght to the evidence. Of course, you must not be misled by any misstatement of the evidence; nor are you bound to accept the inference or theories of counsel. If, after you have considered them, they do not commend themselves to you, you are at liberty to discard them. It is the province of counsel to suggest; but, after all, it is for you to consider and decide the weight and significance to be given to any particular portion or all of the evidence. Not even the Court can deprive you of the right, or relieve you of the responsibility, of determining the facts and passing upon the wieght and credibility of the testimony. That is for you exclusively. While I would have the right, if I saw fit so to do, to comment upon the evidence, and express n.y views relative thereto, you would not be bound to accept my view. But I have no intention of doing so in this case; I am going to leave that responsibility entirely with you, and if I have at any time during the trial inadvertently expressed, or if, in these instructions, I should incidentially express any opinion as to the weight or creditibility of any particular testimony, you are at liberty to disregard such opinion.

Upon the other hand, while you are the exclusive judges of the facts, I, alone, must assume the responsibility of declaring the principles of law by which you should be guided. As my oath of office pledges me to leave to you the determination of the facts, so your oath as jurors, binds you to accept my statement of the law. You may have preconceived ideas, not in harmony with what I may declare the law to be, but even so, it is your sworn duty in this case to apply to the evidence the law as I give it to you. And it is your duty to do this even though counsel upon the one side or the other may entertain, and may in their arguments have stated, views out of harmony with what I explain to you the law to be.

In discussing the facts before a jury, it not infrequently becomes necessary for counsel to advise the jury what, in their judgment, the law is, in order that they may properly analyze and group the evidence in support of their contentions; but it is always to be understood that such statements of the law are not binding upon the jury, and that the jury must look to the Court for the law.

Now, when you go to your jury room, and indeed during your entire deliberations, you will bear in mind and be governed by the general rule that each defendant in this case, as in every criminal case, is presumed to be innocent of the crime charged, until his guilt is proved by competent evidence beyond a reasonable doubt. This humane principle is fundamental in all of our criminal procedure. And closely connected with it is the familiar principle that when a defendant's conduct and acts are such that they can as well be attributed to an honest and lawful purpose upon his part, as to a criminal intent, the jury should assume that his motives and purposes were innocent and not criminal.

I would like to be able to give to you a definition of the phrase "reasonable doubt" which would make the matter entirely plain to you, but obviously it is impossible to describe a mental condition with mathematical certainty. Perhaps, however, I can assist you: You will take note that the phrase is "reasonable doubt." Not every doubt therefore will excuse you from finding guilt. Reasonable doubt is not such a doubt as anyone may conjure up merely for the purpose of escaping the duty of returning an un-

pleasant verdict, or a doubt which one may imagine
or surmise without basis of fact in the testimony.
The doubt which should deter you from finding a
defendant guilty must be based upon reason, and
must be reasonable in view of all the evidence. If,
after you have fairly and impartially considered all
the evidence, with a sincere and reasonable effort to
reach a conclusion, you can candidly say that you are
not satisfied of the defendants' guilt, you have a reasonable doubt. But upon the other hand, if, after
an impartial and earnest consideration and compari-
son of all the evidence, your minds are in such a condition that you can truthfully say that you have an
abiding conviction to a moral certainty that the
charge is true, then you have no reasonable doubt
and it becomes your duty so to declare by your verdict.

You will observe that I have said that *each* defendant is presumed to be innocent, etc. While the
three defendants are jointly charged, and have been
put on trial together, it is not your right to acquit
all, simply because you may not be able to find one
guilty; nor should you convict any one of the defendants simply because you may find another defendant or other defendants guilty. While the three
are being tried together, charged with the same offense, each stands before you in his own right, and
with the same presumptions of innocence and the
same perils and responsibilities as if he were being
tried alone.

Now bearing in mind these general principles, you
should, at the outset, fix clearly in your minds the

exact offense of which the defendants are accused and of which you are to declare their innocence or their guilt. For, as I shall have occasion to explain to you, while in the indictment other offenses may be incidentially alleged, and the evidence may, in your judgment, tend to prove other offenses against one or more of the defendants they are now on trial for *conspiracy* and that alone; not for perjury or subornation of perjury, or any other crime except conspiracy.

The indictment charges against the defendants conspiracy to defraud the United States, in violation of Section 5410 of the Revised Statutes of the United States. This section reads as follows:

"If two or more persons conspire, either to commit any offense against the United States, or to defraud the United States, in any manner, or for any purpose, and one or more of such parties do any act to effect the object of the conspiracy, all the parties to such conspiracy shall be liable to a penalty,"

—and thereupon the penalty is stated.

This statute is the basis of the charge, and it has been incumbent upon the prosecution to show beyond a reasonable doubt that the defendants violated it in the manner substantially as set forth in the indictment.

You will bear in mind that the indictment contains five counts or five accusations, in each of which, however, the defendants are charged with a violation of this section of the statute, that is, a conspiracy to defraud the United States. The several counts are very similar in form, and, with the exception of dates, names of entrymen of the lands, and the descriptions of the lands entered, the five counts are without material distinction; and I will, therefore, fully explain to you only the first count and then call your attention to the difference between it and each of the other counts.

In the first count it is substantially charged that on the 26th day of October, 1904, in Nez Perce County, State of Idaho, the defendants, William F. Kettenbach, George H. Kester and William Dwyer, and other persons to the Grand Jury unknown, did unlawfully conspire, combine, confederate and agree together and among themselves, to defraud the United States of the title and possession of large tracts of land situate in the County of Shoshone and State of Idaho, by means of false, fraudulent and illegal entries of said lands, under the laws of the United States, the same being then and there public lands, of which public lands the North one-half of the Northeast one-fourth and the Southwest one-fourth of the Northeast one-fourth of Section 29, Township 39 North, of Range 5 East, of Boise Meridian *and* was a part.

That according to and in pursuance of such conspiracy and agreement and for the purpose of effecting or consummating the object thereof, the defendants, on the 26th day of October, 1904, fraudulently, unlawfully and corruptly persuaded and induced one Edward M. Lewis to appear at the United States Land Office at Lewiston, Idaho, and there to make and file in said Land Office an affidavit or sworn statement whereby the said Lewis made application to enter and purchase, under an Act of Congress, approved June 3, 1878, entitled "An Act for the sale of timber lands in the States of California, Oregon, Nevada and in Washington ITerritory," as amended by an Act of Congress, approved August 4, 1892, entitled "An Act to authorize the entry of lands, valuable for building stone, under the placer mining law," the land which I have heretofore particularly described, which affidavit or sworn statement was known by said Lewis and the defendants to be false and fraudulent. The indictment further alleges that the said Lewis, in his said affidavit, stated that he did not apply to purchase said land on speculation, but in good faith to appropriate it to his own exclusive use and benefit and that he had not, directly or indirectly, made any agreement or contract, in any way or manner, with any person or persons, whomsoever, by which the title which he might acquire from the Government to said land might inure, in whole or in part, to the benefit of any person except himself. It is charged that these statements were false, and that said Lewis and the defendants well knew that they were false, and well knew that said Lewis did not apply to enter or purchase said lands in good faith and for the purpose of appropriating the same to his exclusive use and benefit, but that, in truth and in fact, he made such application for the use and benefit of the defendants and other persons, and that said Lewis applied to enter said land for the purpose of speculation and not in good faith, for his exclusive use and benefit; and that prior to the making and filing of said affidavit or sworn statement he had entered into a contract or agreement with the defendants whereby he had agreed that the title which he might acquire from the Government of the United States to said land should inure to the benefit of the defendants.

It is further charged that according to and in pursuance of said conspiracy and unlawful agreement and for the purpose of effecting the onject of the conspiracy, the defendants, on the 20th day of January, 1905, fraudulently and corruptly persuaded and induced Lewis to make oath and to testify falsely before the Register of the United States Land Office at Lewiston, in support of his said application to purchase said lands and for the purpose of procuring title thereto from the Government; that at said time, in order to procure title to said land, he falsely testified that he had not, since making his said application on the 26th day of October, 1904, sold or transferred his claim and that he had not, directly or indirectly, made any agreement or contract in any way or manner, with any person whomsoever, by which the title which he might acquire from the Government of the United States might inure, in whole or in part, to the benefit of any other person, and that he made the entry for said land in good faith and for the appropriation of said land exclusively to his own use and benefit and not for the use and benefit of any other person; and that no other person, firm, or corporation, or association had any interest in said entry or the said land or the timber thereon; and, it is charged, that said written affidavit, testimony or sworn statement, was false and fraudulent, as was well known to said Lewis and the defendants; that Lewis was, at the time of making said statement, acting as the agent of and in collusion with the defendants, with the intention of giving to the defendants the benefit of said lands and the timber thereon and that he had entered into an agreement with the defendants whereby he had agreed that the title which he might acquire from the Government, to the land, should inure to the benefit of the defendants.

It is further charged that in pursuance of said conspiracy and for the purpose of effecting the object thereof, the defendants caused to be paid to the Receiver of said Land Office, the price of said land as fixed by law; that thereafter, upon the 20th day of January, 1905, the defendants, in pursuance of said conspiracy and for the purpose of effecting the object thereof, persuaded and induced J. B. West, the Register of said Land Office, to issue and deliver to said Lewis a certificate of purchase and Register's Receipt, in the name of said Edward M. Lewis, for the purchase of said land; and further persuaded and induced said Register to certify that on presentation of said certificate to the Commission of the General Land Office, the said Edward M. Lewis would be entitled to receive a patent for the said land.

The indictment sets forth these matters in great detail, but you will observe that, in substance, the charge is that the defendants and other persons conspired together to procure from the United States the title to public lands under the provisions of what has been frequently referred to in the testimony as

the Timber and Stone Act, by procuring and inducing Lewis to swear falsely to material matters, both
at the time he made his application to enter and at
the time he made his proof upon the land described,
at the United States Land Office at Lewiston, Idaho,
by false statements or oaths, thus deceiving the officers of the United States, authorized to convey title
to public lands, and thus fraudulently procuring the
title thereto.

There have been introduced in evidence several affidavits or sworn statements required to be made at
the time of the application to enter and also the testimony or sworn statements made at the time of what
has been referred to as final proof and you have thus
been made familiar with both the form and substance
of these statements prescribed by law and Department regulations.

In the second count the date of the conspiracy is
alleged to be August 29, 1904, and in said count it is
charged that the defendants in pursuance of such conspiracy and to effect the object thereof, persuaded
and induced one Hyrum F. Lewis to procure title
to the Northwest one-fourth of Section 20, Township 38 North, of Range 5 East, of Boise Meridian,
by fraud and perjury similar to that charge in the
first count.

In the third count of the indictment it is charged
that the conspiracy was entered into on the 23d day
of August, 1904, and in pursuance thereof, and to
effect its object, the defendants persuaded and induced one Charles Carey to procure title to the North
half of the Northeast quarter, and the North half

of the Northwest quarter of Section fifteen, Township 38 North, of Range 6 East, Boise Meridian, by means of perjury and fraud similar to that charged in the first count.

In the fourth count the defendants are charged with conspiring together on April 25, 1904, in pursuance of which conspiracy and to effect the object thereof, they persuaded and induced one Guy L. Wilson to procure title to Lots 3 and 4, and the Northeast one-fourth of the Southwest one-fourth and the Northwest one-fourth of the Southeast one-fourth, Section 19, Township 39 North, of Range 5 East, of Boise Meridian, by fraud and perjury similar to that charged in the first count.

In the fifth count the defendants are charged with having conspired together on the 25th day of April, 1904, in pursuance of which conspiracy and to effect the object thereof, they persuaded and induced one Frances A. Justice to procure title to Lots 3 and 4 and the East one-half of the Southwest one-fourth of Section 19, Township 38 North, of Range 6 East, of Boise Meridian, by fraud and perjury similar to that charged in the first count.

You will observe that the entries referred to in the indictment and, indeed, I think all of the entries referred to in the testimony, were made under what has been frequently referred to as the Timber and Stone Act. By this act it is provided that the surveyed public lands of the United States, which are not included within the military, Indian or other reservations of the United States, and which are chiefly valuable for timber, but unfit for cultivation, and which have not been offered at public sale according to law, may be sold to citizens of the United States and persons who have declared their intention to become such, in quantities not exceeding one hundred and sixty acres to any one person, or association of persons, at the minimum price of $2.50 per acre.   Section 2 of the Act is as follows:

"That any person desiring to avail himself of the provisions of this act shall file with the Register of the proper district a written statement in duplicate, one of which is to be transmitted to the General Land Office, designating by legal subdivisions the particular tract of land he desires to purchase, setting forth that the same is unfit for cultivation, and valuable chiefly for its timber or stone; that it is uninhabited; contains no mining or other improvements; except for ditch or canal purposes, where any such do exist, save such as were made by or belong to the applicant, nor as deponent verily believes, any valuable deposit of gold, silver, cinnabar, copper or coal; that deponent has made no other application under this Act; that he does not apply to purchase the same on speculation, but in good faith to appropriate it to his own exclusive use and benefit, and that he has not, directly or indirectly, made any agreement or contract, in any way or manner, with any person or persons, whomsoever, by which the title which he might acquire from the Government of the United States should inure, in whole or in part to the benefit of any person except himself; which statement must be verified by the oath of the applicant before the Register or the Receiver of the

Land Office within the district where the land is situated; and if any person taking such oath shall swear falsely in the premises, he shall be subject to all the pains and penalties of perjury, and shall forfeit the money which he may have paid for said lands, and all right and title to the same; and any grant or conveyance which he may have made, except in the hands of bona fide purchasers, shall be null and void.

"So much of Section 3 as is material reads as follows:

"That upon the filing of said statement, as provided in the second section of this act, the Register of the Land Office shall post a notice of such application, embracing a description of the land by legal subdivisions, in his office, for a period of sixty days, and shall furnish the applicant a copy of the same for publication at the expense of such applicant, in a newspaper published nearest the location of the premises, for a like period of time; and after the expiration of said sixty days, if no adverse claim shall have been filed, the person desiring to purchase shall furnish to the Register of the Land Office satisfactory evidence, first, that said notice of the application prepared by the Register aforesaid was duly published in a newspaper as herein required; secondly, that the land is of the character contemplated in this act, unoccupied and without improvements, other than those excepted, either mining or agricultural, and that it apparently contains no valuable deposits of gold, silver, cinnabar, copper or coal; and upon payment to the proper officer of the purchase money of said land, together with the fees of the Register and the Receiver, as provided for in the case of mining claims in the twelfth section of the Act approved May tenth, eighteen hundred and seventy-two, the applicant may be permitted to enter said tract, and on the transmission to the General Land Office of the papers and testimony in the case, a patent shall issue thereon.''

Effect is to be given to the provisions of the law by regulations to be prescribed by the Commissioner of the General Land Office at Washington.

You will observe that, under this law and the regulations of the Department, the first step on the part of anyone desiring to acquire lands of the character contemplated in the Act, is the filing in the Land Office of a written statement, sworn to before the Register or Receiver, designating the particular tract which the applicant desires to purchase and setting forth that the land is unfit for cultivation and valuable chiefly for its timber or stone; that it is uninhabited; that it contains no mining or other improvements; and that it contains no valuable deposits of gold, silver, cinnabar, copper or coal; that the applicant has made no other application under the Act, and that he does not apply to purchase the land on speculation, but in good faith to appropriate it to his own exclusive use and benefit; that he has not, directly or indirectly, made any agreement or contract, in any way or manner, with any person or persons whomsoever by which the title which he might acquire from the Government of the United States should inure, in whole or in part, to the benefit of any person except himself.

Anyone swearing falsely in such statement subjects himself to all the pains and penalties of perjury.

After this sworn statement is filed the Receiver posts a notice of the application, embracing a description of the land, in his office, for a period of sixty days, the applicant being furnished with a copy of the notice for publication in a newspaper nearest the location of the premises, for a like period of time.

After the expiration of the said sixty days, the applicant must furnish to the Register of the Land Office, satisfactory evidence that the land is of the character contemplated in the Act; that the applicant has not sold or transferred the land since making his sworn statement, and has not, directly or indirectly, made any agreement or contract, in any way or manner, with any person whomsoever, by which the title he may acquire from the Government may inure, in whole or in part, to the benefit of any person except himself; and that he makes his entry in good faith, for the appropriation of the land for his own exclusive use, and not for the use or benefit of any other person. Certain questions in detail are asked of the applicant which he is required to answer for the purpose of enabling the officers of the Land Department to determine whether or not the entryman has complied with the law in these respects, and the Court advises you that these regulations of the Land Department, made for the purpose of enabling the officers to carry out and execute the law, have the effect of law.

Now, as I have before stated to you, the charge here against the defendants is that they conspired or unlawfully agreed together to defraud the United States out of large tracts of public lands; and it is, in substance, alleged that this fraud, to be perpetrated upon the Government, consisted in procuring entrymen to commit perjury, that is to swear falsely, both in applying for and in entering or making proof upon lands under the act above referred to. What, then is perjury? It is defined thus by statute:

"Every person who, having taken an oath before a competent tribunal, officer or person, in any case in which a law of the United States authorizes an oath to be administered, that he will testify, declare, depose or certify truly, or that any written testimony, declaration, deposition or certificate, by him subscribed, is true, willfully, and contrary to such oath, states or subscribes any material matter, which he does not believe to be true is guilty of perjury."

You will notice that the sworn statement must not only be false but that the person making such statement must, at the time, not believe it to be true; hence, if a false statement is made by a person under oath, by inadvertance, without his knowing or intending it to be false, there is no perjury.

Every person who procures another to commit perjury is guilty of subornation of perjury.

Remembering now, that the indictment charges the defendants with having combined, fraudulently, to acquire public lands by inducing persons to procure such lands from the Government, by falsely representing that they had complied with said Timber and Stone Act; let us, for a moment, turn our attention to this act and see what it means, that is, what it permits and what it prohibits. In explaining to you its meaning I quote language which very aptly expresses my views and which I desire you to accept as a correct exposition of the law;

"The statute in forbidding the applicant to make, directly or indirectly, any agreement or contract in any way or manner with any person by which the title he may acquire from the Government shall inure in whole or in part to the benefit of any person except himself means by the word 'agreement' that there must be a meeting of minds expressed in some tangible way, and must be intended in some way to be binding upon the parties. One party may have intended to sell; the other party may have intended to buy; yet this would not be enough unless the intention of each was in some way communicated from the one to the other and was understood and agreed to by both. An agreement, as the word 'agreement' is used, need not be in writing; it need not be of sufficient formality or of a nature to be enforced in a court. It is enough if it is proved beyond a reasonable doubt that in some way the minds of the applicant and some other person have met definitely, understandingly; that there is a mutual consent upon the point that when the applicant may acquire title to the land from the United States it shall inure to the benefit of such other person for a consideration; that is, that in truth and in fact the applicant is really to acquire the land for the use and benefit of another.   And any words or any acts and words manifesting this mutual consent of the minds of the parties are sufficient to constitute a contract or agreement.

"You will readily appreciate the policy which *pre-*vades the Timber and Stone Act.   It is meant to enable such persons as may be qualified, to acquire by purchase certain classes of public lands unfit for cultivation, subject to entry under its provision which have been read to you; but an entryman must apply for and enter the lands in good faith for his own exclusive use and benefit.   He cannot lend himself to other and become merely an instrument for the acquisition of lands under an agreement that the other shall pay all the expenses of his entry and give him a sum of money, for exercising his right, and that when he may acquire title to the land he shall convey it to them or someone of them.

"The entryman must always deal in good faith with the Government, from the initiation of his claim, that is by an application to purchase, up to and including his deposition or sworn statement at final proof.   Then when he has made payment into the land office of the purchase money for his tract he is permitted to enter it and thereafter to receive patent therefor.

"A person qualified under the law has a right to enter lands under the provisions of the Timber and Stone Act, even though he considers, prior to the time of making his sworn statement and his final proof, a sale of it as soon as he can, after he makes his final proof and obtains the usual Receiver's receipt.

"That is to say, gentlemen, you will understand that the law does not make it obligatory that an entrymen who acquires title under the Timber and Stone Act, shall keep the land, nor does it control his use or right to dispose of it for any period of time after he shall have complied with the provisions of the law in perfecting the right to the claim. But the statute does denounce a prior agreement, the acting for another in the purchase from the Government of the United States. However, if when the title passes from the Government to the entryman, by Receiver's receipt after final proof, no one save the purchaser has any claim upon it or any contract or agreement for it, the law is satisfied.

"The act does not in any respect limit the dominion which the purchaser has over the land after he acquires his final receipt from the Government of the United States, or restrict in the slightest degree his power of alen*i*ation."

There is some evidence tending to show that the defendants Kettenbach and K*a*ster were in the market for the purchase of lands entered under the Timber and Stone Act and that they have acquired the possession of and title to large tracts of such lands and that they loaned money to various entrymen; also that the defendant Dwyer was what is termed by some of the witnesses a timber cruiser and locator.

By themselves these acts would be legitimate and would not imply or suggest any wrong. There is no limit to the amount of land which a man may legally purchase or otherwise acquire after the same has passed final proof and receipt has issued.

"A man may legitimately go or send into a vicinity and make known generally or to individuals a willingness to buy timber lands at a price in excess of that which it would cost, to obtain it from the Government, and any person knowing of that offer, may rightfully go to the Land Office and make application and purchase a timber tract from the Government. Nor do I think that the mere indifinite expectation on the part of a claimant or applicant to give someone a preference in buying the land, if he would give as much as anyone, would be in conflict with the oath required by the applicant. So a man may legitimately undertake, either gratuitously or for hire, to locate persons upon stone and timber claims; that is, he may search out a claim; take upon it a would-be locator; point out to him the lines of the claim; tell him of the character of the ground; and assist him in estimating the amount of timber on the claim and do any and all similar acts to aid and assist him in acquiring title to the land. So it is entirely ligitimate for a person to loan money to persons desiring to enter lands under the Timber and Stone Act for the purpose of defraying the expenses incident to the entry, and to pay for the land, and to agree with the would-be entryman that the loan so made would be secured by a mortgage on the land. But a loan and mortgage, if made, must be in good faith, and not under any prior contract or agreement, direct or indirect, that when the title to the land is secured, the loan and mortgage shall be satisfied by transfer of the title to the land.''

I have now stated to you somewhat in detail the provisions of the Timber and Stone Act; the mode of procedure to acquire title to lands thereunder, and what a person may lawfully do and what he is prohibited from doing, if he desires and undertakes to procure title to lands under and pursuant to its provisions. It is important that you bear in mind all of these matters in considering the conduct and acts of the various entrymen who, it is claimed by the prosecution, were, in effecting the object of the conspiracy, induced by the defendants, or one of them, to violate the law by making false statements in the Land Office in connection with their applica-tions or entries.

But in considering these matters you should con-stantly keep in mind that the offense charged against the defendants and for which they are being tried is not that they or any of them committed perjury; nor is it that they or any of them procured or sub-orned perjury. These are distinct offenses in them-selves, and even though you should find that one or all of the defendants committed perjury or that one or all of the defendants suborned perjury or pro-cured it to be committed, such finding, in itself, would not warrant a verdict of guilty in this proceeding. If such offenses have been committed by the defend-ants they may be indicted and tried therefor.

The charge here, as I have before told you, is not perjury or subornation of perjury, but it is con-spiracy. The object of the conspiracy, as I have before stated, is alleged to be the acquisition of public lands by means of fraud abd perjury statements or testimony; and this offense—that is, conspiracy— might be complete and punishable even though it were unsuccessful and its purpose was not effectuted. Hence, even if perjury was committed by the entrymen and if you find that these defendants procured such perjury to be committed, you must go further and inquire whether or not the defendants had theretofore entered into a combination or conspiracy among themselves to procure such offenses to be committed. In other words, while a large mass of evidence has been put before you in relation to the acts of various entrymen and the connection of the defendants or some of them therewith, the fundemental question for you to determine is whether or not there was a *conspiracy* among the defendants to have such things done; whether there was a *conspiracy* or *understanding* to acquire lands by unlawful methods as set forth in the indictment. Hence, it becomes important that you clearly understand, and that you bear in mind, what is meant by conspiracy.

Conspiracy has been defined as "a combination or agreement, formed between two or more persons, to effect an unlawful end, they acting under a common purpose to accomplish that end."

Under the United States Statute defining conspiracy, and denouncing it as a crime, the gist of the offense is the conspiracy, that is, the combination or agreement, between two or more persons to effect an unlawful end. This unlawful agreement of conspiracy is the fundamental thing. However, that statute further provides that before parties can be prosecuted for a conspiracy one or more of such parties must perform some act to effect the object thereof. This is commonly referred to as an *"overt act,"* and it has been so referred to, more or less frequently, by counsel during the trial of the case. In other words, something more is required than a mere mental purpose to do the unlawful thing intended to be done by the combination. The conspiracy must be really set on foot by a positive act on the part of one of the conspirators. It is only necessary that one such act be done and by one of the conspirators; upon the performance of such an act the crime is complete as to all.

Again using the language of another,I advise you that:

"A common design is the essence of the crime of conspiracy, and this may be made to appear when the parties steadily pursue the same object when acting separately or together, by common or different means, all leading to the same unlawful result. When it is proven that they do so act with a common unlawful design, the principle upon which the acts and declarations of one of the conspirators in the prosecution of the enterprise are admitted in evidence against all the persons prosecuted is that, by the act of conspiring together, the conspirators have jointly assumed as a body the attribute of individuality so far as regards the prosecution of the common design, thus rendering the acts and declarations of one done in furtherance of that design a part of the res gestae, and therefore the acts of all. Men are presumed to intend the natural, usual and probable consequences of their acts, voluntarily done.

"Positive evidence entirely in proof of a conspiracy is not necessary to be had. From the nature of the case, the evidence frequently is in part circumstantial. So, though the common design is the essence of the charge, it is not necessary to prove that all of the parties charged met together and came to an explicit and formal agreement for an unlawful scheme, or that they did directly, by words or in writing, state to each other what the unlawful scheme was to be, and state to each other the details of the plan or means by which the unlawful combination was to be made effective; that is, it is not necessary that that should be shown by direct evidence; the offense is suffuciently proved if the jury is satisfied from the evidence, beyond a reasonable doubt, that two or more of the parties charged, in any manner or through any contrivance, positively or tacitly came to a mutual understanding to accomplish a common and unlawful design, followed by some act done by any one of the parties for the purpose of carrying it into execution; in other words, where an unlawful end is sought to be effected, and two or more persons, actuated by the common purpose of accomplishing that end, work together in any way in furtherance of the unlawful scheme, every one of said persons becomes a part of the conspiracy, although the part he was to take therein was a subordinate one, or was to be executed at a remote distance from the other conspirators. It is not necessary that each of the parties should, in person, commit the unlawful act, if such act is a part of the plan for which the combination is formed; for, if the unlawful agreement has been proven to your satisfaction and beyond a reasonable doubt, the act of one in furtherance of the conspiracy becomes the act of all.

"The Government is not required to furnish direct evidence of a conspiracy or of the knowledge or intent of the defendants, or either of them, but the conspiracy, knowledge, or intent of the defendants may be established by circumstantial evidence, if sufficient for that purpose."

In considering each count of the indictment, the essential questions for you to determine, therefore, are, does the evidence show, beyond a reasonable doubt, that Kettenbach, Kester and Dwyer, or two of them, knowingly and intentionally entered into an understanding or combination to induce or procure persons to appear at the Land Office at Lewiston and make applications to enter and purchase lands under the Timber and Stone Act, as alleged in the indictment, after having first come to an agreement or understanding with such persons that they would convey the title which they might acquire to the defendants, or one of them; and, next, does the evidence convince you, beyond a reasonable doubt, that the defendants, in so conspiring, intended that the persons, or some of the persons, whom they might induce or procure to make such entries, should willfully and deliberately, in making their sworn statements or applications to purchase such lands, at the time of making their first filing, or in making their affidavits or depositions, at the time they submitted proof, commit perjury by swearing falsely that their applications were not made on speculation, but in good faith, to appropriate the lands to the exclusive use and benefit of the applicants; and that the applicants had not, directly or indirectly, made any agreement or contract, in any way or manner, by which the title to be acquired from the United States should inure, in whole or in part, to the benefit of any person other than the applicant. Such combination, conspiracy or agreement, if you find that there was one, must have been formed or entered into in the State of Idaho, prior to the overt acts as charged in each count, and such overt acts, or some of them, you must find, beyond a reasonable doubt, were performed by one or more of the defendants, in pursuance of such conspiracy or agreement and to effect the object thereof and while the same was in existence.

If, after carefully considering all the evidence, you can answer each of these questions affirmatively and beyond a reasonable doubt, then you should convict such defendants as, beyond a reasonable doubt, you find, from the evidence, formed or entered into such conspiracy. If, upon the other hand, you have a reasonable doubt of the truth of any of them, your verdict should be for the defendants.

As I have before indicated to you, in considering your verdict you should determine the guilt or innocence of each defendant separately, and you are not warranted in finding one of the defendants guilty merely because of the guilt of another defendant. Before you can convict any defendant you must be convinced beyond a reasonable doubt that such defendant committed the offense charged.

I have heretofore told you that positive evidence entirely in a proof of conspiracy is not necessary to be had, but that the offense may be established by circumstantial evidence. I do not mean by that that a conviction can be had upon mere suspicion, however strong, or upon conjectures, or even probability, of guilt. Where circumstantial evidence is relied upon, it is not sufficient merely that the circumstances established by the evidence point to the guilt of the defendant. Circumstances may point to the guilt of the defendant and yet be capable of a reasonable explanation entirely consistent with his innocence. Hence, the rule in criminal cases, where circumstantial evidence alone is relied upon, is that, to warrant a conviction upon such evidence, the circumstances, when all taken together, must not only be compatible or consistent with the guilt of the accused, but they must be inconsistent with his innocence. Or, to state it in another way, it is not sufficient that the circumstances proven point to and render probable the defendant's guilt, but they must exclude to a moral certainty and beyond a reasonable doubt every theory or hypothesis other than that of guilt. If such evidence, while it may point to the guilt of the accused, still can be reasonable reconciled with the theory of his innocence, the law requires that he be given the benefit of the doubt and that the theory of innocence be adopted.

In determining the question of the formation or existence of the conspiracy, among other circumstances, the acts and declarations of the persons accused may be looked to and considered by the jury. From time to time during the course of the trial statements, now of one of the defendants and then of another, in the absence of the other defendants, have been given in evidence; letters and written memoranda have also been received, and there has been testimony relative to the acts of first one defendant and then another, in the absence of his codefendants. These statements, conversations, representations and acts were admitted to show the nature, purpose, plan and operation of the conspiracy, if one existed, and to aid in shedding light upon the relation of the defendant speaking, writing or acting, to the transactions. But you will bear in mind that guilt cannot be fixed upon any person by the declarations or statements, either oral or written, of other persons; his guilt must be disclosed by his own conduct, statement and admissions and the connection of anyone of the defendants with the conspiracy charged must be shown by the acts and circumstances, or by his own acts and declarations independent of the acts or declarations of his codefendants. In other words, as I have advised you from time to time during the course of the trial, the admissions or statements of any one of the defendants to the effect that there was a conspiracy or agreement are not binding upon and do not connect the other defendants with such conspiracy, if it existed. As an illustration, the witness Morrison testified that the defendant Dwyer told him that Dwyer had some arrangement with the defendant Kester or the defendants Kester and Kettenbach, which, in substance, was that lands were to be entered, Kester or Kester and Kettenbach were to furnish the money, and Dwyer was to get a portion of the land. If you believe this testimony to be true, you can consider it in determining whether Dwyer, who made the statement, was connected with a conspiracy, if one existed; but such a statement by Dwyer cannot be considered by you, and it should be ignored, when you are considering whether or not the other defendants were connected with a conspiracy, if it existed. In other words, such a statement is no proof at all against any of the defendants except Dwyer. This consideration emphaises the suggestion which I have heretofore made that you take up and consider the evidence as it relates to each defendant on trial separately. For instance, William F. Kettenbach is the first defendant named. In considering whether or not he was a party to the alleged conspiracy or agreement, if you find there was one, you should take into consideration only his own statements, acts, and conduct and his own connection with acts and conduct of others as shown by the evidence, independent of any statements or declarations by others; and unless you find, beyond a reasonable doubt, from such evidence, that he was a party to such conspiracy, if one existed, it would be your duty to acquit him. If, however, you find that he was a party to such conspiracy, then the statements and declarations of his codefendants relative to and in carrying out or effecting the object of the conspiracy, may by considered as if made by him. You can follow the same course in determining the relation of each of the other defendants to the alleged conspiracy.

It being impossible for one person to enter into a conspiracy, you cannot find a single defendant guilty and acquit the others. You must find at least two of them guilty, or else acquit all.

Evidence has been introduced in relation to entries of land other than the entries made by the parties named in the several counts of the indictment, and in relation to the connection, or alleged connection, of the defendants, or some of them, with such entries. Such evidence was admitted solely for the purpose of aiding the jury to infer intent and to establish a prior design or system or conspiracy to defraud the United States, including the doing of the unlawful and wrongful acts charged in the indictment, and to enable the jury to reach a just conclusion as to the particular charge made against the defendant.

It is immaterial to what extent the defendants or any of them may have been guilty in other entries, or however well their criminality in relation to such other entries may be established, if it is established, unless you find, beyond a reasonable doubt, that two or more of the defendants unlawfully combined and conspired together to defraud the United States, substantially as alleged in the indictment, and that pursuant to such conspiracy, as alleged in each count of the indictment, considered separately, they procured and induced the entryman named in such count to commit one or more of the overt acts therein charged.

As I have before explained to you, only Kettenbach, Kester and Dwyer are now on trial. In the indictment, however, it is charged that these three defendants not only confederated among themselves, but combined with other persons whose names were to the grand jury unknown. Before the trial commenced the prosecution, being by the Court required so to do, filed a list of the names of the persons, who, the prosecution might, during the course of the trial, contend acted in *consent* with or were engaged with the defendants in the alleged conspiracy. This list has been read to you and the persons therein named have been frequently referred to. They are Clarence W. Robnett, Jackson O'Keefe, J. B. West, I. N. Smith, W. B. Benton, E. L. Knight, C. W. Colby, Fred Emory, Melvern C. Scott, Edwin F. Bliss and H. J. Steffey.

I advise you that by furnishing this list the prosecution did not undertake or become bound to connect all *of* any of the persons therein named with the alleged conspiracy. Whether the Government was able to do so and chose not to try to connect some of these persons, or whether it was unable to do so, is a matter which is wholly immaterial for your consideration. There is no contention on the part of the Government that there is sufficient evidence in the record to connect with the alleged conspiracy said Steffey, Bliss, Scott, Emory, Colby, *K*night, Benton, Smith, or West. But, while advising you that there is insufficient evidence before you to show such connection, I further instruct you that the failure of the prosecution to make such showing must not be considered by you as affecting your verdict.

As to the other persons so named, that is, Jackson O'Keefe, and Clarence W. Robnett, the prosecution contends that the evidence sufficiently connects them with the alleged conspiracy, which contention is denied by counsel for the defendants. This issue is a material one for your consideration, as I shall point out to you. If there was a conspiracy to defraud the Government, such as is charged in the indictment, was Jackson O'Keefe one of the conspirators? And if there was such a conspiracy, was Clarence W. Robnett one of the conspirators? While these two persons are not on trial, perhaps in considering your verdict, it would be well for you to answer these two questions first. And unless you are satisfied from the evidence, beyond a reasonable doubt, that Jackson O'Keefe was, in the part which you may find he took in and about the entries of C. W. Taylor and E. J. Taylor, and the transfer of the lands entered by them, acting in concert with the defendants Kettenbach, Kester and Dwyer in pursuance of the conspiracy charged in the indictment, then you should discard and wholly ignore the testimony of C. W. Taylor and E. J. Taylor, and all the exhibits relating exclusively to their entries. Even though you should find that the Taylors committed perjury in acquiring title to their land and that O'Keefe induced and procured them to commit such perjury, such facts are wholly immaterial and must be disregarded by you, unless, as I have stated, you find from the evidence as a whole, beyond a reasonable doubt, that said Jackson O'Keefe was a member of the alleged conspiracy and was acting in consert with the defendants now on trial.

And what I have said with regard to the entries with which O'Keefe was connected applies with equal force to the testimony and documentary evidence relating or tending to connect Clarence W. Robnett with certain entries and land transactions. I refer to the testimony of George Ray Robinson, Bertsel H. Ferris, Joel H. Benton, Mary J. Harris, Jeanette Harris, Ethel Harris, R. O. Waldman, P. H. Waldman and Louis Dreckman and the exhibits relating to their entries and to the transfer of their lands or entries. All this evidence was received upon the promise of the prosecution and upon the theory that it would be shown, while Robnett is not now on trial, yet he was acting with three defendants, pursuant to an understanding among themselves and with him to defraud the United States in the manner alleged in the indictment; in other words, that he was a co-conspirator with the defendants and was engaged in the same unlawful combination. Therefore, before you can consider the testimony of any of the witnesses' names or the documents received in evidence relating to their entries and the transfer of their lands or entries, or against these defendants, or any of them, you must be convinced beyond a reasonable doubt, from all of the evidence, that Robnett was, in said transaction, engaged in a conspiracy with the defendants as alleged; and that in and about said entries and matters he was acting in concert with the defendants in carrying out and effecting the object of said conspiracy. It is not enough that you may believe that said entrymen swore falsely in entering said lands; or that Robnett procured or induced them to swear; or that he was engaged in *some* scheme or conspiracy to defraud the Government. You must be convinced beyond a reasonable doubt that he was acting in concert with the defendants, that is in the identical conspiracy charged in the indictment. Unless you do so find, it is your duty to disregard the testimony of all of said witnesses last named and the documentary evidence relating to their entries and the transfers thereof.

There have been admitted in evidence the record in the case of the *United States vs. Clarence W. Robnett,* and the record in the case of the *United States vs. William Dwyer,* for the purpose of establishing the fact that each of these persons, that is Robnett and Dwyer, has been convicted of the crime of subornation of perjury. These records, as I admonished you at the time they were received, you will consider only as establishing the fact of the conviction of these persons of said crime, for the purpose of effecting the weight and credibility which you will give to their testimony in this case. The theory of the law is that if a man has been guilty of such an offense, his testimony is not as worthy of credence, other things being equal, as that of one who has not committed such an offense. The records in the matter of these convictions were not offered for the purpose of proving, and you must not consider them as proving, or tending to prove, the guilt of any one of the defendants, or as tending to establish any allegation of the indictment in this case.

It was intimated to you when you were being examined as to your qualifications to sit as jurors, that the Government would in part rely upon the testimony of persons, who, in acquiring title to the lands referred to in the indictment, testified falsely or committed perjury in the United States Land Office at the time they applied for or made proof for their lands. Several of such persons have testified on behalf of the Government, and have stated before you that they gave false testimony and made false oaths in the United States Land Office, in acquiring title to such lands. And I advise you that if you find that any person who has been a witness here committed perjury, either in applying for or in making final proof upon such lands, in the United States Land Office, in furtherance of and in effecting the object of the conspiracy charged in the indictment, then, while such persons may not, strictly speaking, be an accomplice with the defendants in the conspiracy charged, that is, a coconspirator, yet he would be so implicated that it will be your duty to scrutinize his testimony closely and to receive it with due caution; and it is entirely proper for you to seek for corroborating circumstances. I do not mean by this that you must reject such testimony merely because there may be no corroborating circumstances. I simply mean that it is your duty to receive their testimony with great caution and close scrutiny. The rule that the testimony of an accomplice should be closely scrutinized and received with caution is well founded in reason and experience in that an accomplice testifies to his participation in a crime, the blame for which he is interested in putting upon another. But such witnesses are not rendered incompetent by reason of their connection with the offense; and it was the duty of the Court to receive their testimony, and likewise it is your duty to consider it. It is not infrequently necessary for the Government, in disclosing unlawful acts and in throwing light upon the designs of men, to rely largely upon testimony of this character, and, if it were excluded, it would sometimes be impossible to discover or punish crimes. It is therefore, your duty to fairly consider such testimony, tainted though it may be, and give to it the weight to which under all of the circumstances you conclude it is entitled. You may consider the probable motives prompting such witnesses to testify against the defendants, and you must also consider their demeanor upon the witness-stand, their apparent candor or lack of candor and, indeed, all other circumstances and influences which, in your judgment, may tend to affect their credibility. But after you have so considered their testimony, if you believe it to be truthful, in other words, if you believe that such witnesses testified truthfully relative to any matter in this case, you should then give to such truthful testimony the same force and effect as you would give it had such witnesses not committed perjury in the land office.

The defendants have each testified upon their own behalf, as they were at liberty to do, and you cannot rightfully reject their testimony merely because they are the defendants. In considering their testimony you should apply to their credibility the same tests which are properly applied to other witnesses who have testified. This means that among other things you may take into consideration, in passing upon the credibility of their testimony, their great interest in the result of the prosecution, the reasonableness or unreasonableness of their statements and explanations and the consistency or the inconsistency of their account of the transactions involved.

In short, gentlemen, in calling your attention to a certain class of witnesses for the prosecution and to certain witnesses for the defendants, including the defendants themselves, it has not been my purpose to charge, and I disclaim any attention of advising you, that you should apply one test to one of the witnesses or group of witnesses and a different test to another witness or group of witnesses. I have been compelled to single out certain witnesses only for the purpose of calling your attention to certain circumstances attending their testimony and the principles of law applicable thereto, in order that you may not be left in confusion by the apparently conflicting contentions of counsel.

After all, your primary inquiry must be, Does the witness, whoever he may be, speak the truth? What weight or significance shall be attached to his testimony? And in answer to these questions you may, in relation to all of the witnesses, including the defendants, consider their opportunities for knowing and their capacity for remembering their fairness or unfairness; their reputation for truth and veracity; their interest or lack of interest in the result of the prosecution; their friendliness or hostility to the parties accused and to the representatives of the Government; the influence surrounding them and their probable motives; their proven implication in of their freedom from perjury and subornation of perjury in connection with the conspiracies charged in the indictment; the consistency or inconsistency of their testimony with their past conduct and with statements previously made by them, either sworn or unsworn; their manner of testifying, their apparent candor or lack of candor; and, indeed, all other facts and circumstances in evidence which your common sense and experience teach your influence men and affect the credibility and weight of their testimony.

If you believe that any witness has wilfully sworn falsely to any material matter upon this trial, you are at liberty to reject his entire testimony, except in so far as it may be corroborated by other credible evidence.

One other matter, and that relates to your conduct while you are in the jury-room. The law presumes and I shall assume that you are all fair-minded, reasonable men and that it is the earnest desire of each of you to reach and render a just verdict. I must also assume, that, true to your oath, and in compliance with the admonition which I have so frequently given to you during the course of the trial, you have not finally made up your minds as to what your verdict will be. While you could not help receiving impressions as the trial progressed, and these it was your right to receive, it was, as I have frequently informed you, your duty to withhold final judgment until the evidence was closed and counsel had made their arguments and you had heard my charge. When you now retire to your room and for the first time give expression to your views, it is not impossible that a radical difference between you may be disclosed, and, in view of such contingency, I want to say to you that the law contemplates that you will try in good faith to harmonize your differences and agrees upon a verdict. No juror has the right to enter the jury-room, and, in effect, say: "I have made up my mind and it can't be changed. If you fellows want to agree with me, all right, otherwise we will stay here all summer."

Such an attitude does not comport with an honorable discharge of the duties of a juryman. No man, whether he be a juryman or not, can properly arrogate to himself infallibility or unerring judgment. Every juryman should retire to consider his verdict, not necessarily free from impressions or even well defined views, but with a mind open to reason and argument, with a willingness to discuss differences and to listen to the suggestions and views of his associates. His recollection of some of the evidence may not be correct; the significance of other evidence may not have occurred to him; and in many ways, especially where the record is voluminous, as it is in this case, free and fair discussion in the jury-room may be extremely helpful in enabling you to come to an agreement.

You must reach unanimity, that is, you must all agree, or we shall have only a mistrial and our extended and arduous labros will be entirely lost.

Of course, I do not mean that, in order to avoid a mistrial the monority must or should yield their honest convictions to the majority. It is the right and duty of each one of you, whether standing alone or with a large number, to vote your conscience and your honest judgment. But what I am trying to make clear to you is that you should make earnest and sincere efforts to harmonize conflicting views; and in doing so there must be among you a feeling of mutual deference and respect; and oppenness of mind; patience in listening, and fairness in considering; and a spirit of give and take in matters of minor detail. While, as I have already indicated, it is not expected that one of you, merely because he stands alone, must yield his honest judgment, conscientiously formed, to that of his eleven associates, still, where a man finds himself standing along against eleven others with equal facilities for judging, it is only natural and proper for him, as a prudent and honest man, to search diligently the operations of his own mind and to prove carefully his conclusions in the light of the views of his associates. If, thereafter, his judgment still remains unshaken, by it he may stand.

Sensible you must be of the responsibility resting upon you. The law is no respector of persons. Whether the defendants be rich or whether they be poor, should be a matter of indifference to you; their conduct, not their condition, is on trial. Poverty may appeal to your sympathies but it should not bias you; wealth and social position may excite your envy, but they should not prejudice you. A fair trial you have sworn to give to both the Government and the defendants. This they are entitled to. Your verdict would, under the law, be upon the evidence and that alone. Deliberate disapassionately and decide impartially. The case is now submitted to you.

[Endorsed]: No. 615. In the District Court of the United States, for the District of Idaho, Northern Division. The United States vs. Wm. F. Kettenbach, et al. Instructions by the Court. Filed June 15, 1907. A. L. Richardson, Clerk.

*United States District Court, Northern Division, District of Idaho.*

THE UNITED STATES OF AMERICA,

Plaintiff,

vs.

WILLIAM F. KETTENBACH, GEORGE H. KESTER, and WILLIAM DWYER,

Defendants.

### Verdict.

We, the jury in the above-entitled cause find the defendant William F. Kettenbach, not guilty, as charged in the first count of the indictment; and we find the defendant William F. Kettenbach not guilty, as charged in the second count of the indictment; and we find the defendant William F. Kettenbach, guilty as charged in the third count of the indictment; and we find the defendant William F. Kettenbach guilty as charged in the fourth count in the indictment; and we find the defendant William F. Kettenbach, not guity as charged in the fifth count of the indictment; and we find the defendant George H. Kester, not guilty as charged in the first count of the indictment; and we find the defendant George H. Kester not guilty as charged in the second count of the indictment; and we find the defendant George H. Kester guilty as charged in the third count of the indictment; and we find the defendant George H. Kester guilty as charged in the fourth count of the indictment; and we find the defendant George H. Kester not guilty as charged in the firth count of the indictment; and we find the defendant William Dwyer not guilty as charged in the first count of the indictment; and we find the defendant William Dwyer not guilty as charged in the second count of the indictment; and we find the defendant William Dwyer guilty as charged in the third count of the indictment; and we find the defendant William Dwyer, guilty, as charged in the fourth count of the indictment; and we find the defendant William Dwyer not guilty as charged in the fifth count of the indictment.

M. D. FREEDENBERG,
Foreman of the Jury.

[Endorsed]: No. 615. In the District Court of the United States for the District of Idaho. United States of America vs. William F. Kettenbach, George H. Kester and William Dwyer. Verdict. Filed June 16, 1907. A. L. Richardson, Clerk.

---

## Journal Entries.

At a stated term of the District Court of the United States, for the District of Idaho, held at Moscow, Idaho, on Monday, the 14th day of May, 1906. Present: Hon. JAS. H. BEATTY, Judge.

No. 615—CONSPIRACY.

THE UNITED STATES

vs.

WILLIAM F. KETTENBACH, GEORGE H. KESTER, and WILLIAM DWYER.

### Arraignment, Plea, etc.

On this day the defendants herein came into court in person and appearing by their attorneys, J. H. Forney & I. N. Smith, Esqs., to be arraigned upon the true bill of indictment heretofore presented against them by the Grand Jury. In answer to the Court each defendant stated that he was indicted under his true name. The formal reading of the indictment was waived and each defendant furnished with a true copy thereof by order of court at the expense of the United States. Being asked for their plea, each defendant pleaded separately for himself that he is not guilty of the offense charged in the indictment, and upon application of counsel for defendants ordered that said cause be continued for the term.

Friday, the 9th day of November, 1906.

### No. 615—CONSPIRACY.

## THE UNITED STATES

vs.

## WILLIAM F. KETTENBACH et al.

### Order Setting Cause for Trial.

On motion of the U. S. District Attorney, ordered that this cause be set for trial to follow No. 616. The plaintiff expressly reserves the right to take up either this cause or No. 605 to follow No. 601 or 616, as to the plaintiff may seem best.

Friday, the 17th day of May, 1907.

Present: Hon. FRANK S. DIETRICH, Judge.

### No. 615—CONSPIRACY.

## THE UNITED STATES

vs.

## WILLIAM F. KETTENBACH, GEORGE H. KESTER, and WILLIAM DWYER.

### Trial—May 17, 1907.

Now on this day this cause came regularly on to to be heard and tried before the Court and jury. N.

M. Ruick, U. S. District Attorney, and Miles S. Johnson, Assistant U. S. District Attorney, appearing as counsel on behalf of the United States and Messrs. Forney & Moore and Geo. W. Tannahill, Esqs., appearing on behalf of the defendants, said defendants being in court in person. Before the jury was called the defendants by their counsel moved the Court for an order requiring the plaintiff's counsel to furnish the said defendants with a Bill of Particulars, and by agreement of counsel for the respective parties it is ordered that either party be given sixty days after the entry of judgment herein to prepare, serve and file a Bill of Exceptions in said cause.

The clerk, under direction of the Court, proceeded to draw from the jury-box the names of twelve persons, one at a time, to serve as a jury in said cause, and the names of the following persons were drawn from the box and who took their seats and were first duly sworn on their *voir dire,* to wit:

W. H. Gage,         John Hanley,
F. A. Stewart,        H. Hatki,
John Coverdale,      Ludwig Feldmeir,
J. H. Robinson,       R. E. Thomas,
J. B. Rice,            Geo. W. Follett,
Claude Swank,        W. D. Fredenberg.

The said persons were examined and passed upon for cause by counsel for plaintiff, and during their examination for cause by counsel for the defense said jurors were excused from the court-room for a period of fifteen minutes, and during their absence the Court announced its decision upon defendants' motion in cause No. 637, heretofore submitted, to disqualify Marshal Ruel Rounds and for the appointment of an elisor in their cause, and ordered that said motion be and is hereby denied, to which ruling the defendants by their counsel then and there excepted. Said jury was recalled and all answered to their names; thereupon the Court admonished said jury, ordered that said jury be kept together during the adjournment of court, placed them in charge of Frank M. Johnson, and James Fogel, who were first duly sworn as bailiffs, and ordered that the marshal furnish said jury and two bailiffs with their meals and lodging during the progress of the trial herein, and adjourned the further hearing of said cause until to-morrow, the 18th inst., at 10 o'clock A. M.

Saturday, the 18th day of May, 1907.

## No. 615—CONSPIRACY.

## THE UNITED STATES

### vs.

## WILLIAM F. KETTENBACH et al.

### Trial (Resumed)—May 18, 1907.

The trial of this cause adjourned on yesterday for further hearing was this day resumed. Jury called and found to be present and the respective attorneys of record and the defendants in person being in court. Geo. W. Follett, a person on the panel, was excused for cause upon challenge by counsel for defendants. W. H. Gage, a person on the panel, was excused for cause upon challenge interposed by counsel for plaintiff. The counsel for plaintiff interposed a challenge for cause against James Turner, a person drawn from the box and sworn on *voir dire,* which challenge was opposed by counsel for defendant, and pending a decision thereon the Court admonished the jury, placed them in charge of sworn officials of the Court, and adjourned the further hearing of said cause until Monday, the 20th inst., at 9:00 o'clock A. M. The following are the names of the persons now on the panel who were drawn from the jury-box and sworn on *voir dire,* to wit:

| | |
|---|---|
| J. H. Robinson, | R. E. Thomas, |
| J. B. Rice, | John Coverdale, |
| Ludwig Feldmeir, | C. E. Christanson, |
| John Hanley, | F. A. Stewart, |
| H. Hatki, | Claude Swank, |
| W. D. Fredenberg. | James Turner. |

Monday, the 20th day of May, 1907.

## No. 615—CONSPIRACY.

### THE UNITED STATES

vs.

### WILLIAM F. KETTENBACH et al.

### Trial (Resumed)—May 20, 1907.

The trial of this cause adjourned on Saturday, the 18th inst., for further hearing was this day resumed. Jury called and found to be present, the respective attorneys of record and the defendants in person each being present. Here the Court admonished the jury, placed the same in charge of sworn officers of the Court, and adjourned the further hearing of said cause until 10:30 o'clock this A. M.

## No. 615—CONSPIRACY.

## THE UNITED STATES

### vs.

## WILLIAM F. *K*ETTENBACH et al.

The trial of this cause heretofore adjourned for further hearing this day was resumed at 10:30 o'clock A. M. Jury called and found to be present, the respective attorneys of record and the defendants in person each being present. Here the Court announced its decision upon the challenge for cause heretofore submitted to the juror James Turner, and ordered that said challenge be and is hereby sustained and the said juror was excused from service on the panel. To the ruling of the Court in sustaining said challenge the defendants by their counsel then and there excepted in due form of law, which exception was allowed by the Court. The clerk thereupon, under direction of the Court, proceeded to fill the panel from the jury-box. Claude Swank and Emery Guay persons drawn from the box and sworn on *voir dire* were excused on peremptory challenge by counsel for plaintiff. John B. Foresman and John Hanley, persons drawn from the box and sworn on *voir dire,* were excused on peremptory challenge by counsel for defendants, and the following are the names of the persons drawn from the box, sworn on *voir dire,* passed upon, accepted by counsel for the respective parties and sworn by the clerk to well and truly try said cause and a true verdict render therein according to the law and evidence, to wit:

| | |
|---|---|
| J. H. Robinson, | William Drawford, |
| H. Hatki, | J. B. Kreiger, |
| C. E. Christianson, | F. A. Stewart, |
| Frank Leachman, | Ludwig Feldmeir, |
| R. E. Thomas, | W. D. Fredenberg, |
| John Coverdale, | J. B. Rice. |

The clerk, under direction of the Court, read the indictment to the jury and stated the defendant's plea. After which the Court admonished the jury and placed the same in charge of sworn officers of the court, and adjourned the further hearing of said cause until to-morrow, the 21st inst, at 10 o'clock A. M.

Tuesday, the 21st day of May, 1907.

No. 615—CONSPIRACY.

THE UNITED STATES

vs.

WILLIAM F. KETTENBACH et al.

**Trial (Resumed)—May 21, 1907.**

The trial of this cause adjourned on yesterday for further hearing was this day resumed. Jury called and found to be present. The respective attorneys of record and the defendants in person each being in court. By agreement of counsel it was ordered that all witnesses in this cause be excluded from the courtroom. The following named persons were sworn, examined and cross-examined as witnesses on behalf of the plaintiff, to wit: Guy L. Wilson, Mrs. Ellen Wilson, and Charles Carey, and during the examination in chief of the latter named witness, the Court admonished the jury, placed the same in charge of sworn officers of the Court and adjourned the further hearing of said cause until to-morrow, the 22nd inst. at 10 o'clock A. M.

Wednesday, the 22d inst. of May, 1907.

No. 615—CONSPIRACY.

THE UNITED STATES

vs.

WILLIAM F. KETTENBACH, GEORGE H. KESTER and WILLIAM DWYER.

Trial (Resumed)—May 22, 1907.

The trial of this cause adjourned on yesterday for further hearing was this day resumed. Jury called and found to be present, the respective attorneys of record and the defendants in person each being in court. Charles Carey, sworn on yesterday, was recalled and examined briefly on behalf of plaintiff, then excused for a time and F. M. Goodwin was sworn, examined and cross-examined as a witness on behalf of plaintiff. Charles Carey was recalled, examined and cross-examined on behalf of plaintiff. Frances A. Justice was sworn and examined as a witness on behalf of plaintiff, and during her cross-examination the Court admonished the jury, placed them in charge of sworn officers of the Court and

adjourned the further hearing of said cause until to-
morrow the 23d inst, at 10 o'clock A. M.

Thursday, the 23d day of May, 1907.

No. 615—CONAPIRACY.

THE UNITED STATES

vs.

WILLIAM F. KETTENBACH, GEORGE H. KES-
TER and WILLIAM DWYER.

**Trial (Resumed)—May 23, 1907.**

The trial of this cause adjourned on yesterday for
further hearing was this day resumed. Jury called
and found to be present, the respective attorneys of
record and the defendants in person, each being in
court. The cross-examination of Mrs. Frances A.
Justice was concluded. F. M. Goodwin was recalled
and examined as a witness on behalf of plaintiff. H.
F. Lewis was called, sworn, examined and cross-examined as a witness on behalf of plaintiff Edward
M. Lewis and John P. Roos were sworn, examined
and cross-examined as witnesses on behalf of plaintiff, after which the Court admonished the jur.v,
placed them in charge of sworn officers of the Court,
and adjourned the further hearing of said cause until to-morrow, the 24th inst., at 10 o'clock A. M.

Friday, the 24th day of May, 1907.

No. 615—CONSPIRACY.

THE UNITED STATES

vs.

WILLIAM F. KETTENBACH, GEORGE H. KES-
TER and WILLIAM DWYER.

**Trial (Resumed)—May 24, 1907.**

The trial of this cause adjourned on yesterday for further hearing was this day resumed. Jury called and found to be present, the respective attorneys of record and the defendants in person each being in court. The following names persons were called, sworn, examined and cross-examined as witnesses on behalf of plaintiff, to wit: W. W. Pefley, F. M. Goodwin (recalled), Ivan R. Cornell, Samuel C. Hutchins, Rowland A. Lambdin, A. L. Richardson, Fred W. Schaeffer, and after the examination in chief of the latter named the Court admonished the jury, placed the same in charge of sworn officers of the Court, and adjourned the further hearing of said cause until to-morrow, the 25th inst., at 10 o'clock A. M.

Saturday, the 25th day of May, 1907.

No. 615—CONSPIRACY.

THE UNITED STATES

vs.

WILLIAM F. KETTENBACH, GEORGE H. KESTER and WILLIAM DWYER.

**Trial (Resumed)—May 25, 1907.**

The trial of this cause adjourned on yesterday for further hearing was this day resumed. Jury called and found to be present, the respective attorneys of record and the defendants in person each being in court.

Thomas H. Bartlett was sworn and examined as a witness on behalf of the United States, and during his examination in chief the Court admonished the jury, placed the same in charge of sworn officers of the Court, and adjourned the further of said cause until Monday, the 27th inst., at 10 o'clock A. M.

Monday, the 27th day of May, 1907.

## No. 615—CONSPIRACY.

## THE UNITED STATES

vs.

## WILLIAM F. KETTENBACH, GEORGE H. KESTER and WILLIAM DWYER.

**Trial (Resumed)—May 27, 1907.**

The trial of this cause adjourned on Saturday, the 25th inst., for further hearing was this day resumed. Jury called and found to be present, the respective attorneys of record and the defendants in person each being in court. The examination of Thomas H. Bartlett, a witness on behalf of plaintiff, sworn on the 25th inst., both direct and cross was concluded, and after the introduction of documentary evidence, the Court admonished the jury, placed them in charge of sworn officers, with leave by consent of the attorneys for one of the bailiffs to accompany such members of the jury as desired to attend a lecture this evening to do so, and adjourned the further hearing of said cause until to-morrow, the 28th inst., at 9:30 o'clock A. M.

Tuesday, the 28th day of May, 1907.

No. 615—CONSPIRACY.

THE UNITED STATES

vs.

WILLIAM F. KETTENBACH, GEORGE H. KES-
TER and WILLIAM DWYER..

**Trial (Resumed)—May 28, 1907.**

The trial of this cause adjourned on yesterday for
further hearing was this day resumed.  Jury called
and found to be present, the respective attorneys of
record and the defendants in person each being in
court.  F. M. Goodwin was recalled and examined as
a witness on behalf of plaintiff.

The following named persons were sworn, examined and cross-examined as witnesses on behalf of
plaintiff, to wit: J. M. Molloy, Charles W. Taylor
and E. J. Taylor, after which the Court admonished
the jury, placed them in charge of sworn officers of
the Court, and adjourned the further hearing of said
cause until to-morrow, the 29th inst., at 9:30 o'clock
A. M.

Wednesday, the 29th day of May, 1907.

No. 615—CONSPIRACY.

THE UNITED STATES

vs.

WILLIAM F. KETTENBACH, GEORGE H. KES-
TER and WILLIAM DWYER.

**Trial (Resumed)—May 29, 1907.**

The trial of this cause adjourned on yesterday for
further hearing was this day resumed.  Jury called

and found to be present, the respective attorneys of record and the defendants in person each being in court. The following named persons were sworn, examined and cross-examined as witnesses on behalf of plaintiff, to wit: Stanley P. Fairweather, John G. Fralick, Thomas Jackson, George Ray Robinson, F. M. Goodwin, recalled, W. L. Gifford and Bertsel H. Ferris, and at the conclusion of the examination in chief of said witness, the Court admonished the jury, placed them in charge of sworn officers of the Court, and adjourned the further hearing of said cause until to-morrow, the 30th inst., at 9:30 o'clock A. M.

Thursday, the 30th day of May, 1907.

No. 615—CONSPIRACY.

THE UNITED STATES

vs.

WILLIAM F. KETTENBACH, GEORGE H. KESTER and WILLIAM DWYER.

Trial (Resumed)—May 30, 1907.

The trial of this cause adjourned on yesterday for further hearing was this day resumed. Jury called and found to be present, the respective attorneys of record and the defendants in person each being in court. The examination and cross-examination of Bertsel H. Ferris, a witness sworn on yesterday, was concluded. F. M. Goodwin, recalled, and Joel H. Benton, and during the examination in chief of the latter named witness the Court admonished the jury and adjourned the further hearing of said cause until to-morrow, the 31st inst., at 9:30 o'clock A. M.; the said jury were placed in charge of sworn officers of the Court during said adjournment.

Firday, the 31st day of May, 1907.

No. 615—CONSPIRACY.

THE UNITED STATES

vs.

WILLIAM F. KETTENBACH, GEORGE H. KESTER and WILLIAM DWYER.

**Trial (Resumed)—May 31, 1907.**

The trial of this cause adjourned on yesterday for further hearing was this day resumed. Jury called and found to be present, the respective attorneys of record and the defendants in person each being in court. The examination of Joel H. Benton, sworn, on yesterday, both direct and cross was concluded. The following named persons were sworn, examined and cross-examined as witnesses on behalf of plaintiff, to wit: Mrs. Mary J. Harris, Miss Jeanette Harris, Miss Ethel Harris, F. M. Goodwin (recalled), Robt. Wright, Mrs. Maude Wright, Robert O. Waldman and P. H. Waldman, after which the Court admonished the jury, placed the same in charge of sworn officers of the court, and adjourned the further hearing of said cause until to-morrow, the 1st day of June, 1907, at 9:30 o'clock A. M.

Saturday, the 1st day of June, 1907.

No. 615—CONSPIRACY.

THE UNITED STATES

vs.

WILLIAM F. KETTENBACH, GEORGE H. KES-
TER and WILLIAM DWYER.

**Trial (Resumed)—June 1, 1907.**

The trial of this cause adjourned on yesterday for further hearing was this day resumed. Jury called and found to be present, the respective attorneys of record and the defendants in person each being in court. The following named persons were sworn, examined and cross-examined as witnesses on behalf of plaintiff, to wit: Louis Breckman, M. J. Dowd, J. M. Molloy, recalled, Theodore Fohl, E. N. Brown, Frank Morrison, Andrew J. Sherbourne, Geo. W. Tannahill, and after the introduction of documentary evidence the Court admonished the jury, placed the same in charge of sworn officers of the Court, and adjourned the further hearing of said cause until Monday, the 3d inst., at 9:30 o'clock A. M.

Monday, the 3d day of June, 1907.

No. 615—CONSPIRACY.

THE UNITED STATES

vs.

WILLIAM F. KETTENBACH, GEORGE H. KES-
TER and WILLIAM DWYER.

**Trial (Resumed)—June 3, 1907.**

The trial of this cause adjourned on Saturday, the 1st inst., for further hearing was this day resumed.

Jury called and found to be present, the respective attorneys of record and the defendants in person each being in court. Axel P. Ramstede was sworn and examined as a witness on behalf of plaintiff, and after the introduction of documentary evidence the plaintiff rest, subject to the rights of the defense to recall Mrs. Mary J. Harris and Miss Jeanette Harris for further cross-examination.

The Court here admonished the jury, placed the same in charge of sworn officers of the Court, and adjourned the further hearing of said cause until to-morrow, the 4th inst., at 9:30 o'clock A. M.

Tuesday, the 4th inst. of June, 1907.

No. 615—CONSPIRACY.

THE UNITED STATES OF AMERICA,

vs.

WILLIAM F. KETTENBACH et al.

**Trial (Resumed)—June 4, 1907.**

The trial of this cause adjourned on yesterday for further hearing was this day resumed. Jury called and found to be present, the respective attorneys of record and the defendants in person each being in court. The following named persons were called, sworn, examined and cross-examined as witnesses on behalf of the defendants, to wit: I. E. Cook, Henry Schisler, Jas. A. McBride, R. B. Crouch, J. D. Heritage, M. B. Richey, D. J. O'Brien, Jas. H. Howe, Geo. E. Erb, Samuel D. White, John Ray Morris, Jas. H. Gant, Frank D. Wyllis, R. Clyde Beach, Duncan J. McGildrey, William Schuddt, Martin L. Goldsmith and William B. Benton, after which the Court admonished the jury, placed the same in charge of sworn officers of the Court and adjourned the further hearing of said cause until to-morrow, the 5th inst. at 9:30 o'clock A. M.

Wednesday, the 5th day of June, 1907.

No. 615—CONSPIRACY.

THE UNITED STATES

vs.

WILLIAM F. KETTENBACH, GEORGE H. KESTER and WILLIAM DWYER.

**Trial (Resumed)—June 5, 1907.**

The trial of this cause adjourned on yesterday for further hearing was this day resumed. Jury called and found to be present, the respective attorneys of record and the defendants in person, each being in court. The following named persons were sworn, examined and cross-examined as witnesses on behalf of the defendants, to wit: Charles W. Williams, Curtis Thatcher, James F. Wall, Clarence W. Robnett, Thomas Mullen, Frank Morris, Phillip Nutting, Wm. B. Benton, recalled, after which the Court admonished the jury, placed the same in charge of sworn officers of the Court, and adjourned the further hearing of said cause until to-morrow, the 6th inst., at 9:30 o'clock A. M.

Thursday, the 6th day of June, 1907.

No. 615—CONSPIRACY.

## THE UNITED STATES

### vs.

## WILLIAM F. KETTENBACH, GEORGE H. KESTER and WILLIAM DWYER.

### Trial (Resumed)—June 6, 1907.

The trial of this cause adjourned on yesterday for further hearing was this day resumed. Jury called and found to be present, the respective attorneys of record and the defendants in person each being in court. The following named persons were sworn, examined and cross-examined as witnesses on behalf of defendants to wit: J. Woodworth, Thos. H. Bartlett, recalled, Mrs. William Dwyer, Frank W. Kettenbach, J. B. LeClair, Geo. H. Kester and William Dwyer, and during the examination in chief of the latter named witness the Court admonished the jury, placed the same in charge of sworn officers of the Court, and adjourned the further hearing of said cause until to-morrow, the 7th inst., at 9:30 o'clock A. M.

Friday, the 7th day of June, 1907.

No. 615—CONSPIRACY.

## THE UNITED STATES

### vs.

## F. KETTENBACH, GEORGE H. KESTER and WILLIAM DWYER.

## Trial (Resumed)—June 7, 1907.

The trial of this cause adjourned on yesterday for further hearing was this day resumed. Jury called and found to be present, the respective attorneys of record and the defendants in person each being in court. Thos. H. Bartlett was recalled and further examined as a witness. The examination and cross-examination of William Dwyer was concluded. J. B. West and Wm. F. Kettenbach were sworn, examined and cross-examined as witnesses on behalf of defendant, after which the Court admonished the ʲury, placed the same in charge of sworn officers of the Court, and adjourned the further hearing of said cause until to-morrow, the 8th inst., at 9:30 o'clock A. M.

Saturday, the 8th day of June, 1907.

No. 615—CONSPIRACY.

THE UNITED STATES

vs.

WILLIAM F. KETTENBACH, GEORGE H. KESTER and WILLIAM DWYER.

## Trial (Resumed)—June 8, 1907.

The trial of this cause adjourned on yesterday for further hearing was this day resumed. Jury called and found to be present, the respective attorneys of record and the defendants in person each being in court. The following named persons were recalled and examined as witnesses on behalf of defendants, to wit: Wm. F. Kettenbach, and Geo. H. Kester,

Clarence W. Robnett, was recalled and further cross-examined. Albert A. Perkins was sworn and examined as a witness on the same behalf and the defense rest here.

The following named persons were sworn, examined as witnesses in rebuttal, to wit:

M. L. Goldsmith, James M. Long, Benjamin Long, J. H. Clear, Alfred Stiffle, Thos. Needham, W. T. Gripman, Duncan F. McGilvery, F. V. Blair, N. J. Clemans, Fred M. Hinkley, Charles Carey, recalled, Ivan R. Cornell, recalled, Guy L. Wilson, recalled, Frances A. Justice, recalled, and the plaintiff rest, and the evidence and testimony closed.

Here the Court admonished the jury, placed the same in charge of sworn officers of the court, and adjourned the further hearing of said cause until Monday, the 10th inst., at 9:30 o'clock A. M.

Monday, the 10th day of June, 1907.

No. 615—CONSPIRACY.

THE UNITED STATES OF AMERICA,

vs.

WILLIAM F. KETTENBACH et al.

**Trial (Resumed)—June 10, 1907.**

The trial of this cause adjourned on Saturday, the 8th inst., for further hearing was this day resumed. Jury called and found to be present, the respective attorneys of record and the defendants in person each being in court. The Court and jury were addressed by N. M. Ruick, U. S. District Attorney, on behalf of the United States, during which the Court admonished the jury, placed the same in charge of sworn officers of the Court, and adjourned the further hearing of said cause until to-morrow, the 11th inst., at 9:30 o'clock A. M.

Tuesday, the 11th day of June, 1907.

No. 615—CONSPIRACY.

THE UNITED STATES

vs.

WILLIAM F. KETTENBACH, GEORGE H. KESTER and WILLIAM DWYER.

### Trial (Resumed)—June 11, 1907.

The trial of this cause adjourned on yesterday for further hearing was this day resumed. Jury called and found to be present, the respective attorneys of record and the defendants in person each being in court. N. M. Ruick, U. S. District Attorney, concluded the opening argument on behalf of the United States, followed by Frank L. Moore and Geo. W. Tannahill, Esqs., on behalf of the defendants, and during the argument of the latter named the Court admonished the jury, placed the same in charge of sworn officers of the Court, and adjourned the further hearing of said cause until to-morrow, the 12th inst., at 9:30 o'clock A. M.

Wednesday, the 12th day of June, 1907.

No. 615—CONSPIRACY.

THE UNITED STATES

vs.

WILLIAM F. KETTENBACH, GEORGE H. KESTER and WILLIAM DWYER.

### Trial (Resumed)—June 12, 1907.

The trial of this cause adjourned on yesterday for further hearing was this day resumed. Jury called and found to be present, the respective attorneys of record and the defendants in person each being in court. Geo. W. Tannahill, Esq., concluded his argument on behalf of defendants, followed by J. H. Forney, Esq., on the same behalf. N. M. Ruick, United States District Attorney, then closed the argument on behalf of the United States, after which the Court admonished the jury, placed the same in charge of sworn officers of the Court, and adjourned the further hearing of said cause until to-morrow, the 13th inst., at 8:30 o'clock A. M.

Saturday, the *15th day of May,* 1907.

### No. 615—CONSPIRACY.

### THE UNITED STATES

#### vs.

### WILLIAM F. KETTENBACH, GEORGE H. KESTER and WILLIAM DWYER.

### Trial (Resumed)—May 15 (June 13), 1907.

The trial of this cause adjourned on the 13th inst., for further hearing was this day resumed. Jury called and found to be present, the respective attorneys of record and the defendants in person each being in court. The court delivered its charge and instructions to the jury, thereupon said jury retired to their room to consider of their verdict in charge of sworn officers of the court.

Sunday, the 16th day of June, 1907.

## No. 615—CONSPIRACY.

## THE UNITED STATES

vs.

## WILLIAM F. KETTENBACH, GEORGE H. KESTER and WILLIAM DWYER.

### Trial (Resumed)—June 16, 1907.

Now came the jury all called and found to be present, the respective attorneys of record and the defendants in person each being in court in person. Being asked if they had agreed upon a verdict, *the,* through their foreman, *th*ated that they had, and presented their written verdict in the words following, to wit:

*"United States District Court, Northern Division, District of Idaho.*

## THE UNITED STATES OF AMERICA

vs.

## WILLIAM F. KETTENBACH, GEORGE H. KESTER and WILLIAM DWYER.

### Verdict (In Minutes of Court).

We, the jury in the above-entitled cause, find the defendant William F. Kettenbach Not Guilty as charged in the first count of the indictment, and we find the defendant William F. Kettenbach Not Guilty as charged in the second count of the indictment, and we find the defendant William F. Kettenbach Guilty as charged in the third count of the indictment, and we find the defendant William F. Kettenbach Guilty as charged in the fourth count of the indictment, and we find the defendant William F. Kettenbach Not Guilty as charged in the fifth count in the indictment, and we find the defendant George H. Kester Not Guilty as charged in the first count of the indictment, and we find the defendant George H. Kester Not Guilty as charged in the second count of the indictment, and we find the defendant George H. Kester Guilty as charged in the third count in the indictment, and we find the defendant George H. Kester Guilty as charged in the fourth count of the indictment, and we find the defendant George H. Kester Nor Guilty as charged in the fifth count of the indictment, and we find the defendant William Dwyer Not Guilty as charged in the first count of the indictment, and we find the defendant William Dwyer Not Guilty as charged in the second count of the indictment, and we find the defendant William Dwyer Guilty as charged in the third count of the indictment, and we find the defendant William Dwyer Guilty as charged in the fourth count of the indictment, and we find the defendant William Dwyer Not Guilty as charged in the fifth count of the indictment.

W. D. FREDENBERG,

Foreman of the Jury."

Which verdict was recorded by the clerk and read to the jury, who confirmed the same; at the request of counsel for defendant the said jury was polled and each juror answered separately for himself that the above is his verdict; thereupon said jury was discharged from the further consideration of said cause.

Monday, the 17th day of June, 1907.

No. 615—CONSPIRACY.

## THE UNITED STATES OF AMERICA

vs.

WILLIAM F. KETTENBACH, GEORGE H. KESTER and WILLIAM DWYER.

**Minutes of Court—June 17, 1907.**

Now came the Assistant U. S. District Attorney with the defendants in person and by their respective attorneys of record, and thereupon the said defendants by their said attorneys moved the Court in arrest of judgment herein, and upon consideration the Court ordered that said motion be and the same is hereby denied, to which ruling of the Court the said defendants by their counsel then and there excepted in due form of law; thereupon the Court ordered that the said defendants William F. Kettenbach and George H. Kester be each confined in the County Jail of ——— County, at ———, Idaho, for a period of eight months, and that the said defendants William F. Kettenbach and George H. Kester do each pay a fine of $1000.00, and ordered that the defendant William Dwyer be confined in the County Jail of ——— County, at ———, Idaho, for a period of eight months, and that he do pay a fine of $100.00, and further, that said imprisonment in said County Jail be not concurrent with the imprisonment heretofore adjudged in cause No. 616,

The United States vs. William Dwyer. On motion of the Assistant United States Attorney it is ordered that each of the defendants herein furnish a bond pending appeal in the sum of $2500.00, and on motion of counsel for defendants it is ordered that there be a stay of execution upon the judgment herein until the further order of the Court, the defendants having given notice of intention to move for a new trial and appeal in said cause, and that said defendants be given ninety da,s from this date in which to prepare, serve and file a Bill of Exceptions herein.

------

*In the District Court of the United States Within and for the District of Idaho.*

## THE UNITED STATES OF AMERICA

### vs.

## WILLIAM F. KETTENBACH, GEORGE H. KESTER and WILLIAM DWYER.

### Notice of Intention to Move for New Trial, etc.

To Honorable N. M. Ruick, U. S. District Attorney, for the District of Idaho:

You will please take notice that the defendants in the above-entitled action intends to move the Court to set aside the verdict herein, and for a new trial in the above-entitled cause, for the following causes materially affecting the substantial rights of the said defendant.

1.   Error in law committed during the trial and excepted to by the defendants.

2.   Newly discovered evidence material to the defendants who makes this application, and which they

could not with reasonable diligence have discovered and produced at the trial of the above-entitled cause.

3. Irregularity and misconduct of the jury, and that the jury which rendered the verdict against these defendants was unduly influenced in the consideration of the said cause; the statement of facts as to this ground of this motion will be shown by affidavit hereafter to be prepared and served upon the said United States District Attorney for the District of Idaho.

FORNEY & MOORE,
GEO. W. TANNAHILL,
Attorneys for Defendants.

Service of the within by copy admitted this 28th day of June, 1907.

N. M. RUICK,
U. S. District Attorney.

[Endorsed]: No. 615. In the District Court of the United States, District of Idaho. The United States of America, Plaintiff, vs. Wm. F. Kettenbach, George H. Kester and Wm. Dwyer, Defendants. Notice of Intention to Move for New Trial. Filed this 25th day of June, 1907. A. L. Richardson, Clerk. By M. W. Griffith, Deputy.

*In the District Court of the United States for the Northern Division of the District of Idaho.*

May Term, A. D. 1907.

No. 615.

Present: Hon. FRANK S. DIETRICH, Judge.

CONVICTED OF CONSPIRACY.

THE UNITED STATES

Against

WILLIAM F. KETTENBACH, GEORGE H. KESTER and WILLIAM DWYER.

**Judgment (Against Wm. F. Kettenbach and Geo. F. Kester).**

Now, on this 17th day of June, 1907, the United States District Attorney, with the defendants Wm. F. Kettenbach and Geo. H. Kester, and their counsel, Messrs. Forney & Moore and Geo. W. Tannahill, Esq., came into court; the defendant was duly informed by the Court of the nature of the indictment found against them for the crime of conspiracy committed on April 25, 1904, and Aug. 23, A. D. 1904, of their arraignment and plea of "Not Guilty as charged in said indictment," of their trial and the verdict of the jury on the 17th day of June, A. D. 1907, "Guilty as charged in the indictment." The defendants were then asked by the Court if they had any legal cause to show why judgment should not be pronounced against them, to which they replied that they had none, and no sufficient cause being shown or appearing to the Court.

Now, therefore, the said defendants Wm. F. Kettenbach and Geo. H. Kester having been convicted of the crime of conspiracy:

It is hereby considered and adjudged that the said defendants Wm. F. Kettenbach and Geo. H. Kester each do pay a fine of One ¡Thousand ($1000.00) Dollars, and the costs of this action taxed at ———— Dollars, and that they stand committed until said fine is paid.

And that they each be imprisoned and kept at hard labor in the County Jail of ———— county at ———— for the term of eight months, and it is further ordered that there be a stay of execution on the judgment until the further order of the Court pending appeal.

*In the District Court of the United States for the Northern Division of the District of Idaho.*

May Term, A. D. 1907.

Present: Hon. FRANK S. DIETRICH, Judge.

CONVICTED OF CONSPIRACY.

THE UNITED STATES

Against

WILLIAM F. KETTENBACH, GEORGE H. KESTER and *WILLIAM*

**Judgment (Against William Dwyer).**

Now, on this 17th day of June, 1907, the United States District Attorney, with the defendant Wm. Dwyer and his counsel, Messrs. Forney & Moore & Geo. W. Tannahill, Esq., came into court; the defendant was duly informed by the Court of the na-

ture of the indictment found against him for the
crime of conspiracy, committed on Apr. 25, 1904,
and Aug. 23, A. D. 1904, of his arraignment and
plea of "Not guilty as charged in said indictment,"
of his trial and the verdict of the jury on the 17th
day of June, A. D. 1907, "Guilty as charged in the
indictment." The defendant was then asked by the
Court if he had any legal cause to show why judgment should not be pronounced against him, to which
he replied that he had none, and no sufficient cause
being shown or appearing to the Court.

Now, therefore, the said defendant having been
convicted by the crime of conspiracy: It is hereby
considered and adjudged that the said defendant
William Dwyer do pay a fine of One Hundred
($100.00) Dollars, and the costs of this action taxed
at ——— Dollars, and that he stand committed until said fine is paid.

And that he be imprisoned and kept at hard labor
in the County Jail of ——— County of ———,
Idaho, for the term of eight months, said imprisonment not to be concurrent with imprisonment adjudged this day in cause No. 616, U. S. V. S. Wm.
Dwyer, and it is further ordered and adjudged that
there be a stay of execution on the judgment until
the further order of the Court preceding appeal.

[Endorsed]: In the District Court of the United
States for the District of Idaho. Judgment-roll No.
615. The United States vs. William F. Kettenbach
et al. Filed June 17, 1907. A. L. Richardson, Clerk.

*In the District Court of the United States, Within and for the District of Idaho.*

UNITED STATES OF AMERICA

vs.

WILLIAM DWYER, GEORGE H. KESTER and WILLIAM F. KETTENBACH.

**Order Extending Time in Which to File Bill of Exceptions, etc.**

On the application of Forney and Moore and George W. Tannahill for an extension of time in which to file Bill of Exceptions and affidavits on motion for new trial, and for good cause shown:

It is ordered that the time for filing said Bill of Exceptions and Affidavits be and is hereby extended until the first day of November, A. D. 1907.

Dated Sept. 3d, 1907.

FRANK S. DIETRICH,

Judge.

[Endorsed]: Case No. 615. In the U. S. District Court of the State of Idaho. United States of America, Plaintiff, vs. William Dwyer, George H. Kester and William F. Kettenbach, Defendants. Order Extending Time in Which to File Bill of Exceptions. Filed this 3d day of September, 1907. A. L. Richardson, Clerk of the U. S. District Court.

*In the District Court of the United States, Within and for the Northern Division of the District of Idaho.*

No. 615.

THE UNITED STATES OF AMERICA

vs.

WILLIAM F. KETTENBACH GEORGE H. KESTER and WILLIAM DWYER.

**Order Extending Time in Which to Propose and Serve Amendments to Proposed Bill of Exceptions.**

In the above-entitled cause, pursuant to stipulation this day filed, and it appearing to the Court that there is good cause therefor, it is hereby ordered that the plaintiff, the United States of America, by its counsel, have until and including thirty days from this date in which to propose and serve amendments to defendant's proposed Bill of Exceptions herein.

Dated, Nov. 2, 1907.

FRANK S. DIETRICH,

U. S. District Judge, District of Idaho.

[Endorsed]: No. 615. In the District Court of the United States, Northern Division, District of Idaho. United States vs. William F. Kettenbach et al. Order Extending Time to File Proposed Amendments to Bill of Exceptions. Filed Nov. 2, 1907. A. L. Richardson, Clerk.

*In the District Court of the United States, Within and for the District of Idaho.*

## THE UNITED STATES OF AMERICA

vs.

## WILLIAM F. KETTENBACH, GEORGE H. KESTER, and WILLIAM DWYER.

### Bill of Exceptions.

Be it remembered that this cause came on regularly for trial before Hon. Frank S. Dietrich, United States District Judge for the District of Idaho. N. M. Ruick, United States Attorney, appearing for the plaintiff, and Forney & Moore and George W. Tannahill for the defendants.

That prior to the introduction of any testimony it was stipulated and agreed in open court that either party should have sixty days after the rendition of judgment in which to prepare and serve a Bill of Exceptions in said cause, and thereafter the Court duly allowed the defendants until the first day of November, 1907, in which to prepare for settlement and serve Bill of Exceptions in said cause.

Thereafter the jury was duly empaneled, and the following testimony was introduced, and none other: And the following proceedings were had:

GUY L. WILSON, a witness called and sworn on behalf of the Government, testified as follows, on

Direct Examination by Mr. RUICK.

Q. State your name.

Mr. FORNEY.—The defendants object to the introduction of any testimony under this indictment

(Testimony of Guy L. Wilson.)

on the ground that it fails to state a crime; secondly, we object to each count in this indictment on the ground that it is duplicitous, in this, that various offenses are set up in one count, and are not separately stated. We further move the Court at this time to require the prosecution to elect upon which count in this indictment it will proceed, and further on the ground that the indictment shows on its face the offense is one of conspiracy, and is split up into five alleged separate and distinct offenses. Defendants further object to the introduction of any evidence as to any fraudulent acts set forth in said indictment which post dates the culmination of the conspiracy.

The COURT.—As I understand it, this is an objection and a motion. The objection is overruled, and the motion is denied. To which ruling of the Court the defendants excepted, which exception was duly allowed, and the witness answered:

A. Guy L. Wilson.

(Witness continuing:) I reside in Clarkston, Washington; have resided there six or seven years. I used to live in Palouse before I came there; I have lived in the Northwestern country all my life; I was born at Starbuck, Washington; I an twency-five years of age. I have a family consisting of my wife and baby. My wife is the daughter of Mrs. Francis A. Justice, summoned here as a witness in these cases. My occupation is electric lineman. I am in the employ of the Lewiston-Clarkston Company of Lewiston that furnishes light for the city of Lewiston,

(Testimony of Guy L. Wilson.)

Moscow and Genessee. I am foreman of construction. I have been engaged in this business as a lineman about seven years.

Q. Did you ever file on timber lands under the laws *of the laws* of the United States?

A. Yes, sir.

Q. Where were you residing at the time you made your filings? A. In Clarkston.

Q. Was that before or subsequent to your marriage? A. That was after I was married.

Q. State the circumstances under which you happened to file on these lands.

A. Why, it was my father in law talked about taking timber lands, and suggested that I should go up and set a claim too.

Q. Whom do you refer to as your father in law?

A. Mr. Justice.

Q. Where was he living at that time?

A. In Clarkston.

Q. Mr. Justice is since deceased, is he?

A. Yes, sir.

Q. State who, if anyone, you saw concerning the matter before you made your filing other than Mr. Justice?

A. I saw the defendant here, William Dwyer.

Q. Where did you see him?

A. I saw him several times; one time I saw him in Clarkston.

Q. State the first interview you had with Mr. Dwyer?

A. Mr. Dwyer told me he was going up there—

(Testimony of Guy L. Wilson.)

And be it remembered that then and there the following proceedings were had:

Mr. FORNEY.—Objected to on the ground that before the defendant Kester and Kettenbach could be bound by this testimony, the prosecution should show by prima facie evidence, or at least, by some evidence, that there was a conspiracy.

The COURT.—The objection is overruled, with the understanding that the testimony will be of no avail unless the conspiracy is ultimately shown; the Court will, within reasonable bounds, permit the prosecution to put in proof in such order as may seem to it advisable.

To which ruling of the Court the defendants and each of them excepted, which exception was allowed by the Court, and the witness answered:

A.   Mr. Dwyer told me he was going up to this timber and I could go along with him to the timber claim.

Q.   Where was it he told you this?

A.   I think it was in Clarkston.

Q.   Was it the first inteeview you had with him?

A.   I think it was.

Q.   Did you have later interviews with him before going up to the timber?

A.   No, I don't believe I did.

Q.   What understanding, if any, did you have with Mr. Dwyer relative to your timber claim before going up to the timber?

And be it remembered that the following proceedings were then and there had:

(Testimony of Guy L. Wilson.)

Mr. FORNEY.—I object to that on the ground that before the defendants Kester & Kettenbach could be bound by this testimony the prosecution should show by at least some evidence that there was a conspiracy, which objection was by the Court overruled, to which ruling of the Court the *defendants which* exception was allowed.

Q. Did you have any understanding with Mr. Dwyer concerning your timber claim, or any talk with him before you went up to the timber?

Mr. FORNEY.—Same objection, and further the question calls for the understanding witness ha*f* with Mr. Dwyer, and calls for the conclusion of the witness.

The COURT.—The objection is overruled, with instructions to the witness to answer this yes or no, to which ruling of the Court the defendants then and there e*x*epted, which exception was allowed, and the witness answers:

A. Yes, sir.

Q. State the conversation you had with Mr. Dwyer relative to your timber claim?

A. Why, he told me—how much I would get for it—that is, after he turned these claims over.

Q. Speak a little louder.

A. He told me that our expenses would be paid up there after he turned the claims over; we would get a certain amount of money out of them.

Q. Who was he referring to?

A. He referred to myself.

(Testimony of Guy L. Wilson.)

Q. Now the—give his exact language, as near as you can—as far as you can now recall it?

A. He said that he would pay our expenses up there and back, and after he had turned these claims over, that there would be something like $150 in it for me.

Q. Who did he say would pay your expenses up there and back?

A. I understood he was to pay my expenses.

Q. Did this conversation occur in the first inter view you had with him?    A. Yes, sir.

Q. Do you know if other parties were about to take timber claims under the same arrangement?

A. Yes, sir; I knew it.

Q. Did you know it from anything Mr. Dwyer said to you?    A. No, I don't think so.

Q. Who went up to the timber with you, or were in the same company?

A. There was Mr. and Mrs. Justice and Mr. Hopper and *M* O'Brien, and Mr. Dwyer and my-self.

Q. Mr. Justice and Mrs. Justice?

A. Yes, sir.

Q. And what is Mr. Hopper's name?

A. It is E. H. Hopper, I think.

Q. And his wife?    A. No, sir.

Q. Who made the arrangements for your going?

A. Well, the arrangements were—we were just told we were ready to go—Mr. Dwyer said we were to go up on a certain day.

Q. He fixed the day for you to go?

(Testimony of Guy L. Wilson.)

A.  He said he was going that day; yes, *sr*.

Q.  What did he say*d* concerning it?

A.  He said that they were all going up that day to look up their timber.

Q.  And what further, if anything, led you to go on that day, what fur*h*er, if anything, did he sày?

A.  I don't remember anything fur*t*er being said.

Q.  What did he tell you to do?

A.  He said if I wanted to go, to go with the rest of them the same day.

Q.  That same day?      A.  Yes, sir.

Q.  Where did you see him to have this conversation with him?

A.  I don't remember just where I saw him.

Q.  Did you go up to the timber?

A.  Yes, sir.

Q.  Was Mr. Dwyer with you?      A.  Yes, sir.

Q.  State what you did pursuant to this suggestion of his; state what was done.

A.  We went up as far as Pierce City, and went out into the timber, into Mr. Dwyer's camp; I guess it was Mr. Dwyer's camp, and part of the part\ stayed there and Mr. and Mrs. Justice and myself, we came back to Pierce that same day.

Q.  What did you do toward looking over the timber?

A.  We rode through the timber; that is all that we done toward looking at it as we went to the camp.

Q.  You rode through it; how were you traveling?

A.  On horseback.

Q.  Where did you get your horses?

(Testimony of Guy L. Wilson.)

A.   Orofino.

Q.   Who supplied the horses?

A.   I suppose Mr. Dwyer got them, I don't know.

Q.   Did you supply them?        A.   No, sir.

Q.   Were Mr. and Mrs. Justice travelling the same way as yourself?        A.   Yes, sir.

Q.   On horseback?        A.   Yes, sir.

Q.   How many of them were on horseback?

A.   There were five, besides myself.

Q.   Along what were you traveling—the road, the trail or through the timber or through the woods?

A.   It was through the timber, practically, all the way on a trail.

Q.   On a trail?

A.   There was a wagon raod a ways out of Pierce, practicaly on a trail the most of the way.

Q.   How far out of Pierce did you go, about?

A.   I don't know exactly, somewhere about 12 or 15 miles, I suppose.

Q.   Part way on the road and part way on the trail?

A.   Yes, sir.

Q.   Did you go off the trail and travel through the timber for the purpose of seeing it?

A.   I think not.

Q.   You know whether you did or not?

A.   No, I don't remember of it.

Q.   What did you do when you got up there to the timber?

A.   We rode out as far as his camp and ate dinner and came back.

(Testimony of Guy L. Wilson.)

Q.  Mr. Dwyer had a camp there?

A.  He was stopping there.  I supposed it was his camp.

Q.  You say you supposed it was his camp? What led you to that belief?  What action on the part of Mr. Dwyer made you believe it was his camp?

A.  He was the only one that was there—the rest —he was going to stop there the next few days.

Q.  He remained there, did he?      A.  Yes, sir.

Q.  He didn't come back with you?      A.  No.

Q.  Did you have lunch there at the camp?

A.  Yes, sir.

Q.  Who cooked the lunch or dinner?

A.  I think Mr. Bliss had dinner ready.

Q.  Mr. Bliss?      A.  Yes, sir.

Q.  What Mr. Bliss is that?

A.  A Mr. Bliss who lives in Clarkston.

Q.  A timber locator, a cruiser?

A.  I don't know whether he is a timber locator or not.

Q.  You don't remember his initials?

A.  No, I do not.

Q.  He was there at the camp, was he?

A.  Yes, sir.

Q.  Who came back with you?

A.  Mr. and Mrs. Justice.

Q.  What did Mr. Dwyer say relative to the timber while you were up there?

A.  Why, he told me we had passed through the timber that we were going to file on.

(Testimony of Guy L. Wilson.)

Q. He said you had passed through it?

A. Yes, sir.

Q. Did he show you any of the corners?

A. Why, he didn't show me none; no.

Q. Did you see him showing Mr. and Mrs. Justice any corners?

A. No, I don't think so.

Q. Did you notice whether Mr. and Mrs. Justice went out and around through the timber to look at it?

A. They might have but I don't remember them doing it, though.

Q. How long were you there at the camp altogether, do you think?

A. Probably an hour and a half.

Q. Well, you returned to Orofino?

A. We returned to Pierce that day.

Q. You returned to Pierce that day?

A. *Ye,* sir.

Q. And stopped over night?    A. Yes, sir.

Q. Next day where did you go?

A. To Orofino.

Q. And took the train for Lewiston?

A. Yes, sir.

Q. How long were you gone altogether from Lewiston including the day of your leaving and the day of your return?

A. Altogether about five days, four or five days.

Q. Who paid the expenses of this trip, Mr. Wilson, your expenses?

A. I think Mr. Dwyer.

(Testimony of Guy L. Wilson.)

Q. Did you pay them yourself?    A. No.

Q. Who supplied your railroad ticket, if you know, who handed it to you?

A. I didn't have any.

Q. How did you go on the train?

A. Got on the train and nothing was said about it, about a ticket, or anything to me.

Q. How is that?

A. I got on the train. I don't know who took up the tickets; I didn't have one.

Q. Do you know whether Mr. and Mrs. Justice had a ticket?    A. I do not.

Q. Who paid your other expenses while you were up there?

A. I suppose Mr. Dwyer paid them; I didn't pay them.

Q. What led you to believe Mr. Dwyer paid them?

A. Well, I suppose—I don't think any of the rest of the party paid them.

Q. Did you pay any hotel at Orofino?

A. No, sir.

Q. Or, rather, at Pierce?    A. No, sir.

Q. Nor any livery bills for the use of the horses?

A. No, sir.

Q. Nor any other expenses whatever?

A. No, sir.

Q. None whatever on the trip?    A. No, sir.

Q. How long after you returned to Clarkston was it before you filed?

(Testimony of Guy L. Wilson.)

A. I went up there in October, I think, and filed some time in April.

Q. What was the reason of the long delay between your seeing or going up there and your filing on the land?

A. Why, I don't think this land was ready for filing yet.

Q. You don't think it was yet open to filing at the Land Office?    A. I don't think so.

Q. Had Mr. Dwyer said anything about this, or explained anything about it—the land not being open to settlement yet—what had he said, if anything, yet?

A. I believe he had said it was not open for settlement yet.

Q. What did he say further?

A. That is all I remember of him saying about it, that it was not open.

Q. How did you know when to go and file, go to the Land Office?

A. Mr. Dwyer told me of it—to go and file and get in line.

Q. What did he say as you now recall it?

A. Why, he said, to go and get in the line-up which was forming at the land office—he said, "Be ready to file when the land office is opened up for filing on the land."

Q. Explain what you mean to the jury by the line-up?

A. Well, there were a good many people there, and each one, as you went up there, if a man was

(Testimony of Guy L. Wilson.)

first, he was No. 1, and so on down; each man as you go you were given a number to have that number in the line.

Q. The land was going to be opened up on a certain day? A. Yes, sir.

Q. And parties went there to the Land Office?

A. Yes, sir.

Q. And the first one there got the first number?

A. Yes, sir.

Q. How many days before the land was actually open to settlement was it that this line-up began to be formed, if you remember?

A. I think it was about six or seven days; seven days.

Q. Did you go and get in line as Dwyer told you to do?

A. I got in line for a short time only.

Q. You got in line for a short time only; what number did you get in the line?

A. I don't remember now—fourteen, or something like that.

Q. Who do you remember as having been in the same line-up with you?

A. Well, there was Mr. Hopper, he was in line, I remember him, and Mrs. Justice.

Q. Mr. Justice was not in this line-up was he?

A. No, sir.

Q. Why wasn't he in the line-up?

A. I think he was sick at that time.

(Testimony of Guy L. Wilson.)

Q.  Sick with the illness which later·carried him off?    A.  Yes, sir.

Q.  He never did file, did he?    A.  No, sir.

Q.  Do you remember whether Mr. O'Brien was also?    A.  I don't think he was; no.

Q.  Well, there were three of your party, as you recall, who were in the line-up?    A.  Yes, sir.

Q.  How many do you recall of having been in the line-up?  About how many numbers were issued?

A.  I could not say; there was a good many; there must have been thirty or forty.

Q.  You say you were in the line-up for a short time only?    A.  Yes, sir.

Q.  How did you arrange to hold your place in the line-up without being there?

A.  I got a young fellow to stay in my place.

Q.  Who did you hire?

A.  A young man by the name of Walter Case.

Q.  How long did he have to stand in line for you?

A.  I think it was seven days.

Q.  That is your recollection?    A.  Yes, sir.

Q.  How much did you pay him a day?

A.  Two dollars a day, I think.

Q.  What arrangement did you have, if any, for paying him?

A.  Why, I spoke to Dwyer and told him I could not be away from my work, and he said to get some-one, and so I got this young fellow.

Q.  And he told you get someone?

(Testimony of Guy L. Wilson.)

Mr. FORNEY.—Objected to as leading and suggestive.

The COURT.—Yes; it is objectionable to repeat the answer go on.

Q. What, if anything, did Mr. Dwyer say about the payment of this young man?

A. I don't remember what he—his exact words.

Q. Did you pay this young man?

A. Yes, sir.

Q. How much did you pay him?

A. Fourteen dollars.

Q. At what time relative to the time you filed did you pay him?

A. It was some time afterwards; a couple of weeks afterwards, I should think.

Q. Did you have any talk with Mr. Dwyer afterwards about this payment the matter of payment?

A. Why, I told him this young fellow wanted his money, and he said he would pay him.

Q. Do you know whether he did pay him?

A. Yes, sir.

Q. How and when did he pay him?

A. He paid me, and I paid Mr. Case.

Q. Stte the circumstances under which he paid you?

A. He gave me a check for fourteen dollars, and I went and got the money and paid this young fellow.

Q. Where did you get the money?

A. To the Lewiston National Bank.

Q. On what bank was the check drawn?

(Testimony of Guy L. Wilson.)

A.    The Lewiston National Bank.

Q.    To whose order?    A.    To my order.

Q.    Do you remember whose name was signed to the check?

A.    I think Mr. Dwyer's name was signed to the check.

Q.    You think it was?    A.    Yes, sir.

Q.    Did you get a receipt from the young man for the pay?    A.    No, sir.

Q.    When the day came that the land was open for filing, did you take your place in line?

A.    Yes, sir.

Q.    How did you know the date on which the lands were going to be opened for filing at the land office?

A.    Why, I made— Mr. Dwyer told me what day the land would be open.

Q.    Who made out your filing papers, your sworn statement?

A.    They were made out in Mr. I. N. Smith's office; I couldn't say exactly who made them out.

Q.    Mr. Smith, the attorney at Lewiston?

A.    Yes, sir.

Q.    How did you happen to have them made out in Mr. Smith's office?

A.    I didn't have them made out.

Q.    You didn't have them made out?

A.    No, sir.

Q.    How did they happen to be made out there, if you know?    A.    I don't know.

Q.    Did you give any instructions to have them made out?    A.    No, sir.

(Testimony of Guy L. Wilson.)

Q. How did you know where to go and get the papers?

A. Mr. Dwyer told me to go up there, and that he wanted to get my name, or something, I think.

Q. Again state what he said to you about going up to Smith's office.

A. Ho told me to go up there, that he wanted to see me there and wanted to get my name, I think, and my occupation.

Q. Did you go up with him?

A. No, I don't think I did.

Q. Well, what day was this relative to the day on which you filed?

A. I think it was the day before I filed.

Q. Where did you see Mr. Dwyer on the day before, if you recollect?

A. I think it was in and around the bank building there some place.

Q. Your work took you to Lewiston, did it?

A. Yes, sir.

Q. Did you ever get a description of this land, Mr. Wilson, prior to your filing on it?

A. I don't remember of ever getting one.

Q. Did you ever give the description of the land to Mr. Smith, or any other person for the purpose of having your papers made out?

A. No, sir.

Q. Do you know who did give the description?

A. No, sir; I do not.

Q. Did you know what land you were filing on when you presented this paper in the land office?

(Testimony of Guy L. Wilson.)

A.   Why, only the description which was on this paper was all.

Q.   Did you know whether or not this was the land which you may hqve seen on your trip up there?

A.   No, sir; I do not.

Q.   When did you go to Mr. Smith's office?

A.   The day before I filed.

Q.   By whose direction?     A.   Mr. Dwyer's.

Q.   How long after he had got your name and occupation?

A.   Well, I gave that at the office.   I told him that in Mr. Smith's office.

The COURT.—Told who—Mr. Dwyer?

A.   I told Mr. Dwyer that; yes, sir.

Q.   You said, I believe, that you didn't go up there with Mr. Dwyer?

A.   No, sir; I don't think I did.

Q.   Now, state the transactions that day; that is what I want to get at, without my having to draw them out from you.   State how the thing occurred.

A.   He told me to come up there; that he wanted to get my name and occupation, and I went in and gave it to him and went out again.

Q.   Went what?

A.   I went into Mr. Smith's office and gave it to him, and I want there but a minute and went out again.

Q.   You gave it to Mr. Dwyer?     A.   Yes, sir.

Q.   I asked you whether or not you went up with Mr. Dwyer or went up later?

(Testimony of Guy L. Wilson.)

A. I went up after—after I think he had told me to go up there.

Q. Where did you see Mr. Dwyer when you went up?

A. If I remember, it was around the bank building some place; I was around there that day.

Q. Later you say you saw him and went up to Smith's office. Did you see Mr. Dwyer there?

A. Yes, sir; Mr. Dwyer was there.

Q. Mr. Dwyer was there when you went up?

A. Yes, sir.

Q. Where is Mr. Smith's office located relative to the location of the land office at that time?

A. It was across the hall from the land office.

Q. State whether or not it is on the same floor of the building.    A. Yes, it is on the same floor.

Q. Which floor?    A. The second floor.

Q. The second floor—describe the land office, how it is arranged, and where Mr. Smith's office is relative to the land office, or was at that time.

A. They both front—both—the land office is one front room, so is Mr. Smith's office, as you go upstairs, you turn to the right, and go to the land office, and your turn right around to the left and go to Mr. Smith's office.

Q. Now, where is the Lewiston National Bank located?    A. Why, underneath these rooms.

Q. Now, how do you reach the land office from the street—how did you, I refer to that time?

A. You go around on Fourth Street; there is an entrance, a stairway that you go up.

(Testimony of Guy L. Wilson.)

Q.  That goes up in the bank building?

A.  Yes, sir.

Q.  And when you get up to the top of the stairs, at the second floor, where would you go to go to the land office?

A.  We would turn right around to the right, and it is across.

Q.  And where would you go to go to Mr. Smith's office?      A.  You would turn to the left.

Q.  Now, what is there then between the land office door and the door opening into Mr. Smith's office?

A.  I think there is a room in between there.

Q.  In what?      A.  In between the doors.

Q.  In the hallway what is there between the entrance to the land office and the entrance to Mr. Smith's office?      A.  The stairway.

Q.  What else? *Wh't* do you include in the stairway?      A.  There is a hallway.

Q.  And what else connected with the stairway? What protects the stairway?  What protects parties coming up the stairway?

A.  There is a railing there.

Q.  About how far is the entrance to Mr. Smith's office from the entrance to the land office, in a direct line across the hall?      A.  Probably thirty feet.

Q.  The land office at that time was in the Lewiston National Bank Building?      A.  Yes, sir.

Q.  *Oer* the bank in which Mr. Kettenbach and Mr. Kester are officers?      A.  Yes, sir.

(Testimony of Guy L. Wilson.)

Q. What transpired, Mr. Wilson, when you went up there to Mr. Smith's office? What took place in the office?

A. Why, Mr. Dwyer asked me my name and occupation, and that is all I remember taking plce; I went in there just a minute, and went out again.

Q. Who do you recall was in the office at this time?

A. I don't remember anyone except Mr. Smith; Mr. Smith was in the office.

Q. And Mr. Dwyer?     A. Yes, sir.

Q. You don't remember anyone else?

A. No, sir; I do not.

Do you remember who made out your papers?

A. I don't remember who wrote them out. Mr. Smith was writing on a typewriter—I don't remember whether he wrote those papers out or not.

Q. Did you get your papers at this time?

A. No.

Q. How long were you in the office altogether?

A. Not over five minutes, anyway.

Q. When did you return, if at all, to this office?

A. I went back there the day I filed, I think.

Q. The day you filed—who did you find in the office at this time?

A. I don't remember who was in there at that time, the day I filed.

Q. Who handed you your papers?

A. Mr. Dwyer gave them to me, my filing papers.

Q. Where did he give them to you?

(Testimony of Guy L. Wilson.)

A.  Well, it was around the bank building some place; I couldn't say just where it was.

Q.  Do you recall whether or not it was in Mr. Smith's office?

A.  No, I do not; I do not know.

Q.  What did you do when you got those papers?

A.  Why, after I got those papers—in the morning I went and filed; I filed that morning.

Q.  You filed, then, soon after you got the papers?

A.  Yes, sir.

Q.  And while still in the building?

A.  Yes, sir.

Q.  I have referred to your papers, your filing papers.  I now show you a paper already marked "Plaintiff's Exhibit 1 for Identification," and ask you if you recognize this paper and your signature thereon?

Be it remembered that the following proceedings were then had:

Mr. FORNEY.—The defendant objects to any testimony—

The COURT.—They are not offered yet.

Mr. RUICK.—I have not offered them at all.  I only ask him if he recognizes that.

Mr. FORNEY.—I will put the objection in at this time, anyway.  I object to the introduction of any testimony relative to an overt act set forth in the indictment as connecting these defendants with this case until some evidence of a conspiracy has been introduced, which objection was by the Court overruled; to which ruling of the Court the defendants

(Testimony of Guy L. Wilson.)

excepted, which exception was allowed by the Court and the witness answered:

A. Yes, sir.

Q. Are these the papers you procured at Mr. Smith's office and later filed in the land office?

A. These are the papers Mr. Dwyer gave me.

Q. At the time you mention?    A. Yes, sir.

Mr. RUICK.—In order that the record may be regular and these exhibits appear in their logical order, I will now offer in evidence the paper in duplicate, just identified by the witness purporting to be "sworn Statement Timber and Stone Land" filed by this witness, Guy L. Wilson, April 25, 1904, in the United States Land Office, Lewiston, Idaho.

And be it remembered that then and there the following proceedings were had:

Mr. RUICK.—We offer this paper as it is in duplicate, and ask that it be marked "Plaintiff's Exbibit 1" with to-day's date appended. I take this precaution so that the exhibit may be identified as an exhibit in this case, it already bearing a mark.

Mr. FORNEY.—The defendants object to the introduction of this testimony on the ground it is irrelevant and immaterial and incompetent, and on the further ground that there is no evidence tending to show any conspiracy, no evidence has been introduced tending to show any conspiracy by the defendants, and on the further ground that the evidence is objectionable for the reason that it post dates the consummation of the conspiracy as alleged in the indictment. I will ask your Honor to let this objection

(Testimony of Guy L. Wilson.)

run to the testimony of this witness throughout and we will not renew it.

The COURT.—This is the application of this witness to enter some lands or land referred to in the indictment?

Mr. RUICK.—Yes, to *a*land referred to in the indictment.

The COJRT.—The objection is overruled.

To which ruling of the Court the defendants excepted, which exception was allowed by the Court.

The COURT.—Let it be marked.

Whereupon said documents were admitted in evidence, and marked Plaintiff's Exhibits 1, J. E. B., May 21, 1907.

Mr. RUICK.—For the information of the jury at this time, and in order that you may follow this evidence relating to this sworn statement, I will now read one of them (reads):

"This affidavit can be made only upon the personal knowle*de* of the applicant derived from his own personal examination of the land.

"TIMBER AND STONE LAND.

Sworn Statement

(To be made in duplicate.)

Land Office at Lewiston, Idaho.

Date April 25, 1904.

I, Guy L. Wilson, of Clarkston, ——— County, State of Washington, desire to avail myself of the provisions of the Act of Congress of June 3, 1878, entitled An Act for the Sale of Timber Lands in the States of California, Oregon, Nevada and in Wash-

(Testimony of Guy L. Wilson.)

ington Territory, as extended to all the public lands of the States by Act of August 4, 1892, for the purchase of Lots 3, 4, and the NE. ¼ of the SW. ¼ and the NW. ¼ of the SE. ¼ of Section 19, Township 39 North, range 5, East B. M., in the District of Lands subject to sale at Lewiston, Idaho, do solemnly swear that I am a native citizen of the United States, of the age of twenty-two and by occupation a laborer that I have *personally said* lands and from my personal knowledge state that said land is unfit for cultivation and valuable chiefly for its timber; that it is uninhabited; that it contains no mining or other improvements, nor, as I verily believe, has any valuable deposit of gold, silver, cinnebar, copper, or coal; that I have made no other application under said acts; that I do not apply to purchase the land above described on specu*l*tion, but in good faith to appropiate it for my own exclusive use and benefit, and that I have not edirectly or indirectly made any agreement or contract, or in any way or manner, with any person or persons whomsoever, by which the title I may acquire from the Government of the United States may inure in whole or in part *ot* the benefit of any person except myself, and that my postoffice address is Clarkston, Washington.

GUY L. WILSON,"

"I hereby certify that the foregoing affidavit was read to affiant in my presence before he signed his name thereto, that said affiant is to me personally known (or has been satisfac*tisfac*torily identified before me by ——) and that I verily believe him to

(Testimony of Guy L. Wilson.)

be the person he represents himself to be, and that this affidavit was subscribed and sworn to before me this 25th day of April, 1904.

J. B. WEST,

Register.''

''(NOTE) Every person swearing falsely to the foregoing affidavit is guilty of perjury and will be punished as provided by law for such offense

"In addition thereto the money that may be paid for the land is forfeited, and all conveyance of the land or of any right, title or claim thereto are absolutely null and void as against the United States.

"In case the party has been naturalized, or has declared his intention to become a citizen, a certified copy of his certificate of naturalization or declaration of intention, as the case may be, must be furnished.

"If the residence is in a city, the street and number must be given."

This document is endorsed on the back:

"Timber Lands. Acts of June 3d, 1878, and August 4th, 1892,

"Sworn Statement.

"Land Office at Lewiston, Idaho.

"Section 19, Township 39 N. Range 5 W. B. M.

GUY L. WILSON."

Q. Mr. Wilson, before you presented this sworn statement at the land office for filing—I refer now to Plintiff's Exhibit 1, J.E.B., just identified by you, did you have a conversation with any person in relation to the matters which you would have to swear to in this sworn statement?      A. Yes, sir.

(Testimony of Guy L. Wilson.)

Q. With whom?     A. Mr. Dwyer.

Q. Where did that conversation occur?

. A. Why, it was around the bank building, I think.

Q. Around the bank building?     A. Yes, sir.

Q. At what time relative to the time that he handed you this paper?

A. I think it was when he gave it to me that the conversation took place.

Q. What was tht conversation, what did he say?

A. Why he said that there was—was some things in there I would have to swear to; that it was being done every day, there was nothing unusual about it.

Q. What further, if anything, did he say?

A. I don't remember anything further at that time.

Q. Do you know what things he referred to in this affidavit?     A. No, I don't know now.

Q. You don't know what he referred to in that affidavit?     A. I don't remember.

The COURT.—You may ask him whether he knew at that time.

Mr. RUICK.—I think that would be a proper question.

Q. Did you know at that time what matters he referred to?     A. Yes, sir.

Q. How did you know it?

A. Well, he talked it over with me at that time, I think.

Q. What did he talk over with you?

(Testimony of Guy L. Wilson.)

A.   Well, I don't remember now just what was said at that time.

Q.   Well, do you remember the *m*tters? Do you remember what the conv*e*sation related to?

A.   It related to the filing.

Q.   Now, you say that he talked the matter over with you at that time?     A.   Yes, sir.

Q.   Now, I want you to state to the best of your recollection what matters he called your attention to, if any?

A.   I think the only thing I remember was about being on the land—that—examining the land. I could say I had been over it, as I had passed through it as we went out to the camp that day.

Q.   Refresh your recollection from this paper which you have already identified, P*l*intiff's Exhibit 1, J.E.B, " and state to the jury what matters you recollect as having been talked over with Mr. Dwyer at that time.

A.   That is all I remember of—about being on the land; he told me we had passed through this timber, and I had been on the land; I would answer the question that way.

Q.   When did you read that affidavit over, Mr. Wilson?

A.   I think I read it *ove* when he handed it to me.

Q.   Did you note the statements in that affidavit carefully at the time you read them ov*ee*?

A.   No, I don't th*ik* I did very c*r*efully.

Q.   Do you recall of reading that statement there to the effect: "I do not apply to purchase the land

(Testimony of Guy L. Wilson.)

above described on speculation, but in good faith to appropriate it to my own exclusive use and benefit? Do you remember that?

A.   Yes, sir; I remember that.

Q.   Do you remember whether or not you had any conversation with Mr. Dwyer about it at t*ht* time?

A.   Yes, sir; I think he told me that.

Q.   Now, what did he tell you about that, if anything?

A.   As I remember it, he said that question here you take it up for your own benefit, that I was taking it up for my own benefit, what money I would get when he turned the claims over was merely a verbal agreement that did not apply to that at all.

At that time, you also made this statement "That I have not directly or indirectly made any agreement or contract in any way or *mnner* with any person or persons whomsoever by which the title that I may acquire from the Goveenment of the United *Sttes* may *inur* in whole or in part to the benefit of any person except myself." Do you remember whether or not Mr. Dwyer said anything to you in relation to that part?

A.   As near as I remember he said that I had not made any contract, that was just a verbal agreement, and that when he turned these claims over I would get this money for them.

Q.   How did this conversation between you and Mr. Dwyer come up? How did it start, this conversation relative to the contents of this sworn statement?

(Testimony of Guy L. Wilson.)

A. Why, I think that when he handed me the paper—why I don't just remember, but I expect that I asked him about those things.

Q. And what was your purpose in asking him about those things?

A. I wanted to know how I would answer them.

Q. Did you ever have any experience in these matters before?    A. No, sir.

Q. Stte again and by itself what Mr. Dwyer said to you concerning this part of your application which reads: "That I do not apply to purchase the land above described on speculation, but in good faith to appropriate it to my own exclusive use and benefit"; what did he say about that?

A. Well, he said that I was getting the benefit from it; I was taking it up for myself, and I derived the benefit.

Q. Did he explain to you how you derived the benefit?

A. When this land was turned *ove*, I would get this money for it.

The COURT.—Get what money?

A. This $150.

The COURT.—The Court is not clear as to what the agreement was between this witness and Mr. Dwyer.

Q. Now then, have you and Mr. Dwyer already agreed upon an amount you were to receive?

A. Yes, sir.

Q. State when and where?

(Testimony of Guy L. Wilson.)

A. It was in Clarkston, at time I first talked of going up in the timber.

Q. What was that?

A. He said he would pay our expenses up there and when he turned the claims *ove* there would be about $150 left for me.

Q. Who went to the land office with you when you filed these papers? Who, if anyone, to file this sworn statement?

A. I don't remember; there were several filed that same day.

Q. Who do you recollect as filing the same day?

A. Mrs. Justice, I think, filed the same day

Q. Was she in the land office at the same time?

A. I believe she was.

Q. Was she in Mr. Smith's office at the same time you were?     A. No, sir.

Q. Was anything—or had anything been said up to this time between you and Mr. Dwyer or any other person as to where you were to get the money to pay for the land?

A. He said he would get the money.

Q. Can you tell the Court what Mr. Dwyer said about these matters, stating this agreement to which you refer, what was the understanding, the agreement stated to you by Mr. Dwyer? State what was said by Mr. Dwyer on this subject as to where you were to get the money.

A. I did not know where he would get it; it was to be furnished to me by him.

(Testimony of Guy L. Wilson.)

Q. You say that agreement was had at Clarkston?    A. Yes, sir.

Q. Before you went up to see the land?

A. Yes, sir.

(Adjournment until 2 P. M. to-day, May 21, 1907.) Direct Examination of GUY L. WILSON Resumed.

Q. What, if anything, was said at that time about the dispositon of this land when you got title to it?

A. When I got title to it I was to deed it to him or some one; I don't know just who.

Q. Well, who stated that? What was said about that? That is what I wqnt to know.

A. He said as soon as we proved up we would make out this deed and then I would get my money.

Q. What money?    A. This $150.

Q. Who, if anyone, went with you to the Land Office at the time you filed this sworn statement in duplicate (Plantiff Exhibit 1, J. E. B.) do you recall?

A. I don't recall who was with me, there was several people filing.

Q. Ate the same time?    A. Yes, sir.

Q. This sworn statement appears to have been filled out partially with a rubber stamp, the "Lewiston, Idaho" being a rubber stamp and the remaining blanks with one exception ar filled out on a typewriter. Do you know who inserted the "22" in figures there, referring to your age?

A. No, I do not.

Q. That is with a pen, I am referring to now?

(Testimony of Guy L. Wilson.)

A. I don't know.

Q. Who else was in the Land Office when you filed these papers, if you recall?

A. I don't recall anyone except that I think Mrs. Justice was there about th*q*t time.

Q. Where did you get the money to pay the filing fee? A. Mr. Dwyer gave me the money.

Q. Where did he give it to you?

A. Why, it was some place there in the bank building; I don't know just where.

Q. When, relative to the time that he filed this statement.

A. It was the same morning that I filed.

Q. How much did he give you, do you remember?

A. I don't remember the exact mount; some*ti*ng like $16, I think.

Q. Is that the money that you paid into the Land Office? A. *Ye,* sir.

Q. At the time you filed this application to purchase? A. Yes, sir.

Q. Did you have any money left out of the amount which he had given you?

A. I don'*te* believe I did; I don't remember of any.

Q. Was that statement, the sworn statement to which I have referred and called your attention to bearing your signature?

A. Yes, sir; that is my signature.

Q. And it bears the certificate of Mr. J. B. West, Register, to the effect that you were duly sworn to this affidavit? A. Yes, sir.

(Testimony of Guy L. Wilson.)

Q.   Do you remember the fact of being sworn by Mr. West?

A.   Well, I remember I was sworn; I am not certain whether it *ws* Mr. West or not.

Q.   Sworn to this paper?

A.   Yes, sir.

Q.   There in the land office?     A.   Yes, sir.

Q.   You are not certain that it was Mr. West that swore you?     A.   No, sir.

Mr. RUICK.—(Paper shown witness purporting to be a nonmineral affidavit filed in the United States Land Office on April 25th, in the United Sttes Land Office at Lewiston, Idaho, April 25th, 1904, describing the same land included in sworn sttatement of this witness heretofore referred to and also beairing the signature of this witness.)

Q.   Look at this paper, and see if your signature is on th*t* paper.

A.   Yes, sir; that is my signature.

Q.   Have you any recollection with regard to that paper?     A.   I have not.

Q.   Do you know where that paper was made out?

A.   No, sir; I do not.

Q.   Or who made it out?     A.   No, sir.

Q.   Did you have anything to do with making out that paper, filling out the blanks?

A.   No, sir.

Q.   Do you know whether you got that paper at the same time you got your sworn statement?

A.   No, sir; I don't remember.

(Testimony of Guy L. Wilson.)

Q.  Do you remember of filing this in the Lewiston Land Office?      A.  I do not.

Q.  This other paper purporting to be notice for publication, timber land, Act June 3d, 1878, dated at Lewiston, Idaho, April 25th, 1904, describing the same land as included in your sworn statement, also containing the certificate of the Registee as to the posting of the notice.  Do you remember anything about the paper?      A.  No, sir; I do not.

Q.  Do you reember of having had anyhing to do with it?

A.  No, I never had anything to do with it.

Mr. RUICK.—In this particular case, your Honor, being the first one named, the first one that I have called, I will offer in evidence these documents.  I do not intend to follow this up by offering similar documents in regard to the other cases, but this, as much as anything, by way of illustration, as illustrating the evidence which I shall produce later by other witnesses.

The  COURT.—One is a  non-mineral  affidavit; what is the other?

Mr. RUICK.—The other is notice for publication of the application of Guy L. Wilson, Clarkston, Washington, the non-mineral affidavit we will ask to have the reporter mark Plaintiff's Exhibit 1-A, J. H. P., 5/21/07.

And be it remembered the following proceedings were then and there had:

Mr. FORNEY.—We object to it on the ground it is incompetent, irrelevant and immaterial, not prop-

(Testimony of Guy L. Wilson.)

erly authenticated, no proper foundation having been laid for their introduction.

The COURT.—The non-mineral affidavit was made by him, was it not?

Mr. RUICK.—Yes.

The COURT.—I will overrule the objection as to the non-mineral affidavit. Is there any identification to the other?

Mr. RUICK.—No, there is none; there is no signature. We will have to wait until Mr. West comes.

The COURT.—The non-mineral affidavit may be received in evidence.

To which ruling of the Court the defendants excepted, which exception was allowed, and said paper was admitted in evidence and marked Plintiff's Exhibit 1-A, J. H. P., 5/21/07.

(Omitted here—appears elsewhere.)

Q. Who procured your witnesses, Mr. Wilson, if you know?     A. I don't know who procured them.

Q. Did you have anything to do with naming them?     A. No, sir.

Q. I am now referring, of course, to the witnesses that are used in making final proof under the law. That is what you understand me to be referring to?

A. Yes, sir.

Q. Now, before you had occasion to make final proof, Mr. Wilson, did you have any further conversation with Mr. Dwyer in relation to this subject?

A. Yes, sir.

Q. Where did that conversation occur?

(Testimony of Guy L. Wilson.)

A. Out at my home in Vineland.

Q. Where is Vineland relative to Clarkston? You said *yo* resided in Clarkston?

A. It is on the outskirts of the town—a suburb.

Q. A suburb of Clarkston?     A. Yes, sir.

Q. Then when you said you reside in Clarkston you mean in the suburbs of C*l*rkston?

A. Yes, sir.

Q. You have property th*4*re?

A. Not at present.

Q. You had at that time?     A. Yes, sir.

Q. State the circumstances under which this conversat*i*on between you and Dwyer occur*rd*?

A. Mr. Dwyer drove out to my place and he was there at the house when I came home, and said he came out there to give me some pointers how to answer some of those questions that would be asked when I proved up.

Q. Now, before I go into that I desire to complete *me* examination with regard to this sworn statement so that the testimony may go in in proper order. as I am in the habit of introducing it. Take that duplicate of your sworn statement heretofore identified and offered in evidence. (Hands paper to witness.) To the question in this statement here, or to that clause in this affidavit which reads "That I do not apply to purchase the land above described on speculation, but in good faith to appropriate it to my own exclusive use," was that statement so subscribed by you true or untrue at the time you made it?     A. It was untrue.

(Testimony of Guy L. Wilson.)

Q. Did you know it to be untrue at that time?

A. Yes, sir.

Q. To the statement, "I have not directly or indirectly made any agreement or contract or in any way or manner with any person or persons whomsoever, by which the title I may acquire from the Government of the United States may inure in whole or in part to the benefit of any person except myself," was that statement true or untrue at the time you made it?    A. It was untrue.

Q. You may explain to the jury how you came to make those statements.

A. The way it was argued to me that this was nothing unusual; that other people did it, and it was just a custom, and there would be nothing wrong about doing this.

Q. Who, if anyone, so stated to you?

A. That was Mr. Dwyer told me.

Q. You say he argued to you. What did he say to you? Give what that argument consisted of; that is what we want.

A. Well, as far as the making of the contract, that it was a verbal agreement, that when we turned these cliams over, when we got proved, I was to turn these over to him and I would get this money; that that was a benefit to me as well as a benefit to him.

Q. And how about the contract?

A. That the contract was verbal between him and I, and it didn't amount to anything.

Q. This was at the time you have already testified to?    A. *Ye,* sir.

(Testimony of Guy L. Wilson.)

Q. Did you know, Mr. Wilson, at the time you made these statements that they were untrue?

A. Yes, sir.

Q. Now, returning to the incident at Vineland and the conversation with Mr. Dwyer, state the circumstances under which that conversation occurred?

A. He and his wife were already at my place. They had arrived there a few minutes before I got home, and he told me he wanted to give me a few pointers, and told me that I was to prove up on a certain day and he would give me a few pointers on how to answer some questions, which he did.

Q. What time of the day was it?

A. I should judge about six o'clock in the evening.

Q. Where were you at the time they were there?

A. I was just returning from my work.

Q. Where did you find them when you got home?

A. They were sitting in the buggy.

Q. Or find Mr. Dwyer, I mean?

A. They was still in the buggy, in front there.

Q. Who was with Mr. Dwyer?

A. Mrs. Dwyer was with Mr. Dwyer.

Q. Did you know Mrs. Dwyer at that time?

A. Yes, sir.

Q. Did they get out of the buggy?

A. No, sir.

Q. Who was present at this conversation?

A. Well, there was—my wife was there.

Q. And yourself and Mr. and Mrs. Dwyer?

A. Yes, sir.

(Testimony of Guy L. Wilson.)

Q. Now state how the conversation opened, what was first said?

A. Yes, sir; as near as I can remember he said that he came to give me a few pointers on how to answer some of those questions that would be asked when I proved up.

Q. Did you know what he referred to?

A. Well, I didn't know what questions would be asked; no.

Q. Look at this paper, purporting to be testimony of claimant and signed by you and certified as having been sworn to before J. B. West, Register of the United States Land Office at Lewiston, Idaho. Have you ever seen that paper before?

A. Yes, sir.

Q. Is th*t* your signature to that paper, Mr. Wilson? A. Yes, sir.

Now, this purports to be your final proof paper. Do you remember of being sworn to that paper?

A. Yes, sir.

Q. By whom? A. I believe by Mr. West.

And be it remembered that then and there the following proceedings were had:

Mr. RUICK.—We now offer in evidence this paper, and ask that it be marked Plaintiff's Exhibit 2.

Mr. FORNEY.—The defendants object to the introduction of this testimony on the ground it is irrelevant and immaterial and incompetent, on the further ground there is no evidence tending to show any conspiracy, no evidence has been intro-

(Testimony of Guy L. Wilson.)

duced tending to show any conspiracy by the de-
fed*n*ant, and on the further ground that the evidence
post-dates the consummation of the conspiracy as alleged in the indictment; which objection was by the
Court overruled—and to which ruling of the Court
the defendants then and *te*re excepted, which exception was allowed by the Court, and said paper was
admitted in evidence and marked Plaintiff's Exhibit
2.

Q. I now show you this other paper purporting to
be cross-examination of claimant, in connection with
direct examination on form 4-370, timber and stone
lands, and ask you if that is your signature to that
paper on the second page? A. Yes, sir.

Mr. RUICK.—We ask that this paper may be
marked Plaintiff's Exhibit 3 for identification (so
marked.)

Q. Do you identify this paper as the paper that
you signed at the time you *m*de your final proof as a
part of your final proof? Just look it over.

A. I think it is; it has my signature.

Q. Well, just read that over, and see if you *c*an
recognize that as the paper and your answers thereon? A. Yes, sir; that is the same.

Q. Is this the paper? A. Yes, sir.

Mr. RUICK.—I ask that this may be ma*k*red Exhibit 3 of plaintiffs. (Paper so marked.)

Be it remembered that then and there the following proceedings were had:

Mr. RUICK.—We offer it in evidence.

(Testimony of Guy L. Wilson.)

Mr. FORNEY.—The defendants object to the introduction of this testimony on the ground it is irrelevant and immaterial and incompetent, and on the further ground that there is no evidence tending to show a conspiracy; no evidence has been introduced tending to show any conspiracy by the defendants, and on the further ground that the evidence is objectionable for the reason that it post-dates the consummation of the conspiracy as alleged in the indictment; which objection was by the Court overruled, and to which ruling of the Court the defendants then and there excepted, which exception was allowed by the Court; and said paper was admitted and marked Plaintiff's Exhibit 3. Admitted.

Mr. RUICK.—I will read these papers, your Honor, first. They will all be in the same form substantially, and I will read them to the jury so tht they may understand the application of the testimony. This is on form 4-370, and states in parenthesis on the top:

"Testimony of Claimant and Witnesses must be taken at the same time, and before the Receiver or Register of the Land Office of the Land District in which the land is situate.

"Timber and Stone Lands. Testimony of Claimant.

Guy L. Wilson, being called as a witness in support of his application to purchase lots three and four and the northeast 4 of southeast 4 and northwest four of southwest 4 of Section Nineteen, Township 39, North of Range 5, East Boise Meridian, testifies as follows:

(Testimony of Guy L. Wilson.)

Question 1: What is your age, postoffice address and where do you reside?

Answer 22: Clarkston, Washington; same.

Question 2: Are you a native-born citizen of the United States, and if so in what State or territory were you born?

Answer: Yes, Washington.

Question 3: Are you the identical person who applied to purchase this land on the 25th day of April, 1904, and made the sworn statement assigned by laws before the Register or Receiver on that day?

Answer: Yes.

Question 4: Are you acquainted with the land above described by personal inspection of each of its smallest legal subdivisions?

Answer: Yes.

Question 5: When and in what manner was such inspection made?

Answer: October 9, 1903; walked over it.

Question 6: Is the land occupied or are there any improvements on it not made for ditch or canal purposes, or which were not made by or do not belong to you?      A.  No, was not at that time; none.

Question 7: Is the land fit for cultivation or would it be fit for cultivation if the timber was removed?

Answer: No, no.

Question 8: What is the situation of this land and what is the nature of the soil and what causes render the land unfit for cultivation?

A.  Rough and covered with timber.

(Testimony of Guy L. Wilson.)

Question 9: Are there any salines, or any indication of deposits of gold, silve*e*, cinnabar, copper or coal on this land, if so state what they are, and whether the springs or mineral deposits are *vl*uable?

Answer: No.

Question 10: Is the land valuable for minerals or any other purposes than for the timber and stone thereon, or is it chiefly valuable for timber or stone?

Answer: Chiefly for timber.

Question 11: From what facts do you conclude that the land is chiefly valuable for timber or stone?

Answer: Covered with timber, and is not fit for cultivation.

Question 12: What is the estimated value of the timber standing upon this land?

Answer: One thousand dollars.

Question 13: Have you sold or transferred your claim to this land since making your sworn statement, or have you directly or indi*r*ctly made any agreement or contract in any way or manner with any person whomsoever by which the title which you may acquire from the Government of the United States may inure in whole or in part to the benefit of any person except yourself?

Answer: No.

Question 14: Do you make this entry in good faith for the appropriation of the land exclusively for your own use and *nto* for the use or benefit of an*y* other person?    Answer: Yes.

Question Fifteen: Has any other person than yourself, or has any firm, corpor*t*ation or associa-

(Testimony of Guy L. Wilson.)

tion any interest in the entry you are now making, or in the land or in the timber thereon?

Answer: No.

GUY L. WILSON.

I hereby certify that the above-named Guy L. Wilson personally appeared before me; that I ver*y*ly believe affiant to be the person he represents himself to be; and that each question and answer in the foregoing testimony was read to him in my presence before he signed his name thereto, and that the same was subscribed and sworn to before me at Lewiston, Idaho, this 13 day of July, 1904.

J. B. WEST, Register.

Note: Every person swearing falsely to the above deposition is guilty of perjury, and will be punished as provided by law for such offense. In addition thereto, money that may be paid for the lands is forfeited and all conveyances of the lands or of an*y* right, title or claim thereto *ar* absolutely null and void as against the United States.

I hereby certify that I have tested the accuracy of affiant's information and the bona fides of this entry by a close and sufficient oral cross-examination of the claimant and his witnesses directed to ascertain whether the entry is made in good faith for the appropriation of the land to the entryman's own use and not for sale or speculation and whether he has conveyed the land or his right thereto, or agreed to make such conveyance, or whether he has directly or indireclty entered into any contract or agreement in any manner with any person or persons whomso-

(Testimony of Guy L. Wilson.)

ever by which the title that may be acquired by the entry shall inure in whole or in part to the benefit of any person or persons except himself, and am satisfied from such examination that the entry is made in good faith for entryman's own exclusive use, and not for sale or speculation nor in the interrsts nor for the benefit of any other person or persons, firm or corporation.

J. B. WEST, Register.

Note: In case the *prty* is of foreign birth, a certified transcript from the court records of his declaration of intention to become a citizen or naturalization or a copy thereof certified by the officer taking proof must be filed with the case.

(Endorsed:) Timber Lands. Acts of June 3d, 1878, and August 4th, 1892. Testimony of Claimant; Land Office at ————.''

Plaintiff's Exhibit 3 is as follows:

''Form 4-370A. Timber and Stone Land.

Cross-examination of Claimant in Connection with Direct Examination on form 4-370. Note.—Before taking the testimon*e* the Register and Receiver should read or cause to be read to the witness Section 2392 of the Revised Statutes in regard to perjury. See bottom of page on form 4-370, and see that witness understands *sme*.

Question 1: Are you an actual bona fide citizen of this State? A. No.

Question 2: Are you married or single?

Answer: Married.

(Testimony of Guy L. Wilson.)

Question 3: Where did you reside prior to becoming a resident of this State, and what was your occupaition?

Answer: Am a resident of Washington. Lineman.

Question 4: How long have you been an *actul* resident of Washington, and where have you lived during all of this time?     A. All my life.

Question 5: What has been your occupation during the past year, and where and by whom have you been employed and at what compensation?

Answer: Lineman, employed by Lewiston Water and Power Company. $75.

Question 6: How did you learn about this particular tract of land, and that it would be a good investment to buy it?

Answer: Through William Dwyer.

Question 7: Did you pay or agree to pay anything for this information? If so to whom, and the amount?

Answer: Yes; William Dwyer; $100.

Question 8: Have you made a personal examination of each smallest subdivision of said land? If so, state when and under what circumstances, and with whom?

Answer: Yes; October 9, 1903, with William Dwyer and Edwin Bliss.

Question 9: How do you identify said land? Describe it fully.

Answer: By going to the section corner, lies rough, and is covered with timber; rocky.

(Testimony of Guy L. Wilson.)

Question 10: How many thousand feet board measure of lumber did you estimate that there is on this entire tract, and what is the stumpage value of the same?        Answer: One million feet; $1000.

Question 11: Are you a practical lumberman, or woodsman?   If not, how did you arrive at your estimate of the quantity and value of the lumber on the land?        Answer: Took estimate of locator.

Question 12: What do you expect to do with this land and the lumber on it when you get title to it?

Answer: Hold it for the future.

Question 13: Do you know of any capitalist or company which is offering to purchase timber land in the vicinity of this entry; if so, who are they, and how did you know of them?        Answer: No.

Question 14: Has any person offered to purchase this land after you acquire title?   If so, who and for what amount?        Answer: No.

Question 15: What is the nearest and best market for the timber on this land at the present time?

Answer: Lewiston, Idaho.

Question 16: Did you pay out of your own individual funds all the expenses in connection with making this filing, and do you expect to pay for the land with your own money?

Answer: Yes; yes.

Question 17: Where did you get the money with which to pay for this land, and how long had you had same in your actual possession?

Answer: I saved it from my earnings two and a half years.

(Testimony of Guy L. Wilson.)

Question 18: Have you kept a bank account during the past six months, and if so, where?

Answer: No.

"GUY L. WILSON.

Note: In addition to the foregoing the officer before whom the proof is made will ask such questions as seem necessary to bring out all the facts in the case."

Q. Now, Mr. Wilson, refreshing your recollection from any paper which you may have filed or subscribed to in this case, or from any other source, please state what the conversation was between you and Mr. Dwyer at the time he visited you at your home in Vineland on the occasion last referred to in your testimony?

A. Why, he told me all this, that I would be asked where I got this *mone,* and he said to tell them that I had saved it, and I had it or its equivalent for two and a half years, that I had a place over there in Vineland, and had had it that long, and that would be all that would be necessary.

Q. How would that place in Vineland cut any figure as stated by him, is what I mean?

A. I had it that long; it would be equivalent to this amount of money.

Q. Well, what other questions, if any, did he refer to that would be asked of you?

A. Well, if I had sold or transferred it; that was an agreement we had, was just a verbal agreement we had, and it didn't amount to anything in this case.

(Testimony of Guy L. Wilson.)

Q. Was Mrs. Wilson where she could hear this conversation?    A. Yes, sir.

Q. Where was Mrs. Wilson at the time these statements were made?

A. We was standing by the fence, and they was out in the road.

Q. How far from the fence?

A. Up against the fence, I guess.

Q. You was standing near her?

A. Yes, sir.

Q. Did Mr. Dwyer have a blank with him at that time?    A. No, sir; I don't think that he did.

Q. At least you did not see any?

A. No, sir.

Q. How long was this before you wet to the land office to make final proof?

A. Just a few days; I don't remember just the exact number; it was not more than a week, I don't think.

Q. Where did you get the money with which to pay for the land; I mean now at the United States Land Office?    A. Mr. Dwyer gave it to me.

Q. Where did Mr. Dwyer give it to you?

A. It was in the back room of I. N. Smith's office.

Q. In the Leiwiston National Bank Building?

A. Yes, sir.

Q. How did you know the day on which you were required to make final proof?

A. Well, as near as I can remember the evening Mr. Dwyer came to my house, he told me what day we would make proof.

(Testimony of Guy L. Wilson.)

Q. And what instructions, if any, did he give you in addition to what you have already testified; what, if anything, did he tell you to do is what I want to know, what were you to do? How did you happen to go to the land office on the day on which you made final proof?

A. Well, I went there that morning with the expectation of proving up; he had told me out at my home we would prove up that day, and my wife and I went there.

Q. How is that?

A. I say, my wife and I went to the land office that morning.

Q. You went to the land office together?

A. Yes, sir.

Q. And did you see Dwyer on that morning?

A. Yes, sir.

Q. Where did you see him?

A. I saw him around the building and I also seen him when he gave me the money in Mr. Smith's office.

Q. How much money did he give you in Mr. Smith's office at that time to pay for the land?

A. I don't remember the exact amount; I don't think. $411—it was over $400; I don't remember just how much over.

Q. In what shape was the money?

A. Part of it was in gold, and some of it in bills.

Q. Did you count it at the time he gave it to you?

A. I don't remember whether I did or not.

Q. Did he say anything to you about it when he gave it to you?      A. No, sir.

(Testimony of Guy L. Wilson.)

Q. How did you know what the money was for?

A. Well, I knew that was what he was giving it to me for.

Q. Well, how did you know that? State how you knew.

A. Well, I knew that he was going to furnish me the money. That is what I went there for to get the money.

Q. How did you know to go there on that morning to get the money?

A. Well, I don't remember whether—just how I happened to know, whether he told me or whether I had asked him.

Q. Did you know that you were going to get the money there?

A. I knew that he was going to give me the money.

Q. To pay for the land at the land office?

A. Yes, sir.

Q. What did you do with this money?

A. I paid for this piece of land.

Q. Did you have any further talk with Dwyer at about this time in relation to making your final proof —did he have any further talk with you at this time about the questions that were to be asked you in the land office?

A. I don't remember of anything said there.

Q. Did Dwyer go with you to the land office?

A. I think he was in the land office; I don't remember of him going in with me.

Q. Who were your witnesses, do you remember?

A. Mr. Dwyer and Mr. Bliss.

(Testimony of Guy L. Wilson.)

Q. Mr. Edwin Bliss?

A. Yes, sir; I guess that is his first name.

Q. Was it the same man that was up to Dwyer's camp the day you visited there?     A. Yes, sir.

Q. Did you have anything to do with procuring either Mr. Dwyer or Mr. Bliss to act as your witnesses?     A. No, sir.

Q. Was Mr. Dwyer there when you were answering these questions, do you remember?

A. I remember him being in the room; I remember he was in the room.

Q. Did you see Mr. Dwyer sign his testimony given at that time?

A. I don't remember whethe I did or not.

Q. Mr. Wilson, referring to your final proof, the papers, testimony of claimant, Plaintiff's Exhibit 2, J. H. P., do you recall this question being read over to you in the land office at the time you made your final proof, and your answer thereto as follows: Question 13: Have you sold or transferred your claim to this land since making your sworn statement, or have you directly or indirectly made any agreement or contract in any way or manner with any person whomsoever, by which the title which you may acquire from the Government of the United States may inure in whole or in part to the benefit of any person except yourself? Do you remember that question?

A. Yes, sir.

Q. To which you answered, No; do you remember your answer?     A. Yes, sir.

(Testimony of Guy L. Wilson.)

Q. Was that answer true or false at the time you made it? A. It was false.

Q. Did you know *i* to be such at that time?

A. Yes, sir.

Q. Question 14: Do you make this entry in good faith for the appropriation of the land, exclusively to your own use and not for the use or benefit of any other person? Do you remember that question?

A. Yes, sir.

Q. To which you answered, Yes. Do you remember that answer? A. Yes, sir.

Q. Was that statement true or false when you made it? A. It was false.

Q. Did you know it to be such at the time?

A. Yes, sir.

Q. Question 15: Has any other person than yourself, or has any firm, corporation or association any interest in the entry you are now making or in the land or in the timber thereon?" Do you remember that question? A. Yes, sir.

Q. And your answer, No; do you remember that answer? A. Yes, sir.

Q. Was that answer true or false at the time you made it? A. It was false.

Q. Had you any talk with Mr. Dwyer concerning these matters embodied in these questions before they were asked you? A. At the time, at my home.

Q. That was the time to which you referred?

A. Yes, sir.

Q. Now, going specifically into the matter of these questions, I want to ask you this: Question 13, to

(Testimony of Guy L. Wilson.)

the effect, "Have you sold or transferred your claim to this land since making your sworn statement, and have you any agreement, etc., whereby the title which you may acquire from the Government of the United States may inure to the benefit of any other person?" How did you make answer to that question "No"?

A. Well, the way he talked to me that it was a verbal agreement, and that it would not make any difference; it would be all right to answer it that way.

Q. That is, inasmuch as it was not in writing?

A. Yes, sir.

Q. Now, this question 14, which is: "Do you make this entry in good faith for the appropriation of the land exclusively to your own use, and not for the use or benefit of any other person?" Did you have any talk with Mr. Dwyer concerning that question before you answered it?     A. *Ye,* sir.

Q. What did he say to you relative to that question?

A. Well, he said I was taking it for my own benefit, and I would derive the benefit from it.

Q. Did he tell you how you were to derive a benefit from it?

A. Well, we would get this money at the time we turned these claims over.

Q. What money?     A. This $150.

Q. Question 15: Has any other person than yourself, or has any firm, corporation or association any interest in the entry you are now making, or in the land or in the timber thereon? Do you remember that question?     A. Yes, sir.

(Testimony of Guy L. Wilson.)

Q.    To which you answered, No; do you remember your answer to it?    A.    Yes, sir.

Q.    Now, what did Dwyer say about that, if anything?

A.    Well, he said that this was—this verbal agreement between he and I did not amount to anything, that I was taking this up for my own benefit.

Q.    You have already stated something concerning his conversation with you relative to where you got the money, but I call your attention now specially to question 17, in what is denominated cross-examination of Claimant, being a part of your final proof.    The document itself being Plaintiff's Exbibit 3, J. H. P.    This question reads: "Where did you get the money with which to pay for this land, and how long have you had it in your actual possession?"    As to the first part of that question, "where did you get the money with which to pay for this land" you answered, "I saved it from my earnings."    Do you recall that?    A.    Yes, sir.

Q.    And as to the latter part of the question, "And how long had you had the same in your actual possession," you replied two and a half years.    Do you remember this answer?    A.    Yes, sir.

Q.    Now, what, if anything, did Mr. Dwyer state to you relative to how you should answer this question?

A.    He said that I could say I saved it; that I had this piece of property, and *tat* it was equal to this amount of money; that I had had it or its equivalent for that number of years.

(Testimony of Guy L. Wilson.)

Q. Had it or its equivalent: Had you had this piece of property for that length of time?

A. Yes, sir.

Q. This other question, 16: "Did you pay out of your own individual funds all the expenses in connection with making this filing, and do you expect to pay for the land with your own money?" to which you answered, "Yes," to each of those questions. Do you recall that question and those *answer*?

A. I remember the question; I don't—I don't—

Q. Don't remember how you answered it?

A. No, sir; I do not.

Q. Well, did you pay out of your own individual funds all the expenses in connection with making the filing? A. No, sir.

Q. Who, if anyone, was present there in Smith's office where this $411.00 or thereabouts was paid over to you by Dwyer?

A. Albert Kester was in the front room, and we back in another room.

Q. Which room were you and Dwyer in?

A. We were in the back room.

Q. Of how many rooms did Smith's office consist?

A. At that time there were two.

Q. Describe those rooms.

A. One was a large room in front, and the other was a small room in the back; I don't remember whether it had a door or not. I don't believe it did. There was a door going in, but I don't know whether it was an archway or a door.

(Testimony of Guy L. Wilson.)

Q. In which room did Dwyer give you this money?    A. It was in the back room.

Q. Was anyone besides you and Dwyer in the room at the time?ʻ    A. Not in that room.

Q. Was it where any person could see you or that was in the office at that time, did he see?

A. I don't know whether he could see me or not.

Q. Was anything said?

A. He gave me this money, and I signed a note there.

Q. Who was the note payable to, if you remember?    A. Payable to Kettenbach and Kester.

Q. Do you remember the amount of the note?

A. No, I don't; I know it was something over 400; I don'te remember the exact amount.

Q. Do you remember how long the note was to run?

A. The best I can recollect, I think it was on demand, or after date, or something.

Q. Have you got that note now?

A. No, sir; I have not.

Q. What became of it?

A. I think my wife burned it up.

Q. Where was that note drawn up?

A. I think that he drew it up there.

Q. That is your recollection?

A. Well, that is the best of my recollection that he made it out there.

Q. What explanation did he give of this note, or what did he say about it, if anything?

(Testimony of Guy L. Wilson.)

A. He said that was to secure the loan until we had proved up.

Q. Was there any security for the note?

A. No, sir.

Q. Did he ask an endorser?    A. No, sir.

Q. Or any other security?    A. No, sir.

Q. Had he said anything about you giving a note at any time before this?    A. No, sir.

Q. This was the first that you knew about a note?

A. Yes, sir.

Q. To whom did you deliver this note?

A. I returned it to him after I had signed it.

Q. And when next did you see the note, when was it returned to you?

A. I don't know as I ever seen it after that myself.

Q. You know of the note having been returned?

A. Yes, sir.

Q. But you don't know whether you ever saw the note afterwards?

A. I don't know that I did; I don't remember of ever seeing it.

Q. Who, if anyone, did you authorize to get the note?    A. My wife.

Q. On what date?

A. The same day that we proved up.

Q. The same day that you made the note?

A. Yes, sir.

Q. State the circumstances under which you authorized your wife to procure this note?

A. After we had proved up and we had made out a deed and been paid, why she stayed in the room

(Testimony of Guy L. Wilson.)

there and was to get this note.  It was to be returned back to her.

Q.  Well, who made the arrangement for turning back the note, that is what I want to get at; how did you know where to go to get the note?

A.  Well, we turned the note to Mr. Dwyer.  I didn't know where to go to get it; I supposed the note had been made out to Kettenbach—

Q.  Of course we don't want your supposition. What I want to know is this:  You say the note was to be returned to you?    A. Yes, sir.

Q.  With whom did you have this understanding that the note was to be returned to you?

A.  Mr. Dwyer said it was to be returned to me.

Q.  Now, then, you say at the time the deed was executed there, was something said about the note, was there?

A.  I think he said when—the best of my recollection was when I gave him this note, that it would be returned to me at the time we settled up with him.

Q.  When you and your wife executed this *ded* there was something said about your wife getting the note was there?    A. Yes, sir.

Q.  Thats what I want to get at; state it.

A.  I told her to stay there and get the note.

Q.  Did you know where the note was at that time?    A.  No, I did not at that time.

Q.  You didn't know where she would have to go to get it?    A.  No, sir.

(Testimony of Guy L. Wilson.)

Q. When did you get your final receipt from the land office? How long after you made your final proof?

A. I don't remember exactly; I got it that day, though.

Q. And then what did you do after you got the final *r*receipt?　　A. I gave it to Mr. Dwyer.

Q. Where was Mr. Dwyer when you gave it to him?　　A. I don't remember where he was.

Q. For what purpose did you give it to Mr. Dwyer if it was stated there at that time?

A. To get this deed made out.

Q. State about what you said, how you came to give it to Mr. Dwyer, and what was said?

A. He said if I would give him the receipt, he would go to a notary public, and have this deed made out, and we would be through.

Q. What instruction did he give you in regard to it?

A. That is all that I remember him saying.

Q. Was your wife with you at that time?

A. I don't remember whether she was or not.

Q. YOur wife was with you when you executed the deed?　　A. Yes, sir.

Q. Where was the deed executed.

A. *I* the Idaho Trust Building.

Q. In whose office?

A. Otto Kettenbach's office.

Q. A notary public?　　A. Yes, sir.

Q. Where is that from the Lewiston National Bank?

(Testimony of Guy L. Wilson.)

A.   About a block and a half on the Main Street west.

Q.   By whose instructions, if any, did you go up to Otto Kettenbach's office?

A.   I went as Mr. Dwyer told me to come up there to make this deed out and sign it.

Q.   Did he tell you when to come?

A.   Yes, sir.

Q.   How long after you had handed him the final receipt before you went up there?

A.   When I gave him the receipt, as I remember, it was in the morning, and we went up after dinner.

Q.   You gave him the receipt, however, after you made your final proof?    A.   Yes, sir.

Q.   Did you execute your deed while there in the office?    A.   Yes, sir.

Q.   Do you remember who the deed was executed to?    A.   Yes, sir.

Q.   Who was it?

A.   Kettenbach & Kester was the way it read.

Q.   Just Kettenbach & Kester, you think?

A.   Yes, I think that was all there was.

Q.   Did you read the deed?

A.   I don't remember of only reading a part of it; I might have read it all; I don't remember.

Q.   *Wha* part of it do you remember of reading?

A.   I remember of reading it conveyed a certain lot to these parties, Kettenbach and Kester; that is all that I remember that was in the deed.

Q.   Certain lots?    A.   Yes, sir.

Q.   The description of your land?

(Testimony of Guy L. Wilson.)

A. *Ye,* sir.

Q. Do you remember something, then, of the description? A. Yes, sir.

Q. Do you remember what the consideration named in the deed was?

A. I don't remember it.

Q. Was the deed signed by yourself and wife?

A Yes, sir.

Q. Who paid over this money and where was it paid aver to you?

A. It was paid in a room right off of that office.

Q. State the circumstances of the payment.

A. Mr. Dwyer called me in this room and gave me $136.

The COURT.—Gave you how much?

A. $136.00.

Q. Where was this room relative to the room in which the notary was?

A. Why it was right off of his office in the back room.

Q. In another room? A. Yes, sir.

Q. Was there anybody in there when he gave you the $136?

A. No, sir; not in that room where we were.

Q. How did he give it to you? In what shape was the money.

A. I don't remember. It was money, might have been gold and might have been currency; I don't remember just that.

Q. Why didn't you get $150, if you remember?

(Testimony of Guy L. Wilson.)

A.   Well, he was deducting this $14 that was paid to this young fellow for running this line; he had taken that out of this $150.

Q.   Then you were out that $14, or did you afterwards get it from him?

A.   No, that was all I got, $136.00.

Q.   Did your wife leave Otto Kettenbach's office with you?

A.   No, sir; I went to work right after I signed this deed and she—I left her there in the office.

Q.   Dwyer did not state to you*a* at that time in your presence or hearing where this note was?

A.   Not that I remember of.

Q.   Do you remember of his saying anything there as to the note at all, or making any reference to it?      A.   I don't remember that.

Q.   Did he at the time Dwyer had you up in *I.* . Smiths' office, and gave you $411, or thereabouts, did you have another transaction with Mr. Dwyer?

A.   Yes, sir.

Q.   What kind of a transaction did you have.

A.   I paid him for locating me on this timber.

Q.   Describe to the jury how you paid him, and with what.

A.   Oh, he gave me this money, why he—

Q.   What money?

This money to pay for the land, If I remember, it was before he gave me this money, he gave me a one hundred dollar bill, and he said, "You hand this back to me," and as I did he said, "You have paid me for locating you, so it will be all right."

(Testimony of Guy L. Wilson.)

Q. Did you have any interest in that one hundred dollar bill that Mr. Dwyer handed you at that time? A. No, sir.

Q. Have you ever paid Dwyer anything at all for locating you? A. No, sir.

Q. I call your attention to this paper which purports to be a register's final receipt, and ask you if you recall getting a paper like that?

The COURT.—Answer the question

A. I remember of getting a receipt.

Q. You remember getting a receipt? To whom did you give that receipt that you got?

A. To Mr. Dwyer.

Q. You are not sure whether this is the one or a duplicate of it or not? A. No, sir.

Q. Was this one hundred dollars that you received from Dwyer, and handed back to him, as you have stated, included in this note? A. No, sir.

Q. Did you ever execute any note or obligation for this $100? A. No, sir.

Mr. RUICK.—That is all; take the witness.

Cross-examination by Mr. TANNAHILL.

Mr. RUICK.—Pardon me just a moment, Mr. Tannahill. I am reminded of a question to ask.

By Mr. RUICK.—Q. Do you remember about the time, Mr. Wilson, that Mr. O'Fallon, an inspector of the Interior Department, and Mr. Goodwin, a special agent were over there in Clarkston, interviewing people in regard to these matters?

(Testimony of Guy L. Wilson.)

A.   Yes, sir.

Q.   Did you have your final receipt in your possession at the time they were first over there?

A.   No, sir.

Q.   Was it afteerwards placed in your possession?    A.   Yes, sir.

Q.   By whom?    A.   By Mr. Dwyer.

Q.   And what did Mr. Dwyer say to you at that time.

A.   Why he told me there was some inspectors around, and that they would probably be to see me, and he said that—

Q.   Speak louder.

A.   He said if they came to ask me anything about it to tell them that I had timber, and ask them if they wanted to buy some.

Q.   What about the final receipt?

A.   Well, he gave it to me at that time.

Q.   What, if anything, did he say relative to the final receipts, or any reasons why he gave it to you?

A.   He said they might want to see it.

Q.   How long was this after you had deeded away the land?

A.   That was the same fall, I guess.

Mr. RUICK.--That is all.

Be remembered that then and there the following proceeding was had:

Mr. FORNEY.—If your Honor please, we object to all this testimony, and move your Honor to withdraw it from the jury for the reason that this testi-

(Testimony of Guy L. Wilson.)

mony relates to a transaction that occurred long after this conspiracy, if any can be shown, was consummated, and on the further ground that the testimony of this witness does not connect Kester or Kettenbach with any conspiracy, or show that there was any conspiracy formed by either of the defendants.

The COURT.—I don't know whether that is in the form of a motion, or an objection. It is rather late for an objection.

Mr. FORNEY.—This is a motion to withdraw it.

The COURT.—The motion will be denied.

To which ruling of the Court the defendants then and there excepted, which exception was allowed by the Court.

Mr. RUICK.—(Continuing.) Q. What did you do with this final receipt that Dwyer returned to you? A. I afterwards gave it back to him.

Q. Where? A. At my house.

Q. How long did you have it in your possession at that time, do you think?

A. Probably two or three months.

Q. How did you happen to give it back to him?

A. He asked me for it.

Q. What did he say at that time?

A. He said he would like to have it, and I returned it to him.

Mr. RUICK.—Take the witness.

(Testimony of Guy L. Wilson.)

Cross-examination by Mr. TANNAHILL.

Q. Mr. Wilson, how old are you now?

A. Twenty-five years.

Q. How old were you at the time you made this filing?    A. I was twenty-two years old.

Q. How long have you been married?

A. Five years.

Q. How long were you married at the time you made this filing?    A. Two years.

Q. And you say you have one child?

A. Yes, sir.

Q. Did you have thqt child at the time you made this filing?    A. No, sir.

Q. Did you have a child at the time Mr. Goodwin and O'Fallon came to see you?

A. I don't remember exactly—no, sir; I didn't have any child.

Q. How long after they were there to see you was it before your child was born?

A. The following Spring.

Q. Mr. Wilson, are you a man of some education.    A. Not so very much.

Q. Have you attended school?

A. Attended school up to the time I was fourteen. I attended schools in the country and also a school in town.

Q. Did you ever attend a high school?

A. No, sir; I finished the common branches.

Q. Where did you attend school.

(Testimony of Guy L. Wilson.)

A. I attended school in several different places. I was in school probably three or four years.

Q. What had been your occupation prior to taking up your present calling?

A. I followed most anything—laborer's work.

Q. Are you a member of any church?

A. No, sir.

Q. Do you belong to any secret orders?

A. Yes, sir; the Odd Fellows.

Q. Now, Mr. Wilson, do you understand that you should tell the truth about the questions I am going to ask you?    A. Yes, sir.

Q. And will you tell me the truth in answering the questions I ask you?

A. To the best of my ability, I will.

Q. Now, when Mr. Goodwin and Mr. O'Fallon were there did they ever talk to you about this matter?    A. They talked to me about it; yes.

Q. When did they first talk with you about it?

A. I talked to them about it.

Q. When did you talk with them about it?

A. I don't remember the exact time.

Q. When? About when was the first time you talked with them about it?

A. I don't remember that either.

Q. Can't you give me some idea about when it was?

A. Well, it might have been that same summer. or it might have been the next summer; I don't remember.

(Testimony of Guy L. Wilson.)

Q.   Haven't you any better recollection about it that*n* that, Mr. Wilson?

A.   No, that is the best I can do on that; I don't remember just what year it was.

Q.   Will you give us the month as near as you can?

A.   If I remember right, I think it was before I was called before the grand jury.

Q.   Where did you talk to them about it?

A.   Why, in Mr. Johnson's law office.

Q.   How did you come to go there?

A.   I went there to see Mr. Johnson.

Q.   What did you go there to see him about?

A.   I went to see a lawyer.

Q.   Did you go to see a lawyer about this matter?

A.   Yes, sir.

Q.   How did you come to go to see Mr. Johnson?

A.   Mr. Johnson is a personal friend of mine, and I have known him a long time.

Q.   And you and Mr. Johnson were good freinds, were you?

A.   Well, not any better than any other people I know around there, any other lawyers I happen to know.

Q.   Was Mr. Johnson Deputy United States Attorney at that time?      A.   No, sir.

Q.   Are you and Mr. Johnson both political friends as well as personal friends?

A.   I have no interest in the politics in Idaho.

Q.   What are your politics?

A.   I am a Republican.

Q.   And Mr. Johnson is also a Republican?

(Testimony of Guy L. Wilson.)

A. Yes, sir.

Q. Where have you been living during the last four or five years?    A. Clarkston.

You say you saw Mr. O'Fallon in Mr. Johnson's office?    A. Yes, sir.

Q. And was he there when you went there?

A. No, I don't think he was.

Q. How long had you been there before Mr. O'Fallon came in?

A. I don't remember exactly; a few minutes, I suppose.

Q. How did you come to go to Mr. Johnson regarding these matters?

A. Well, I wanted to see some attorney, and I went to him.

Q. How did you come to go there at all? How did you come to get to thinking about it?

A. Well, I went to find out just what I would do in case somebody did get hold of me.

Q. And did Mr. Johnson call up Mr. O'Fallon after you went there?

A. Well, he told me he had arrnaged for me to meet Mr. O'Fallon, and I could tell Mr. O'Fallon what I wished.

Q. How long were you there before you met Mr. O'Fallon ?

A. A few minutes—I don't know just exactly. I had been there once before. I came back twice. I went to see Mr. Johnson and came back afterwards.

Q. What did Mr. O'Fallon say to you about it?

(Testimony of Guy L. Wilson.)

A.   Why, he just told me that he knew all about it anyway, and I could tell the same story, and tell what I knew, and I told him.

Q.   What did you tell him?

A.   About the same thing as I have said here to-day.

Q.   Did you make a statement for Mr. O'Fallon?

A.   Yes, sir.

Q.   Was it a written statement?

A.   Yes, sir.

Q.   And was it signed by you?

A.   Yes, sir.

Q.   And was it sworn to?

A.   Yes, sir; I think it was.

Q.   What did you do with that statement?

A.   Why, Mr. O'Fallon took that statement.

Q.   And did Mr. Goodwin have that statement too?

A.   I don't know whether he did or not.

Q.   When did you last see that statement?

A.   I don't ever remember seeing it after that. I might have; I don't remember it.

Q.   Has your attention ever been called to it?

A.   Yes, sir; I think it has.

Q.   When was your attention called to that statement?

A.   I think I read it over before I went before the grand jury.

Q.   You read that statement ovec before you went before the grand jury?     A.   Yes, sir.

Q.   And you don't know where it is now?

A.   No, sir.

(Testimony of Guy L. Wilson.)

Q. W*el,* Mr. Wilson did you ever make any other statement in writing than that one? A. No.

Q. Where did you make that statement?

A. In Mr. John*osn'x* office.

Q. Who drew it up?

A. Why, if I remember, Mr. Goodwin wrote it.

Q. Were there any corrections in it ?

A. I don't believe there was.

Q. You signed it as Mr. Goodwin wrote it up?

A. It was read to me and I signed it.

Q. Who was the notary that you signed it before?

A. If I remember, if there was a notary, Mr. O'Fallon was he.

Q. And you read that statement before you went before the grand jury? A. Yes, sir.

Q. Whom did you receive the statement from at that time?

A. From Mr. Johnson in his office, in this court— in this District Attorney's office.

Q. What was said by Mr. Johnson to you regarding that statement?

A. He just told me to read it over if I wanted to.

Q. And did you tell him that there were statements in there that were not true? A. No, sir.

Q. You read the statement over?

A. Yes, sir.

Q. And read it over so you could tell the same story before the grand jury?

A. No, I don't think I read it for that fact; I just read it over.

(Testimony of Guy L. Wilson.)

Q. You read it over so you could refresh your memory?    A. Yes, sir.

Q. That is the way of it; did you know you could be indicted for making those false statements?

A. Yes, sir.

Q. And did Mr. Goodwin and Mr. O'Fallon tell you that you would not be—if you made that statement? He never told you anything of that kind?

A. No, sir.

Q. But you understood you would not be?

A. Nothing was ever said about that.

Q. Did you understand that if you made that statement you would be indicted?    A. No, sir.

Q. And did you understand that if you did not make the statement, you would not be indicted?

A. No, sir.

Q. You did not understand anything of that kind?

A. No, sir.

Q. But you felt very sure you would not be indicted if you made the statement?

A. I didn't know whether I would or not.

Q. Were you ever inter*fi*ewed again by Mr. Goodwin or Mr. O'Fallon?

A. I don't believe I *eve* was.

Q. What did Mr. Johnson say to you about your evidence?

A. I don't remember of his ever saying anything about it.

Q. Did Mr. Goodwin or Mr. O'Fallon ever talk about it, either one of them?

(Testimony of Guy L. Wilson.)

A. I never talked to either one of them very much since then.

Q. Have you ever talked to either of them at all?

A. No, sir.

Q. What?

A. I don't think I have on that subject.

Q. Did you talk to either of them on any other subject connected with this transaction?

A. I might have.

Q. What did you talk to them abot?

A. I don't remember; I couldn't tell you.

Q. When did you talk with them?

A. I don't remember that; I don't remember the day when I met them. I might have talked to them to-day if I met them; I don't know.

Q. What?

A. I might have talked with them to-day.

Q. Did you ever talk to them about this case?

A. No, sir. ,

Q. Have you ever said anything to them about this case?    A. No, sir.

Q. You have read your evidence over?

A. Yes, sir.

Q. When did you read your eveidence over?

A. Last night.

How many times did you read it over?

A. Once.

Q. It was in typewritten form, was it not?

A. Yes, sir.

Q. From whom did you receive that evidence?

A. From the District Attorney's office.

(Testimony of Guy L. Wilson.)

Q.    How long did it take you to read it over?

A.    Probably twenty minutes.

Q.    Did you read over your cross-examination?

A.    Yes, sir.

By the COURT.—What is meant by this evidence which you refer to? His testimony as given on the former trial?

Mr. TANNAHILL.—Yes.

Mr. RUICK.—It would be well enough to identify it—let it appear—it might appear—

The COURT.—It does appear.

Mr. Wilson, when you went to see Mr. Johnson, isn't it a fact that Mr. Johnson told you if you would make that statement for Mr. O'Fallon, you would be exonerated?

A.    I don't ever remember him telling me that.

Q.    He might have told you something of that kind?

A.    He might have; he might have but I don't remember it.

Q.    You felt, though, you would be exonerated, didn't you?

A.    I didn't feel *vey* good any of the time.

Q.    Did you show Mr. Goodwin and Mr. O'Fallon or either of them your receipt?    A.    No.

Q.    They never have seen your receipt?

A.    They may have seen it; I never gave it to them.

Q.    Did you tell them you had a final receipt?

A.    I don't remember whether I did or not; I might have.

(Testimony of Guy L. Wilson.)

Q. Have you ever talked this matter over with your mother in law? A. Yes, sir.

Q. How many times have you talked it over with her? A. Quite a few times, I think.

Q. Have you ever talked it over with your wife? A. Yes, sir.

Q. Have you ever talked it over with anyone else? A. I might have.

Q. Now, have you ever talked with your wife about what she knew about it?

A. Have I ever talked with my wife as to what she knew about it?

Q. Yes, about what she knew about this transaction?

A. Why, she has told me what she knew.

Q. How many times did she tell you what she knew? A. I don't remember.

Q. Did you tell Mr. Goodwin and Mr. O'Fallon what she knew about it? A. No, sir.

Q. Did you tell Mr. Johnson what she knew about it? A. No, sir.

Q. Was your wife's name mentioned?

A. It might have been mentioned; I don't remember whether it was or not.

Q. But your wife has told you all about what she knew about it?

A. I already knew what she knew.

Q. You had talked it over a great many times. Where did Mr. Dwyer give you this receipt?

A. It was on 7th Street in Clarkston; that is where I was living at the time.

(Testimony of Guy L. Wilson.)

Q.   When was it he gave you the receipt?

A.   It was along in the latter part of the summer; it might have been early fall.

Q.   W*ht* year was it?

A.   It was the fall of 1904.

Q.   Now, Mr. Wilson, when was it that you first conceived the idea of taking up a timber claim?

A.   Why, it was some time before I went up into the timber.

Q.   How long before?

A.   I don't remember exactly; it might have been a month.

Q.   What year was it?      A.   It was 1903.

Q.   How did you come to get that idea into your head?

A.   Mr. Justice had talked to me about it, my father in law.

Q.   Your father in law, Mr. Justice, was from a timber country, was he?

A.   He was from Wisconsin.

Q.   And he knew considerably about timber?

A.   I couldn't say whether he did or not.

Q.   And he talked to you about taking up a timber claim?      A.   Yes, sir.

Q.   How many times did he talk to you about taking up a timber claim?      A.   I don't remember.

Q.   Did your mother in law, Mrs. Justice. also talk to you about taking up a timber claim?

A.   I expect she has.

(Testimony of Guy L. Wilson.)

Q. How many times has she talked to you about taking up a timber claim?

A. I don't remember.

Q. A great many times?

A. No, I don't think a great many times—it was—I didn't see them very often in those days.

Q. How many times did your father in law talk to you about taking up a timber claim before you saw Mr. Dwyer?

A. I could not say; not so very many times.

Q. Now, Mr. Wilson, isn't it a fact that your mother in law is the one who solicited you to take up your timber claim?

A. She spoke to me about it; I don't remember whether it was her or Mr. Justice, but I think it was Mr. Justice that spoke to me first.

Q. Isn't it a fact, Mr. Wilson, that Mr. Dwyer didn't know for sure that you wanted to take up a timber claim or was going to take up a timber claim until he met you at the train the day you went to look at this land?

A. Well, it might have been; the only conversation I ever had was te one I have just told you about—that is, some time before I went.

Q. And he didn't know that you wanted to take up a timber claim until you met him at the train?

A. I don't know whether he did or not.

Q. Didn't you hear him state to your mother in law at the train, and ask if you were going along, and she said yes, and he said, "How do you know

(Testimony of Guy L. Wilson.)

Guy will get a claim," or words to that effect? Did you hear that conversation?

A. I don't remember that.

Q. Do you remember Mrs. Justice having a conversation with Mr. Dwyer there?

A. Her and—Mr. Dwyer and Mr. Justice were together; they might have had a conversation.

Q. You were not with them?     A. No, sir.

Q. As far as you know, Mr. Dwyer did not know positively that you wanted to take up a timber claim, or was going with them until you met at the train?

A. He knew, as I said before, at this conversation I had with him at Clarkston, I told him I would go.

Q. How long before this was it that you had that conversation with him?

A. I couldn't say how long it was.

Q. Who directed your attention to that conversation, or asked you about it?

A. I remembered it when I was asked, when I first had a conversation with him; I remembered this conversation.

Q. Is that the conversation mentioned in the statement which you made for Mr. Goodwin and Mr. O'Fallon?

A. I don't remember whether it is or not.

Q. Is the fact that you did not know for sure that Mr. Dwyer knew you were going to take up a claim until you met him at the train, mentioned in this statement you made for Mr. Goodwin and Mr. O'Fallon?

(Testimony of Guy L. Wilson.)

A. I don't know whether—as I said before, I don't know whether Mr. Dwyer knew for—I supposed he knew I was going to go, after this conversation we had had.

Q. In so far you don't know whether he did or not?

A. He might not have expected me; I don't know.

Q. Who was it propounded these questions to you from which this statement was made?

A. Mr. O'Fallon*g* asked me the questions.

Q. How many pages did the statement cover?

A. I could not tell you.

Q. Was it a typewrit*en* st*t*cment or a statement writen out in longhand?

A. It was a typewritten statement, I think.

Q. A typewritten statement. Did you say you read that over before you went into the grand jury room and yet you don't know how many pages it consisted of?     A. Yes, sir; I read it over.

A. Yes, sir; I read it over.

Q. About how man*y* pages?

A. Well, I could not tell you exactl*y*; it is not ver*y*—not so very awfully many.

Q. How long did it take you to read it over?

A. I don't remember that either.

Q. Now, who interrogated you in the grand jur*y* room?     A. Mr. Ruick.

Q. How man*y* times have you been before the grand jury?     A. Twice.

(Testimony of Guy L. Wilson.)

Q.   Now, Mr. Wilson, where did you go to after you got on the train before you got off the train, starting to look over this land?

A.   Where did I go?

Q.   Yes, where did you get off the train?

A.   At Orofino.

Q.   You had had a conversation with Mr. Dwyer regarding your location fee, or have, haven't you?

A.   At that time in Clarkston; that is all.

Q.   What did he tell you it would cost you for a location fee?

A.   There wasn't nothing said about location fee at that time.

Q.   There was nothing said about location fee at that time?      A.   No, sir.

Q.   Now, was there anything said about what it would cost to make your final proof at that time?

A.   All that was said was that the money would be furnished to me; that is all that I knew that took place.

Q.   He asked you if he wanted to take up a timber claim at that time?

A.   I remember I went along with him and went into the timber and looked at it.

Q.   What?

A.   At the time I was in the train do you refer to?

Q.   No, this time in Clarkston.

A.   Yes, sir; he told me if I wanted to take up a claim and look at the timber, to take one up and go up with him.

(Testimony of Guy L. Wilson.)

Q. That is all that was said in Clarkston, if you wanted to take up a timber claim to go up with him and look at the timber?

A. The proposition was made then to me about the money.

Q. What money?

A. The money which was to be paid for the timber when filed.

Q. The money to file?    A. Yes.

Q. What did he tell you about it?

A. He said at the time that my expenses would be paid up there, and when the timber was turned over—when he turned this timber over, there would be about $150 in it for me.

Q. You don't know whether this was included in your statement to Mr. Goodwin and Mr. O'Fallon or not?

A. I don't remember whether it was or not.

Q. Now, Mr. Wilson, is it not a fact that Mr. Dwyer and you talked over what it would cost to prove up at Clarkston at that ime?

A. We might have, but I don't remember of it.

Q. Isn't it a fact that you talked over what the expense would be in going to look at the land, and the publication fee?

A. I don't remember of it.

Q. You may have talked that over?

A. Might have.

Q. And isn't it a fact you talked over the location fee at that time?

(Testimony of Guy L. Wilson.)

A.   I don't remember of talking anything about location fee at that time.

Q.   But you might have talked over the location fee?     A.   It might have been spoken of.

Q.   You do know that the location fee was $100, don't you?

A.   That is what some loctors charged.

Q.   And then Mr. Dwyer said, if you wanted to turn over the claim you could undoubtedly get $150 over and above these?

A.   As near as I can remember that was the prpos'sitiou that when these timber claims were turned ovee, I would get $150.00.

Q.   Didn't he say these claims ought to be worth $700 or $800 according to the timber?

A.   He might have said it; I don't remember him saying it.

Q.   Don't you remember, Mr. Wilson, after you figured up the location fee and the publication fee, and the expenses for going to look over the timber that he figured, and that you figured that ovee and above these expenses, there would be at least $150 for you?

A.   As I said before, there might—he might have done that: I don't remember.

Q.   He might have done that, but after you had figured ovec all these expenses, and figured up all of these expenses, they ran a little bit higher than you and Mr. Dwyer had figured on by $14.00, didn't they, Mr. Wilson, and you got $136.00 instead of $150?

(Testimony of Guy L. Wilson.)

A.   I don't think that I ever figured—that we ever figured, but that one time.

Q.   Mr. Wilson, don't you remember *tut* your expenses ran a little higher than you had figured on by about $14?          A.   No, I don't remember that.

Q.   But it did run higher, *dd* it not?   And you had only $136, instead of $150?

A.   This paying for this fellow waiting in line was $14.

Q.   And if it had not been for paying this fellow for waiting in line out of the $700, you would have had $150; is that right?        (No response.)

Q.   You say you had a little above *$*160 acres, a fraction above that?

A.   I don't remember; it was above 160, I think.

Q.   Wasn't the Government price $412?

A.   I don't remember ab*ot* those details.

Q.   It was little bit over $400, you remember that?

A.   It was over $400; I remember that.

Q.   Assuming, then, that it was $412, that would make you a little more than *$*160 acres, wouldn't it?

And be it remembered the following proceeding was then had:

Mr. RUICK.—Objected to; my objection is that the question of counsel assumes a *s*state of facts not in evidence.

The COURT.—The Court will sustain the objection.   I do not care to take up time in arguing the matter.

To which ruling of the Court the defendant excepted, which exception was by the Court allowed.

(Testimony of Guy L. Wilson.)

Q. The advertising fee was $8, wasn't it, Mr. Wilson?

A. That is something I didn't know anything about.

Q. And the expenses to the land and the expenses in making your final proof, including making our your papers, was in the neighborhood of $30, wasn't it?

A. I don't know just what my expenses were up there.

Q. Don't you know, Mr. Wilson, that the price that was paid for this land including the final proof and the advertising and the expenses incurred, was $700?

A. I don't know what the expenses were.

The COURT.—That is not the question.

Mr. TANNAHILL.—To make myself clear, the price it cost to acquire title from the Government and the location fee was $550, wasn't it, Mr. Wilson, as figured up by you and Mr. Dwyer?

A. I don't remember of figuring the thing up.

Q. That might have been the case?

A. We might have figured it up some time or other; I don't remember.

Be it remembered that then and there the following proceeding was had:

Q. Then, if you have received $700 for your claim, your portion of it would be $150?

Mr. RUICK.—Objected to on two grounds; one is, it is arguing the question to the witness; the second is, it is a matter of computation which counsel

(Testimony of Guy L. Wilson.)

and the other members and the jury are just as competent to make as the witness himself.

Mr. TANNAHILL.—The dividing line is very indistinct, and the witness says he does not know just what the agreement was. If he turned the land over, he ought to have $150 out of it as his part; I believe the witness is trying to tell the truth about it; now then, I am trying to find out how they arrived at $150; that is the only object of my question; I am not trying to confuse the witness, and I think the witness understands it thoroughly; I am simply asking him if those figures are correct.

The COURT.—The Court will sustain the objection in the present form with the explanation that the witness, as the Court understands, has stated several times, in response to counsel for the Government, that he was to have, as he understood, about $150, after Mr. Dwyer stated to him he would realize about $150 out of it. I have no objection, and will permit counsel for defendant to cross-examine the witness upon that subject, and find out what he meant by that, and what was said relative to that.

To which ruling of the Court the defendants then and there excepted, and which exception was allowed by the Court.

Q. Mr. Wilson, it has been some time since you and Mr. Dwyer have had a conversation regarding this matter, hasn't it? A. Yes, sir.

Q. And the exact conversation is not very clear in your mind now in detail, is it?

A. I made it as clear as I could remember.

(Testimony of Guy L. Wilson.)

Q. That is, just as you remember it?

A. Yes, sir.

Q. But you would not say that Mr. Dwyer understood it, that if you wanted to turn your claim over, you ought to have about $150 out of it?

A. I don't catch your meaning quite.

Be it remembered that the follow*ig* proceeding was then and there had:

Q. You would not say that Mr. Dwyer did not understand that if you wanted to turn your claim over, you ought to have $150 out of it?

Mr. RUICK.—That is objected to as calling for the understanding of Mr. Dwyer.

The COURT.—I sustain the objection.

To which ruling of the Court the def*ndz*nts then and there excepted, which exception was allowed by the Court.

Q. Mr. Wilson, who else did you say went with you to this land?

A. There was Mr. and Mrs. Justice, Mr. O'Brien, Mr. Hopper and Mr. Dwyer and myself.

Q. Now, when did you have a conversation, or did you have a conversation with Mr. Dwyer on this trip regarding his location fee?

A. I don't remember having any; I might have had.

Q. You might have had?    A. *Ye,* sir.

Q. You understood you were to pay Mr. Dwyer $100 for locating?

(Testimony of Guy L. Wilson.)

A. No, I don't remember of having an understanding, anything about the location fee at all at that time.

Q. But it was understood that Mr. Dwyer was to have $100 for locating you?

A. I don't—no, I don't remember anything about that.

Be it remembered that the following proceedings were then had:

Q. Don't you know that Mr. Hopper also paid him $100 for locating him?

Mr. RUICK.—Objected to as incompetent, irrelevant and immaterial and hearsay.

The COURT.—The objection is sustained.

To which ruling of the Court the defendants excepted, which exception was allowed by the Court.

Q. Did you have any conversation with Mr. Dwyer on this trip regarding this loction fee?

A. None that I remember of.

Q. Now, Mr. Wilson, in your final proof you swore in answer to question 7, "Did you pay or agree to pay anything for this information, if so, to whom and amount?" "Yes, William Dwyer, $100"; you swore to that, did you?    A. Yes, sir.

Q. And you also, in response to question 6, "How did you first learn about this particular tract of land, and that it would be a good investment to buy it?" your answer was "Through William Dwyer"; do you remember swearing to that?

A. Yes, sir.

(Testimony of Guy L. Wilson.)

Q.  And you did first learn this through William Dwyer?

A.  About that particular piece of land, I first learned it from him.

Q.  And he located you on that particular tract of land?    A.  Well, I suppose he did.

Q.  Now, who else did you say went with you?

A.  There was Mr. and Mrs. Justice, Mr. O'Brien, Mr. Hopper and Mr. Dwyer and myself.

Q.  And *di* you go back together?

A.  No, sir.

Q.  Did Mr. Justice go out and look at the timber?

A.  I don't know whether he did or not.

Q.  You don't think you did, do you?

A.  I don't believe he did.

Q.  And he concluded not to take a claim, didn't he?

A.  I don't know what was his reason except he was sick at the time we filed.

And be it remembered that then and there the following proceeding was had:

Q.  He didn't go out and look at the timber? Didn't you hear him say that he didn't think the timber was worth it?

Mr. RUICK.—Objected to as incompetent, irrelevant and immaterial, and hearsay.

The COURT.—Objection sustained.

To which ruling of the Court the defendants excepted, which exception was allowed by the Court.

Q.  You came back with Mr. and Mrs. Justice, did you?    A.  Yes, sir.

(Testimony of Guy L. Wilson.)

Q. And who else came back at the same time?

A. There were three of us; that is all.

Q. And who remained there?

A. Mr. Hopper, and Mr. O'Brien, they were still there yet with Mr. Dwyer.

Q. Mr. Hopper remained there to look over the timber?     A. Yes, sir.

Q. And did Mr. Hopper report to you after he returned about the timber?

A. He told me he had taken a claim.

Q. Who was it paid your expenses back on your return?

A. I don't know whether they were paid or not; if they were, Mr. Justice must have paid them.

Q. Did you buy a ticket to come back?

A. I did not.

Q. Who was it paid your hotel bill?

A. I don't know who did, or whether he did or whether it was paid or not.

Q. Didn't you see him pay your hotel bill?

A. No, I did not.

Q. Did you see Mr. Justice leave the hotel?

A. I can't remember whether we left the hotel together or whether I went out first.

Q. Did you see him buy tickets for your return?

A. No, I don't believe I did.

Q. Now, as a matter of fact, Mr. Wilson, didn't Mr. Justice pay your expenses both going and coming, with the exception of the livery horses which you rode out to the claim?

(Testimony of Guy L. Wilson.)

A. If he did I didn't know anything about it.

Q. How long was it after you went up to look at the claims before you filed?

A. This was in October, and I fie*l*d some time in April.

Q. That is four or five months af*te* you went to look at the claim before you filed?     A. Yes, sir.

Q. Why didn't you file earlier?

A. My understanding was that this land—you could not file upon it yet.

*Q.*—

Q. And your understanding was that the plats had to be filed before you could file on it?

A. Yes, sir; I think the State had a right, or something.

Q. The S*tte* had a sixty day prior right?     *A*

A. Yes, sir.

Q. Now, Mr. Wilson, did you have a conversation with Mr. Dwyer after you returned from the timber and before you filed your sworn statement or made your application?

A. I might have had; the onl*y* one I remember is the time he gave me the papers.

Q. Where did you have that conversation?

A. That was around in the bank building there some place; I could not tell you the exact place.

Q. Is *tht* in the statement you made for Mr. Goodwin and Mr. O'Fallon?

A. Why, I expect it is; I don't know for sure.

Q. You don't know whether that is in your statement or not, do you?     A. No.

(Testimony of Guy L. Wilson.)

Q. Your best recollection is it is not in that statement, isn't it, Mr. Wilson?

A. My best recollection is I would say it was; I expect it is.

Q. You don't know whether it is or not?

A. No, not for sure.

Q. Now, Mr. Wilson, you say that you went to Mr. Johnson's office before you saw Mr. O'Fallon; had you talked with them about going to see Mr. Johnson?

A. No; I might have. I don't remember any particular person that I have talked to.

Q. Have you talked with anyone about going to see a lawyer at all?  A. I talked with my wife.

Q. Did you talk with anyone else?

A. I might have; I don't remember anyone.

Q. But you might have talked with other people about it?  A. Yes, sir.

Q. And some one might have suggested to you to go and see Mr. Johnson?

A. No, I don't think anyone suggested that to me.

Q. How many trips did you make to see Mr. Johnson before you made the statement to Mr. O'Fallon?  A. I mde one.

Q. You made one and then you left the office and went back before O'Fallon came?

A. I didn't make that statement. I went to see him one time; it was several days, or two or three days before I went there again, I think.

Q. And that statement was made out for you when you went there again?

(Testimony of Guy L. Wilson.)

A.   It was made out at the time I was there, at the second time.

Q.   *How did you come to go there at that particular time?*

A.   *I had an appointment with Mr. Jonson to be there.*

Q.   *You, made arrangements the first time you were there to*

Q.   It was made out the second time you went there?     A.   Yes, sir.

Q.   Was it made out when you got there?

A.   No, sir.

Q.   Did you meet Mr. O'Fallon there by appointment?     A.   Yes, sir.

Q.   How long a consultation did you have with him the first time?

A.   That was the only time I met him, the second time I went to Mr. Johnson's office.

Q.   You went to Mr. Johnson's office first and then you went there about a week or two afterward to meet Mr. O'Fallon there?

A.   I went there afterward, I could not say how long it was between the times.

Q.   It was sometime afterwards, was it?

A.   Yes, sir.

Q.   And did Mr. Johnson tell you you would better make a statement for Mr. O'Fallon? *and*

A.   He did not say I better make one; he advised me it would be well to tell the truth.

Q.   He told you you better make a statement for Mr. O'Fallon?

(Testimony of Guy L. Wilson.)

A.   Well, he didn't mention any names; he said I could do as I like; he advised me that way.

Q.   And how did you come to go back to see Mr. O'Fallon?

A.   Mr. Johnson had told me I would be there when he came.

Q.   When did he tell you he would be there?

A.   I don't know.

Q.   How did you come to go at that particular time?

A.   I had an appointment with Mr. Johnson to be there.

Q.   You made arrangements the first time you were there to meet him the second time?

A.   Yes, sir.

Q.   On a particular day?

A.   I don't remember that—it was to be at a certain tim4, I think.

Q.   And he was to have Mr. O'Fallon there at that time?        A.   Yes, sir.

Q.   And you didn't see Mr. O'Fallon and Mr. Goodwin there the first time you went there?

A.   No, sir.

Q.   How long were Mr. Fallon and Mr. Goodwin making out this statement?

A.   Why, I couldn't say exactly; it was probably an hour.

Q.   And they were asking you questions during that time, weren't they?        A.   Yes, sir.

Q.   I believe you said you did not know where Mr. Dwyer was to get the money?

(Testimony of Guy L. Wilson.)

A.　No, I don't know where he was to get it.

Q.　And you don't know of anything that Mr. Kester and Mr. Kettenbach had to do with this matter?

A.　Only their names; I don't know anything more.

Q.　How do you know that note was payable to Kester and Kettenbach?

A.　I remember seeing that name on the note; I remember reading the note.

Q.　Was this fact stated in your statement to Mr. Goodwin and Mr. O'Fallon?　　A.　I think so.

Q.　Are you sure of it?

A.　I am not positive.

Q.　Did they ask you if there was anything that Kester and Kettenbach's name appeared on?

A.　They might have asked me that.

Q.　How do you know this note was for four hundred dollars?

A.　Well, I don't know—but I remember—all I can remember, it was more than four hundred dollars; I don't remember the exact amount.

Q.　It was more than four hundred dollars, but you don't know just what amount it was for?

A.　No, not exactly.

Q.　It may have been for five hundred?

A.　I don't believe it was.

Q.　Do you wish to be understood as swearing positively that it was not?

(Testimony of Guy L. Wilson.)

A.  I could not swear positively it was not, but to the best of my knowledge I think it was something over four hundred dollars.

Q.  Do you know what became of that note?

A.  I never seen it after my wife burned it up.

Q.  You don't think there was anything particularly wrong in Mr. Dwyer having your papers made out for you, and helping you to get that filing, did you?

A.  At that time I supposed it was all right.

Be it remembered that then and there the following proceeding was had:

Q.  Don't you know that it is a very usual thing for anyone to do to help another to get a filing on a piece of land, and have papers made out for him?

Mr. RUICK.—Objected to as incompetent, irrelevant and immaterial.

The COURT.—Objection sustained.

To which ruling of the Court the defendats excepted, which exception was by the Court allowed.

Q.  You didn't think there was anything particularly wrong in Mr. Dwyer locating you on this piece of land, did you?

A.  I thought it was all right at that time.

Be it remembered that the following proceedings were then had:

Q.  In so far as the locating of you on this piece of land—the locating of you on a piece of land, you don't think there would be anything wrong in that, do you?

(Testimony of Guy L. Wilson.)

Mr. RUICK.—Objected to as incompetent, irrelevant and immaterial, and as calling for a conclusion.

The COURT.—Objection sustained.

To which ruling of the Court the defendants excepted and which exception was allowed.

Q. Now, I believe you said that Mr. Dwyer told you that you would have to be able to answer those questions in your final proof a certain way in order to make the proof pass, or something to that effect, didn't he?

A. Yes, sir; they would have to be—I would have to know how to answer them.

Q. In order to make your proof pass?

. A. Yes, sir.

Q. And also told you that you had made no contract with him which would be in violation of these answers, didn't he?    A. Yes, sir.

Q. And he also told you that there was no contract which you had made with him for the conveyance of this land, didn't he?    A. Yes, sir.

Q. I believe you also said *tha* Mr. Dwyer told you that when you turned this land *ove* you were getting a benefit, or something to that effect, didn't he?

A. Yes, sir.

Q. Now, isn't it also a fact that Mr. Dwyer referred to this agreement with you for this location fee and the borrowing of your money—of the money with which to make final proof and told you there was nothing wrong in that?    A. Yes, sir.

(Testimony of Guy L. Wilson.)

Q. And he also told you that you had a perfect right to borrow the money to make your final proof, didn't he?

A. I don't remember of that convesation taking place.

Q. He may have made that statement?

A. He might have.

Q. Now, Mr. Wilson, was the fact of Mr. and Mrs. *Dwiers* visti to you t your home, which you testified to, included in your statement to Mr. Goodwin and Mr. O'Fallon?    A. I think it was.

Q. You are not sure it was?

A. I am pretty sure it was.

Q. And you don't wish to be understood as swearing positively it was, do you?

A. I think I would swear that we was not there.

Q. You wish to be understood as swearing he was not there?    A. Yes, sir.

Q. Do you remember Mr. Goodwin and Mr. O'Fallon calling your attention to that particular question, and asking you if he came ovec to see you just before you made your final proof?

A. They might have asked me that.

Q. Don't you remember that they did ask you that?

A. No, I don't know as I remember that?

Q. And you don't remember that Mr. O'Fallon told you that he had the evidence and knew just what occurred and you had just as well tell it, or words to that effect?

Testimony of Gu L. Wilson.)

A.   I don't remmber just what he did say, just t that time.

Q.   You don't rmemer he called your attention to 'at particular cirumstance and asked you about 1at?

A.   No, sir; I cnot say that I do remember.

Q.   You cannot say you do remember it? What uses you to think that that particular statement in the statement ou made to Mr. Goodwin and Mr. 'Fallon—what imoressed it upon your mind more ·an the other statments which I have called your tention to, which you say you cannot remember?

1.   Well, I remmber of him asking me if they ·d ever been in m house.

Q.   Ever been in your house?

A.   Been to my ouse.

Q.   And you tolt them they had or had not?

A.   I told them hey had.

Q.   And didn't e tell you he had information ey had been to yur house?

A.   He might hae; I don't remember that.

Q.   And didn't Ir. Goodwin and Mr. O'Fallon ll you they had te whole *thin* anyway, and you s well tll it?

A cannot say I remember them telling me

What did thy tell you about that?

.  I don't remenber much of what was said at · time.

.  Didn't you sa a while ago that Mr. Goodwin

(Testimony of Guy L. Wils n.)
tion anyway, and you might ust as ell tell it and
tell it all, or words to that e ct?

A. I don't remember ans ering ch a question
as that.

Q. What, don't you rem ber swering that
question? A. No.

Q. Or any question simil to th ?

A. I might have.

Q. Now, is it not a fact, M Wilso that the only
thing that bothered you in a swerin the questions
of Mr. Goodwin and Mr. O'I llen w that you had
sworn in your final proof p ers th you had had
this money for two and a hall ears, words to that
effect? A. That was of t m.

Q. And didn't they tell u tha you had committed perjury by making t t sta ent?

A. They might have told ne tha

Q. And didn't they tell r that u could be indicted and sent to the peniter ary f t. or words to
that effect?

A. I don't remember any ing of at kind being
said to me.

Q. Did not Mr. Johnson t l you u might be indicted for it and sent to the itent ry?

A. He might have.

Q. Don't you remember . Wil n that he did
tell you that?

A. If he did, I asked him don' kn w whether
he did or not.

Q. You think he did tell y that

(Testimony of Guy L. Wilson.)

A.   I don't remember just what he did say, just at that time.

Q.   You don't rememcr he called your attention to that particular circumstance and asked you about that?

A.   No, sir; I cnnot say that I do remember.

Q.   You cannot say you do remember it? What causes you to think that that particular statement is in the statement you made to Mr. Goodwin and Mr. O'Fallon—what impressed it upon your mind more than the other statements which I have called your attention to, which you say you cannot remember?

A.   Well, I remember of him asking me if they had ever been in my house.

Q.   Ever been in your house?

A.   Been to my house.

Q.   And you told them they had or had not?

A.   I told them they had.

Q.   And didn't he tell you he had information they had been to your house?

A.   He might have; I don't remember that.

Q.   And didn't Mr. Goodwin and Mr. O'Fallon tell you they had the whole *thin* anyway, and you might just as well tell it?

A.   No, I cannot say I remember them telling me that.

Q.   What did they tell you about that?

A.   I don't remember much of what was said at the time.

Q.   Didn't you say a while ago that Mr. Goodwin and Mr. O'Fallon told you they had all the informa-

(Testimony of Guy L. Wilson.)

tion anyway, and you might just as well tell it and tell it all, or words to that effect?

A. I don't remember answering such a question as that.

Q. What, don't you remember answering that question? A. No.

Q. Or any question similar to that?

A. I might have.

Q. Now, is it not a fact, Mr. Wilson, that the only thing that bothered you in answering the questions of Mr. Goodwin and Mr. O'Fallon was that you had sworn in your final proof papers that you had had this money for two and a half years, or words to that effect? A. That was one of them.

Q. 'And didn't they tell you that you had committed perjury by making that statement?

A. They might have told me that.

Q. And didn't they tell you that you could be indicted and sent to the penitentiary for it, or words to that effect?

A. I don't remember anything of that kind being said to me.

Q. Did not Mr. Johnson tell you you might be indicted for it and sent to the penitentiary?

A. He might have.

Q. Don't you remember Mr. Wilson that he did tell you that?

A. If he did, I asked him; I don't know whether he did or not.

Q. You think he did tell you that?

(Testimony of Guy L. Wilson.)

A.   I don't remember just what he did say, just at that time.

Q.   You don't remember he called your attention to that particular circumstance and asked you about that?

A.   No, sir. I cannot say that I do remember.

Q.   You cannot say you do remember it?   What causes you to think that that particular statement is in the statement you made to Mr. Goodwin and Mr. O'Fallon—what impressed it upon your mind more than the other statements which I have called your attention to, which you say you cannot remember?

A.   Well I remember of him asking me if they had ever been in my house.

Q.   Ever been in your house?

A.   Been to my house.

Q.   And you told them they had or had not?

A.   I told them they had.

Q.   And didn't he tell you he had information they had been to your house?

A.   He might have; I don't remember that.

Q.   And didn't Mr. Goodwin and Mr. O'Fallon tell you they had the whole thing anyway, and you might just as well tell it?

A.   No, I cannot say I remember them telling me that.

Q.   What did they tell you about that?

A.   I don't remember much of what was said at the time.

Q.   Didn't you say a while ago that Mr. Goodwin and Mr. O'Fallon told you they had all the informa-

(Testimony of Guy L. Wilson.)

tion anyway, and you might just as well tell it and tell it all, or words to that effect?

A. I don't remember answering such a question as that.

Q. What, don't you remember answering that question?    A. No.

Q. Or any question similar to that?

A. I might have.

Q. Now, is it not a fact, Mr. Wilson. that the only thing that bothered you in answering the questions of Mr. Goodwin and Mr. O'Fallon was that you had sworn in your final proof papers that you had had this money for two and a half years, or words to that effect?    A. That was one of them.

Q. And didn't they tell you that you had committed perjury by making that statement?

A. They might have told me that.

Q. And didn't they tell you that you could be indicted and sent to the penitentiary for it. or words to that effect?

A. I don't remember anything of that kind being said to me.

Q. Did not Mr. Johnson tell you you might be indicted for it and sent to the penitentiary?

A. He might have.

Q. Don't you remember Mr. Wilson that he did tell you that?

A. If he did, I asked him; I don't know whether he did or not.

Q. You think he did tell you that?

(Testimony of Guy L. Wilson.)

A.   He might have asked me that; I went to him for advice.

Q.   And he told you if you went ahead and told all you knew, you would not be bothered?     A.   No.

Q.   Mr. Ruick told you if you went ahead and told all you knew you would not be bothered?

A.   No, he never told me anything like that.

Q.   You were not afraid of being bothered yourself, were you?

A.   No, I didn't think they were after me.

Mr. RUICK.—We have not been after the entrymen; I frankly admit that fact.

Q.   Now, did you hear your father in law say anything about taking up a claim after he came back from the timber?

A.   I don't remember of hearing him; he was sick after he came back, and I was busy working.

Q.   How long after you came back was it he took sick?

A.   He was sick at the time he came back.

Q.   How long was he ill before he died?

A.   Lets see; we had filed and proved up; it was a year from October—a year from the February after we went up into the mountains.

Q.   He was not sick then when you came back from the mountains?

A.   He was not exactly sick in bed, but he was not feeling good.

Q.   He was not feeling well, but that was not the sickness from which he died?

(Testimony of Guy L. Wilson.)

A. I don't know whether it was or not. I think it was, though.

Q. He was up and around a great deal?

A. He was up and around after he came back, yes, but then he was—he was up and around but he was sick at the same time.

Q. It was more than a year after you came back before he died, wasn't it? A. Yes, sir.

Q. Then he was not sick at the time you proved up, was he?

A. Yes, sir; he was able to be around but he was a sick man.

Q. He was able to be around but there was not anything to prevent him coming *ove* and making his filing if he wanted to; he was well enough to do that, wasn't he? A. Possibly he might have.

Q. After your father in law *cae* back from the mountains he never said anything more about taking up a claim up there, did he?

A. I don't remember any conversation I had with him after that.

Q. He never made any other statements to you about your taking up a claim?

A. He might have, but I don't recollect any.

Q. Didn't he tell you the timber was not worth anything like the amount he would have to pay for it?

A. I don't remember of his telling me that.

Q. Did you hear him tell Mrs. Justice, his wife?

A. No, I don't believe I did.

(Testimony of Guy L. Wilson.)

Be it remembered that then and there the following proceedings were had:

Q. Did you hear Mrs. Justice, or do you know anything about her making arrangements to get the money to make final proof from Mr. Hopper?

Mr. RUICK.—Objected to as incompetent, irrelevant and immaterial and hearsay, and not cross-examination.

The COURT.—Objection sustained.

To which ruling of the Court the defendants then and there excepted, which exception was allowed by the Court.

Be it remembered that then and there the following proceeding was had:

Q. Is it not a fact, Mr. Wilson, that Mrs. Justice told you she was making arrangements with Mr. Hopper to get the money for you to get the timber claim?

Mr. RUICK.—Objected to as incompetent, irrelevant and immaterial.

The COURT.—If the Court recollects, the testimony of the witness, it is improper cross-examination. Have you in mind any testimony of which it is proper cross-examination?

Mr. MOORE.—I suggested to my associate that he bring out the fact that this witness and his mother in law had been endeavoring to get the money elsewhere to make proof on these claims.

The COURT.—The objection is sustained.

(Testimony of Guy L. Wilson.)

To which ruling of the Court the defendants then and th*ee* excepted, which exception *wa* allowed b*y* the Court.

Q. Mr. Wilson, do you know Fred Justice?

A. Yes, sir.

Q. Fred Justice was then on the day you made your proof, was he not? A. I think he was.

Q. Didn't you know Fred Justice was the man who had charge of that line-up, and had the book and kept the names and numbers?

A. Yes, sir; I knew he kept the numbers.

Q. And didn't you know Fred Justice was the man who had had your papers made out?

A. If he supplied the information I didn't know anyth*ig* about it.

Q. And didn't you know he also paid I. N. Smith for making out your papers?

A. Not that I know of.

Q. But Fred Justice was there and looked after the matters for you and was tr*y*ing to help you out, wasn't he?

A. I don't know as he was trying to help me out; he was there.

Q. He was helping all of you, wasn't he, seeing you kept your places in line, and had your papers?

A. I don't ever remember him having m*y* papers; he had some.

Q. He had some of your papers, didn't he?

A. Not that I know of.

Q. You don't know anything about that?

(Testimony of Guy L. Wilson.)

A.  No, sir.

Q.  Who was it gave you your number when you went up and got in line and put your name on the book?     A.  I think he did, Fred Justice.

Q.  And he is a son of Mrs. Francis A. Justice and your brother in law, is he not?     A.  Yes, sir.

Q.  What day was this you filed, do you remember?

A.  I think it was on Monday; I am not sure about that.

Q.  What did you do in relation to this matter the day before you filed—anything?

A.  I went into the office there to—I was asked in there by Mr. Dwyer for some information about making out those papers.

Q.  Now, Mr. Wilson, it is not a fact that Fred Justice told you to go up to Mr. Smith's office?

A.  I think that Mr. Dwyer is the man who told me to go up there.

Q.  That is your remembrance of it, is it?

A.  That is the best of my remembrance.

Q.  Is the fact that Mr. Dwyer told you to go up to Mr. Smith's office in the statement you made to Mr. Goodwin and Mr. O'Farron?

A.  I could not say whether it is or not.

Q.  You don't know whether that is there or not?

A.  No, it has been a long time ago; I have forgotten.

Q.  Did Mr. O'Brien get a claim?

A.  Not that I know of.

Q.  He was not in line that day, was he?

(Testimony of Guy L. Wilson.)

A. No, sir.

Q. Was Mr. Hopper in line t*ht* day?

A. Yes, sir.

Q. Do you know what he did with his claim?

A. I don't.

Q. You know he didn't sell it to Mr. Dw,er, don't you?      A. I don't.

Q. Now, Mr. Wilson, do you know t*ht* Mr. Dw,er made any arrangements for the payments of your expenses other than the livery bill?

A. I don't know what arrangement he had made.

Q. You don't know anything about that?

A. Except I didn't pay any expenses.

Q. Do you know that he paid any of your expenses other than ,our liver, bill, either going or coming?

A. All I know is he told me my expenses would be paid up there and back.

Q. I am asking you what you know of ,our own knowledge what he did do?

A. I didn't see him pay an,thing.

Q. Now, you say that Mr. Dwyer said you passed through or over the timber; you had no reason to believe you did not pass over the land, did you?

A. No, sir.

Q. You believe now you were upon the land?

A. Well, I am not sure I was or was not.

Q. Well, Mr. Wilson, did you read that statement over which you gave Mr. O'Farron and Mr. Goodwin before you signed it?      A. Yes, sir.

Q. How many times did you read it ovce?

(Testimony of Guy L. Wilson.)

A.  Once.

Q.  Did you read it yourself, or did Mr. Goodwin or Mr. O'Farron read it to you?

A.  I think I read it myself.

Q.  You are sure you read it yourself?

A.  Yes, sir.

Q.  How many times before you say you testified before the grand jury?    A.  Twice.

Q.  Where was the first time and when?

A.  It was in this building—it was—it must have been two years ago.

Q.  I believe you said you read this statement over at that time before you testified before the grand jury?    A.  Yes, sir.

Q.  When was the next time?

A.  I never read it after that.

Q.  When was the next time you testified before the grand jury?    A.  It was in Boise.

Q.  Did you read your evidence over at that time, taken in the trial last fall before testifying at Boise?

A.  Yes, sir.

Q.  How many times did you read it over then?

A.  Once.

Q.  You read your testimony over last night, did you?    A.  Yes, sir.

Q.  You had a talk with Mr. Ruick and Mr. Johnson during the noon recess about your evidence, didn't you?

A.  Why, we talked some about it, yes, sir.

(Testimony of Guy L. Wilson.)

Redirect Examination by Mr. RUICK.

Q. In a question which counsel asked you on cross-examination, Mr. Wilson, there is embodied in it an assumption that something was agreed upon or understood between you and Mr. Dwyer relative to a location fee. Do you wish to be understood as stating there was an agreement at any time between you and Mr. Dwyer relative to a location fee?

A. There is nothing that I ever remember of. I don't remember ever having a conversation about location fees; there might have been something said about it, but I don't remember of it.

Q. Fred Justice has been referred to. Is Fred Justice now loving? A. No, sir.

Q. When did he die?

A. Two years ago last April.

The COURT.—Is this the brother in law?

Mr. RUICK.—Yes, the brother in law; the father in law and the brother in law are both dead.

Q. What the cause of Fred's death?

A. Why, he was killed while working on live wires in Lewiston.

Q. An electric shock? A. Yes.

Recross-examination by Mr. TANNAHILL.

Q. You knew you gave that statement and made your answers to Mr. O'Fallon and Mr. Goodwin under oath, didn't you? A. Yes, sir.

(Witeness excused.)

ELLA WILSON, a witness called and sworn in behalf of the Government, testified as follows on

Direct Examination by Mr. RUICK.

Q. Mrs. Wilson, what is your given name?

A. Ella Wilson.

(Witness continuing:) I am the wife of Guy L. Wilson, and a daughter of David Justice, deceased, and Mrs. Francis A. Justice. Fred Justice is my brother.

In 1903 and 1904 I was residing in Clarkston, Washington, I was marreid to Mr. Wilson in 1901. I was residing with my husband in Clarkston. In 1903 and 1904, I believe it is Clarkston. We have moved around so much, I don't know exactly. We have resided in Vineland, a suburb of Clarkston.

I rrmember the occasion of my husband filing on a stone and timber claim. I am acquainted with Mr. and Mrs. William Dwyer; have known them about eight years and a half in Clarkston, Washington.

Q. Do you recall an instance of Mr. and Mrs. Dwyer, either or both of them, coming to the home where you then lived to see Mr. Wilson, your husband?　A. Yes, sir.

Q. About what time in the day was this?

A. About six o'clock in the evening.

Q. Was your husband there at the time that they arrived?　A. No, sir.

Q. How long after they came did your husband come?　A. About 15 minutes.

Q. What inquiries, if any, did Mr. Dwyer make when he came to the house?

(Testimony of Ella Wilson.)

A. He wanted to know if Mr. Wilson was at home; he wanted to see him.

Q. How were he and Mrs. Dwyer journeying?

A. They had a horse and buggy.

Q. Did they get out of the buggy at your home on that occasion?    A. No, sir.

Q. What, if any, reply to them did you make when they asked if your husband was at home?

A. I told them no.

Q. Where was your husband just at that time?

A. He was on his way home from work.

Q. How long before he arrived was it, do you say?    A. Abot ten or fifteen minutes.

Q. Did they remain until he came?

A. Yes, sir.

Q. Did you see your husband coming before he reached the house?    A. Yes, sir.

Q. What, if anything, did Mr. Dwyer say before your husband came up as to what he wanted, or did he state what he wanted regarding your husband?

A. I don't remember.

Q. Did you hear any conversation between your husband and Mr. Dwyer after your husband came?

A. Yes, sir.

Q. Did you hear the entire conversation?

A. Yes, sir.

Q. What did that conversation relate to?

A. About the questions which Mr. Wilson had to answer at the land office.

Q. State what Mr. Dwyer and your husband said, either one or both of them in the conversation; in

(Testimony of Ella Wilson.)

other words, relate the conversation as you heard it, Mrs. Wilson?

A. Mr. Dwyer said that he wanted to give Mr. Wilson some pointers on the questions he had to answer, and he said to tell them that he had the money or its equivalent to pay for this claim, and Mr. Wilson asked if he had to perjure himself when he answered the question, and Mr. Dwyer said not to worry about that, it was a thing which was being done every day.

Q. Do you recall anything else that he said relative to matters between him and Mr. Wilson, your husband?

A. He said that the agreement between them was only verbal, but that he would get the money just the same.

Q. That who would get the money?

A. Mr. Wilson.

Q. Do you know what money he referred to?

A. Why, the money for the claim.

Q. Did you know what money he referred to?

A. Yes, sir.

Q. What money did he refer to?

A. The money he was to get for his timber claim, for the right.

Q. For his right?     A. Yes, sir.

Cross-examination by Mr. TANNAHILL.

Q. Who have you talked to about your evidence?

A. My evidence?

Q. Yes.

(Testimony of Ella Wilson.)

A.   Why, I don't know as I have talked with any-one about it.

Q.   You *hv*en't talked with anyone about your evidence?   A.   No, sir.

Q.   How many times have you read your evidence over which you gave at the last trial before going upon the stand?

A.   Why I have remembered that.   I only had a ver, little to say.

Q.   And you haven't read it over at all?

A.   Why, I have had a chance to glance it over.

Q.   Didn't you read it very carefully?

A.   No.

Q.   How long did it take you to read it over ?

A.   About two seconds.

Q.   You did read it over, though?

A.   I just glanced at it.

Q.   And you haven't talked with anyone about your evidence?   A.   No, sir.

Q.   Have you made a statement for Mr. Goodwin or Mr. O'Fallon?   A.   No, sir.

Q.   You *hv*en't signed any statement for them or anyone else?   A.   No, sir.

Q.   You haven't signed any for Mr. Ruick?

A.   No.

Q.   And he has not talked with you about your evidence ?

A.   He did the last time I was up here.

Q.   Hasn't he talked to you about the evidence before you went before the grand jur, ?

A.   I wasn't before the grand jury.

(Testimony of Ella Wilson.)

Q. Has Mr. Johnson talked to you about your evidence?    A. No, sir.

Q. Has anyone talked to you about your evidence at all since coming to Moscow?    A. No.

Q. Have you talked with your mother, Mrs. Justice, about your evidence since coming to Moscow this last time?    A. No, sir.

Q. You haven't mentioned it?

A. No, only that I was here to testify.

Q. When did you come to Moscow?

A. Sunday night.

Q. Sunday night; did you talk to her about your evidence before you came to Moscow?

A. I didn't see her for six weeks.

Q. Did you talk to your husband about what you were going to testify to this time?

A. I don't remember whether I did or not; I suppose I did.

Q. You think you did?

A. I imagine so.

Q. Who gave you your evidence to look over?

A. I don't know where I *dd* get it; I suppose from Mr. Ruick; I don't know.

Q. You think Mr. Ruick gave you your evidence to look over?    A. Yes, sir.

Q. When did he give it to you?

A. I believe to-day I saw it.

Q. To-day you have seen it?  Have you seen it at the noon hour?

A. Since the noon hour.

Q. At the noon hour?

(Testimony of Ella Wilson.)

A. No, sir; not at the noon hour.

Q. This morning?    A. No.

Q. This forenoon? `    A. No, sir.

Q. Last night?

A. No, I didn't see it last night

Q. When did you see it?

A. This afternoon.

Q. How long before you went upon the witness-stand?    A. About three hours or four.

Q. Was it after court convened this afternoon?

A. No, sir.

Q. What day was it Mr. and Mrs. Dwyer were at your house?

A. I don't remember the exact day. It was just a few days before Mr. Wilson filed.

Q. What kind of a day was it?

A. I guess it was a bright, sunshiny day; it didn't seem to be raining.

Q. A pretty warm day, wasn't it?

A. I don't know.

Q. What kind of a horse was Mr. Dwyer driving?

A. I don't remember now.

Q. You don't remember anything about that?

A. I think it was a sorrel horse; I would not swear to it, though.

Q. Was it two horses or one?    A. One.

Q. Was Mrs. Dwyer with him?

A. Yes, sir.

Q. Do you remember how she was dressed that day?    A. No, I don't remember.

(Testimony of Ella Wilson.)

Q.  Which way did they come from?

A.  They came from Clarkston up Eighth Street.

Q.  W*ht* time of day did they get there?

A.  About six o'clock in the evening.

Q.  Was it sundown?    A.  I don't remember.

Q.  Had it been raining that da,?

A.  Not that I know of.

Q.  Was it cloud,?

A.  I don't remember about the weather unless it was a bright day.

Q.  You don't know whether *ii* was sundown or not?    A.  No, sir.

Q.  Mrs. Wilson, did you ever talk to Mr. Goodwin and Mr. O'Fallon about your evidence?

A.  No, sir.

Q.  Did you ever see Mr. Goodwin and Mr. O'Fallon?    A.  Yes, sir; I have seen them.

Q.  Where *di* ,ou see them?

A.  Each time I have been to Moscow.

Q.  Did ,ou see them when they *wer* at Lewiston?

A.  I saw them once in Cl*a*kston, at my home.

Q.  When?    A.  Last fall.

Q.  What mo*j*th was it?

A.  I believe it was November.

Q.  And who else was with them?

A.  Mr. O'Fallon was not there with Mr. Goodwin.  It was Mr. Gorman.

Q.  Mr. Gorman and Mr. Goodwin were there?

A.  Yes, sir.

Q.  And did they talk to you at the time?

(Testimony of Ella Wilson.)

A. They didn't say anything about my evidence.

Q. Did they talk to you at all?     A. Yes, sir.

Q. Did they talk to your husband?

A. No, sir.

Q. Where was your husband?

A. At work.

Q. Did they see him during that time at that trip?     A. I don't know.

Q. Did they inquire for him?     A. No, sir.

Q. What did they come to your house for?

A. They wanted to know where Mrs. Justice was.

Q. Did you tell them where she was?

A. Yes, sir.

Q. And they went to see Mrs. Justice?

A. She was not in Washington at the time; she was in Canada.

Q. Were you at home when Mr. Goodwin and Mr. O'Fallon went to see Mrs. Justice and got a statement from her?     A. No, sir.

Q. Do you know anything about that?

A. No.

Q. Did she ever say anything to you about it?

A. She told me they were there.

Q. Did she tell you she made a statement?

A. Yes, sir.

Q. And that she did not know what was in it?

A. She knew what was in it.

Q. Did she tell you she didn't read it over?

A. I don't remember.

(Testimony of Ella Wilson.)

Redirect Examination by Mr. RUICK.

Q. Mrs. Wilson, when you were asked as to the day or date on which Mr. and Mrs. Dwyer were up there, you said you didn't know the date, but it was some time before your husband filed. What do you mean by that, that your husband filed?

A. Why filed on his claim.

Q. I want to ask you whether or not or what this conversation had between you husband and Mr. Dwyer related to, whether it related to his filing, or to his final proof at the land office?

A. Why, it must have been the final proof; I couldn't swear to that.

Q. As fixing the date I simply want to know the date, what time was it relative to the time that he got a final receipt from the land office, and you went and joined him in a deed for this land, about how long before that occurrence was it?

A. I believe two or three months; I am not certain.

Q. Do you remember of joining your husband, or rather do you remember going to Lewiston with your husband the day he made his final proof?

A. Yes, sir.

Q. What did you do while over there relative to the land which he proved up on?

A. I signed a paper while there.

Q. In whose office did you sign the paper?

A. In Mr. Otto Kettenbach's.

Q. Did you know what the paper was? Did you understand what it was?

(Testimony of Ella Wilson.)

A. I supposed it was a contract for a deed or a deed; I didn't know.

Q. And who was there at the time that you executed this deed?

A. My husband and Mr. Justice and Mrs. Justice, Mr. David Justice.

Q. Did you see Mr. Dwyer?

A. Yes, Mr. Dwyer was there.

Q. For what purpose did you go to the office?

A. To sign this deed.

A. After you had signed the paper there in Otto Kettenbach's office did you get any other paper or papers from any place or from anyone?

A. Yes, sir.

Q. What did you get?

A. I got Mr. Wilson's note from the bank.

Q. From what bank?

A. The Lewiston National Bank.

Q. How did you happen to go to the bank for it? By whose direction?

A. By my father's and Mr. Wilson's.

Q. How did you know to go to the bank to get the note?

A. Mr. Wilson said his note was there in the bank.

Q. Do you remember whether Mr. Dwyer said anything there at that time?

A. I don't remember.

Q. In other words, do you know how your husband knew that his note was in the Lewiston National Bank?    A. I don't know.

(Testimony of Ella Wilson.)

Q. You went to the bank to get the note?

A. Yes, sir.

Q. Who passed it over to you, do you remember?

A. I don't remember.

Q. Were you alone?

A. No, my mother was with me.

Q. What did you ask for?

A. For Mr. Wilson's note.

Q. Did you have any order in writing for the note?    A. No, sir.

Q. How did you expect to get that note if you didn't have any order in writing?

A. Why, Mr. Wilson told me to get it.

Q. And you simple went to the bank and asked for Mr. Wilson's note?    A. Yes, sir.

Q. And it was turned over to you?

A. Yes, sir.

Q. How long after you had executed this deed or contract for a deed in Otto Kettenbach's office was it before you appeared at the bank to get this note and received it?

A. It was less than an hour.

Q. Did you go direct from Otto Kettenbach's office direct to the bank, or did you go somewhere else in the meantime?

A. I think I went right to the bank.

Q. That is your recollection, is it?

A. Yes, sir.

Q. Did you read the note which you got, did you see the note?    A. Yes, sir.

(Testimony of Ella Wilson.)

Q. Did you look at it?    A. Yes, sir.

Q. Did you see your husband's signature oj the note?    A. Yes, sir.

Q. What become of the note?

A. I burned it up.

Q. Now, state what was in the note as you remember; describe the note just so much of it as you remember.

The COURT.—That is the amount, and to whom payable?

Q. The date and the amount, and to whom payable.

A. I don't remember that; I could not answer that.

Q. Do you remember what the note was?

A. No, sir; I do not.

Q. Were you acquinted with the officers or the employees of the bank there, at the Lewiston National Bank at the time?

A. I had met Mr. Kester; that was all.

Q. It wasn't Mr. Kester that handed you out the note, you think?

A. I don't remember who it was.

Q. So far as you know, were you known to any other one connected with the bank except Mr. Kester?

A. I believe not.

Q. You had no difficulty in getting the note?

A. No, sir.

Q. Now, you have been asked concerning a visit of Mr. Goodwin and Mr. Gorman to your home in

(Testimony of Ella Wilson.)

Clarkston last fall in November. What was their errand there at that time, as stated by them as you ascertained?

A. It was merely to ask where Mrs. Justice was.

Q. For what purpose did they want Mrs. Justice?

A. To bring her here as a witness.

Q. Where was Mrs. Justice at *tis* time?

A. She was in Vancouver.

Q. For what point, do you know, had Mrs. Justice left when she left Clarkston?

A. I don't know.

Q. Did you give them the last address of *yor* mother?

A. I gave them the address I knew, the last address I knew.

Q. How long had your moteher been gone before this visit of the officers?

A. I don't remember the exact time; it was a week or ten days; perhaps more.

Q. Did Mr. and Mrs. Dwyer *eve* visit you at any other time in a vehicle other than the time you referrd to at your place?    A. No, sir.

Recross-examination by Mr. TANNAHILL.

Q. When did you burn this note, Mrs. Wilson, that you refer to?    A. When I got home.

Q. The same day you went home?

A. Yes, sir.

Q. I believe you say you never got the note from Mr. Kester?    A. I say I got it *gtom* the bank.

Q. You were acquainted with Mr. Kester?

(Testimony of Ella Wilson.)

A. Yes, sir.

Q. You didn't get it from him?

A. I don't remember who handed it to me?

Q. Now, you know what kind of instrument your mother signed when she proved up on her claim, do you?

A. I don't know anyth*ig* about her claim.

Be it remembered *tht* then and there the following proceeding was had :

Q. Did you think you and your husband were making the same disposition of your claim as your mother did of hers?

Mr. RUICK.—Object*d* to as incompetent, irrelevant and immaterial.

The COURT.—Objection sustained.

To which ruling of the Court the defend*ats* excepted, which exception was allowed by the Court.

Q. I understand you to say, Mrs. Wilson, that you supposed the paper was either a contract for a deed, or a deed. What do you mean b*y* a contract for a deed?    A. A contract *c*lling for a deed.

Q. You knew it was either a deed or a mortgage, didn't you?

A. No, I didn't know it was a mortgage; I didn't know anything about a mortgage; I supposed it w*aa* a contract for a deed or a deed.

(Excused.)

CHARLES CAREY, a witness called and sourn on behalf of the plaintiff, testified as follows, on

Direct Examination by Mr. RUICK.

Q. Where do you reside, Mr. Carey?

A. Pierce City.

Q. (Continuing.) Nez Perce County, formerly Shoshone County. Have resided in that locality since July, 1906. Prior to that time, the summer of 1903 and 1904, prior to 1906 I was around Spokane, Lewiston and different places. I worked different places in the country. For an occupation have followed the butcher business some, and had a shooting-gallery in Lewiston one year. While I resided there I had a shooting-gallery and cigar-stand. I am acquainted with William Dwyer and Melvern C. Scott, known as Scotty. I was acquainted with them while a resident of Lewiston.

I have known Mr. Dwyer since some time in the summer of 1904. I got acquainted with Scotty in 1903, at the Hotel De France in Lewiston. He worked for me a little in the gallery. I do not remember just what he was doing other than that about that time. Mr. Scott introduced me to Mr. Dwyer.

Q. Well, what was the business you had with Mr. Dwyer which led to the introduction?

A. Well, he located me on timber land.

Q. You filed on a stone and timber claim, didn't you, at the Lewiston Land Office? A. Yes, sir.

Q. State to the jury, Mr. Carey, how you came to

(Testimony of Charles Carey.)

file upon that claim. Begin at the begi*i*ng and detail your knowledge of the facts.

A. The conversation I had with Mr. Scott?

Q. No, the conversation which you had with Scotty would not be competent evidence as against these defendants if not made in their presence. Now you can state for what you met Mr. Dwyer?

A. Why, it was to file on a homestead, on a timber claim, rather.

Q. With whom have you been talking about this prior to meeting Mr. Dwyer? A. Mr. Scott.

Q. Where did you meet Mr. Dwyer on this occasion?

A. Why, it was right by the bank, the stairways which lead up to the land office.

Q. What bank?

A. The Lewiston National, the one where the land office was.

Q. The bank of which Mr. Kettenbach here is president and Mr. Kester cashier?

A. Yes, sir; I believe that is the gentleman.

Q. And it is in the building where the land office was at that time? A. Yes, sir.

Q. And you met Mr. Dwyer at the stairs leading up to the land office?

A. Right there on the stone steps by the door, just on the outside.

Q. These were the steps which led to the hall, these stone steps?

A. Yes, sir; they stepped up into the building, one or two steps.

(Testimony of Charles Carey.)

Q. Did you have any conversation there with Mr. Dwyer? Was there anything said?

A. I was introduced to him.

Q. State what was said there in the presence of Mr. Dwyer.

A. Mr. Scotty told him I was looking for a timber claim; that I was all right, and he told me there would be $125 for me.

Q. Who?    A. Mr. Dwyer.

Q. What did you say to that, if anything?

A. I accepted it; I told him it was all right; something to that effect; I don't remember just the words I used. He said the less said about it would be the better, and I don't remember very much more that he *sid* and we walked down to the Bollinger together, and went to the bar and Mr. Dwyer treated us, and I think he told me he would see me the next day, or something like that, and that was all there was to it at that time.

Q. Did he tell you where he would see you the next day?

A. Well, he said I would find him around the corner there somewhere.

Q. Did you see Mr. Dwyer te next day?

A. Yes, sir.

Q. What business did you transact with him on that day, if any?    A. I filed on this claim.

Q. Did you go up to the timber before or after you saw Mr. Dwyer, and before you made your filing?

A. No, I had been on it previous to that time, to the time I filed.

(Testimony of Charles Carey.)

Q. For what purpose—for the purpose of looking at timber lands?

A. No, I was up there fishing, and I happened to be right on the ground, what I supposed was the ground anyhow from the blue prints and things that I looked up afterwards.

Q. So you didn't deem it necessary to go to the land?

A. No, I was satisfied I had been on the land.

Q. Well, where did you get your papers made out Mr. Carey? Who made out your filing papers?

A. Mr. Dwyer himself.

Q. Where did Mr. Dwyer make them out?

A. It was in one of those offices up there in the bank building.

Q. Do you remember on what floor of the bank building this office was where he made out your filing papers?

A. It was the same floor that the land office was on.

Q. In what direction was it from the land office relative to the stairway?

A. It would be just north of the land office.

Q. Would it be across the hall?

A. You have to go around the stairs; yes, it would be across the hall.

Q. Where was the door of the office where he made out the papers relative to the door of the land office, the entrance to the land office?

A. It was just about the same, only just on the opposite corner, just about in the same locality.

(Testimony of Charles Carey.)

Q. Mr. Carey I will ask you to illustrate merely by a sketch, just draw a line showing approxim*tely* the door the hallway upstairs, and the relative position of these doors. (Witness draws d*a*gram.) Before I ask you about that, let me ask you a question: Do you know where I. N. Smith's office is or was at that time? A. No, sir.

Q. Now, that (referring to diagram) is on rather a small scale for the jorors to see, but explain to them what this is, Mr. Carey.

Mr. MOORE.—That ought to be in evidence I think first, and become a part of the record.

Mr. RUICK.—No, it is only for the sake of illustration.

Be it remembered that then and there the following proceeding was had:

Mr. TANNAHILL.—It is objected to as irrelevant and immaterial, and not properly before the jury.

Mr. RUICK.—And as showing it only for the purposes of illustration.

The COURT.—The Court cannot see how it is very material, but does not see how it can do any harm;

To which ruling of the Court the defendant then and there excepted, which exception was allowed by the Court.

Q. Explain the relative position of the doors, relative to the stairs?

A. (Indicating on diagram.) This represents the north and south street; this is the east and west street; this is the building, and this is the stairway

(Testimony of Charles Carey.)

leading up to the land office; this represents the landing at the top of the stairs, there is where the door opens to the different offices around, and this is the land office, and that is where I went in and got those papers.

Q. The land office which you refer to, and the door of the office where your filing papers were made out, are opposite one another, and right across the stairs?

A. Yes, sir; as near as I can remember.

Q. Now, coming up this stairway into the building, when you arrive at the second floor, to which hand would you turn to go to the land office?

A. Let's see; that would be facing east; I would turn around here to my left—no, to my right to the land office.

Q. And if you were going to the office where you got these papers?

A. You would turn to the left.

Q. And would have to go around the stair railing to reach the door?      A. Yes, sir.

Q. Where did you meet Mr. Dwyer on this occasion before going up to this office? Where di you first meet him?

A. I think he was around on the four corners some place, or around town; I don't remember just where; he told me to come over, but some time in the forenoon he would be around there.

Q. One thing more about this, Mr. Carey. I want to ask you what was said between you and Mr. Dwyer, if anything more than what you have testi-

(Testimony of Charles Carey.)

fied to relative to the arrangement under which you should take up this land? Was there anything more said at any time or prior to your filing?

A. I don't know there was much; I had understood it through other parties; I think it was Scotty told me.

Q. Now was the arrangement that Scotty had made or told you of afterwards carried out by Mr. Dwyer as Scotty had told you?

A. No, not in every part it was not.

Q. Well, you may state then what transpired after you met Mr. Dwyer on that morning?

A. Mr. Dwyer made out the papers and gave me—

Q. I want to know—you met Mr. Dwyer there—what did you do, and where did you go?

A. We went up to this office, the papers were made out there, and he gave them to me to file in the land office, and with them was a relinquishment, and he gave me money to pay in the land office.

Q. To pay what in the land office?

A. I suppose filing, or whatever it was; whatever it was for.

Q. What did he instruct you to do with the money?

A. To take it into the land office and have it filed, or something to that effect; I don't remember what words he used.

Q. To take what in the land office?

A. The paper I had.

(Testimony of Charles Carey.)

Q. And what were you to do with the money he gave you?    A. Pay it into the land office.

Q. Did you see Dwyer write out these papers and fill them out?    A. Yes, sir.

Q. Who else was in the office if anyone at the time?

A. I think Melvern Scott was in there some of the time; I don't know whether he was there all of the time.

Q. How much money did Mr. Dwyer give you at the time, if you recollect?

A. I don't remember just how much it was.

Q. What did you do with the money?

A. I paid it into the land office.

Q. Did you have any left of that which Dwyer had given you after you paid it into the land office?

A. I don't remember whether I did or not.

Q. You paid the fee, whatever it was?

A. Yes, sir.

Q. Where did you sign these papers, your filing papers?

A. I think it was in the land office; I don't know.

Q. Did you know Mr. J. B. West at that time?

A. No, sir.

Q. You didn't know him? Do you recollect whether or not you were sworn to these papers, Mr. Carey, after taking them in the land office?

A. I would hate to say positively one way or the other.

Q. What is your recollection now, Mr. Carey, in regard to it?

(Testimony of Charles Carey.)

A.   My recollection is that I was not sworn to it.

Q.   I will ask you to look at these papers which are now shown you and which are denominated "Sworn statement" and are in duplicate, and state whether or not those papers bear your signature?

A.   Yes, sir; that is my signature.

Q.   Refreshing your recollection, do you recognize these papers as having seen them before?

A.   Yes, sir; I must have seen them because that is my signature on them all right.

Q.   Do you remember whether or not you read over these papers?

A.   No, I didn't read them over; Mr. Dwyer read them over to me.

Q.   Where?

A.   In his office, when he made them out.

Q.   And before you went into the land office?

A.   Yes, sir.

Be it remembered that then and there the following proceeding was had:

Mr. RUICK.—We now offer in evidence these papers, or this paper in duplicate, the sworn statement of this witness, and we ask that it be marked Plaintiff's Exhibit 6.

Mr. FORNEY.—The defendants object to the introduction of this testimony on the ground it is irrelevant, immaterial and incompetent; it is not properly authenticated, and no proper foundation has been made for the same; on the further ground that there is no evidence tending to show any conspiracy, no evidence has been introduced tending to show any

(Testimony of Charles Carey.)

conspiracy, and on the further ground that the evidence is objectionable for the reason that it postdates the consummation of the conspiracy as alleged in the indictment, on the further ground that this testimony does not connect or tend to connect the defendants Kester and Kettenbach with any conspiracy or agreement.

Which objection was by the Court overruled, and to which ruling of the Court the defendants then and there excepted, which exception was allowed by the Court, and the said documents were received in evidence, and marked Plaintiff Exhibit 6, J. E. B., 5/21/07, and were and are in words and figures as follows:

(Omitted, the same being identical with Plaintiff's Exhibit 1, J. E. B., May 21, 1907, except as to the name of the entryman, age and occupation, description of the land, and date).

Q. Read over one of these papers, Mr. Carey (handing witness Plaintiff's Exhibit 6. After reading paper).

Q. Mr. Carey calling your attention particularly to that part of this sworn statement which reads: "That I do not apply to purchase the land above described on speculation but in good faith to appropriate it to my own exclusive use and benefit," did you notice that paragraph when Mr. Dwyer read it over to you?

A. I did; but I had a different understanding; I understand that I was talking it for my own benefit.

(Testimony of Charles Carey.)

Q. Where had you gotten that understanding?

A. Well there had been talk that way, and if I was receiving a certain sum for it, why it would be for my benefit.

Q. With whom had you talked relative to what you would have to swear to in the land office before you went there to file?     A. The first papers?

Q. Just before you went to file your second statement?

A. There wasn't any talk with anybody before I made my first papers, what I would swear to.

Q. You went to the land office and filed these with any understanding of your own?

A. This first paper was the paper, the first paper written out by Mr. Dwyer and the questions were answered by him.

Q. What?

A. The same questions were answered by him; he simply read the questions over and wrote it out here, and would answer and tell his reasons for answering; he would read this question here about taking it up for your own benefit, and say, "Certainly for your own benefit; you are going to get so much money."

The COURT.—Who said that?

A. Mr. Dwyer.

Q. Are you now refferring to the paper you now hold in your hand?

A. The first paper, if it is the first paper.

Q. Yes, sir; that is it; that is what I want to get at.

(Testimony of Charles Carey.)

Mr. TANNAHILL.—Read some of those questions and answers on that paper?

Mr. RUICK.—I am not referring to the final proof.

A. Yes, I understand.

Q. But the paper you hold in your hand.

A. Yes, sir; this is the first paper; he made this out for me.

Q. That was the first paper which was made out?

A. Yes, sir.

Q. The one filled out in this handwriting, you say he read it over to you. What we want to know is—

The COURT.—Let the witness state just exactly what occurred there.

The WITNESS.—Why, we went in there in just a friendly way; I thought I *ws* selling my right—going in to sell my right, and he fixed these papers; I didn't know whether I had a right to or didn't have a right; I was ignorant in the business and he wrote out these things, and read them over as he wrote them, and put down the answer to it at the same time like this, where it says, Have you got any agreement with anybody—why, no, I haven't any agreement. It carried the idea—the idea was it had to be a written agreement, and I didn't have any written agreement with anybody.

Q. Go with the next proposition.

A. He said it was taken up for my own benefit. I thought it was too; if I got any money out of it, I got some benefit.

(Testimony of Charles Carey.)

Q. He said it was taken over for your own benefit.

A. He read it over and the agreement was passed up to me and it looked very reasonable to me that it was right.

Q. You say an agreement was passed up to you; by whom was it passed up to you?

A. Mr. Dwyer read these things over to me.

Q. What did he say; that is what we want?

A. He would say: You have not sold it to anybody; you have not made no written agreement with nobody; you are going to get the money; it will be for your own benefit.

QQ. Did you have that talk with him before you went into the land office to file that paper?

A. No, sir—before I filed it—yes, sir.

Q. That is what I meant.

A. Yes, sir; this was in the office where he was making them out at the time.

Q. I understand you as he would fill out these blanks here, he would talk this matter over as he went along?    A. Yes, sir.

Q. As he read it over to you?

A. Yes, sir, as he came to others—the only question I think in there is that he asked my age.

Q. And you remember giving him your age?

A. Yes, sir.

The COURT.—What exhibit is he reading from, Mr. Ruick?

Mr. RUICK.—Plaintiff's Exhibit 6.

(Testimony of Charles Carey.)

Q. Now, Mr. Carey, we want you to be careful and take your time, so that your testimony may be correct. I want to call your attention now to the matter of your final proof, made late, and I show you your final proof to see if there is a possibility that you might have confounded this sworn statement that you first filed with the testimony which you afterward gave; now, here is a paper which I will later identify as your final proof paper, bearing your signature and it is the Testimony of Claimant. Now, do you still remember that Mr. Dwyer talked to you as he was filling out this sworn statement of yours?   A. Yes, sir.

Q. So you are not confounding the two at all?
A. No, I am not at all.

Q. You are perfectly clear on that score?
A. Yes, sir.

Q. And later you did have a talk with him, did you, with regard to the testimony of claimant, this paper here?   A. Yes, sir.

Be it remembered that then and there following proceedings were had:

Q. Now, state, Mr. Carey, everything t*u*t Melvern Scott may have said to you leading up to your introduction to Mr. Dwyer?

Mr. FORNEY.—We object to that, on the ground that any statements made to Melvern G. Scott would not be binding on these defendants, he not being connected with the case. In this count in the indict-ment where it charges that these defendants agreed

(Testimony of Charles Carey.)

to defraud the Government by inducing this witness
to file his sworn statement—in the first part of the
indictment here, reference is made to other persons,
but after that, you will see an absence of the other
persons in this count—when he comes to the latter
part of that count.

The COURT.—What page of the indictment?

Mr. FORNEY.—This indictment I have is not
numbered as to the page. It is about the middle of
the count. After the first one or two allegations in
this count, he omits the name of other persons and
simply accuses Dwyer, Kester and Kettenbach of
doing these things; so I say it is not properly charged
in regard to other persons; there is no allegation
here that other persons were connected to the overt
acts in this indictment in this count.

(Jury excused.)

The COURT.—Mr. Ruick, I would like to call
your attention to the condition of this indictment,
of the indictment upon that matter as a general
proposition. The Court would not care for very
much argument, but as to whether or not the allegations of this indictment do not preclude your use
of this kind of testimony.

(Adjournment until 9:30 A. M., May 22d, 1907.)

May 22d, 1907.

CHARLES CAREY on the stand.

The COURT.—We will admit the testimony upon
the statement of the Government that he will show
that this man Scott was a representative of the de-

(Testimony of Charles Carey.)

fend*at* Dwyer; the testimony to be considered as against the defendant Dwyer only, unless it is further made to appear that the acts of this man Scott were authorized by the other defendants.

To which ruling of the Court the defendants excepted, which exception was by the Court allowed, and the witness answered:

A. Well, I told Mr. Scotty that I wanted to take up some land, and if he ever saw any t*ht* I could take, to let me know—

Q. First, when did you tell him this?

A. Well, suppose on several oc*s*ions; we were quite well acquainted.

Mr. FORNEY.—This is going in under our objection?

Mr. RUICK.—It is so understood.

Q. Where had you been, or where did you come from shortly before you told him this, made this statement?

A. I *hd* been up in the Pierce country, Pierce timber country, there fishing.

Q. And you had returned to Lewiston?

A. Yes, sir.

Q. Now, what was the conversation you had with Scotty after you returned from Lewiston that you refer to?

A. He came down to my place of business the same day I came there from the woods, and wanted to know if I wanted to take up some land, and I asked him about it, and he told me that there would be so much in it for me, and my expenses would be paid, and so on and so forth, and I told him I thought I would do that, and we walked up to Mr. Dwyer.

Q.  How much did Mr. Scott tell you there was in it for you?        A.  $150.00.

Q.  What did he say about the payment of your expenses?

A.  He said my expenses would be paid; he said would get $150 for my right.

Q.  Where were you to get the money with which to pay the Government for the land?

A.  I don't know as he gave me any name; I was to be furnished with the money.

Q.  It was after this conversation, then, that you went to Dwyer?        A.  Yes, sir.

Q.  Now, what else, if anything, did Scott tell you?  Just repeat the full conversation that occurred when he came to you, and asked you if you wanted to take a timber claim?

A.  He asked me if I wanted to take a timber claim, and said there would be $150 in it for me for my right, and he wanted to know if I knew anybody else; he said there was another claim or two that he wanted to get somebody for; then we walked up together, right at that time, and we didn't part, but we went up and met Mr. Dwyer.

Q.  Immediately following the conversation and before you separated you went up and saw Mr. Dwyer?        A.  Yes, sir.

Q.  Mr. Carey, did you have any further conversation with Mr. Dwyer in relation to this subject on

(Testimony of Charles Carey.)

the day on which you filed your application—your sworn statement?

A. Nothing different from what I stated last night, I don't think.

Q. Who furnished the names of the witnesses—or did you furnish the names of the witnesses to the land office?

A. No, Mr. Dwyer put them down.

Q. That is the witnesses who would be witnesses for you on your final proof? A. Yes, sir.

Q. I will ask you right here who were the witnesses for you when you made final proof?

A. Melvern Scott and Mr. Dwyer.

Q. And you recall, do you, what other witnesses were named?

A. Mr. Bliss and Mr Kester, I think.

Q. What Mr. Kester?

A. I don't know; I am pretty sure it was Mr. Kester; I don't know the gentleman.

Q. Mr. Albert Kester?

A. Well, I wouldn't say as to that now; I know it was Kester and Mr. Bliss.

Q. It was not Mr. George Kester, the defendant here? A. I don't know.

Mr. RUICK.—We will admit to save proof, that it was Mr. Albert Kester, and not Mr. George H. Kester.

Q. You recall the circumstances of your making final proof in the land office, do you, Mr. Carey? Do you remember the circumstances, the occasion?

A. I remember going there, yes, sir.

(Testimony of Charles Carey.)

Q. Did you see Mr. Dwyer there, and have any conversation with him prior to the day you made final proof?          A. Yes, sir.

Q. In relation to your final proof?

A. Yes, sir.

Q. Where did those—where did you see him concerning it?

A. Why, it was around there on the street somewhere that I met him, and he asked me, when is the day you prove up, Charlie, and I told him, and then he says, I will get you a blank, so you can read it over and see the questions you have got to answer.

Q. How long was this before the date you actually made final proof?

A. It was four or five days, or something like that.

Q. Was anything more said at that time which you now recall?

A. I think he said he would get it for me next day; that he didn't have one with him that day.

Q. Did you see him the next day?

A. I think it was th next day that he gave me the paper. It was very soon, anyhow.

Q. Where did you see him?

A. I think it was in Wiggins' cigar store he gave me the paper. It is on the north side of the street there in Lewiston.

Q. Wht occurred there between you and Mr. Dwyer at that time?

(Testimony of Charles Carey.)

A. Well, we walked in there, and he handed me this paper and told me not to show it to anybody, but to take it home and read it over, so that I could answer the questions, and he said that if I didn't understand any of them, that either he or Mr. Scotty would try and tell me—enlighten me on them.

Q. Whereabouts in the Wiggins cigar store did he give you this paper?

A. In the stairway that leads downstairs in the cigar store.

Q. Describe to the jury in a general way the arrangement of this cigar store, and where he gave you this paper.

A. Well, the store faces the south, and there is a stairway on the west side of the storeroom leading upstairs, and right around that under this stairway there is the stairway leading dowstairs, and I walked in there with him; he walked right around into the door leading downstairs and he handed me this paper.

Q. What did he say to you at the time he handed the paper to you?

A. Nothing more than not to show it to people, and told me to return it to him when I read it over.

Q. When next did you see—I will now ask you to identify this paper—Now what did you say to him, and what was said by him about Scotty at this time?

A. He said—Mr. Scotty here would show me the questions, and assist me with the answers here, if there was any here that I didn't understand, and I

(Testimony of Charles Carey.)

said I don't think there is any questions but what I would be able to answer them.

Q.   Well, did you go to Mr. Scotty?

A.   I asked him about some of them.

Q.   Now, I show you a paper purporting to be your testimony, testimony of claimant, in your application here to enter certain timber and stone lands at the United States Land Office at Lewiston; this being the paper you already identified in your testimony yesterday, and I will ask you first this question, would you be able to identify a blank similar to the one that Dwyer furnished you with at that time?    A.   Yes, sir.

Q.   I now ask you to look at this testimony of claimant, which you have identified and ask you whether or not this is the blank, whether or not this is the paper?

A.   It is just like the one—

Q.   This is just like the one that he had?

A.   Yes, sir.

Q.   Did he have the questions answered on it?

A.   No, it was a blank form.

Q.   I will ask you if that is your signature to that paper?    A.   Yes, sir.

Q.   And were you sworn to this paper?

A.   Yes, sir.

Q.   By whom?

A.   By some Colonel something—what do you call him there in the land office.

Q.   Do you mean Mr. West—do you know Mr. West?    A.   Yes, sir.

(Testimony of Charles Carey.)

Q. Were you sworn to it by Mr. West?

A. I ain't sure whether it was Mr. West or this man that filled out the papers in the land office. I was sworn to it in the land office.

Mr. RUICK.—If the Court please, I will withdraw this witness.

The COURT.—Temp*r*arily?

Mr. RUICK.—Yes, your Honor, temporarily.

(Excused.)

Mr. F. M. GOODWIN, a witness called and sworn on behalf of the Government, testified as follows, on

### Direct Examination by Mr. RUICK.

Q. Where *d* you reside, Mr. Goodwin?

A. Spokane, Washington.

(Continuing.) I am chief of one of the field divisions of the General Land Office—Department of the Interior, and as such have charge of the land offices of my division. I am acquainted with J. B. West, former Register of the Lewiston Land Office. I have had occasion to visit that office frequently in line with my official duty. I have been acquainted with Mr. West about two years and a half, I think. I have conducted some investigations with the so-called North Idaho Land Frauds in the Lewiston Land Office.

Q. Are you familiar with the signature of Mr. J. B. West, the Register of the Lewiston Land Office, so as to be able to identify it? A. I think so.

Q. Do you know whether you can or not?

(Testimony of F. M. Goodwin.)

A.   I would know his signature almost any place
I am positive.

Q.   (Handing witness Plaintiff's Exhibit 1, J. E.
B., sworn statement of Guy L. Wilson in duplicate.)

Q.   State whether or not that is the signature of
J. B. West? Register of the Lewiston Idaho Land
Office?       A.   Yes, sir; they are both.

Q.   (Plaintiff's Exhibit 1-A, shown witness.)
State whether or not that is the signature of Mr. J.
B. West, Register of the Lewiston Idaho Land office?

A.   Yes, sir.

Q.   Now, I show you Plaintiff's Exhibit 1-B for
Identification, and ask you to state whether or not
that is the signature of Mr. J. B. West, the Register
of the Lewiston Idaho Land Office?

A.   Yes, sir.

Be it remembered that then and there the following
proceeding was had:

Mr. RUICK.—We now offer in evidence this
paper marked Plaintiff's Exhibit 1-B for Identification, being the notice for publication for Guy L. Wilson.

Mr. FORNEY.—We object to it as irrelevant and
immaterial, as we understand that it is nothing more
or less than a notice for publication made out by the
register or receiver of the land office, and sent out by
him for publication to give notice to the world of this
application; neither of the defendants nor the claimant had anything to do with it.   It was simply an act
of the officers of the land office.

(Testimony of F. M. Goodwin.)

The COURT.—Objection overruled.

To which ruling of the Court the defend*n*t then and there excepted, which exception was allowed by the Court.

The document was admitted and marked Exhibit 1-B in evidence.

Q. (Witness is shown Plaintiff's Exhibit 2 J. H. P.) Examine this paper and state whether or not that is the signature of Mr. J. B. West, whether or not those are the signatures of Mr. J. B. West, Register of the U. S. Land Office at Lewiston, Idaho?

A. They are.

Q. Now, I will ask one general question—on the date appearing on those papers, Mr. Goodwin, was Mr. West the Acting Register of the United States Land Office at Lewiston, Idaho? A. He was.

Q. Now, I will show you a paper that purports to be the testimon.\ of the witness William Dwyer, called as a witness in support of the application of Guy L. Wilson, to purchase certain of the lands, described in the indictment in this case, and ask you to state whether or not this paper bears the signature of J. B. West, former Register of the United States Land Office at Lewiston, Idaho?

A. It bears his signature to the jurat.

Be it remembered that then and there the following proceeding was had:

Mr. RUICK.—The Government offers in evidence this paper and asks t*ht* it be—with a suggestion to the Court that it be limited according to the order made by your Honor this morning to the defendant

(Testimony of F. M. Goodwin.)

William Dwyer, unless we later connect it with the other defendants—it is the testimony of the witness William Dwyer in support of the application of Guy L. Wilson to purchase certain timber lands, being a portion of the land described in the indictment in this case.

Mr. FORNEY.—The defendants object to the introduction of this testimony on the ground that it is irrelevant and immaterial and incompetent, and on the further ground that there is no evidence showing or tending to show any conspiracy or combination upon the part of or between the defendats, or either of them, upon the further ground that it post-dates the consummation of the conspiracy as alleged in the indictment, on the further ground that it does not connect or tend to connect any of the defendants with the alleged offenses set forth in the indictment, or any of them.

The COURT.—The objection will be overruled.

To which ruling of the Court the defendats then and there excepted, which exception was by the Court allowed and said paper was admitted in evidence, and marked Plaintiff's Exhibit 3-A, and is as follows:

(Omitted; appears elsewhere.)

Q. (Showing witness paper purporting to be the Register's final certificate, subscribed by J. B. West, Register, issued to Guy L. Wilson from the United Sttes Land Office at Lewiston, Idaho, July 13th, 1904.)

(Testimony of F. M. Goodwin.)

Q.  State whether or not that is the signature of Mr. J. B. West, Register of the United States Land Office at Lewiston?    A.  Yes, sir.

Be it remembered that then and there the following proceeding was had:

Mr. RUICK.—We offer this in evidence.

Mr. FORNEY.—The defendants object to the introduction of the testimony offered on the ground that it is irrelevant and immater*il*, and incompetent, and on the further ground that there is no evidence showing, or tending to show, any *c*nspiracy or combi*nt*ion upon the part of or between the defendants or either of them, as alleged in the indictment; upon the further ground that it post-dates the consummation of the conspira*t*y, as alleged in the i*dn*ictment; on the further ground that it does not connect or tend to connect any of the defendants with the alleged offenses set forth in the indictment or any of them.

The COURT.—It may be received.

To which ruling of the Court the defendants then and there excepted, which exception was by the Court allowed, and s*ad* paper was admitted and marked Plaintiff's Exhibit 4, and is as follows:

(Omitted—copy appears elsewhere.)

Q.  And the prosecution of your duties as chief of this division of the land office including the general land office—including the Lewiston, did you become familiar with the signature of Mr. Charles M. Garby, Receiver of the Land Office at Lewiston?

A.  Yes, sir.

Q.  So as to be able to identify it?

(Testimony of F. M. Goodwin.)

A. Yes, sir.

Q. I now show you what purports to be a re-ceiver's receipt, number*d* 4770, issued out of the United States Land Office *a* Lewiston, Idaho, to Guy L. Wilson, and ask you to state whether or not that is the signature of Mr. Charles M. Garby, former Receiver of the United States Land Office at Lewis-ton?	A. Yes, sir.

Be it remembered that then and there the follow-ing proceeding was had:

Mr. RUICK.—We now offer in evidence this paper last identified by the witness and ask that it be marked Plaintiff's Exhibit 5.

Mr. FORNEY.—The defendants object to the in-troduction of this testimony on the ground that it is irrelevant and immaterial and incompetent, and on the further ground that there is no evidence show-ing or tending to show any conspiracy or combina-tion upon the part of or between the defendants or either of them; upon the further ground that it post-dates the consummation of the conspiracy as alleged in the indictment; on the further ground that it does not connect or tend to connect any of the defend-ants with the alleged offenses set forth in the indict-ment, or any of them; on the further ground that it does not prove or tend to prove any of the offenses charged in the indictment.

The COURT.—The objection is overruled; it will be received in evidence.

To which ruling of the Court the defendants then and there excepted, which exception was by the Court

(Testimony of F. M. Goodwin.)

allowed, and the paper admitted in evidence and marked Plaintiff's Exhibit 5, and is as follows:

(Omitted; cop.v appears elsewhere..)

Mr. RUICK (Continuing.)—Q. (Witness is shown Plaintiff's Exhibit No. 6 in duplicate.) State whether or not that paper in duplicate there bears the signature of J. B. West, former Register of the Land Office at Lewiston, Idaho? A. They do.

Q. Was he a Register of the United States Land Office at the date mentioned in this place?

A. Yes, sir.

Q. Is that the signature of Mr. J. B. West, former Register of the United States Land Office, Lewiston, idaho? (Showing witness nonminer*l* affidavit of Charles Carey, made at the Lewiston United States Land Office *t* Lewiston, Idaho, August 23d, 1904.) A. Yes, sir.

Q. State whether or not those are the signatures of Mr. J. B. West, formerly Register of the United States Land Office at Lewiston, Idaho, on th*t* paper (showing witness what purports to be testimony of claimant, Charles Carey, on his application to purchase land from the United States, being a part of the lands described in the indictment.)

A. They are.

Be it remembered that then and there the following proceeding was had:

Mr. RUICK.—We now offer the paper in evidence. (The last *p*per identified.)

Mr. FORNEY.—The defendants object to the introduction of this testimony on the ground that it

(Testimony of F. M. Goodwin.)

is irrelevant, immaterial and incompetent on the furthee ground that it does not prove or tend to prove any of the allegations in the indictment; on the further ground tht there is no evidence showing or tending to show any conspiracy or combination upon the part of or between the defendants or either of them upon the further ground that it post-dates the consummation of the conspiracy as alleged in the indictment, on the further ground that it does not connect or tend to connect any of the defendants with the alleged offenses set forth in the indictment, or any of them.

The COURT:—The same ruling; it may be admitted.

To which ruling of the Court the defendants excepted, which exception was allowed by the Court, and the document received in evidence, and marked Plintiff's Exhibit 7, and is as follows:

(Omitted; copy appears elsewhere.)

Mr. RUICK (Continuing.)—Q: I show you a paper purporting to be testimony of witness William Dwyer, called in support of the application of Charles Carey, to enter certain lands at Lewiston, Idaho, Land Office under the Stone and Timber Act, is that the signature of Mr. J. B. West, the former Register of the United States Land Office at Lewiston, Idaho? A. It is.

Q. Was he acting Register on the date which the certificate bears? A. He was.

Be it remembered that then and there the following proceeding was had:

(Testimony of F. M. Goodwin.)

Mr. RUICK.—We offer this in evidence and ask that it may be marked Plaintiff's Exhibit 8; we also ask for the admission of this under the statement heretofore made as applying only to the defendant Dwyer, unless later connected with the other defendants.

Mr. FORNEY.—The defendnt Dwyer objects to its introduction on the grounds we make in the general objection and the defendnts object to the introduction of this testimony on the ground that it is incompetent, irrelevant and immaterial; on the further ground that it does not prove or tend to prove any of the allegations in the indictment; on the further ground that there is no evidence showing or tending to show any conspiracy or combination upon the part of or between the defendants, or either of them; on the further ground that it post-dates the consummation of the conspiracy as alleged in the indictment; on the further ground that it does not connect or tend to connect any of the defendants with the alleged offenses set forth in the indictment, or any of them.

The COURT.—Objection overruled.

To which ruling of the Court the defendants excepted, which exception was by the Court allowed, and the said document admitted in evidence, marked Plaintiff's Exhibit 8, and is as follows:

(Omitted; copy appears elsewhere.)

Mr. RUICK (Continuing).—Q. I show you a paper purporting to be notice for publication on the application of Charles Carey, made at the United

(Testimony of F. M. Goodwin.)

States Land Office, Lewiston, Idaho, August 23d, 1904, to enter certain land under the Stone and Timber Act; State whether or not the signatures appearing on the paper are the signatures of J. B. West, former Register of the United Sttes Land Office at Lewiston, Idaho.

A.   They are.

Q.   And state if he was acting Register of the Land Office at Lewiston, Idaho, at the date mentioned in this paper?      A.   He was.

Be it remembered that then and there the following proceeding was had:

Mr. RUICK.—We offer this in evidence under the same limitation heretofore stated.

Mr. FORNEY.—The defendant Dwyer individually and the defendats generally object to the introduction of this testimony on the ground that it is irrelevant, immaterial and incompetent, on the further ground that it does not prove or tend to prove any of the allegations in the indictment; on the further ground that there is no evidence showing or tending to show any conspiracy or combintion upon the part of or between the defendants, or any of them; upon the further ground that it post-dates the consummation of the conspiracy as alleged in the indictment; on the further ground that it does not connect or tend to connect any of the defendants with the alleged offenses set forth in the indictment or any of them; on the further ground that it is matter pertaining solely and exclusively to the duties of the Register in

(Testimony of F. M. Goodwin.)

giving notice of the application of the entryman, Charles Carey.

The COURT.—The objection is overruled; it may be admitted.

To which ruling of the Court the defend*n*ts except, which exception was*b* allowed by the Court, and the document was received in evidence and marked Plaintiff's Exhibit 9.

Cross-examination by Mr. TANNAHILL.

Q. You stated in response to a question from the prosecutor that you had been engaged in investigating alleged fraudulent entries in the Lewiston Land Office. Did I understand you right?

A. Yes, sir.

Q. How long have you been engaged in that business?

A. You mean in the Lewiston District?

Q. Yes.

A. I think my first investigation in the Lewiston District was in May, 1905.

Q. How long have you been engaged in the investigation of entries with which these defendants are connected?    A. Since that time.

Q. Have you been continuously engaged in that investigation?    A. No. Occasionally.

Q. How much of the two and a half years have you confined your attention to these defendants?

A. It would be impossible for me to state; I spent about three months that summer at the work, and then occasional periods off and on. It might come up to-day, and might come up to-morrow; a trip now

(Testimony of F. M. Goodwin.)

and again; I could not give you any approximate idea of the time.

Q. You have no idea how much time you have spent in that investigation?

A. I have not the slightest.

Q. How many assistants have you had assisting you in that investigation as far as it relates to these particular defendants?

A. I could not tell you without consulting my records. Sometimes I had had one, sometimes two and sometimes as many as half a dozen different parties working with me on these cases.

Q. About how many?

A. I could not tell you exactly.

Q. How many statements have you taken from entrymen in your efforts to connect these defendants with these particular entries?

A. I could not tell you.

Q. You don't know?     A. I don't.

Q. Have you the statement of Guy L. Wilson in your possession?     A. I have not.

Q. Who has it?     A. I could not tell you.

Q. You don't know anything about that?

A. I do not.

Q. You wrote that statement did you?

A. I did.

(Witness excused.)

CHARLES CAREY, recalled.
(By Mr. RUICK.)

Q. I will show you a paper purporting to be the cross-examination of claimant in connection with

(Testimony of Charles Carey.)

your direct examination in the United States Land Office in support of your application to purchase lands under the Stone and Timber Act, and will ask you if that paper bears your signature?

A. Yes, sir.

Q. As a part of your final proof?

A. Yes, sir.

Q. You identify the paper, do you?

A. Yes, sir.

Q. Were the answers taken to that in the United States Land Office at Lewiston?

Be it remembered that then and there the following proceedings were had:

Mr. RUICK.—In order to complete the record in the Carey case, we offer this paper and ask that it may be marked Plaintiff's Exhibit 7-A.

Mr. FORNEY.—The defendants object to the introduction of this testimony on the ground that it is irrelevant, immaterial and incompetent; on the further ground that it does not prove or tend to prove any of the allegations in the indictment; on the further ground that ther is no evidence showing or tending to show any conspiracy or combination upon the part of or between the defendants, or any of them, upon the further ground that it post-dates the consummation of the conspiracy as alleged in the indictment, on the further ground that it does not connect or tend to connect any of the defendants with the alleged offenses set forth in the indictment, or any of them.

The COURT.—The objection is overruled.

(Testimony of Charles Carey.)

To which ruling of the Court the defendants excepted, which exception was by the Court allowed, and said document was admitted in evidence, and marked Plantiff's Exhibit 7-A, and is as follows:

(Omitted; copy appears elsewhere.)

Q. Now Mr. Carey, coming back to the point ehre you said that you had received a blank identical with the blank shown you purporting to be the testimony of claimant and containing the same questions, but without answers, you say that you received such a paper from Mr. Dwyer on the occasion you have mentioned?     A. Yes, sir.

Q. And what did you do with the paper?

A. I took it home with me and read it over.

Q. When next did you see Dwyer?

A. Well, it was the next day, or right away after, I don't know just—

Q. Where did you see him?

A. The first time I saw him that I had a chance to talk to him was right in front of my place of business.

Q. Under what circumstances did you see him?

A. I went out and spoke to him about some questions I didn't understand.

Q. Where was he?

A. He was in his buggy, coming over from Clarkston, I guess.

Q. Where is Clarkston relative to Lewiston?

A. Just across the Snake River.

Q. He crossed on the bridge?     A. Yes, sir.

Q. In what direction was he driving?

(Testimony of Charles Carey.)

A.   Driving east on Main Street.

Q.   Into or from Lewiston?

A.   Into Lewiston.

Q.   What was said there? Relate the conversation.

A.   I just mentioned two or thre questions, and he told me how I was to answer them.

Q.   Did you have your blank with you at the time?

A.   I had it, but I didn't have it out so that anybody could see it at all.

Q.   It was in your pocket?

A.   Yes, or it was in the room, I don't know which.

Q.   What matters did you talk over with him at that time?

A.   I asked him about the contract, and he said, Well, you haven't got any contract, and about the contract to sell it and about taking it up for my right, or for my own benefit, and he said, Well, you are getting it for your own benefit.

Q.   Did he explain how you were getting it for your own benefit?      A.   Yes, sir; he did.

Q.   What did he say?

A.   He said, inasmuch as I was receiving a certain sum of mone, for it, I was taking it for my own benefit.

Q.   What did he say with reference to the matter of contract?

A.   He said we haven't got no contract.

Q.   Did he explain to you about the contract?

A.   Yes, sir.

Q.   What did he say about the contract?

(Testimony of Charles Carey.)

A.   He said that we didn't have no contract.

Q.   Did he give you any reason why you didn't have any contract, that is what I want to get at? Answer, yes or no.

A.   He didn't say anything further; I don't remember anything, only we didn't have any contract; we didn't have no written contract.

A.   What I want to get at is what he said about the contract? Did he make any explanation why you didn't have any contract? That is what I want.

A.   I will not be positive at present.

Q.   Well, you had a talk with Mr. Dwyer you say on this occasion?

Q.   When next did you see Mr. Dwyer in relation to this business?

A.   Why, it was the day before I proved up, I believe was the next time.

Q.   Where did you see Mr. Dwyer?

A.   I met him down around the corners, or upstairs, I don't just remember where; around there somewhere.

Q.   How did you happen to meet him on that day, do you remember?

A.   I believe we had an appointment.

Q.   Well, state how it came about and what was said and how you happened to be there at that time; give us your recollection; that is all we want.

A.   He gave me some money, and told me to go and deposit it in the bank.

Q.   I will ask him the question direct: State what took place between you and Dwyer?

(Testimony of Charles Carey.)

A. We met down there and he gave me $400 and told me to go and place it in the bank to my credit, or get a certificate of deposit and bring it back to him. He said that would show I had money in the bank. He asked me if I had a bank account; I told him I had. I went and got a certificate of deposit and brought it back to him.

Q. Where did you deposit the money?

A. In the Idaho Trust Company.

Q. And where did you find Mr. Dwyer when you came bqck?

A. Why, I think he was around on the street there by the cornee some place.

Q. You say this was *fo* four hundred dollars?

A. Four hundred dollars.

Q. Now what did you do with the cetificate of deposit? A. I gave it to Mr. Dwyer.

Q. And did he keep it or return it to you at that time? A. He kept it at that time.

Q. What other transactions or what other business did you transact with him on that day?

A. I signed some papers up over the bank.

Q. Where did you sign them?

A. Up over the Idaho Trust Company's Bank.

Q. Before that time?

A. It was on the same day I got the money.

Q. I don't want you to get transactions mixed; did you sign some papers in connection with the four hundred dollars on the same day you got it?

(Testimony of Charles Carey.)

A. I don't know whether it was in connection with the four hundred dollars or not; I signed a paper.

Q. Where did you sign the paper?

A. That was up over the Idaho Trust Company's Bank.

Q. Did you sign two papers up in the office over the Idaho Trust Copany's Bank?

A. Yes, sir; I signed one the day I got the money and one the day I proved up.

Q. I will ask you where was that paper you signed on the day you got the money drawn up?

A. I don't know. It was up there in the office when I went up there.

Q. How did you happen to go up there?

A. At Mr. Dwyer's suggestion.

Q. Do you know what kind of a paper that was?

A. I don't remember him telling me; he might have. I won't say he did.

Q. Did you read it over?     A. No, sir.

Q. You didn't know the contents of it then?

A. No, sir; I didn't.

Q. What did it look like? Or have the appearance of?     A. Oh, it was a long paper.

Q. Part of it—was it written or printed?

A. It was printed and then filled in or wrote in, filled in with the typewriter, I don't remember which paper, when did you see that paper again?

Q. In order that we may not lose sight of that now.

(Testimony of Charles Carey.)

A. Why, I think at the time I proved up; it was the same paper.

Q. Where did you see it?.

A. It was up there in the same office.

Q. State the circumstances under which you saw it.

A. I went up there and signed some other paper and after I signed it, I started to walk out, and Mr. Dwyer said, "Wait a minute," and he stopped at the desk and picked up a paper and tore my name out of it, and left the paper there.

Q. That was after you had executed some other paper? A. Yes, sir.

Q. And after you had your final proof?

A. Yes, sir.

Q. Do you know whether it was the same paper you executed the day you got your money?

A. No, I don't know; but it had my signature on it.

Q. Had you executed—or did you execute at Mr. Dwyer's request—more than two papers?

A. No, not that I know of.

Q. Now, then, coming down to the day on which you made your final proof, what happened on that day? Start in at the beginnigg and tell us all that happened on that day?

A. I met Mr. Dwyer on the morning of the day I made my final proof. He handed me this certificate of deposit and a roll of money, and told me to go and get Mr. Scotty, who was one of my witnesses, who was working up on the hill. I went and got

(Testimony of Charles Carey.)

him. He never told me what the money was for or how much there was, and while I was away on the hill, I counted the money, and I found $150 in it, and I kind of thought that it was the money I was to get for my right; I didn't know, and when we came down to the land office and went in there, the final papers were made out. I took this certificate and offered it to the —in the land office.

The COURT.—You mean *th* certificate of deposit.

A. Yes, sir; they would not accept it; said they didn't do their banking with that bank, and so I went and got it cashed.

Q. By whose direction, if anyone's, had you tendered the certificate to the land office?

A. Mr. Dwyer.

Q. What had Mr. Dwyer said to you?

A. He said it would show that I had money of my own in a bank account.

Q. To whom, if anyone, did you pay the money?

A. To some one in the land office.

Q. What did you do with the money that you got on the certificate of deposit?

A. I paid it into the land office.

Q. And did you have occasion to pay any other money than the four hundred dollars into the land office at that time?

A. Yes, some fees in there; I don't remember just how much I had $15 extra to pay that with; I don't know what they amounted to.

Q. Where had you got the fifteen dollars?

A. From Mr. Dwyer.

(Testimony of Charles Carey.)

Q. When did Mr. Dwyer give it to you?

A. On the day I proved up.

Q. This one hundred and fifty doolars, where did Mr. Dwyer hand that to you?

A. Well, that was around the hall thère somewhere in that building.

Q. What did you do with it when he handed it to you? How did he hand it to you? Describe that?

A. It was just a roll of bills; he handed it to me and I put it in my pocket.

Q. Was Mr. Dwyer there in the land office and Mr. Scotty while you were giving your evidence on your final proof?

A. Well, they were my witnesses; they might not have been standing right near me, but they were not far away.

Q. Now, did you get a final receipt that day from the land office after you made your final proof?

A. Yes, sir.

Q. What became of the receipt, what did you do with it?     A. I gave it to Mr. Dwyer?

Q. When did you next see that receipt, if at all?

A. I don't think I ever saw it.

Q. Was there anything said at the time you gave it to him at the time by either of you why he wanted it, or why you gave it to him?

A. I don't think there was.

Q. How did you happen to give it to him?

A. I had understood previously that I had to deed it óver to somebody and I thought that was all there was to it.

(Testimony of Charles Carey.)

Q. What I want to get at is whether or not any request was made for this receipt at the time when you got it from the land office, how you came to give it to Dwyer?

A. Why, he asked me for the receipt.

Q. Now, what else? What did you do then with the land or the title to the land? Go on and state what you did with regard to that?

A. I don't know what I did with it; I signed some papers and got a receipt.

Q. Where did you sign those papers?

A. Up over the Idaho Trust Company.

Q. What time relative to the time you made your final proof? A. On the same day.

Q. Now, before getting to that, I will ask you about another transaction. What became of this one hundred and fifty dollars that Mr. Dwyer handed you? Did you find out later the purpose for which Mr. Dwyer had given it to you?

A. Yes, sir; when I came out of the Receiver's office he said to me, Give me the one hundred and fifty dollars, and I will give you a receipt for location fees or locator, or something like that, and he stepped inside the land office and wrote out the receipt in the land office for $150 for location.

Q. Where did he get the paper from?

A. There in the land office.

Q. Did you give him this money?

A. Yes, sir.

Q. The same $150 he handed you earlier in the day? A. Yes, sir.

(Testimony of Charles Carey.)

Q. You say he gave you a receipt?

A. Yes, sir.

Q. Written out by himself?     A. Yes, sir.

Q. In whose writing is that receipt?

A. Mr. Dwyer.

The said paper was offered and reeived in evidence without objection, read to the jury, and is as follows:

"DEPARTMENT OF THE INTERIOR,
UNITED STATES LAND OFFICE.

Lewiston, November 18th, 1904.

Received of Charles Carey One hundred and fifty dollars in full for location fee.

WILLIAM DWYER.

Q. After you had delivered to Mr. Dwyer this receipt you went ovee to Mr. Kettenbach's office, or rather to the office over the Idaho Trust Company and executed some papers?     A. Yes, sir.

Q. Why did you go to the office over the Idaho Trust Company at the time, for what purpose?

A. To sign some paper, I don't know that he told me the nature of the paper; he might have; I would not be positive.

Q. What did you do while there?

A. I went over there and signed some papers.

Q. At whose instance did you go over there?

Q. Who requested you to go ovee, or requested you to go?     A. Mr. Dwyer.

Q. Did you go with him?     A. Yes, sir.

(Testimony of Charles Carey.)

Q.  Were the papers already made out when you got there?     A.  Yes, sir.

Q.  Where were they in the office?

A.  They lay on the desk.

Q.  What did you do while there in the office?

A.  I signed them.

Q.  Did you acknowledge any paper there?

A.  I think I did.

Q.  Was Mr. Dwyer there at the time?

A.  Yes, sir.

Q.  State whether or not this was the time Mr. Dwyer picked up the other paper and tore your signature out of it.     A.  Yes, sir.

Q.  Did he hand you any paper there?

A.  No, sir.

Mr. TANNAHILL.—All of these questions are very leading.

The COURT.—Yes; the witness is not a reluctant witness particularly, Mr. Ruick.

Q.  What happened after you signed this paper up there in the office?

A.  We walked down to the California Wine House together, and Mr. Dwyer bought a glass of wine—he handed the bar-keeper a ten dollar bill, and got five and some silver and put a five dollar bill back in the roll of bills, and took me out two more tens, and handed me the roll, and he walked out.

Mr. TANNAHILL.—The Court understands this is all objectionable.

The COURT.—Yes.

(Testimony of Charles Carey.)

Be it remembered that then and there the following proceeding was had:

Mr. FORNEY.—We ask it be stricken out as irrelevant, immaterial and incompetent and as post-dating the culmination of the conspiracy.

The COURT.—Motion overruled.

To which ruling of the Court the defendants excepted, which exception was by the Court allowed.

Q. Where did he take this money from?

A. Out of his pocket.

Q. In what form was the money?

A. A roll of bills.

Q. And what did he do? Now state that again a little plainer.

A. He bought the drinks and paid for them with a ten dollar bill.

Q. Out of his roll?

A. Yes, sir; and afterwards took out two tens more and added one five back and handed me the roll of bills.

Q. You saw him do that did you?

A. Yes, sir.

Q. How much money was there in the roll of bills he handed you?

A. I took the roll of bills and went to the bank with them. After I got to the bank, I counted them over, and there was $125, and I deposited it there in the bank that day.

Q. And that was the day you got the final proof?

A. Yes, sir.

(Testimony of Charles Carey.)

Q. Now, how much then was there in this roll that Mr. Dwyer had taken out of his pocket at that time?

A. There must have been one hundred and fifty dollars.

Q. Have you ever been called upon to execute any other or further paper in connection with this land?     A. No, I never have done it.

Q. Have you even been called upon to do it?

A. I think he told me at some time he would want me to, but he never did.

Q. You say you didn't read this paper you signed there in that office on that day?     A. No, sir.

Q. And it was not read over to you?

A. No, sir.

Be it remembered that then and there the following proceeding was had:

Q. Well, what was your understanding at that time as to the nature of this paper. What did you understand that you were doing at that time relative to this land?

Mr. TANNAHILL.—Objected to as calling for the conclusion of the witness and not a statement of fact.

Mr. RUICK.—That comes right directly to the proposition, your Honor. It is claimed this man was acting under the direction of Mr. Dwyer.

The COURT.—I think the Court understands your position and does not care to go into it. In regard to the Court's ruling, as a matter of general rule, it is not proper to ask a witness what his understanding is, but in this case, it is charged that the

(Testimony of Charles Carey.)

defendants entered into a conspiracy to defraud the Government, and it becomes necessary or at least proper for the Government to prove that charge, that is, the acts constituting a fraud upon the Government, and it is charged in that connection that certain persons were used as instruments, otherwise as agents, of the defendants in doing certain things, and it appears to the Court that in view of the elements in this charge it is proper under some circumstances to require the witness to state what the intention and understanding was. This witness, to be more specific, if the charge in the indictment is true, was used as an instrument or agent of the defendant in carrying out this purpose. I state this much in order to indicate to counsel for the defendants the theory upon which the Court admits such statements. The Court is aware of the general rule, but in the Court's view the understanding of the witness. after stating the facts as they occurred, is proper evidence in this action. Proceed Mr. Ruick.

To which ruling of the Court the defendants then and there excepted, which exception was allowed by the Court, and the witness answered:

A. I don't know what the nature of the paper was.

Q. That isn't it; what was your purpose and intention, or what was the intention and purpose you had in going there to that office?

A. I went up there to sign some paper.

(Testimony of Charles Carey.)

Q. What was to be the nature of the paper? What were you to do with this land? That is what we want to get at?

A. I had to deed it over to somebody.

Q. That is what we want to get at. Then what did you go there for the purpose of doing relative to this land?

A. I went up there and signed that paper, but I don't know that I was deeding it.

Q. You don't know that you were?    A. No.

Q. What were you to do in order to get this $150 or this $125.00?

The COURT.—It appears to the Court that you have covered the ground, but you may go into it briefly?

A. I was to take up a piece of land and sell my right.

Q. That is what you call it, selling your right?

A. Yes, sir; that is what I understood I was to get, $125.00 for selling my right?

A. Yes, sir; that is what I understood I was to get, $125.00 for selling my right.

Q. How were you going to sell your right? What were you going to do to sell it?

A. Use my right of land, however you do it.

Be it remembered that then and there the following proceeding was had:

Q. How were you going to do it?

Mr. FORNEY.—It is understood we have the same objection to all this?

The COURT.—Yes.

(Testimony of Charles Carey.)

To which ruling of the Court the defendants then and there excepted, which exception was by the Court allowed.

Q. What were you going to do with the land?

A. I suppose sell it, or sell my right anyhow, whatever it means.

Q. I want to know what you were going to do before you could get the $125.00?

A. I had to use my right.

Q. And what disposition, if any, did you have to make of the land before you could get the $125.

A. I understood that I had to deed it to somebody.

Q. Calling your attention, Mr. Carey, to your testimony in Exhibit No. 7, in support of your application to purchase, in other words your final proof, you familiarized yourself with the questions which were to be put to you in the land office?

A. Yes, sir.

Q. Now, Mr. Carey, this question 13, I will read it to you, "Have you sold or transferred your claim to this land since making your sworn statement, or have you directly or indirectly made any agreement or contract in any way or manner with any person whomsoever by which the title you may acquire from the Government of the United States may inure in whole or in part to the benefit of any person except yourself." Did you read that question over before you went to the land office?     A. Yes, sir.

Q. You remember that question being asked you at the land office?

(Testimony of Charles Carey.)

A. Why, I remember reading it over lots of times; I don't know as I particularly remember it in the land office.

Q. Refresh your recollection from this paper which bears your signature. Do you remember it?

A. Yes, sir; it was all read over there, that paper.

Q. You answered that question no, didn't you?

A. Yes, sir.

Q. Was that answer true or untrue at the time you made it? A. It was untrue.

Q. You knew it was untrue, didn't you?

A. Yes, sir.

Q. How did you come to make *that* answer in that way at that time? A. I was told to.

Q. By whom were you told to?

A. Mr. Dwyer told me how I would have to answer those questions.

Q. Well, what, if anything, did Mr. Dwyer say about this relative to the contract?

A. He said we didn't have no contract, to just answer that No; we didn't have no contract.

The COURT.—You have been over that several times with this witness.

Mr. RUICK.—Not specially on those questions.

The COURT.—I have no objection to your asking if the statement there is true. He explained two or three times, saying he told him inasmuch a the agreement was an oral one, it is not a contract. Unless there is something in addition to that, the Court will not permit you to take up further time with it.

(Testimony of Charles Carey.)

Mr. RUICK.—I wanted, if your Honor please, as formerly, to be specific in this matter, so that the defense as well could have the benefit of knowing just what directly we charge him with, the having induced the witness to it, he having testified falsely; I don't regard it as necessary that I should be, perhaps so particular in establishing these facts as I was upon a former trial of the defendant Dwyer, wherein he was charged with subornation of perjury, and where it was necessary I should prove specifically that he had procured the witness to testify falsely as laid in the indict*nemtn,*—in the language of the indictment, and that the witness knew that he was testifying falsely, and Dwyer knew the witness knew that. However the same charge is made—

Mr. TANNAHILL.—We object to that statement, and ask an exception to it for the reason it is not proper for him to so state before the jury in this trial.

Exception allowed.

Mr. RUICK (Continuing.)—The same language is used in this indictment as was used in the former indictment wherein were alleged these facts. I think it is set out specifically, is it not? It says it then and there became a material question, a question material to the issue as I recall the indictment—

The COURT.—I am familiar with the indictment in the other case, and also the record. The Court does not want to dictate to counsel what course he should pursue, but the Court is trying to limit this to some extent, a little too much time has already been taken.

(Testimony of Charles Carey.)

Mr. RUICK.—I am glad your Honor will have it limited. It is not a pleasure to me to go over these matters, and yet I have been compelled to try these cases with extreme care in order that there might not be, in my judgment any oversight or failure to perform my duty.

The COURT.—Proceed, and we will try to reach these questions as they come up.

Q. I now read question 14 from your testimony on final proof: "Do you make this entry in good faith for the appropriation of the land exclusively to your use, and not for the use or benefit of any other person"? You recollect that question?

A. Yes, sir.

Q. And you answered that yes?

A. Yes, sir.

Q. Now, how did you come to answer that?

A. Mr. Dwyer told me that inasmuch as I was going to get money for it, that it was for my benefit.

Q. Was the answer true or false at the time you made it?      A. I got money for it.

Q. But was the answer you made to this true or false at the time you made it? It says "Do you make this entry in good faith for the appropriation of the land exclusively to your own use and not for the use or benefit of any other person"? I am now referring to the land and not to the money. Was the answer you gave true or untrue at the time you made it?

(Testimony of Charles Carey.)

A. It was untrue, at least part of it, because outside of the $100, or so odd dollars, I would have no interest in it.

Q. Now, I will read the other question, question 15: "Has any other person than yourself, or any firm, corporation or association any interest in the entry you are now making or in the land or the timber thereof," to which you answered "No." Was that answer true or untrue at that time?

A. That was false.

Q. Did you know it to be so? A. Yes, sir.

Q. And how did you come to make that answer in that way?

A. Mr. Dwyer said as long as there was no writing there was nobody had any interest in it.

Q. Nobody had any interest in it? Now taking up your cross-examination, Mr. Carey, Plaintiff's Exhibit 7-A, I want your attention particularly to questions 16 and 17. Question 16: "Did you pay out of your individual funds all the expenses in connection with the making of this filing, and do you expect to pay for the land with your own money to which you answered, Yes. In the light of your testimony what explanation have you got for the reason—or what induced you to make these answers?

Q. Was that true?

A. I understood it was my money.

Q. Your money how?

A. It was in my possession.

Q. How did you come to understand that?

(Testimony of Charles Carey.)

A. Mr. Dwyer told me that the money is in your *ps*session and it is your own.

Q. Question 17, next: "Where did you get the money with which to pay for this land, and how long have you had it in your actual *ps*session? You say you "earned it in my business" and "had it in my possession 12 years" is what this means. How did you come to make that statement?

A. Well, Mr. Dwyer told me to say that I had it in my business for the twelve years—I don't think—I had been in business twelve years, not that I had had the money twelve years.

Q. That you had been in business twelve years?

A. Yes, sir.

Q. Not that you had had the money twelve years?

A. No, sir.

Cross-examination by Mr. TANNAHILL.

Q. Mr. Carey, how old are you?

A. Thirty-three years old.

Witness continuing:

I was born in Michigan and first came west in 1900. I was then twenty-six years old. I first lived in Spokane for a while after coming west and then went to Wallace. I stayed in Spokane about three months. I did not work in Spokane at all at that time. I stayed at the cottage hotel while there. My business is jeweler, or was up to that time. I worked for the butcher in Wallace, for about a year and a half, and then I came back to Spokane and stayed there something like a year and a half, and worked in a furniture store. Then I came to Lewis-

(Testimony of Charles Carey.)

ton. There I had a shooting-gallery and made wire jewelry and one thing and another. I burned out in Lewiston the year following the time I went there. I was there two summers and then I went back to Spokane in the fall of 1903. I first thoug*h* of taking up a timber claim in 1904.

Q. Where were you when you first thought of taking up a timber claim?

A. Around Lewiston.

Q. How did you come to think of that?

A. Everybody was taking up land there, it was common talk on the streets.

Q. Do you know of any particular person you talked with about the time you thought of taking up a timber claim?

A. Every day somebody would be along talking about it and I ta*l*ed with several people and they would tell me how they had taken up claims, and I got interested. And I thought I would like to take one up and talked to Scotty about it.

Q. And you talked to Scotty about tr*y*ing to get you a claim? A. Yes, sir; I asked him to.

Q. And he told you he would tr*y* to find you one?

A. Yes, sir; if he saw anything he thought was good.

Q. When he was tr*y*ing to get you a claim, he was acting for you, wasn't he?

A. I told him to look me up a claim.

Q. And he did try to get you a claim?

A. He came to me and wanted to know if I wanted a claim; he said he had one.

(Testimony of Charles Carey.)

Q. He finally succeeded in finding you a claim?

A. Yes, sir.

Q. And you didn't think there was anything wrong about it?    A. No, I did not.

Q. And you intended to pay for the claim with your own money?

A. I thought this money was my own that they gave me.

Q. When you spoke to Scotty and asked *you* to find you a claim, you intended to pay for the claim with your own money or borrow it didn't you?

A. He told me that I could get money out of it; he didn't tell me at that time though.

Q. I am asking you what you did when you told Scotty to find you a claim? How you expected to pay for it?

A. I told him to try to get somebody who would furnish me the money.

Q. You told him to get you a claim, and to try and get someone to furnish you the money so you could borrow the money and make proof?

A. Yes, sir; I understood there was lots of them doing that in the town.

Q. Your understanding was that one could take up a claim, get located on a claim, find someone they could borrow the money from to make the final proof and to pay the Government price and location fee, didn't you?

A. I understood I could take up a claim and use my right on them—they said a law would soon be passed so that we could not use our right and we

(Testimony of Charles Carey.)

had better have a little money out of it than nothing.

Q. Then you thought that in order to take up a claim and pay the Government price for it, and pay your location fee, you could sell your claim and turn it over? You understood that was selling your right, didn't you?     A. Yes, sir.

Q. And that was the arrangement which you made in this case as you understood it?

A. Yes, sir, I was to sell my right.

Q. And you understood that you were selling your right in that way in this particular case?

A. Yes, sir.

Q. And that is your understanding about it now?

' A. Well, I have learned a lot since these cases started.

Q. Now then, Mr. Carey, you had this talk with Scotty about locating you on a timber claim before you burned out, didn't you?

A. Yes, sir; the first time.

Q. Now where were you when you first thought of taking up a timber claim, or first talked with Scotty about finding you a claim?

A. I could not say the first time; we were friendly and I suppose I talked with him dozens of times, as far as that goes.

Q. Did you ever talk with him in any place except Lewiston?

A. Yes, sir; I met him up in the woods.

Q. You met him in the woods?     A. Yes, sir.

Q. And talked to him about it there?

(Testimony of Charles Carey.)

A. I asked him if he knew of anything yet.

Q. What did he tell you?

A. I think he told me he didn't at that time.

Q. And what did you say to him?

A. Well, I didn't talk very long; we had horses and just met him, and I asked him if he had a claim for me, or to watch for one, or something to that effect.

Q. And where were you at that time?

A. We were at what is called Brown's cabin, that is on Deer Creek over there.

Q. And you were rather combining business and pleasure and fishing a little, and looking out for a claim too?

A. No, I didn't look out for any claims while I was up there.

Q. You were what we call commonly keeping your eye peeled for a gold claim?

A. If there had been any pointed out to me, I would probably have taken it up all right.

Q. And you were trying to get a claim located for the purpose of using your right on a timber claim before the Government repealed the law, when you could not use your right on a timber claim?

A. Yes, sir; we had talked it over about using my right.

Q. Whom did you talk it over with?

A. Scotty.

Q. And you talked it over with others?

A. Yes, sir.

(Testimony of Charles Carey.)

Q. A kind of general topic of discussion in thqt section of the country was it?

A. Yes, sir; it seemed that they all took claims. You were not in it if you didn't take a timber claim.

Q. You have stated various places in regard to the proceedings between yourself and Scotty and Mr. Dwyer, and you have given your understanding about it; now you don't wish to be understood as swearing to the jury that that was Mr. Dwyer's and Scotty's understanding do you?

A. I don't know as I understand the question.

Be it remembered that then and there the following proceedings was had:

Q. You don't wish to be understood as swearing that Scotty and Mr. Dwyer had the same understanding that you did about these various steps which you have testified to do you?

Mr. RUICK.—That is objected to on the ground it is incompetent, irrelevant and immaterial; and for the same reason as I stated yesterday; this witness is not a mind reader, and it would be wholly irrelevant what his understanding of Mr. Dwyer and Scotty would be. It would be wholly incompetent as against the defendants, or in their favor.

The COURT.—I think the Court will permit him to answer the question if his attention is directed to what counsel designate as to his understanding.

Mr. RUICK.—It is too general a proposition, I think, your Honor.

The COURT.—You understand, Mr. Ruick, he says whether or not Mr. Dwyer had the same under-

(Testimony of Charles Carey.)

standing he did.   If he doesn't know, he can so state.

Mr. RUICK.—My objection is chiefly it not only includes Scotty and Dwyer, but includes the whole subject.

The COURT.—Objection sustained.

To which ruling of the Court the defendants then and there excepted, which exception was allowed by the Court.

Q.   (Continuing.)   Who did you first talk with regarding the taking up of this timber claim?

A.   Scotty.

Q.   I mean after you took up the claim and this investigation was set on foot, who first talked to you? Which of the Government officers first talked to you?

A.   I think Mr. Johnson and Mr. Goodwin, and some of those.

Q.   Where did they talk to you?

A.   Here in the office.

Q.   In what office?

A.   This office out here.

Q.   I will ask you Mr. Carey if you made a statement for anybody?      A.   Yes, sir.

Q.   Whom did you make that statement for?

A.   For the Government.

Q.   Who was present at the time that statement was made?

A.   I would not be positive as to all parties, but I think Mr. O'Fallon, I am pretty sure he was there; the others I could not say certainly.

Q.   Was Mr. Ruick present at the time?

A.   I don't think so.

(Testimony of Charles Carey.)

Q. Was Mr. Goodwin present at the time?

A. I think he was in the room some of the time, anyhow, he might have been there all of the time.

Q. Who was it interrogated you and asked the questions when that statement was being made up?

A. Well, I was asked questions by different ones, I don't know whether anyone present asked me all the questions or not.

Q. First one and then another asked you questions?

A. I was asked by different ones.

Q. And they asked them pretty fast?

A. Some of them.

Q. A stenographer took them down?

A. Yes, sir.

Q. Was there any corrections made in your statement?    A. I don't know.

Q. Did they tell you unless you answered certain questions a certain way, you would be indicted?

A. No; I went in there and tried to tell them another lie and found it wouldn't work.

Q. Who told you to say you tried to tell them another lie?

A. I didn't say it was a lie; I am saying it myself; I went to tell a story and tried to protect Mr. Dwyer.

Q. Who told you to say you tried to tell a story to protect Mr. Dwyer?

A. I came up here and I was pretty badly scared myself, when I read the second papers over and went before the land office I saw that I done wrong by

(Testimony of Charles Carey.)

going to the land office and swearing to that, and didn't know but what I would be indicted the same as anybody else.

Q. They told you you would be liable to be indicted?

A. They told me the best thing to do was to tell the truth.

Q. Did they change your statement any from what you first told it?

A. I told him the truth as near as I could.

Q. You say you didn't tell them the truth the first time?    A. I started in to try to avoid it.

Q. What did they tell you?

A. They had other statements and proof that I was not telling the truth.

Q. And they let you read over the final proof which you made and this statement in the other paper which you have just identified here?

A. I think they read some of it over afteeward and asked me how I answered them.

Q. And before they showed you the papers?

A. Well, that was after I made the statement; they read over some of them.

Q. And told you you were liable to be indicted?

A. Well, they told me they knew I was not telling the truth.

Q. Who told you that?

A. I don't know which one.

Q. And did they tell you you were liable to be indicted?

A. Yes, if I didn't tell the truth.

(Testimony of Charles Carey.)

Q. And how long was it before you told a different story after you started in to tell them a lie, as you say?

A. Right away; I decided I would tell the truth.

Q. The same day?

A. And take the consequences.

Q. They told you if you told the truth you were not liable to be hurt?

A. No; I don't know as they made me any promises.

Q. You felt that way?

A. I thought that was the best way out of it.

Q. You thought the best way was to let them draw up a statement and you sign it?

A. No; they asked the questions and I answered them.

Q. Who wrote the statement out?

A. Some of those stenographers, or whatever you call them.

Q. And when the statement was written you signed it?     A. Yes, sir.

Q. And you didn't read it over any more?

A. I read it over before I signed it.

Q. You read it over before you signed it? How many times have you read it over?

A. Just that once.

Q. Just that once? Have you seen it since then?

A. No, sir.

Q. To whom did you give that statement?

A. They kept it.

Q. Who kept it?

(Testimony of Charles Carey.)

A.   The people in the office there.

Q.   Whom do you mean by the people in the office?

A.   Well, the Government officers, whoever they may be.

Q.   Did Mr. Ruick keep it?

A.   I don't know whether he ever saw it or not.

Q.   It was left in Mr. Ruick's office, wasn't it?

A.   It was left in the office with them.

Q.   And Mr. Johnson was there?

A.   Part of the time.

Q.   And after you made the statement you were taken before the grand jury and you made another statement there?        A.   Yes, sir.

Q.   And then you went before the grand jury at Boise?        A.   Yes, sir.

Q.   And you didn't see that statement there?

A.   No, sir; I don't know as I did.

Q.   And you have not seen it since?

A.   No, not that I know of.

(Recess until 2 P. M. of this day.)

Mr. RUICK.—If the Court please, just before coming into court at this time, the witness, Mr. Carey, came to me and stated that he was in error in one part of his testimony, and he desired to be given an opportunity to correct it, and I ask that he be given that opportunity now.  It is in regard to the execution of certain documents.

Q.   (By Mr. RUICK.)  Mr. Carey, is there some statement in your testimony that you desire upon reflection to change?        A.   Yes, sir.

(Testimony of Charles Carey.)

Q. State what it is.

A. I stated this forenoon that I made out two papers, that one of them was made out the day I got $400 and the other one was made out the day I proved up. I was wrong in that statement. The first paper was made out the day I proved up, and the latter paper was made out some little time after I proved up; I was thinking of leaving Lewiston and I went— he told me when I made out the first paper I would have to make out another when I got the patent or receipt from the Government, and as I was leaving Lewiston, and I didn't know I would ever return, I went to him and told him that fact, and he said he would have it fixed up and I could sign it.

Q. Did he ever have it fixed up?

A. Yes, sir; he had some papers ready for me; it was some time after that and either that day or next day I signed them and at that time he destroyed the first paper by tearing my name out as I stated this morning; the only difference was in regard to time.

Q. Were the last papers executed the same place?

A. The first place.

Q. And about how long after you had made final proof?

A. I could not say, it was some little time afterwards.

Cross-examination Continued by Mr. TANNAHILL.

Q. Who have you talked with about your evidence since you left the stand this forenoon?

A. I just spoke to Mr. Ruick about this question.

Q. Did anyone else speak to you about it?

(Testimony of Charles Carey.)

A.   No, sir.

Q.   Did Mr. Ruick call your attention to any part of your evidence?    A.   N sir.

Q.   He never asked you any questions about it? A.   No, sir.

Q.   And you now remember that you made  out some kind of paper on the day you proved up?

A.   Yes, sir.

Q.   You don't know what date it was, do you?

A.   No, sir.

Q.   I will ask you, Mr. Carey, if you don't know that that paper was an option to purchase?

A.   It might have been; I don't know what it was.

Q.   Isn't it your best recollection now it was an option given to Dwyer to purchase that land—

A.   I never knew what the paper contained.

Q.   —— at a specified time?  That might  have been the case?

A.   It might have been; yes, sir.

Q.   And don't you know when the option expired you made a deed to him?

A.   I don't know what the second papers were.

Q.   Then you don't wish to  be  understood  as swearing you conveyed your land on the day you made final proof, do you?

A.   Well, I don't know as I did.

Q.   It may have been five or six months after you made final proof before you conveyed your land?

A.   It was not as long as that; it was some time afterward though.

Q.   How long afterwards was it?

(Testimony of Charles Carey.)

A. I should think in the neighborhood of one month; I don't know; it is a long time ago; I am liable to be mistaken.

Q. You made your final proof in November, '904, didn't you, Mr. Carey?

A. Yes, sir; I believe so.

Q. And isn't it a fact you conveyed your land on April 15th, 1905?

A. No, I don't think it was as long ago as that; I don't think so.

Q. I will ask you to look at this paper, Mr. Carey, and state whether or not that is your signature. (Handing witnes paper.)

A. Yes, sir; I believe that is my signature all right.

Q. And is that the deed you made out at that time? At the time you speak of?

A. Well, I signed a paper; the paper was already laying there; I never read it; I would not say it was the deed even. I could not positively swear it was a deed.

Q. Did the paper look like the one you held in your hand?

A. I could not just remember. I know it was some legal paper; it had this kind of writing in here, you know.

Q. Had typewriting in here?

A. I could not say about that; I remember this all printed here.

Q. You say part was printed and part in writing?

A.   Yes, sir; but I don't remember just what it was.

(Testimony of Charles Carey.)

Q.   What part was printed?

A.   I mean such things as this (indicating).

Q.   Then the printed portion of this deed is simi-lar to the printed portion of the  instrument  you signed, the last instrument you signed; is that right?

A.   I don't remember further than that the paper looked something of that nature which I signed.

Q.   And that is your signature?

A.   Yes, sir; that is my signature.

Q.   To the best of your knowledge,  recollection and belief after refreshing your memory from that paper, is that paper the last paper you signed?

A.   I only signed the two and that is my signature.

Q.   Now do you think now that is the last paper you signed?        A.   Yes, sir.

Q.   Now, after refreshing  your  memory,  Mr. Carey, don't you know that the other instrument you signed was an option wherein you agreed to sell this land to Mr. Dwyer in six months?

A.   It might have been; I don't know what it was.

Q.   And isn't it also a fact that you were going away and closed this option by giving this deed about five months after the date of the option?

A.   It don't seem to me right, that part don't.

Q.   It don't seem to you right?

A.   I think it was the fall of 1904 I signed my last paper.

Q.   The fall of 1904; will you look at the date of this deed?        A.   I know the date of the deed.

(Testimony of Charles Carey.)

Q. And also the acknowledgment?

A. The date of the deed seems to be that way.

Q. Now look at the date of the acknowledge-ment.

A. I would like to know what some of these things erased on here mean before I answer.

Q. That is all right; look at the date of the deed, and the date of the acknowledgment. Has any date been erased?

A. The date seems to be the 16th of April, 1905.

Q. Now, Mr. Carey, don't you remember that that was about the time you left Lewiston, the 15h of April, 1905?

A. No, I was trying to think where I was at that time.

Q. Take your time and think, Mr. Carey, and while you are doing that, we will have this instrument marked Defendant's Exhibit A for identification.

A. That might be it was April.

Q. It might be it was April?

A. Yes, because at the time I spoke to him, I went over to Asotin and ran a market up there for Mr. Schaffer, and it was near Lewiston and I suppse it was when I came back from Asotin.

Q. That you made this deed?

A. I know I left there, I left Mr. Shaffer's in the spring, and it might be possibl it was in April.

Q. You think now it was in April.

A. Yes, sir, since I have referred to my diary.

Q. That is your best recollection?

(Testimony of Charles Carey.)

A.   Yes, sir; that is my best recollection.

Q.   You haven't a diary to refresh your memory as to all the facts you testified to?

A.   No, some of the diaries were burned up during the fire.   I had diaries before.

Q.   Was it a fact as you testified to on your direct examination that you closed this mat*tr* up by *rr*ason of the fact that you were going away.

A.   Yes, sir; I was going to leave.

Q.   Where were you going to?

A.   You see I went to— I believe I went up into the hills up into the Pi*ece* City country.

Q.   It is your best recollection now that the paper that you signed on the day you made final proof was either an option or contract?

A.   I don't know what the nature of the paper was and never did.

Q.   Your best recollection of that matter is not that it was a deed, since I have handed you this deed?

A.   I could not truthf*uly* say what the paper was; I signed a paper.   I don't know what any of them was.

Q.   Your best recollection, though, is that the last instrument signed was this deed here, isn't it?

A.   Yes, sir.

Q.   And your best recollection after refreshing your memory from your diary is that it was about the 15th of April? that you executed this deed?

A.   I say I was around Lewiston up until about that time.

(Testimony of Charles Carey.)

Q. I am asking you for your very best recoolection about it, Mr. Carey?    A. Yes, sir.

Q. That is your best recollection?

A. Yes, sir.

Q. Now, Mr. Carey, before noon I was asking you about this statement that you made for Mr. Goodwin and Mr. O'Fallon abd Mr. Johnson and Mr. Ruick and several others. Will you tell us who was present at the time you made that statement.

A. My best recollection is Mr. O'Fallon, Mr. Goodwin, and the stenographer, and I believe Mr. Johnson part of the time. I would not say that Mr. Johnson was there all of the time, though.

Q. Now, did the stenographer take down your statements as you made them?    A. Yes, sir.

Q. And were there any changes made in your statement by the stenographer?

A. Not that I discovered.

Q. Were there any changes requested by any of the gentlemen who were there?    A. No, sir.

Q. There were no corrections made in your statement after it was shown to you as extended by the stenographer?

A. Not that I remember of now.

Q. You signed it as it was written, did you?

A. Yes, sir.

Q. You have never seen it since that time?

A. I think not.

Q. You appeared before the grand jury at Boise, didn't you, Mr. Carey?    A. Last month.

(Testimony of Charles Carey.)

Q. Did you have any conversation with Mr. Ruick or Mr. Johnson there at that time?

A. Not to speak of; I just met them.

Q. Did you have any talk with Mr. Johnson and Mr. Ruick relative to your evidence at that time?

A. No, sir.

Q. None at all?　　A. No, sir.

Q. Mr. Carey, do you remember of being in Pierce City shortly after you came back from Boise?

A. Yes, sir; I went to Pierce City.

Q. Do you remeber seeing Mr. H. J. Steffy there at that time?　　A. Yes, I met him.

Q. Did you make any statement there at the time? in Pierce City in the presence of Mr. Steffy and the lady who runs the hotel regarding what took place at Boise?　　A. Not that I remember of.

Q. You don't remember of making any statement?　　A. No, *isr.*

Q. I will ask you, Mr. *Steffy,* if you didn't say in the presence of Mr. Steffy and a lady, and I think possibly someone else, the lady I think who rant the hotel in Pierce City, in the month of April, 1907, shortly after your return from Boise, yourself and Mr. Steffy and others being present, "I have been to Boise to appear before the grand jury in the Kester-Kettenbach cases. If I said anything in favor of the defendants, they"—if you said anything in favor of the defendants, they will send you home, and if you don't say what they want you to they will swear at you, or words in substance and to that effect?

A. No, I didn't make any such statement as that.

(Testimony of Charles Carey.)

Q. Did you make a statement at that time, or about that time, that if you said anything in favor of the defendants, they will send you home, and if you don't say what they want you to they will swear at you, or words in substance and to that effect?

A. I didn't say anything which I know of which would indicate anything of the kind.

Q. You said nothing of the kind?

A. I might have said I was at Boise, but I don't know what cases I was on even to-day.

Q. Now, again, referring to the matter of Mr. Scott trying to find you a timber claim, isn't it a fact that you at one time talked to Mr. Scott about mortgaging your business there for the purpse of raising the money with which to pay for a timber claim?    A. No.

Q. You never talked to him about that?

A. No, there wouldn't be anybody give me fifteen cents on my business.

Q. You never had any such conversation as that?

A. No, sir.

Q. But you did say to Mr. Scott at one time you would have to borrow the money with which to make your proof?

A. No, I never did, because I knew where the money was coming from.

Q. Didn't you testify in response to my questions this forenoon that you did at one time tell Mr. Scott you would have to borrow the money to make your final proof?

(Testimony of Charles Carey.)

A.   Well, I might have on the first papers, but I don't remember.

Q.   You might have done what?

A.   On the first conversation, long before I was ever located, I might have said something to that effect.

Q.   Now, Mr. Carey, you do not wish to be understood as swearing that Mr. Scott was in the employ of Mr. Dwyer at that time, do you?

A.   I don't know that he was, I am sure.

Q.   You don't know whether he was in his employ or not?

A.   I cannot say; he never told me he was.

Q.   Didn't he tell you he was not in the employ of Mr. Dwyer?

A.   I don't know as he ever told me either way; I knew he worked at several different things around town.   I never knew he was working for any particular person; he worked for me, even.

Q.   He worked at anything he could get to do?

A.   Yes, sir.

Q.   You knew he was not engaged with Dwyer in the location business, didn't you?

A.   I don't know as I knew anything about his business.   I knew he was up in the timber there that day.

The COURT.—Up in the timber with whom?

A.   With Dwyer.

Q.   When was it he was up in the timber with Dwyer?

(Testimony of Charles Carey.)

A.   It was in the summer of 1904.   I saw him up there in Brown's cabin.

Q.   All that Mr. Scott did was to make a few trips up there for Mr. Dwyer and take the horses and carry people up the*r,* wasn't it?

A.   I don't know what he did, sir.

Q.   He worked for him by the day?

A.   Possibly; I don't know anything about that.

Q.   You *You* don't know anything about that?

A.   No, sir; I know I asked him once if he could not get me a job with him.

The COURT.—With whom?

A.   With Mr. Dwyer.

Q.   You asked whom?

A.   I asked Mr. Scott if he could.

Q.   When was that?

A.   I think it was about the same time; it may be the same day.

Q.   What did he tell you?

A.   I don't remember now.   I guess he told me he would see.

Q.   You don't wish to be understood as swearing that Mr. Dwyer's or Mr. Scott's understanding as to what constituted the sale of your right or a right on a timber claim, was the same understanding that you had about it, do you?

A.   I don't know what their understanding was.

Q.   Now, Mr. Carey, have you given us all the conversations that you remember of having with either one of them, Dwyer or Scott, regarding this transaction?

(Testimony of Charles Carey.)

A.   Well, that would be pretty hard for me to answer, particularly with Scotty, because I have talked
a good deal with him; in fact, if there was anybody
in Lewiston I wanted a favor of, I would go naturally to Scotty; we were very intimate friends:

Q.   And Scotty interested himself in trying to get
a timber claim for you because you were a friend of
his?      A.   Yes, sir; I think he did.

Q.   And you didn't consider there was anything
wrong in it?

A.   No, I thought I had a right to sell my right.

Q.   Now, will you give us the conversation again
which you say you had with Mr. Dwyer when he
made out your first papers, your filing papers?

A.   Yes, sir; they were very brief.   Scotty
brought me down and introduced me to him and said:
Mr. Carey wants to take up a claim; he is all right.

Q.   I mean when you went up to make out your
filing papers in the office up on the same floor where
the land office is, where he was and explained it to
you, these questions.

A.   He read over the papers and done the writing there, and talked over the matter as we went
along about what was in there.   He stated: "You
are not making any contract with anybody."   I
didn't have any written contract, and I don't just
remember all the questions in that paper; but whatever they are, anyhow, he read them over and I
signed my name.

Q.   Is that all you want to say about it?   Do you
think of anything else he said?

(Testimony of Charles Carey.)

A. I don't know as he said anything except read the paper over.

Q. Have you stated now all the conversation which you remember which took place between you and Mr. Dwyer at the time your filing papers were made out? That is, the papers which you took into the land office to file, not your final proof papers?

A. He instructed me to take them into the land office and file them, and gave me money to file them, and a relinquishment and all that.

Q. And he told you that you had no contract with him to sell the land except a verbal contract?

A. He said I had no contract, and I knew that as well as he did.

Q. You knew you had no contract with him to purchase the land?    A. No written contract.

Q. Now, Mr. Carey, do I understand you to say that he told you—explained all of this to you about you had no written contract, and you were taking it for your own exclusive use and benefit by reason of your getting the $125 for your right?

A. Yes, sir.

Q. And he made that explanation to you there at the time—at the time you made out and signed your filing papers and took them into the land office?

A. Yes, sir; he read them over just as you state.

Q. What happened when you took them into the land office?

A. There was something wrong with the reliuquishment, and I had to return them and have Mr.

(Testimony of Charles Carey.)

Dwyer fix them over in some particulars, and then I returned them there and they were filed, I suppose. I don't know what was done with them.

Q. How long were you in Mr. Dwyer's office when you took them back for correction?

A. I could not say just how long.

Q. Now, Mr. Carey, you testified in this court in the case of the United States vs. William Dwyer, charged with subornation of perjury, didn't you?

A. Yes, sir.

Q. And do you remember of testifying as to what took place between yourself and Mr. Dwyer when your papers were made out at that time?

A. No, I don't know as I remember the partienlars.

Q. Do you remember when it was that you testified in that case?    A. As to the date?

Q. Yes.

A. No, I don't know as I remember the date now; it was along the last of August, I think.

The COURT.—Counsel asks you whether you remember the date when you testified in the case of the United States vs. Dwyer for subornation of perjury, the case tried in this court?

A. It was in November, I believe sometime, in 1906.

Q. I will ask you, Mr. Carey, if you remember this question being asked you. You may state the conversation which you had at this time, this being the second time that you met *M* Dwyer, as I under-

(Testimony of Charles Carey.)

stand, to which you answered, Well, he handed me those papers to take in and file. Do you remember making that statement?

A. He handed me the papers and I took them in and filed them.

Q. Do you remember making that statement, Mr. Carey?

A. Why, if it is there, I must have made it; I don't know as I remember making it.

Q. Do you also remember testifying as follows: "Q. State what was said." To which you answered, "There was something about the papers not being filled out right, and Mr. West sent me back with them"; do you remember making that statement?

A. I don't remember particularly, though I just stated there was something wrong with the papers; he sent me back with the papers to have them fixed over.

Q. I ask you to state if you remember of so testifying at the trial of that case?

The COURT.—How could it be material whether he remembers that or not? For what purpose do you ask him the question?

Mr. TANNAHILL.—His testimony is different now from what it was then.

The COURT.—Yes, but how could that affect this question? If you desire to impeach him by the testimony he gave before, the Court will permit you to do that, but it will be remarkable if he remembered just what he testified to six or eight months ago.

(Testimony of Charles Carey.)

Mr. TANNAHILL.—I was doing it with the intention of being fair with the witness in asking him the preliminary question. Of course, if he remembers it, all right; if he doesn't, all right.

The COURT.—The Court has no objection to your showing him the testimony, and asking him if it is the testimony he gave, and if it impeaches his present testimony you can offer it in evidence.

Mr. TANNAHILL.—I will show you your evidence given upon that trial of the United States vs. Dwyer, on page 40 of the cros-examination, and page 41, and direct your attention especially to that prtion of your examination enclosed in that pencil mark.

Mr. RUICK.—Read it right into the record. I have no objections to your asking him if he did so testify.

Mr. TANNAHILL.—(Reading):

"Q. State what was said. A. There was something about the papers not being filled out, znd Mr. West sent me back with them; I don't know anything about that.

"Q. What did Mr. Dwyer say to you when he handed you the papers; state fully what was said?

"A. He said, take them in the land office and file them.

"Q. Did he read them over to you?

"A. Why, he read some of the questions.

"Q. There were not any questions, were there?

"A. One asked how old I was."

(Testimony of Charles Carey.)

Q. Do you remember of those questions being asked you at the last trial?

A. I don't remember particularly.

The COURT.—Just ask him if he was asked such questions, and if he made such answers.

Mr. RUICK.—He should have done that with each question and answer as far as *ps*sible.

A. I can't remember all those questions.

Q. Do you remember making such answers to those questions?

A. I don't remember what I did; if it is there, I suppose I answered them.

Q. You have a perfect right to examine it. I will let you look it *ovee* if you desire; I do not want you to doubt its being here.

A. I don't doubt it, but of course I might be mistaken in those particulars.

Q. I will read another question: "Q. Did he state how old you are?"

"A. He said, 'How old are you, Charlie,' and he put that down." Do you remember so answering that question?

A. I remember him asking me *tat,* but I don't remember particularly about last fall.

"Q. He read that to you?" to which you answered, "Yes, sir." Do you remember that?

Mr. RUICK.—Just read further.

Mr. TANNAHILL (Reading):

"Q. What else did he read to you? A. I don't know whether he read all the questions or not; I

(Testimony of Charles Carey.)

sup*pse* he did, though." Have you any recollection of any particular part of the papers coming up for discussion at that time? "A. The first papers?

"Q. Yes.

"A. No, don't know as I recall anything specially."

Do you remember of so testifying?

A. No, I don't remember the testimony; I don't remember there being anything said specially.

Mr. TANNAHILL (Reading): "Q. And then immediately upon his giving you these papers you took it into the land office and Mr. West sent you back? "Yes, sir.

"Q. Do you remember what the correction was?

"A. No, I don't; I do not know."

Q. Now, Mr. Carey, did you so testify at that trial? At the trial of the case of the United States vs. William Dwyer, last fall?

A. I don't know what I testified to at that time.

Q. You don't know what you testified to?

A. No, sir.

Q. Mr. Carey, if you did so testify at the time of that traial, which statements were true, the one you made then, or the one you are making now?

A. I am testifying to the best of my knowledge— in both of them I aimed to tell the truth. I don't know.

Q. Both of them? You realize both of your statements could not be true, don't you?

The COURT.—In what respect?

(Testimony of Charles Carey.)

A.   I didn't think they varied any.

The COURT.—The Court would like to be advised.

Mr. TANNAHILL.—The statement he makes now:

"Q.   Have you any recollection of any particular part of the papers coming up for discussion at that time?   "A.   The first papers?

"Q.   Yes.   A.   No, I don't know as I recall anything special"—and now he says they were discussed, and Mr. Dwyer explained to him how these answers were to be made, and that he was taking it for his own use and benefit because he had sold his right for one hundred and twenty-five dollars, and that he was taking it for himself, and he states in detail that was all gone over by Mr. Dwyer and explained to him at that time and that is the reason that I say that that evidence is in conflict with it.

The COURT.—He made that kind of answer here; he says he don't remember what he testified to, and he don't remember anything special being said at that time.

The WITNESS.—I think further in that statement I made last fall that you will find there is a similar question there.

The COURT.—I think the Court will require you to read the question and answer to him, and ask him whether, if he so testified, it was true.

Mr. TANNAHILL.—I went back a little further than was necessary in order to get the connection, but he has it at this time.

(Testimony of Charles Carey.)

The COURT.—You may start anywhere.

Q. Was this question asked you at that time:

"Q. There were not any questions, were there?

"A. One asked how old I was."

Q. Was that question asked you, and did you so answer at the last trial of Mr. Dwyer?

Mr. RUICK.—Wait until we find where you are reading from.

Q. Mr. Carey, you were a witness at the trial of the United States vs. William Dwyer, had in November, 1906, in this court, were you not?

A. Yes, sir.

Q. And you were sworn at that time?

A. Yes, sir.

Q. And gave testimony in that case?

A. Yes, sir.

Q. I will ask you if this question was asked you at that time:

(Reading.) "Q. What did Mr. Dwyer state to you when he handed you the papers, state fully what you said?

"A. He said, take them in the land office and file them."

Q. Did you make that answer to that question at that time?

Mr. RUICK.—That is calling for his recollection.

The COURT.—Mr. Carey, the Court wants to ask you one or two questions: Do you remember any question or answer which was asked you, or which you made at the trial of this case? Do you recollect what was said or was asked you?

(Testimony of Charles Carey.)

A. No, not positively; it is quite a while ago. I don't remember exactly the questions asked me or the way they were asked me.

Q. That is, at the term of court when you testified here?

A. I don't remember just the questions.

The COURT.—The witness *ha* answered this in this way two or three times, and I don't think the Court will permit you to ask this question in that way. You may take your exception if the ruling is objectionable. The Court is not ruling now on the testimony he gave before; perhaps you don't understand the Court's view of the way in which the witness may be impeached; there is no objection to impeaching him if his testimony was different on the last trial from what it is now, and the Court will permit you to prove contradictory testimony, but it is not proper to ask him if he made such an answer and was asked such a question, because the Court knows ordinarily a witness could not remember that, and he says positively he does not remember.

Mr. TANNAHILL.—If the Court desires I will read this to the witness again and give him an opportunity of correcting any answers he desires, or I will have it identified, so we can offer it in evidence.

Mr. RUICK.—It will not be necessary to have him identify it.

The COURT.—Put it in this way, Mr. Tannahill. simply read into the record that it is agreed for the prosecution that it is the testimony of this witness

(Testimony of Charles Carey.)

given by this witness at the last term of court and that will get it before the jury.

Mr. TANNAHILL.—Counsel for the defendant now reads into the record the following portion of the evidence of the witness now upon the stand, given in the case of the United States vs. William Dwyer, in the month of November, 1906, in this court:

"Q. What did Mr. Dwyer say to you when he handed you the paper? State fully what he said?

"A. He said to make them—to take them in the land office and file them.

"Q. Dd he read them over to you?

"A. Why, he read some of the questions.

"Q. Well, there wasn't any questions, was there?

"A. One asked me how old I was.

"Q. It simply said how old you were?

"A. He said, 'How old are you Charlie,' and he was writing it down and answering them.

"Q. He read that to you?     A. Yes, sir.

"Q. What else did he read to you?

"A. I don't remember as he read all the questions or not, I suppose he did.

"Q. Have you any recollection of any particular part of the application coming up for discussion at that time? Was there anything said to you about any particular part of it?

"A. The first papers?

"Q. Yes.

"A. No, I don't know as I recall anything special.

(Testimony of Charles Carey.)

"Q. And then immediately upon his giving you this paper you took it into the land office and Mr. West sent you back? A. Yes, sir.

"Q. Do you remember what the correction was?

"A. No, I don't.

"Q. Was there any conversation took place between you and Mr. Dwyer when Mr. West sent you back?

"A. I just told him what Mr. West said.

"Q. And he filled it in there?

"A. Yes, sir; I suppose he did.

"Q. And you went back? A. Yes, sir.

"Q. And then you filed? A. Yes, sir.

"Q. Now, Mr. Carey have you stated the only two conversations that you had with Mr. Dwyer prior to your filing your first papers, have you?

"A. Yes, sir.

"Q. And you have stated all the conversations which you have any memory of?

"A. Yes, sir."

Mr. TANNAHILL (Continuing examination).—

Q. You say that Mr. Dwyer told you to take the four hundred dollars and put in the bank?

A. Yes, sir.

Q. Isn't it a fact you said to Mr. Dwyer and asked him what he should do with it, that you didn't want to carry it in your pocket and keep it till next day?

A. No, he told me to take it and put it in the bank.

(Testimony of Charles Carey.)

Q.   And you took it and put it in the bank and then brought the draft back to Mr. Dwyer?

A.   Yes, sir.

Q.   Didn't he tell you to keep the draft?

A.   No, he said to bring it back to him.

Q.   The certificate of deposit of which you testified in your direct examination that is what I am referring to?        A.   Yes, sir.

Q.   Now, Mr. Carey, do you remember what it was you signed the day you got your money?

A.   I don't remember of signing any*h*ing.

Q.   You signed nothing the day you got your money?        A.   *No* that I recollect now.

Q.   Didn't you sign a note the day you got your money?        A.   Not that I know of.

Q.   A promissory note?

A.   Nothing that I know of.

Q.   Do you wish to be understood as swearing you didn't sign a note?

A.   I don't remember signing anything.

Q.   You might have signed a note?

A.   I might have but not probably, I don't think I did.

Q.   And you say you saw Mr. Dwyer just before you proved up?

A.   Yes, sir; some few days.

Q.   And he told you you had no contract with him for the sale of the land, if I understand you right?

A.   We looked over the papers, and I think that question appears in there, and when I asked him

(Testimony of Charles Carey.)

about it again, he told me that I had no contract, and he said "You have got no contract."

Q. He said, "You have got no contract"?

A. He said, "We have got no contract," or some such words to that effect.

Q. And he *told* you you had no contract with him? that was in conflict with the questions you had to answer, didn't he?

A. I don't know as he used them words.

Q. But substantially?

A. He said we had no contract.

Q. In substance, that is what he said, was it?

A. Yes, sir.

Q. Now, Mr. Carey, do you remember whether or not the question of this contract and the statement that Mr. Dwyer made that you had no contract with him, that would conflict with your answers there, was put into the statement you made to Mr. Goodwin and Mr. O'Fallon?

A. I don't remember the question.

Q. You don't remember whether it was or not?

A. I don't remember whether it was or not.

Q. Do you remember whether or not the fact that you made this deed to Mr. Dwyer or for Mr. Dwyer, long after you made your final proof? was included in your statement you made for Mr. Goodwin and Mr. O'Fallon?

A. I don't remember how that was; it is possible I made the same mistake I made this morning, but I would say not. I don't remember what I said at that time, as to that deed.

(Testimony of Charles Carey.)

Q. Do you remember you included in your statement to Mr. Goodwin and Mr. O'fallon that Mr. Dwyer and you had a discussion about your first papers, and that Mr. Dwyer explained it to you that there was no contract with him, that was in conflict with your first papers? Do you remember that that was in your statement which you made for Mr. Goodwin and Mr. O'Fallon?

A. No, I don't remember that.

Q. You don't remember very much about what was in your statement that you made for Mr. Goodwin and Mr. O'Fallon, do you?

A. No, I don't remember but very little.

Q. Did you ever read over your evidence here before going on the witness-stand?

A. Yes, sir.

Q. When did you read it over?

A. The night before last, I think.

Q. Did you read it over carefully?

A. Oh, I just read it over.

Q. From whom did you get your evidence?

A. From Mr. Ruick.

Q. How long were you reading it over?

A. I was probably one-half or three-quarters of an hour.

Q. Did you read over your cross-examination?

A. I read it all over, the whole thing.

Q. And you studied it over carefully did you?

A. No, I just ran it over the once.

Q. You have talked with Mr. Ruick about your evidence have you before going on the stand?

(Testimony of Charles Carey.)

A. No, sir.

Q. Did you talk with Mr. Johnson about it?

A. No, sir.

Did you talk with anyone else about your evidence?

A. No, sir; I did not talk about it.

Q. You have not mentioned your evidence to anyone since you came to Moscow? A. *N*, sir.

Q. I mean since you came to Moscow the last time to attend this trial, that is what I mean?

A. No, I don't know as I have in particular; I might have said some words to somebody.

Be it remembered that then and *the* the following proceeding was had:

Q. I will ask you Mr. Carey, if you had any conversation with Mr. Goodwin or Mr. O'Fallon regarding Mr. Dwyer's stating to you that there was no agreement *bt*ween you except the verbal agreement, or words to that effect?

Mr. RUICK.—Objected to as incompetent, irrelevant and immaterial.

The COURT.—Objection sustained.

To which ruling of the Court the defendants then and there excepted, which exception was allowed by the Court.

Q. I will ask you Mr. Carey if you also testified on direct examination in the case of the United States vs. Wiliam Dwyer in November, 1906, in this court as follows:

(Testimony of Charles Carey.)

Mr. RUICK.—I think we can agree so as to sim-
plify this matter very much.  Is this Mr. Carey's
testimony?

Mr. TANNAHILL.—I think I would be justified
in simply reading this into the record, because it is
practically the same as the other (the cross-examination) except it is direct examination, and unless the
Court requires me, I will not ask the question.

The COURT.—The Court would prefer to have
you read it into the record, when it is agreed upon
that it is his testimony.

Mr. TANNAHILL.—The defense reads into the
record the following prtion of the direct examination of the witness Carey, taken at the trial of the
United States vs. William Dwyer in the month of
November, 1906, in this court:

"Q.  Where did you get this paper, this sworn
statement?        A.  Mr. Dwyer gave it to me.

"Q.  Mr. Dwyer gave it to you?

"A.  Yes, sir.

"Q.  Where did he give it to you?

"A.  He gave it to me in one of these offices there.

"Q.  He gave it to you in one of those offices there?

"A.  Yes, sir.

"Q.  Do you now recollect who it was made out
this sworn statement for you?

"A.  Mr. Dwyer.

"Q.  Was anyone in the office at the time that
you recollect?        A.  Melvern Scott.

"Q.  At the same time it was made out, you say?

"A.  Yes, sir.

(Testimony of Charles Carey.)

"The COURT.—Who did he say?

"A. Melvern Scott.

"Q. Scotty? A. Scotty.

"Q. Do you know whether he was there all the time or not?

"A. I cannot say, I believe he was. I could not say for sure.

"Q. Have you an idea? Or do you know in whose handwriting this is filled out?

"A. Mr. Dwyer's.

· "Q. Now, what was said between you and Mr. Dwyer there—I will withdraw that question—was this sworn statement read over to you Mr. Carey— or did you read it—read it over now and see if you recollect the circumstances of reading tat or of it having been read to you?

"A. I remember the questions asked me in regard to how old I was and my occupation. It was read to me by Mr. Dwyer.

"Q. Read to you by Mr. Dwyer?

"A. Yes, sir.

"Q. Do you recollect this prtion of your sworn statement (reading): 'That I do not apply to purchase the land above described on speculation, but in good faith to appropriate it to my own exclusive use and benefit.' Do you remember that subject having come up between you?

"A. I don't remember that question being asked.

"Q. This was not a question; it was simply a part of your affidavit or sworn statement which you

(Testimony of Charles Carey.)

filed; you say this was read over to you by Mr. Dwyer?

"A.   Part of it was anyhow.   This part in here I know was.

"Q.   The part that was—that is where the blanks occur?          A.   Yes, sir.

"Q.   And where the writing occurs, that you are certain o; you are certain of that?

"A.   Yes, sir; I am certain of that.

"Q.   You are certain that was read over to you?

"A.   Yes, sir.

"Q.   You are not certain about this portion down here (indicating).

"A.   I am not so certain about those.

"Q.   I will go a little further and read from this blank. *t*hat provision that is as follows: 'A*A*nd that I have not directly or indirectly made any agreement or contract in any way or manner with any person or persons whomsoever, by which the title I may acquire from the Gove*n*ment of the United States may inure in whole or in part to the benefit of any person except myself.'   Do you remember that subject coming up between you and Mr. Dwyer?

"A.   Not at that time; not in this paper.

"Q.   Not at that time?          A.   No, sir.

"Q.   You may state to the jury what occurred there, just as you remember it between you and Mr. Dwyer on that day?

"A.   I was handed the paper and money to go and take to the land office and file."

(Testimony of Charles Carey.)

Mr. TANNAHILL.—That is all of that record, and that is all of the cross-examination unless we desire to cross-examine for some isolated fact.

Redirect Examination by Mr. RUICK.

Q. You have heard your testimony given at the last therm of the court upon the trial of William Dwyer for subornation of perjury read to you, a portion of it. Now, I will ask you what explanation you have to make concerning this testimony and the facts which you have now testified to upon this trial. On yesterday you testified concerning certain statements made to you by Mr. Dwyer at the time he filled out your original application or sworn statement as it is called? A. Yes, sir.

Q. Make any explanation you desire with regard to this matter.

A. Well, some of it has come more fresh to my recollection as the time passed by, and it makes some little difference in the words of it, at least, in regard to that first paper.

Q. What do you now recollect with regard to the matter?

A. It is as I stated this morning as near as I can recollect it; it was read over to me and I was asked my age and occupation, and Mr. Dwyer read them over in a nice friendly way and told me to sign it, and there was nothing in there but what was perfectly all right, in other words that I had no agreement, he said, "You have got no agreement that is written agreement, which I didn't have any, You are getting the land for your own benefit, it looked

(Testimony of Charles Carey.)

to me that I was getting it for my own benefit too; I was getting money for it.

Q. When, Mr. Carey, was this matter of your recollection with regard to this conversation with Mr. Dwyer?

A. It has been since the last trial.

Q. When was it first made known to myself or to the prosecution at all?

A. I don't know as it was ever until right here.

Q. I want to ask this witness this question: When you first made known the fact that he recollected?

A. It was right here on the witness-stand.

Q. When he first made the fact known?

The COURT.—He *ha* already stated that it was yesterday when he was on the witness-stand.

Q. Th*ee* is one other question I overlooked, Mr. Carey. You brought the subject of relinquishment on cross-examination. Did you file a relinquishment at the time you filed your sworn statement?

A. Yes, sir; there was something like that I had to take in and file; I believe they call it a relinquishment.

Q. From whom did you get it?

A. From Mr. Dwyer.

Q. You said there was a mistake in some paper which you had to go back?

A. Something wrong with it.

Q. Which paper was that?

A. I don't know positively but 1 think the reliuquishment.

(Testimony of Charles Carey.)

Q. You say that Mr. Dwyer corrected it and you took it back to the land office?

A. He fixed it up some way, and I took it back and handed it in there.

Q. And you filed another paper besides the sworn statement at that time?

A. Yes, sir; this relinquishment or whatever it is called.

Q. Now, with regard to your having executed a deed to this property, in April, 1905, to which your attention has been called. You say that you brought the subject up yourself of executing that deed?

A. I told him I was going away.

Q. You told Mr. Dwyer?

A. Yes, sir. He told me previously there would be some other papers to sign, or something.

Q. And they you went and executed a paper?

A. Yes, sir; I signed some paper.

Q. Did you ever get any more money from Mr. Dwyer or any other person for this land other than the $125, which you have already testified to?

A. No, sir.

Q. And that was paid to you on the day on which you made final proof? A. Yes, sir.

Recross-examination by Mr. TANNAHILL.

Q. You say Mr. Dwyer made this statement to you and you and he discussed your declaratory statement, or your first papers.

Be it remembered that then and there the following proceeding was had:

(Testimony of Charles Carey.)

The COURT.—That is already in the record.

To which ruling of the Court the defendants then and there excepted, which exception was by the Court allowed.

Q. (Continuing.) You say you remember more about it as time goes by, do you?

.A. I say those things have kind of refreshed me, different questions as these suits have come up, I have kept thinking about them and I remember some particulars of them a great deal better than others. On the first papers I remember now he explained them to me, and how I kind of got them mixed up with some other papers lying around which had substantiall᷄ the same questions in them.

Q. How many times have you testified and gone over ᷄our evidence since you filed?

A. I went over it last fall.

Q. You went over it last fall?

A. I was here last fall.

Q. Did you appear before the grand jury?

A. I don't think I did last fall.

Q. Did you ever appear before the grand jur᷄ and go over your evidence before the grand jur᷄?

A. I was here once before the grand jur᷄.

Q. You were once here before the grand jur᷄?

A. Yes, sir.

Q. And did ᷄ou go over ᷄o*u* evidence at Boise before the grand jur᷄?

A. I looked it over some. I didn't read it all over; I read a few pages.

(Testimony of Charles Carey.)

Q. And then did you appear before the grand jury?    A. Yes, sir.

Q. And then you read over your evidence here before you went on the stand, if I understand you?

A. Yes, sir.

Q. And you also testified in Mr. Dwyer's case last November?    A. Yes, sir.

Q. Now, Mr. Carey, you spoke about a relinquishment which you had that Mr. Dwyer gave you. Do you remember Mr. Dwyer telling you he had a relinquishment for this tract of land?

A. I said I didn't know what the paper was; I said I thought it was a relinquishment. I don't know positively what kind of a paper this was.

Q. Don't you remember the reason this remark was made by Mr. Dwyer, "The less said about it the better," was because he had that relinquishment and said, "The less said about it the better?"

A. I remember his saying "The less said about it the better," I don't know for what purpose it was said.

Q. It may have been said in connection with this relinquishment might it not?

A. Yes, it might have been.

Q. And didn't he also tell you that if it was made public before you got your filing, that possibly someone would come in and test the legality of the entry, and you would lose it?

A. I don't know whether he explained himself at all or not. He said the less said about the matter the better, and we walked down to the Bollnger.

(Testimony of Charles Carey.)

Q. But some reference had been made to the relinquishment?

A. I don't think it had been mentioned at the time; I don't think I knew anything about the relinquishment until the first papers had been made out.

(Witness excused.)

Be it remembered that then and there the following proceeding was had:

Mr. FORNEY.—The *defendants to* withdraw all testimony of the witness pertaining to Melvern Scott from the jury on the ground it will not bind Kettenbach and Kester or either of the defendants, for the reason the witness himself testified that Scott was acting as his agent, and not as an agent of Dwyer.

The COURT.—The motion will be denied.

To which ruling of the Court the defendants then and there excepted, which exception was allowed by the Court.

Mrs. FRANCES A. JUSTICE, a witness called and sworn for the plaintiff, testified as follows, on

Direct Examination by Mr. RUICK.

Q. Your name is Frances A. Justice?

A. Yes, sir.

(Witness Continuing:) I claim Clarkston, Washington, as my home; I have been temporarily absent from home.

Q. From what point or at what point were you subpoenaed for attendance upon this trial?

A. From Touma, Wisconsin.

(Testimony of Mrs. Frances A. Justice.)

Q. What were you doing there?

A. I was visiting a sick brother.

(Witness Continuing:) I have resided in Clarkston eight and a half years; I am the widow of David Justice, who died the 5th day of February, 1905; I am the mother of Mrs. Guy L. Wilson and Fred Justice, who died April 1st, 1905, shortly after my husband's death.

Prior to coming to Clarkston, my husband and I resided at Greenwood, Clarke County, Wisconsin; I resided there nearly all my life.

I am acquainted with Mr. and Mrs. William Dwyer; have known them over eight years at Clarkston, Washington. My acquaintance with them was an intimate one. Mrs. Dwyer and myself were members of the same secret order. We sometimes visited one another. I remember the circumstanc of taking up a timber claim. I went up into the timber to look at a timber claim. Mr. O'Brien, Guy Wilson, Mr. Hopper, Mr. Justice, Mr. Dwyer and myself were in the party.

Q. Who was in charge of the party?

A. Mr. Dwyer.

Q. Had you had any talk with Mr. Dwyer about timber or timber claims before you went up to the timber? A. Yes, sir; several times.

Q. Where had those conversations occurred?

A. Well, at different places; I talked to him at my home and at his home in Lewiston.

Q. Now, then, state what those conversations were? State what was said about timber?

(Testimony of Mrs. Frances A. Justice.)

A.   Why, to go up there and get a claim up above Pierce.

Q.   Who was going to show you the claim?

A.   Mr. Dwyer was the locator.

Q.   Did you pay your own expenses on the way up there and back?

A.   My expenses were all paid.

Q.   By whom, if you know?

A.   By Mr. Dwyer.

Q.   Have you had any talk with Mr. Dwyer about this matter of expenses before going up there?

A.   Yes, sir.

Q.   Can you state what was said about the matter and the matter of taking up a timber claim?

A.   Well, I didn't have money to take a claim with, and I asked Mr. Dwyer if he would get the money for me to take a claim, and he said he thought he could get the money for me, and he got the money.

Q.   What do you mean, what money do you mean you had him get for you?

A.   The money to pay all expenses for a claim for locating and my expnses there and back and for filing and for paying for the timber.

Q.   Now, state everything in relation to that, Mrs. Justice.   Did you have any understanding with Mr. Dwyer before going up to the timber about your timber claim?

The COURT.—Answer yes or no?

A.   Yes.

Be it remembered that then and there the following proceeding was had:

(Testimony of Mrs. Frances A. Justice.)

Q. Now state what that understanding was?

Mr. FORNEY.—Objected to as calling for a conclusion of the witness.

The COURT.—Objection overruled.

To which ruling of the Court the defendants then and there excepted, which exception was allowed by the Court, and the witness answered:

A. That he would get the money for me for a claim and then I would go up there and take a claim. It was a verbal agreement. I thought I would get one hundred and fifty dollars clear of all my expenses.

Q. What were you to do with your claim to get one hundred and fifty dollars?

A. I was to file on the claim and prove up on it.

Q. And then what were you to do after you proved up, if anything, in order to get the one hundred and fifty dollars.

A. I gave a contract of a deed for the timber.

Q. I am asking you with regard to the understading between you and Mr. Dwyer before you went up there? What were you to do with this land when you got title to it?

A. I would sell it; I would get $150 for my chance in the claim.

Q. For your chance. Who did you get the $150 from?

A. Well, he paid me the $150 and I don't know—the claim was made over to the bank, if I remember right, to pay for the note which I had in the bank.

(Testimony of Mrs. Frances A. Justice.)

Q. What I want to know is whether or not you had any agreement or understanding with Mr. Dwyer before you went up to the timber as to what you were to do with the land after you got title to it?

A. Why, he would find a buyer for it; I was to sell it.

Q. What were you to get out of it?

A. I was to get one hundred and fifty dollars claer of all expenses.

Q. You went up to the timber did you?

A. I did.

Q. How did you travel, how did you go?

A. I went up as far as Orofino on the train and then went horseback from there above Pierce.

Q. You went on horseback?     A. Yes, sir.

Q. To what place did you go?

A. Well, it was to a camp away above Pierce; I don't know the name of the camp.

Q. Was Mr. Dwyer with you?     A. Yes, sir.

Q. And your husband and the other parties?

A. Yes, sir.

Q. Did you leave the trial or road in which you were traveling from Pierce up to the camp, either going or coming to look at the timber?

A. Why, we rode through the timber in going and there were several trails through it.

Q. Did you ride on several trails, or one trail?

A. One trail.

Q. Then you rode through the timber?

A. Ye, sir.

(Testimony of Mrs. Frances A. Justice.)

Q. Did you know whether or not you rode through the tim*br* you afterward filed on?

A. Mr. Dwyer showed me the corner stake to the timber.

Q. Where?

A. Above Pierce going to the cabin.

Q. Were you still on horseback on the trail?

A. Yes, sir.

Q. You didn't get off the trail did you?

A. No, sir.

Q. To go *an* look for corners?

A. No, sir.

Q. He pointed out the corners to you?

A. Yes, sir.

Q. How far from the trial?

A. Not very far.

Q. How many corners did he point out?

A. I don't remember.

Q. How long were you gone on that trip altogether?    A.  Five days.

Q. How long after you had come back was it before you filed, if you recollect, about how long?

A. It was about the 9th of October, I believe that I went to the timber, and it was the 25th of April the next spring that I filed.

Q. Do you know why you delayed so long in filing?

A. I don't know; there was something about the land that we could not file just then; I don't know what the reason was.

(Testimony of Mrs. Frances A. Justice.)

Q. Did you go to the land office in person to file?

A. I did.

Q. To file your application?     A. Yes, sir.

Q. Were you in a line-up at the land office?

A. I was.

Q. How did you come to get in the line-up?

A. Mr. Dwyer told me I had better stand in line so as to take my chance in filing.

Q. What number did you get in the line, do you remember?

A. I have forgotten; I think it was 16, but I am not positive.

Q. Did you stand in line during all the time of the line-up?

A. No, sir; my daughter was there one day in line for me.

Q. *Sis* you see Mr. Dwyer before you filed?

A. Yes, sir.

Mr. RUICK (showing witness paper purporting to be sworn statement of Frances A. Justice under Timber and Stone Act).—Mrs. Justice, look at this paper in duplicate and see if your signature is attached to it?     A. Yes, sir.

Q. You recognize those papers?     A. I do.

Q. Where were those papers made out?

A. In I. N. Smith's office.

Q. In what building? Whereabouts from the land office at that time?

A. It was in the main building on the same floor as the land office.

(Testimony of Mrs. Frances A. Justice.)

Q. Did you remember in what direction from the door of the land office it was to the door of Mr. Smith's office relative to the hall?

A. No, sir; I don't remember.

Q. It was on the same floor?    A. Yes, sir.

Q. How did you happen to go to Mr. Smith's office to have the papers made out?

A. Mr. Dwyer said we could have them made out there.

Q. Did you pay anything for having those papers made out?    A. Yes, sir.

Q. How much did you pay if you remember?

A. I am not positive; I think it was $7.50.

Q. I am speaking now not of the papers—the filing fee in the land office, but did you pay anybody for filling out these blanks?

A. I don't remember.

Q. Who made out the paper, if you recollect?

A. Mr. I. N. Smith.

Q. Who did the typewriting in the paper, if you remember?    A. I don't know.

Q. Mr. I. N. Smith you say was there when the paper was made out?

A. Yes, sir; if I remember right he was there.

Q. Do you know who filled in the paper with a pen, your age in this blank?

A. I am not *p*sitive.

Q. Who asked you the question which it was necessary for you to answer?

A. Mr. I. N. Smith.

(Testimony of Mrs. Frances A. Justice.)

Q. Who else was in the office at this time that you recall? Any members of your family?

A. Yes, sir; Fred Justice and Guy Wilson.

Q. Were they having papers made out also?

A. Yes, sir.

Q. I will ask you to read over this paper, Mrs. Justice, to see if you recollect, or have any recollection of the statements that are contained in that papr? A. I don't remember.

Q. Did you have any talk with anyone before you filed this paper as to the contents of the paper, and the statements which are made therein?

A. Yes, sir.

Q. With whom? A. With Mr. Dwyer.

Q. Where did this conversaiton or these conversations occur?

A. I talked wih him at his home and also at my own home about it.

Mr. RUICK.—May it please the Court, we will withdraw the witness temporarily for the purpose of introducing the papers. I suppose you have no objection to Mrs. Justice—

Mr. TANNAHILL.—That will be introduced as identified by Mr. Goodwin, with our objections going to them.

Mr. RUICK.—Defense admits the signature of J. B. West—

Mr. TANNAHILL.—We will admit that Mr. Goodwin will swear that is the signature of J. B. West, and it can go in subject to the general ob_jection and not to the form of the offer.

(Testimony of F. M. Goodwin.)

Mr. RUICK.—Why not admit it is his signature?

Mr. TANNAHILL.—We make the objection right along that the documents are not properly authenticated or identified.

(Witness withdrawn.)

F. M. GOODWIN, a witness recalled in behalf of the Government, testified as follows on

Direct Examination by Mr. RUICK.

(Paper shown witness purporting to be sworn statement in duplicate of Francis A. Justice, being an application to enter stone and timber lands at the United States Land Office at Lewiston, Idaho, the application bearing date April 25th, 1904.)

Q. Mr. Goodwin, is that the general signature of J. B. West, the former Register of the United States Land Office at Lewiston, Idaho?

A. Yes, sir; they are.

Q. Was he such register on the date named in that sworn statement? A. He was.

Be it remembered that then and there the following proceeding was had:

Mr. RUICK.—The Government offers in evidence the sworn statement and asks that it be marked Plintiff's Exhibit No. 11.

Mr. FORNEY.—The defendants object to the introduction of this testimony on the ground that it is incompetent, irrelevant and immaterial; on the further ground that it does not prove or tend to prove any of the allegations of conspiracy alleged in the indictment; on the further ground that there

(Testimony of F. M. Goodwin.)

is no evidence showing or tending to show any conspiracy or combination upon the part of or between the defendants or any of them; upon the further ground that it post-dates the consummation of
the conspiracy as alleged in the indictment; on the
further ground that it does not connect or tend to
connect any of the defendants with the alleged offenses set forth in the indictment, or any of them.

The COURT.—Objection overruled.

To which ruling of the Court the defendants then
and there excepted, which exception was allowed by
the Court, and the said documents were admitted in
evidence and marked Plaintiff's Exhibit 11.

(Omitted; appears elsewhere.)

(Paper shown witness purporting to be the testimony of the claimant Frances A. Justice on her application to purchase timber lands at the Unied
States Land Office, Leeiston, Idaho, under the Stone
and Timber Law.)

Q. Are the signatures upon that paper, J. B.
West, the genuine signatures of J. B. West, former
register of the United States Land Office, at Leeiston, Idaho? A. They are.

Q. Was he the acting register at the date named
in that certificate or paper? A. He was.

Be it remembered that then and there the following proceedings were had:

Mr. RUICK.—The Government offers in evidence
this paper and askes that it be marked Plaintiff's
Exhibit No. 12.

(Testimony of F. M. Goodwin.)

Mr. FORNEY.—The defendants object to the introduction of t*h*s testimony on the ground it is incompetent, irrelevant and immaterial; on the further ground that it does not prove or tend to prove any of the material allegations in the indictment; on the further ground that there is no evidence showing or tending to show any conspiracy or combination upon the part of or between the defendants or any of them, upon the further ground that it postdates the consummation of the conspiracy as alleged in the indictment; on the further ground that it does not connect or tend to connect any of the defendants with the alleged offenses set forth in the indictment or any of them.

The COURT.—The objection is overruled.

To which ruling of the Court the defendants then and there excepted, which exception was allowed by the Court, and said document was admitted in evidence, and marked Plaintiff's Exhibit 12, and is as follows:

(Omitted; appears elsewhere.)

Q. I now present to the witness for identification the signature of J. B. West, appended to the testimony of the witness, William Dwyer, in support of the application of Mrs. Frances A. Justice, herein before referred to, and ask the same question; is that the signature of Mr. J. B. West*l* form*e* Register of the United States Land Office, Lewiston, Idaho?

A. It is.

Be it remembered that then and there the following proceeding was had:

(Testimony of F. M. Goodwin.)

Mr. RUICK.—I desire to offer this in evidence, and ask that it be marked Plaintiff's Exhibit 13.

Mr. FORNEY.—The defendants object to the introduction of this document on the ground that it is irrelevant, immaterial and incompetent, in that it does not prove or tend to prove any of the material allegations in the indictment; on the further ground that there is no evidence showing or tending to show any conspiracy or combination upon the part of or between the defendants or any of them; upon the further ground that it post-dates the consummation of the conspiracy aleged in the indictment; on the further ground that it does not connect or tend to connect any of the defendants with the alleged offenses set forth in the indictment, or any of them.

The COURT.—Objection overruled; to which ruling of the Court the defendats then and there excepted; which exception was by the Court allowed, and said document admitted in evidence, marked Plaintiff's Exhibit 13, and is as follows:

(Omitted; appears elsewhere.)

Q. I will now present for identification to the witness the testimony of the witness Edwin Bliss, called as a witness in supprt of the application of Frances A. Justice, hereinbeofre referred to, and ask the witness if that is the general signature of J. B. West, former register of the United States Land Office, at Lewiston, Idaho? A. It is.

Be it remembered that then and there the following proceeding was had:

(Testimony of F. M. Goodwin.)

Mr. RUICK.—I offer this paper in evidence and ask that it be marked Plaintiff's Exhibit 14.

Mr. FORNEY.—The defendants object to the introduction of this testimony on the ground that it is ireelevant, immaterial and incompetent, in this, that it does not prove or tend to prove any of the material allegations in the indictment; on the further ground that there is no evidence showing or tending to show any conspiracy or combination upon the part of or between the defendants or any of them; upon the further ground that it post-dates the consummation of the conspiracy as alleged in the indictment, and on the further ground that it does not connect or tend to connect any of the defendants with the alleged offenses set forth in the indictment or any of them.

The COURT.—Objection overuled.

To which ruling of the Court the defendants then and there excepted, which exception was allowed by the Court, and the said document was admitted in evidence and marked Plaintiff's Exhibit 14, and is as follows:

(Omitted; appears elsewhere.)

Q. I present a paper purprting to be the notice for publication of the application of Frances A. Justice for final proof in support of her stone and timber claim herein referred to, bearing date April 25th. 1904. Is that the genuine signature of J. B. West, the former register of the United States Land Office, Lewiston, Idaho, appeneded thereto? A. It is.

Be it remembered that then and there the following proceedings were had?

(Testimony of F. M. Goodwin.)

Mr. RUICK.—The Government offers in evidence Exhibit No. 15 above identified.

Mr. FORNEY.—The defendants object to the introduction of thsi testimony on the ground' it is incompetent, irrelevant and immaterial, in that it does not prove or tend to prove any of the material allegations in the indictment; on the further ground that there is no evidence showing or tending to show any conspiracy or combination upon the part of or between the defendants or either of them; *non* the further ground that it post-dates the consummation of the conspirac\ as alleged in the indictment; on the further ground that it does not connect or tend to connect any of the defendants with the alleged offenses set forth in the indictment or an\ of them.

The COURT.—Objection overruled.

To which ruling of the Court the defendants then and there excepted, which exception was by the Court allowed, and said paper was admitted in evidence, marked Plaintiff's *marked Plaintiff's* Exhibit 15 and is as follows:

(Omitted; appears elsewhere.)

Q. I show witness a paper purporting to be register's certificate No. 4771, issued at the United States Land Office of Lewiston, Idaho, to Frances A. Justice, July 13th, 1904. Is that the signature of J. B. West, former register of the United States Land Office at Lewiston, Idaho.

A. Yes, sir.

Mr. RUICK.—We offer in evidence Exhibit 16 as above identified.

(Testimony of F. M. Goodwin.)

Mr. TANNAHILL.—The same objection.

The COURT.—Same ruling. Exhibit admitted.

Mr. TANNAHILL.—An exception.

(Exhibit omitted, here appears elsewhere.)

Q. I now present to the witness a paper purport· ing to be the receiver's final receipt issued to Frances A. Justice, dated July 13th, 1904, bearing number 4771, and ask that the witness if this is the genuine signature of Charles H. Garby, former receiver of the United States Land Office at Lewiston, Idaho?

A. It is.

Be it then and there remembered that the following proceeding was had:

Mr. RUICK.—We offer in evidence Exhibit 17, last above identified.

Mr. FORNEY.—The defendants object to the introduction of the exhibit offered, on the ground that it is irrelevant, immaterial and incompetent; on the further ground that it does not prove or tend to prove any of the material allegations in the indictment; on the further ground that there is no evidence showing or tending to show any conspiracy or combination upon the part of or between the defendants or either of them; upon the further ground that it post-dates the consummation of the conspiracy as alleged in the indictment, and on the further ground that it does not connect or tend to connect any of the defendants with any of the alleged offenses set forth in the indictment.

The COURT.—The objection is overruled.

(Testimony of F. M. Goodwin.)

To which ruling of the Court the defendants then and there excepted, and the exception was allowed and said paper was admitted in eividence, and said paper was marked Plaintiff's Exhibit 17, and is as follows:

(Omitted; appears elsewhere.)

Q. What is this paper signed here by Mr. Garby termed?

A. It is termed the receiver's receipt, or cash receipt.

Q. That is what you refer to as the final receipt?

A. The final receipt—they usually call that the register's receipt, the one given by the register.

Q. What time were these issued relative to the time that the final proof was made?

A. They should be issued the same date, ordinarily.

Q. With the final proof?    A. Yes, sir.

(Witness excused.)

Mrs. FRANCES A. JUSTICE recalled.

Direct Examination (Resumed) by Mr. RUICK.

Q. Ppaper shown witness purporting to be the cross-examination of the claimant Frances A. Justice, taken in connnection with the proof offered in support of her claim to enter the lands hereinbefore referred to in her sworn statement, Plaintiff's Exbibit 11. Is that your signature, Mrs. Justice, to that paper?    A. Yes, sir.

Q. You remember that paper on looking it over— do you remember that paper as having been signed

(Testimony of Mrs. Frances A. Justice.)

by you and delivered into the land office at the time you made your final proof? You don't need to read it through. Just read down over it enough so that you can know and identify the paper. Do you recollect that paper? A. Yes, sir.

Be it remembered that then and there the following proceeding was had:

Mr. RUICK.—We *ofcr* this paper in evidence and ask that it be marked Plaintiff's Exhibit 12-A.

Mr. FORNEY.—The defendants object to the introduction of the exhibit offered, on the ground it is irrelevant, immaterial and incompetent; on the further ground that it does not prove or tend to prove any of the material allegations in the indictment; on the further ground that t*hr*e is no evidence showing or tending to show any conspiracy or combination on the part of or between the defendants, or any of them; on the further ground that it post-dates the consummation of the conspirac*y* as alleged in the indictment, and on the further ground that it does not connect or tend to connect any of the defendants with any of the alleged offenses set forth in the indictment.

The COURT.—The objection is overruled.

To which ruling of the Court the defendants then and there excepted, which exception was allowed by the Court, and the said document admitted in evidence and marked Plaintiff's Exhibit 12-A, and is as follows:

(Omitted; appears elsewhere.)

(Testimony of Mrs. Frances A. Justice.)

Q. Now, Mrs. Justice, taking this sworn statement of yours in duplicate, I will read it through.

"I, Frances A. Justice, of Clarkston, County of Asotin, State of Washington, desiring to avail myself of the Acts of Congress of June 3rd, 1878, entitled 'An Act for the sale of timber lands in the State of California, Oregon and Nevada, and in Washington Territory, as extended to all of the public lands, states, by Act of August 4th, 1892, for the purchase of lots three and four, and the east one-half of the southwest one-fourth of Section nineteen, tp. 38 north, Range*d* 6 E. B. M., in the District of land subject to sale at Lewiston, Idaho, do solemnly swear that I am a native citizen of the United States, of age forty-nine, and by occupation housewife." Can you follow me?     A. Yes.

(Continuing:) "That I have personally examined said *land is* unfit for cultivation, and valuable chiefly for its timber, and that it is uninhabited; that it contains no mining nor other improvements, nor, as I verily believe, any valuable deposits of gold, silver, cinnabar, copper or coal; that I have made no other application under said acts. That I do not apply to purchase the land above described on speculation but in good faith to appropriate it to my own exclusive use and benefit, and that I have not directly nor indirectly made any agreement or contract, or in any way or manner, with any person or persons whomsoever, by which the title I may acquire from the Government of the United *State* may

(Testimony of Mrs. Frances A. Justice.)

inure in whole or in part to the benefit of any person except myself, and that my postoffice address is Clarkston, Washington.

Signed, FRANCES A. JUSTICE.''

I read this over for the purpose of asking you certain questions. You have already stated that you had an agreement and understanding with Mr. Dwyer before you went up to the timber relative to this land. Is that correct?

A. I had a verbal agreement; yes, sir.

Q. Now, at the time you made this affidavit, you stated in there that "I do not apply to purchase the land above described on speculation, but in good faith to appropriate it to my own exclusive use and benefit." Now, at that time when you made that statement, was it true or untrue? A. Untrue.

Q. And this statement "That I have not directly nor indirectly made any agreement or contract, or in any way or manner with any person or persons whomselver, by twhich the title I may acquire from the Government of the United States may inure in whole or in part or the benefit of any person except myself." Now, at the time that statement was made by you, Mrs. Justice, was the statmenent true or untrue? A. Untrue.

Q. Now, how did it happen—now, what explanation have you to give for having made these false statements at the time you filed your application to enter these lands?

(Testimony of Mrs. Frances A. Justice.)

A.   I was told it would be a benefit to me in one way, that I would get the $150 out of it, and that that was a benefit to me from the land.

Q.   Who stated this to you?

A.   Mr. Dwyer.

Q.   Before I go any further, I will ask you, Mrs. Justice, if this statement was sworn to by you in the land office, this sworn statement.

A.   Yes, sir.

Q.   Now, this statement, "That I have not directly or indirectly made any agreement or contract, or in any way or manner, with any person or persons whomsoever, by which the title I may acquire from the Government of the United States may inure in whole or in part to the benefit of any person except myself." How did you come to make that statement?

A.   Why, I was told how to answer those questions; that it would be all right to make that statement that way; that it was to be—that it was to benefit me, the money I was to get out of it, and I answered the questions that way.

Q.   What about the agreement, what, if anything, was said to you about the agreement? You stated here in there in the affidavit that you had no agreement directly or indirectly?

A.   Well, it was just a verbal agreement that I would sell my land—my interest in it, for $150.

# No. 1605

# NITED STATES CIRCUIT COURT OF APPEALS

## FOR THE NINTH CIRCUIT

---

# TRANSCRIPT OF RECORD

### (In Six Volumes.)

---

ILLIAM F. KETTENBACH, GEO. H. KESTER,
AND WILLIAM DWYER,

Plaintiffs in Error,

vs.

HE UNITED STATES OF AMERICA,

Defendant in Error.

---

## VOLUME II.

### (Pages 401 to 816, Inclusive)

---

pon Writ of Error to the United States District Court
for the District of Idaho.

---

FILMER BROS Co., PRINT, 330 JACKSON ST., S. F., CAL.

# No. 1605

# UNITED STATES CIRCUIT COURT OF APPEALS

## FOR THE NINTH CIRCUIT

---

# TRANSCRIPT OF RECORD

(In Six Volumes.)

---

WILLIAM F. KETTENBACH, GEO. H. KESTER,
AND WILLIAM DWYER,

Plaintiffs in Error,

vs.

THE UNITED STATES OF AMERICA,

Defendant in Error.

---

## VOLUME II.

(Pages 401 to 816, Inclusive)

---

Upon Writ of Error to the United States District Court
for the District of Idaho.

---

FILMER BROS CO., PRINT, 330 JACKSON ST, S. F., CAL

(Testimony of Mrs. Frances A. Justice.)

Q. That's what I want to know; what we want to know is who, if anyone, suggested to you at that time that you could answer it this way?

A. Mr. Dwyer told me how to answer the questions; I don't know *w*how I answered that.

Q. What did Mr. Dwyer say to you about this matter of the agreement? Do you recall what he said to you or what explanation or argument he made or gave to you?

A. I don't just understand.

Q. Do you know that you stated here in this paper that you had no agreement, directly or indirectly, or any contract, in any way or manner with any person whomsoever. Now then, did you have an agreement at that time?

A. Why, that is not an agreement, is it? If it is, just a verbal agreement.

Q. Did you have a verbal agreement at that time?

A. I did with Mr. Dwyer.

Q. Now, then, you had some agreement, we will say. How did you come to answer that question that you had no agreement directly or indirectly, no agreement?

A. Why, I was told that that was no agreement, a verbal agreement. A verbal agreement was no agreement.

Q. Who told you that?

A. Mr. Dwyer told me that that was no agreement, a verbal agreement.

Q. That a verbal agreement was no agreement?

A. No, sir.

(Testimony of Mrs. Frances A. Justice.)

Q. How long before you went to the land office do you recall that you had these conversations with Mr. Dwyer?     A. Before I went to take the claim.

Q. Before you went to take the claim?

A. Yes, sir; it was there I made the agreement.

Q. Where did you get the money, Mrs. Justice, to pay the fee at the time you filed this paper?

A. Mr. Dwyer gave me the money.

Q. At the time you filed this first paper? At the time you filed these papers?     A. Yes, sir.

Q. Do you recall what the amount was?

A. I think it was $7.50, if I remember right.

Q. Who went with you to the land office at the time you filed this paper, who was in the land office at the time you filed the first paper? Who went with you to the land office, if anyone?

A. Fred Justice and Guy Wilson.

Q. Where, if you know, was Mr. Dwyer at that time?

A. I saw him at the land office that day.

Q. How about the time you swore to this statement, the first paper, at the time you made the filing? What I want to know is, where was Dwyer?

A. He was around the land office, but I don't remember now just where.

Q. Did you have anything to do with naming the witnesses, Mrs. Justice? Who arranged for the witnesses?

A. Mr. Dwyer did, and I don't know who I got, who arranged for the witnesses.

(Testimony of Mrs. Frances A. Justice.)

Q. Who were your witnesses when it came to final proof? A. Mr. Dwyer and Mr. Bliss.

Q. Now, in making up these papers for the first filing papers, Mrs. Justice, who caused these papers to be made up, if you know? How did they come to be made up?

A. Mr. Dwyer said we would go to Mr. I. N. Smith's and have these papers made out.

Q. Where did they get the description of the land to put in this paper, if you know? Did you furnish it?

A. I don't know whether I did or not.

Q. Well, did you see Dwyer between the time that you filed on this land and the time you made final proof? A. Yes, sir.

Q. Where did you see him?

A. I saw him several times between the time I filed and the time I made the final proof.

Q. Did you have anything to do with procuring the notice to be published in the land office of your intention to make proof? A. No, sir.

Q. Did you have to pay any of the expenses in connection with it? A. No, sir.

Q. How did you know the date on which that final proff would be made?

A. Mr. Dwyer gave notice.

Q. Did you have any talk with Dwyer before going up to the land office on the day you made final proof? A. Yes, sir.

Q. Did you transact any business with him before going to the land office to make final proof?

(Testimony of Mrs. Frances A. Justice.)

A.   I did after I went to the land office.

Q.   Well, now, then state the circumstances, how you happened to go over there from your home at all.  What did Dwyer tell you?

A.   I went over there to make final proof, and I met him upstairs and he gave me the money to prove up with on the land.

Q.   And where did he give you the money?

A.   When I was in Mr. I. N. Smith's office when he gave me the money.

Q.   How much money did he give you?

A.   I can't remember the eact amount; my claim was not a full claim; it was less than 160 acres.

Q.   What was this money for?

A.   It was paid for the land.

Q.   Where, in the land office, do you mean?

A.   Yes, sir.

Q.   The Goverment price for the land?

A.   Yes, sir.

Q.   State whether or not the amount he gave you was sufficient to pay for the land.

A.   Yes, sir; it was more than sufficient, six dollars more.

Q.   What did you do with the six dollars.

A.   I gave it back to him.

Q.   Who was in the office at the time he gave you this money?

A.   Fred Justice and Guy Wilson.

Q.   In what part of the office did he give you this money, if you remember?

(Testimony of Mrs. Frances A. Justice.)

A.   In I. N. Smith's office; I don't remember; it was in the main office.

Q.   In w*ht* form was the money, if you recall, bills —or gold or silver?

A.   It was gold some of it, $100 was in bills. I remember there was a hundred dollar bill for locating.

Q.   We will get to the hundred dollar bill later. I am asking you particularly with regard to the money that went to pay for the land?

A.   I am not *ps*itive whether it was all gold or not.

Q.   Did you sign any papers at that time when he gave you this money?     A.   I signed a note.

Q.   Signed a note?

A.   Yes, I gave a note for the money.

Q.   To whom did the note run, if you remember?

A.   It ran to the bank, the National Bank.

Q.   'The Lewiston National Bank?

A.   Yes, sir.

Q.   Do you remember whether it was the bank or to individuals connected with the bank? What is your recollection?

A.   W*el*, I can't swear positive, but I think it was to the bank.

Q.   Do you remember for what amount this note was?

A.   I can't remember the full amount; it was to cover my expenses up to the timber, and I *c*an't remember the exact amount that I paid on that timber.

Q.   Where was that note made out, do *y*ou know?

(Testimony of Mrs. Frances A. Justice.)

A.   I don't know; it was brought to me and I signed it.

Q.   Where did you sign it? Where was it brought to you? Where were you when you signed it?

A.   At the land office.

Q.   Was your husband there?

A.   No, sir; he was very sick at the time.

Q.   Did your husband sign the note?

A.   No, sir.

Q.   Was security required or demanded of you?

A.   No, sir.

Q.   You didn't give any mortgage?

A.   No, sir.

Q.   Or any other security?    A.   No, sir.

Q.   Did you get any endorser on the note?

A.   No, sir.

Q.   Was any asked for?    A.   No, sir.

Q.   To whom did you deliver the note after you signed it?    A.   Mr. Dwyer.

Q.   No, there was another transaction that occurred there that day, wasn't there, something about a location fee?    A.   Yes, sir.

Q.   State that transaction to the jury.

A.   Well, Mr. Dwyer gave me a hundred dollar bill that I could pay him for locating on the timber; that was his charge for locating, was $100.

Q.   What did you do? State the whole circumstances.

A.   Well, I gave him back the $100 bill.

Q.   Wht did Dwyer say to you when he handed you the hundred dollar bill?

(Testimony of Mrs. Frances A. Justice.)

A.  He said I could pay him that for locating me on the timber?

Q.  And you handed it back to him?

A.  Yes, sir.

Q.  Did that occur before you went into the land office to make your final proof?    A.  Yes, sir.

Q.  You recall making your final proof in the land office, do you, Mrs. Justice?    A.  Yes, sir.

Q.  Do you remember whether or not your witnesses were there at the same time that you made your final proof?    A.  Yes, sir.

Q.  They were?  Where was Mr. Dwyer?

A.  He sat at the table with me at my right, and Mr. Bliss on my left.

Q.  What part did Mr. Dwyer take in the proceedings?

A.  Well, when I didn't know how to answer the questions he prompted me.

Q.  I will ask you if before going to make your final proof you had a talk over these matters with any person as to how you should answer these questions or any of them?    A.  Yes, sir.

Q.  Do you recall when and where and how long before you made your final proof?

A.  It was—I don't remember how long before I was—Mr. Dwyer had a blank, and he told me the question and how to answer it.

Q.  Where was this?

A.  At his home or at my home.

Q.  You say he had a blank with him?

(Testimony of Mrs. Frances A. Justice.)

A.   I think he had a blank.  He told me what the questions were and told me how to answer, and I wouldn't be positive about the blank.

Q.   You say he told you about the questions you would have to answer?      A.   Yes, sir.

Q.   When—at the time you made your final proof?

A.   Before.

Q.   I mean the questions you would have to answer?      A.   Yes, sir.

Q.   Now, I will read from this final proof of yours, question thirteen:  "Have you sold or transfered your claim to this land since making your sworn statement, or have you directly or indirectly made any agreement or contract in any way or manner with any person whomsoever, by which the title which you may acquire from the Government of the United States may inure in whole and in part to the benefit of any person except yourself?"  Now, that part of it which reads, "Or have you directly or indirectly made any agreement or contract," etc.  To that you answered no in the land office.  Now, was that answer made by you true or untrue at the time it was made?      A.   Untrue.  .

Q.   Did you know it was untrue?

A.   Yes, sir.

Q.   How did you come to make that answer in that way?  What explanation have you to give?

A.   Well, that it would be all right to answer the questions that way, being only a verbal agreement, a verbal contract.

Q.   Who told you that?      A.   Mr. Dwyer.

(Testimony of Mrs. Frances A. Justice.)

Q. Now, this question number fourteen, "Do you make this entry in good faith for the appropriation of the land, exclusively to your own use, and not for the use or benefit of any other person?" To that you answered yes. Was that answer true or untrue at the time it was made?

A. Not exactly true.

Q. Not exactly true? How did you come to answer that question in that way that you made the entry in good faith for the appropriation of the land exclusively to your own use?

A. Well, money that I would get for the land would be to my benefit.

Q. Yes; who told you that it would?

A. Mr. Dwyer told me that it would be to my benefit.

Q. This question 15, "Has any other person than yourself or has any firm, corporation or association any interest in the entry you are now making or in the land or the timber thereon? To that you answered No. Now, *q*was that answer true or untrue at the time you made it? You understand the question was, Has any firm, cor*p*ration or association any interest in the entry you are now making? In the *f*act of the entry was that statement true or false at the time it was made?

A. Well, I haven't sold it.

Q. Now, I know you hadn't sold it, but had some person an interest in it, the entry that you were making?

(Testimony of Mrs. Frances A. Justice.)

A.   I don't see how there could be an interest till I sold it.

Q.   What I want to know here is this: You already testified that you took *up* this land under the understanding that you were to get one hundred and fifty dollars for it over and above all expenses?

A.   Yes, sir.

Q.   The expenses you were put to, and you were to be supplied with money; is that right?

A.   Yes, sir.

Q.   Now, question sixteen of your cross-examination reads, Mrs. Justice, "Did you pay out of your own individual funds all the expenses in connection with making this filing and do you expect to pay for the land with your own money?"   Now, the first part of the question, "Did you pay out of your own individual funds all of the expenses in connection with the making of this filing?"   You answered "I did"; was that true or untrue at the time it was made?    A.   Untrue.

Q.   And the other part of the question, "Do you expect to pay for the lands with your own money?"   Your answer to that, "I do"; was that true or untrue?

A.   Well, in one way true and in another way untrue.   I gave a note for the money.

Q.   How did you come to make that entry?

A.   I was told to answer the questions that way.

Q.   By whom?     A.   Mr. Dwyer.

Q.   Question seventeen, "Where did you get the money with which to pay for this land, and how long

(Testimony of Mrs. Frances A. Justice.)

have you had same in your actual possession?" To that part of the question reading, "Where did you get the money with which to pay for this land?" you answered "sold fruit." How did you come to answer that question in that way?

A. I thought it wouldn't matter where I got the money. I *w*was told it didn't matter where I got the money so I *dad* it.

Q. That you sold fruit, was that true or untrue?

A. That was untrue.

Q. How did you come to make it, Mrs. Justice?

A. I thought it wouldn't make any difference where I got the money so I had it.

Q. Who told you that, if anyone?

A. Mr. Dwyer said it didn't make any difference where I got the money, so I had the money; so the answer read that way.

Q. How did you come to put the answer down there, "Sold fruit?"

Mr. TANNAHILL.—She has answered twice.

The COURT.—I suppose that counsel desires to know whether or not that was her own idea or at the suggestion of someone else.

Mr. RUICK.—That's the point.

Q. Whether or not anybody suggested that to you?

A. No, sir; that was not suggested. I answered it that way as long as it didn't matter how I got it; I answered it that way.

Q. That was not true?     A. No, sir.

(Testimony of Mrs. Frances A. Justice.)

Q. "How long have you had same in your actual possession"? to which you answered, "One month in my possession." What we want to know is this, Mrs. Just*ic,* what we want to know is whether or not you answered these questions on your own responsibility, or on the suggestion of someone else?

A. I answered that as I was told to answer them. Mr. Dwyer told me how to answer the questions.

Q. And all of these questions you *hay* have been talked over between you and Mr. Dwyer prior to your making final proof?

A. Yes, sir; with the exception that I sold fruit; he didn't tell me to say that.

Q. He didn't suggest that answer?

A. No, sir.

Q. I don't know tha I asked you—were you sworn at your final proof, your testimony when you gave your final proof?    A. Yes, sir.

Q. And to this cross-examination?

A. Yes, sir.

Q. Now, Mrs. Justice, when did you get your final receipt and certificate out of the Land Office?

A. The day I proved up.

Q. What did you do with that re*c*ipt when you got it?

A. Why, I made out a contract or deed to secure the money that I had had, and I handed over the final receipt to Mr. Dwyer.

Q. What do I understand you to say?

(Testimony of Mrs. Frances A. Justice.)

A.   When I made out the deed or contract, which-
ever it was, after I had proved up I handed the final
receipt over to Mr. Dwyer.

Q.   Did you say to secure the money?

A.   I suppose it was to secure the money.

Q.   Where was this paper executed?

A.   In Mr. Otto Kettenbach's office.

Q.   The notary?      A.   Yes, sir.

Q.   On the same day you made final proof?

A.   Yes, sir.

Q.   Who was there when you executed this paper?      A.   Fred Justice and Guy Wilson.

Q.   Was your husband there?

A.   We sent for him, he wasn't there when I
first went there.   He came afterwards.

Q.   And executed the paper with you?

A.   Yes, sir.

Q.   Did you read the paper that was executed?

A.   No, sir.

Q.   Was it read ove*e* to you?

A.   I don't remember that it was.

Q.   Do you remember what the paper looked
like?

A.   It was a large sheet of paper, *te* same as you
make a deed on.

Q.   Printed matter in it?      A.   Some.

Q.   You signed the papers there, did you?

A.   Yes.

Q.   Was Dwyer present at that time?

A.   He was in the next room.

Q.   In the same office, but in the next room?

(Testimony of Mrs. Frances A. Justice.)

A.   Yes, sir.

Q.   Now, when you signed this paper, what, if anything did you recive there?

A.   I received one hundred and fifty dollars.

Q.   When next did you see, when did you see this note you had signed in the morning of that day, earlier in the day?

A.   After I signed that paper.

Q.   Where did you get the note?

A.   I went over to the bank and got it.   The Lewiston National Bank.

Q.   How did you happen to go to the Lewiston National Bank to get it?

A.   Because it was in the bank.

Q.   How did you know it was in the bank?

A.   Mr. Dwyer had told me it was in the bank.

Q.   Did you get any written order from Dwyer to get this note?      A.   No, sir.

Q.   Who went with you to the bank?

A.   My daughter, Mrs. Wilson.

Q.   Wwere you acquainted at that bank, kin the bank?

A.   No, sir; I had never met any members of the bank to know who they were.

Q.   So you are a total stranger to them?

A.   Yes, sir.

Q.   What did you ask for?

A.   I asked for the note in the bank.

Q.   Did you have any difficulty in getting it?

A.   No, sir.

Q.   Did they ask you to be identified?

(Testimony of Mrs. Frances A. Justice.)

A. No, sir.

QQ. Was you there when Mrs. Wilson got Guy Wilson's note?     A. Yes, sir.

Q. Did they ask her to be identified?

A. No, sir.

Q. Was this the same note that you had executed earlier in the day?     A. No, sir.

Q. Now, was anyone with you and Mrs. Wilson at the time you got these papers?

A. My husband was; yes, sir.

Q. Did you make any payment, have to pay anything to get this note from the bank?

A. No, sir.

Q. Did your daughter pay anything when she got Guy(s note from the bank?     A. No, sir.

Q. Mrs. Justice, you are—were you visited by inspector O'Fallon and Mr. Goodwin some time on one occasion in relation to these matters?

A. Yes, sir.

Q. Did they have a conversation with you?

A. Yes, sir.

Q. Well, after they had that conversation with you did you see Dwyer and have a conversation with him?     A. Yes, sir.

Q. Where did that conversation occur?

A. At my home.

Q. Do I understand that Dwyer came to your home?

A. He and his wife came up to my home.

Q. What was said there about it by Dwyer, about the mater relating to the conversation there?

(Testimony of Mrs. Frances A. Justice.)

A. I told him that Mr. O'Fallon and another man had come there and asked for a statement, and he said I didn't need to give the statement to anyone in regard to their timber business.

Q. Who said that?　　A. Mr. Dwyer.

Q. Go right along and give the rest of the conversation?

A. I told him I had given the statement to them, and that they wanted my final receipt, but I didn't have it and he said I could have the final receipt again, and I afterward got it.

Q. What did Dwyer say, if anything at that time as to the*r* whereabouts of that receipt?

A. He said they were in the bank.

Q. Did he mention any bank?

A. Lewiston National Bank.

Q. State if you did afterwards get the receipt?

A. I did.

Q. Where did you get it?

A. Well, I am not positive whether I got it of Mr. Dwyer or at the bank, but I think I got it out of the bank?

Q. About how long after this first visit from Mr. O'Fallon and Mr. Goodwin?

A. It was not very many days, but I can't remember the length of time.

Q. Did you finally deliver up that receipt later?

A. Yes, sir.

Q. To whom?

A. Well, afterwards I made a deed.

Q. To whom did you deliver the receipt?

(Testimony of Mrs. Frances A. Justice.)

A. Well, I gave the receipt, when I made out the deed; when I made the deed to Mrs. Dwyer for my timber claim, I gave her the receipt then.

Q. How did you come to make the deed to Mrs. Dwyer? State the circumstances.

A. She wanted to buy my timber claim, and I sold it to her.

Q. State the circumstances. You haven't stated the circumstances.

A. Well, we went over to Lewiston, and had the deed made out.

Q. How did it come about that you went over to Lewiston? What led up to this thing?

A. She asked me to go to Lewiston with her and make out the deed.

Q. Now then, state the whole conversation, how she broached the subject to you—how did she first communicate with you about the matter?

A. Over the telephone.

Q. That is what I want to get at; I am going to ask it again.

A. She called me up over the phone and wanted to buy my timber claim and wanted I should go to Lewiston with her and make out the deed, and I did.

Q. Where did you go to make it out?

A. Well, I can't remember the man's name where I made the deed.

Q. Whom did you see over there when you came over to Lewiston?

A. I went to Lewiston with Mr. and Mrs. Dwyer with a horse and buggy.

(Testimony of Mrs. Frances A. Justice.)

Q.   They called for you?

A.   Yes; I was—I had been in Clarkston and so I came down there and waited for them, and I rode from Clarkston to Lewiston with them and went up to Mr. Dwyer's office, and from there we went to anot*hr* office and I can't remember the man's name that made out the deed; I can't remember.

Q.   You went to Mr. Dwyer's office first?

A.   Yes, sir.

Q.   *Wa* Mr. Dwyer there?        A.   Yes, sir.

Q.   What took place there—what was said there?

A.   Well, we was talking about making out the deed, and I said that if it was—I considered it was a contract—I always thought the first was a contract, that it was a contract that I made out, but Mr. Dw*ζ*er said it was a deed.

Q.   The first paper that you made out?

A.   No, sir, I thought it was a contract calling for a deed, the first one. If it was a deed it never was on record, and I gave another deed.

Q.   What did Dwyer say about it never having been put on record?

A.   He didn't say anything about it; he didn't say anything about it not being on record.

Q.   What did you say about it *o*not being on record?

A.   I said it never was on record, and so I made another deed.

Q.   How *dd* you know it never was on record? How did you learn it never was on record?

(Testimony of Mrs. Frances A. Justice.)

A. I said to Mrs. Dwyer, I don't know how I could make out a deed if it was on record, but it wasn't on record.

Q. How did you know it wasn't on record?

A. Well, they said it was not on record.

Q. That is what I want to know? He said it was not on record?

A. I can't remember whether it was Mr. or Mrs. Dwyer.

Q. It was in the presence of Mr. Dwyer?

A. Yes, it was in his presence, if it was in his office.

Q. Did they give you back the first paper?

A. No, I never had the first paper back.

Q. Did they offer to give it back to you?

A. Mrs. Dwyer said she would give it back to me but I never went after it.

Q. Did Mr. Dwyer draw up the deed or did you go to this other office to have the deed drawn up?

A. I went to the other office to have the deed drawn up and I paid the taxes on the timber claim and made out the deed.

Q. How much taxes did you pay?

A. Seventeen dollras and something.

Q. Where did you get the money to pay the taxes?

A. They took it out of the money I was to get for the claim there in making the second deed.

Q. They held out seventeen dollars?

A. Yes, sir.

(Testimony of Mrs. Frances A. Justice.)

Q. What amount did they pay you at the time you executd the deed?

A. The second deed called for nine hundred and fifty dollars, if I remember right the amount.

Q. I will ask the witness, Mrs. Justice, did I misundersand, did you or did you not state before *tha* you were getting under the new deed that you were to get seventy-five dollars for it? Was I in error, did you state how much you were to get for the claim?

A. Do you mean the first time or this time?

Q. Yes, this time?

A. No, not this time.

Q. Then that is my mistake; how much was they to pay you at this time?

A. Well, I got seventy-five dollars for making out the deed.

Cross-examination by Mr. TANNAHILL.

Q. Mrs. Justice, you said you had been away on a visit?    A. This spring?

Q. Yes.    A. Yes, sir.

Q. When did you go away?

A. I can't remember the exact date.

A. Can you tell what time I went to Asotin? If you can, I can tell you the exact date I went away.

Q. That was about the 16h of April?

A. Tht is when I went then. When I left Asotin, I went that day.

Q. How long was it after you proved up on your place before you sold out to Mrs. Dwyer?

A. I proved up on the 13th of July, two years ago, last July.

(Testimony of Mrs. Frances A. Justice.)

Q. Then when did you sell to Mrs. Dwyer?

A. Last summer.

Q. Something over a year after you proved up?

A. Yes, sir.

Q. In what way did she pay you? Mrs. Justice, in a check or cash?     A. It was a check.

Q. Do you remember of endorsing the check?

A. Yes, sir.

Q. I will ask you to look at this check and also at the endorsement on the back, and state whether or not that is the check you received from Mrs. Dwyer in payment for your timber claim?

A. Yes, sir.

(Paper marked Exhibited "B" for identification.)

Q. This check bears date March 30th, 1906? Is that the time you sold the claim to Mrs. Dwyer?

A. I can't remember the exact date; I think likely that is right.

Q. That is your best recollection, after refreshing your memory from this check?

A. Yes, sir.

Q. Who paid for the abstract, Mrs. Justice, when you sold to Mrs. Dwyer?     A. Mrs. Dwyer did.

Q. Did not you order the abstract from Jay Woodworth the abstractor?

A. I didn't pay anything for it.

Q. Did you order the abstract?

A. Not that I remember of.

Q. Were not you and Mrs. Dwyer—did not you and Mrs. Dwyer go up in the abstract offife and order the abstract?

(Testimony of Mrs. Frances A. Justice.)

A. Mrs. Dwyer and I went up in the office the day I had the deed made out, but I don't remember that I order any paper at all.

Q. Where did you find out what the taxes were?

A. Well, if I remember right, the man that made out the deed telephoned and found out; I can't remember how we found out what the taxes were; he found out what the taxes were, and took it out of the money, but I don't know; I don't remember how we found out.

Q. Is it not a fact that the price of the abstract was deducted from this $900? Mrs. Justice, the taxes and abstract were deducted from the amount you were to get from Mrs. Dwyer for the timber claim?

A. Yes, the taxes were taken out; I don't know about the other; I don't remember.

Q. The price of the abstract may have been taken out?

A. It may; I don't know; I don't remember.

Q. (Handing the check to witness—Defendant's Exhibit 2 for identification.) Look at that check and see the amount?

A. I see the amount that is here.

Q. After deducting the amount of the taxes and the abstract, if any, and the various other items including the amount of money you borrowed for the purpse of proving up, you had about seventy-five dollas left, at least that much, did you not?

A. What money I had out of this check was $75 less the taxes.

(Testimony of Mrs. Frances A. Justice.)

Q. How much were the taxes?

A. I told you I couldn't remember the exact amount of the taxes.

Q. And I believe you said you didn't remember where you went to find out what the taxes were?

A. We found out what the taxes were right where we made the deed out.

Q. How?

A. Where the deed was made out, we found out what the amount of the taxes, and it was deducted; the tax was to be taken out of the $75.

Q. Mrs. Justice, to refresh your recollection, I will ask you if it was not a trust deed you first gave for the purpose of securing the money to prove up.

A. I stated that I wasn't *psitive* whether it was a *contrct* or a deed; I can't tell the exact nature of it.

Q. You understood you had borowed this money to prove up and pay the location fee. Have you any recollection that you gave something to secure it?

A. Yes, sir.

Q. That was your understanding?

I supposed it was to insure them for the money, whatever that was a contract or a deed. and I supposed it was to the bank for them; I didn't know.

Q. You supposed it was to secure the money that you had from them?     A. Yes, sir.

Q. And then you knew a year later when you sold *you* claim to Mrs. Dwyer. you knew, then. that you had parted with your claim, and that you had

(Testimony of Mrs. Frances A. Justice.)

sold it, didn't you; when this check was made out, you knew that you had deeded your claim at that time?

A.   Yes, I knew that I had deeded it away.

Q.   To Mrs. Dwyer?      A.   Yes, sir.

Q.   Now, Mrs. Justice, you state that you had some conversation with Mr. Dwyer regarding the taking of a timber claim? You first went to Mr. Dwyer and solicited him to locate you on a timber claim, and it may have been to Mrs. Dwyer. Did you first go to Mr. or Mrs. Dwyer and ask them about getting a timber claim for you?

A.   I asked Mr. Dwyer about taking a timber claim.

Q.   How long was that before you went up into the timber to look at this claim, and what was it you said to Mr. Dwyer about taking a timber claim?

A.   It was a long time ago; first we were talking about a claim in California, but they had trouble down there about their claim, and we didn't go down there because we didn't want any trouble, but afterwards we were talking about a claim in Oregon, and then we couldn't take one there, and then we talked about going up to Pierce and taking one.

Q.   Who talked about going up to Pierce?

A.   Mr. Dwyer said he could locate me on a claim at Pierce.

Q.   How many times did you talk to Mr. Dwyer about locating you on a claim before he located you?

A.   I don't know.

Q.   A great many times, did you not?

(Testimony of Mrs. Frances A. Justice.)

A. Several times.

Q. And at that time he had no claim he could locate you on, had he?

A. No, he went down in California to look up claims, but on account of the trouble there we didn't go down.

Q. When he finally succeeded in finding a claim for you he took you up to get you a location, did he not?      A. Yes, sir.

Q. Now, I will ask you if it is not a fact that Mr. Dwyer gave you an estimate at that time, gave you his valuation of those claims, and what they would be worth?

A. I can't remember what he told me they would be worth.

Q. Don't you remember that Mr. Dwyer told you in one of these conversations when you were talking to him about it, and what you would be able to make out of the claim that the claim ought to be worth seven hundred or eight hundred dollars according to the timber that was on the claim, and that he would try and locate you on a good claim?

A. I remem*be* him saying that the claims that had been located on, that the parties couldn't get a thousand dollar for them.

Q. Couldn't get a thousand dollars for them?

A. No, some of the parties that had located couldn't sell their claims for a thousand dollars.

Q. But he told you that they ought to sell for seven or eight hundred dollars at any time, didn't he, Mrs. Justice?      A. Yes, sir.

(Testimony of Mrs. Frances A. Justice.)

Q. And he told you he would locate you on a good claim, did he not?

A. Yes, sir; he told me he would get me a good claim.

Q. And that you ought to be able to seel if for at least seven hundred hundred or eight hundred dollars, without having to hold it?

A. Well, I can't remember how much.

Q. To refresh your memory, Mrs. Justice, I will ask you if you do not remember his making that statement to you at one time when you told him that you had to have the money out of your claim soon, and that you were not able to carry it for a long time?

A. I told him I wouldn't.

Q. When you told him that you would have to have the money out of your claim because you wouldn't be able to hold it for a long time?

A. I told him I wouldn't be able to hire the money to pay for the claim and hold it for any length of time; that I was poor.

Q. Then don't you remember the conversation you had *wit* Mrs. Dwyer about it wherein you asked her if you thought you could sell your claim for as much as she sold hers for, and when she stated to you that you could not, as she got an extra good claim, and you said. "Do you think I can get my money out of it right away," or words to that effect?

A. Yes, we had several conversations about claims and about selling them, and Mr. Dwyer

(Testimony of Mrs. Frances A. Justice.)

thought I could get a chance to sell my claim right away.

Q. Do you not remember that Mrs. Dwyer told you that Mr. Dwyer was dealing with people who were investing in timber, and that he would locate you on a good claim so that you would have no trouble is disposing of it, or words to that effect?

A. He said hè didn't think I would have to hold my claim long to sell it.

Q. He thought that you could sell it right away?

A. Yes, sir.

Q. You told both Mr. Dwyer and Mrs. Dwyer that you were not able to hold the claim and pay interest on the money?     A. Yes, and I wasn't.

Q. And do you remember, Mrs. Justice, that there was something said in one of those conversations about Charlie Woulflin, who was located upon a claim up there and couldn't sell it? Do you remember that that was referred to in one of those conversations?

A. Yes, sir; I remember that Mr. Wolflin held his claim some time trying to sell it.

Q. That was referrred to in one of the conversations with Mr. and Mrs. Dwyer?     A. Yes, sir.

Q. Now, Mrs. Justice, when you went up to look over that claim, your husband went with you, did he not?     A. *Ye,* sir.

Q. Your husband and you were from a timber country before you came to Idaho?

A. Yes, sir.

(Testimony of Mrs. Frances A. Justice.)

Q. Your husband was a man pretty well posted in timber?　　A. Yes, sir.

Q. And you had some considerable knowledge of timber ,ourself, did you not, Mrs. Justice?

A. Well, a little.

Q. And Mr. Justice went to Piece City with you?

A. Yes, sir.

Q. And did he go out and look at the timber?

A. Yes, sir.

Q. And Mr. Justice was not very favorably impressed with the timber, was he, Mrs. Justice?

A. I cannot remember what he thought of the timber.

Be it remembered that *then there* the following proceedings were had:

Q. Don't you remember, Mrs. Justice, that your husband said he did not feel like taking a timber claim there because he would have to hold it too long *because* before he could sell it.

Mr. RUICK.—Objected to as immaterial and incompetent.

The COURT.—Objection sustained.

To which ruling of the Court the defendants then and there excepted, which exception was by the Court allowed.

Q. Did Mr. Justice take a claim?

A. No, sir.

Q. Mr. Justice was not ill at the time you filed, was he?

(Testimony of Mrs. Frances A. Justice.)

A.   Yes, sir; he was very ill at the time, and I expected every minute to get a telegram or telephone message that he was gone.

Q.   But he was able to come over to make out the deed?    A.   That was afterwards.

Q.   And signed it?

A.   That was afterwards.

Q.   He was able to come over to Lewiston at a subsequent time after you had filed to file, was he not?    A.   No, sir.

Q.   He could have filed when he came over to make out the deeds, could he not?

Q.   How many times was your husband over at Lewiston or Clarkston after you filed and before he died?

A.   He was over to Lewiston once after I filed.

Q.   He was up and around the house the most of the time, was he not, Mrs. Justice?

A.   No, sir; he wasn't.

Q.   When did he die?

A.   The 5th of February.

Q.   When did you make your final proof?

A.   The 13th of July, 1904.

Q.   Now, Mrs. Justice, you saw those corners to your *cl* claim?

A.   I said that Mr. Dwyer showed me some corner s stakes when we were going through the timber.

Q.   You had no reason to believe that Mr. Dwyer did not show you the correct land, did you?

A.   I didn't have any reason to think that when he told me those were corner stakes.

(Testimony of Mrs. Frances A. Justice.)

Q. You suppoed you were on the land?

A. I supposed that that was the land.

Q. Now, did Mr. Dwyer return with you?

A. No, sir.

Q. Who did you return with?

A. Guy Wilson and Mr. Justice.

Q. Who bought your tickets on your return?

A. Mr. Dwyer gave Mr. Justice the money to get the tickets to return.

Q. He got the tickets?  He paid your way back, did he?        A.  Yes, sir.

Q. Where did you leave Mr. Dwyer?

A  At the camp above Pierce.

Q. Who was there with Mr. Dwyer?

A. Mr. Hopper and Mr. O'Brien.

Be it remembered that then and there the following proceeding was had:

Q. Why did they remain there?

Mr. RUICK.—Objected to as incompetent, irrelevant and immaterial.

The *COUR.*—Objection sustained.

To which ruling of the Court the defendants then and there excepted, which exception was by the Court allowed.

Q. How long was it before they returned?

A. That is something I don't know.

Q. Now, Mrs. Justice, did you say that you made a statement oto Mr. Goodwin and Mr. O'Fallon?

A. Yes, *sr*.

Q. When was it you made that statement?

A. When they came up to my house.

(Testimony of Mrs. Frances A. Justice.)

Q. How many statements did you make?

A. I made one.

Q. Did you make a verbal statement to them before you made the one in writing?

A. No, sir; the satement I made was in writing.

Q. Do you remember anything that was in that statement—that is, generally, I am not asking you to state any particular thing? Have you a fair recollection of what was contained in that statement?

A. No, sir; I don't remember.

Q. I will ask you to state if you don't remember that there was included in that statement a statement that you had gone to Mr. Kester to borrow the money to make the proof on that claim, and that he arranged to loan it to you?

A. I don't remember.

Q. That may have been in the statement?

A. I don't remember anything in that statement.

Q. You don't remember?

A. I had never met Mr. Kester before this.

Q. Mrs. Justice, you testified in this Court in the case of the United States vs. William Dwyer in November, 1906, as a witness?    A. Yes, sir.

Q. You were sworn at that time?

A. Yes, sir.

Q. I will ask you, Mrs. Justice, now, after you made your final proof and proved upon your land, you went over to Otto Kettenbach's office and made out what you supposed was a contract to secure the money you had borrowed, did you not?

A. Yes, sir; I had supposed it was a contract.

(Testimony of Mrs. Frances A. Justice.)

Q.   And then you received $150.

A.   Yes, sir.

Q.   You received that when you made out the paper, whatever it was, a trust deed or whatever *i* was, you received that at that time?

A.   Yes, sir.

Q.   Did you understand that that contract was to secure the entire amount you were getting at that time, did you not?

A.   Yes, it was to secure all the money that I had had up to—

Q.   All the money you had had?   A.   Yes.

Q.   Your son Fred was th*er* at the time you made your proof and the contract, these papers were made, the trust deed or w*ah*tever it was to secure this money?   A.   He was in the building.

Q.   Now, did not Fred Justice get your papers at the land office, the final receipt?

A.   I got the final receipt when I proved up.

Q.   Did not Fre*e*d Justice stay there and get your final receipt from the land office a little after you had proved up?   A.   No, sir.

Q.   At that time you got it yourself, did you?

A.   Yes, sir.

Q.   Now, Fred Justice was there at the time you were standing in line, was he not?

A.   Yes, sir.

Q.   He looked after getting your papers made out, did he not?   He got-Mr. I. N. Smith to make out the papers?

(Testimony of Mrs. Frances A. Justice.)

A.  I went to the office myself and got the papers made out?

Q.  Do you know whether or not Fred Justice paid I. N. Smith for it?

A.  I don't know what Fred Justice did.

Q.  Fred Justice had charge of the line and gave out the numbers?

A.  He gave the numbers in the line.

Q.  He had the names in a book?

A.  Yes, he had a book; he kept the names in a book.

Q.  And you and Fred and Guy all went into-gether and got your filing papers, did you not?

A.  Yes, sir.

Q.  And Fred Justice was there at the time you made—at the time you got the declaratory statement from I. N. Smith, was he not?     A.  Yes, sir.

Q.  Now, your husband was present at the time you had these various conversations with Mr. Dwyer, or one of these conversations with Mr. Dwyer, where you told him you would have to turn the claim pretty soon, that you wouldn't be able to hold it and pay the interest?

A.  I don't remember whether he was there or not.

Q.  You understood you were to pay Mr. Dwyer a location fee?     A.  Yes, sir.

Q.  Who was it took the testimony when you made your final proof?

The COURT.—In the *lan* office?

Mr. TANNAHILL.—Yes, your Honor, in the land office.

(Testimony of Mrs. Frances A. Justice.)

A. Mr. J. B. West.

Q. He wrote it down, did he? A. Yes, sir.

Q. Who else was present?

A. Mr. Dwyer and Mr. Bliss.

Q. They were there, were they?

A. Yes, sir.

Q. Mr. Dwyer made some suggestions to you about the way you were to answer these questions in making the final proof? A. Yes, sir.

Q. And he told you there was no contract that you had made *tht* was in conflict with these questions, did he, when he made these suggestions?

A. He told me a verbal contract had nothing to do with it. The contract would be in writing and that a verbal contract had nothing to do with it.

Q. Now, Mrs. Justice, he also told you that you had made no contract that *wa* in conflict with those statements, did he not?

A. Well, the verbal contract he said had nothing to do with it.

Q. That was his contention? A. Yes, sir.

Q. Now, Mrs. Justice, how did you receive notice of the time you were to make your final proof?

A. Mr. Dwyer told me.

Q. How did he notify you?

A. I can't remember whether he came to my house, or whether he came or whether I was downtown or where I saw him, but he let me know at any rate when I was to come.

Q. He either told you at the house or downtown, did he not?

(Testimony of Mrs. Frances A. Justice.)

A. I don't remember where or what the circumstances was, but he let me know where to come.

Q. Did he write to you?

A. I told you I couldn't remember how he let me know.

Be it remembered that then and there the following proceeding was had:

Q. Do you remember testifying in the former trial of the United States vs. William Dwyer that you received the notice of the time through the mail?

Mr. RUICK.—We object.

The COURT.—The objection sustained.

To which ruling of the Court the defendants then and there excepted, which exception was allowed.

Be it remembered that then and there the following proceeding was had:

Q. I will ask you, Mrs. Justice, if you didn't make the following answer to the following question when you were testifying in the case of the United States vs. William Dwyer in this Court in November, 1906?

Mr. RUICK.—Objectd to for two reasons; One is we would like to have counsel read from the other record so that we can follow him, and the other is that the Court ruled expressly that to read from this record and ask the witness if sher remembered it was not competent, and was not the proper way by which to impeach the witness.

The COURT.—That was after the witness has stated she did not remember. This witness has not stated that and if she remembers what she testified to, that is all right.

(Testimony of Mrs. Frances A. Justice.)

Mr. RUICK.—He would have to ask different questions. He might ask these questions and have her answer. I don't remember clear through the entire record.

The COURT.—I wouldn't permit that.

To which ruling of the Court the defendants then and there excepted, which exception was allowed by the Court.

Q. Mrs. Justice, how did you receive notice of the time on which you would be required to make your final proof, which you answered, "I received notice through the mail." Do you remember so testifying?

A. No, I don't remember.

Be it remembered that then and there the following proceeding was had:

Mr. TANNAHILL.—I will ask to read into the record that *prtion* of page 9 of the direct examination of Mrs. Justice—

The COURT.—For what *purpse*?

Mr. TANNAHILL.—For the purpose of showing she so testified in the other case.

The COURT.—For the purpose of impeachment?

Mr. TANNAHILL.—She now says that Dwyer notified her personally either at Clarkston or at her home, while she testified before it was by mail.

The COURT.—I understood her to say that she didn't know how he notified her.

Mr. TANNAHILL.—No, *se* says here it was—

The COURT.—The Court will exclude the testimony.

(Testimony of Mrs. Frances A. Justice.)

Mr. TANNAHILL.—The Court will consider that as an offer.

The COURT.—Yes.

To which ruling of the Court the defendants then and there excepted, which exception was by the Court allowed.

Q. Mrs. Justice, you stated that Mr. Dwyer arranged for your witnesses because you didn't know them. Is that right, that you were not acquainted with the witnesses?

Mr. RUICK.—That was not *hat* she stated at all.

Q. Did Mr. Dwyer arrange for the witnesses?

A. I can't remember just how it was; he was my witness and Mr. Bliss, but I can't remember just how we arranged it with the witnesses.

Q. Then you don't know whether Dwyer arranged for your witnesses or whetheer your son Fred Justice arranged for them, do you?

A. I can't remember who it was arranged for my wintesses.

Q. Mrs. Justie, you went east about the middle of April, 1907, did you not?

A. Yes, sometime about that time.

Q. You had been at Boise before you went away?

A. Yes, sir.

Q. And Mr. Ruick told you to go east and go as far as you wanted to, and he would send for you and pay your way back, did he not?

A. I didn't say anything to Mr. Ruick about my going away.

(Testimony of Mrs. Frances A. Justice.)

Q. Did you say anything to anybody else about going east?    A. Yes, sir.

Q. Who?

A. The United States Marshal; I told him—

Q. I will ask you to state whether or not the marshal or anyone else told you that your mileage east— that you would get your mileage on the way back?

A. No, they did not.

Q. You have been promised that you would not be prosecutè if you testified in th*si* case, have you not, Mrs. Justice?    A. I have not.

Q. There was nothing said to you about it?

A. No, sir.

Q. You fe*l*l, though, that you will not be prosecuted?

A. I don't know any reason why I should be.

Q. Do you know Mrs. and Mr. Hopper?

A. I do.

Q. I will ask you, Mrs. Justice, if you did not ask Mr. Dwyer to get Mrs. and Mr. Hopper a timber claim also?    A. I cannot remember that I did.

Q. I will ask you, Mrs. Justice, if you did not state to Mrs. Dwyer in Clarkston about the month of July, 1903, yourself and Mrs. Dwyer and Mrs. Hopper and none others being present, "Is it not p*s*sible for Mr. Dwyer to get two more claims for Mrs. and Mr. Hopper? I have made an arrangement for the money for Mr. Hopper to prove up on my claim as soon as I can get a claim," or words in substance and to that effect, this being before you had gone up to the mountains to look at the land?

(Testimony of Mrs. Frances A. Justice.)

A. I can't remember the exact convesation.

Q. Did you have any scuh conversation as that in substance?

A. I remember of going with Mrs. Hopper down to Mr. Dwyers. She wanted to get a timber claim and Mr. Hopper wanted to get one, and I went with her to see if she could get one, but I don't remember the exact conversation and I would not try to repeat it by saying yes or not to any conversation, because I don't remember.

Q. Had you had a talk with Hoppers in regard to getting money to make proof on a timber claim, had you not?

A. Yes, when they first came here.

Q. I will ask you, Mrs. Justice, if you did not state to Mrs. Dwyer in Clarkston, Asotin County, Washington, immediately after you had field your declaratory statement yourself and Mrs. Dwyer, and none other being present, "I have made an arrangement to get the money to prove up on my claim," and didn't Mrs. Dwyer then say, "Is that so?" to which you replied, "I went to the bank and saw Mr. Kester at the window and asked him if I could borrow the money of him to prove up on my timber claim, and he said, "Yes, if the estimate is satisfactory to them, I think they can let me have it. And I asked Mr. Kester whose estimate he would take, and if he would be satisfied with Mr. Dwyer's estimate, and he said yes, he would take Mr. Dwyer's estimate, and I saw Mr. Dwyer and he said he would

(Testimony of Mrs. Frances A. Justice.)
give Mr. Kester the estimate so I could get my money,
or words in substance and to that effect?

A.   I never met Mr. Kester and I didn't know
him.   What I said then before I filed—

Mr. RUICK.—Answer the question whether that
was stated to her in substance?      A.   No, sir.

Q.   I believe you stated, Mrs. Justice, that you
did have a conversation with Mrs. Dwyer wherein
you asked her if she thought you could sell your
claim for as much as Mrs. Dwyer's sold for, or words
to that effect?

A.   We talked about the claim, if it was *ps*sible
to get one, if I could sell it for as much, but I don't
remember the exact conversation.

Q.   I will ask you if you did not in the spring of
1904 in Clarkston, Asotin County, W*z*shington,
yourself and Mrs. Dwyer being present, and none
others, state to Mrs. Dwyer: "Mrs. Dwyer, can I
sell my claim for as much as you sold yours for," to
wh*c*h Mrs. Dwyer replied, "No, you cannot do
that, as my claim was an extra good claim and you
cannot get that kind of a claim now, to which you
replied: "Well, do you think I could sell it for $700
or $800," to which Mrs. Dwyer replied, "No doubt
you could sell it for that much," or words in substance
and to that effect?

A.   We had some such conversation, but I can't
tell exactly what it was.

Q.   It might have been that kind of a conver*s*tion?

A.   It might have been.   I am not positive.

(Testimony of Mrs. Frances A. Justice.)

Q. I believe, Mrs. Justice, you said you went to Lewiston with Mrs. Dwyer when you sold your claim to her and when the deed was made?

A. I went with Mr. and Mrs. Dwyer to Lewiston.

Q. Mr. Kester was in the bank at the time, was he not? A. Yes, sir.

Q. You and Mrs. Dwyer went to the window and arranged it, and you passed Mrs. Dwyer's check, this check, in evidence through to Mr. Ketser?

A. Yes, sir.

Q. *n*And he figured out the amount of money you owed, and taxes, and the abstract, and deducted it from the amount of this check, and paid to you the balance? It was something like $75 or $75 less the amount of the taxes as you testified; is that right?

A. He took out the amount that is on that check, and I took out what was coming to me.

Q. You took out what was coing to you?

A. Yes, sir.

Q. You saw Mrs. Dwyer in Clarkston about a week before you made the deed, did you not? You began talking about her buying about a week before you made the deed, did you not?

A. I can't remember seeing her in Clarkston.

Q. Do you remember what was said between you and Mrs. Dwyer about the buying of your claim?

A. No, sir, I can't remember to repeat the conversation exact. She wanted to buy it and I sold it to her, but I can't repeate the conversation.

Q. To refresh your memory, I will ask you this question: Did you not see Mrs. Dwyer in Clarkston,

(Testimony of Mrs. Frances A. Justice.)

Asotin County, Washing*to,* about a week before you made her the deed to your claim, and did not Mrs. Dwyer state to you at that time and place, yourself and Mrs. Dwyer and none others being present, "Mrs Justice, do you want to sell your claim?" to which you rep*led,* "Yes," and did not Mrs. Dwyer say, "Land is going to be a better price up there now, and I can give you $900 for it if you want to sell it," and you replied, "I'll be glad to sell it, as I am paying interest on the money I got to prove up with, and I want to get it all settled up now," or words in substance and to that effect?

A.   No, sir; I don't remember any such conversation.

Q.   Did you go to the Lewiston National Bank and get that receipt when Mr. O'Fallon asked you about it?

A.   I said I couldn't remember for sure whether I got it out of the bank or not.

Q.   I will ask you, Mrs. Justice, if you didn't telephone Mrs. Dwyer immediately after Mr. Goodwin and Mr. O'Fallon were there?

A.   No, sir; I didn't; not that I remember of.

Q.   Don't you remember after Mr. Goodwin and Mr. O'Fallon left your place that you called Mrs. Dwyer up over the telephone, that the Government officers had been there and that you wanted to see her?

A.   I don't remember any such thing.

Q.   You may have done that?

A.   I don't remember.

(Testimony of Mrs. Frances A. Justice.)

Q. Will you say you did not do that?

A. I can't remember.

(Continuing:) I can't recollect any such thing at all. Mr. and Mrs. Dwyer drove up there afterwards and I told them, but I don't remember ever calling her over the telephone to tell her.

Q. And don't you remember that Mrs. Dwyer replied to you, "Can't you come down?" or words to that effect?

A. I don't remember any such statement.

Q. And you told her I am too busy?

A. No, sir; I don't remember.

Q. I will ask you this question, Mrs. Justice, did you not telephone Mrs. Dwyer, just after Mr. Goodwin and Mr. O'Fallon went away the first time, and didn't you state to Mrs. Dwyer in substance the Government officers have been here, and I want to see you, to which Mrs. Dwyer replied, "Can't you come down," to which you replied, "No, I am too busy," or words in substance and to that effect?

A. I don't remember any such thing at all.

Q. Did not you tell Mr. and Mrs. Dwyer when you went down to see them, after Mr. Goodwin and O'Fallon were there, that the Government officers had been there, and did not Mrs. Dwyer say, "What did they say to you?" to which you replied, I don't hardly know what they did say, they said so much they nearly scared me to death, and I was feeling so badly over the death of my son; to which she replied, "What did you say to them?" to which you replied,

(Testimony of Mrs. Frances A. Justice.)

"I said the same as I told them in the Land Office," or words in substance and to that effect?

A. I can't remember what I told Mr. O'Fallon when he was there. I can't remember what I told him. I was scared most to death, and I can't remember what I told him, and I can't remember what I told Mrs. Dwyer that I told him either.

Q. You may have made that statement to Mrs. Dwyer?

A. I don't remember of saying what I told him.

Q. Did you not also state to Mrs. Dwyer that he told me that he knew I was telling a lie, and that they had talked to the others, Mrs. Miller and Mrs. Stevens, and knew how I got the money and all the particulars?

The COURT.—When was this?

Mr. TANNAHILL.—That was at the same time. My object in dividing the conversation was to make it easier.

The COURT.—The telephone conversation?

Mr. TANNAHILL.—No, when Mrs. Dwyer went up to her place after Mr. O'Fallon and Goodwin were there. (Continuing question.) Do you remember making that statement?

A. Mr. O'Fallon said I was evading the truth when I didn't answer his question; he said he understood that part of it. I remember that.

Q. Had they told you that they had the statement of Mrs. Miller and Mrs. Stevens against you?

A. I don't remember.

Q. Did you tell Mrs. Dwyer that?

(Testimony of Mrs. Frances A. Justice.)

A.  I don't remember what I told her, but there were no names; I don't remember that I told her of any names that they mentioned at all.

Q.  I will ask you this question: Did you not at the same time and place, state to Mrs. Dwyer that "They told me that they knew that I was telling a lie, and that they had talked to the others, Mrs. Miller and Mrs. Stevens, that they, Goodwin and O'Fallon, had talked to the others, and that they knew I got the money and all the particulars, and I had as well come out and tell them and save trouble for myself, or words in substance and to that effect?

A.  They said I was evading the truth, and it would be better for myself to make a statement.

Q.  And didn't they say you had better do that and save yourself trouble?

A.  I can't remember.

Q.  Did you not, at your home, at the time when Mr. and Mrs. Dwyer were there, just after the Government officers were there, as you term them, or Mr. Goodwin and Mr. O'Fallon, state to Mrs. Dwyer, "They told me they knew I was telling a lie and that they had talked to the others, Mrs. Miller and Mrs. Stevens, and knew where I got the money, and all the particulars, and that I had as well tell the truth and save myself trouble, and I asked, "If I am not telling the truth, what do you want me to say?" So they read a statement and I signed it, to which Mrs. Dwyer replied "A statement? What kind of a statement?" And you said, "They told me the same as several others have made, that got

(Testimony of Mrs. Frances A. Justice.)

the money from Kester and many other things," to which Mrs. Dwyer replied to you "Did you not read it over?" To which you replied, "No, I have worried over that statement ever since I made it; I am afraid I am going to have trouble; I am going to see an attorney, and see if they had a right to come over and compel me as they did to sign a statement," or words in substance and to that effect?

Be it remembered that then and there the following proceeding was had:

WITNESS.—Please, did you say, Judge, that I am to answer it? I don't know how to answer it?

The COURT.—Just on what condition do you conceive this to be proper or material?

The WITNESS.—I have already—

The COURT.—Just a moment, Mrs. Justice. She stated here several times that she didn't remember what was in the statement. I know she has stated repeatedly that she didn't know what was in the statement. The Court cannot see the materiality of this matter. If counsel will point out anything in the statement which is inconsistent with, or tends to contradict any statement of the witness as now made on the stand at this trial, then the Court might take a different view of it. The objection  is  sustained. You may pass on to the next question.

To which ruling of the Court the defendants then and there excepted, which exception was allowed by the Court.

Q.  *Dd* you not, at your home in Clarkston, Washington, at the time that Mr. and Mrs. Dwyer went

(Testimony of Mrs. Frances A. Justice.)

ot see you, after Mr. Goodwin and O'Fallon were
there, or the Government officers, as you call them,
state to Mrs. Dwyer, "The officers asked me if I had
made a prior agreement, and I told them positively
that I had not made a prior agreement to sell the
land," or words in substance and to that effect?

A.   I can't remember of making the statement at
all.

Q.   You may have made that statement?

A.   I can't remember of making such a statement.

Mr. TANNAHILL.—I think under the rule
adopted where the witness has stated she does not
remember, that entitled us to prove it.

The COURT.—Yes, that is as far as the witness
can go.

Be it remembered that then and there the follow-
iny proceeding was had:

Q.   Did you at the home of Mrs. Dwyer, in Clarkston, Asotin County, Washington, late in the fall of
1905, yourself and Mrs. Dwyer and none others being present, state, "I told the officers, meaning Mr.
O'Fallon and Goodwin, distinctly that I had no prior
agreement; I don't know what they wrote down, but
I did tell them distinctly I had no prior agreement,"
or words in substance and to that effect?

Mr. RUICK.—We think this has gone to the point
where we have the right to object.

The COURT.—I don't think the Court cares to
hear anything further on the matter, and I cannot see
how this would be material; I will sustain the objec-

(Testimony of Mrs. Frances A. Justice.)

tion.    To which ruling the defendants then and there excepted, which exception was allowed by the Court.

Be it remebered that then and there the following proceeding was had:

Q.    Did you not, at the same time and place, in February, 1905, I think I said in the fall of 1904 in the other question, and it should be the fall of 1905, yourself and Mrs. Dwyer being present, state to Mrs. Dwyer, "I don't know what those Government officers put down, but one thing I do know, I never did make any prior agreement, and told them so," or words in substance and to that effect?

Mr. RUICK.—Same objection.

The COURT.—Same ruling.

To which ruling of the Court the defendants then and there excepted, which exception was by the Court allowed.

(Court adjourns until 10 o'clock A. M. May 23, 1907.)

May 23d, 1907, *1* o'clock A. M.

Trial resumed.    Mrs. FRANCES A. JUSTICE on the stand.

(By Mr. RUICK.)

Be it remembered the following proceeding was had:

Q.    Mrs. Justice, you have—you were questioned on yesterday by counsel for the defendants—or rather you were asked as to whether or not you had had certain conversations in relation—or with other parties than Mr. Dwyer in relation to getting the

(Testimony of Mrs. Frances A. Justice.)

money with which to file on and prove up on the claim, in which the names of the Hoppers were introduced and a conversation with Mr. Dwyer himself other than the one you had already tesitfied to besides the one you had already testified to.. Now, will you kindly go back and give the history of your relation, or in relation to your filing on the timber claim, and bringing it up to the time that you had this agreement or understanding as you have testified; go back to the beginning.

Mr. FORNEY.—We object to the question as a useless repetition and because it may necessitate another cross-examination taking her over the entire field again.

Mr. RUICK.—This was not gone over in chief, but it has been gone over indirectly in the questions that have been propounded to Mrs. Justice.

The COURT.—You mean the history up to the time she made her filing, the history and convesations up to that time?

Mr. RUICK.—Yes, sir.

The COURT.—She may do so, not later than the time of the first filing.

To which ruling of the Court the defendants excepted, which exception was allowed by the Court, and the witness answered as follows:

A. I shall start at that time we first talked?

Q. Yes, start at the beginning.

A. It was some time ago we talked about talking claims. At first we were going to California—

(Testimony of Mrs. Frances A. Justice.)

Q. I beg your pardon. You say "Some time ago." A. Long before I filed on it.

Q. How long after you come to the country, in order to fix the date?

A. I can't tell just how many years.

Q. This was before you had this arrangement with Mr. Dwyer that you testified to?

A. Yes, sir.

Q. State if that occurred prior—state everything that occurred prior to that time.

Mr. MOORE.—Who do you mean by "we"? Tell us who you mean by "we."

A. I was mistaken in that. Mr. Justice and myself were wanting to take claims.

The COURT.—Go ahead.

A. We talked about talking claims and I tried to get the money of my brotaher in the east to take a claim, and he didn't care to put money into it and then afterward I went east, and when I was east I saw my brother again about getting money, and he didn't care then about putting money into a claim, and I was visiting at the Hoppers in Milwaukee. And we were speaking about people taking claims out here, and they thought it would be nice to take a claim, and after I came back the Hoppers stopped here at my house. They was to my house about two months, I don't know the exact time they were there, and we talked about claims then. At that time we was talking about going to California to take claims, and I asked the Hoppers about the money to get a

(Testimony of Mrs. Frances A. Justice.)

claim and they thought when they first came that they would furnish the money for Mr. Justice and myself and themselves to take claims, and then we didn't go to California, and we talked some of going to Oregon, but we didn't go down there, and then Mr. Hopper's people stayed at Mr. Dwyers for some time before we took claims, and before we could take claims, and they thought then they didn't have the money to spare for us and temselves too.

Q. Who thought that?

A. Hoppers; they concluded not to let us have the money to take the claims, and then I saw Mr. Dwyer and told him that I couldn't get the money to get a claim, and I asked him if he could get the money for me, and he said he could, and on this one condition—that he could get the money—he furnished all the money and then gave me $150 for the claim. That is all I can tell you about it.

Q. That he could get the money on that condition? A. Yes, sir.

Q. You have already testified that on the date that you made final proof and executed this paper in the office of Otto Kettenbach, that you received from Dwyer $150. A. Yes, sir.

Be it remembered that then and there the following proceeding was had:

Q. I want to ask you if there was any more money coming to you after you received that $150?

Mr. FORNEY.—Objected to as a repetition, having been gone into before, and calling for the conclusion of the witness.

(Testimony of Mrs. Frances A. Justice.)

Mr. RUICK.—This is simply in explanation of this question.

The COURT.—Objection overruled.

To which ruling of the Court the defendants then and there excepted, which exception was by the Court allowed and the witness answered:

A.  No, sir.

Be it remembered that then and there the following proceeding was had:

Q.  Did you expect to receive anything more for those lands?

Mr. FORNEY.—Objected to on the ground that it is irrelevant and immaterial; she might have thought she ought to have more for the lands, that she expected to receive any more would not change the condition of the parties in the least.

The COURT.—Objection verruled.

To which ruling of the Court the defendants then and there execpted, which exception was allowed by the Court.

And the witness answered:

A.  I said, no, sir.

Be it rememberd that then and there the following proceeding was had:

Q.  Did you have at that time any understanding that you were to receive any more for those lands?

Mr. FORNEY.—Objected to as calling for a conelusion.

Mr. RUICK.—As part of the res gestae.

The COURT.—The Court understands the matter; objection overruled.

(Testimony of Mrs. Frances A. Justice.)

To which ruling of the Court the defendant then and there excepted, which exception was allowed by the Court, and the witness answered:

A.   No, sir.

Be it rememberd that then and there the following proceeding was had.

Q.   Now, Mrs. Justice, I want you to begin and relate any conversations you had with Mrs. Dwyer or Mr. Dwyer, or both of them, leading up to your getting $75 more out of this claim, less the amount of taxes.

Mr. FORNEY.—Objected to as irrelevant and immaterial, and repetition of the testimony already given by the witness on both direct and cross examination.

Mr. RUICK.—It ocovers only the questions propounded.

The COURT.—Objection is overruled; he asks her to relate the conversation.

To which ruling of the Court the defendants then and there excepted, which exception was allowed by the Court and the witness answered:

A.   Mrs. Dwyer said that she had concluded to buy my claim and pay me more than I had had; that she would give me $75 more, and I make out a deed to her, $75 less the taxes.

Be it remembered that then and there the following proceeding was had:

Q.   What explanation, if any, did Mrs. Dwyer give for getting the second deed?   What did she say with reference to that, if anything?

(Testimony of Mrs. Frances A. Justice.)

Mr. FORNEY.—Same objection, and also that it is not binding on the defendants Kettenbach or Kester.

The COURT.—Objection overruled.

To which ruling of the Court the defendant then and there excepted, which exception was by the Court allowed and the witness answered:

A. She said she had concluded to buy my claim and givé me that much more.

Q. You had sold and given one deed, had you not, or contract for a deed?

A. A contract or a deed.

Q. What explanation, if any, did she give for making out the second deed, or for making out this second paper?

A. Well, I can't remember any explanation.

Q. Now, then, we will get to the check; tell what you know about that check. Just relate the whole thing, Mrs. Justice; just take your time to it and do some thinking and answer the questions; the jury want to know the whole of it; just tell them in your own way what occurred.

A. I went with Mrs. Dwyer to make out the deeed, and when they was making out the deed they asked how much it would call for, and Mrs. Dwyer told them the amount it called for, and the deed was made out, and then she gave me the check on the bank, and I went to the bank and had it cashed, and took out what was coming to me, that $75 less the taxes.

(Testimony of Mrs. Frances A. Justice.)

Q. Who went to the bank with you?

A. Mrs. Dwyer.

Q. What conversation, if any, was had about the amount of the check and what, if anything, did Mrs. Dwyer say about the check?

A. I don't remember her saying anything about the check only the amount I was to have out of it.

Q. Who passed the money out to you?

A. If I remember right, I got the check cashed by Mr. Kester.

Q. And this money was handed out to you?

A. Yes, sir.

Q. Did you count it?

A. I just took out what was coming to me; I didn't count the money..

Q. You didn't count the rest?

A. No, sir.

Q. Was Mrs. Dwyer standing right there?

A. Yes, sir.

Q. Who took the balance of the money?

A. Mrs. Dwyer had it placed to her credit, the balance of it.

Q. Do you know whether she did or not?

A. I heard her say place that money to her credit.

Q. What became of the money? That's what I want to know.

A. She gave it back to the bank, put it back in the bank.

Q. Did Mrs. Dwyer handle the money herself?

(Testimony of Mrs. Frances A. Justice.)

A.  The money was lying on the desk, and she pushed the money back and said, "Place that to her credit"; that is all I know about it.

Q.  The record shows that final proof and payment for the claim was made on the 13th day of July, 1904; now, I understood and the testimony shows that this interview with Mr. Goodwin and O'Fallon occurred in the fall of that same year; now, Mrs. Justice, is that your recollection, or what is your recollection?

A.  Well, it was between the time I made the final proof and the fall some time; I don't know when they came.

Q.  That is your recollection?    A.  Yes, sir.

Q.  Then this check transaction took place when— last July sometime?

A.  Last spring sometime.

Be it remembered that then and there the following proceedings were had:

The COURT.—Was the check put in evidence, Mr. Tannahill?

Mr. TANNAHILL.—No, but it was dated March 30t, 1906.

Mr. RUICK.—That was in March, 1906?

The WITNESS.—Last spring.

The COURT.—Very well.

Mr. FORNEY.—Our same objection, if the Court please, goes to this, and in addition I offer an objection to any part of the entire transaction which postdates the culmination of the conspiracy.

(Testimony of Mrs. Frances A. Justice.)

Mr. RUICK.—This is in regard to a fact that was brought out by the defense.

The COURT.—Objection overruled.

To which ruling of the Court the defendants then and there excepted, which exception was allowed by the Court.

Mr. RUICK.—At this time I will read the testimony of William Dwyer, a witness on behalf of this claimant, Mrs. Francis A. Justice, in suport of hei application to purchase under the stone and timber act land described in the indictment in this case. I now read Plaintiff's exhi*bt* 13· "The testimony of two witnesses in this form taken separately required in each case. Testimony of witness under Acts of June 3d, 1878, and August 4th, 1892. William Dwyer being called as a witness in sup*prt* of the application of Francis A. Justice to purchase the lots three, four and the east half of the southwest fourth of section nineteen, township thirty-eight north of range 6, E. B. M., testifies as follows:

"Q. 1. What is your age, postoffice address and where do you reside.

"Ans*er*: Age 45; Clarkston, Wash, *Clarkston Wash.*

"Qu*e*tion two: Are you acquainted with the land above described b.ı personal inspection of each of the smallest legal subdivisions.

"A. Yes.

"Question 3: When and in what manner was such inspection made?

(Testimony of Mrs. Frances A. Justice.)

"An*s*er:  The last time June 30th, 1904; went on foot.

"Question 4:  Is it occupied or are there any improvements on it not made for ditch or canal purposes, or which were not made or do not belong to the said applicant?     "Answer:  No; no.

"Question 5:  Is it fit for cultivation?

"An*s*er:  No.

"Question 6:  What causes render it unfit for cultivation?

"Answer:  Rough and mountainous, and covered with timber; "the climatic conditions render it unfit for cultivation.

"Question 7:  Are there any salines or indications of deposits of gold, silver, cinnabar, copper or coal on this land?  If so, state what they are, and whether the springs or mineral deposits are valuable.

"Answer:  No.

"Question 8:  Is the land more valuable for mineral or other purposes than for the timber or stone thereon, or is it chiefly valuable for timber or stone?

"Answer:  No, chiefly val*a*uble for the timber.

"Question 9:  From what fact do you conc*u*de that the land is chiefly valuable for timber?

"Answer:  Rough character of the land; heavy growth of timber, seasons too short.

"Question*s* 10:  Do you know whether the applicant had directly or indirectly made any agreement or contract in any way or manner whatever with any person whomsoever by which the title he may acquire from the Government of the United

(Testimony of Mrs. Frances A. Justice.)
States may inure in whole or in part to the benefit
of any person except herself?

"Answer: No.

"Question 11: Are you in any way interested in
this application, or in the lands above described, or
the timber or stone salines, mines, or other improvements of any description whatever thereon?

"Answer: No; no.

"(Signature)   WILLIAM DWYER."

"I hereby certify that each question and answer
in the foregoing testimony was read to the witness
before he signed his name thereto, and that the same
was subscribed and sworn to before me this 13th day
of July, 1904.

"J. B. WEST, Register."

Mr. RUICK.—And the note at the bottom which
I will now read, and I may not have occasion to read
again:

"Note.—The officer before whom the testimony
is taken shall call the attention of the witness to the
following section of the Revised Statute, and state
to him that it is the purpose of the Government, if
it be ascertained that he testifies falsely to prosecute
him to the full extent of the law.

"TITLE LXX—CRIMES—Chap. IV."

"Section 5392—Every person who, having taken
an oath before a competent tribunal, officer or person, in any case in which a law of the United States
authorizes an oath to be administered that he will
testify, declare, depose or certify truly, or that any
written testimony, declaration, deposition or certifi-

(Testimony of Mrs. Frances A. Justice.)

cate by him subscribed is true, willfully and contrary to such oath, states and subscribes any material matter which he does not believe to be true, is guilty of perjury, and shall be punished by fine of not more than two thousand dollars, and by imprisonment at hard labor not more than five years, and shall moreover thereafter be incapable of giving testimony in any court of the United States until such time as the judgment against him is reversed (Sec. 1750).

This endorsed:

"Timber Lands—Acts of June 3rd, 1878 and August 4th, 1892. Testimony of witness.

Recross-examination by Mr. TANNAHILL.

Q. Who have you talked with about your evidence since you were on the stand yesterday evening?

A. I haven't talked about my evidence.

Q. You haven't talked with anyone since you were on the stand yesterday evening about your evidence?

A. About the evidene here?

Q. Yes.　　A. No, sir.

Q. Did you not talk to Mr. Ruick at all?

A. I talked to Mr. Ruick a few minutes this morning.

Q. You taled to Mr. Ruick a few minutes this morning before you went on the stand?

A. Ye, sir.

Q. You talked with him about these questions he asked you, some of them?

(Testimony of Mrs. Frances A. Justice.)

A.   What do you mean?

Q.   These questions that Mr. Ruick asked you here this morning, were not some of these questions referred to?     A.   They might have been.

Q.   Was that gentleman over there with his hair parted in the middle, who nodded to you a while ago, with Mr. Ruick?

A.   I haven't seen that gentleman since I came from Canada.

Q.   You saw him nod to you a while ago?

A.   Yes, and that's all right.

Q.   Didn't you talk to this gentleman here the other day?

Q.   That man? (Indicating.) Didn't you talk to him right here, when you were sitting right here the other day?     A.   No, sir.

Q.   You didn't speak to him?     A.   No, sir.

Q.   Didn't he talk to you?     A.   No, sir.

Q.   Mrs. Justice, is it not a fact that you had a conversation with A. S. Burnett in Clarkston, Washington, in the month of March, 1906, in which you talked of this contemplated sale of your timber claim to Mrs. Dwyer,

A.   Not that I remember of.

Q.   You know Mr. Burnett, don't you?

A.   Yes, sir.

Q.   I will ask you if you don't remember having a conversation with Mr. Burnett about a sale of the timber claim to Mrs. Dwyer in March, 1906, before you made the sale and before you signed the deed?

(Testimony of Mrs. Frances A. Justice.)

A.  I don't remember any such conversation with Mr. Burnett.

Q.  I will ask you if in Clarkston, Washington, in the month of March, 1906, you did not state to A. S. Burnett yours*l*ef and Mr. Bur*n*tt being present, "I am going to sell my timber claim to Mrs. Dwyer for $1000, and when I get the money I am going back east on a trip, or on a visit," or words in substance and to that effect?

A.  No, sir; I never said any such thing.

Q.  Nothing of the kind?      A.  No, sir.

Q.  You had no such conversation?

A.  No, sir.

Redirect Examination by Mr. RUICK.

Q.  I will ask a preliminary question, it it is not already in the record:

Q.  Mrs. Justice, you were a witness here in this court at the last term?      A.  Yes, sir.

Q.  In the month of November last upon the ti*r*al of William Dwyer charged with the subornation of perjury?      A.  I was.

Q.  Did you testify at the time of that trial as a witness on behalf of the government?

A.  I did.

Mr. RUICK.—Now, we offer in evidence certain of the testimon\ of this witness, Mrs. Francis A. Justice, given at the time of the trial referred to and pertaining to the same identical transaction, and consultation to which her attention has been called upon the witness-stand this morning: We

(Testimony of Mrs. Frances A. Justice.)

offer this in evidence for the purpose of corroborating her statement, *ad* in sup*pr*t of her testimony given here upon this trial this morning, and without reading it in the presence of the jury until after your Honor shall have ruled, and if your Honor shall rule that it is competent, we will then offer it in evidence. I would say to counsel, the p*r*tion we shall offer in evidence begins on page marked "Justice x 38," beginning *q*t line 29, and going down to and including line 25 on the next page marked "Justice x-39."

Mr. TANNAHILL.—Objected to on the ground that it is incompetent, irrelevant and immaterial. (After argument at length.)

The COURT.—The Court will sustain the objection; I do not think this testimon\ is proper.

(Witness excused.)

F.. M. GOODWIN, a witness recalled in behalf of the Government, testified further as follows, on

Direct Examination by Mr. RUICK.

Q. Mr. Goodwin, I show you now certain papers purporting to be the original papers and application of Hiram F. Lewis, made before the land offi*c*e at Lewiston, Idaho, to purchase certain land referred to in the indictment in this case, to wit:

The northwest quarter of section twent\, township thirt\-eight north, of range fi\e east, of the Boise Meridian, of District of land subject to sale at Lewiston, Idaho; the first paper I call your attention to purp*r*ts to be the sworn statement in duplicate of

(Testimony of F. M. Goodwin.)

the said Hiram F. Lewis, signed by J. B. West, Register, of date August 29th, 1904; the next paper is the notice of publication in the same case.

The next is the testimony of the claimant Hiram F. Lewis in support of his application to purchase.

The next is the corss-examination of the claimant Hiram F. Lewist in connection with his proof offered in support of such application.

The next is the testimon₃ of the witness Melvern C. Scott, in supprt of said application of said Hiram F. Lewis.

The next, the testimon₃ of Edwin Bliss, a witnss in supprt of the application of the said Lewis.

The next, a letter dated Lewiston, Idaho, May 19th, 1905—I will change the order of that—I will withdraw that.

The next, what purports to be the final certificate issued to Hiram F. Lewis, by J. B. West, describing lands referred to in said indictment.

The next, the receiver's final receipt issued to Hiram F. Lewis, and subscribed by Charles H. Garby, Receiver of the United States Land Office.

The number of this final certificate and final receipt being 5046 and bearing date March 8th, 1905. Examine these papers that I have referred to, and state whether or not the signature of J. B. West appearing thereon on each of thse papers respectively is the grnuine signature of J. B. West, former Register of the United States Land Office, Lewiston, Idaho. I do not include in that the cross-ex-

(Testimony of F. M. Goodwin.)

amination of the witnesses which has not yet been identified, but I do include the cross-examination of the claimant?

A. The signatures are all those of J. B. West, except the Receiver's receipt; and that is the signature of Charles H. Garby.

Q. Was Mr. West the acting register of the Lewiston Land Office at the time these papers bear date respectively? A. He was.

Q. Was Mr. Garby on the date on which the final receipt bears date the acting receiver of the land office at Lewiston, Idaho? A. He was.

Q. Is that his genuine signature to this receipt?

A. Yes, sir.

Q. I now call your attention to the letter dated Lewiston, Idaho, May 19th, 1905, and purprting to have been addressed by J. B. West, Register of the United States Land Office at Lewiston, Idaho, to the Hon. Commissioner of the General Land Office, Washington D. C., and will ask you if that is Mr. West's signature? A. It is.

Q. As former Register of the United States Land Office Lewiston, Idaho? A. Yes, sir.

Whereupon the following proceeding was had:

Mr. RUICK.--We now offer in eivdence the sworn statement of Hiram F. Eewis, in Duplicate.

Mr. FORNEY.—The defendants made the same general objection heretofore made to the same papers pertaining to other entries, that is irrelevant, immaterial, in that it does not prove or tend

(Testimony of F. M. Goodwin.)

to prove any of the material allegations of the indictment; on the further ground that there is no evidence showing or tending to show any conspiracy or combination upon the part of or between the defendants or either of them; upon the further ground that it post-dates the consumation of the conspiracy as alleged in the indictment; on the further ground that it is not properly authenticated, and on the further ground no foundation has been laid, and that it does not connect or tend to connect any of the defendants with the alleged offenses set forth in the indictment, or any of them.

The COURT.—Objection overruled.  Exhibit admitted.

To which ruling of the Court the defendants then and there excepted, which exception was allowed by the Court, and said document in duplicate was admitted  in evidence and marked Plaintiff's Exhibit 18.

Mr. FORNEY.—It is now understood, is it not, that this same objection goes to all of the documents pertaining to the acquisition of title to this land by Hiram F. Lewis.

Mr. RUICK.—That is understood.

The COURT.— The ruling will be the same.

Mr. FORNEY.—We will reserve our exceptions thereto.

The COURT.—Exceptions will be allowed you.

Mr. RUICK.—We next offer the notice of publication of Hiram F. Lewis, and ask that the same be marked Plaintiff's Exhibit **19.**

(Testimony of F. M. Goodwin.)

We offer the testimony of the claimant Hiram F. Lewis*t,* and ask that it be marked Plaintiff's Exbibit 20.

We offer the cross-examination of the plaimtiff Hiram F. Lewis, in connection with the final proof, and ask that it be mark*ee* Plaintiff's Exhibit 21.

We offer the testimony of Melvern C. Scott, a witness in support of the application of Hiram F. Lewis, on final proof, and ask that the same be marked Plaintiff's Exhibit 22.

We offer in evidence the testimony of Edwin Bliss, a witness on behalf of the claiman*d* Hiram F. Lewis, in sup*p*rt of the said application, and ask that this be marked Plaintiff's Exhibit 23.

We offer the final certificate of the Register of the United States Land Office at Le*i*ston, Idaho, issued to the said Hiram F. Lewis, and ask that it be marked Plaintiff's Exhibit 24.

We now offer the receiver's final receipt subscribed by Charles H. Garby, Receiver of the Lewiston Land Office, issued to Hiram F. Lewis, and ask that the same be marked Plaintiff's Exhibit 25.

To which offers, and each of them, the defendants objected, which objection was by the Court overruled, and to which ruling of the Court the defendants then and there excepted, which exception was by the Court allowed, and said documents were admitted in evidence, and exhibits number 18 to 25 are as follows:

(Testimony of F. M. Goodwin.)

(Omitted; copies appear elsewhere in ths transcript.)

Mr. RUICK.—We ask that this letter which was identified by this witness be marked Plaintiff's Exhibit 25-A for Identification; the letter will not be offered now.

Q. Mr. Goodwin, you are familiar with the customs and rules and regulations of the United States Land Office in reference to the issuance of final certificates and final receipts? A. Yes, sir.

Q. State whether or not these are issued in duplicate? A. They are.

Q. Is one given to the entryman?

A. Yes, and one sent into the General Land Office with the proof.

Q. Then these certificates and receipts which we produce are the ones that were sent in to the General Land Office? A. Yes, sir.

Q. And they are—these papers are a part of the original papers in the case? A. Ye, sir.

Q. And part of the files in the general aLand Office of Washington? A. Yes, sir.

Cross-examination by Mr. TANNAHILL.

Q. Mr. Goodwin, has patent issued for this tract of land? A. I can't tell you.

Q. You don't know whether it has or not? Had patent issued to the Francis A. Justice tract?

A. I can't tell you without consulting the record.

Q. Have you made an investigation as to whether or not it has issued?

(Testimony of F. M. Goodwin.)

A. I believe I have, but I cannot state from memory whether or not it was issued.

Q. Will you learn whether the paternt has issued for this tract and for the Mrs. Francis A. Justice tract and the Guy L. Wilson tract of land or not?

QA. I think those records will be here.

Mr. RUICK.—The proper custodian will be here that will be the register and receiver of the land office, and they have tlqt information. I expect Mr. Bartlett of the Lewiston Land Office here on the train to-night.

(Witness excused.)

HIRAM F. LEWIS, a witness called and sworn on behalf of the Government, testified as follows, on

Direct Examination by Mr. RUICK.

The COURT.—These records that you offered in evidence and received in evidence here, are they to be considered before the jury unless they are read?

Mr. MOORE.—I think we have a statute requiring all documentary evidence to be read while the witness is on the stand, and if not so read, it cannot be read to the jury unless the reading is waived at that time. We have no particular objection to waiving the reading until the argument to the jury.

Mr. RUICK.—We are prepared to read them at any time unless the reading of them is waived.

The COURT.—The usual practice in my observation has been to have them considered as read before the jury, so the record will show they are read, and

(Testimony of Hiram F. Lewis.)

then counsel can read them or such part of them as they desire.

Mr. RUICK.—We want to read them before the jury and if they want them read at the time they are introduced we will read them now.

The COURT.—I simply asked this question at this time that there may be no misunderstanding. The Court does not see why the time of the Court should be taken up in reading in particular every one of these papers with all of the printed matter. I suppose some of the papers introduced are only to show some certain fact.

Mr. RUICK.—A certain line of procedure.

The COURT.—Yes; I understand, but these receipts, for instance, the Court cannot at this time see their materiality. It may be they are material to show a line of procedure, but even then it is difficult to see how they bear on the charges made in the indictment. The Court would prefer that you make a stipulation that they should be considered as having been read, and then counsel can actually read such portions of them as they consider are material for the consideration of the jury; cannot you proceed, Mr. Ruick?

Mr. RUICK.—I will proceed with*e teh* examination.

Q. What is your name?

A. Hiram F. Lewis.

(Witness continuing:)

Lewiston, Idaho, is my home; I have resided at Lewiston about five years; before coming to Lewiston

(Testimony of Hiram F. Lewis.)

I resided on the Pend O'Reille river in Norhtern Idaho; have resided in Lewiston in all six years. I came from Waverly, Washington, to Idaho. I was there two years.

I have been in the West altogether twenty-two years last fall. I am a native of Minnesota. I am now working for Naylor & Norlin, contractors on the Chicago and Milwaukee railroad, at what they call Crab Creek, on this side of the Columbia River in Adams County, Washington.

I am working as carpenter at present. When I first went down to Lewiston, I worked as city engineer about two years. I worked with Mr. Briggs, who was city engineer, and after that when Mr. Maxon was elected, I was with him.

I was employed by the city of Lewiston altogether two years and a half. I am acquainted with W. F. Kettenbach; have known him for about five years.

I have known George H. Kester about the same time. I became acquainted with them in Lewiston, Idaho. I am acquainted with Mr. Dwyeer and have known him for three years last fall.

Q. Did you file on a stone and timber claim at one time at the Lewiston Land Office?

A. *Ye,* sir.

Q. (Paper, being Plaintiff's Exhibit 18, shown witness, purporting to be his sworn statement.) Look at this paper in duplicate, and say whether or not you recognize those papers, and whether or not your signature to them or to that paper in duplicate, whether or not you signed that paper in duplicate?

(Testimony of Hiram F. Lewis.)

A.  *Ye,* sir.

Q.  You identify those papers, do you?

A.  Yes, sir.

Q.  Do you remember of filing those papers in the Land Office, this paper in duplicate?

A.  Yes, sir.

Q.  Do you remember of being  sworn  to  this paper?      A.  Yes, sir.

Q.  Do you remember by whom you were sworn?

A.  J. B. West.

Q.  Now state, Mr. Lewis, what led up to your filing this application or sworn statement in the Land Office? What led up to your application for the timber claim?

A.  Shortlay after I became acquainted with Mr. Dwyer he asked me one day if I had used my stone and timber right.  I told him I had not.  He wanted to know if I wanted to take a claim, and I told him I didn't know.  He told me that they had some good claims, and if I hadn't used my right that he could get a claim for me which he afterwards did.

Q.  Where did you meet Mr. Dwyer, if you recall?      A.  On the streets in Lewiston.

Q.  Did you have any further conversation with Dwyer or with anybody else prior to your filing the application?      A.  Yes, sir.

Q.  With whom did you have that conversation?

A.  Mr. Dwyer.

Q.  Where did you have that conversation? '

A.  I think it was at my home in East Lewiston or near my home, east of Lewiston.

(Testimony of Hiram F. Lewis.)

Q. State the conversation.

A. He came up there one evening and told me they had some claims, and that he would go up and show me one, and I could file on it, and also what they would give me for my right for the claim.

Q. What did he say he would give you for your right? A. $150.00.

Q. Did you have a conversation prior to your filing your applcation at which any of the other defendants were present besides Dwyer?

A. Why, Mr. Kester was with Mr. Dwyer one time, but I would not say positive which time it was, whether it was the first or the second time that I met them.

Q. Where did you meet them?

A. On the street in Lewiston.

Q. Well, you may go ahead and state where you met him?

A. I think I was coming down town at the time from home, and I met them; they were in a buggy; Mr. Dwyer and Mr. Kester.

Q. What conversation, if any, did you have there relative to your proposed timber filing?

A. They wanted to know when I could go up and I told them almost any time they would set a date. Mr. Dwyer said he would go up with me and he did. We took the train to Lenore and then got horses and went out and saw the timber claim and came back to Lewiston.

Be it remembered that then and there the following proceeding was had:

(Testimony of Hiram F. Lewis.)

Q. Had there been any understanding between you and the defendant Dwyer, or Dwyer and the other defendants, or either of them, prior to your going up to this timber as to the disposition you were to make of this claim, when you should procure the title to it? Answer the question yes or no?

Mr. TANNAHILL.—Objected to as calling for the conclusion of the witness and as incompetent.

Mr. RUICK.—It is preliminary merely.

The COURT.—The Court so understood. I will permit the answer to the question yes or no; the objection is overruled.

To which ruling of the Court the defendants then and there excepted, which exception was allowed, and the witness answered:

A. Yes.

Be it remembered that then and there the following proceeding was had:

Q. State what your understanding and agreement was, when and where it was made, and how; state everything in relation to it.

Mr. TANNAHILL.—The same objection, please.

The COURT.—State the conversation; state what was said.

To which ruling of the Court the defendants then and there excepted, which exception was allowed by the Court. And the witness answered:

A. Well, I told them they wanted—Mr. Dwyer wanted to know if I had any money of my own, and I told them I did. He wanted to know where it was, and I told him it was in the Idaho Trust Company's

(Testimony of Hiram F. Lewis.)

bank, and he said as I stated, that I could take up a claim, and they would pay all the expenses and they would furnish the balance of the money for me. I was to give my note for it, and I would pay all of the expenses out of the money*k*, that is, when I drew checks on it, on the Idaho Trust Company for expenses, they procured the money from the Lewiston National Bank, and I gave my note for it as I say, and deposited it in the Idaho Trust Company.

Be it remebbered that then and there the following proceeding was had:

Q. What I asked you in particular—you anticipated a little, Mr. Lewis, what I want to know particularly is the terms of the agreement; in other words, what was said in the conversation between you and Dwyer, start in at the first conversation and go through and then go *l*on with the later conversation you had with him before going to the timber with him, or with him and Kester.

Mr. TANNAHILL.—Objected to as a repetition.

The COURT.—Objection overruled.

To which ruling of the Court the defendants then and there excepted, which exception was allowed, and the witness answered:

A. He told me what they would give me for the claim, allow me for my right, and they would furnish all money and pay all expenses, and I was to deposit the money in the Idaho Trust Company and draw upon it to defray all the necessary expenses, and all expenses on account of that filing and proving up on the claim.

(Testimony of Hiram F. Lewis.)

Q. At which of these conversations or at what conversation was Mr. Kester present, or have you already testified?

A. I think it was the second time that I met them.

Q. Yes, what arrangement, if any, was made that time when you met, when he and Dwyer were together?

A. That was the time I was to go upon the claim when I met Mr. Kester with him.

Q. Who was present when the arrangement was made and you were to procure the money, when the arrangement by which you were to procure the money was made and agreed upon?    A. Mr. Dwyer.

Q. Who?

A. Mr. Dwyer and Mr. Kester were together.

Q. What?    A. Mr. Dwyer and Mr. Kester.

Q. Were together?    A. Yes, sir.

Q. At the time the money matters were talked over?    A. Yes, sir.

Q. You went up, did you, to the timber?

A. Yes, sir.

Q. Who went with you?    A. Mr. Dwyer.

Q. How did you travel, how did you go?

A. We went on the cars to Lenore and then procured horses and went on the timber claim on horses and came back to Lenore and then took the cars back to Lewiston.

Q. Where is Lenore? What line of railroad? On the Clearwater Branch?

A. Yes, sir; on the Clearwater branch.

Q. How far did you have to travel on horses?

(Testimony of Hiram F. Lewis.)

A.   It took us two days to get into the timber and back from there.

Q.   Who paid the expenses of that trip?

A.   Mr. Dwyer.

Q.   Did he give you the money or did he pay it out of his own pocket?

A.   He paid it out of his own pocket.

Q.   You say you were gone two days *form* Lei*w*oton?

A.   Three days—no, four days from Lewiston; it took four days, one day out and one day we took the horses after we left the train and was gone two days and come back and we had to wait for the train and come back the third day and got back to Le*w*iton right after dinner.

Q.   How long after you were up to the timber was it approximately before you filed?

A.   It was about two weeks.

Q.   What?

A.   Some little time after I came back I know I was delayed for a while after I came back, I forget now, something about two weeks before I filed, something like that.

Q.   Where did you go to have your papers made out?     A.   Mr. I. N. Smith's office.

Q.   How did you happen to go to I. N. Smith's office?

A.   I asked Mr. Dwyer where we could have them made out and he suggested that I go there and have them made out.

(Testimony of Hiram F. Lewis.)

Q.    Where was this office relative to the location of the land office at that time.

A.    It was on the same floor with the land office.

Q.    Whereabouts from the land office?

A.    Right across on the opposite side of the building just around the *hea* of the stairs.

Q.    Across the hall, and around the head of the stairs?    A.    Yes, *si*.

Q.    Who was there when you went to get your filing pape*es*?    A.    Mr. Smith.

Q.    Do you remember who wrote this out?    Who filled in the ba*l*nks in your sworn statement or did you see it filled out?    A.    Yes, sir.

Q.    Who filled out the blanks?

A.    Mr. Smith.

Q.    In your presence?    A.    Yes, sir.

Q.    What did you say to Mr. Smith when you went up there, or was Mr. Dwyer there?

A.    I went in and told him that I had some papers; I would like to have him fill out for me and he took them and looked them over and filled them out.

Q.    Did you have the blank with you?

A.    Mr. Dwyer gave me the blank.

Q.    And you took the blank with you to Mr. Smith's office?    A.    Yes, sir.

Q.    Did you tell him who had sent you there?

A.    No, sir.

Q.    Did you pay Mr. Smith anything for making out these pape*es*?    A.    Yes, sir.

Q.    How much did you pay him?

(Testimony of Hiram F. Lewis.)

A. Six dollars for those papers, and the subsequent ones made out after that, I paid him six dollars.

Q. When did you pay him, at a later date?

A. At a later date, I forget just when it was.

Q. What did you do with the papers after they had been made out?

A. I took them to the United States Land Office.

Q. And paid the fee?    A. Yes, sir.

Q. Where did you get the money to pay this fee?

A. *drew* it out of the Idaho Trust Company.

Q. Your own money?

A. Money I had deposited there, yes, sir.

Q. Prior to this time had you got the money out of the Lewiston National Bank which you had deposited in the Idaho Trust Company?    A. Yes, sir.

Q. You had? How did you come to get that?

A. Mr. Dwyer told me to get the money there and deposit it with the other, which I did.

Q. Deposit it with your money?

A. With the Idaho Trust Company, yes, sir; with the money I had there.

Q. Before you filed your application you went to the Lewiston National Bank and got the money?

A. Yes, sir.

Q. Do you remember how much you got at that time?

A. No, sir; I don't remember just what the amount was.

Q. For what purpose did you get the money, if you remember?

(Testimony of Hiram F. Lewis.)

A.  F filing purposes and the expenses of the claim.

Q.  Did you give any note or other obligation for it?    A.  Yes, sir.

Q.  How long before you filed your application qwas it you put this money in the Bank of the Idaho Trust Company?

A.  Two weeks, I think, or something like that.

Q.  I am speaking of your original application, you understand, not the final proof?

A.  Yes, sir.

Q.  You understand this was before your first papers?    A.  Yes, sir.

You say you took the blank to I. N. Smith's office?    A.  Yes, sir.

Q.  That Dwyer had given you?

A.  Yes, sir.

Q.  Did you have a tl*a*k with Mr. Dwyer before you went to the land office, before you went to I. N. Smith's office respecting the contents of this application?    A.  Yes, sir.

Q.  Where did that talk occur?

A.  I think it was on the street.

Q.  Where had Dwyer given you these blanks?

A.  There in the hallway of the bank buildi*j*g on the floor where the land office is.

Q.  What did Dwyer say to you at the time he gave you these blanks?

A.  He said to take them into Smith and have them .filled out and then take them to the land office, and file them.

(Testimony of Hiram F. Lewis.)

Q. When did you, or did you have a talk with Dwyer respecting the contents of this sworn statement, or of these blanks that he had given you?

A. It was that same day I filed them; I think it was.

Q. Where did that conversation occur?

A. It was, I think, on the floor of the land office in the hallway.

Q. That is your recollection? A. Yes, sir.

Q. Now, I will call your attention to the statement contained in your application or sworn statement you had filed.

"That I do not apply to purchase the land above described on speculation, but in good faith to appropriate it to my own exclusive use and benefit." Did you read this statement over before you signed it and swore to it? A. Yes, sir.

Q. You knew that was in there?

A. Yes, sir.

Q. Now, when you stated under oath at this time that you "did not apply to purchase the land above described on speculation, but in good faith to appropriate it to your own exclusive use and benefit, now was that statement when you made it, and so made by you, Mr. Lewis, true or untrue?

A. Untrue.

Q. Did you know it was untrue at the time you made it? A. Yes, sir.

Q. I call your attention to this other statement in the filing immediately following: "That I have not directly or indirectly made any agreement or con-

(Testimony of Hiram F. Lewis.)

tract, or in any way or manner, with any person or persons whomseover by which the title I may acquire from the Government of the United States may inure in whole or in part to the benefit of any person except myself," you recall having read that do you?    A.  Yes, sir.

Q.  Now, was that statement true or untrue at the time that you made it?    A.  Untrue.

Q.  Please explain to the jury what led up to your making these false statements at the time they were made, Mr. Lewis?

A.  Well, I was told, after I read them over, and swore to them, that there was nothing in there that would be illegal, or out of the way in any manner.

Q.  Who told you?    A.  Mr. Dwyer.

Q.  And when?

A.  At the time I got the blank.

Q.  What further did Dwyer say about these matters or what if anything did he say about that propositiou that you were taking this up fcr your own benefit?

A.  Why he said there was nohing out of the way, nothing illegal about it; it was being done right alohg, and if I swore to those papers it would be all right.

Q.  Well, how was this to be for your benefit? How did you understand this to be fore your benefit?

A.  Well, I was to receive $150 for my right.

Q.  What I want to know is, whether or not that was your own suggestion, or the suggestion of somebody else and if so, who suggested it?

(Testimony of Hiram F. Lewis.)

A.   It was Mr. Dwyer's suggestion.

Q.   Now, with regard to the proposition down here that you had not made any agreement, directly or indirectly with an*d* persons, etc., what, if anything, was said about that?

A.   Well, I was told that when I had procured this money, I hav*d* some of the money and I borrowed the rest on my own personal note, was a legal transaction and nothing out of the way.

Q.   Who told you this?      A.   Mr. Dwyer.

Q.   You said here, "That I have not directly or indirectly made any agreement or contract or *a*in any way or manner with any person or persons whomsoever," now you have already testified here as to the understanding which you had before you filed th*s* paper; now why did you state under oath here that you had no contract in view of the understanding that you had?

A.   Well, as I *sadi sad* before, I supposed it was a legal transaction, and I had a right aft*e* I acquired the land in this was to transfer it and it would be a legal transaction.

Q.   What I want to know, what I want to get at is this: What was said concerning that, if anything, in this conversation with re*t*gard to your not having any contract?

Why, we didn't have any*hh*ing only a verbal contract; there was no papers drawn up or anything that way.   All the contract I did have was simply by orally and giving my note for this money.

(Testimony of Hiram F. Lewis.)

Q. Was anything said about that between you and Dwyer in that conversation? I am referring now *t* the verbal contract proposition; where *di* you get the idea *that a* verbal contract? That is what I want to know?

A. I don't just catch what you want, Mr. Ruick.

Q. You testified, you swore here at this time that you had not made any contract?     A. Yes, sir.

Q. And you now say it was only a verbal contract, and I say where did you get the idea prior to this time that a verbal contract was no contract?

A. I don't know particularly that I had or did have that idea, that it was not a contract at all.

Q. Well, you stated that at that time that you had no agreement or contract?     A. Yes, sir.

Q. Well, did you have more than one talk with Dwyer concerning these matters before you went in the land office, this paper, I mean?

A. No, sir; I don't think I did.

Q. I mean now with regard to the contents of this affidavit?     A. Yes, sir.

Q. Who attended to the matter of procuring witnesses for you, Mr. Lewis?     A. Mr. Dwyer.

Q. Did you have anything to do with it yourself?

A. Why, I asked him who I would have as weitnesses and he suggested the names.

Q. Do you recall what names he suggested?

A. Melvern Scott and Edwin Bliss, I had as witnesses to prove up.

Q. Who was the others suggested?

A. Albert Kester and I forget the other one.

(Testimony of Hiram F. Lewis.)

Q. Dwyer himself, wasn't it?

A. I think William Dwyer himself.

Q. Now, there was some—there is another matter right now, what other paper did you file in the land office Mr. Lewis at the same time you filed the sworn statement that I have just asked you about?

A. A relinquishment.

Q. Where did you get that relinquishment?

A. Dwyer gave it to me.

Q. You filed that at the same time, did you?

Q. Where did Dwyer give that to you, if you remember?

A. He gave it to me the same time that he gave me the blank.

Q. Was Dwyer in the land office when you went to file these papers, your first papers?

A. Yes, sir.

Q. Was he in Smith's office while the papers were being made out?    A. No, sir.

Q. Where was he then when you started to go to the land office?

A. I think he was in the hallway whilst I got the papers made out.

Q. Was he present when you swore to your sworn statement?

A. He was in the hallway to the land office, right inside; I don't know as he was right there in hearing at the time in the land office.

Q. You remember of the occasion of your making final proof and giving your testimony in support of your claim, what we call the final proof, do you?

(Testimony of Hiram F. Lewis.)

A.   Yes, sir.

Q.   Did you see Dwyer and have a talk with him before going up to make your final proof?

A.   Yes, sir.

Q.   Where did you see him?

A.   On the street in Lewiston.

Q.   What was said there or done?

A.   He wanted to know if I had everything fixed to prove up when the time came and I told him I hadn't yet; it was about two weeks before I proved up; he said, You better get fixed up and have eveything ready then, and he wanted to know what was the matter and I told him I didn't have quite money enough, and he said I better get enough so as to be ready, and he wanted to know how much I needed, and I told him, and went to the Lewiston National Bank and got it, and deposited it in the Idaho Trust Company.

Q.   Did Dwyer go there with you?

A.   No, sir; I don't think he went in the bank with me.

Q.   Who did you get the money from, if you remember?     A.   Mr. Kester.

Q.   Did you give your note for it?

A.   Yes, sir.

Q.   Do you recall how much you got at that time?

A.   Something over four hundred dollars, I think $450, or something like that, enough to pay up for the land, and, the expenses and witness fees, and so forth.

(Testimony of Hiram F. Lewis.)

Be it remembered that then and there the following proceeding was had:

Q. Now, were these—I will ask you about another proposition: Did you have an understanding with these parties whom you have referred to about your brother, E. M. Lewis taking up a claim? Answer yes or no.

Mr. TANNAHILL.—Objected to on the same ground; it calls for a conclusion and not the statements of the facts.

The COURT.—Objection overruled.

To which ruling of the Court the defendants then and there excepted, which exception was allowed by the Court, and the witness answered:

A. Yes, sir.

Q. And now state what was said by them and what the arrangement was. State what was said and done.

A. I met Mr. Dwyer one day and he wanted to know if my brother, E. M. Lewis, had used his stone and timber right, and I told him no; if he had used his right, and I told him he had not. He said if he wanted to take one under the same conditions, that we could probably fix it up.

Be it remembered that then and there the following proceeding was had:

Mr. TANNAHILL.—I move to strike out the last part of the answer on the ground that it is not binding upon the defendats Kester and Kettenbach.

Q. The COURT.—I do not care to hear any argument; the motion is denied.

(Testimony of Hiram F. Lewis.)

To which ruling of the Court the defendants Kester and Kettenbach then and there excepted, which exception was allowed by the Court.

Q.  Was this before you filed your sworn state·ment that this conversation occurred?

A.  Yes, sir.

Q.  Have you repeated all the conversation you had with Dwyer that you had at that time, as you recall it?

A.  Why, I told him that I would see my brother and if it was all right he would come up and take a claim.

Q.  Did you see your brother?    A.  Yes, sir.

Q.  Did you tell him what Dwyer told you?

A.  Yes, sir.

Q.  Well, then, what did your brother do in connection with it, or what did you do in connection with it?

A.  Why, I told my brother he could go up and take a claim and all the business was to be transacted through me.

Q.  That is something you have not yet stated.  I think you forgot that before when you stated the conversation between you and Dwyer.  You had better go back and state the full conversation you had with Dwyer, relative to your brother taking the claim.

A.  Why, he said if he wanted the claim that he could fix it up, but that I was to transact all the business for him.

Q.  For whom?    A.  For my brother.

(Testimony of Hiram F. Lewis.)

Q. I will ask you as a matter of fact, did you transact all the business for your brother?

A. Yes, sir.

Q. Relative to his claim?     A. Yes, sir.

Q. I am referring to this part of his business?

A. Yes, sir.

Q. Where *dd* you get the money to pa\ the expenses of your brother, and to pay the Government for his land?

A. In the way that I had the prior money.

Q. Was your brother known in the transaction at all, that is, at the bank?

A. No; no, sir.

Q. The money was all obtained through you, was it?     *Q.* Yes, sir.

Q. And upon your note?     A. Yes, sir.

Q. You made all the arrangements?

A. Yes, sir.

Q. I want to ask you if these amounts you got from the Lewiston National Bank at different times included your brother's expenses as well as your own?     A. Yes, sir.

Q. You stated that you, about two weeks before you made your final proof, you met Dwyer on the street and had this conversation with him relative to the money; now, we will go back to that. What other conversation did you have with Dwyer prior to going to the land office to make final proof?

A. In regard to the papers do you mean?

Q. Yes, in regard to anything?

(Testimony of Hiram F. Lewis.)

A. Why, he told me that I would have to take the papers and get them, take the papers up there and file them, and there would be nothing that would be illegal in the transaction. It would be all right.

Q. Now, I will go back a little bit. What, if anything, did Dwyer give you in this connection or at this time? What, if anything, did he supply you with? I will put the question to you direct. Did you have any conversation with Dwyer prior to your going to the land office to make the final proof about what your testimony would be? A. Yes, sir.

Q. What did he do in relation to that?

A. Well, he told me to swear to the papers just as they were and there would be nothing illegal about the transaction.

Q. What I want to know is, did he supply you with any*h*ing in that connection for your information?

The COURT.—You mean supplied any blanks?

Mr. RUICK.—*D*e doesn't quite understand.

Q. Witness now shown Plaintiff's Exhibit 20, testimony of claimant, also Plaintiff's Exhibit 21, cross-examination of claimant. Do you recognize those papers as what is termed yo*u* final proof papers? *Do* they bear your signature do the*y* not?

A. Yes, sir.

Q. Have you ever seen any papers like that before you went to the land office to answer these questions? A. Yes, sir.

Q. Where did you get them?

A. Mr. Dwyer had them.

(Testimony of Hiram F. Lewis.)

Q. Where did you meet Dwyer that day?

A. In his room over the Lewiston National Bank.

Q. Wher is his room over the Lewiston National Bank? A. On the third floor.

Q. Did you see the papers there?

A. Yes, sir.

Q. Now state what was done in his room in relation to those blanks? Did he have the blanks there?

A. We looked over the blanks.

Q. You and he looked ovee the blanks?

A. Yes, sir.

Q. Now you say you recognize these papers as your testimony given in support of your application to purchase this claim; now I want to ask you this: I read from question 13 on the blank testimony of claimant: "Have you sold or transferred your claim to this land since making your sworn statement, or have you directly or indirectly made any agreement or contract in any way or manner with any person whomsoever by which the title which you may acquire from the Government of the United States may inure in whole or in part to the benefit of any person except yourself"? You remember that question being asked in the land office? A. Yes, sir.

Q. And you answered that question, No; was that answer true or untrue at the time you made it?

A. Untrue.

Q. Did you know it to be untrue at the time you made it? A. Yes, sir.

Q. This other question number 14, "Do you make this entry in good faith for the appropriation of the

(Testimony of Hiram F. Lewis.)
land exclusively to your own use, and not for the use or benefit of any other person," do you remember that question? A. Yes, sir.

Q. You answered that question "Yes." Now was that answer true or untrue at the time it was made? ,Q. Untrue.

Q. "Question 15. Has any other person than yourself or any firm, corporation or association any interest in the entry you are now making or in the land or in the timber thereon," your answer to that was "No." Was that answer true or false at the time it was made? A. False.

Q. Did you know it to be so? A. Yes, sir.

Q. Now, I want to ask you how you came to answer those questions in the way that you did in the land office at tht time? What explanation have you to give?

A. Well, as I said before, we had a copy of the blank and looked them over and Dwyer said that if I swore to them just as they wasl there would be nothing illegal about the transaction.

Q. Well, with regard to this matter as to whether you had any contract or agreement in any way or manner with any person by which the title might inure to their benefit you answered that question "No." How did you come to answer that no?

A. I was given to understand that this money and the way I procured it was legal, and everything would be a legal transaction in swearing to the papers as I did.

Q. Who told you that? A. Dwyer.

(Testimony of Hiram F. Lewis.)

Q. I asked how you came to say you didn't have an agreement, in other words to answer the question no?

A. I was told it was legal, or I wouldn't have done it.

Q. What was said about the agreement? *Ws* anything said about the agreement between you and Dwyer at the time you went over these blanks?

A. Nothing only to read over the blanks there, the questions there.

Q. Were these questions answered in the blanks he showed you?     A. No, sir.

Q. How did you know what these answeres were then, how to be drawn up?   How did you know whether to answer no or yes?   What I want to know is what Dwyer said to you there about how you were to answer these questions, *Mr. Ruick*?

A. Well, he said just to answer the questions, where it said no, to answer no.

Q. The answers weren't there?     A. No, sir.

Q. I read you a part of question 13, "Have you directly or indirectly made any agreement or contract in any way or manner with any person whomsoever by which the title which you may acquire from the Government of the United States may inure in whole or in part to the benefit of anyone except yourself," and to which you answered, No."

A. Yes, sir.

Q. Who, if anyone, suggested that answer, No?

A. Well, I say I think I did that myself, for after reading the question I had already been told to an-

(Testimony of Hiram F. Lewis.)

swer them as they had been drawn up, which I did. If I had answered them contrary, it would have been contrary to the laws of the land office, and I was told to answer them right so as to get the claim.

Q. That is what I am getting at, what would be answering them right so that you would get the claim?

A. If the answer came on that form to be answered one way, to answer it so.

Q. Who suggested that, that you answer that no, so as to get the claim?

A. I think I done that on my own suggestion.

Q. You said you talked the matter over *wih* Dwyer?    A. Yes, sir.

Q. What was the purpose of Dwyer in taking you up to his room with these blanks, if you know?

A. To *llok* them over, I suppose, and see if I understood them.

Q. To look them over and see if you understood them?    A. Yes, sir.

Q. This question here, "Do you make this entry in good faith for the *p*appropriation of this land exclusively to your own use, and not for the use or benefit of any other person," you answered, Yes, and say that was untrue. What I want to know is, who, if anyone, suggested that you answer that question as you did, Yes, that you took this for your own benefit and not for the benefit of another? Who, if anyone, suggested that you answer that the way it was answered?    A. Dwyer.

Q. What did he say about it?

(Testimony of Hiram F. Lewis.)

A. Well, he read over all the questions and I suppose, I don't remember that one in particular, but they were suggested that I answer them just as they were drawn up there in the blank.

Mr. RUICK.—Have you got back to that again?

Mr. TANNAHILL.—Don't dispute him; let him finish his answer.

Q. What I want to know is who, if anyone, suggested the answer to that final proof?

Mr. MOORE.—The sectinn of the code to which I called your Honor's attention this morning is 6085 of the Revised Statutes of 1887.

The COURT.—Now, can't we have some understanding about it; I don't know what the practice of counsel has been, but there are a large number of exhibits being admitted practically duplicated along the same line; it is for consel to agree that the exhibits should be read in evidence, and in the argument to the jury counsel may emphasize such parts as are set forth in the written instruments as they desire to. The Court wants to know when any paper is offered in evidence, whether it shall be considered as read to the jury. It is simply to save time. It is immaterial to the Court, of course, except that it will take so very much time to read all of these papers.

Mr. TANNAHILL.—We have no objection to that calling the Court's attention to the statement we make, so that no particular part will be read at some time to emphasize a part of a witness' testimony. The Court can control that. We have no objection

(Testimony of Hiram F. Lewis.)

to making a stipulation that any of these exhibits offered may be considered as read in evidence.

The COURT.—Very well, then; proceed with the evidence.

Q. Showing witness Plaintiff's Exhibit 21, purporting to be the cross-examination of claimant, Hyrum F. Lewis. I think you have identified that paper. That is your cross-examination.

A. Yes, sir.

Q. You identify it as such? A. Yes, sir.

Q. Mr. Lewis, Question 16 on this blank, "Did you pay out of *yor* own individual funds all the expenses in co*j*nection with making this filing, and do you expect to pay for the land with your own mone; to the first part of that question read as follows: "Did you pay out of your own individual funds all of the expenses with making this filing," to that question you answered "Yes." Now, was that answer true at the time you made it? A. No, sir.

Q. Where did you procure the funds to pay the expenses?

A. I drew it out of the Idaho Trust Company.

Q. From whom did you receive it?

A. From the Lewiston National Bank.

Q. From whom? Who paid it to you at the Lewiston National Bank? A. Mr. Kester.

Q. And to the other part of the question "and do you expect to pay for the land with your own money," is your answer to that true or untrue?

A. Untrue.

Q. Did you have any such expectations?

(Testimony of Hiram F. Lewis.)

A. No, sir.

Q. "Question 17: Where did you get the money to pay for this land, and how long have you had the same in your actual possession?" To the first part of that question reading, "Where did you get the money with which to pay for this land," you answered, "Saved it from my earnings." Was that answer true or untrue at the time it was made?

A. Untrue.

Q. Did you know it was untrue at the time?

A. Yes, sir.

Q. And you were further asked "How long have you had the same in your actual possession?" to which you replied "three months." Was that answer true or untrue? A. Untrue.

Q. How did you come to make these replies as you made them here?

A. Mr. Dwyer told me to answer those questions in that way and it would be all right.

Q. Did you go over this blank with Mr. Dwyer before you went to the land office the same as the other blanks? A. Yes, sir.

Q. I believe you have already stated that you were sw*on* at the time you made your proof?

A. Yes, sir.

Q. In support of your claim, sworn by Mr. West?

A. Yes, sir.

Q. How many times? Do you recollect, did you have occasion to go to the Lewiston National Bank to get money in connection with proving up on these two claims?

(Testimony of Hiram F. Lewis.)

A.　Why*k* it was four or five different times, I think.

Q.　What did you leave at the bank as an evidence of your having received the money?

A.　My note.

Q.　Payable to whom, and for what?

A.　Payable to the First National Bank.

Q.　From whom did you get this money when you went to the bank?　　A.　Mr. Kester.

Q.　On each of these occasions?

A.　Yes, sir.

Q.　Where did you get the money to pay the location fee?　　A.　In the same way.

Q.　How did you happen to go to the bank to get the money to pay the location fees?　State the circumstances.

A.　Mr. Dwyer came to me and told me he had not received his location fee, and we better fix it up.　We did so, and I paid him.

Q.　Do you remember of anything—in the first place, I will ask you of whom did you get the money to pay the location fee?

A.　From the Lewiston National Bank.

Q.　From what individual in the bank?

A.　Mr. Kester.

Q.　How did you happen to go to the Lewiston National Bank for this purpose at this time?

A.　At the instigation of Mr. Dwyer.

Q.　Who did you see there, if anyone, to talk to about this location fee?　　A.　Mr. Dwyer.

Q.　At the bank?

(Testimony of Hiram F. Lewis.)

A.   Mr. Kester, that is all.

Q.   What was said between you and Mr. Kester?

A.   I told him that Mr. Dwyer wanted his location fee, and he gave me the money, and I gave him the note for it.

Q.   How much money did you get at that time for that purpose?

A.   I think I got both fees, $300, I think it was.

Q.   What did you do with that money?

A.   Gave it to Mr. Dwyer.

Q.   Did you get any receipt for it, do you remember?     A.   No, sir.

Q.   Do you recall where Mr. Dwyer was when you gave it to him?

A.   I think he was on the street; I am pretty sure he was.

Q.   Where and when was this money which you were to recive for your right paid to you, if at all, and how was it paid?

A.   It was after I proved up on the claim, I received the money; it was given me, and I deposited it in the Idaho Trust Company the same as the other.

Q.   Where was it given to you?

A.   At the Lewiston National Bank.

Q.   By whom?     A.   Mr. Kester.

Q.   What transaction occurred there at that time, at the Lewiston National Bank, at or about the time you got that money that was coming to you?   How much did you get by the way?

A.   Three hundred dollars.

Q.   That covered both locations, did it?

(Testimony of Hiram F. Lewis.)

A. Yes, sir.

Q. Both claims. Now what transaction occurred there at that time?

A. I went to the bank myself and told Mr. Kester what I wanted, and he gave me the money and I gave him my note for it the same as I had before.

Q. When did you have then an adjustment with the bank?    A. For all these?

Q. Yes.

A. It was after I had some time afterwards.

Q. How long afterwards?

A. Some time after my brother proved up that I went there and took up the samall notes and merged them all into one.

Q. How long after you proved up did your brother prove up if you remember?

A. I think it was two or three months anyhow; I know there was a contest on his claim, and it was after that was settled before he got proved up, something like that, two or three months.

Q. You think it might have been two or three months after you proved up before he proved up?

A. Yes, sir.

Q. And after he proved up and got his final certificate then you went and took up these notes witnh a single note?    A. Yes, sir.

Q. Now state something about the cause of the delay in getting title to your brother's claim?

A. There was a contest on one forty of it.

Q. There was a contest? Did that delay his proving up?    A. *Ye,* sir.

(Testimony of Hiram F. Lewis.)

Q. What do you know about that contest? Did you have any talk with any one of these defendants about the matter? A. No, sir.

Q. Did you later have some talk with them?

A. I think all the conversation I had with them was through my brother when he had the contest; he was out thirty dollars or thirty-five dollars; I forget just what it was, and I went to Mr. Dwyer.

Q. What was that for; I don't understand what you said?

A. I said my brother had a contest and he was out the moeny for this contest; it was thirty dollars or thirty-five dollars, and I had been down town to work, and when I got home he told me about it and said he wished I would get the money for it as he needed it.

Q. What did you do?

A. So I saw Mr. Dwyer and he said that they would refund the money, and I went with him to the bank, and Mr. Kester paid me the thirty dollars and I gave it back to my brother.

Q. Where were you during the time this contest was going on?

A. I think I was at work in town at that time.

Q. You had nothing to do with the contest yourself or defending it? A. No, sir.

Q. You had yourself made no arrangement with the parties to defend the contest? A. No, sir.

Q. Now, when you made your final proof, Mr. Lewis, did you get a final receipt? A. Yes, sir.

Q. What did you do with it?

(Testimony of Hiram F. Lewis.)

A.   I think I have got it; I would not be sure, but I think I have got it in my possession yet at home.

Q.   The same?      A.   Yes, sir.

Q.   You are not sure about that?

A.   No, I would not say for certain.

Q.   When you had made final proof, or after your brother made final proof, then what transaction did you have at the bank?   What transaction did you have at the bank after your brother had made final proof?

A.   Why, we settled up for both claims, and it was then that I merged these small notes all into one, and they paid me the final balance which was due us both.

Q.   The balance of what?

A.   Of our location fee, or what we were to receive for our right.

Q.   And it was all balanced up and paid up, was it?      A.   Yes, sir.

Q.   And you say it was all included in the note— was it all included in the note?      A.   Yes, sir.

Q.   Why, if you know, did you not convey the land over at that time?   What, if anything, was said by you to the parties concerning it?

A.   Why, Mr. Kester told me there was no particular hurry about it, to just let it lay as it was.

Q.   Said what?

A.   There was no particular hurry about it; we would just leave it as it was.

Q.   When did you finally execute the papers in relation to it?

(Testimony of Hiram F. Lewis.)

A. About a year afterwards, I think.

Q. State the transaction, how you came to have it?

A. I went to work on the ditch, and I got through, I think it was in May last year, and when I went into town one day I happened to be in the bank and Mr. Kester said that we might as well transfer those papers, and so I went to work and made a transfer to the bank of both claims. I had previous to this had my brother's claim transferrd to me.

Q. At whose suggestion, if anyone's?

A. Mr. Kester's.

Q. What had Mr. Kester told you about having your brother's claim transferred to you?

A. He wanted to know if it would be all right to have it transferred over to me, and then have them transferred over to him. I said that I didn't see as there would be anything out of the way if he did; I did so.

Q. You had your brother's claim transferred to you? A. Yes, sir.

Q. It was held in your name, then?

A. Yes, sir.

Q. How long after your brother made final proof was it before this claim was transferred to you, his claim?

A. I think it was about a year or something like that, ten months, maybe.

Q. Then it was transferred to you shortly before --did you transfer it shortly before you executed this deed to Mr. Keser? A. Yes, sir.

(Testimony of Hiram F. Lewis.)

Q. Did Mr. Kester give you any reason why he thought it best to have your brother's claim transferred to you and then have you transfer them both?

A. No, sir.

Q. What paper was this that you executed at this time which you have now referred to your claim and your brother's claim?    A. He got a deed.

Q. Did you receive any other or further consideration when you executed that deed?

A. No, sir.

Q. You had received it all more than a year before, had you?    A. Yes, sir.

Whereupon the following proceedings were had:

Q. Did you consider yourself as having any interest in these lands whatever after you had that settlement *iwth* the bank?

Mr. FORNEY.—Objected to as incompetent, irrelevant and immaterial.

Mr. RUICK.—It is as to his understanding to whom the land belonged to.

Mr. TANNAHILL.—That is for the jury.

The COURT.—Objection overruled.

To which ruling of the Court the defendants then and there excepted, which exception was allowed by the Court, and the witness answered as follows:

A. After I had made the deeds, you mean?

Q. No, after you had got your pay, did you consider you had any interest or further interest in those lands or own anything in the lands?

(Testimony of Hiram F. Lewis.)

A. Well, yes, as long as I had not transferred or made any deeds to the parties, I claim I had an interest in it.

Q. That would be the legal title?

A. Yes, sir.

Be it remembered that then and there the following proceedings were had:

Mr. Lewis, did you consider that you owned these lands after you got this money for them at the bank?

A. No, sir.

Mr. TANNAHILL.—We object to that as leading and suggestive and we move to strike the answer out.

The COURT.—If the witness had not answered before the Court would pass on the objection the Court would have sustained the objection. These questions are pretty near the border line and the Court will not permit counsel to ask leading questions. I think this particular question should not be put in a leading form; inasmuch as he has answered the question, the Court w*k*lll permit it to stand, because the Court considers it a proper question except as to its form, that is, it is objectionable because it is leading.

To which ruling of the Court the defendants then and there excepted, which exception was b\ the Court allowed.

Q. Where did you go to execute this deed for \our lands? A. The Lewiston National Bank.

Q. Where was the deed prepared, if \ou remember? A. By Charles McDonald.

Q. What?

(Testimony of Hiram F. Lewis.)

A.    Charlie McDonald made out the deed, I think.

Q.    Where did you go to execute it?

A.    To Charlie McDonald.

Q.    You went to his office?    A.    Yes, sir.

Q.    Where did you go before you went to his office to execute the deed?    By whose direction did you go to McDonald's office?    A.    By Mr. Kester's.

Q.    How did you come to go there?

A.    Why, I happened to be at the bank, and he said he thought it would be all right now to transfer that property to them, and I asked him where I should go to make out the papers, and he said to McDonald's office.

Q.    Did anybody go with you?    A.    No, sir.

Q.    And who had made the arrangements with McDonald, if anyone, to have the papers made?

A.    Not anybody as I know of.

Q.    Were the papers made out by him at your request after you got there?    A.    Yes, sir.

Q.    You acknowledged them?    A.    Yes, sir.

Q.    And then what did he do with the deed?

A.    I brought them back— No, I took them to the courthouse to have them put on record.

Q.    How did you happen to take them to the courthouse and put them on record?

A.    Mr. Kester asked if I would do it.

Q.    And to whom did that deed read?

A.    I think it was the Lewiston National Bank.

Q.    This was after that portion of Shoshone County in which the lands lay had been taken into

(Testimony of Hiram F. Lewis.)

Nez Perce County, wasn't it?  Did you have it re-corded?

A.  Before that time or after?  I think it was be-fore that time.

Q.  Did you have the deed recorded at Lewiston?

A.  Yes, sir.

Q.  Did you receive any consideration or any money for your brother or for his use at the time you executed this deed?     A.  No, sir.

Q.  When did you receive the money for him?

A.  Well, it was at the time I received my own, pretty nearly a year before.

Q.  Do you know of your brother's ever having received any other money for this land other than the money which you received for him?

A.  No, sir.

Q.  Did you have a conversation with the defend-ant William Dwyer on the streets of Lewiston some time last fall after a subpoena had been served upon you as a witness?     A.  Yes, sir.

Q.  Will you please state what that conversation was?

A.  He asked me if I had been subpoenaed to go to Moscow, and I told him I had, that I had my sub-poena in my pocket, and I took it out and showed it to him.

Q.  Now go on and state what further was said as you recollect it?

A.  I think he said it wasn't much of a case, and if we had some good lawyers we would come out all right, or words to that effect.

(Testimony of Hiram F. Lewis.)

Q. ' He said what?

A. That it wasn't much of a case, and if they had some good lawyers, and if they stood together everything would come out all right, or words to that effect.

Q. Give us his expression.

A. "We," I think it was.

Q. Give us his expression as he used it.

A. He said if we stand together, we will come out all right.

### Cross-examination by Mr. TANNAHILL.

Q. Mr. Lewis, have you talked with anyone about your evidence to-day?　　A. No, sir.

Q. Did you talk to anyone last night about your evidence?　　A. No, sir.

Q. Who was it talked with you about this particular part of your evidence at any time regarding what Mr. Dwyer said to you?

A. I don't understand what you mean, Mr. Tannahill.

Q. Who was it talked to you about this part of your evidence as to what Mr. Dwyer said to you? Has anyone talked to you about it? About what Mr. Dwyer had said to you, "We" would all stand together if we had some good lawyers?

A. I don't think anybody has since last fall.

Q. Who talked to you about it last fall?

A. The matter was brought up in court then.

Q. Did you ever make a statement for the prosecution in this case?　　A. Yes, sir.

Q. And you signed it, did you?

(Testimony of Hiram F. Lewis.)

A.  I don't know whether you would call it a statement or not.

Q.  Did you sign a statement for the prosecution?

Q.  Yes, sir.

Q.  And was that particular question in that statement?

A.  I don't know whether it was or not.

Q.  Who did you make that statement for?

A.  I made it for Mr. Dwyer.

Q.  I mean for the prosecution, or for Mr. Ruick? Did you make a statement for Mr. Ruick?

A.  Make it for him?

Q.  Yes.          A.  Yes, I made it to Mr. Ruick.

Q.  And did you sign that statement?

A.  To Mr. Ruick?

Q.  Yes.          A.  There is my evidence here.

Q.  It was your evidence?          A.  Yes, sir.

Q.  Before you went on the stand last fall did you have any conversation with anyone about your evidence, or did anyone ask you about what you were going to testify to?          A.  No, sir.

Q.  No one at all?

A.  No, sir; not outside of that.

Q.  You had no talk with Mr. Ruick about it?

A.  Well, I reviewed my testimony which I had given in before the grand jury.

Q.  Now, did you appear before the grand jury before you were brought in here and put on the witness-stand?          A.  Yes, sir.

Q.  And did you have a talk with Mr. Ruick there before you went before the grand jury?

(Testimony of Hiram F. Lewis.)

A.   Yes, sir.

Q.   How long after you appeared before the grand jury was it you were brought in here and put on the stand?

A.   I think it was about a year if I am not mistaken.

Q.   About a year?

A.   I think it was two years ago.   I was before the grand jury, and I think it was last fall.

Q.   You were not before the grand jury last fall?

A.   No, sir.

Q.   Now, Mr. Lewis, how long was it after you proved up on your claim before you sold it?

A.   It was over a year, anyhow.

Q.   And you sold it to Mr. Kester?

A.   Yes, sir.

Q.   And you sold your brother's claim to him too?

A.   Yes, sir.

Q.   And when you sold it to him you got your notes in return?     A.   Yes, sir.

Q.   And what was the undersanding when you sold it to him?   You were to get your notes, were you not, and you were not to have anything in addition?     A.   Yes, sir.

Q.   Now, Mr. Lewis, you stated your understanding was that when you proved up on your claim and deeded it, and got your $150 over and above expenses, you were selling your right.   As a matter of fact, your understanding about selling your right was that when Mr. Dwyer located you on the claim, and you proved up on it, and got your final receipt and sold

(Testimony of Hiram F. Lewis.)
the land, that was your understanding of selling your right, was it not? A. Yes, sir.

Q. You don't know whether that was Mr. Dwyer's understanding of selling your right, do you?

A. No, I don't know as I do.

Q. Now, then, Mr. Lewis, did not you and Mr. Dwyer have a talk about the expenses, about what it would cost for the location fee, and for the amount which was necessary to prove up on the land, and the general expenses, and also have a talk about what the land would be worth after title was acquired?

A. Yes, sir*p* I think we did.

Q. And did not Mr. Dwyer say that you ought to get at least $150 clear out of that *f*laim in case you wanted to sell it after you proved up?

A. Yes, sir.

Q. And *tat* was the understanding between you?

A. Yes, sir.

Q. And you understood that as selling your right?

A. Yes, sir.

Q. Now, you went to Mr. Kester and talked to him about money to prove up after you had filed on your claim, and before making final proof, did you not, Mr. Lewis? A. Yes, sir.

Q. And told him you wanted to borrow a sufficient amount of money to finish paying for your claim. You had some money you say?

A. Yes, sir.

Q. And Mr. Kester told you he would lend you enough money to enable you to pay for your claim if

(Testimony of Hiram F. Lewis.)

you would give your note for it; that is correct, is it not?

A. Well, yes, they said if I would give them a note they would furnish the money.

The COURT.—What is the answer?

A. They said they would furnish the money to prove up with if I would give a note for it.

Q. And your note was drawing interest, was it?

A. Yes, sir.

Q. You understood you had a right to sell that land to some one else any time after you had proved up, did you not?

A. Yes, sir; I guess I could have done it all right.

Q. And you did try to sell it to someone else?

A. Yes, sir.

Q. Whom did you try to sell it to?

A. To Potlatch Lumber Company.

Q. Did you try to sell it to anyone else?

A. Yes, sir; I went to *Jo* Malloy; I forget what company he was representing at the time.

Q. How long was that after you proved up?

A. About four or five months.

Q. About four or five months? And how long after you proved up was it that you tried to sell it to the Potlatch Lumber Company?

A. About the same time, I think.

Q. I will ask you also if you did not try to sell it to Charles W. Williams, who has an office in the Lewiston National Bank on the third floor?

A. I think I did.

(Testimony of Hiram F. Lewis.)

Q. I will ask you if you did not go to Mr. Kester and tell him you could not sell it and wanted him to take the land and give you back your notes?

A. No, I don't know as I did do that.

Q. What? A. No, sir; I don't think I did.

Q. Don't you remember, Mr. Lewis, you went to Mr. Kester and told him you wanted to deed over the land to him and wanted to take up your notes, and he asked you if you could not sell it to someone else, or words to that effect?

A. Mr. Kester told me if I could get any more money than a certain amount for the claim, I was at perfect liberty to do so.

Q. And you understood you had a perfect right to do so?

A. I tried to do so, and could not do it.

Q. You could not do it?

A. No, I could not do it.

Q. And you came back and told him you wanted to deed it to him? A. Yes, sir.

Q. And that is how you came to deed them over to Mr. Kester at that time? A. Yes, sir.

Q. Now, Mr. Lewis, you got your brother's notes in return at the same time you deeded this land to Mr. Kester, did you not?

A. My brother never gave him any notes; they were all given in my name.

Q. You gave the notes for the whole amount?

A. Yes, sir.

(Testimony of Hiram F. Lewis.)

Q. Now you also had these notes taken up, the samall notes taken up, and gave one large note for the full amount, did you not?    A. Yes, sir.

Q. And that large note is the one you took up when you made the deed?    A. Yes, sir.

Q. How much was that note for?

A. I could not tell you how much it was, but I think I have the note at home.

Q. Have you either of these notes with you?

A. I have not now. I have not been home since January; one is in Lewiston, I think I have that note at Lewiston.

Q. You have none of the notes here?

A. No, sir.

Q. Do you know about how much it was, Mr. Lewis?

A. It was $1600 or something like that, of $1700; I forget just how much it was.

Q. You think about $1600 or $1700?

A. Yes, sir.

Q. And that is the one returned to you?

A. Yes, sir.

Q. And that is the one you think you have at Lewiston?    A. Yes, sir.

Q. Then Mr. Lewis, you understood you had an interest in those claims up to the day you made a conveyance to Mr. Kester did you not?

A. Yes, sir.

Q. And if you could have sold those claims for $2500 or $3000, you would have gone and paid your notes off and the balance would have been yours,

(Testimony of Hiram F. Lewis.)

would it not, according to your understanding about it? A. Yes, sir.

Q. Now, Mr. Lewis, you testified here at the former trial of United States against Dwyer, did you not?

A. Yes, sir.

Q. And you saw Mr. Dwyer after you went to Lewiston, after you returned to Lewiston?

A. Yes, sir.

Q. And had a talk with him? A. Yes, sir.

Q. Where did you see Mr. Dwyer?

A. I think I met him on the street in Lewiston.

Q. Do you know about where?

A. I think I met him right near the postoffice, if I remember.

Q. Don't you remember of going across to Mr. Dwyer where his horse was tied just before he started for home?

A. It might have been that way; I don't recollect just now.

Q. Do you recall what you said to Mr. Dwyer at that time? A. I don't know.

Q. Do you remember saying anything to him about the fact that you wanted to make a statement?

A. No, sir; not at that time.

Q. Do you remember saying anything to him about it at any other time?

A. I think after that he spoke to me something about it.

Q. Don't you remember at that time you said something to him about your maming a statement, and that you would come to his office in a few days?

(Testimony of Hiram F. Lewis.)

A.  I don't recall just now.

Q.  T*k*o refresh your memory Mr. Lewis, I will ask you if you did not come up to Mr. Dwyer, on the corner of Fourth and Main Street, by the Lewiston National Bank Building, where Mr. Dwyer's horse was tied? Do you remember coming up to Mr. Dwyer there at that place?

A.  I don't remember that I did; no, sir.

Q.  And do you remember saying to him, Bill, I am sorry about what took place up at Moscow, or words to that effect?

Mr. RUICK.—I object to the evidence as incompetent, irrelevant and immaterial.

The COURT.—Mr. Tannahill, is this all of the conversation you intend to call his attention to?

Mr. TANNAHILL.—Yes, your Honor.

Mr. RUICK.—Why not let him give the conversation, if you want it?

Mr. TANNAHILL.—That is not all of the conversation.

The COURT.—The Court will require you to give the entire conversation.

Be it remembered that then and there the following conversation was had:

Q.  In November, 1906, just after you had re*utn*red to Lewiston, after the trial of the case of the United States vs. William Dwyer for subornation of perjury, did you not go up to Mr. Dwyer at the corner of Fourth and Main Street at the corner of the Lewiston National Bank Building where *m*r. Dwyer's horse

(Testimony of Hiram F. Lewis.)

was tied, and state to Mr. Dwyer, "Bill, I am sorry about what took place up at Moscow," to which Mr. Dwyer replied, "Why then didn't you tell the truth?" To which you replied, "I just could not do it; Miles Johnosn and Ruick just browbeated me so that I could not do it; I started to tell the truth and they stopped me, and would not let me say anything only what they wanted me to. I want to make a statement to that effect; that is the reason I came up to see you now. I met you over on the other side and you would not speak to me, and I want to tell you the position I was placed in; I will come to your office and will put it in writing just as it was, so I will never have to be bothered again," or words to that effect?

The COURT.—Now, what is the purpose of this question? Suppose he stated this, or suppose he did not. Assuming he now states he did not, how would it be material or relevant at this time?

Mr. TANNAHILL.—It would be material if the Court please to show it is in conflict with the evidence which he has given here.

The COURT.—If counsel desires to say the witness has been intimidated, or subjected to any influences of an improper nature, the Court will admit it; but the Court will exclude this question. The objection is sustained.

To which ruling of the Court the defendants then and there excepted, which exception was allowed by the Court.

Q. You did sign a statement did you not, Mr. Lewis.

(Testimony of Hiram F. Lewis.)

The COURT.—Show him the statement; that is the proper way.

Q. You can read it over, and look at the signature both on that page and on this one, and after you read it over, state whether or not you signed, state whether or not you signed that statement? You swore to that?

A. There is some things in there I didn't.

Q. That is your signature?     A. Yes, sir.

Q. And you swore to it before Charles L. McDonald, a notary public.

A. I did, but I think there are some things in there I never stated.

(The paper is marked Defendant's Exhibit "C" for Identification, J.E.B., May 22n, 1907).

Q. Mr. Lewis, did I understand you to say there were some things in this affidavit which were not in there when you signed it?

A. No, I didn't say that, but then I think there are two or three statements in there I didn't make.

Q. Did anyone go with you to Mr. McDonald's office to swear you to this or did you go alone?

A. I think Mr. Dwyer; I don't know whether he went along or not; I would not swear positively.

Q. Don't you know whether you went alone or not, Mr. Lewis, and signed that?

A. I would not say positively whether I did or not.

Q. Don't you know whether Mr. McDonald read it over to you?     A. No, sir.

Q. Don't you know he did read it over to you?

A. No, sir; I don't know he did.

(Testimony of Hiram F. Lewis.)

Q. Will you swear he did not?

A. Yes, sir; I think I would.

Q. Do you know Mr. Mullan?     A. Yes, sir.

Q. Do you not know that you took that affidavit to him and wanted him to swear you to it before you swore to it, before Mr. McDonald, and he would not swear you to it?

A. At Mr. Dwyer's instigation I took it to Mr. Mullen.

Q. He took it and read it over?     A. Yes, sir.

Q. And handed it back, and would not swear you to it?

A. He handed it back to me and said he did not want to do it.

Q. And then you took it to Charlie McDonald?

A. I didn't take it that day; it was another day.

Q. You afterwards took it to Charlie McDonald and he swore you to it?

A. Yes, sir; he swore me to it all right I don't swear I went alone, Mr. Tannahill.

Q. The COURT.—I think impeaching a witness by showing him a statement at some different time, which are contrary to or inconsistent with the statements made on the stand, I think that should be done while the witness is on the stand, to give the other side an opportunity of asking for an explanation.

Mr. TANNAHILL.—I will offer this affidavit in evidence.

The COURT.—There is no objection. It will be admitted.

(Testimony of Hiram F. Lewis.)

And the same is admitted and marked Defendant's Exhibit "C," and is as follows:

### Defendant's Exhibit "C."

State of Idaho,
County of Nez Perce,—ss.

Hiram F. Lewis, being duly sworn says: That he is the identical Hiram F. Lewis who testified in the United States Court for the Northern Division, District of Idaho, in the case of the United States of America, Plaintiff, vs. William Dwyer, defendant; that prior to testifying in said cause I was interrogated by N. M. Ruick, U. S. District Attorney, and told the said U. S. District Attorney many things regarding my purchase of the tract of land in question, which the said Ruick ordered his stenographer to strike from his notes with the statement: "We don't want that," and this was always the case when any statement was made which was unfavorable to the government's case or favorable to the defendants. Mr. Ruick also told me three or four times if I did not make certain statements he would take me before the judge and have me impeached, and many other things which caused me to fear the consequences if I did not leave out of my evidence certain statements which he requested the stenographer to strike out, and add others at his request.

I told Mr. Ruick, among other things, prior to being placed upon the stand as a witness in said case that I owned my land and showed him tax receipts, and that I had tried to sell to other parties, Mr. Will-

(Testimony of Hiram F. Lewis.)

iams and *Jo* Malloy, and there was nothing to prevent me from selling to anyone. I also stated to Mr. Ruick I did not borrow the money from the Lewiston National Bank expressly for the purpose for paying for the land, and I had done business with the bank before this timber matter ever came up; that I came to Lewiston for the purpose of getting some timber claims, and using my rights. All this he had the stenographer strike out with the statement: We don't want that. All these statements I aver and swear to be true as herein stated.

I told Mr. Ruick I never made a prior agreement with Mr. Dwyer or Mr. Kester*l* or anyone else; that Mr. Dwyer only told me if I took the claim I could make a little money out of them, and he did not care who I sold them to; so he got his location fee, which is true, and the statements made by Mr. Dwyer to me.

I owned the land fourteen or fifteen months, and tried to sell to other parties, among them being Mr. Williams and Joe Malloy, but no one seemed to want to buy that class of timber at that time.

Mr. Ruick wanted me to make the statement that Mr. Dwyer looked me up, but that is not true. I was looking for timber and a chance to locate, and went to Mr. Dwyer myself and offered to pay him his location fee if he would find me a timber claim.

In regard to leaving Mr. Dwyer before I went to Moscow, Mr. Ruick made the suggestion that the defende had good attorneys; I said, Mr. Dwyer told me that if everybody told the truth it would come out all right. Mr. Ruick says, "Did he not say you would all have to stand together," but that is not what Mr. Dwyer said. He said, "If everybody tells *th* truth, everything will come out all right." He never said anything about attorneys.

I also state that nothing was said about money being procured from Mr. Kester or the Lewiston National Bank, prior to making my declaratory statement, or filing my application to purchase the land, and we had not discussed money affairs until a short time prior to time for making final proof. In fact, I supposed I would have a sufficient amount of money to make the payments, and *dd* not think I would have any trouble raising it if I did not.

A short time prior to making final proof, I went to Mr. Kester, and asked him for a loan of the balance of the money necessary to make the payments, and promised to pay him when I sold the claims. Mr. Kester loaned me the money, and I gave my notes for same, taking it over and depositing it in Idaho Trust Co. We had no arrangement for the purchase of the claims either by Mr. Kester or Mr. Dwyer or anyone else up to this time.

Some time after making final proof, Mr. Dwyer asked me for his location fee. I again went to Mr. Kester for the money and told him I would pay him as soon as I found a purchaser for the claim. I gave my note for the money, took same to the Idaho Trust Co., and deposited it, and in about two weeks thereafter, I drew out money to pay Mr. Dwyer his loca-

(Testimony of Hiram F. Lewis.)

tion fee, and paid him the first time I saw him which was about a week after I drew it from the Idaho Trust Company. I had no agreement with Mr. Dwyer or Mr. Kester or anyone else to purchase these claims at this time.

Later on, after I had tried to sell the claims to different parties without success, I went to Mr. Kester and asked him if he would not buy the claim. He (Kester) says, I do not care to buy them, and asked me if I could not sell them to someone else. I told him no, I had tried and cannot do so; I want to pay my note, and you had better buy them. We had some conversation regarding price, and finally reached an agreement and I sold the claims. This is the only arrangement I had with Mr. Kester or Mr. Dwyer or anyone else regarding the purchase of these claims. I further aver that I made this statement of my own free will and not at the request or suggestion of anyone; that I have carefully read the foregoing affidavit, know its contents and aver the same to be true as therein set forth.

HIRAM F. LEWIS.

State of Idaho,
County of Nez Perce,—ss.

On this 17th day of December, A. D. 1906, before me Chas. L. McDonald, a notary public in and for said county, personally appeared Hiram F. Lewis, known to me to be the person whose name is subscribed to the foregoing affidavit, who, after carefully reading the same to the said deponent, and explain-

(Testimony of Hiram F. Lewis.)
ing to him its contents stated to me that he subscribed
his name there*ott* for the uses and purposes therein
set forth.

### HIRAM F. LEWIS.

In witness whereof, I have hereunto set my hand
and affixed my official seal the day and year in this
certificate above written.

[Notarial Seal]  CHARLES L. McDONALD,
Notary Public in and for Nez Perce County, Idaho.

Q. Mr. Lewis, do you know William Schultz?

A. Yes, sir.

Q. Dou you know where he is at the present time?

A. Yes, sir.

Q. Did you see him in the fore part of this month,
the month of May, 1907?     A. Yes, sir.

Q. Where did you see him, at Crab Creek?

A. Yes, sir; I saw him on the Chicago & Milwaukee railroad?

Q. I will ask you, Mr. Lewis, if you did not state
to William Schultz at Crab Creek in Naylor & Norlin's camp about the month of May, 1907, in the State
of Washington, yourself and William Schultz being
present, did you not state to him as follows:  George
Kester did not know that I had filed on a timber claim
until I applied to him for the money to make final
proof, or purchase the land, or words in substance
and to that effect?  Did you make such a statement
as that to William Schul*dt*?     A. No, sir.

Q. Mr. Lewis, in regard to these statements which
you say Mr. Dwyer talked to you about, and discussed
with you relative to your final proof, Mr. Dwyer al-

(Testimony of Hiram F. Lewis.)

ways contended and told you that you had made no contract that was in violation of these questions and answers, did he not? A. Yes, I believe he did.

Mr. TANNAHILL.—That's all.

Redirect Examination by Mr. JOHNSON.

Q. Mr. Lewis, you are working for the contracting firm of Naylor & Norlin, are you not?

Q. Yes, sir.

*Mr.* Be it remembered that then and there the following proceeding was had:

Q. That contracting firm of Naylor & Norlin is financially backed by George H. Kester.

Mr. TANNAHILL.—Objected to as irrelevant and immaterial and incompetent.

The COURT.—Objection overruled.

To which ruling of the Court the defendants then and there excepted, which exception was allowed, and which was answered as follows:

A. Yes, sir.

Q. I will ask you if it was not a fact that George H. Kester came to you after you were a witness and under oath, and examined, and told you that unless you signed a document that he prepared for you, that you would lose your job? A. No, sir.

Q. Didn't he induce you to make a statement here similar to that? A. Mr. Kester?

Q. Yes, or some one for him?

A. No, sir; Mr. Kester never did.

Q. Mr. Dwyer spoke to you for him?

A. Yes.

Q. What did he tell you in relation to that?

(Testimony of Hiram F. Lewis.)

A.   He kind of ripped me up the back for the way the case had gone here.

Q.   What portion of this statement is it that you say is not true?

A.   I said this:  That the statement I made Mr. Dwyer took down in his *w*own hand writing.

Q.   This statement?

A.   Afterwards this was taken somewhere and typewritten and I never read it afterwards, the statement.

Q.　Did you tell him that Mr. Ruick took your statement?  Did you tell Mr. Dwyer that Mr. Ruick took your statement?

A.   Here before this Court?  Yes, I think so.

Q.   The first time you were here?

A.   Yes, I think I did.

Q.   You told him that did you?       A.   Yes, sir.

Q.   That is not a fact, is it?

A.   Yes, I think it is.

Q.   Is it not a fact that when you first came here to the grand jury that you were brought up and made a statement before you came, before the last day you made a statement to myself voluntarily, and voluntarily in the presence of Mr. Goodwin, and either Mr. *Pl*letier or Mr. Greb, and that Mr. Ruick was in the grand jury room at this time?

A.   I think it was Mr. Ruick, Mr. Johnson; I think Mr. Ruick took my statement.

Q.   Did you make any statement to Mr. Dwyer that Mr. Ruick had made any suggestion to you in reference to your first statement that you made?

(Testimony of Hiram F. Lewis.)

A. No, sir; I don't think I did.

(Here Mr. Johnson retires, and Mr. Ruick begins the redirect examination.)

Q. Mr. Lewis, when were you first summoned as a witness in this court, either before the Court or before the grand jury?

A. Two years I think before the grand jury, two years last fall.

Q. Not two years last fall; it must have been in the fall of 1905? A. Yes, that's right.

Q. The same term of court at which the indictments were returned against these defendats?

A. Yes, sir; a year ago last fall.

Q. Now, do you recall this circumstance, that your brother E. M. Lewis appeared here before you had, and that he had made a statement, and when you came up, we requested you to make a statement in my office, and you did make a statement in my office; don't you remember? A. Yes, sir.

Q. And that statement was taken down by some stenographer who was there, if you recollect?

A. Yes, sir.

Q. You remember who you were interrogated by, who it was that asked the questions?

A. I was thinking it was you, Mr. Ruick, but I may have been mistaken.

Q. I am not referring to last fall; I am referring to a year ago last fall?

A. That is what I mean, a year ago last fall. I thought it was yourself, but I may have been mistaken.

(Testimony of Hiram F. Lewis.)

Q. You remember that I did interrogate you last fall prior to the Dwyer trial?　A. Yes, sir.

Q. I am asking now about the fall of 1905 when you made a statement?

A. I think I made a request of you Mr. Ruick but I won't say positive that you took my statement.

Q. Don't you remember at that time that I was engaged continuously before the grand jury from day to day, while these statements were being taken from the witnesses in my office, and that it was my assistant who took them at the time?

A. I know the grand jury was in session at the time.

Q. Don't you recall that I was continually before the grand jury and that the statements were being taken by Mr. Johnson or by Mr. O'Fallon or by Mr. Goodwin?

A. Mr. O'Fallong I know was there at the time.

Q. And pssibly Mr. Goodwin?

A. Yesk sir.

Q. And quite probably Mr. Johnson?

A. I know Mr. Johnson was in the room, but I got it in my head that I made a request of you, and that you took my statement. I may be mistaken on that point.

Q. You say now that you may be mistaken about that?　A. Yes, sir.

Q. Do you recall this circumstance, that when you came up here last fall as a witness that I did interrogate you on two occasions at least before you testified?　A. Yes, sir.

(Testimony of Hiram F. Lewis.)

Q. And that I had before me the typewritten statement you had made before, do you recall that?

A. Yes, sir.

Q. And I interrogated you from that typewri*t*een statement, didn't I? A. Yes, sir.

Q. Do you recall any intimidation used upon you when you made the statement a year ago in my office.

A. A year ago last fall?

Q. Yes. A. No, sir.

Q. You have no recollection of any intimidation of any sort? A. A year ago last fall?

Q. Yes, sir.

A. No, sir; not a year ago last fall, but there was last fall.

Q. At the time you made this statement, you recall no intimidation at all? A. No, sir.

Q. This statement was made free and involuntarily was it? A. Yes, sir.

Q. Do you think you could identify your signature to this statement? A. Yes, sir.

Q. (Showing witness paper.) Is that your signature? A. Yes, sir.

Q. Sworn to before Mr. Goodwin, special agent?

A. Yes, sir.

Q. That is also your signature?

A. Yes, sir.

Q. Also sworn to before Mr. Goodwin?

A. Yes, sir.

Q. On the first day of November, 1905?

A. Yes, sir.

(Testimony of Hiram F. Lewis.)

Q. Mr. Lewis while they are reading that statement, do you recall who the stenographer was?

A. A year ago last fall?

Q. Yes.　　A. I think it was Mr. Greb.

Q. Did we have a stenographer last fall? Was one here when you made your statement?

A. Yes, sir.

Q. *D* you recall who the stenographer was?

A. He was the present stenographer if I am not mistaken.

Q. Mr. Oppenheim?　　A. Yes, sir.

Q. At that time Clerk of the United States Judge?　　A. Yes; I think so.

Q. Now, Mr. Lewis, was that original statement made at the request of Mr. Dwyer? How was it taken? State the circumstances under which it was taken.

A. You mean this statement?

Q. I mean this statement produced here and put in evidence to which you refer; I understand that after you left, after the Dwyer trial was concluded last fall that you were approached by Mr. Dwyer, is that corrct?　　A. Yes, sir.

Q. Now, state the whole thing, all about it?

A. I say I met him on the street, I think there one day, and as I said, he was feeling kind of sore, the way the case had gone, and he said he didn't think I had done him justice, or something to that effect.

The COUT.—I didn't understand that remark.

Q. Did you say that he stated that you hadn't done him justice? He said who *hadn't him* justice?

(Testimony of Hiram F. Lewis.)

*A*A.   He said I hadn't done him justice.

The COURT.—Tell the whole thing; how it occurred without waiting for the counsel to interrogate.

.   A.   Also that I met him going up to his office and he took down the statement, wrote it down himself and afterwards had it typewritten and in regard to just what was said there, I couldn't state fully to what was said, but he took it down so*em*where and had it t)pewritten and afterwards brought up this, as I say, I never read it after that was copied.

*A*.   You never read it after it was typewritten?

A.   No, sir; which I should have done. It was taken in that form.

Q.   You swore to it you think in this form?

A.   Yes, sir.

Q.   You say that the only statement that you made was taken down by Mr. Dwyer himself?

A.   Yes, sir.

Q.   And he procured it to be typewritten?

A.   Yes, sir.

Q.   And when was it brought to you?

A.   I think at Mr. Dwyer's room, if I am not mistaken.

Q.   In Mr. Dwyer's room where?

A.   In *th* First National Bank on the third floor.

Q.   On the third floor, do you mean where you had gone with the question?   A.   Yes, sir.

Q.   How long was Dwyer writing down the statement?

(Testimony of Hiram F. Lewis.)

A. I don't know; not a great while; I don't think I was up there over fifteen or twenty minutes.

Q. You don't think you were over fiteen or twenty minutes that you were up there?

A. No, sir.

Q. Here is a statement containing 700 or 750 words and you say that Dwyer wrote this out in fifteen minutes?

A. It don't seem to me I was up there that long; it was a *vey* short time.

Q. He wrote it with a pen did he?

A. With a pencil.

Q. He is not a stenographer is he?

A. No, sir.

Q. Nor a typewriter?    A. No, sir.

Q. Did you see what he wrote it on?

A. I think he had a tablet, a commom sized writing tablet.

Q. Did you notice how many pages he wrote?

A. No, sir, I didn't.

Q. Your recollection is that you were up there about fifteen minutes to the best of your recollection?

A. Yes, sir; I think about fifteen or twenty minutes.

Q. Who do you remember afterwards brought *ki* for you to sign?    A. Mr. Dwyer.

Q. Where did you sign it, do you remember?

A. I think in this room.

(Testimony of Hiram F. Lewis.)

Q. You say you never read this over? after when it was typewritten? A. No, sir.

Q. You never read this document?

A. No, sir.

Q. Now I think the quickest way to get after it, Mr. Lewis, you say some of the things in here, you said some of the things, you did not say. I think the best way to do in fairness to you is to let you go through it and read it and state what you did and what you did not say, so that you can know what you have got from me. (Handing witness affidavit.)

The COURT.—If you find anything there that you want to call attention to that you did not say, the Court gives you the privilege of marking the affidavit by enclosing the lines or by a check-mark.

A. Yes, I think so. (Reading) "I told Mr. Ruick among other things—

Mr. RUICK.—What's that?

I told Mr. Ruick among other things—

The COURT.—He is reading from the affidavit now.

The WITNESS.—"Prior to being placed upon the satand as a witness in said case that I owned my land and showed him tax receipts."

Q. What about that?

A. That is one that I don't think I ever said.

Q. How?

A. That one, that one thing I don't think I ever said, two or three places here, as I say, I marked them.

Q. Read them out, just read them out.

(Testimony of Hiram F. Lewis.)

A.   Also that "I told **Mr.** Ruick I never made a prior agreement with Mr. Dwyer or Mr. Kester."

Q.   You want to strike that out?    A.  Yes.

The COURT.—He answered, yes, nodded his head.

WITNESS.—"I also state that nothing was said about money being procured from **Mr.** *K*ester or the Lewiston National Bank."

Q.   Want to strike that out?    A.   Yes.

Q.   Is that all?

A.   Yes, that's all.

Q.   Mr. Lewis, last fall, will you let me have that statement please—last fall when I was interrogating you as a witness before you testified in the case, I have your—I had the typewri*teen* statement that bore your signature didn't I?    A.   Yes, sir.

Q.   In other words, I had this *stt*ment didn't I?

A.   Yes, sir.

Q.   And you began*t* to tell me a different story from that contained in this statement, didn't you?

A.   Well, I don't remember about all the things word for word *for word.*

Q.   Didn't you, don't you think you did?

A.   Perhaps a little.

Q.   Began*t* to talk differently and tell me a different story from what you had sworn to one year before?

A.   It was not my intention to do so, but I didn't remember it.

Q.   Don't you rec*l*ll the circumstance *tha* you began to tell me a different story?    A.   Yes, sir.

(Testimony of Hiram F. Lewis.)

Q. And I asked you how it happened, your story was so different from what you had testified to before? A. Yes, sir.

Q. And I asked you which one of the statements was correct, and which one you proposed `to stand on, the one you had made the year before, or the one you now made? You remember my asking you that? A. Yes, sir.

Q. And which statement did you decide to stand on? A. The former statement.

Q. You decided to stand on the former statement and did I not tell you that if the former statement was true I should insist on you testifying as you did in the former statement? A. Yes, sir.

Q. Didn't I tell you that I would not permit you to make one statement under oath and then go and attempt to change? A. Yes, sir.

Q. *DI* did that? A. Yes, sir.

Q. I told you that if the facts you had stated in the affidavit of November 1905 were not true that you were subject to indictment, didn't I?

A. Yes, sir.

Q. I went through every one of those questions *wih* you didn't I? A. Yes, sir.

Q. And you made a still further statement, didn't you? A. Yes, sir.

Q. And they were taken down by Judge Beatty's stenographer? A. Yes, sir.

(Testimony of Hiram F. Lewis.)

Q. And which reiterated the same facts you testified to and which you stated in November, 1905, didn't it?    A. Yes, sir.

Q. Did I use any pressure on you other than tell you that if your statements contained in this affidavit made in 1905, and you testified to any other state of facts that you would subject yourself to an indictment for perjury? Did I use any other pressure than that?    A. Yes, sir.

Q. What was it?

A. You told me you would take me before the judge and have me impeached.

Q. Before the judge?    A. Yes, sir.

Q. You mean by that, that if you went on the witness-stand here and testified to a different stte of facts than these, if these facts were true?

A. Yes, sir.

Q. That I would impeach you, didn't you?

A. Yes, sir*i*

Q. Did you regard that as a threat?

A. Somewhat, yes, sir.

Q. We went over this statement that was made by you in 1905, and which was sworn to by you, and you admitted to me, did you not, that the facts stated in thzt statement were true?    A. Yes, sir.

Q. And I told you if you went on the witness-stand and testified to a different state of facts that I would impeach you?    A. Yes, sir.

Q. You remember that distinctly do you not?

A. Yes, sir.

(Testimony of Hiram F. Lewis.)

Q. And when you started in and told me a whole lot of stuff and I told you that that—when I asked you a question and you tried to tell me something on another subject, I pinned you right down to the question, didn't I?     A. Yes, sir.

Q. I required you to say whether a certain fact was or was not true?     A. Yes, sir.

Q. Have I ever told you or asked you or solicited you Mr. Lewis at any time to, or intimated to you that I wanted anything out of you except the absolute straight truth?     A. No, sir.

Q. Never by any intimidation. Did I at noon to-day decline to have you interview me during recess?     A. Yes, sir.

Q. Did I tell you at that time as I told you before that all I desired you to do was simply to testify the truth?     A. Yes, sir.

Q. I don't know whether—I will go to the other matter. Now Mr. Lewis, I went through this statement of yours as you already testified, I went through this statement of yours, and I referred to your statement, made in 1905 before you testified upon the trial?     A. Yes, sir.

Q. When, and you are familiar with that, and in a way familiar with the evidence you gave last fall?     A. Yes, sir.

Q. You made the statement in your affidavit to the following effect: "I told Mr. Ruick among other things prior to being placed on the stand as a witness in said case that I owned my land, and

(Testimony of Hiram F. Lewis.)

showed him tax receipts." I now read from the affidavit which you made before McDonald which has been produced by counsel as your statement, and you say you have no recollection as having made such a statement as that?

A.   I think I told you that I had some tax receipts at home.

Q.   But I am speaking about the affidavit now. You say you desire that stricken out of this affidavit?

A.   Yes, sir.

Q.   As not having been said by you?

A.   Yes, sir.

Q.   The next paragraph? "I told Mr. Ruick I never made a prior agreement with Dwyer or Mr. Kester, or anyone else." You ask to have that stricken out also?    A.   Yes, sir.

Q.   That you didn't say?    A.   No, sir.

Q.   You never made that statement to Mr. Dwyer?

A.   No, sir.

Q.   And the next statement: "Mr. Ruick wanted me to make the statement that Mr. Dwyer looked me up." Do you recall that or do*w* you withdraw that statement? Do you ask to have that statement withdrawn?    A.   Is it marked?

Q.   It is marked with a cross.

Mr. TANNAHILL.—Let him examine it.

Mr. RUICK.—Yes, you examine it and look at the paragraph there which is checked with lead pencil?

A.   Yes, sir.

Q.   Do you want to withdraw that?

A.   Yes, sir.

(Testimony of Hiram F. Lewis.)

Q. I understand you to say that this statement reading, "Mr. Ruick wanted me to take the statement that Mr. Dwyer looked me up" that that was not true, you want to withdraw that statement as not having been made by you?    A. Yes, sir.

Q. Now this further statement, "I also state that nothing was said about money being procured from Mr. Kester or the Lewiston National Bank prior to making my declaratory statement, or filing my application to purchase lands." You also state you desire to withdraw that statement as not having been made?    A. Yes, sir.

Q. Now you say these statements that have been withdrawn by you—    A. Never made.

Q. You never swore to this statement knowingly?    A. No, sir.

Q. You never read over this affidavit after it was typewritten?    A. No, sir.

Q. And these statements were never known or made by you?    A. No, sir.

Recross-examination by Mr. TANNAHILL.

Q. I understand you to say you told Mr. Ruick you had tax receipts at home, is that right?

A. Yes, sir.

Q. And you have tax receipts at home, have you?

A. Yes, sir; I think I have.

Q. The change you desired was that you told Mr. Ruick you had tax receipts at home, and not that you showed the tax receipts to Mr. Ruick?

A. Yes, sir.

(Testimony of Hiram F. Lewis.)

Q. Now, how long did you have this affidavit before you signed and swore to it? How long did you have it in your possession, this affidavit which you swore to before Charles L. McDonald?

A. Only a few minutes, I think, just the time I got it, I think.

Q. Didn't you get it two or three days before you swore to it?    A. No, sir.

Q. You think you didn't?    A. No, sir.

Q. Don't you remember that Mr. Mullen read the affidavit over to you?    A. No, sir; I don't.

Q. He did not?    A. No, sir.

Q. You are positive of that?    A. Yes, sir.

Q. Don't you remember you gave Mr. Mullen the affidavit and you sat down on his right and he read the affidavit over to you?

A. I sat down in the same room, certainly, but he read it over to himself; he didn't read it to me.

Q. He didn't read it to you?

A. No, sir; he didn't read it to me.

Q. Don't you remember he read it aloud to you?

A. No, sir; he didn't.

Q. And you sat there beside him and looked at the affidavit?

A. No, sir; I wasn't close enough to him when he had it in his possession.

(Witness excused.)

F. M. GOODWIN, a witness recalled on behalf of the prosecution, testified as follows, on

Direct Examination by Mr. RUICK.

Q. I show this witness the following papers pertaining to the application of Edward M. Lewis, of Lewiston, Idaho, to enter at the United States Land Office at Lewiston, Idaho, under the Stone and Timber Act, the North half of the northeast quarter and the southwest quarter of the northwest quarter of section twenty-nine (29), Township thirty-nine (39) north, range five (5) east, of the Boise Meridian, District of lands subject to sale at Lewiston, Idaho, the first paper being sworn statement in duplicate; the second being notice for publication; the third—I won't number them at all, the testimony of claimant Edward Mr. Lewis, the cross-examination of claimant, Edward M. Lewis, the testimony of the witness William C. Helkinburg, the testimony of the witness Edwin Bliss, the final certificate signed by J. B. West, Regiser of the United States Land Office at Lewiston, and the final receipt isssued by Charles H. Garby, Receiver of the United States Land Office at Lewiston, Idaho, both certificate and receipt having been issued to Edward M. Lewis, of Lewiston, Idaho, and each of them numbered 5016. Examine the papers referred to which I now hand you, Mr. Goodwin, and state whether or not the signature of J. B. West, former Register of the United States Land Office at Lewiston, Idaho, is the genuine signature of Mr. J. B. West?

(Testimony of F. M. Goodwin.)

A. They are, with the exception of the cross-examination.

Q. I didn't present that to you.

A. And the certificate of the Receiver's receipt. That is of Mr. Garby.

Q. The cross-examination of Lewis in his own behalf, that is the cross-examination of claimant, isn't it signed?　　A. There is a blank there.

Q. The other papers bear his signature?

A. Yes, sir.

Q. And was Mr. West acting receiver at the Lewiston Land office at the time mentioned in those papers?　　A. He was.

Q. And was that the genuine signature of Charles H. Garby, former receiver of the Unied States Land Office at Lewiston?　　A. Yes, sir.

Be it remembered that then and there the following proceedings were had:

Mr. RUICK.—We now offer the sworn statement in duplicate and ask that it be marked Plaintiff's Exhibit 26.

Mr. FORNEY.—The defendants object to the introduction of this testimony on the ground it is incompetent, irrelevant, and immaterial; on the further ground that it does not prove or tend to prove any of the material allegations of the indictment; on the further ground that there is no evidence showing or tending to show any conspiracy or combination upon the part of or between the defendants, or any of them; upon the further ground that it post-dates the consummation of the conspiracy as alleged

(Testimony of F. M. Goodwin.)

in the indictment, and on the further ground that it does not connect or tend to connect any of the defendants with any of the alleged offenses set forth in the indictment.

The COURT.—The objection will be overruled.

To which ruling of the Court the defendnats excepted, which exception was allowed by the Court, and said documents were admitted in evidence, marked Plaintiff's Exhibit 26, and are as follows:

(Omitted—appear elsewhere.)

Be it remembered that then and there the following proceeding was had:

Mr. RUICK.—We now offer in evidence notice for publication of Edward M. Lewis, and ask that the sae be marked Plaintiff's Exhibit 27.

Mr. FORNEY.—The defendants make the same objection as made to the last document offered.

The COURT.—Objection overruled.

To which ruling of the Court the defendants then and there excepted, which exception was allowed by the Court. Said document was received in evidence and marked Plaintiff's Exhibit 27, copy of which appears elsewhere in this record.

Be it remembered that then and there the following proceedings were had:

Mr. RUICK.—I offer in evidence the testimony of claimant Edward M. Lewis, together with the cross-examination attached thereto and ask that these papers be marked as follows:

(Testimony of F. M. Goodwin.)

Testimony of claimant, Plaintiff's Exhibit 28.

Cross-examination attached thereto, Plaintiff's Exhibit 28A.

Testimony of the witness Wm. E. Helkinburg, and ask that it be marked Plaintiff's Exhibit 29.

Mr. FORNEY.—The defendants make the same objections to each of these documents offered as made to the last documents admitted in eviddnce.

The COURT.—The same ruling; they will be admitted in evidence.

To which ruling of the Court the defendants then and there excepted, which exception was allowed by the Court, and said exhibits were admitted in evidence, and marked respectively Plaintiff's Exhibits 28, 28-A, and 29, copies of which appear elsewhere in this transcript.

Be it remembered that then and there the following proceeding was had:

Mr. RUICK.—I offer next the testimony of Edwin Bliss, a witness on the application of Edward M. Lewis, and ask that it be marked Plaintiff's Exhibit 30.

Mr. FORNEY.—We make the same objection, please.

The COURT.—The same ruling.

To which ruling of the Court the defendants then and there excepted, which exception was allowed by the Court, and said document was admitted and marked Plaintiff's Exhibit 30, and is as follows:

(Omitted—appears elsewhere in this transcript.)

(Testimony of F. M. Goodwin.)

Be it remembered that then and there the following proceeding was had:

Mr. RUICK.—I next offer the final certificate *of* issued to Edward M. Lewis by the United States Land Office, at Lewiston, Idaho, being number 5016, and ask that the same be marked Plaintiff's Exhibit 31.

Mr. FORNEY.—Defendants make the same objection as heretofore made to these offers.

The COURT.—The same ruling.

To which ruling of the Court the defendants then and there excepted, which exception was allowed by the Court. Said document was received in evidence and marked Plaintiff's Exhibit 31, copy of which appears elsewhere in this transcript.

Be it remembered that then and there the following proceedings were had:

Mr. RUICK.—And the next is the final receipt issued to Edward M. Lewis, at the United States Land Office, Lewiston, Idaho, signed by Charles H. Garby, receiver, and ask that it be marked Plaintiff's Exhibit 32.

Mr. FORNEY.—We make the same objection to its introduction.

The COURT.—The same ruling.

To which ruling of the Court the defendants then and there excepted, which exception was allowed by the Court, and said document was receied in evidence, and marked Plaintiff's Exhibit 32, copy of which appears elsewhere in this transcript.

(Excused.)

EDWARD M. LEWIS, a witness called and sworn on behalf of the prosecution, testified as follows on

Direct Examination by Mr. RUICK.

Q. Where do you reside?

A. Lewiston, Idaho.

Q. How long have you resided there?

A. About four years.

Q. Are you a brother of Hiram F. Lewis?

A. Yes, sir.

Q. Did you file on a stone and timber claim under the stone and timeber law?    A. I did.

Q. Plaintiff's Exhibit No. 26 shown witness. Look at this paper in duplicate and see if it contains your signature.    A. Yes, sir.

Q. You recognize the paper, do you?

A. Yes, sir.

Q. How did you come to take up a stone and timber claim, Mr. Lewis?

A. By request of my brother.

Be it remembered that then and there the following proceeding was had:

Q. Did your brother state to you anything which Mr. Dwyer had said to him about taking up a timber claim, Mr. Dwyer or Mr. Kester?

Mr. FORNEY.—Objected to as immaterial and hearsay. And for the further reason that there is no evidence connecting Kester and Kettenbach with this transaction, and especially the transaction with this witness.

The COURT.—Let him answer.

(Testimony of Edward M. Lewis.)

To which ruling of the Court the defendants then and there excepted, which exception was allowed by the Court, and the witness answered:

A. Yes, sir.

Q. Well, you took up a timber claim?

A. Yes, sir.

Q. Who attended to the business for you?

A. My brother attended to most of it.

Q. What part of it did you attend to?

A. Just the filing, I think it was. The proving up.

QQ. What?

A. The filing and proving up was all I did.

Q. That is everything you did about it?

A. Yes, sir.

Q. You didn't have anything to do with making any arrangement concerning it?     A. No, sir.

Be it remembered that then and there the following proceeding was had:

Q. How much did you get out of this claim, Mr. Lewis?

Mr. FORNEY.—We object to that as immaterial.

The COURT.—The objection is overruled.

To which ruling of the Court the defendants then and there excepted, which exception was allowed, and the witness answered:

A. $150.00.

Be it remembered that then and there the following proceeding was had:

Q. Did you know before you filed you were going to get $150.00 out of it?

(Testimony of Edward M. Lewis.)

Mr. FORNEY.—Objected to as calling for a conclusion of the witness and not a fact, and in no way binding on the defendants.

Objection overruled.

To which ruling of the Court the defendants excepted, which exception was allowed.

And the witness ansered: No, sir.

Be it remembered that then and there the following proceeding was had:

Q. How much did you expect to get out of it?

Mr. FORNEY.—Objected to as immaterial.

The COURT.—Objection overruled.

To which ruling of the Court the defendants then and there excepted, which exception was allowed by the Court, and the witness answered:

A. Well, I didn't know how much I was to get out of it at the time, not until afterwards.

Q. No one said anything to you about how much you were to get out of it?     A. No, sir.

Q. At that time?

A. No, sir; not at that time.

Q. When did you learn you were going to get $150 out of it?     A. About the 16th day of January.

Q. What year.

A. I think it was the same year I proved up in that I made final proof.

Q. The 16th day of January?

A. I think it was when I first learned about it.

Q. You knew your brother was conducting all negotiations with reference to that claim, did you?

A. Yes, sir.

(Testimony of Edward M. Lewis.)

Q. Everything in relation to it?

A. Yes, sir.

Q. Did he advise you or inform you of the arrangement he had made in relation to your claim?

A. No, sir; not at that time.

Q. Or what he was going to do?

A. No, sir.

Q. Your claim was contested, wasn't it, Mr. Lewis?     A. Yes, sir.

Q. Did you have any talk with Mr. Dwyer or any of these parties in relation to the contest?

A. *Ye,* sir; I spoke to him about it and—

Q. What did you say to Dwyer?

A. I spoke to him about the contest on the claim.

Q. What did you tell him? That is what I want to know?

A. I told him the claim had been contested.

Q. What did Mr. Dwyer say?

A. He said for me to look after it; it was worth looking after.

Q. He said it was worth looking after?

A. Yes, sir.

Q. What did he tell you or what did he direct you to do or advise you to do?

A. He said I would have to have an attorney to take it through.

Q. Whom did he tell you to get?

A. Well he said, I think he said, it was Mr. Mullen should take *te* case.

Q. What attorney did you go to?

A. I went to Mr. Mullen.

(Testimony of Edward M. Lewis.)

Q. Who directed you to go to Mr. Mullen, if anyone? A. Mr. Dwyer.

Q. How much were you out on that contest?

A. I was out thirty dollars altogether.

Q. About thirty dollars? A. Yes, sir.

Q. Who first notified you that your claim had been contested? A. Mr. Dwyer.

Q. Who, if anyone, told you how much an attorney would cost you to conduct this contest?

A. Mr. Dwyer.

Q. Did you have any conversation with the defendants, or either of them, about the return of the thirty dollars to you that you had expended in this contest? A. No, sir.

Q. How is that? A. No, sir.

Q. Did you have any conversation with your brother about the $30 you had expended in this contest? I am calling for the conversation. I am asking you merely the fact: Did you have any conversation with him about the $30?

A. Not at that time, no.

Q. Not at that time, but later? A. Yes.

Q. Was that $30 ever returned to you?

A. Yes, sir.

Q. By whom? A. My brother.

Q. At what time relative to the time you made your final proof if you remember? Before or after you made your final proof?

A. It was after I made my final proof.

Q. Can you tell us about how long after, Mr. Lewis.

(Testimony of Edward M. Lewis.)

A. I think it was only about two months or so afterwards.

Mr. RUICK.—This witness I will state to the Court is not called to prove any of these overt acts alleged in the indictment at this time; he is simply called for the purpose of confirming the testimony of his brother, Hiram F. Lewis, in the particulars wherein E. M. Lewis was involved. We understand the entire business was transacted by his brother, Hiram F. Lewis, and this witness did not come in contact with the defendants or either of them, except in the one instance to which his attention has been called.

Mr. TANNAHILL.—We object then to this evidence as incompetent, because you cannot call a witness to corroborate the evidence of another witness by some witness who did not come in contact with the defendants.

Mr. RUICK.—I will use the word explain.

The COJRT.—Is there anything before the Court, gentlemen?

Mr. TANNAHILL.—I think not. I was simply replying to Mr. Ruick.

Q. Mr. Lewis, you filed a relinquishment in the land office at the same time you filed your sworn statement didn't you at the time you made your application to file?

A. Sworn statement, I don't understand.

Q. At the time you filed your original papers, the first papers, you filed a relinquishment didn't you?

A. Yes, sir.

(Testimony of Edward M. Lewis.)

Q.   Where had you procured that? Who had furnished that relinquishment to you?

A.   I don't remember just where that was now.

Q.   But you remember there was a relinquishment, don't you?

A.   Yes, sir, on this contest afterwards, was all.

Q.   And then there was a contest afterwards?

A.   The relinquishment first, and the contest afterwards was filed against me.

Q.   But what I mean to say is that at the time you filed your application to enter these lands, to purchase these lands, you filed another paper with that, a relinquishment?

A.   I don't remember as to that.

Mr. RUICK.—By way of explanztion it should be understood that this will be all shown by record evidence in the course of this trial.

Q.   Didn't you understand the land had been previously *been* contested and filed upon, and that it had to be relinquished before you filed?

A.   No, it don't seem like as if I remember anything like that, anything being said about it at all. I don't remember of any such thing.

Q.   Do you remember now the filing of a paper known as a relinquishment at the time you filed your original application?

A.   Well, I could not say for sure whether I did or not now; I don't remember.

Q.   Who was with you when you filed your papers in the land office?

(Testimony of Edward M. Lewis.)

A.   Oh, Mr. Mullen I think was the only one who was with me or went in with me.

Q.   When you filed your original papers?

A.   Yes, sir; the filing papers.

Q.   And who made out the papers if `you remember? I speak now of your sworn statement which I now show you? Where were those papers made out?

A.   I think the*ye* were made out in Mr. Mullen's office, the attorney, at that time.

Q.   Do you remember whether anyone was w*ih* you when they were made out?

A.   No, I don't think there was a*nb*ody there only myself.

Q.   You don't think there was?

A.   I know there was not; Mr. Mullen went into the office with me.

Q.   If you went to Mullen's office to have these papers made out, by whose direction did you go there?

A.   By Mr. Dwyer's.

Q.   Do you remember, Mr. Lewis, whether it was the fore part of January or the latter part of January that you got your $150?

A.   Well, it was on or before the 26th day of January; that I know.

Q.   Of what year?       A.   1905, I think it was.

Cross-examination by Mr. TANNAHILL.

Q.   Are you sure it was in 1905?

A.   I think it was; I was married in the same year.

Q.   You were married in the same year?

(Testimony of Edward M. Lewis.)

A. I was married on the 27th day of January, 1905.

Q. You say Mr. Dwyer told you your claim had been contested? A. Yes, sir.

Q. Where were the contest papers first served on you and is that the way you found out the claim was contested?

A. I think I received notifications of the contest through the mail, but as to who sent them, I don't recollect.

Q. And didn't you take that notice of contest to Mr. Dwyer and tell him your place had been contested after you received it, through the mail?

A. Yes, sir.

Q. And did not Mr. Dwyer tell you you had better employ an attorney and look after it*k* that it was worth looking after? A. Yes, sir.

Q. And you considered you had an interest in it sufficin*t* to justify you in looking after it?

A. Yes, sir.

Q. And you did look after it? A. Yes, sir.

(Excused.)


JOHN P. ROOS, a witness called and sworn on be*hl*f of the prosecution, testified as follow, on

Direct Examination by Mr. RUICK.

Q. Where *d* you reside Mr. Roos?

A. Lewiston, Idaho.

Q. What is your age? A. Twenty-six.

Q. How long have you resided at Lewiston?

A. About 24 years.

(Testimony of John P. Roos.)

Q. Are you acquainted with the defendants here, W. F. Kettenbach, George Kester and William Dwyer, and each of them? A. Yes, sir.

Q. How long have you known Mr. Kester?

A. I suppose I have known Mr. Kester since I have been old enough to know anyone.

Q. What have your relations been with Mr. Kester, intimate or what?

A. I term it so, yes, sir.

Q. You were boys together? A. Yes, sir.

Q. Went to school together?

A. Mr. Kester is somewhat older than I am I suppse we both attended the same school.

Q. How long have you known Mr. Kettnbach?

A. About the same length of time.

Q. How long have you known Mr. Dwyer?

A. Perhaps two or three years, or such a matter.

Q. Did you ever take up a stone and timber claim, or timber claim?

A. I filed on a claim once, but it was rejected; my filings were rejected.

Be it remembered that then and there the following proceeding was had:

Q. Did you have or did you ever have any conversation with the defendant George H. Kester relative to your using your right to take up timber land?

Mr. FORNEY.—Objected to upon the ground that no time has been specified and it is not shown that if any conversation was had it is within the time embraced within the indictment.

(Testimony of John P. Roos.)

The COURT.—The objection is overruled; answer yes or no*t*.

To which ruling of the Court the defendants then and there excepted, which exception was allowed and the witness answered:

A.  Yes, sir.

Q.  Now fix the time of that conversation as near as you can approximately?

A.  Well, it was during the year 1902, I would not say positively.

Q.  Could you give us an idea about the time you recollect it was in 1902?

A.  Well, it was later in the year than July, it was after July in 1902, I believe.

Be it remembered that then and there the following proceeding was had:

Q.  Where did this conversation take place?

Mr. TANNAHILL.—Objected to if the Court please, on the ground that it is irrelevant, immaterial and incompetent, not within the time embraced in the indictment.

The COURT.—The Court will not confine the prosecution to the time in the indictment; the question is whether this is in such proximity to that time as to make it admissible.

The COUR*T*.—I will ask the District Attorney the purpose of the testimony. The Court can't anticipate what the purpose is.

Mr. RUICK.—The purpose of this testimony and that of succeeding witnesses will be to connect the

(Testimony of John P. Roos.)

defendants Kettenbach and Kester and Dwyer directly together as having formed the conspiracy for the acquiring of timber lands, and we propose to trace this right down to the overt acts alleged in the indictments. We propose to connect it—to connect the defendants together with the testimony of this and other witnesses.

Mr. FORNEY.—On the ground of similarity of offenses?

Mr. RUICK.—No, not on that ground; this is for the purpose of proving acts going to show the conspiracy; this is a circumstance going to show the conspiracy, the concerted action or combination; this is a circumstance on that, and also it will be competent, we *clim*, for the purpose of showing other similar acts on the part of the defendants, or one or more of them, going to show the motive and purpose with which they acted.

The COURT.—Of course, the Court cannot anticipate what a witness is going to testify to or will testify to if permitted to testify; I assumed however, that it was for the purpose of showing motive, and counsel states it was for the purpose of showing motive, also for showing concerted action.

Mr. RUICK.—That is usually shown by circumstantial evidence and it is to show the conduct of the parties, and the declarations of the parties, as going to prove the concerted action. Now, I am well aware of the rule that the declaration of one co-conspirator *canot* be relied upon to prove the conspiracy. I am well aware of that rule, but that is not the purpose in

(Testimony of John P. Roos.)

offering this. We propose to show, and we offer the witness for the purpose of showing, the acts and conduct of two of the defendants named here, showing their concert of action. We will offer later, or propose to offer later, evidence showing concerted action on the part of three defendants, and then of another two of the defendants and so forth, as showing their acts, going to show pur*ps*e and motive, the circumstance showing, as I say, these concerted actions from which the jury are to infer that a combination, agreement and conspiracy existed between these parties; that is the evidence usually relied upon to show other and similar acts, acts similar to those which were laid in this indictment for the pur*ps*e of showing motive.

Mr. MOORE.—Which are you offering it for?

Mr. RUICK.—For all purposes for which it is-competent, and we say it is competent for those two purposes; we will offer it under the rule which your Honor has announced.

The COURT.—We probably all agree as to the rule. The rule is somewhat familiar, and the only question with the Court at this time, is, as I cannot anticipate—

Mr. RUICK.—Well, your Honor pardon me one moment more; we propose to offer evidence of a series of acts on the part of the defendants, two of them, two or more of them, acting in concert at a time prior to the time laid in the indictment, to show that the conspiracy, at the time laid in the indictment was or had been formed.

(Testimony of John P. Roos.)

The COURT.—The Court has never ruled upon the general question that you refer to, nor has it had any opportunity to mature a judgment upon the general question. That really involves a question of the statute of limitation and you are referring to that questons discussed in the newspapers and suggested by some pleas in this District, but I will state to you the question now in the Court's mind is, saying that your contention is correct, Mr. Ruick, that is, to the contention, or as to the conspiracy being a continuing offense, and that it may be prosecuted within three years after an overt act, or any overt act has been performed consummating the conspiracy. The real question in my mind at the present time is whether or not you are going to connect this testimony by referring to an incident occurring two or three years prior to the earliest date referred to in the indictment, whether or not you are going to show a continuous concerted action, so that that act would or could be made to relate to some continuing conspiracy.

Mr. RUICK.—That is what we propose to do.

The COURT.—That is what I have been asking you.

Mr. RUICK.—That is what we offer to do, and what we intended to offer to do.

The COURT.—If the District Attorney promises the Court that that is what will be done, or in good faith he will endeavor to do that, the Court will permit the testimony to go in, without, however, prejudicing or foreclosing the question as to whether or not the conspiracy is a continuing crime, or when

the only promise the Court expects of the Di
rney is that he will in good faith endeavor to
these incidents with a series of incidents to
the concerted action was continuous.

r. RUICK.—That is our suggestion, your H
he COURT.—This may ultimately be or may
aterial but I do not see how the Court car
e it on the District Attorney's promise to cor

Last question read with the objection.)
r. TANNAHILL.—Allow us the further o
that it is not within the time embraced w
statute of limitations or within three year
and a half years of the charge alleged in th
ment as to the conspiracy, and as too remo
the defendants notice of such evidence
1 evidence would be offered or relied upon by
ecution.
he COURT.—The ruling will apply to the a
ction. And the objection will be overrulec
k I will say further, if ultimately this inci
ot properly connected with the charges, as
he indictment, the Court will strike it out
er instructions to the jury.
o which ruling of the Court the defendants
there excepted, which exception was allowe
Court. And the witness answered:

A.   On the main street in Lewiston.

Be it remembered that then and there the fo
proceeding was had:

Q.   How did the conversation occur?

A.   Mr. Kester spoke to me on the str
asked me the question—

Mr. FORNEY.—Wait a moment.

Mr. RUICK.—You may state the convers

Mr. FORNEY.—We now offer the same o
last offered.

The COURT.—Objection overruled.

To which ruling of the Court the defenda
and there excepted, which exception was allow
the witness answered:

A.   Mr. Kester asked me if I had been up
a certain body of timber, giving the section a
bers and so forth, and I told him I did no
and asked him if that timber was the timbe
between Southwick and the Clearwater river,
said it was.   I said I had passed through it
wagon road, that is all.   He asked me what
take for my right, and I answered I didn't ki
asked him what he would be willing to gi
said he would give me, I think it was, $200.
not positive as to the amount.   I told him I
my right was worth more to me than that

(Testimony of John P. Roos.)

Mr. FORNEY.—We move to strike out the testimony of the witness for the reasons set forth in the objections to the question.

The COURT.—Motion denied.

To which ruling of the Court the defendants then and there excepted, which exception was allowed by the Court.

Cross-examination by Mr. TANNAHILL.

Q. Who have you talked with about your evidence?

A. I talked with Mr. Johnson and also Mr. Ruick.

Q. Have you talked with Mr. Goodwin or Mr. O'Fallon?

A. I think I talked with Mr. Johnson and Mr. Ruick in Mr. Goodwin's office, but not to him though.

Q. And how many times did you *tlak* to him?

A. Well, the first time I was called to Mr. Johnson's office in Lewiston in the matter, I think it was in 1905, and was asked in regard to these things, which I tried to avoid, but I found out that Mr. Johnson was posted more than I was in the matter and then again before the grand jury, before which I appeared; I think I spoke with Mr. Johnson before I went into the grand jury.

Q. Did you make a statement for them, or sign a statement?

A. I never signed any statement, no, sir.

Q. You and Mr. Kester had some discussion about the expense of proving up, didn't you?

A. No, sir.

(Testimony of John P. Roos.)

Q. You say you don't remember just exactly what you were to get out of it?

A. I think he said the amount was $200; I am not positive.

Q. Didn't he say what the claim was worth?

A. What?

Q. Did not he say the claim was possibly worth $200?

A. Not to the best of my knowledge at present.

Q. You don't wish to be understood as swearing positively he did not say that to you?

A. No, sir; I don't.

Q. Mr. Kester might have told you that the claim ought to be worth $200 over the cost of proving up?

A. I don't think he did.

Q. You won't swear *pstively* he did not?

A. No, sir; it has been some time ago.

The COURT.—Can we agree as to the date this occurred, what day it was?

Mr. RUICK.—He said it was after July, 1902.

Redirect Examination by Mr. RUICK.

Q. Did you mention the fact of this conversation to any other person?

A. I believe I did. I kept it no secret whatever.

Q. Will you state one or more persons to whom you mentioned it?

A. I could not as to that. I perhaps mentioned it to several, but as to any certain one, I could not say because I could not swear to it.

(Testimony of John P. Roos.)

Recross-examination by Mr. TANNAHILL.

Q. What is your best recollection as to the date of this conversation?

A. Well, I think it was in the fall of 1902.

Q. About what time in the fall?

A. It is pretty hard to say.

Q. About October or November?

A. I could not say as to that; I had already been up through the timber; I went up into the timber in July, 1902.

Q. Your recollection is now it was somewheres close to July, 1902?    A. I think so.

Q. Mr. Roos, you did not follow that up and take a claim, did you?    A. No, sir.

Redirect Examination by Mr. RUICK.

Q. You stated there to the best of your recollection and judgment it was in the fall of 1902?

A. Yes, sir.

Q. And yet—

Mr. TANNAHILL.—Finish your answer.

The WITNESS.—Yes, I did. But I always thought *g*that fall immediately followed summer, June, July and August is summer and fall follows.

Q. You mean, then, that it was in the fall, the beginning of September?

A. Practically late in the summer or early in the fall; I could not tell you as to that. We sometimes have a late and sometimes an early fall.

Friday, May 24th, 1907, 10 o'clock A. M.

WYNN W. PEFLY, a witness called and sworn for the prosecution, testified as follows on

Direct Examination by Mr. RUICK.

Q. What are your initials?     A. W. W.

(Witness continuing:)

I reside at present at Boise. At one time I was a resident of the city of Lewiston; from 1899 up three months ago. I was born in Boise; I am past thirty years of age.

I acted as assistant special agent of the General Land Office for almost two years, that is occasionally, off and on. I was in the Spanish War, in the Idaho regiment. I am acquainted with Mr. W. F. Kettenbach, have known him ever since I have been in Lewiston, I think. I am acquainted with George H. Kester; have known him about the same length of time. I have known William Dwyer by sight for some years, I can't imagine how many. I never was personally acquainted with him.

I made a preliminary filing on a timber claim under what is known as the stone and timber law.

Q. Did you have any conversation with the defendants here whom I have named, or either of them, relative to filing on a timber claim?

A. Yes, sir.

Q. With which of the defendants, if more than one of them?     A. With Mr. Kester.

Q. When did the conversation occur?

A. It was in the fall of 1903.

Q. And where did it occur?

(Testimony of Wynn W. Pefly.)

A. In Lewiston.

Q. Whereabouts in Lewiston?

A. On Main Street.

Q. How did you come to go to Mr. Kester?

A. I was—there was several of use that would like to get timber claims, and Mr. Roos informed me that Mr. Kester was locating people, and I stopped him and asked him on the street one day concerning it.

Q. Was that Mr. J. B. Roo*d*, who testified here yesterday?    A. Yes, sir.

Be it remembered that then and there the following proceeding was had:

Q. Now, state the conversation that you had with Mr. Kester at that time?

Mr. FORNEY.—Objected to as incompetent, irrelevant and immaterial, and too remote and not tending to prove any issue in this case.

The COURT.—The Court will permit him to testify with the same understanding and on the same theory as applied to the testimony of the witness Roos yesterday.

Mr. FORNEY.—That is, that it is conditionally admitted, do I understand the Court?

The COURT.—Yes, it is admitted upon the promise that it will be connected.

Mr. FORNEY.—We will then ask your Honor to let the testimony of this witness go under our general objection also so that we will not be compelled to renew it again.

(Testimony of Wynn W. Pefly.)

The COURT.—Yes, sir.

To which ruling of the Court the defendants then and there excepted, which exception was allowed by the Court, and the witness answered:

A. I saw Mr. Kester on the street, and I asked him if it was a fact that he was locating people on timber claims and that there were several that would like to go in with me, if we could make satisfactory arrangements and he said it was so. I asked him concerning the particulars. He said all the expenses would be paid, and the money furnished to prove up on the land and *tat* it would net us about $150 apiece, and he said there was a party going out in a few days, and that he would be able to accommodate all of us, if we wanted to go.

Q. Did he name that party at that time?

A. No, sir.

Q. Did you see either of the defendants after that in relation to the subject? A. No.

Q. Well, did you meet either of the defendants— I will withdraw that question, and I will ask you this question: Did you file on a timber claim under this arrangement? A. No, sir.

Q. Well, did you notify the defendants, or either of them of that fact? If so, when and where?

A. Three or four days afterwards Mr. Dwyer came along in a buggy and asked *e* if we would be ready to go that afternoon on the train, and I told him we had decided to let the matter drop.

Q. Had you spoken to Mr. Dwyer concerning the subject your*slf*? A. No, sir.

(Testimony of Wynn W. Pefly.)

Q. Do you know how he knew or came to know that you had this talk that this matter had been mentioned to you? A. I do not.

Mr. RUICK.—That is all.

Be it remembered that then and there the following proceeding was had:

Mr. FORNEY.—We ask the Court to strike out the testimony of this witness on the ground that it is incompetent, irrelevant and immaterial, no connection having been shown between the defendants, and on the further ground that it does not tend to prove any offense alleged in the indictment or any continning offense. I submit to the Court that where a party has a conversation with any party and no action has been taken under it, that it is inadmissible to prove any intent or design or motive on the part of the defendant.

The COURT.—Well, this might, as the Court has said, it is somewhat remote, but the Court assumes that the District Attorney will claim that it is one circumstance in a chain of circumstances, and of course the chain cannot be introduced all at once; it comes from different persons. Of course the Court cannot anticipate whether the District Attorney will be able to connect it or not. I think the motion will be denied.

To which ruling of the Court the defendants then and there excepted, which exception was allowed by the Court.

(Testimony of Wynn W. Pefly.)

Cross-examination by Mr. TANNAHILL.

Q. Mr. Pefly, you do not remember all that took place in that conversation?

A. I don't remember all the details; I remember the main points.

Q. Don't you remember that Mr. Kester told you to go to Dwyer?    A. No, sir.

Q. He may have told you that?

A. I don't think that he did.

Q. Will you swear positively that he did not?

A. To the best of my memory he did not.

Q. You are not swearing positively that he did not tell you that?    A. I am satisfied that he did not.

Q. You say you are an employee of the Government at this time?    A. I did not say that, no.

Q. What are you doing now?

A. I am in the mining business now.

Q. And when was you in the employ of the Government?    A. In the years 1899 and 1900.

Q. Have you been in the employ of the Government since then?

A. I am in the employ of the Government now.

Q. You are?    A. Yes, sir.

Q. That is what I asked you?

A. You asked me what I was doing.

Q. Well, what are you doing now?

A. I am acting for the Government here.

Q. How long have you been in the employ of the Government?    A. For five or six days.

Q. What have you been employed to do?

(Testimony of Wynn W. Pefly.)

A.   As a guard for the attorneys, United States Attorney's office.

Q.   You have been in their employ for five or six days you say?    A.   Yes, sir.

Q.   And how many times have you talked about your evidence with these officials?

A.   Why, twice, I believe.

Q.   How many times did you talk about your evidence with the officials before you came to Moscow?

A.   Not at all.

Q.   Have you ever been in the employ of the Government looking after forest reserve patrol, or anyh-ing of that kind?

A.   Only as assistant, assistant to the special agent.

Q.   Assistant to the special agent.   When were you in that employment?    A.   In 1899 and 1900.

Q.   Have you been so engaged since that time?

A.   No, sir.

Q.   Now, who did you talk with about your evidence?    A.   Lately?

O.   Yes.    A.   Mr. Ruick and Mr. Johnson.

Q.   Who else?

A.   Why, I don't know whether I said anything to Mr. Goodwin or not; that was all.

Q.   Whom did you first tell of this conversation you had with M, Kester?

A.   After it happened?

Q.   Yes.

A.   Well, I don't remember; it has been several years ago.

(Testimony of Wynn W. Pefly.)

Q. Who did you first talk with about it?

A. The probabilities are that I talked with my associates that were going out in the timber with me.

Q. Who was the first government official that you talked with about it?

A. Mr. Johnson I believe.

Q. When?

A. Two years, two or three years ago.

Q. What was said?

A. Well, he asked me about what I knew about it and I told him.

Q. Did you make a statement at that time?

A. I did.

Q. You swore to it did you?    A. I did.

Q. Have you seen that statement since?

A. I have not.

Q. Never looked it over since that time?

A. No, sir.

Q. Now, as a matter of fact, there were a great many of you people around there who came to Mr. Kester for the purpose of getting him to assist you in getting timber claims, were there not?

A. I was the only one that I know of; of course I was acting for several others; they were all wanting to know concerning it.

Q. How many others were you acting for?

A. There was four or five; I don't remember exactly.

Q. And you and Mr. Kester discussed the details and the values of the claims, didn't you?

A. We did not.

(Testimony of Wynn W. Pefly.)

Q.	And you.discussed the question as to the expenses *an* costs of making final proof?

A.	Only in that he said that the money would be advanced for the final proof.

Q.	For the final proof?

A.	That is all the details there was.

Q.	That he would furnish the money for the final proof?	A.	Yes, sir.

Q.	There was something said about what the claims would be worth after you made final proof?

A.	There was somethi*g* said about how much it would net us clear.

Q.	Something about what it o*8*ught to net you clear?	A.	What it would net us clear.

Q.	And you and Mr. Kester discussed that, did you?	A.	Well, just about that much.

Q.	And Mr. Kester said it ought to net you about $150 or $200?

A.	He said it would net us $150 apiece.

Q.	You are positive about that now, are you?

A.	Yes, sir; I am, yes, sir.

Q.	You were not positive of it when you testified on direct examination?	A.	I was.

Q.	Now, Mr. Pefly, did not you testify on direct examination that Mr. Kester told you it would net you about $150 apiece clear?

A.	Well*l* it was about $150.

Q.	That is what you remember he said, now, is it not?	A.	Yes.

Q.	Then he did not say positively that it would net you $150?

(Testimony of Wynn W. Pefly.)

A. I don't remember whether he said it would net us $150 or about $150; it is about the same thing.

Q. You have been in the timber a good deal, haven't you, Mr. Pefley?

A. Quite a bit; yes, sir.

Q. You had been in the employ of the Government before you talked with Mr. Kester?

A. Yes, sir.

Q. And had been in the employ of the Government for some *tme* before? A. Yes, sir.

Q. And you knew enough to know that you could not make a prior agreement for the purchase of a timber claim, did you not?

A. I knew it was not lawful to.

Q. But that was not the reason you abandoned your purpose, was it? A. Yes, sir.

Q. How long after that was it before you took up a timber claim?

A. I did not take up one; I only made a preliminary filing on one.

Q. How long after that was it?

A. It was not after that; it was before that.

Q. And you had not got your right restored?

A. Yes, sir.

Q. And you say now that you remember that Mr. Kester told you it would net you about $150?

A. Yes.

Q. And you knew that it was unlawful?

A. I knew it was; yes.

Q. You never told Mr. Kester it was unlawful?

A. No, I did not.

(Testimony of Wynn W. Pefly.)

Q. What wages are you drawing now for the services you render the Government?

A. $5 a day.

Q. Drawing double pay, pay as a witness and pay as a doorkeeper?

A. No, sir; I am not drawing any pay as a witness.

Q. You are on very friendly terms with the Government officials, are you not?

A. Well, with Mr. Johnson I am; I have known him a good many years.

Q. You and Mr. Johnson are particular friends?

A. Not intimate, no.

Q. When did you quit the services as a special agent of the Government?

A. I never was a special agent, only an assistant.

Q. Well, as an assistant? A. I quit in 1900.

Q. What were the circumstances under which you quit?

A. Well, there was no quitting about it.

Q. You were discharged?

A. Just Mr. Meyendorf was *th* special agent at the time and he was transferred to some other part of the country, and the new special agent got somebody else, that was all.

Q. Do you know Miss Kistler living *k*in town here? A. Yes, sir.

Q. Did you have a conversation with her about this case and about the conviction of these boys?

A. I don't think so; not that I know of.

Q. Had no such conversation?

(Testimony of Wynn W. Pefly.)

A. Not to amount to anything; I might have expressed an opinion, or something like that.

Q. You expressed an opinion that this case would at least break the boys up, if it did not convict them, didn't you?

A. No, I don't think so; I don't remember all that I have said to Miss Kessler.

Q. I will ask you, Mr. Pefley, if you didn't state*y* to Miss Kessler in Moscow, Latah County, Idaho, 'since you came to Moscow to attend this trial yours*l*ef and Miss Kessler being present that ''We will either convict them, or will break them up before this trial is over,'' or words in substance and to that effect?

A. I don't believe I ever said anything of the kind.

Q. Did you say anything like that?

A. I probably said that they would, if not convicted, be broken up, but I did not say that we would, because I had nothing to do with it.

Q. But you remember that you may have said that if not convicted they would be broken up?

A. Well, I was repeating the words of others that had been said to me.

Q. *D*ome of the Government officials had told you that?

A. No, sir; the Government officials had not.

Q. But you made that statement to her?

A. Not that I remember of; I might have. I do not say that I did not.

Q. You won't say that you did not?

(Testimony of Wynn W. Pefly.)

A.   No, sir.   But not as you *sad* it though, that "we" said it.

Q.   You and Mr. Johnson are *plitical* friends also, are you not?      A.   No, sir.

Redirect Examination by Mr. RUICK.

Q.   You have moved out of Mr. Johnson's neighborhood, haven't you?      A.   Yes, sir.

Q.   Moved out of his part of the State?

A.   Yes, sir.

Q.   Your home was for years in Boise, wasn't it?

A.   Yes, sir.

Q.   The old home of the Pefly family is in Boise?

A.   Yes, sir.

Q.   And you have returned to the old home?

A.   Yes, sir.

Q.   Where all your relatives are?

A.   Yes, sir.

(Witness excused.)

F. M. GOODWIN, a witness recalled on behalf of the prosecution testified further as follows on

Direct Examination by Mr. RUICK.

Mr. RUICK.—What are these remarks made for? For my benefit or for the benefit of the District Attorney?   Do you remember when the District Attorney's office was broken into in Portland for valuable papers?   I am guarding my papers.   The Government has furnished a watchman for my office to guard my papers.   Do you understand the purpose now?   When I am followed home at 11 o'clock at

(Testimony of F. M. Goodwin.)

night, when I am leaving my office, by one of your employees—

The COURT.—Now, Mr. Ruick. Let us proceed—

Mr. RUICK.—and my footsteps are dogged, I will see that my papers are protected.

Mr. TANNAHILL.—We have no objection to your seeing that you have all the protection you want. In our little community nobody is going to do you any harm, Mr. Ruick.

The COURT.—Proceed with the case, gentlemen.

Q. Now, Mr. Goodwin, I show you paper purporting to be a sworn statement of Ivan R. Cornell, filed in making his application to purchase from the United States at the Lewiston, Idaho Land Office certain lands referred to in the indictm*netn* in this case, this paper being in duplicate; I next show you paper purporting to be testimony of claimant of Ivan R. Cornell, given—in order that it may be in the regular order, I will next show you the notice of publication of the intention of Ivan R. Cornell to give evidence in support of his said application; I next show you the testimony of claimant, Ivan R. Cornell, in the same proceeding and the cross-examination of claimant Ivan R. Cornell. Next the testimony of witness William F. Kettenbach in support of the application of Ivan R. Cornell; next the cros-examination of William F. Kettenbach, in *conc*tion with his direct examination; next the testimony of William Dwyer in support of the application of Ivan R. Cornell; next the cross-examination of William Dwyer in connection with the direct ex-

(Testimony of F. M. Goodwin.)

amination in support of the application of Ivan R.
Cornell. I next show you the register of final certificate No. 4,508, issued at the Lewiston, Idaho, Land
Office to Ivan R. Cornell. I next show you receiver's receipt number 4508, issued at the Lewiston, Idaho Land Office to Ivan R. Cornell, and purporting to bear the signature of C*hr*les H. Garby,
receiver of the United States Land Office. I ask
you to examine .those papers and each of them, and
state whether or not, with the exception of the receiver's receipt, these papers bear the genuine signature of J. B. West, former register of the United
States Land Office at Lewiston, Idaho?

A. They do.

Q. Was Mr. J. B. West the acting register of the
United States Land Office at the dates mentioned in
those papers?     A. He was.

Q. This receiv*r's* final receipt? Do you identify
this as the genuine signature of Charles H. Garby,
former receiver of the United States Land Office
there?     A. Yes.

Q. And was he acting as such receiver at the
time of this receipt?     A. He was.

Be it remembered that then and there the following proceeding was had:

Mr. RUICK.—We now offer in evidence the paper first identified, being the sworn statement of Ivan
R. Cornell, bearing date June 19th, 1903; this statement being in duplicate, and ask that it may be
marked Plaintiff's Exhibit 3.

(Testimony of F. M. Goodwin.)

Mr. FORNEY.—The defend*n*ts object to the introduction of this testimony as incompetent, irrelevant and immaterial, and not properly authenticated; no proper foundation having been laid and on the further ground that this party has not been charged as one of *te* co-conspirators in the indictment, nor was his name furns*i*hed in the bill of particulars and on the further ground that the acts alleged to have been committed here are long prior to the time alleged in the indictment that this conspiracy was formed. And that it tends to unduly prejudice the rights of these defend*n*ts before the jury, and on the further ground that it does not prove or tend to prove any of the allegations in the indictme*n*, on the further ground that there is no evidence showing or tending to show any conspiracy or combination upon the part of or between any of *any of* the defendants, and upon the further ground that it does not connect or tend to connect any of the defendants with any of the alleged offenses set forth in the indictment; on the further ground that it tends to unduly prejudice the rights of these defendants before the jury, and confuse them in their defense.

The COURT.—This is not one of the tracts of land connected with the parties named in the indictment.

Mr. RUICK.—This evidence is offered for the purpose for which the testimony of witness Pefley and Roos was offered, *fr* the purpose of showing a circumstance, showing combination or concert of action on the part of the defendants also.

(Testimony of F. M. Goodwin.)

The COURT.—These papers will be followed by the testimony of the entryman, Mr. Ruick?

Mr. RUICK.—Yes, your Honor, this is only preliminary.

The COURT.—Objection overruled.

To which ruling of the Court the defendant then and there excepted, which exception was allowed, and said documents were admitted and marked Plaintiff's Exhibits 32, and are as follows:

(Omitted; appear elsewhere in transcript.)

Mr. FORNEY.—Now, may the same objection go to each and all of the papers in connection with this entry?

The COURT.—Yes.

Mr. RUICK.—We now offer in evidence the testimony of claimant Ivan R. Cornell, and ask that it may be marked Plaintiff's Exhibit 33.

Mr. FORNEY.—To which offer the defendants make the same objection.

The COURT.—Same ruling.

To which ruling of the Court the defendants then and there exceped, which exception was allowed by the Court, and said paper was admitted in evidence, and marked Plaintiff's Exhibit 3, a copy of which appears at page —— of transcript.

Be it remembered that then and there the following proceeding was had:

Mr. RUICK.—I now offer in the same connection, cross-examination of Ivan R. Cornell, taken in connection with his direct examination, and ask that this may be marked Plaintiff's Exhibit 33-A.

(Testimony of F. M. Goodwin.)

Mr. FORNEY.—We make the same objection.

The COURT.—Objection overruled.

To which ruling of the Court the defendants then and there excepted, which exception was by the Court allowed.

Said paper was admitted in evidence marked Plaintiff's Exhibit 33-A, a copy of which appears elsewhere in transcript.

Be it remembered that then and there the following proceeding was had:

Mr. RUICK.—We next offer the testimony of William F. Kettenbach in support of the application of Ivan R. Cornell and ask that this be marked Plaintiff's Exhibit 34.

Mr. FORNEY.—We make the same objection.

The COURT.—Objection overruled; to which ruling of the Court the defendants then and there excepted, which exception was by the Court allowed, and said paper was admitted in evidence and marked Plaintiff's Exhibit 34, a copy of which appears elsewhere in the transcript.

Be it remembered that then and there the following proceeding was had

Mr. RUICK.—We now offer in evidence cross-examination of witness William F. Kettenbach, taken in connection with his direct examination, and ask that this be marked Plaintiff's Exhibit 34-A.

Mr. FORNEY.—The defendats make the same objection.

The COURT.—The same ruling.

(Testimony of F. M. Goodwin.)

To which ruling of the Court the defendants then and there excepted, which exception was by the Court allowed, and said paper was admitted in evidence and marked Plaintiff's Exhibit 34-A, a copy of which appears elsewhere.

Be it rememberrd that then and there the following proceeding was had:

Mr. RUICK.—We next offer in evidence the testimony of William Dwyer in *sp*port of the app,*i*cation of Ivan R. Cornell to enter the lands referred to and ask that this be marked Plaintiff's Exhibit No. 35.

Mr. FORNEY.—We submit the same objection.

The COURT.—The objection will be overruled.

To which ruling of the Court the defendants then and there excepted, which exception was allowed by the Court, and said paper was admitted in evidence, and marked Plaintiff's Exhibit 35, a copy of which appears elsewhere.

Be it remembered that then and there the following proceeding was had:

Mr. RUICK.—We next offer in evidence cross-examination of William Dwyer taken in connection with his cross-examination referred to and ask that it be marked Plaintiff's Exhibit 35-A.

Mr. FORNEY.—We submit the same objection, if your Honor please.

The COURT.—Objection overruled; to which ruling of the Court the defendant then and there excepted, which exception was allowed by the Court, and said document was admitted in evidence and

(Testimony of F. M. Goodwin.)

marked Plaintiff's Exhibit 35-A, a copy of which is set forth elsewhere in this transcript.

Be it remembered that then and there the following proceeding was had:

Mr. RUICK.—We offer in evidence the register's final certificate, No. 4508, issued to Ivan R. Cornell and ask that it may be marked Plaintiff's Exhibit 36.

Mr. FORNEY.—Same objection.

The COURT.—Same ruling.

To which ruling of the Court the defendants then and there excepted, which exception was by the Court allowed, and said certificate admitted in evidence, and marked Plaintiff's Exhibit, a copy of which appears elsewhere.

Be it remembered that then and there the following proceeding was had:

Mr. RUICK.—We next offer in evidence the receiver's final receipt issued to Ivan R. Cornell, No. 4508, and ask that this be marked Plaintiffs' Exhibit 37.

Mr. FORNEY.—The defendants make the same objection to this offer.

The COURT.—Objection overruled.

To which ruling of the Court the defendants then and there excepted, which exception was allowed, and said receipt was admitted in evidence and marked Plaintiff's Exhibit 37, a copy of which appears elsewhere in the transcript.

(Witness excused.)

IVA'N R. CORNELL, a witness called and sworn for the prosecution, testified as follows on

Direct Examination by Mr. RUICK.

Q. Mr. Cornell, where do you reside?

A. Portland, Oregon.

(Witness continuing:)

I was born in Portland; I am thirty-four years of age; I have resided in Lewiston, Idaho. I was first in Lewiston in the spring of 1897, for a short time I was in the employ of the O. R. & N. Company as freight clerk at the wharf.

I was there I think over three or four weeks.

I next went to Lewiston in the fall of 1902. There was more or less talk at that time about work being started on the railroad between Riparia and Lewiston, and there was some surveying being done at the time and I was in hopes they would start the construction work, and I thought there was a chance of getting employment as time-keeper on the construction work. That was the occasion of my going there at that time. I came from Kendrick to Lewiston on that occasion.

I had probably been in Kendrick two months and a half previous to this. I had been down on the Snake River south of Pullman before I came to Kendrick. I had been in Pullman from probably about the first of September, 1901, until the 10th or 12th of July, 1902. I am acquainted with the defendant William F. Kettenbach. I got acquainted with him the second time I was in Lewiston. I used to see him quite often on the street. I afterward be-

(Testimony of Ivan R. Cornell.)

came slightly acquainted with him. I have known the defendant George H. Kester probably about seventeen or eighteen years.

Q. Where had you known him?

A. Why, I first saw him in Portland, while I was attending the Bishop Scott Academy. He was also a student at the academy.

Q. You were both students at Bishop Scott's academy in Portland? A. Yes, sir.

Q. That is where you first formed your acquaintance with Mr. Kester? A. Yes, sir.

Q. So you knew Mr. Kester when you came to Lewiston? A. Yes, sir.

Q. When did you get acquainted with Mr. Dwyer? A. Why, during June, 1903.

Q. You filed on a stone and timber claim one time did you? A. Yes, sir.

Q. Please relate to the jury the circumstances leading up to your filing on this claim? Go ahead and relate in narrative form all the incidents which preceded it.

A. Well, one afternoon Mr. Kester came up to my room and asked me if I had ever used my stone and timber right, and I told him I hadn't. He then asked me if I would like to and I told him no, that I didn't think so; that I had made arrangements to go down the river the next day to Kelly's bar, and that I did not care to change my plans. And then he said if I did, he knew of a good place where I could use it—my right—and then he told me he would pay me $100 for my right, and all my expenses of filing on the land and going up to see it.

Q. Give the conversation in full as you remember it, Mr. Cornell?

A. Then another remark he made was this proposition which he had made to me was stretching the law somewhat, and also that this sort of thing was going on all the time, soliciting entrymen in this manner. Well, I was not in favor of it, and he urged me somewhat, and another remark that he made was that $100 would look pretty big to me he thought, and then after we had been up there a few minutes longer he asked me if it was agreed, and I finally said "I guess so," and then he said, "You know who Bill Dwyer is, don't you?" and I said "Yes," and he told me to go down to the depot the following morning, and Mr. Dwyer would meet me there and go with me to look at the land, so—

Q. Just a moment; pardon me for interrupting you there. Do you know how Mr. Kester came to know your financial condition at tha time?

A. Yes, sir.

Q. Relate the circumstances.

A. In the forenoon of the day before he had this talk with me I went into the Lewiston National Bank and asked him if he would let me have ten dollars until the first of July and I would repay it. After thainking the mattr over for a few minutes he finally let me have it and that was in the forenoon of the day before he had the talk with me in regard to the timber lands.

(Testimony of Ivan R. Cornell.)

Q. Now you can resume your narrative.

A. Then the following day after I had had this talk with him, I went down to the depot and took the train and Mr. Dwyer didn't arrive in time enough. He was late, a few minutes, and we could not make the trip that day, and he asked me then if I would go the following day and I said, All right.

Q. Who asked you? A. Mr. Dwyer.

Q. Relate that conversation, how it occurred and what occurred?

A. Why, when he came over he had driven over in his buggy, his wife was with him, and I met him as I was going back from the depot, probably about a block away, and he called to me and asked me what time it was. I told him it was about two minutes after nine I think; I think that was the time his train left and then he remarked that his watch must have been slow, or he would have been over in time, and then he asked me if I would go the following morning, and I said, Yes, and he said then he would be over to go with me.

Q. Now, in order *tat* the narrative may be in order, chronological order, I will ask you where you had first come to know Mr. Dwyer. Relate all the circumstances of your first meeting him, and becoming acquainted with him?

A. Well, I had seen him a number of times in Lewiston on the street, and I knew who he was by name, but the afternoon before during this talk with Mr. Kester in regard to the timber claim, I went over to Mr. Dwyer's place to pick cherries for the White

(Testimony of Ivan R. Cornell.)

Brothers and it was there that I first talked with Mr. Dwyer.

I asked him where the men were working on the place picking fruit and he told me it was at—pointed out the place, and at that time he was standing just behind the house, I think.

Q. At his place in Clarkston? A. Yes, sir.

Q. That was the first acquaintance you had had with Mr. Dwyer?

A. The first conversation I ever had with him, yess, sir.

Q. Now proceed with the conversation.

A. Well, he came over the following morning, and I met him at the depot.

Q. You mean the morning following his failure to reach the depot?

A. Yes, sir; and he bought two tickets, one for himself and one for me, and we got on the train— first he handed me one of the tickets himself, to me, and I noticed then—

The COURT.—A little louder.

A. I noticed then that the destination was Troy. Up to that time I didn't know exactly which direction it was; I was under the impression it was in that direction from the fact the train would go up that way. We then went up to Troy and from there we went in a buggy which Mr. Dwyer hired, and in going out to the claim I think we passed through the village of Jansville this claim was located I think about eighteen miles from Troy, proabbly, I should judge, east of there, and it was close to the Big Pot-

(Testimony of Ivan R. Cornell.)

latch Creek, that is, it slopes—it slopes towards the creek east, I should judge, but after we had driven onto the claim, why we drove onto it near the northwest corner, and just after getting onto it, why Mr. Dwyer remarked that this was the land we had come to see and I got out then and he drove on down to the bottom of the hill and I walked on down near the creek; there was a log cabin and also a small potato patch fenced in.

Q. Just a little louder; talk so the gentlemen furthest from you can hear you, talk as if you are talking to them and then your voice will reach.

A. Well, when we got down to this cabin Mr. Dwyer felt in his pocket for a key to unlock the door and wanted to get in for some purpose or other, but he found that he didn't have the key to the door, then he explained to me that this was a homestead on which he had filed, and that he intended to relinquish it and he—

Q. Well, what did you do next?

A. Well, then he turned the buggy around and went back up the hill, and there I got into the buggy and we drove back to Troy.

Q. Did you have any conversation on the way relative to these matters or anything connected with it?

A. Why, I think in going out he made the remark that the parties interested with him had got possesson of considerable land in that vicinity; they had scripped some and got it in other ways, and—

(Testimony of Ivan R. Cornell.)

The COURT.—Is that all he said? If it is, say so?

A. Well, that is, as I remember it, that is all he said along that line.

Q. Go ahead and relate the incidents and we will draw out the details afterwards; go right ahead.

The COURT.—You mean from the time he returned to Troy?

Mr. RUICK.—Yes, after getting back to Troy?

A. Well, first in going out from Troy, we stopped at a rancher's house for lunch, and Mr. Dwyer paid the expense of that, and also the feed of the horses; then afterwards we got back to Troy; why it was about six o'clock I think, and we went into a restanrant and had supper, for which Mr. Dwyer also paid, and while we were eating supper a freight train came in from the north, and after we got supper we went down to the depot and took that train for Lewiston, and Mr. Dwyer paid the fare for that trip, also on return; then afterwards when we had got back to Lewiston, it was I think about half past ten, Mr. Dwyer told me he would come over the following day, the next morning and make out a relinquishment blank and fill it out, and would give it to me. He didn't come over in the forenoon, but came over in the afternoon, I think, and I met him at the Leiston National Bank, and we went inside and he had a tin box which he opened there and looked, I think, for a paper which would give the description of the land of this homestead.

Q. A little louder; we can't hear.

(Testimony of Ivan R. Cornell.)

A. As I remember it he didn't find it in this tin box and he went out of the bank I think, upstairs I think, up the stairway, I was under the impression.

Q. You need not state your impression. What stairway did he go up?

A. The stairway leading up stairs to the second floor of the bank building.

Q. To the Lewiston National Bank?

A. Yes, sir.

Q. Did the stairs go up *and go up* to the Land Office up there?  A. Yes, sir.

Q. Now, go ahead and don't state what you thought or surmised, but state what occurred or happened?

A. Well, he soon returned from upstairs, and about that time Mr. Kester and Mr. Kettenbach had returned from lunch, and then the three of them went into the president's private office, where they all sat down around a desk there and were engaged in conversation and did some figuring; I don't know what it was about, but they were there about an hour and during that time I was seated in the lobby of the bank.

Q. Where was the president's private office relative to the lobby of the bank?

A. Why, it was—it is in the southeast corner of the banking-room, pertitioned off by itself, with windows around it, so you can see into it from any part of the banking-room.

Q. Do I understand by looking through glass you can see right into the president's room?

(Testimony of Ivan R. Cornell.)

A.  Yes, sir.

Q.  Parties standing in the public part of the bank can see right into it?    A.  Yes, sir.

Q.  Where were you then while this consultation was going on?

A.  Why, I was in the front part of the lobby.

Q.  Well, go on and state.

A.  Well, after they got through with their talk in there Mr. Dwyer came out and I noticed that he had a relinquishment blank in his hand.

The COURT.—Had what?

A.  Had a relinquishment blank in his hand, and then he said he was ready to go upstairs with me to the Land Office, and then he handed me eight dollars in silver and explained to me that that was the amount it would cost for my filing fees.  Then he went out of the door into the hallway leading upstairs, and on our way upstairs we overtook Mr. Thomas Mullen, who is a lawyer and has an office on the same floor as the Land Office, and Mr. Dwyer said to him: "Fix this up," and at the same time handed him this relinquishment blank, and then Mr. Mullen asked him what he wanted, and he replied to make out a timber and stone application for this man.  So we proceeded up and Mr. Mullen and I went into his office and Mr. Dwyer went into the Land Office.

Q.  Describe this hallway out of which you went from the bank into this hall and upstairs?  Describe

(Testimony of Ivan R. Cornell.)

it to the jury, its connection with the bank, and its relation to the bank?

A. Well, there is a side door which opens into the bank, and from this hallway the hallway—

Q. You mean the public part of the bank?

A. Yes, sir; this hallway is at the bottom of the stairs, going up to the second floor.

Q. That is all in the building, is it?

A. Yes, sir.

Q. You didn't go out of the building?

A. No, sir; not at all.

Q. To go into this hallway and upstairds?

A. No.

Q. While you were on that you may as well described where the director's room of the bank is relative to this?

A. It is on the north side of the hall; then there is a door opposite this door whch goes from the banking-room into the hallway, the door opposite that, which leads into the director's room from this hallway.

Q. And is there another door leading into the director's room from any other part?

A. There is a door at the rear of the banking-room which leads into the director's room.

Q. So you can go in there, into the director's room from the banking-room or private part of the bank, and also from the hall?    A. Yes, sir.

Q. Now go ahead; what occurred in Capt. Mullen's office?

A. Well, after we went in there Mr. Mullen asked the clerk in the office to get out two timber and stone

(Testimony of Ivan R. Cornell.)

application blanks, and the cler did so and handed
them to Mr. Mullen and then Mr. Mullen asked my
name and age and my occupaiion and then proceeded to ask me the usual questions in making a
timber and stone entry.

Q.  Go ahead.  You are relating the conversation
with Capt. Mullen now, are you?        A.  Yes, sir.

Q.  And were either of the defendants present?

A.  No, sir.

Be it remembered that then and there the following proceeding was had:

Q.  Then you need jot state what Capt. Mullen
said.

Mr. MOORE.—Let it go in.

Mr. RUICK.—If you will let the rule apply all
the way through, yes.

Mr. MOORE.—We have not made any objection
to the conversations.

Mr. RUICK.—I don't care to have my witness
relate a lot of hearsay, and I am not going to let him
say it.  You need not state what Capt. Mullen said.

The COURT.—The Court will instruct you you
need not say that.

To which ruling of the Court the defendants then
and there execped, which exception was allowed by
the Court.

Q.  Go on and state what was done?

A.  Why, he took my answers to the question.

Q.  Well, state what else was done; what else did
you do then?

(Testimony of Ivan R. Cornell.)

A. Then, after he had finished taking my answers, he pinned this relinquishment to the timber and stone application which he had filled out, and then we went into the land office.

Q. Where was Mr. Dwyer at this time?

A. He was in the land office.

Q. Who named the witnesses for you in your final proof?

A. Well, when we came to that question, Mr. Mullen asked me—

Q. You need not state how Mr. Mullen asked you; how did you procure the names of the witnesses? You may state that.

A. I named Mr. Dwyer, and then—that is the only one I knew of, and Mr. Mullen then explained that the law required—

Q. Whom did you go to to get the names of the others, that is the circumstance I wish to know?

A. Why, I got those from Mr. Dwyer.

Q. Where was Mr. Dwyer at this time?

A. He was in the land office.

Q. Could you see him from where you were?

A. Yes, sir.

Q. What did you do then to get the names of the witnesses.

A. Why, I went in and told him, asked him whom I could get for witnesses, and he came back into Mr. Mullen's office and gave the names of three other parties.

Q. Do you remember who they were?

(Testimony of Ivan R. Cornell.)

A. One was William F. Kettenbach and the other two were strangers, people I was not acquainted with.

Q. You don't recall their names?

A. No, I don't now.

Q. You say two were strangers, William F. Kettenbach was one, and who was the other of those you knew?

The COURT.—Mr. Dwyer?

A. Mr. Dwyer.

Q. Mr. Dwyer?     A. Mr. Dwyer.

Q. Now then, state what occurred after you had done this.

A. Then Mr. Mullen and I went into the land office and Mr. Mullen handed the papers to the Register, and he looked at the first page, which was the relinquishment, and he remarked that—

Q. In the presence of Mr. Dwyer—was Mr. Dwyer present?

A. I don't remember whether he was.

Q. If he was not present do not state what the Register said; you may state what occurred, if anything; you may relate that, you can state the facts if there was anything wrong sgate the facts of what was done, not what Mr. West said or Capt. Mullen said, which was not in the presence of either of the defendants, but just state what occurred there, what happened there in the land office; you can. Understand?

The COURT.—If the register said there was something wrong with the relinquishment, or made

(Testimony of Ivan R. Cornell.)

some suggestion in regard to it, he may state what he told him.

Mr. RUICK.—Go ahead under the permission of the Court.

A. He remarked there was the relinquishment, and Mr. Mullen said yes, and then asked him to turn that over and look at the second page, and he did so; then he saw that there was a timber and stone application filled out, and he looked that over and then he asked me what my name was, and I told him.

Q. State what was done in the land office; don't relate the conversation; what I want to know is what was done.

The COURT.—That is all we care for.

A. Well, the application was accepted, and then Mr. Mullen and I returned to his office.

Q. What did you do with the money? Did you pay any fees at the time?

A. Yes, sir; I did.

Q. How much did you pay?

A. I paid $8.00.

Q. Where did you go then after leaving the land office.

A. After leaving the land office we returned to Mr. Mullen's office, and he told me that—

Q. Now, Mr. Cornell, I want to state to you once and for all, so that you will understand, guard against giving any conversations with anyone except in the presence of one of the defendants. Do you understand? Don't give any conversations unless they were had in the presence of one of the de-

(Testimony of Ivan R. Cornell.)

fendants, nor u/less they directed you to go to someone for a certain purpose; that is, one of the defendants directed you. Mr. Cornell state what you did
after you left the land office, having filed your application in the first place. I will show you Plaintiff's
Exhibit 32, and ask you if that is the paper which
you filed there at this time.     A.   Yes, sir.

Q.   You recognize that, do you, as the paper
which you filed?     A.   Yes, sir.

Q.   Now, then, go ahead and relate what you did
after this, and any conversations you had with Mr.
Dwyer or Mr. Kester, or any of the defendants.

A.   Well, that afternoon, I met Mr. Dwyer driving over to Lewiston from Clarkston, and I stopped
him and told him that Mr. Mullen's fee or charge
was $1.50, and he stated that—I got into the buggy
with him, and rode back to Lewiston. I met him
on the bridge, and I had started to go over to
his house, and on the way back he said that he was
going to the bank, to the Lewiston National Bank,
and after he got throught there he would go upstairs
and pay Mullen. Well, I went up to Mullen's office
after I left Dwyer, and—

Q.   What did you learn there? You need not
state what was said, but what did you learn there?
For what purpose did you go there?

A.   To t/ell Mr. Mullen that Mr. Dwyer would
come in to pay it. Mr. Mullen was not in the office
at the time, but I told the clerk. In about two days
after that, I think it wans, I learned that the fees
had not been paid, so I spoke to Mr. Kester in re-

(Testimony of Ivan R. Cornell.)

gard to it, and he handed me $1.50, which I paid to Mr. Mullen.

Q. Now, go right along and state what next transpired with regard to this claim. State any conversation you had now with the defendants, or either of them after this.

A. Well, a few days later I met Mr. Kester, and he asked me if I knew the description of the land, and I told him that I did not; that I would go to the land office and get it, and then he also asked me if I knew in which paper the notice of application had been published, and I said no, and I went up to the land office then and found out—got the description and also learned in which paper the advertisement would appear, and I afterwards told him, and then shortly after that he asked me if I knew on what day I was to make final proof, and I told him I didn't, and I went up to the land office and asked the register in regard to that, and he told me the 10th of September, and then I told Mr. Kester that afterwards.

Q. Well, what next occurred in relation to it? Did anything more occur till you come to make final proof or along about that time?

A. Yes, sir; about a week before I was to make the final proof, I met Mr. Kester on the streets, and he told me to come in on the morning of the 10th and he would go over with me a list of questions that I would have to answer in making final proof, but I think at that time I asked him if W. F. Kettenbach would be back by the 10th and I would—that I wanted him to come as one of the witnesses, and

(Testimony of Ivan R. Cornell.)

he told me he would arrange that matter, that part of it, all right, and a few days before that, though, I had seen Mr. Dwyer in Lewiston, and I had asked him that queestion also whether Mr. Kettenbach would be back, and he said he thought he would, and then he remarked that he and Kettenbach would act as m) wit*h*esses, but that if Kettenbach was not back by that time, that I could get someone else. Well, on the morning of the 10th, I went to the bank and met Mr. Dwyer outside—

The COURT.—Was that the time for the final proof?

A. Yes, sir; we both went into the bank and Mr. Kester remarked I had better go up into the land office and see if there were entries ahead of me to make proof on that day. I did so, and found that there were not, and then I went down and told him, and he handed a paper with the printed questions on it asked in making final proof at the land office, handed this paper to Mr. Dwyer, and Mr. Dwyer and I went into the private office of the president.

Q. Whose office?

A. W. F. Kettenbach's office, and there I looked over this list of questions and answers.

Q. You would identif) a b*a*lauk similar to that? You could identif) a blank?    A. Yes, sir.

Q. You afterwards made final proof, didn't you?

Λ. Yes.

Q. How did this blank which Dw)er had at this time compare with the blank on which )ou made final proof later?

(Testimony of Ivan R. Cornell.)

A.   Why, the questions were the same.

Q.   I will show you Plaintiff's Exhibit 33, purporting to be and already identified as testimony of claimant.   Is that your signature?

A.   Yes, sir.

Q.   Do you recognize that as the testimony which you gave at that time? when you made your final proof?      A.   Yes, sir.

Q.   Now, looking at that, I will ask you if you identify this next paper, Plaintiff's Exhibit 33-A as cross-examination given in connection with your direct examination at that time?      A.   Yes, sir.

Q.   Now, looking at this, state what blank Mr. Dwyer—Mr. Kester handed to Mr. Dwyer.

A.   Why, it was this one.   (Indicating Plaintiff's Exhibit 33.)

Q.   Did he hand him more than one blank, if you remember?      A.   No, I think not.

(Court takes recess till 1:30 P. M., May 24th, 1907.)

1:30 P. M., May 24th.

Direct examination of witness Cornell resumed.

Q.   Will you please read the last two or three questions.   (The last three questions read.)

The WITNESS.—I want to correct that last.   I think there were two; the cross-examination blank also.

Q.   What do you mean, the cross-examination blank.   The one I called your attention to just before dinner?

(Testimony of Ivan R. Cornell.)

A.   Yes, this one.   (Indicating Plaintiff's Exhibit 33-A.)

Q.   Now, then, you were stating, Mr. Cornell, when you digressed, you were stating that Dwyer or Mr. Kester you think handed those papers to Dwyer?

A.   Yes.

Q.   In the bank?      A.   Yes, sir.

Q.   On the morning of the 10th of September?

A.   Yes.

Q.   The day you made final proof?

A.   Yes, sir.

Q.   Now, go on from there and give your narrative.

A.   Tehn we went into the President's private office, Mr. Kettenbach's office, and sat down there and I looked over the papers, those that Kester handed Dwyer, and read over the questions and also the anssers that had been written to those questions.

Q.   What do you mean by that?

A.   I mean we sat down in the president's private office, and I looked over a list of the questions on the two blanks, read them over, and saw what they were, and also some answers that had been written in to those questions.

Q.   What written on these blanks that you refer to?      A.   Yes, sir.

Q.   How were they written in?

A.   Why, I—it seems to me with a lead pencil.

Q.   Well, go ahead?

A.   And I looked over them, and when I came to the question in regard to the amount of timber

(Testimony of Ivan R. Cornell.)

on the claim, why, Dwyer told me to say one million and a quarter feet; then, after that, we had been in the private office for a few minutes—

Q. Let me ask you a moment right there, Mr. Cornell. Now, do I understand you to say that the questions had been answered in these blanks which you had at that time? A. Yes, sir.

Q. Had all of the questions been answered in some form or other?

A. I think so as I remember it; yes.

Q. Had this question, I call your attention particularly to questions 13, 14 and 15 of your direct examination, and ask you whether or not these questions had been answered and the answers were written in on the blank?

A. That is my recolection.

Q. And how had they been answered?

A. Why, in the same manner as these are.

Q. Now, calling your attention particularly to the cross-examination blank, the questions 13 and 14, questions 16 and 17. I will ask you if the answers to those questions were discussed at that time there?

A. Well, in the talk I had with Kester, I said that the question might arise in the land office as to where I got the funds from to pay for it, and I told him that I thousght I would answer from my folks. Then he told me that that question would be asked.

Q. Is that all the conversation you remember about them?

A. Yes, I think so on that point.

(Testimony of Ivan R. Cornell.)

Q. Now, go ahead, and relate what else occurred there. Relate everything that occurred.

A. After we had been in the private office a few minutes I think Mr. Kettenbach came in. As I remember it, he was not in there when we went in there in the first place, and he sat down at his private desk, and then in a few minutes later, why some man came into the bank, and started down the lobby towards his office, and he saw him coming, and he spoke to Dwyer and he said, Billy, take him into the directors' room. He referred to me.

Q. What were you and Dwyer doing there in Mr. Kettenbach's office after Mr. Kettenbach came in before this man came in?

A. Why, he was sitting there, and so I was, and I was reading over these questions and answers.

Q. Did you discuss them or exchange any words there with Mr. Dwyer?

A. Why, I think not, except in regard to the amount of timber.

Q. Well, what did you do next?

A. Well, then Dwyer and I went into the directors' room, as Kettenbach requested.

Q. How did you go in going into the director's room?

A. We passed out a door leading into the private entrance of the bank, and through that, through another door into the director's room.

Q. You passed from the president's private office into the business portion of the bank?

A. Yes, sir.

(Testimony of Ivan R. Cornell.)

Q. And then through the door into the director's room?    A. Yes, sir.

Q. Where was Mr. Kester at that time, do you recollect?

A. Why, I think he was probably at his desk.

Q. Not probably, if you recollect. I am only asking for your recollection, whether you saw him there.

A. He was in the private part of the bank.

Q. Well, what occurred when you got into the director's room?

A. Well, in there, I finished looking over the questions and answers, and after I had done so I said I was all through, and then we stepped into the banking-room and told Kester, and then he figured out the amount of money it would take to pay for the land, and also the other fees.

Q. Can you recollect any of the figuring that he did?

A. Why, he put down the number of acres of land in the claim, and multiplied it by two fifty, the price of each acre, and in *tht* way he got the amount of *te* price of the land, and then he added the other fees; I think that amounted to $11.20.

Q. The fees?

A. Yes; in addition to the price of the land.

Q. How much more? How much money did he give you? Pardon*t* me; I am anticipating.

(Witness continuing:) A. Then, after he had found out the amount it would take, he walked right

(Testimony of Ivan R. Cornell.)

to the money counter and picked up eighteen twenty dollar gold pieces and brought them over and handed them to me. Then he went back into the director's room, and out through the door that led into the hallway.

Q. Who did?

A. Dwyer and I, and from there we went upstairs into the land office and there we were both sworn by the register.

Q. State what occurred there in the land office, what you did there.

A. Well, after we had been sworn, the register stepped out for a few minutes and then he returned and told me to step inside, on the inside of the office, inside of the counter, and he then took my answers.

Q. Who was this, do you remember?

A. The register, Mr. West.

Q. Well, go right on; you gave testimony there did you?    A. Yes, sir.

Q. Were your witnesses there when you gave your testimony?

A. Why, Dwyer was. Kettenbach was not; he was busy at the time we went up stairs, and after I gave my testimony then Dwyer gave his, and as I remember it the register then said to ask Kettenbach to come up in about twenty minutes. I went down stairs then and told him they would want him in about twenty minutes, and then I returned to the land office and was there during Dwyer's testimony and also Kettenbach's.

(Testimony of Ivan R. Cornell.)

Q. You waited until Kettenbach came up, didn't you? A. Yes, sir.

Q. When did you get your final certificate from the register? A. The record receipt?

A. *Ye,* sir; your final receipts?

A. Why*k,* it was the afternoon of the 10th, probably about three o'clock.

Q. That same day? A. Yes, sir.

Q. What did you do with that?

A. Why, I mailed it.

Q. I will ask you— I did not intend to say what did you do with it, but where did you go after you got your receipt, what occurred after that?

A. I went down stairs and up *m*ain street. Then I walked east on Main street probably about a block when Dwyer overtook me.

Q. Pardon me a moment. Who left the office with you? Anybody at all?

A. No, I was alone.

Q. Did you go direct out onto Main Street?

A. Yes, sir; then when I had gone about a block, why Dw,yer overtook me, and he said, "Here is the deed to the land. I wish you would take it over to Otto Kettenbach and have him witness and acknowledge it." And then I should sign it up ther*r*, and then I told him that I would do so, but I wanted to see Kester and have a talk with him in regard to it and I also told him that I was going to insist on Kester not having the deed *tht* I gave him recorded for six months, and he remarked that that was all right; then that same afternoon, why, I mailed the receipt, the

(Testimony of Ivan R. Cornell.)

record receipt I got from the receiver to the county clerk of Latah County.

Q. Do you remember whether it was the register's final certificate or the final receipt you recorded or both of them or which? Do you remember which one it was? Was it the paper that you got at the land office? A. Yes, sir.

Q. It was either the final certificate or the final receipt? A. Yes, sir.

Q. Why did you have that recorded, or what caused you to have that recorded?

A. Why, the land was apparently sold to me, and I thought that it should be recorded in my name, as I got the receipt from the land office myself.

Q. So that there would be a record of it in your name? A. Yes, sir.

Q. Then what did you do?

A. Then that evening while I was eating supper in the restaurant, Kester came in and asked me if I had the deed that Dwyer gave me, if I had signed it, and had it witnessed and acknowledged, and I told him that I had not. Then I told him that I wanted to see him and have a talk with him, and asked him where I could meet him in about a half an hour, and he told me that he would be on the street probably for some time. He was waiting, I think, for the mail to be distributed, and then I saw him afterwards, met him near the bank, and I told him that there was— that I did not—that I would request him not to have it—to have the deed that I gave him recorded for six months. Well, he said that that is all right; I am not

(Testimony of Ivan R. Cornell.)

going to have this deed recorded, but later on I want another one from you, and then he remarked that he had already bargained to sell the land.

Q. Already what?

A. Had already bargained to sell the land, and I told him of a remark or two that the receiver had made just before he gave me the receipt, something like this: That—

Q. You told Kester this?

A. Yes, sir, the receiver remarked or told me it looks to a man up a tree very much as if Dwyer had furnished the money, advanced the money to you and that you are going to deed it back to him after you get this receipt, and he further said that there is a man here now in Lewiston who is here for the very purpose of looking into this transaction and others like it, and then when I told Kester that, he remarked, Oh, all he is here for is to investigate some cutting of timber lands, cutting timber on Government land, or soemthing of that kind.

Q. Was there any name mentioned in this conversation between you and Kester?    A. No, sir.

Q. Well, when did you execute the deed, if at all?

A. Well, then during that talk I had with Kester at that time, he asked me to come in the following morning, when he said he would like to change the date of the deed, and I went in, and we went into Kettenbach's private office, and he sat down at Kettenbach's desk and changed the date. Then as I remember it, I went over to Otto Kettenbach's as he asked me to and signed it there, and it was witnessed. Then

(Testimony of Ivan R. Cornell.)

I did not see Kester again for probably three or four days, and I met him on the street one evening, and he asked me if I had the deed with me then, and I told him I had not but—

The COURT.—But what?

. A.   Had the deed with me, and I replied that I had not, and that I was waiting to—waiting for the return of the receipt from Moscow, when I would bring that in also with the deed and give them both to him.   Well, he said that is not necessary; you come in in the morning with the deed and I wil pay you what is due you according to the agreement.

Q.   Well, what did you do?

A.   I went in.   After the bank opened, and he figured out how much was still due me, and he asked me if I wanted cash and I told him I would like to have thirty dollars of it in money and the balance in a certificate of deposit, so he turned to Bradbury, as I remember, and asked him to hand me $30 and to make out a certificate of deposit for the balance.

Q.   You owed the bank something, did you, at that time?

A.   Why, I was indebted to Kester for the $10 he had furnished me in June; the understanding was that that was to be taken out of the $100.

Q.   When was that understanding had?   You say there was an understanding?

A.   When he first talked to me about taking up the timber land in June, and then the money that I paid to the receiver was not quite $360, and—

Q.   How is that?

(Testimony of Ivan R. Cornell.)

A.   The amount that I paid to the receiver of the land office was not quite $360.

Q.   Oh, you mean including the fees?

A.   Yes, so that left a few dollars in change, which I had kept and that was added to the $10, and then the fee for having the receipt recorded here in Moscow, I think was 35 cents, and so Kester added that to the $100 and deducted the $10, plus whatever change I got back from the land office.

Q.   To whom did that deed—to whom did you convey that land at that time?

A.   To W. F. Kettenbach and George H. Kester.

Q.   You testified to you and Dwyer having these blanks in the director's room, and of your stepping out into the banking-room when you concluded and saying to Kester you were through.   What became of those blanks then, if you know?

A.   Why Dwyer or Kester took them and handed them to Robnett.

Q.   Do you know what was done with them?

A.   Not after that, no.

Mr. RUICK.—Take the witness.

Be it remembered that then and there the following proceeding was had:

Mr. FORNEY.—I suppose all the testimony of this witness goes under our general objection.

The COURT.—Yes.

Mr. FORNEY.—We move that all the testimony of this witness be stricken out for the reasons specified in our objection.

The COURT.—Motion denied.

(Testimony of Ivan R. Cornell.)

To which ruling of the Court the defendants then and there excepted, which exception was allowed by the Court.

### Cross-Examination by Mr. TANNAHILL.

Q.   Mr. Cornell, how old are you?

A.   Thirty-four years.

Q.   And you have known Mr. Kester for some time?     A.   Yes, sir.

Q.   You have been very good friends, have you?

A.   Why, I was pretty well acquainted with him, yes.

Q.   Mr. Kester has loaned you money from time to time, hasn't he, small amounts of money?

A.   He did on one occasion, one other occasion, I think, yes.

Q.   Didn't he loan you small amounts of money on two or three other occasions?

A.   Not that I recollect of.

Q.   He may have loaned you small amounts of money?

A.   One other time I did ask him if he would let me have some money, but I didn't get it; I found it was not necessary.

Q.   He was always ready to accommodate you whenever he could, was he not?

A.   Yes, I think so.

Q.   Now, you and this W. W. Pefley have been together considerable since you came to Moscow, haven't you?     A.   Who?

Q.   This witness Wynn Pefley?

A.   No, sir; I don't know that man at all.

(Testimony of Ivan R. Cornell.)

Q.   Did you talk to him just after he left the witness-stand and went outside this morning?

A.   No, sir; I may know the man by sig*n*t, and not by name, but I am sure I had no talk with him.

Q.   In what business are you engaged now?

A.   Why, I am not engaged in any particular business.

Q.   Have you been employed for any purpose since you came to Moscow as door-keeper for the District Attorney's office or anything of that kind?

A.   No, sir.

Q.   Nothing of that kind?     A.   No, sir.

Q.   Now, Mr. Cornell, you say you know Capt. Mullen, or Mr. Mullen?

A.   Why, slightly, yes; I know him by sight.   He is sitting over there.

Q.   That is he over there?     A.   Yes, sir.

Q.   And you say he made out your first papers for you?     A.   The application?

Q.   Yes.     A.   Yes, sir.

Q.   You had a talk with him at the time?

A.   Why—

Q.   That is just a few words of conversation, such as was necessar\ for him to get the information to make out your papers?     A.   Yes, sir.

Q.   You remember that distic*n*tly, do you?

A.   Yes, sir.

Q.   Now, where was that?   Where were those papers made out?     A.   In his office.

Q.   Where *as* his office *i*situated?

(Testimony of Ivan R. Cornell.)

A.  On the second floor of the Lewiston National Bank Building.

Q.  On the same floor that the land office is on?

A.  Yes, sir.

Q.  Were there any other offices on that floor?

A.  I think there was; I think Mr. Kroutinger had an office on that floor, but I am not certain.

Q.  Mr. Kroutinger was a land attorney, was he not?    A.  I think so.

Q.  He had an office adjourning the land office?

A.  Yes, sir.

Q.  Was there another office there?

A.  I don't know; there might have been.

Q.  No, where was Mr. Mullen's office with reference to the land office?

A.  Well, it was as I remember it, it was sort of diagonally across the hall.

Q.  And you remember that distinctly that his office is diagonally across the hall from the land office?

A.  I should think that was the direction, yes.

Q.  And you know that Mr. Mullen was in there?

A.  Yes, sir.

Q.  And you know that he made out your papers?

A.  Yes, sir.

Q.  You *ar* positive of that?    A.  Yes, sir.

Q.  Cannot possibly be mistaken?

A.  No, sir.

Q.  Now, Mr. Cornell, when did you first talk this matter over regarding your transaction with Mr. Kester?

(Testimony of Ivan R. Cornell.)

Mr. RUICK.—With whom do you mean?

Mr. TANNAHILL.—With anybody.

Mr. RUICK.—You mean—

Q. After you made your proof; I am examining this witness Mr. Ruick.

Be it remembered that then and there the following proceeding was had :

Mr. RUICK.—I have a right to know to what conversation he directs the attention of this witness; I will ask that the qustion be read, whatever particular conversation, because he had referred to so many different conversations. (Last question read.)

The COURT.—Yes, the witness' attention should be directed if it is the purpose of counsel to call his attention to some particular conversation, his attention should be directed to it; I assume that it is for the purpose of laying the foundation for an impeachment.

To which ruling of the Court the defendants then and there excepted, which exception was allowed by the Court.

Q. When did you first talk these matters over after you made your final proof?

A. With other parties you mean?

Q. Yes, with other parties? (No answer.)

Q. I will ask you when you first talked them over with any Government official or with the District Attorney?

A. Oh them—why, that was in Boise, in 1905.

Q. Who did you talk them over with then?

(Testimony of Ivan R. Cornell.)

A.    Mr. Ruick, and Mr. Goodwin and Mr. O'Fallon.

Q.    Who else was presend at the time?

A.    Why there was a lady stenographer came afterwards, after I had been in there a few minutes.

Q.    How long had you been in there before the stenographer came in?

A.    I don't know; might have been four or five minutes.

Q.    Four or five minutes?

A.    Possibly that long; I don't remember just the length of time.

Q.    Who asked you the questions?

A.    Why, Mr. Ruick asked me; I talked with him first.

Be it remembered that then and there the following proceeding was had:

Q.    Did you give him a statement?    Now what did you tell Mr. Ruick about it?

Mr. RUICK.—Objected to as incompetent, irrelevant and immaterial.

The COURT.—Objection sustained.

Ti which rulinf of the Court the defendants then and there excepted, which exception was allowed by the Court.

Q.    And how many times did you go over your evidence there with Mr. Ruick, Mr. Goodwin and Mr. O'Fallon?

A.    As I remember it, it was only once.

(Testimony of Ivan R. Cornell.)

Q. Only once? And did you sign a statement at that time? A. I don't remember that I did.

Q. Did you tell the same story that you have told here on the stand at that time?

Mr. MOORE.—O speak up, you know whether you did or not.

Mr. RUICK.—Answer the question Mr. Cornell; answer them out freely; that is what you are there for, is to answer questions.

A. Well, not entirely.

Q. You didn't tell them the same; then was you afterwards taken before the grand jury?

A. No, sir.

Q. You was not taken before the grand jury?

A. Not the second time.

Q. Did you appear before the grand jury before?

A. Wait a moment; you asked me if the story I told before the grand jury was what I—

Q. No, the story you told to Mr. Goodwin, Mr. Ruick and Mr. O'Fallon, was that the same story that you are telling now is what I asked you, and then I asked you if you afterwards went before the grand jury?

A. Well, I misunderstood you then; the story that I told Goodwin and Mr. O'Fallon and Mr. Ruick, was not exactly the same as I have told here.

Q. Then you did afterwards go before the grand jury? A. Yes, sir.

Q. And did you tell the same story before the grand jury that you are telling here?

A. Not exactly, no.

(Testimony of Ivan R. Cornell.)

Q.  Then you were indicted, were you not?

A.  Yes, sir.

Q.  And you are under indictment at the present time?

A.  Yes.

Q.  Is that right?        A.  Yes, sir.

Q.  And you filed an affidavit in support of a motion to quash that indictment did you not?

A.  My attorney did for me.

Q.  I will ask you to look at the signatures to this affidavit and state whether or not that is your signature?        A.  *Ye,* that is mine.

Q.  I will also ask you to look at the signature to the other affidavit, the second affidavit, under the same cover and ask you if that is your signature?

A.  Yes, sir.

Mr. TZNNAHILL.—If the Court please, I would like to have this marked for identification.

The COURT.—*Tey* may be marked.

Said affidavits are marked Defendant's Exhibit "D," and "E," respectively for identification.

Q.  Your case has never been called for trial has it Mr. Cornell?        A.  No, sir.

Q.  And you never told the story that you are telling now until after you were indicted?

A.  Not just as I have told it now, no.

Q.  At whose request did you come here to attend this trial?

The COURT.—The Court will exclude that: the Court does not think that question is proper unless you can give the Court some reasons for asking it.

(Testimony of Ivan R. Cornell.)

Mr. RUICK.—Tell him how you happened to come here, Mr. Cornell? A. I was subpoenaed.

Q. Did you have any talk with any Government officials before you came here for trial?

A. Just immediately before?

Q. Yes. A. No.

Q. Did you have any talk with any Government officials some time before you came here for trial, within the last six months? A. No.

Q. Have you had a talk with any Government official since you were indicted? A. Yes.

Q. Who did you talk with? A. Mr. Ruick.

Q. And you was assured that if you would come here and appear as a witness against Mr. Kester that you would not be prosecuted? A. I was not.

Q. You never have been prosecuted though, have you, that is, you never have been called upon to stand trial? A. No, sir.

Q. Where did you have that talk with Mr. Ruick?

A. In Portland at the Portland Hotel.

Q. Mr. Ruick sent for you did he?

A. Why, my attorney notified me that Mr. Ruick would be in Portland on a certain day and that he would like to see me.

Q. When was it that you saw Mr. Ruick in Portland? A. It was in October, 1905.

Q. Your attorney arranged for the interview did he? A. Yes, sir.

Q. And your attorney's name was—

(Testimony of Ivan R. Cornell.)

A.   J. C. Moreland.

Q.   Is he any relation to you?

A.   No, sir.   You are thinking of my uncle probably, but he was not the attorney named there.

Q.   Now, what was the part*ies* name who arranged with Mr. Ruick for the interview?

A.   Mr. Moreland.

Q.   And did no one else have anything to do with it?        A.   No, sir.

Q.   How long an interview did you have with Mr. Ruick there?

A.   Why, probably three-quarters of an hour.

Q.   Then you admit that you swore falsely when you swore to your sworn statement that was made out by Capt. Mullen, do you?        A.   I presume so.

Q.   These papers here.   (Indicating Plaintiff's Exhibit 32.)

A.   I presume so.

Q.   These are the ones that were made out by Capt. Mull*e* are the*y*?        A.   Yes, sir.

Q.   And you also admit you swore falsely when you swore to your final proof papers?

A.   I suppose so, yes.

Q.   And you swore falsel*y* when you appeared before the grand jur*y*, is that right?

A.   I presume so.

Q.   And you made a false statement to Mr. Ruick when he took your statement, is that right?

A.   I suppose so.

(Witness excused.)

SAMUEL C. HUTCHINGS, a witness called and sworn on behalf of the prosecution, testified as follows on

Direct Examination by Mr. RUICK.

Samuel C. Hutchings is your name?

A. Yes, sir.

(Witness continuing:)

I reside in Lewiston, Idaho; have lived there since 1877; I am acquainted with W. F. Kettenbach; have known him ever since he was a boy; I have known George H. Kester ever since he was a boy; went to school with him in the same school; I have known Mr. Dwyer ever since he has been in Idaho. I don't know how long ago that was. I was clerk in the Hotel de France when he came to this country.

As a matter of fact, his home is in Clarkston, Wahington. I mean I have known him ever since he came to that section of the country.

I never took up a stone and timber claim under what is known as the Timber and Stone Act.

Q. Were you ever solicited to do so?

A. Yes, sir.

Q. Well, about when was this, Mr. Hutchings, do you remember? A. No, sir.

Q. Do you recall what year it was, if you dojt remember the exact year, you can tell—

A. It was five or six years ago or four or five years ago.

Q. Well, fix the date after this conversation, did you talk to any other person about it?

(Testimony of Samuel C. Hutchings.)

A. Yes, sir.

Q. How soon after the conversation occured?

A. I think it was either that day or the day following.

Q. Who was that person you talked to about it?

A. R. A. Lambdin.

Q. State where that converstion occurred?

A. When I was talking to Lambdin?

Q. No, these other parties, when you were solicited to file on a timber claim, where was it?

A. It was on the sidewalk by the Lewiston National Bank.

Q. Who, if you remember, talked to you about it?

A. I don't remember who it was.

Q. Do you remember whether or not it was one of these defendants?

A. I think it was; yes, sir.

Q. Well, do you know whether it was or not?

A. Yes, sir.

Q. State whether or not it was one of these defendants?     A. I am sure tha it was.

The COURT.—How is that?

The WITNESS.—I am sure that it was one of them.

Q. Do you recall now which one of the defendants it was?     A. No. sir.

Q. Did you tell any other person at that time or about that time who it was that had talked to you?

Mr. FORNEY.—We object to that if your Honor please—

(Testimony of Samuel C. Hutchings.)

Be it remembered that then and there the following proceeding was had:

Q. In other words did you carry any message from this person who had talked to you?

Mr. FORNEY.—Objected to as incompetent, irrelevant and immaterial.

The COURT.—Objection overruled; it may be answered by yes or no.

To which ruling of the Court the defendants then and there excepted, which exception was allowed by the Court.

(Last question read to the witness.)

Mr. RUICK.—That proposition is not the way I put it at first.

Q. Did you tell any other person at or about that time of this conversation that you had had?

Mr. FORNEY.—Same objection.

The COURT.—Objection overruled.

To which ruling of the Court the defendants then and there excepted, and which exception was allowed by the Court, and the witness answered:

A. *Ye,* sir.

Q. Who was that person? A. Lambdin.

Q. Be it remembered that then and there the following proceeding was had:

Q. Did you give him the name of the party who had talked to you concerning the taking up of the timber claim?

Mr. FORNEY.—Same objection.

The COURT.—Objection overruled; to shich ruling of tje Court the defendants then and there ex-

(Testimony of Samuel C. Hutchings.)
cepted, which exception was allowed by the Court
and the witness answered:

A.  I am not sure that I gave him the name, but I
told him to go down there.

Q.  Did you tell him who to go and see?

A.  I think I did.

Q.  Who did you tell him to go and see?

A.  I don't know.

Be it remembered that then and there the following
proceeding was had:

Q.  Well, what I want to know, Mr. Hutchings,
is this: I will first ask you with regard to the conversation and then come down to this later.  What
did this party state to you relative to taking up a
timber claim?  You say it was one of the defendants,
go ahead and state.

Mr. FORNEY.—Object to this as incompetent, irrelevant and immaterial; it is too remote, no time
fixed.  He said it was five or six years ago.

Mr. RUICK.—Or four or five years ago.

The COURT.—Objection overruled.

To which ruling of the Court the defendants then
and there excepted, which exception was allowed, and
the witness answered as follows:

A.  He wanted me to take up a timber claim, and
if I am not mistakedn he offered me $100—I told him
that I had a friend and I would send him down.

Q.  How did he address you when the subject was
first brought up?  Give his language as near as you
remember how he approached you?

(Testimony of Samuel C. Hutchings.)

A. It has been too long ago. I don't believe I could do it.

Q. How is that?

A. I don't believe I could give his exact language.

Q. I am not asking for the exact language; I am asking you for the substance? How did this party open up this subject to you that morning; what did he say, don't you remember? A. No, sir.

Q. Don't you remember how they addressed you on that morning? A. No, sir.

Q. How did they call you? How did they open up the subject?

A. Why, I just happened to be going along there and I don't know how they did come up to it*k* but they came up and that is what I told them.

Q. Well, how were you to get this $100?

A. By taking up a timber claim.

Q. And what were you to do with it when you took it up to get the $100?

Mr. TANNAHILL.—Objected to as leading and suggestive.

Mr. RUICK.—The Court can see that this witness is a reluctant witness, very reluctant to testify or his memory is not good.

The COURT.—Objection overruled.

Mr. TANNAHILL.—Exception.

Exception allowed by the Court.

Mr. RUICK.—I am satisfied the witness himself intends to tell the truth; I don't intend to reflect upon him, but he is either frightened or very reluctant; he happens to be a lifelong friends of your cleint.

(Testimony of Samuel C. Hutchings.)

Mr. TANNAHILL.—You are not scared, are you, Sammy?    A. No, sir.

Q. Then if you are not scared, I want you to give the conversation. You act like a scared man.

Mr. TANNAHILL.—He is giving it the best he can.

The COURT.—Mr. Hutchings, you understand you are sworn to tell the truth and the whole truth here do you?    A. Yes, sir.

The COURT.—The Court is impressed with the idea that either you are very much frightened or else you are answering the questions very reluctantly. The Court desires that you answer the questions that are put to you. That is, such facts as you remember. Proceed. You need not be frightened; there will be no harm come to you here if you tell the truth.

The WITNESS.—I will not tell anything but that.

The COURT.—No, nothing but the truth.

(Question read.)

A. I supposed I was to turn it over to them as soon as I had proved up on it, but I told them that I would not do it.

Q. Well, now you say—who did you refer to when you said you had a friend, whom did you have in mind?    A. R. A. Lambdin.

Q. He is a freind of yours, is he?

A. Yes, sir.

Q. How long after this before you saw Lambdin and told him?

A. I seen him either that night or the following day, I am not sure.

(Testimony of Samuel C. Hutchings.)

Q. And how did Lambdin know who to go to see?

A. Because I sent him down there.

Q. Did you send him to the person who had made this proposition to you? A. Yes, sir.

Be it remembered that then and there the following proceeding was had:

Mr. FORNEY.—If your Honor please, we move that the testimony of this witness be stricken out on the ground that it is incompetent, irrelevant and immaterial; too remote, and it does not connect or has not connected the defendants or either of them the matters in issue.

The COURT.—The Court will deny the motion at the present. We will see whether it is connected by the other witness.

To which ruling of the Court the defendants excepted, which exception was allowed by the Court.

Cross-examination by Mr. TANNAHILL.

Q. Mr. Hutchings, I believe you said it has been some time since you had this conversation?

A. Yes, sir.

Q. And the details of it are not very clear in your mind at this time? A. No, sir.

Q. Now, you do not know which one of these defendants it was who talked to you, do you?

A. No, sir.

Q. You do not remember *tat*? A. No, sir.

Q. Now, Mr. Hutchings, whoever it was talked to you about it may have stated to you that you could take up a timber claim, *taked* to you or spoke to you

(Testimony of Samuel C. Hutchings.)
about taking up a timber claim and how much it would be worth?

A.  No; they told me they would give me $100.

Q.  And they told you that the claim was a good one, or a poor one, or anything said about that?

A.  I don't remember about that.  I told them they were too cheap; I wouldn't do it.

Q.  And you don't remember what else was said?

A.  No, sir; only I told them that I had a friend and that I would send him down.

Q.  And you do not know which one of the defendants you were talking to at the time?

A.  No, sir.

(Witness excusd.)

F. M. GOODWIN, a witness recalled on behalf of the Prosecution, testified as follows on

Direct Examination by Mr. RUICK.

Q.  I show this witness the following papers for the purpse of having the signature of J. B. West and of C. H. Garby, respectively register and receiver of the United States Land Office at Lewiston, Idaho, identified, formerly register and receiver, I mean.

The first paper I show you, Mr. Witness, is a sworn statement of Rowland A. Lambdin, made at the United Sttes Land Office, April 25th, 1902, on his application to enter and purchase the southwest quarter of section 29, township 42 north, of range 1 West, Boise Meridian, in the District of lands subject to sale at lLEwston, Idaho.  This paper is in duplicate.

(Testimony of F. M. Goodwin.)

I next submit to you testimony of claimant R. A. Lambdin in connection with said application. Next the cross-examination of claimant R. A. Lambdin, in connection with his direct examination; next the testimony of the witness William Dwyer in supprt of the applcation of R. A. Lambdin; next the cross-examination of William Dwyer in connection with his direct examination; next the testimony of witness Charles Graves in support of said application, and the cross-examination of said Charles Graves in connection therewith, next the register's final certificate, 3786, bearing date July 22d, 1902, issued to said Rowland A. Lambdin, next the receiver's final receipt, bearing number 30786 issued to said Rowland A. Lambdin, on the date last mentioned.

Examine these papers specifically, except the receiver's receipt, and state whether or not these papers, whether or not the signature attached thereto is the genuine signature of J. B. West, former Register of the United States Land Office, referred to? A. *Yeh,* they are.

Q. Was Mr. West such acting register during the time mentioned in these papers? A. He was.

Q. I now show you receiver's final receipt, and ask you if that is the genuine signature of Charles H. Garby, formerl̥ receiver of the United States Land Office of Lewiston, Idaho? A. Yes, sir.

Q. And was he such acting reciver on the day on which this bears date? A. He was.

Be it remembered that then and there the following proceeding was had :

(Testimony of F. M. Goodwin.)

Mr. RUICK.—We offer in evidence the sworn statement just identified; the offer is in duplicate.

Mr. FORNEY.—What is the date of it?

Mr. RUICK.—The date is April 25th, 1902.

Mr. FORNEY.—If your Honor please, we object to it as incompetent, irrelevant and immaterial in that it does not tend to prove any of the material allegations of the indictment; it is too remote, long prior to the formation of this conspiracy as alleged in the indictment, none of the papers have been properly authenticated, no proper foundation having been laid, nor does this evidence tend to prove any issue before the Court relative to the overt acts alleged to have been committed and the evidence offered shows upon its face that each act as an offense, is barred.

Mr. RUICK.—Let that stand to each and all of these papers which shall be offered.

Mr. FORNEY.—Yes, to each and all of the papers and to the testimony of the witness following as to each exhibit.

The COURT.—The Court will make the same ruling for the same reasons that apply to this other earlier case. The Court cannot anticipate just what connection will be made.

To which ruling of the Court the defendants excepted, and which exception was allowed by the Court, and Plaintiff's Exhibits numbered 38 to 43 inclusive, were admitted over such objection of the defendant; copies of which appear elsewhere in this transcript.

(Testimony of F. M. Goodwin.)

Mr. RUICK.—We ask that this sworn statement in duplicate be marked Plaintiff's Exhibit 38, and it is so marked and admitted.

Mr. RUICK.—We next offer the testimony of R. A. Lambdin, and ask that it be marked Plaintiff's Exhibit 39, and it is so admitted and marked over plaintiff's said objection.

Mr. RUICK.—Next the cross-examination of claimant, in connection with the direct examination, and ask that it be marked Plaintiff's Exhibit 39-A, and it is admitted and so marked over defendant's said objection.

Mr. RUICK.—I next offer paper, testimony of William Dwyer, and ask that it be marked Plaintiff's Exhibit 40, and it is admitted and so marked over plaintiff's said objection.

Mr. RUICK.—Next the cros-examination of the witness Dwyer in connection with his direct examination, and ask that it may be marked Plaintiff's Exhibit 40-A.

And it is admitted and so marked over defendants' said objection.

Mr. RUICK.—We next offer the testimony of witness Charles Graves in support of the application of Charles A. Lambdin, and ask that it be marked Plaintiff's Exhibit 41, and the same is admitted and marked over the defendant's said objection.

Mr. RUICK.—Next the cross-examination of witness Charles Graves, and ask that it be marked Plaintiff's Exhibit 41-A, and the same is admitted and so marked over plaintiff's said objection.

(Testimony of Rowland A. Lambdin.)

Mr. RUICK.—Next offer the register's final receipt No. 3786, issued to R. A. Lambdin, and ask that it be marked Plaintiff's Exhibiit 42, and the same is admitted in evidence and so marked over defendants' said objection.

Mr. RUICK.—Next offer the receiver's final receipt, No. 3786, and ask that it be marked Plaintiff's Exhibit 43, and the same is admitted in evidence, and so marked over defendant's objection.

(Witness excused.)

ROWLAND A. LAMBDIN, a witness called and sworn for the prosecution, testified as follows, on

Direct Examination by Mr. RUICK.

Q.   Where do you reside, Mr. Lambdin?
A.   Potlatch, Idaho.

(Witness continuing.)

I am in the employ of the Potlatch Mercantile Company, have been there since to 10th of January, about two years at one time, and one year at another time, I resided in Lewiton, Idaho; I was there in 1902.

I am acquainted with the defendant W. F. Kettenbach, and have known him for about five or six years. I don't know as I was ever introduced to him; I have often spoken to him. I have had some business transactions with Mr. Kettenbach through which we became acquainted.

I have known George H. Kester since about the spring of 1902. I got acquainted with him in the

(Testimony of Rowland A. Lambdin.)

Lewiston National Bank. I had dealings with him so that we became acquainted.

I have known the defendant Dwyer about the same length of time at Lewiston, Idaho.

Q. Did you at any time file upon a timber claim under what is known as the stone and timber law?

A. I did.

Q. Where were you residing at that time?

A. Lewiston, Idaho.

Q. State in your own way the circumstances leading up to your filing on this timber claim and then go ahead and relate the incident in your own way?

Mr. FORNEY.—I will ask the Court that he fix the time.

Mr. RUICK.—I will.

Q. I show Plaintiff's Exhibit No. 38 to the witness purporting to be his sworn statement filed at the time he applied to purchase the lands referred to therein. Look at this paper in duplicate and see if your signature is on the same in duplicate?

A. Yes, sir.

Q. You recognize this paper?    A. Yes, sir.

Q. Is that the paper you filed in the land office at Lewiston, the time you appied to purchase these timber lands?    A. Yes, sir.

Be it remembered that then and there the following proceeding was had:

Q. Now you may go ahead and state the circumstances leading up to this, how you came to be attracted to the subject.

(Testimony of Rowland A. Lambdin.)

Mr. FORNEY.—We object to it on the ground it is incompetent, irrelevant and immaterial, and further that it is too remote and does not tend to connect the defendants with this transaction or any of the offe*s*nes alleged in the indictment, and does not come within the time alleged in any count of the indictment, and does not prove or tend to prove any of the material issues set forth in the indictment and that if it could tend to prove an offense, it is barred by the statute of limitation, and we will ask your Honor to let this objection run to all the other testimony of this witness.

The COURT.—Yes, sir.

Mr. RUICK.—I *d*sire to change the question and counsel can renew his objection. I would like to ask him one or two direct questions.

The COURT.—Very well.

Q. Did any person come to you and mention the subject of your taking the timber claim?

A. Yes, sir.

Q. Who was that person?

A. Samuel C. Hutchings.

Q. Did he tell you the name of the person from whom he came?     A. Yes, sir.

Q. Who was it?     A. George H. Kester.

Q. Did he relate to you the conversation he had had with Kester in relation to it, and what had been said to him by Kester?

A. He told me I could get a claim through Mr. Kester.

(Testimony of Rowland A. Lambdin.)

Q. Now what did *yo* do after Hutchings told you about this?

A. I went to the bank and saw Mr. Kester.

Be it remembered that then and there the following proceeding was had?

Q. All right, now go ahead and state what occurred?

Mr. FORNEY.—We now renew our objection, the same as we made before.

The COURT.—Yes, the objection made by Mr. Forney *a*may be understood as going to these questions and all subsequent questions. Objection overruled.

To which ruling of the Court the defendants then and there excepted, which exception was allowed by the Court.

And the witness answered:

A. I went around *an* introduced myself to Mr. Kester and told him Mr. Hutchings had sent me around there and I understood he wanted me to take up this timber claim, and I would get $100 for taking it up, he to pay all expenses of the transaction. We came to an agreement, and he told me that Dwyer was going up in a few days and he would notify me when he was going and to meet him at the train and go up with him into the timber.

Q. You came you say, to an agreement; what was that agreement?

A. The agreement was I should go out and take up a stone and timber claim and they would pay all the expenses, and I was to receive one hundred dollars *whn* I made my final proof and turned over the deed to them.

Q. Was anything said about the money to make the final proof on the land?

A. They were to furnish all the expenses in the transaction.

Q. Including the money to pay for the land?

A. Including everything.

Q. Well, now, go right ahead and relate it?

A. Well, I think it was about ten days later I was notified; I don't remember just who notified me. Anyway I was notified to go up with Dwyer the following morning. He would be going up and to meet him at the train. I think it left at 7:30 in the morning. I went up to Vollmer, what is now called Troy. There we procured saddle horses, Mr. Dwyer got two, and from there we got on into the timber, I should think about twenty miles.

Mr. RUICK.—You speak pretty rapidly for the reporters.

Mr. TANNAHILL.—Go right ahead, they will get it.

Q. Talk to the jury, turn to the jury and go ahead in your own way.

A. We got up there the following day; we stayed over night at a place, we stayed there one night; I had a kind of an accident, and I had to return to Vollmer and back again, proceeding on the next day, and got there along in the afternoon about three o'clock, between three and four and put up at a party's house, I don't remember the name. The

(Testimony of Rowland A. Lambdin.)

next morning we went up to the timber. I went over the claim, I was to file on, I supposed I did, looked at the corners on the stake. I also went over some other timber at that time, and the next day after that I returned to Vollmer, .and Mr. Dwyer stayed up in the timber. He rode back probably about fifteen miles with me, and then he had some other business to look after and he left me there, and I came back to Lewiston that afternoon and got there about 3:30, and went up to the land office and was directed to go to Mr. Mullen, in Anderson's office I believe at the time, I forget which one of them made out my papers, and from there I went in and filed on the timber claim.

Q. Where did you get the money? to file or pay the filing fees? A. Kester.

Q. Did you pay Mullen anything?

A. Yes, sir.

Q. Or whoever made out the papers?

A. I paid for filing the papers, and also for recording them; paid Mr. West.

Q. How much did you get for that?

A. I don't remember how much; just enough to cover it. I gave him the exact amount.

Q. Now, Mr. Lambdin, before you file these papers in the land office, did you have any conversation with any person, any of the defendants, relative to the matters in the land office, and the profits which you would be apt to make?

A. Mr. Dwyer and I had talked the matter over quite a little up in the timber; I didn't know what

(Testimony of Rowland A. Lambdin.)

was expected of me so I had to make inquiries to find out.

Q. Was the matter discussed between you and Dwyer at all relative to what you would have to answer in the land. office and how you would have to answer in the land office?        A.  Yes, sir.

Q. I will show you the testimony given by you upon your final proof, and will call your attention to the sworn application filed by you on the 25th of April, 1902, and the statements contained therein to the effect: I do not apply to purchase the land above described on speculation, but in good faith to appropriate it to my own exclusive use and benefit, and that I have not directly or indirectly made any agreement or contract in any way or manner with any person or persons whomsoever by which the title I may acquired from the Government of the United States may inure in whole or in part to the benefit of any person except myself," also these questions particularly in your final proof: "Have you sold or transferred your claim *t* the lands since making your swoun statement," or have you directly or indirectly"—this is the part to which I call your attention particularly—"directly or indirectly made any agreement or contract in any way or manner with any person whomsoever by which the title you may acquire from the Government of the United States may inure in whole or in part to the benefit of any person except yourself"?  And "Do you make this entry in good faith for the appropriation of the land exclusively to your own use and benefit, and not for

(Testimony of Rowland A. Lambdin.)

the use or benefit of any other person?'' And this other question "Nor has any other person than yourself, or has any firm, corpration or association any interst in the entry you are now making, or in the land or in the timber thereon"; also these other particular questions in your cross-examination, "Did you pay out of your own individual funds all the expenses in connection with making the filing, and do you expect to pay for the land with your own money?" That was question 16 of the cross-examination. Question 17: "Where did you get the money with which to pay for this land, and how lng have you had the same in your actual pssession, to which you answered: "I borrowed $100 of it on my personal note, and no way involved this land to secure the loan. Most of it ha not yet"—etc. Now, I will ask you, Mr. Lambdin, whether or not these subjects embodied in these questions were talked over between you and Dwyer or eithr of the defendants at any time before you made your filing or your final proof?

A. Most of them were talked over between Mr. Dwyer and myself.

Q. Now you have stated about your filing and having papers made out and your filing; now go ahead and state what else occurred in relation to this subject?

*Q.* You mean in regard to filing or final proof?

Q. Yes, anything to any feature of it?

A. I think it was lacking two or three days of three months when I was notifieid through the land

(Testimony of Rowland A. Lambdin.)

office of the day I was to prove up would arrive, and in the meantime Mr. Dwyer had sent to have my weitnesses down for me. I forget his name, one of the men we stopped with the night we was up in the timber. He lived close there and he came down on the morning train on the day to prove up. I think about ten o'clock in the morning. Before I went to proe up I went into the director's room of the bank, and Mr. Kester gave me the money to prove up with, and I went upstairs.

Q. Did you execute any papers there at the time he gave you the money? A. No, sir.

Q. Give him any note or other security?

A. No, sir.

Q. Did he ask you for any?

A. Not to my knowledge. I also got $20 to pay the witness with and I went upstairs and made my final proof and paid the money over and got a deed and came down to the bank, and Mr. Kester and Mr. Dwyer, I think, and myself went across to Mr. H. K. Barnett's office, and there was a deed made out and I signed it, and Mr. Barnett and myself got into a hack and went up to the house and my wife signed the deed, and we came back down town.

Q. You spoke of getting $20 from Mr. Kester to pay a witness with. What witness do you refer to there?

A. The gentlemen that came down to witness my final proof.

Q. Did you know that this witness was clming and had been secured for the purpose?

(Testimony of Rowland A. Lambdin.)

A.   Yes, sir.

Q.   Did you have any convesation with either of the defendants about it before he came there, before he got there?

A.   Yes, Mr. Dwyer told me I would have to have four witnesses and he gave me the four, had the four names that I got from him, and he seen to this witness coming down so that I had nothing to do with it.

Q.   What conversation, if any, did you have with him relative to the witnesses failing to appear or anything of *tha* sort?

A.   Well, not much, if any.   The morning that I was to prove up, I went up and saw Mr. West, I didn't know maybe he might not get down, and I went up to see Mr. West, to see if I could get a stay of proceedings for two or three days if the witness did not get down.   I found that I could, but the witness got down on the morning train and I didn't need it.

Q.   I want to know who suggested it?

A.   I forget who suggested it, but it was suggested to me by either Mr. Dwyer or Mr. Kester.

Q.   You say Mr. Kester gave you this $20 to go and pay the witness?     A.   Yes, sir.

Q.   Did he have any conversation with you at the time he handed you this money?

A.   Before I was handed the money I had to find out what the witness wanted.

(Testimony of Rowland A. Lambdin.)

Q. I want you to tell what Mr. Kester *d*aid, what, if anything, he said to you about it at the time he gave you this money?

A. When he gave me the money he told me so much of it would be to pay for the filing and filing: proof, and pay for the land, and $20 for the witness, but before I got the $20 I found out what the witness was going to charge and reported it to Mr. Kester.

Q. Did you discuss the matter with either of the defendants relative to what you would say as to where the money had come from, or anything of that sort?

A. We had some talk on the matte, but I don't remember just what was said. I know I was supposed to have the money myself, or that it would come up anyway where I got the money from.

Q. Do you remember with whom you had this talk?

A. I had almost all my talk on that part of it with Mr. Dwyer.

Q. When you came down from the land office with them, you stated you got your final receipt. Did you get a final receipt when you made your final proof?    A. I got a receipt, yes, sir.

Q. From the Land Office?    A. Yes, sir.

Q. Where did you take it to?

A. Took it right into the bank and gave it to Mr. Kester.

Q. What, if anything, did Kester say to you when you came down into the bank?

(Testimony of Rowland A. Lambdin.)

A. I think he just asked me if I got any receipt, and I told him yes, and turned it over to him, and he asked me to come over to Mr. Barnett's office and went with me there, and there got a deed and took it along, or else Mr. Barnett had it already. Any-way it was *already* for me to sign.

Q. This was the same day you made your final proof?    A. Yes, sir.

Q. Who did this deed run to?

A. I didn't know at the time who it did run to; I never looked at it.

Q. Did you learn later who it run to?

A. Yes, sir.

Q. Who to?

A. W. F. Kettenbach and George H. Kester.

Q. Have you ever paid any location fee to anyone at all?    A. No, sir.

Q. Never agreed to pay any attorney fee?

A. No, sir.

Q. Were you ever asked to pay any?

A. No, sir.

Q. Any talk about a location fee?

A. None whatever that I remember of.

Q. When, if at all, did you get this $100?

A. Between the time of filing on the claim and proving up on it.

Q. How had you got it?

A. Went to the bank and got it in dribbles of $10 or $15, one time $35.

Q. From whom?    A. From Kester.

(Testimony of Rowland A. Lambdin.)

Q.    State the circumstances of those different payments, Mr. Lambdin?

A.    Well, I think one time I got $10 or $15. No, it was $20, I gave my note I guess, and then a man by the name of Schroeder, I think, signed a note—

Q.    Was there an understanding in regard to that note, at the time it was executed as to its payment?

A.    Why, Mr. Schroeder was given to understand he would never be called upon to pay it.

Q.    By whom?

A.    By myself and Mr. Kester.

Q.    What were the reasons given there at the time?

A.    Why, I think it was just simply that the note would be taken care of and was simply a matter of form, that somebody else would have to be on the note with me.

Q.    Well, now, what other payments did you receive that you recall?

A.    I drew a check once I think for $35 and it was cahsed.

Q.    Did you have any money at the bank at the time?    A.    No, sir.

Q.    Was the check paid or honored?

A.    Yes, sir.

Q.    Well, how much of. this money had been paid at the time you made final proof?

A.    I think the whole thing was paid at the time I made final proof.

Q.    You think there was nothing coming to you at the time?

(Testimony of Rowland A. Lambdin.)

A. I don't remember of any*y*hing coming to me when I proved up.

Q. Was there anything paid to you at that time when you executed the deed?

A. No, sir; I don't think so.

Q. How much then did you ever receive?

A. Received $100.

Cross-examination b*y* Mr. TANNAHILL.

Q. You say you borrowed some money from the bank at one time? A. No, sir.

Mr. RUICK.—We object to it; he said he did not borrow it. I want to ask a further question.

Direct Examination (resumed).

Q. Mr. Lambdin, at the time you first went down to the bank to see Mr. Kester about filing on the timber claim what did Kester say to you a*b*out the proposition of filing on a timber claim?

A. I was given to understand by Mr. Kes*tr* if I went up and took a timber claim that the ex*e*penses would be all paid, and I would receive $100 when I made final proof.

Q. What, if anything, was said about—was anything further said about the scarcity or plentitude of timber claims at that time, if anything of that sort?

A. Well, I was given to understand that timber was being taken up.

Q. Not what you were given to understand, but *wht* Kester told *y*ou?

A. He said the timber *wa* being taken up very rapidl*y* and would soon be all gone and if I did not

(Testimony of Rowland A. Lambdin.)

take up a claim now, I would not be able to get one if I waited.

### Cross-examination (resumed) by Mr. TANNA-HILL.

Q. You say you were given to understand if you went up and took a timber claim that the money would be furnished you to *ake* final proof and save expenses?     A. Yes, sir.

Q. That was your understanding?

A. That was my understanding.

Q. And that if you did go up and take the claim and make final proof you would be able to make $100 out of it?     A. Yes, sir.

Q. That was your understanding of it?

A. Yes, sir.

Q. And you did go up and take a timber claim?

A. I did.

Q. And you went up because they were getting scarce, and you thought you would not have very many opportunities to use your timber right?

A. No, sir, not so much that as I wanted the $100; I needed it.

Q. You needed the $100?     A. Yes, sir.

Q. And you felt you would be able to make $100 if you took up a timber claim?

A. I had Mr. Keser's word for it and I took that.

Q. Where did you say you had been working last here recently?

A. Potlatch Mercantile Company.

Q. How long have you been working there?

(Testimony of Rowland A. Lambdin.)

A. Since the 10th of January of this year.

Q. Where was you before that?

A. In Spokane.

Q. How long have you been there?

A. A year ago last November I went there.

Q. Where were you in April, 1905?

A. I believe I was in Lewiston.

Q. Were you in Spokane in April, 1905?

A. Well, I was in Lewston just a year before I went to Spokane; I was in Spokane a year.

Q. What were you doing in Spokane?

A. I was in both Spokane and Lewiston, but not in April; I think I was in Lewiston in April. I think I left in 1905, in the fall.

Q. You think you left Spokane?

A. No, Lewiston. I think I left there and went to Spokane in the fall of 1905.

Q. Were you in Spokane any of the time during the time you were in Lewiston? Did you go back and forth to Spokane?     A. I don't think I did.

Q. Now, were you at Lewiston all the time?

A. The *lat* time I was there for abo*y*t a year; I think it was a year.

Q. When did you first come to Lewiston?

A. I think I came there in the fall of 1900.

Q. And how long were you there at that time?

A. About two years.

Q. About two years? You left then the fall of 1902?     A. About that, yes, sir.

Q. Then where did you go?

(Testimony of Rowland A. Lambdin.)

A.  I went to Spokane and from Spokane to Seattle.

Q.  When did *yo* go to Spokane?

A.  I *wnt* to Spokane I believe in the fall of 1902.

Q.  When did you leave Spokane to go to Seattle?

A.  I was in Spokane a few days, about ten days or two weeks probably.

Q.  Then where did you go?

A.  I *s*went right to Seattle.

Q.  Where *dd* you go when you left Seattle? How long did you stay in Seattle?

A.  I stayed in Seattle about a year and a half, along in July I think, or the first of August.

Q.  Then where did you go?

A.  Then I came down, came down to Spokane and stayed there u*j*til about the 20th of November.

Q.  Of the same year, 1904?

A.  Of the same year.

Q.  Then where did you go?

A.  Came to Lewiston and stayed one year.

Q.  That would be until the 20th of November, 1905?     A.  That would be *te* fall of 1905.

Q.  I will ask you Mr. Lambdin if you recognize that handwriting (showing witness paper).

A.  That is my writing.

Q.  That is your writing?     A.  Yes, sir.

Q.  You addressed that envelope did you?

A.  I believe I did.

Q.  I will ask you to look at this letter (showing witness paper) and state whether or not that is in your handwrting?

(Testimony of Rowland A. Lambdin.)

A. That is my handwriting.

Q. You mailed that to George H. Kester?

A. I did, sir.

Mr. TANNAHILL.—We ask that these be identified and each marked for identification.

(Envelope marked Defe*nn*t's Exhibit "G" for Identification; L*t*ter marked Exhibit "H" for Identification.)

Q. Look at this letter I now hand you and state whether or not that is your signature? to the letter?

A. That is my signature, yes, sir.

Q. You mailed that to Mr. Kettenbach, did you not?

A. Mr. Kester I think, I don't remember—no, Mr. Kettenbach.

Mr. TANNAHILL.—We ask that this be marked Defendants' Exhibit "I" for Identification.

(Letter so marked.)

Q. I will ask you Mr. Lambdin to look at this copy of a complaint and state whether or not that is the paper that you refer to in this letter, marked Defendants' Exhibit "I" for Identification?

A. Yes, sir; that is the same one.

Mr. TANNAHILL.—We ask that this cop\ of a complaint be marked Defendants' Exhibit "J" for Identification.

(The same is so marked.)

Q. Mr. Lambdin, *yo* wrote Mr. Kettenbach a letter a few days before you sent this one in which you enclosed a copy of the complaint, did you not?

(Testimony of Rowland A. Lambdin.)

A.   You mean a lettr previous to this one you have now?

Q.   The one with which you enclosed the copy of the complaint?

A.   You mean a letter previous to this one you have now?

Q.   Yes, you wrote a lettr previous to this one did you not?    A.   Not that I remember of.

Mr. TANNAHILL.—I offer these documents in evidence, being the envelope and letter referred to as Defendants' Exhibit "G" and "H," already identified; the envelope bears the postmark, Spokane, Washington, April 5th, 6:30 P. M., 1905, and is addressed to George H. Kester, Lewiston, Idaho.

And the same was thereupon marked respectively Defendants' Exhibit "G" and "H," copies of which appear elsewhere n this transcript.

Mr. TANNAHILL.—We also offer in evidence Defendants' Exhibit "I" and "J" for Identification, which said documents were received in evidence and marked Defendants' Exhibits "I" and "J" respectively, copies of which appear elsewhere in this transcript.

Q.   Mr. Lambdin, you stated that you returned to Troy after you and Mr. Dwyer left Troy, or Vollmer as you call it?

A.   Yes, sir; I returned to Troy.

Q.   What did you return for?

A.   To take the train to Lewiston.

Q.   Did you have any other mission?

A.   Did I have any other mission?

(Testimony of Rowland A. Lambdin.)

Q. Yes; after you went away from Troy you went back for something, did you not?

A. Because I lost my *pc*ket-book.

Q. Did it have any money in it?

A. Yes, sir.

Q. How much money did you have?

A. One hundred dollars.

Q. Did you not have two hundred dollars in it?

A. I don't know. I had enough money in it so that I was anxious to get back and find it; I don't think that I had more than a hundred.

Q. Did you not tell Mr. Dwyer on this trip, yourself and Mr. Dwyer being present, that you had money to pay him his location fee, or words in substance and to that effect? A. No, sir.

Q. You didn't tell him that? You never had any conversa*ton* with Mr. Dwyer regarding the location fee? A. Not that I remember of.

Q. Now Mr. Lambdin, you state in this letter that you wrote Mr. Kester a letter and rec*iv*ed no reply from him. What letter did you refer to?

A. That is the letter I wrote from Spokane is it?

Q. Yes. (Reading:) "I wrote you a letter Saturday evening telling you of conditions and that I needed $75 by Friday. I received a letter *frm* my brother to-night, stating that he had not seen you." You wrote that sort of a letter?

A. Yes, sir; I did, prior to that one.

(Testimony of Rowland A. Lambdin.)

Redirect Examination by Mr. RUICK.

Q.  What money was this that was in your purse which you lost on that trip?

A.  Money given me by Mr. Schroeder for another mission.

Q.  Was the money yours, any part of it?

A.  No part of it was mine only for use on this certain mission.

Be it remembered that then and there the following proceeding was had:

Q.  What was your financial condition  at  that time?

Mr. FORNEY.—Objected to as immaterial.

The COURT.—Objection overruled, to which ruling of the Court the defendants then and there exce*pe*d, which exception was allowed by the Court, and the w*ti*ness answered:

A.  I was broke and out of work.

Q.  Who is Mr. Schroeder?

A.  He is the gentleman I had been working for, but his laundry burned and throwed me out of work.

Q.  What threw you out of work?

A.  The burning of his laundry.

Q.  State about this paper?

Mr. TANNAHILL.—Pardon Mr. Ruick, I forgot a question.

Cros-examination  (resumed).

(Mr. TANNAHILL.)

Q.  You have been indicted, have you not?

A.  Have I been indicted?

Q.  Yes?        A.  Not that I know of.

(Testimony of Rowland A. Lambdin.)

Q. You don't know whether you have been indicted or not?

A. I had never heard of it, except it was in the paper, the "Lewiston Tribune," that, of course, is just Lewiston newspaper talk.

Q. You have never been arrested?

A. Have I ever been arrested?

The COURT.—That is upon the indictment here?

A. No, sir.

Q. With whom did you talk about your evidence Mr. Lambdin? Who was the first Government official you talked with regarding any transactions with Mr. Kester.

A. I ta*l*ed with two parties at once.

A. I talked with two parties at once.

Q. Who?

A. Mr. Goodwin and Mr. O'Fallon.

Q. Where did you talk *wih* them?

A. In my house and at the Bollinger Hotel.

Q. Do you remember about when that was?

A. No, it was prior to the grand jury at Boise; I think it was in the spring or early summer of 1905.

Q. Did you give them a statement at the time?

A. I did.

Q. And have you seen that statement since?

A. I have.

Q. When did you see it?

A. I saw it last night.

Q. You read it ov*e* last night, did you?

A. Yes, sir; I *rad* it over.

(Testimony of Rowland A. Lambdin.)

Q.  And when did you see it? prior to last night and since you gave it to the officers?

A.  I could not answer that question positively; I might have seen it down at Boise, but I don't remember seeing it.

Q.  You appeared before the Grand Jury at Boise?    A.  I did.

Q.  And had a talk with Mr. Ruick, Mr. Goodwin and Mr. O'Fallon?

A.  I believe we had some conversation, but what it amounted to I don't remember.

Q.  And then you went over your statement last night?

A.  I read my statement over last night.

Redirect Examination by Mr. RUICK.

Q.  When you testified in Boise, and when you were before the grand jury in Boise, do you remember what month that was?

A.  I think it was June; I know it was in the summer anyway.

Q.  Wasn't it in July?

A.  It possibly was, it was along in the warm weather, I know, June or July.

Q.  Was it before or after you had made this written statement to Mr. Goodwin and Mr. O'Fallon?

A.  It was after.

Q.  When had you made that statement to Mr. Goodwin and Mr. O'Fallon?

A.  Sometime in May, I believe.

Q.  Of what year?    A.  1905, I think.

Q.  Well, was it before you went down to Boise?

(Testimony of Rowland A. Lambdin.)

A.   It was before I went to Boise, yes, sir.

Q.   Is that your signature to that document?

A.   Yes, sir.

Q.   Is that the affidavit that you made the sworn statement that you made in the presence of Mr. Goodwin and Mr. O'Fallon in relation to the facts of this particular case?      A.   Yes, it is.

Q.   Was it made on the day on which it bears date as you recollect it?      A.   About the time of it.

Q.   Mr. Lambdin, this skeleton complaint, this unsigned complaint, which you sent to Mr. Kester—that you sent to Mr. Kettenbach, accompanied by the letter addressed to him, when was that time relative to the time that you made this statement to Mr. Goodwin and Mr. O'Fallon, do you remember?

A.   Why, about a week I should judge prior to my statement to Mr. Goodwin and Mr. O'Fallon.

By permission of the Court the witness Lambdin is withdrawn and A. L. RICHARDSON, clerk of the above-entitled court, was called and sworn on behalf of the prosecution and testified as follows, on

Direct Examination by Mr. RUICK.

Q.   On what date was the indictment returned against the witness R. A. Lambdin, filed in this court?

A.   The 13th day of July, 1905.

Q.   And what is the charge laid in the indictment under the Statutes of the United States, what section of the United States statutes?

A.   5392, perjury.

(Testimony of Rowland A. Lambdin.)

Mr. TANNAHILL.—One thing more, may we know who the witnesses are?

Mr. RUICK.—We have no objection to the entire indictment going in. We have no objection to that.

The WITNESS.—The names of the witnesses are, R. A. Lambdin, H. K. Barnett, S. F. O'Fallon, Samuel C. Hutchings and F. M. Goodwin.

Witness excused.

ROWLAND A. LAMBDIN? *Recalled.*
(By Mr. RUICK.)

Q. Now, MrL Lambdin, you may explain this transaction in these letters and this blank complaint to which your attention has been called.

A. In the first place, my wife was taken very seriously ill and had to be taken up to Spokane to be operated upon and we didn't know whether she would live or whether she would die.

Be it remembered that then and there the following proceeding was had:

Mr. TANNAHILL.—Wait; we object to that, to any such statement as that *an* move the Court to strike that part of the witness' answer out as irrelevant and immaterial.

The COURT.—Objection is overruled; motion denied.

To which ruling of the Court the defendants then and there excepted, which exception was allowed, and the witness continued:

I went to Dr. Phillips and to the First National Bank, and saw Mr. Kester and Mr. Kettenbach, and

(Testimony of Rowland A. Lambdin.)

told them what I wanted the money for, and that I had to have it as she had to be taken very soon, and explained the situation and had the doctor there with me, so he would know and I wanted to borrow the money so I could take her up and they flatly refused me; so later I went to Mr. Frank Kettenbach of the Idaho Trust Company, so he gave me his personal check for three hundred dollars after I stated the case to him.

Be it remembered that then and there the following proceeding was had:

Mr. TANNAHILL.—The Court understands we object to all of this statement as to what he did, or Frank Kettenbach did, as not binding on the defendants, and not being in their presence, or either of them, and as immaterial and hearsay.

Objection overruled.

To which ruling of the Court the defendants then and there excepted, which exception was allowed by the Court.

Q. W. F. Kettenbach? Did W. F. Kettenbach, the defendant, later refer to the transaction between you and Frank Kettenbach? A. He did.

Q. Go ahead and state the conversation between you and Frank Kettenbach?

A. I told Frank Kettenbach the circumstances, the reason I wanted the money, and he told me to come back at 7 o'clock that evening.

Q. Relate the entire conversation you had with him? We want it all.

(Testimony of Rowland A. Lambdin.)

A.   I told Mr. Frank Kettenbach my wife was very
seriously ill; that I had been up to the other bank and
had seen Mr. W. F. Kettenbach about it, and Mr. Kester, and tried to make a loan, and they had refused it,
and that she had to go to the hospital and be operated
on and she would have to go at once, for the  reason
that the surgeon who wanted to operate on her was
going East, and she had to be leaving that night to be
operated on next day.   Mr. Kettnbach said—

Be it remembered that then and there the following proceeding was had:

Q.   State what you told him.   State the conversation in full.

Mr. TANNAHILL.—I object to that if the Court
please, as incompetent, irrelevant and immaterial; he
haas already detailed the conversation.

The COURT.—State what you said.

To which ruling of the Court the defendants then
and there excepted, which exception was allowed.

And the witness answered: A.   I came out at the
time flatfooted and told Frank Kettnbach that if I
didn't get the money, Kester and Kettenbach would
have cause to regret it.

Q.   Now, go ahead and state the facts, the conversation.

A.   And Mr. Kettenbach said he would take the
matter up with Mr. W. F. Kettenbach, his brother, or
anyway a relation, and have me to call at the bank at
seven o'clock that evening.   He also told me, he asked
me who I would get to sign the note with me, and I
said my brothers.   He also wanted my brother's wife

(Testimony of Rowland A. Lambdin.)

on the note, and I objected to bringing her in the deal and he said it wasn't necessary. I got a party by the name of Ralph Chapman in place of her, in place of my brother's wife; I got the note signed up and met him at 7 o'clock, or near 7:30 that evening, and he gave me his personal check for $300, and took the note as security.

Q. What talk did you have with either of the defendants concerning that note later?

A. Later I went first to Spokane anyway, and of course $300 was very little over the operating expenses; in fact the operating expenses were $275 and I had to have a trained nurse and other incidental expenses and I wrote Mr. Kettenbach this letter.

Q. Mr. Kettenbach or Mr. Kester?

A. Mr. Kester. I stated the reasons and told him—told him to see my brother and he would sign a note for $75, and *wehn* I returned, which would be on the Sunday following, Sunday I would sign the note, and for him to send me the money at once.

Q. Pardon me, Mr. Lambdin; I was mislead by your statement. You are now referring to the letter that is not here?

A. I am referring to another lett*r* not here. The first letter they asked me about.

Q. That was written to him?

A. The 17th of August, the same as the second one that was wrote to Mr. Kester.

The COURT.—The letter introduced in evidence was written to Mr. Kester.

Mr. RUICK.—Yes, go ahead.

(Testimony of Rowland A. Lambdin.)

A.  Mr. Kester didn't answer and I telephoned to my brother.  Mr. brother said he hadn't seen him, so I wrote this next letter, stating, as has been read before the Court, that I must have this money.  He already knew from the previous letter just the situation I was in.  I was up there broke, with my wife in the hospital and nothing to do, and I must have the money or stay there.

Q.  Did you see either one of the defendants later concerning this $300 note at the Idaho Trust Company?

A.  Afterwards I was in Mr. Gaut's barber-shop in Lewiston, and Mr. Kettenbach came in and he took a chair in the rear and I went over and sat down beside him, and brought up or mentioned the $300 note, but he gave me to understand it was through his doings that I received the money from Frank Kettenbach, and also that he expected that it would be taken care of.

Q.  What did he say?  You say "the understanding," we want the statements as near as you can give them.

A.  I know money matters were brought up.  I don't know exactly the circumstances, but anyway I believe I asked him for another loan, $25 I believe it was, and he told me that he had already secured me this $300 and that he had done all he needed to, and also in the conversation I understood that he intended to take care of it.  Later we had another conversation after I was notified by F. W. Kettenbach the note

(Testimony of Rowland A. Lambdin.)

was due and ought to be paid at once, or he would serve notice on the other signers, or soemthing to that effect, and I went to him again about it and he denied saying anything about it, and plainl\ told me to attend to m\ own bus*n*ess and he would attend to his, or to that effect, that he didn't care anything about me, or how I came out.

Q. In regard to this skeleton complaint, Mr. Lambdin?

A. The skeleton complaint I got up and sent to Mr. Kettenbach, simply as a matter of form, to see whether he would send this mone\ or not. I found out in the meantime I had onl\ got $100, whereas the warrant\ deed called for $800 for the claim, and that left a difference of $700 for the deed or claim, which I have never received; I got up a skeleton complaint and sent it to Mr. Kettenbach to see what he would do about it. He never said an\thing more to me, and I never said anything to him. It ended right there excepting I saw him, I believe, the next da\ and found out that he didn't intend to do an\thing.

I dropped the matter and he had—

Q. What did you say to him?

A. I could not recall our conversation, it was simpl\—he mentioned something about he had me for blackmail, and he didn't need to bother an\ more about me. He told me, I think. I. N. Smith had it in his hands.

Q. State what he said?

A. He told me the paper I sent him was in his attorney's hands, I. N. Smith's hands, and he guessed

(Testimony of Rowland A. Lambdin.)

he had me where they wanted me or something to that effect. I never signed it or recorded it, or anything of that kind, and I didn't think they did—and I dropped the matter and that has been the end of it.

Q. You had the notes to pay and you paid them?

A. I had the notes to pay; I don't know whether they are all paid or not. I have not been notified of any back payments due on them anyway.

Q. Did you have any transactions with either of these defendants after the grand jury met down there in Boise in relation to this subject, to these mattes at all? A. I don't believe I did.

(Witness excused.)

F. M. GOODWIN, a witness recalled for the prosecution, testified as follows, on

### Direct Examination by Mr. RUICK.

Q. Showing witness certain papers purporting to constitute the original papers relating to the application of Fred W. Shaeffer, of Lewiston, Idaho, made at the United States Land Office at Lewiston, Idaho, to prcbase the east half of the northwest quarter, and certain other lands which ar immaterial, and only given for the purpose of identifying the application to purchase the lands made in the papers themselves; Mr. Goodwin, I show you the sworn statement in duplicate first; next the notice for publication; next the testimony of the claimant, Fred W. Schaeffer, next the cross-examination of Fre W. Schaeffer in connection with this direct examination; next the testimony of the witness William F. Kettenbach as a wit-

(Testimony of F. M. Goodwin.)

ness on said application of Fred W. Schaeffer; next the cross-examination of the witness Kettenbach in connection with said direct examination; next the testimony of the witness William Dwyer in support of said application of said Fred W. Schaeffer; next the cross-examination of said witness William Dwyer in connection with said application; next the final receipt No. 2795, issued at the Lewiston Land Office and signed by J. B. West, Register. Look at these papers, Mr. Goodwin, and see if the signature of J. B. West is attached there to each and every of these papers, and if it is the genuine signature of J. B. West as such register of the land office?

A.   Yes, sir.

Q.   Was Mr. West Acting Register of the United States Land Office at Lewiston, Idaho, at the time stated in these *paper*?     A.   He was.

Be it remembered the followi*g* proceeding was had :

Mr. RUICK.—We now offer in evidence the first papers of this witness, the sworn statement in duplicate.

Mr. FORNEY.—What is the date of that?

Mr. RUICK.—May 5th, 1902.

Mr. FORNEY.—We object to this as irrelevant and immaterial and incompetent, no proper foundation having been laid, and further, it does not tend to prove nor does not relate to one or any of the overt acts set out in the indictment; further, it shows upon its face, if any offense at all, it is barred by the statutes of limitation, owing to the time the matters and transactions referred to relating to the time not em-

(Testimony of F. M. Goodwin.)

braced in any count of the indictment, and in fact was more than three years prior to the filing of the indictment; and further, it is barred by the statute of limitations, and the other grounds I mentioned in the other objections; further, there is no mention made of these transactions or of this party in the bill of particulars furnished us.

The COURT.—Objection overruled.

To which ruling of the Court the defendnats then and there excepted, which exception was allowed by the Court, and the said documents were admitted in evidnce, and marked Plaintiff's Exhibit 45, a copy of which appears elsewhere in this transcript.

Mr. FORNEY.—Will you allow this objection to run to each separate paper offered?

The COURT.—Yes. And you may have your exception.

Mr. RUICK.—I next offer in evidence notice for publication and ask that it be marked Plaintiff's Exbibit 46, and the same was admitted over defendant's said objection and was so marked.

Mr. RUICK.—We next offer in evidence testimony of Fred W. Shaffer and ask that the same be marked Plaintiffd's Exhibit 47, and the same was admitted over defendants' said objection, and was so marked.

Mr. RUICK.—We next offer in evidence the cross-examination of the claimant in connection with the direct examination and ask that it be marked Plaitff's Exhibit 47-A, and the same was admitted over defendants' said objection, and was so marked.

(Testimony of F. M. Goodwin.)

Mr. RUICK.—We next offer the testimony of William F. Kettenbach, a witness on behalf of the claimant Fred W. Shaffer, and ask that it be marked Plaintiff's Exhibit 48, and the same was admitted over defendants' said objection, and was so marked.

Mr. RUICK.—We now offer in evidence the cross-examination of William Kettenbach, in connection with his direct examination just referred to, and ask that it be marked Plaintiff's Exhibit 48-A, and it was admitted over plantiff's said objection, and was so marked.

Mr. RUICK.—We next offer the testimony of William Dwyer in support of the appliction of Fred W. Shaffer, and ask that it be marked Plaintiff's Exhibit 49, and it was admitted over defendants' said objection and was so marked.

Mr. RUICK.—We next offer in evidence the cross-examination of the witness William Dwyer in connection with the direct examination just referred to, and ask that it be marked Plaintiff's Exhibit 49-A, and the same was admitted over the defendants' said objection and was so marked.

Mr. RUICK.—We next offer in evidence the register's final receipt, No. 3795, issued to Fred W. Shaffer, from the Unied States Land Office at Lewiston, Idaho, and ask that it be marked Plaintiff's Exhibit 50, and the same was admitted in evidence over defendants' said objection and was so marked. (Copies appear elsewhere in transcript.)

Mr. FORNEY.—It is understood now that our objection goes to each of these papers offered.

(Testimony of F. M. Goodwin.)

The COURT.—Yes; the objection is overruled.

To which ruling of the Court the defendant then and there excepted, which exception was allowed by the Court.

Q. Mr. Goodwin, look at the paper purporting to be issued to Fred W. Shaffer and see if the signature thereto appended is that of Charles H. Garby, former Receiver of the United States Land Office at Lewiston, Idaho?        A. It is.

Q. Was he such acting receiver at the time mentioned in this final receipt?

A. Yes, sir; he was.

Be it rememberd that then and there the following proceeding was had:

Mr. RUICK.—We now offer the receipt in evidence and ask that it be marked Plaintiff's Exhibit 51.

Mr. FORNEY.—We object to that; we make the same general objection tot that we have made to all other papers connected with this entry.

The COURT.—Yes, I understand; objection overruled.

To which ruling of the Court the defendants then and there excepted, which exception was allowed by the Court, and said paper was admitted in evidence and marked Plaintiff's Exhibit 51. (Copy appears elsewhere.)

FRED W. SHAFFER, a witness called and sworn for the prosecution, testified as follows on

Direct Examination by Mr. RUICK.

Q. Where do you reside? A. Lewiston.

(Witness continuing.) As to occupation I have worked at one thing and another; last fall I worked at the hotel and this spring I have been tacking down carpets. I do a little of everything; sometimes I am a general laborer by occupation, but then I clerked in the hotel last fall.

I have resided in Lewiston pretty close to seven years. I came there in March, and most of that summer I was on Camas Prairie, but came back here in the fall.

I am acquainted with W. F. Kettenbach; have known him about five years, I guess, somewhere along there; I could not tell just exactly how many years. I was at one time janitor at the Lewiston National Bank. I was there a little over a year, I think; I went there in March and was there until the next spring.

I was janitor at the bank at the time I took up my stone and timber claim and when I proved up. I am acquainted with George H. Kester; I got acquainted with him when I went to work for the bank, went to be janitor. If my filing or proving up on my timber claim occurred in 1902, I was employed as janitor at the Lewiston National Bank during the year 1902, or a portion of that year; I am acquainted with the defendant William Dwyer; I met him there

(Testimony of Fred W. Schaffer.)
while I was working in the bank; I became acquainted
with him there.

Q.  Now, you took up a stone and timber claim, did
you?     A.  Yes, sir.

Q.  Did you have any talk with anyone before
you*t* took it up?

A.  Well, I think I mentioned it to somebody, that
I would like to get a timber and stone claim, but there
wasn't much said about it.

Be it remembered th*t* then and there the followi*j*g
proceeding was had:

Q.  Who first mentioned the subject to you which
led to your taking the timber claim?

Mr. FORNEY.—Will the Court allow us an objection to this testimony upon the same grounds as we
have made to other testimony of like nature, that the
transaction is too remote, etc?

Mr. RUICK.—The same general objection as that
previously set forth.

Mr. FORNEY.—Yes, as irrelevant, immaterial
and incompetent, no proper foundation having been
laid, that it does not prove or tend to prove any of
the material allegations of the indictment; th*a* it is
not one of, nor is it connected with, any of the overt
acts set out in the indictment; that it shows upon its
face that it is barred by the statutes of limitation,
and further, that there is no mention made of these
transactions or of this party in the bill of particulars
furn*si*hed us.

The COURT.—Yes, the same ruling.

(Testimony of Fred W. Schaffer.)

To which ruling of the Court the defendants then and there excepted, which exception was allowed, and the witness answered:

A. Mr. Kester.

Q. Where did the conversation occur?

A. It occurred in the front part of the bank where the entrance is, where the peope come in to collect.

Q. The public part of the bank?

A. Yes, sir.

Q. What did Mr. Kester say to you about it?

A. Well, he asked me if I ever took up a timber claim, and I told him no, and then he told me I could make $100 or something of that kind if I would take up a claim, and I said all right.

Q. Did he tell you how you were going to make it?

A. No, sir.

Q. What? A. No, sir.

Q. You said all right? A. Yes, sir.

Q. What were you to do?

A. Well, it was not mentioned at that time.

Q. It was not mentioned at that time?

A. No; that was all that was said, to my recollection.

Q. Now, did you have any further talks with him or with any of the other defendants about it?

A. No, sir; not at that time; it was a short time afterwards he told me to go to Kendrick, and I would meet Mr. Dwyer there and I would go out along and see the claim. I shaped up all my work one day so that I could leave it and I went to Kendrick

(Testimony of Fred W. Schaffer.)

and met Mr. Dwyer there and he had a saddle pony for me and there were some others.

Q. On what conditions were you to take up this claim? How were you going to get the $150, or this $100? What provisions, or where were you going to get the money to pay the excpnses, etc., and pay for the lands?

A. Well, I think that the exepnses were not mentioned until I went up to Kendrick, but at any rate I got the money to pay for the excpnses from Mr. Kettenbach.

Q. Mr. Kettenbach?    A. Mr. Kester.

Q. Before you went?

A. Well, on that trip, before I went, we didn't know what the expenses would be, only I went up on the railraod and I just paid that out of my own pocket, but when I went up there, then all the other pxpenses were paid by Mr. Kester.

Q. Where did you get the money to prove up on the claim to pay for it?

A. I got it from Mr. Kester.

Q. The full amount?    A. Yes, sir.

Q. What were you to do? You had this talk with Kester, you say?    A. Yes, sir.

Q. What were you to do to get this $100? What did you have to do to get this $100?

A. Take up a claim.

Q. What did you have to do to get the $100?

A. It was not expressed just what I should do with it, but he said I could make $100 by taking up a claim, and I didn't know. I had really no idea

(Testimony of Fred W. Schaffer.)

at that time just how it was to be done, but I felt like I could make $100 out of it.

Q. And who were you reying upon? Whose word were you relying upon that you would make $100?

A. I trusted Mr. Kester; I had confidence in him.

Q. Who notifeid you when to go up to Kendrick?

A. Mr. Kester.

Q. You received your instructions from him?

A. I was to go with him out to the claim.

The COURT.—Go with whom?

A. Mr. Dwyer.

Q. He told you to go to Kendrick, and that you were to meet Mr. Dwyer?    A. Yes, sir.

Q. What did you do?

A. We went to Kendrick and met Mr. Dwyer and we went out to his claim and had dinner, and I think it was his homestead, the piece of land he had, and then we went down on the piece of land, and he showed me the line; it was down oj the Potlatch a little—a little across the Potlatch, part of it.

Q. A little louder; we can't hear.

Q. (Witness continuing.) And we went back, and I started with the boy in the buggy, and I think we stayed at a house down below, all night; I think it was at Jansvile Postoffice, and next mornijg we drover into Kendrick and we came down to Lewiston.

Q. Did Mr. Dwyer come back with you?

A. No, sir.

Q. Then what occurred? Where did you go to get uyour papers made out?

(Testimony of Fred W. Schaffer.)

A.   I came down and made my filing.   That part of it I had lost out, just about the papers; I don't recollect just what was done about making those filing papers.

Q.   Do you remember your papers being made out for you?

A.   Yes, sir; I think they were made out for me, but I don't remember just who made them out.

Q.   Do you know, or how did you happen to go to the party to get them made out, who directed you where to have them made out, if anyone?

A.   Well, I think Mr. Kester directed me, because I hadn't no conversation with nobody else in regard to it.

Q.   Mr. Dwyer wasn't there at that time?

A.   No, sir.

Q.   At least you didn't see him?

A.   No.

Q.   Who gave the money to you to pay for the filing fee?      A.   Mr. Kester.

Q.   Who gave you the money to pay the man for making out the papers?

A.   Mr. Kester; Mr. Kester paid for everything; he furnished me all the money.

Q.   Then, if anyone gave you the direction to go and told you who to go to to have the papers made out?

A.   Of course, I knind of followed *Me.* Kester in that regard; I don't remember just what occurred in that line, but I know that—

Q.   You know what?

(Testimony of Fred W. Schaffer.)

A.   I know it was made out through his directions in some way; I disremember how.

Q.   Do you recognize your signature on this sworn statement, Plaintiff's Exhibit 45?

A.   Yes, sir.

Q.   And on the duplica*e* of it?

A.   Yes, sir; that is my signature on it.

Q.   And do you recognize your signature in there— do you recognize those first papers which your—

A.   Yes, sir; I guess it must be.

Q.   Which you filed in the land office? You say you guess it must be?       *Q.*   Yes, sir.

Q.   But you don't remember who *ade* them out?

A.   No, sir; it has been so long ago.

Q.   Do you remember what building *i* was?

A.   I don't remember, really; I don't remember anything about those papers, because I was pretty busy at the time, and had a good deal of work to do, and have been pretty busy since, and not thinking much about them; they slipped my mind, and I forget about that part of it.

Q.   Do you know who named the witnesses for you? Do you know how they came to be named?

A.   I don't remember that.

Q.   Well, when it came time to prove up, what did you have to do with any of the defendants? What do you know about that—

A.   Well, I —on the morning of the time to prove up I went down to the bank, and Mr. Kester gave me the money to pay for it, through the window.

Q.   How much did he give you, about how much?

(Testimony of Fred W. Schaffer.)

A. He gave me, it must have been—well, that land, 160 acres—168 or 170, something like that, about $430; something like that.

Q. Did he give you money enough to pay for the land and fees in the land office? A. Yes, sir.

Q. What, if anything, did Mr. Kester say to you at the time he gave you this money?

A. Well, my recollection is that it was suggested that I was to have half of that money, that is, of my own money, to pay for the land.

Q. I don't quite understand that, Mr. Shaffer?

A. Well, I borwed half and had half, as my recollection is it was.

Q. I want to ask you here, did you borrow any of this money? A. Well, I got $430.

Q. From the bank? A. Yes, sir.

Q. All at one time? A. Yes, sir.

Q. Did you give any note? A. No, sir.

Q. Or any security? A. No, sir.

Q. What did Mr. Kester say to you, if anything, as how you were to answer a certain question, a certain question here as to how you got this money?

A. Well, all there was to it, I was to—I borrowed half of it.

Q. I want to know what Mr. Kester told you about that, what you were to say with regard to where you got the money.

A. Well, I don't remember how it was worded, but all there was to it, I borrowed half the money and the other half I had myself.

(Testimony of Fred W. Schaffer.)

Q. "I was to have borrowed half the money, and the other half I was to have myself"; are those the words?

A. I don't know that it was worded that way, but that was the substance of it.

Q. Now, when you went to the land office and you were cross-examined—I will fi*srt* show you cross-examination, being Plaintiff's Exhibit 47-A, and ask you if it is your signature?

A. It looks like it.

Q. It appears when you were asked where *di* you get the money with which to pay for this land, and how long have you had it in your actual possession, you say, "I earned it, about half I earned, about half of it laboring, the balance I borrowed from the Lewiston National Bank." Now, was that answer true or untrue at the time you made it?

A. Well, I borrowed all the money from the bank. I got the money from the bank.

Q. It wasn't true you had earned any portion of this *omoney* laboring?

A. I got all the money from the bank.

Q. What?

A. I got all the money from the bank.

Be it remembered that then and there the following proceeding was had *:t*

Q. How did you come to answer that question in that way?

Mr. FORNEY.—Objected to as leading and suggestive and as cross-examination *lf* his own wit*h*ess.

Objection overruled.

(Testimony of Fred W. Schaffer.)

To which ruling of the Court the defend*n*ts then and there excepted, which exception was allowed by the Court.

And the witness answered:

A.   It was sort of suggested, or a suggestion made to me.

Q.   By whom?      A.   By Mr. Kester.

Q.   Well, you went up and proved up, didn't you?

A.   Yes, sir.

Q.   (Witness is shown Plaintiff's Exhibit 47, purporting to be testimony of claimant Fred W. Shaffer.)   Mr. Shaffer, look at the signature on the second page of this and see if it is your signature?

A.   Yes, sir.

Q.   Now, when you made final proof did you get a receipt?      A.   Yes, sir.

Q.   What did you do with the receipt?

A.   Well, I went downstairs and went into the front part of the bank and went to the window, and Mr. *K*ester was there, and I just passed the receipt in to the window and he picked it up and looked at it, and then he laid it aside, and he gave me $100.

Q.   Paid it to you right there?      A.   Yes, sir.

Q.   When, if at all, did you execute a deed to this

wards.

Q.   Where did you first see the deed?
land?

A.   Well, I don't remember whether it was the same day or the next; it wasn't long afterwards, not very long.   I don't remember just how long after-

(Testimony of Fred W. Schaffer.)

A. Well; my recollection is that it was lying in on his desk; I am not sure about it, but I feel satisfied, too, that that is where I first saw it.

Q. On Mr. Kester's desk?    A. Yes, sir.

Q. In the bank?    A. Yes, sir.

Q. Is that what I understand you?

A. Yes, sir. I think tha is where it was.

Q. Now, what occurred—what did you do?

A. Well, I think I put my name to that and it was taken from—I don't remember just what was done, but my recollection is that is where I first saw the deed; it was there on his desk.

Q. What do you recollect you did?

A. I think I put my name to it, or signed it, or something; that is my recollection about it.

Q. Do you remember whether you acknowledged it, or went before some notary and acknowledged it?

A. I am not sure what was done—I think—I don't know whethr as that was acknowledged before Mr.—I don't know whether it was or not. I guess I must have. I forget about it; I don't remember what was done about that.

Q. That is all you had to do with it, is it?

A. Yes, sir.

Q. You had got your $100?    A. Yes, sir.

Q. Have you ever executed any papers in relation to it since?    A. No.

Q. Did you ever get any more money?

A. No.

Q. Do you ever expect to get any more money?

A. No, sir.

(Testimony of Fred W. Schaffer.)

Be it remembered that then and there the following proceeding was had:

Q. Did you consider when you got the $100 you had parted with your title to the land, your interest in the land?

Mr. FORNEY.—Objected to as calling for a conclusion of the witness.

The COURT.—Objection overruled.

To which ruling of the Court the defendants then and there excepted, which exception was allowed by the Court and the witness answered:

A. Yes, sir.

Q. Do you know to whom you conveyed this land?

A. I don't remember; I might have known at the time. I don't remember now.

Q. And you have no recollection of it?

A. No, sir.

Be it remembered that then and there the following proceeding was had:

Mr. RUICK.—While the witness is on the stand, I am reading the testimony of the witness William F. Kettenbach. I will read one portion of it only at this time, unless counsel insist that it all be read, and they are at liberty to read any or all of it if they desire; I will read this entirely:

(Reading from Plaintiff's Exhibit 48-A.)

"CROSS-EXAMINATION OF WITNESS WILLIAM F. KETTENBACH, TIMBER AND STONE LANDS.

"Cros-examination in connection with Direct Examination on form 4-371. (Before taking the tes-

(Testimony of Fred W. Schaffer.)

timony the Register and Receiver will read or cause to be read to the witness Section 2392, of the Revised Statutes in regard to perjury. See bottom of page on form 4-471.)

(And see that the witness understands the same.)

"Question 1. Where is your actual plae of residence and how long have you been a resident of the State of Idaho?

"Lewiston, Idaho, 24 years.

"Question 2. Have you ever made a timber and stone filing or entry in the Lewiston, Idaho, Land Office? If so when and for what land?"

"A. Yes; S. ½ NW. ¼ NE. ¼ SW. ¼ Sec. 35, Tp. 40, N., R. 1 W.

"Question 3. Explain the circumstances under which you made a personal examination of this land?

"I examined the land July 4th, 1902, E. ½ NW. ¼ SW. ¼ NE. ¼ NW.¼ SE. ¼, Sec. 27, Tp. 40 N., R. 1 W.

"Question 4. What has been your occupation during the past six months? "Banker.

"Question 5. By whom have you been employed during the past six months?

"Lewiston Nat'l Bank.

"Question 6. How long have you known the applicatn?

"One year.

"Question 7. What is his financial condition so far as you know?

"Good.

(Testimony of Fred W. Schaffer.)

"Question 8. Do you know of your own knowledge that the applica*tn* has sufficient money of his own to pay for this land, and hold it for six months without mortgaging it?

"I don't know.

"WILLIAM F. KETTENBACH."

"Subscribed and sworn to before me this 25*h* day of July, 1902.

J. B. WEST,

Register."

Mr. RUICK.—I will also read from the testimony of the witness William F. Kettenbach:

"Question 10. Do you know whether the applicant has directly or indirectly made any agreement or contract in any way or manner with any person whomsoever by which the title which he may acquire from the Government of the United States may inure in whole or in part to the benefit of any person except himself?

"Ans. No.

"Question 11. Are you in any way interested in this application or in the lands above described, or the timber or stone, salines, mines or improvements of any description whatever thereon?

"Ans. No.

"WILLIAM F. KETTENBACH.

"I hereby certify that each question and answer in the foregoing testimon*\* was read to the witness before he signed his name thereto, and *tat* the same was

(Testimony of Fred W. Schaffer.)

subscribed and sworn to before me this 25*h* day of July, 1902.

"J. B. WEST, Register."

Mr. RUICK.—I wil read from this, the names of the witnesses, or I *wll* read one of these because there has none of them yet been read to the jury, and hereafter it will not be necess*r*y to read them unless counsel insists upon it. It purports to be a notice for publication, and is Plaintiff's Exhibit 46.

"(4-357)

## "TIMBER LAND ACT JUNE 3, 1878, NOTICE FOR PUBLICATION UNITED STATES LAND OFFICE,

"Lewiston, Idaho, May 5th, 1902.

"Notice is hereby given that in compliance with the provisions of the Act of Congress of June 3rd, 1878, entitled 'An Act for the Sale of Timber Lands in the States of California, Oregon, Nevada and Washington Territory, as Extended to all the Public Land States, by Act of August 4th, 1892, Fred W. Shaffer, of Lewiston, County of Nez Perce, State (or Territory) of Idaho, had this day filed in this ofice his sworn statement No. for the purchase of the E. ½ NW. ¼ SW. ¼ NE. ¼ and NW. ¼ SE. ¼ of Sec. No. 27 in Township No. 40 N., Range No. 1 W., B. M., and will offer proof to show *tht* the land sought is more valuable for its timber or stone than for agricultural purposes, and to establish his claim to said land before Register and Receiver of

(Testimony of Fred W. Schaffer.)

this office at Lewiston, Idaho, on Friday, the 25th day of July, 1902.

He names as witnesses:

William Dwyer, of Jansville Idaho;

Henry C. Whetstone, of Janesville, Idaho.

Edgar Lampher, of Janesville, Idaho.

William F. Kettenbach, of Lewiston, Idaho.

Any and all persons claiming adversely the above described lands are requested to file their claims in this office on or before said 25 day of July, 1902.

"J. B. WEST, Register.

"This notice must be published once a week for ten consecutive weeks in a newspaper published nearest the land, and must also be posted in a conspicuous place in the land office for the same period."

Be it remembered that then and there the following proceeding was had:

Mr. FORNEY.—I move to withdraw from the jury the testimony of the witness on the ground it is immaterial and incompetent, and further, it does not tend to prove any of the issues in this case and the matters and things referred to in this testimony do not prove or tend to prove any of the overt acts set forth in any count of the indictment, and on the further ground that the acts referred to in this testimony occurred more than three years prior to the finding of the indictment, and there is no connection between the acts referred to and these defendants, or the matters alleged in the indictment, and further, the other objection, that we have not been

(Testimony of Fred W. Schaffer.)

apprised of the testimony of this witness and he is not referred to in the bill of particulars.

The COURT.—The motion is denied.

To which ruling of the Court the defendants then and tebere excepted, which exception was allowed by the Court.

Cross-examination by Mr. TANNAHILL.

Q. Mr. Schaeffer, how old did you say you was?

A. 52.

Q. Just speak out, Mr. Schaeffer *e* can't hear you? A. I am 53.

Q. Have you any relatives in this country?

A. Yes, sir.

Q. Who are they?

A. Mr. J. L. Eckert, and Mr. Simons of Cottonwood; George Simons.

Q. Have you an aunt here, Mr. Schaeffer?

A. Yes, sir.

Q. Who is she? What is her name now?

A. Well, her name is—her name was Schaeffer, but she is married to Mr. Eckert.

Q. How long have you known Mr. Kester?

A. Wel, I was her, I have been here abot 7 years; I don't know what it is, just exactly how long, but I think I—the first time I met him was when I went down to see him about working there at the bank. Mr. Skipworth had told me about the place; they wanted somebody and he spoke to me and I went down there to see him.

Q. How long have you known Mr. Kettenbach?

(Testimony of Fred W. Schaffer.)

A.   Well, I have known him about that time, and probably before; I seen him around.

Q.   How long have you known Mr. Dwyer?

A.   Well, I couldn't say exactly; I used to see him about the building there.

Q.   I believe you said, Mr. Schaeffer, it had been so long since this transaction occurred that you did not have a very distinct recollection about it. Is that true?     A.   What did occur?

Q.   About this transaction, relative to your filing on this timber claim, and your arrangements with Kester?

A.   Well, I remember just the beginning of it, but it was about the papers or something I think at that time.

Q.   You don't remember all the conversation you had with Mr. Kester?

A.   Well, we never had very much conversation.

Q.   Never had very much conversation?

A.   No, in regard to—

Q.   You remember of asking Mr. Kester something about a timber claim, do you?

A.   No, sir.

Q.   Now, do you remember of talking with Dwyer something about a timber claim in the Lewiston National Bank building, talking with Dwyer about getting a claim for yourself and your relatives?

A.   I know I talked with somebody, I spoke of getting one; I spoke about a claim, I think, for— I don't remember that I spoke for myself at that time, but I did speak to him of getting a claim for

(Testimony of Fred W. Schaffer.)

my sister; I had a sister coming out here just about that time.

Q. You spoke to him abot getting a claim for yourself and your sister instead of your aunt?

A. For my sister?

Q. Now, do you remember when that was?

A. Well, that was just about the time that—well, my sister came here on the train, I think, on the day that I returned from Kendrick; she was on that train when I came back, but I didn't know it, and it was after that time that I spoke to him about a claim for my sister.

Q. And do you remember of having a talk with Mr. Dwyer in the Lewiston National Bank Building about the time you wanted Mr. Kester to take up this claim—about the time you wanted Mr. Kester to make arrangements to take up this claim? Do you remember of having a talk with Dwyer in the Lewiston National Bank Building regarding the taking up of a timber claim, just about the time you and Mr. Kester had a talk about taking up this claim?

A. It must have been after this, because—because—because my sister did not get here until that day that I was up to Kendrick. It must have been after that.

Q. Now, you knew that your sister was coming before she arrived, did you not?

A. Yes, but then there was nothing at all about the claim until after my sister was here a while.

Q. How long before your sister arrived did you know that she was coming?

(Testimony of Fred W. Schaffer.)

A.  It was just a few days.

Q.  Where did your sister come from?

A.  She came from Kansas City.

Q.  And you did not know she was coming for a week before she arrived?

A.  Well, I don't remember that, but it was a short time before that I—

Q.  Do you remember of seeing Mr. Dwyer in the Lewiston National Bank Building, just a few days before your sister had arrived?

A.  Well, I don't remember that, but I know *tht* I had talked to him about getting a claim for my sister; I know that.

Q.  You were satisfied of that?

A.  But I was under the impression that it was after my sister came here, because I know that my aunt and I spoke about it at the house, about getting a claim, and I went up there and spoke about it, and asked her if she would like to go out in the timber, and she was naturally timid, and, well, she said she didn't like to go out into the woods.

Q.  Mr. Shaeffer, you don't wish to be understood as swearing positively that you did not have a conversation with Mr. Dwyer regarding theis before your sister arrived?

A.  I didn't say positive—I don't say positive, but my impression is that I had not said anything about it until probably after she came, but I know I talked to her after, but then I would not be sure about it.

(Testimony of Fred W. Schaffer.)

Q. You would not be sure about it? It has been a long time ago, and you do not remember all these details?

A. It has been a long time ago, and it is hard to remember these many details.

Q. Mr. Schaeffer, all you think you can remember of your conversation and arrangement with Mr. Kester is that he could locate you on a timber claim, or you could take up a timber claim, and you could make about $100 out of it? That was the substance of it?

A. Well, that was the idea, that I could make $100 by taking up a claim. Of course, ther wasn't much to it, there wasn't much said about it.

Q. You did not really have a prior agreement that you should deed it to him, did you?

A. If it was not said, that is the idea I got, that I could make $100 or I could get $100 to take up by taking up a claim.

Q. Now, Mr. Schaeffer, you had talked with Mr. Dwyer something about the value of claims there on your trip up to the mountains to look at this claim, had you not?

A. Well, he—I don't know just what it was, but I got the impression that the claim was not of much value, but I don't know just where I got it; I don't know if I got that from Mr. Dwyer or who.

Q. Now, then, to refresh your memory, Mr. Schaeffer, I will ask you if Mr. Dwyer did not tell you that such claims were worth all the way from

(Testimony of Fred W. Schaffer.)

$600 to $800, and that they were about fifth-class claims?

A.  Well, I think he kind of claimed that this claim was not a first-class claim.  I don't know; I got that idea from somewhere; probably I did from Mr. Dwyer, but I don't just recollect where I got it.

Q.  And you did not have any agreement in that many words with Mr. Kester, or anyone else, that you was to sell your claim before you made your proof, did you?

A.  Well, I don't know that you would call it an agreement or not, but he said I could make out of the claim $100, and I says, "All right," and then when it came to the time to go to Kendrick, he told me to go to Kendrick and I would meet Mr. Dwyer, and I went there and back and made the proof, and that is all there was to it; there didn't seem to be any conversation further than just what was done.

Q.  No agreement about it whatever?

A.  That is all that was said; I don't know as to that.  Of course I understood I would get $100 out of it.

Q.  You never conveyed your claim until after you had made final proof?

A.  No, sir; I couldn't convey it until after I got it proved up.

Q.  Now, Mr. Schaeffer, did you ever have any talk with Mr. O'Fallon regarding this matter?

A.  Yes, sir.

Q.  Where did that conversation take place the first one, I mean now*k*, Mr. Schaeffer?

(Testimony of Fred W. Schaffer.)

A.   Well, Mr. O'Fallon came out one evening; I had just gone to bed, and there was a rap at my door—

The COURT.—Who came?

A.   Mr. O'Fallon, and that was the first time I ever saw Mr. O'Fallon.  I didn't know who he was.

Q.   Don't make it too long; tell us if it was in Nez Perce County, or Lewiston, Idaho.

A.   It was in Lewiston, and he wished me to make a statement, but I can state right now that I never made *M* O'Fallon a statement, and told him what I knew of this case until I went to Boise before the grand jury, and then is when I made my statement, but I never made any statement of the facts of it to even him or anybody, or to my best friends, or anybody, of what happened in this case before I went before the grand jury in Boise, and here in court.

Q.   How many conversations did you have with Mr. O'Fallon?

A.   Well, I don't remember, but we talked about it, but I did not mention any of the facts to anybody, because I tried to get out from coming into court. I did not want to appear in this case at all, if I could possibly have avoided it, and I tried to get out from making any statement whatever to anybody, and I can state here now that I would not have come here as a witness if I could have helped it.  Of course I came in willingly and waived any rights of anything and told just what happened, but I would rather not have come in as a witness in the case at all.

(Testimony of Fred W. Schaffer.)

Q.  Did you not, in Lewiston, Nez Perce County, Idaho, in the spring or summer of 1905, state to Mr. O'Fallon yourwelf, and Mr. O'Fallon being present, that you had no prior agreement with Mr. Kester or Mr. Kettenbach, or anyone else, to sell your land before you proved up. or words in substance or to that effect?

A.  I don't know what it was, but I know I tried to get out of—tried to get out of Mr. O'Fallon—I did not tell him anything—that is all I could—I tried to get out of appearing in the case.

Q.  Answer yes or no.

Mr. RUICK.—Are you going to call Mr. O'Fallon?

The COURT.—What is the purpose of this?

The WITNESS.—I don't know; I couldn't answer yes or no.

The COURT.—What is the purpose in asking this, Mr. Tannahil? He has not stated that there was a prior agreement?

Mr. TANNAHILL.—Does the Court so understand it?

The COURT.—He ha stated the conversation; now, as to his interpretation of it, he has not stated to counsel for either side, as I understand the witness, that there was an agreement; he stated what occurred, and it would be for the Court, perhaps, and the jury, to determine if it was an agreement.

Be it remembered that then and there the following proceeding was had:

(Testimony of Fred W. Schaffer.)

The COURT.—This does not refer to the O'Fallon conversation at all.

Mr. RUICK.—I so understand.

Mr. TANNAHILL.—Yes, that is the conversation.

The COURT.—Read the last question.

(Question read.)

Mr. TANNAHILL.—I understand, if the Court please, that this rests on very thin ground there, and the dividing line is very close, but we desire to make it a matter of record, if the Court please.

The COURT.—You have a perfect right to make your record in that way. The Court will exclude the question. I do not know if any objection is made, but the Court will exclude the question as not being an impeaching question.

To which ruling of the Court the defendants then and there excepted, which exception was allowed by the Court.

Q. Are you acquainted with Fred Emery?

A. Yes, sir.

Q. Do you remember of having a conversation with Fred Emery in Mr. Dwyer's office on the third floor of the Lewiston National Bank Building. in Lewiston, Idaho, in the fore part of July, 1905?

A. I don't think I ever talked to Mr. Emery, because I was pretty careful who I talked to. I have talked to Mr. Dwyer, but just what—

The COURT.—Just answer the question.

A. I don't think I ever talked to Emery.

(Testimony of Fred W. Schaffer.)

Q. Do you remember of talking or having a conversation with Mr. Dwyer in the presence of Mr. Emery about that same time and at the same place?

A. I don't think so; I don't remember.

Q. Do you remember of seeing Mr. Emery and Mr. Dwyer in Mr. Dwyer's office about the fore part of July, 1905? A. No, sir.

Q. Will you say that you did not see them there?

A. I don't remember of seeing Mr. Emery there, and I don't think I ever talked to Mr. Emery about the case.

Q. Did you talk to Mr. Dwyer in Mr. Emery's presence?

A. I don't remember of ever talking to Mr. Dwyer in Mr. Emery's presence, because I have been pretty careful who I talked to outside of Mr. Dwyer. I know that.

Q. Mr. Schaeffer, I will ask you the question, did you not state to Fred Emery and William Dwyer, to either one or both of them, in Mr. Dwyer's office, on the third floor of the Lewiston National Bank Building, in Lewiston, Nez Perce County, Idaho, about the last of June or the 1st of July, 1905, yourself, Fred Emery and William Dwyer, and none others being present, "I never at any time had any agreement or understanding with Kester or Kettenbach, or either of them, prior to *te* time of proving up," or words in substance and to that effect?

A. Well, I don't think that I had a conversation of that kind at that time.

(Testimony of Fred W. Schaffer.)

Q. Will you say that you did not have such a conversation?

A. I don't think I did, because I did not know anything—of anything that would be going wrong that way. I didn't know of anything. I had no occasion to talk at that time, before I proved up on this claim with Mr. Emery or Mr. Dwyer in that way.

Q. Then you did not have any such conversation?

A. I don't think I did. I don't remember of it, and I feel satisfied that I did not. I don't remember of it.

Mr. TANNAHILL.—I think, if the Court please, that is not a sufficient answer to enable us to *enable us to* offer impeaching testimony.

The COURT.—That is as far as the witness can go. If he says he doesn't remember it, the Court cannot compel him to say it was not so. That would not be fair.

Be it remembered that then and there the following proceeding was had:

Q. Did you at the same time and place, and the same parties being present, s*tae* to Fred Emery or William Dwyer, or both of them, "Mr. O'Fallon insisted that I make a statement that I had an agreement or understanding to sell my land, before I proved up, and if I did not give him a statement or affidavit he would make it cost me my home, or words in substance and to that effect?

Mr. RUICK.—That is objectionable on the ground it is incompetent, irrelevant and immaterial. Now,

(Testimony of Fred W. Schaffer.)

we claim that this does not tend to impeach the witness, that it does not contradict any facts that he has testified to here upon this trial, and therefore it is incompetent, irrelevant and immaterial.

The COURT.—Objection sustained. To which ruling of the Court the defendants then and there excepted, which exception was allowed by the Court.

Be it remembered that then and there the following proceeding was had:

Q. Did you not, at the same time and place, and the *sme* parties being present, state to Fred Emery or William Dwyer, or both of them, "I told Mr. O'Fallon I had no agreement to sell my timber claim before proving up," or words in substance and to that effect?

Mr. RUICK.—We object.

The COURT.—Objection sustained.

To which ruling of the Court the defendantds then and there exceped, which exception was allowed by the Court.

Q. I will ask you, Mr. Schaeffer, if youi did not have a letter from R. E. McFarland to Mr. Ruick in regard to those matters, stating you had no agreement or understanding?

A. No, sir. That did not read that way.

Q. And did you not show that letter to Mr. Emery and Mr. Dwyer at that time? A. No.

Q. Mr. Schaeffer, do you remember showing Mr. Emery and Mr. Dwyer that letter?

A. I never did.

(Testimony of Fred W. Schaffer.)

Be it remembered that then and there the following proceeding was had:

Mr. RUICK.—Objected to as incompetent, irrelevant and immaterial.

The COURT.—Don't answer the question so quickly.

Mr. RUICK.—The Court, as I understand it, has ruled out that evidence.

The COURT.—Objection sustaiened; strike it out.

To which ruling of the Court the defendants then and there excepted, which exception was allowed by the Court.

Mr. TANNAHILL.—I want to ask another question along this line.

The COURT.—Yes.

Be it remembered that then and there the following proceeding was had:

Q. Did you not, at the same time and place, state to Fred Emery and William Dwyer, or both of them, "I had no prior agreement or understanding to sell my claim before proving up; Mr. O'Fallon told me if I didn't make an affidavit, I would be indicted and lose my home; they tried to scare me; they used to come to my home nights and talk to me," or words in substance and to that effect?

The COURT.—Do you contend, Mr. Tannahill, that you have asked this witness relative to those matters before, and that the witness has denied the facts as implied in that statement?

Mr. TANNAHILL.—No, I don't know what the witness had denied the facts, if the Court please, but

(Testimony of Fred W. Schaffer.)

I can ask him these questions and if he denies them, I can produce the other parties to show that he made these statements.

Mr. RUICK.—I object to it as incompetent, irrelevant and immaterial.

The COUR.—I think the Court will sustain the objection.

To which ruling of the Court the defendants then and there excepted, which exception was allowed.

Mr. RUICK.—Notwithstanding counsel's argument in the presence of the jury tht he (witness) had no prior agreement, we are willing to stand upon the statements of the witness, and to go to the jury on that propositon.

Mr. TANNAHILL.—Then if it is as counsel states, the questions are entirely proper, because they tend to contradict the presumption which counsel would draw from the witness' evidence.

The COURT.—No, the Court could not conceded that contention. As a rule, an oral agreement or understanding may be inferred from the facts. Now, it may be contended by counsel for the prosecution that what occurred there implied an agreement, and I assume counsel for the defense will argue that there was no agreement. It is for the jury to determine that. I will sustain the objection.

Q. Are you acquainted with J. B. West?

A. Yes, sir.

Q. Do you remember seeing J. B. West in Lewiston, or on the streets lin front of the Lewiston Na-

(Testimony of Fred W. Schaffer.)

tional Bank, after you had been subpoenaed as a witness to go to Boise in July, 1905?

A. I have seen him a great many times on the street; I don't know the particular time you have reference to.

Q. I will ask you if you remember seeing him at one time just after you received your subpoena to go to Boise as a witness before the grand jury?

A. I might have, but I don't remember of it.

Be it remembered the following proceeding was had:

Q. I will ask you if you remember speaking to Mr. West about a letter which you received from Bob McFarland to Mr. Ruick about that time?

Mr. RUICK.—Objected to as incompetent, irrelevant and immaterial, and as having been ruled upon lready.

Mr. TANNAHILL.—It is for the purpose of calling his attention to a partocular conversation.

Q. (FContinuing:) A letter which Mr. McFarland had written for you and addressed to Mr. Ruick at Boise?

The COURT.—What is this new question?

Mr. TANNAHILL.—It is just a part of the other one.

Mr. RUICK.—We object to it.

The COURT.—Objection sustained.

To which ruling of the Court the defendants then and there excepted, which exception was allowed by the Court.

(Testimony of Fred W. Schaffer.)

Be it remembered that then and there the following proceeding was had:

Q. I will ask you, Mr. Schaeffer, if you did not state to Mr. J. B. West, in Lewiston, Nez Perce County, Idaho, just after you received your summons to go to Boise, before the Grand Jury and about the 1st of July, 1905, on the street in front of the Lewiston National Bank, yourself and J. B. West, and none others being present: "I have received a summons to go to Boise as a witness. I had no agreement or understanding with Kester, Kettenbach or anyone else to sell my claim before I made final proof, or before I proved up on it," or words in substance and to that effect?

Mr. RUICK.—That is objected to on the same grounds as before; it does not tend to impeach the witness.

The COURT.—Objection sustained.

To which ruling of the Court the defendants then and there excepted, which exception was by the Court allowed.

Be it remembered that then and there the following proceeding was had:

Q. Did you not, at the same time and place state to Mr. J. B. West, yourself and Mr. J. B. West, and none others being present, "I have received a summons to go to Boise before the Grand Jury. Mr. O'Fallon has been up to my house to see me and talk with me, and told me he wanted me to testify against Kester and Kettenbach. I told Mr. O'Fallon that I didn't know anything to swear against them (Kes-

(Testimony of Fred W. Schaffer.)

ter and Kettenbach), and Mr. O'Fallon said if I did not appear as a witness I would be indicted and lose my home," or words in substance to that effect.

Mr. RUICK.—Objected to upon the same ground.

The COURT.—The same ruling; the objection sustained.

To which ruling of the Court the defendants then and there excepted, which exception was by the Court allowed.

Q. Mr. Schaeffer, did you *eve* make a statement for Mr. O'Fallon or Mr. Ruick, or anyone else in connection with this matter?     A. No.

Q. You never signed a statement at all?

A. No, sir; I never did.

Q. For anyone?

A. No, sir; I went before the grand jury as I told you before. When I went to Boise, that is the first time I ever made a statement as to the facts in this case, and I went there when I went before the grand jury, I made up my mind to tell the truth about the matter.

Q. Did you ever sign a statement for Mr. Ruick, Mr. O'Fallon or anyone else?

A. No, sir; I did not.

Q. You were indicted at Boise weren't you after the 5th day of July, 1905?

A. The papers told me so.

The COURT.—Just a moment. I want to ask counsel how that could be material?

Mr. TANNAHILL.—We think it would be material to show that the witness is under indictment for

(Testimony of Fred **W. Schaffer.**)

perjury and he has not even been arrested, and no proceedings have been taken to prosecute him, and he is giving his testimony under these circumstances. We consider it very material that the jury should have all the circumstances under which he is giving his testimony.

Mr. RUICK.—I don't know whether we have any particular objection to that fact coming out; the defendants are all in the same position.

The COURT.—Very well.

Q. You are under an indictment for perjury and were indicted at the July, 1905, term of court by the grand jury at Boise, were you not?    A. 1905?

Q. Yes.

A. Not as I know of. I never knew anything of it. I saw it in the papers; that is all I know.

Q. It was at the term of the grand jury that you saw it in the papers—*tht* you were indicted?

A. I think I saw it that the paper in Moscow said so.

Q. And you have never been called upon to plead to this indictment?    A. No, sir.

Q. It was the same grand jury you went before to testify and give your evidence, was it not, that indicted you?

A. I don't know; I was before the grand jury in Boise the first time.

Q. And that was in July, 1905?

A. It was in July, I guess it was in 1905.

Did I understand you that you never had pleaded to that indictment, that you never had been

(Testimony of Fred W. Schaffer.)

called before the court in connection with that indictment?      A.   No, sir.

Mr. RUICK.—That is a matter of record.

Mr. TANNAHILL (Reading from the indictment.)   The names of the witnesses called before the grand jury in this case of the United States of America vs. Fred W. Schaeffer on an indictment for perjury in connection wth a volation of section 5392 of the Revised Stateutes of, the United States were: Fred W. Schaeffer, F. M. Goodwin and S. F. O'Fallon.

Q.   Who is F. M. Goodwin?   Is he the same F. M. Goodwin you see around here as Special Agent of the Land Office?      A.   I think so.

Q.   And Mr. S. F. O'Fallon, is he the man who was out to your home and tried to get you to make a statement?      A.   Yes, sir.

Mr. TANNAHILL (Reading.) —This indictment (of Fred W. Schaeffer) is endorsed "Presented by the foreman in the presence of the grand jury and filed in open court this 13th day of July, 1905.   A. L. Richardson, Clerk," and is signed by J. C. Johnson, Foreman of the Grand Jury.

Be it remembered that then and there the following proceeding was had:

Q.   I believe you testified in your direct examination, Mr. Schaeffer, that you borrowed $430 from Mr. Kester with which to make final proof?

Mr. RUICK.—Objected to as assuming a fact not in evidence.

(Testimony of Fred W. Schaffer.)

The COURT.—That is merely calling for a repetition of testimony.

Mr. RUICK.—And another reason it has all been gone over several times.

The COURT.—There is no objection to counsel examining upon it, but the question is objectionable in form, and the Court will sustain the objection.

To which ruling of the Court the defendants then and there excepted, which exception was allowed by the Court.

Q. You did borrow $430 from Mr. Kester? to prove up on your claim?

A. I got $430 from him, I don't know whether you call it borrowing or not. I went down there and he gave it to me, and I went up then and proved up on the land; I don't know what you call it.

Redirect Examination by Mr. RUICK.

Q. This indictment has been identifie and reference has been made to it, your Honor, and there is no objection offered in relation to the facts in relation to the indictment, and we now offer in evidence this indictment returned against the witness Fred Schaeffer at the time referred to. This is with the understanding that a certified copy may be substituted on the record.

Mr. TANNAHILL.—We have no objection to that.

And said document is received in evidence and marked Plaintiff's Exhibit 52.

Be it remembered then the following proceeding was had:

(Testimony of Fred W. Schaffer.)

Mr. FORNEY.—We renew our objection and move to strike out all the testimony of th*w*is witness on the grounds set forth in our general objection and motion heretofore made.

The COURT.—Objection overruled, and motion denied.

To which ruling of the Court the defendants then and there excepted, which exception was allowed by the Court.

(Witness excused.)

THOMAS HERODITUS BARTLETT, a witness called and sworn for the Prosecution, testified as follows on

Direct Examination by Mr. RUICK.

Q. You are *te* register of the Lewston Land Office? A. Yes, sir.

Q. How long have yo*j* been such register?

A. Since January 5th, 1906.

Q. As such register you have now in your possession in the court the records of the office showing the contests inaugurated before the Lewiston Land Office for land subsequently filed upon under the timber and stone law by Edward M. Lewis, Hiram F. Lewis and Charles Carey respectivel*\*?

A. I have, sir.

Q. What book will that book be found in?

A. In the contest record, No. 6. This is No. 5.

Q. Referring to homestead entry No. 10,495; have you the record there of contests inaugurated by William D*w*er as contestant in the Lewiston Land Office? A. A portion of them.

(Testimony of Thomas Heroditus Bartlett.)

Be it rememebred that then and there the following proceeding was had:

Q.  Go ahead Mr. Bartlett and state.

Mr. TANNAHILL.—State what?

Q.  State what the record shows concerning these contests.

Mr. TANNAHILL.—Objected to as immaterial and irrelevant.  We insist that Mr. Dwyer or any other citizen has a right to inaugurate contests against any entrymen under the laws of the United States, and regardless of the outcome of the contest, as decided by the Department of the Interior, and regardless of *wat* the outcome of the contest might be, for it can in no way affect the criminal action of these defendants or in any way establish motive or intent, or any fact from which this crime with which they are charged might be presumed.

The COURT.—Objection overruled.

To which ruling of the Court the defendants then and there excepted, which exception was allowed by the Court*a* and the witness answered as follows:

A.  Do you desire all to be related here?

Mr. RUICK.—Take them up as they appear in the record, give all the data shown by the books in relation thereto.

The COURT.—That should be limited to some time.  Perhaps those you have in mind are within a certain period?

Mr. RUICK.—They are.  I think the very first one will clearly indicate they are within the period.

(Testimony of Thomas Heroditus Bartlett.)

The COURT.—What is the earliest one you have there?

The WITNESS.—It is inaugurated May 24th, 1904.

The COURT.—Very well; proceed.

Q. What entry is that? A. H. E. 10,469.

Q. Give us the record?

A. Page 72 of Homestad Docket 5; that contains the following—

Mr. FORNEY.—As a beginning now, is it the later contest or an earlier one?

A. The earliest one in this book.

Mr. FORNEY.—Is it the earliest or the latest you intend to introduce in evidence?

Mr. RUICK.—It begins with 1904.

The COURT.—The Court will hold this contest is close enough to the dates laid in the indictment; it will be admitted.

Q. State what the record shows?

A. On the page named appears the following:

"H. E. 10459, filed May 24th; name of party, William Dwyer."

Q. Name of what?

A. William Dwyer, vs. George G. James, involving the north half of the southwest quarter of section nine, and the north half of the southeast quarter of section 8, township 38 north, range 6 East, date of entry, February 24th, 1904.

Q. What is the date of the homestead entry?

A. Yes, sir. Notice was issued June 8th, 1904. Do you wish me to read all the notes?

(Testimony of Thomas Heroditus Bartlett.)

Q.  Everything.

A.  Continued until September 6*h* at request of contestant.  Affidavit asking for service by publication filed August 6th, 1904; published in "Pierce City Miner" and it is dismised on motion of contestant September 21st, 1904; pencil mamorandum made by me on this docket as follows: 10469, February 24th, 1904, entry cancelled by relinquishment September 21st, 1904, 1:15 p. m.  On page 74 of the same volume, H. E. 10484.

Q.  What does H. E. mean there?

A.  Homestead entry, and the number of the contest.

Q.  What was the number of the contest?

Mr. MOORE.—Don't repeat it.  He has already read it in H. E. so and so.

Mr. RUICK.—The only purpose of asking these questions is that they won't have to be repeated. This explanation may go into the record, and later we will not have to interrupt him.

Mr. Bartlett, where abbreviations are used with regard to this, you need not, after having once stated them, you need not repeat them, but if you have not already explained, explain the meaning of the abbreviation; kindly do so as you go along, so you won't have to repeat it later.

A.  H. E. 10494, filed May 25*h,* 1904, hearing August 3d, description of tract North half of the north half section 15, Township 38 North, Range 6 East; name of party William Dwyer, vs. Walter Williams.  Date of entry, meaning the date of the

(Testimony of Thomas Heroditus Bartlett.)

homestead entry, February 24th, 1904; remarks, Notice issued June 8th, 1904; contest dismissed at conte*nstatns* request, Aug. 23d, 1904, 3 P? M. Pencil memoranda 10,484, February 24th, 1904. Cancelled by relinquishment August 23rd, 1904; T. & S. meaning timber and stone No. 1492, August 23rd, Charles Carey—

Q. What does that indicate as to Mr. Carey?

A. It in*i*dicates that Mr. C*q*rey on Aug. 23rd, 1904, filed a timber and stone claim 1492 upon the same described tract.

Page 75; H. E. 10,638, filed May 25th, hearing September 8th, description of tract, S. E. ¼ Section 19, Township 38 North, Range 6 East, name of party, William Dwyer vs. John McHardy.

Q. How is that spelled?

A. Capital M-c capital H-a-r-d-i-e, date of entry April 18, 1904, notice issued June 8th, 1904; case continued at request of contestant until September 8th, 1904; case dismissed September 8th, on motion of contestant.

Pencil memorandum, 10,638, April 18, 1904; relinquished September 8th, 1904. The same day T. & S. filing No. 1515 made by Edwin Bliss, Cash entry, C. E. is entered here 4850 November 23, 1904, which indicates that cash entry 4950 was issued to the party filing the timber claim, Edwin Bliss, on November 23, 1904.

That means that final proof was made and payment made for the land?

A. Yes, sir; final proof.

(Testimony of Thomas Heroditus Bartlett.)

Q. And payment for the land?

A. Payment *wa* made, yes, sir.

Q. And a final receipt issued?

A. Receiver's receipt was issued to him on that date.

Q. Mr. Bartlett, one question right here. What is issued to the entryman at the time that he makes payment for the land under the Timber and Stone Act?

A. He receives a receipt from the receiver of the land office.

Q. A receiver's final receipt?    A. Yes.

Q. That is the paper which he receives?

A. Yes, sir; that is not called a final receipt in this case because it is the only receipt given. It is the only paper he receives until he receives his patent.

Q. It is a receiver's receipt?

A. It is a receiver's receipt.

Q. What do they do with that paper when they get their patent?

A. They produce it, or it may be surrendered to the land office on evidence of ownership so they may receive their patent.

Q. They receive their patent on production of that receiver's receipt?    A. Yes, sir.

Q. Can any person but the entryman get the patent?    A. Oftentimes.

Q. Simply upon the production of the receipt?

A. Yes, on showing made, on proper showing made.

(Testimony of Thomas Heroditus Bartlett.)

Q. And the production of the receipt.

A. I don't think the production of the receipt is always insisted upon, Mr. Ruick.

A. Page 76, 10,486, H. E., that is filed May 26th, hearing August 1st—these are all in 1904.

Q. Mr. Bartlett, does that hearing indicate the date that the hearing was actually had, or the date set for the hearing?

A. I presume this means the date set for the hearing.

Q. Does not the record show in these cases there was no hearing? A. No.

Q. In most of them?

A. Well, in this way; it shows that the contest has been dismissed as to most of them, and we would infer from that no hearing was had when it was dismised on motion of contestant.

Q. Then does this date of hearing—it must have referred to the date of hearing?

A. When the case is filed. The north half of the south half of section 15, townsnip 38 north, range 6 east, name of party William Dwyer, against William R. Lawrence, date of entry February 24th, 1904; notife issued June 8th, 1904; contest dismissed July 11th, 1904, on motion of contestant. Pencil memorandum, 10486, February 24th, 1904, cancelled by relinquishment July 11th, 1904, T. & S. timber and stone, 1050. Benjamin F. Rowland. C. E. 4878. September 23d, 1904.

Q. That indicates that he made proof for a timber and stone claim on what date?

(Testimony of Thomas Heroditus Bartlett.)

A.  It indicates that B. F. Rowlan filed a timber and stone claim for the same premises and made final proof and received his receipt No. 4878, September 23d, 1904.

(Continuing:)   Page 77, H. E. 10,485, filed May 25h, hearing July 30th, description of tract south half of the south half of section 15, township 38 north, range six east; names of parties William Dwyer vs. Albert J. Flood; date of entry February 24th, 1904. Notice on June 8th, 1904; contest to dismiss July 11th, 1904, on motion of contestant; pencil memorandum 10,485, February 24th, 1904, cancelled by relinquishment July 11th, 1904; same date T. & S. No. 1451, Albert G. Kester, C. E. 4879, September 23rd, 1904.

Q.  Indicating what?

A.  Which indicates that Albert G. Kester upon th4 date of relinquishment, July 11th, 1904, filed his timber and stone claim 1451 for the same tract, and subsequently, and upon September 23d, 1904, made his proof and received final receipt No. 4879.

Page 78: H. E. 10,488, filed May 25th, hearing October 14th, description the northeast quarter of section 34, township 38 north, range 5 east.  Parties William Dwyer vs. Geo. W. Miller.  Date of entry, February 24th, 1904.  Notice issued June 8th, 1904, cause continued at the request of contestant until September 9th, affidavit asking for service by publication filed August 17th, 1904, published in Pierce City Miner.  As the defendant is sick, this case is hereby continued until October 24th, 1904.  Contest with-

(Testimony of Thomas Heroditus Bartlett.)
drawn October 24th, 1904. Pencil memoranda: 10,488, February 24th, 1904, cancelled by relinquishment October 26th, 1904. Same date, T. & S. 1544, Mabel K. Atkinson. Upon the date of relinquishment, viz., October 24th, 1904, filed a timber and stone claim 1544, and upon January 16th, 1905; made proof and receiver her final receipt No. 5010.

Q. Mr. Bartlett, do you know who Mabel K. Atkinson, what relation she bears to either of the defendants?

A. Only by hearsay, in a general sort of way.

Q. The same way that any*d*body knows relationship?

A. No, I cannot say who Mabel K. Atkinson is. I know a Mrs. Atkinson. I don't know that it is Mabel K. or not.

(Continuing:) Page 79, H. E. 10,512, filed May 25; hearing October 12th; description of tract the east half of the east half of section 13, township 38 north, range 5 east; names of parties, William Dwyer vs. Antone Wohlen, date of entry February 24th, 1904; notice issued January 8th, 1904; cause continued until September 12th, 1904, at request *f* contestant, and an entry here through which a line is run, cause dismissed October *L*2th, 1904, 11 A. M., for want of prosecution. After that, this remark: It was error to dismiss this case, and all parties agreed to continue the case until October 25th, 1904, and it is so ordered.

Page 80. H. E. 10,477, filed May 25th, hearing October 13th, Description:

(Testimony of Thomas Heroditus Bartlett.)

Mr. MOORE.—(Interrupting.)   Did you read all of your notes with reference to that former contest?

A.   Everything that is there.

Mr. MOORE.—You don't know, then, at this time how it stands?        A.   No.

Mr. MOORE.—Your record does not show?

A.   No, nothing shows but what I read.

Mr. MOORE.—We move to strike out all with reference to tht entry.

Mr. RUICK.—It may be stricken out later on if we don't connect the entry.   I will look it over at the noon recess and if it does not apply I will ask to withdraw it.

(Court takes recess till May 27, 1907, 10:00 A. M.)

Witness BARTLETT on the stand:

Direct Examination Resumed by Mr. Ruick.

The COURT.—Mr. Bartlett was testifying as to some contest.

Mr. RUICK.—Page 79, Homestead entry, 10,512, you had completed.   No, on page 80, hoestead entry 10,477.

The WITNESS.—The book reads as follows: 1904.   H. E. 10,477; filing May 25th; hearing October 13th; description of tract, north half northwest quarter section 25, south half southwest quarter section 24, township 38 north, range 5 east.   William Dwyer vs. Charles C. Rigler; date of entry, February 24th, 1904.   Below that in pencil, I. N. Smith attorney, W. M. Morgan, attorney for Rigler.   Remarks: Notice issued June 8th, 1904.   Case continued at reauest of contestant until September 13th, 1904;

(Testimony of Thomas Heroditus Bartlett.)

affidavit asking for service by publication filed August 17th, 1904; published in Pierce Miner; case continued until November 15, 1904; new affidavit for publication filed September 23d, 1904; case by stipulation continued until December 12th, 1904. The following with a line drawn through it; Dismissed December 12th, 1904, for lack of prosecution. Decision of R. & R. May 2d, 1905.

Q. This last statement is written underneath what?

A. Underneath that which I read. One line, with a line drawn through it, appears the following: Without any line drawn through it. Decision of R. & R. May 2d, 1905, in favor of entryman; appeal filed May 22d, 1905; sent up appeal August 21st, 1905, December 28th, 1905, decision of Hon. Commissioner G. L. O. in favor of contestee, subject to rright of appeal by contestant; service on contestant February 8th, 1906; March 10th, 1906 contestant filed written withdrawal of contest. Finis. Pencil memorandum 10,477 on February 24th, 1904, cancelled by relinquishment March 10th, 1906, page 81.

Mr. TANNAHILL.—Who filed on that?

A. It does not appear here.

(Wintess continuing:) Page 81, 1904, H. E. 10,493, filed May 25, hearing July 25, with a line drawn throught it, and then September 7th, description of tract, southeast quarter of section 30, township thirty-eight north, range 6 east, William Dwyer vs. Albert Anderson, date of entry February 24th, 1904; remarks, notice issued June 8th, 1904. Case

(Testimony of Thomas Heroditus Bartlett.)
continued on motion of contestant until September
7th.   Decision October 1st, 1904, of R. & R. in favor
of contestant.   No appeal, sent up November 21st,
1904; contest dismissed December 12th, 1904, at the
request of contestant William Dwyer.   Pencil memorandum 10,493, February 24th, 1904; relinquished
December 12th 1904.   T. & S. same date; 1564.
Mary E. Sherman, see cash entry 5042, March *6h,*
1905.   Which indicates that Mary E. Sherman filed
upon this same tract of land on the date of relinquishment, to wit, December 12th, 1904, and subsequently upon March 6th, 1905, made proof and received her receipt No. 5042.

Page 82, 1904, H. E. 10,495, filed May 25th; hearing July 23d; that is scratched out with a line *drwn*
through it; August 23d description of tract, northeast quarter section 29, township 39 north, range 5
east.   William Dwyer vs. Susan C. Comstock; date
of entry February 24th, 1904; notice issued June
8th, 1904; contest is dismissed October 26th, 1904, at
request of plaintiff, William Dwyer.   Pencil memorandum, H. E. 10,495, February 24th, 1904.   October 26th, 1904, T. & S. 10,542.   William E. Helkenburg, filed on southeeast quarter of northeast quarter of section twenty-nine, C. E. 5015, January 20th,
1905; October *26h,* 1904, T. & S. 1543.   Ed. N. Lewis
north half northeast quarter southwest quarter of
northeast quarter, C. E. 5016, *Jauary* 20th, 1905,
*whcih* memorandum indicates that upon the date of
relinquishment on October 26th, 1904, Helkenburg
filed upon a portion of the tract, namely, the south-

(Testimony of Thomas Heroditus Bartlett.)

east quarter of the nor*ht*east quarter of 29, and upon the same day Ed. M. Lewis filed up*nn* the north half or the northeast quarter and the southwest quarter of the northeast quarter, and that they subsequently and u*pn* January 20th, 1905, made proof respectively and received thei*f* respective receipt for said subdivisions of number 5015 and 5016.

Page 82, 1904, H. E. 10,501, filed May 25th, hearing July 22d with a pen run through it August 2*6h,* pen run through that, October 11th. Description of the tract, southeast quarter section 7, township thirty-nine north, range 5 east; William Dwyer vs. Charles G. Vogelman; date of entry February 24th, 1904. Remarks: Notice issued June 8th, 1904; affidavit asking for service by publication filed August *6h,* 1904; published in Pierce Miner; case continued until November 14, '04· New affidavit for publication filed September 23, 1904; decision of R. & R. February 16th, 1905, in favor of Dwyer. Appeal filed March 4, 1905, sent up March 31st, 1905; pencil memorandum 10,501, February 24th, 1904, cancelled by relinquishment, November 24th, 1905; same day T. & S. 1757, Frank L. Moore. Receipt 5308, February 26th, 1906, which indicates that Frank L. Moore on the day of relinquishment, to wit*h,* November 29th, 1905, filed his timber and stone claim No. 10,757, and subsequently and upon February 26th, 1906, made proof and received his receiver's receipt No. 5308.

Page 84, 1904. H. E. 10,496. Filed May 25th, hearing July 21st, line through that, August 25th,

(Testimony of Thomas Heroditus Bartlett.)

line through that. September 23d; sdescription of tract: Northwest quarter section 29, township 39 north, range 6 east. William Dwyer vs. Charles D. Thornberg. Date of entry, February 24th, 1904. Remarks: Notice is issued June 8th, 1904; affidavit for publication filed July 25th, 1904; published in Pierce Miner; case contineud until November 9th; new affidavit for publication filed September 23d, '04; affidavit for publication filed July 25h, 1904; September 23d, 1904; new affidavit for publication filed; new date set for November 9th, 1904; case heard November 9th, 1904; decision of R. & R. January 11th, 1904, in favor of contestants; no appeal; sent up April 14th, 1905. Cancelled by "H" of September 28th, 1905, on October 5th, 1905, at 3 P. M. That, I will explain, means that it was cancelled authority of a lettr form the Department Letter "H" of September 28th, 1905. Pencil memorandum: 10,496, February 24, 1905, cancelled by letter from H. September 28th, 1905.

Page 85, 1904. H. E. 10,481. Filed May 25th, hearing June 20th, line through that; August 25th; description of tract, norhteast quarter of section 29, township 38 north, range 6 east; William Dwyer vs. Charles F. Schuemaker; date of entry, February 24th, 1904; notice issued January 8th, 1904; decision of R. & R. January 26th, 1905, in favor of entryman. No appeal. Sent up August 21st, 1905; contest withdrawn by Dwyer on September 6h, 1905. Sent up to Department September 6h, 1905, pencil mem-

(Testimony of Thomas Heroditus Bartlett.)

orandum 10,481 February 24, 1904, cancelled by relinquishment September 66h, 1905; same day T. & S. 10,698, Josep*f* F. Atkinson, C. E., 5231; November 22d, 1905, which indicates that Joseph F. Atkinson, upon the day of relinquishment September *6h,* 1905, filed his tim*e*ber and stone claim number 1698, and subsequently and upon November 22d, 1905, made proof and received his final receiver's receipt number 5231.

Page 86, 1904. H. E. 10,579, filed May 25. Hearing July 19. Pen through that. August 29th, Description of tract: North*e*west quarter section 20, township thirty-eight north, range 5 east. William Dwyer vs. Will*ai*m B. Walker. Date of entry April *6h,* 1904. Notice issued June 8th, 1904; case dismissed on motion of contestant August 29th, 1904. Pencil memorandum: 10,579. April 1, 1904, cancelled by relinquishment August 29th, 1904. T. & S. 1567. December 13, 1904, Hiram F. Lewis, C. E. 5046. March 8th, 1905, which indicates that Hiram F. Lewis, on the day of relinqui*a*hment, namely, no, which indicates that Hiram F. Lewis upon December 13th, 1904, filed his timber and stone claim upon the same tract number 1567, and on March 8th, 1905, made proof and received final receipt 5046.

Page 127, 1904. H. E. 10,461. Filed September 21st, hearing November 7th, line through that, December 15; description of tract, southwest quarter section 20, township thirty-eight north, range six east. William Dwyer vs. Frank A. McConnell; date of entry February 24th, 1904. Remarks. Noti*f*e

(Testimony of Thomas Heroditus Bartlett.)
issued September 30th, 1904; case continued to December 15th, 1904, on motion of contestant.*C*ntestant dismissed contestant De*cm*ber 12th, 1904. At request of contestant, William Dwyer contestant. Pencil memorandum, 10,461. February 24, 1904. Cancelled by relinqui*a*hment December 12th, 1904; same day T. & S. 1566. Marguerite E. Miller. C. E. 5045. March 7, 1905, which indic*z*tes that upon the date of the relinquishment December 12th, 1904, Margaret E. Miller filed. her timber and stone claim No. 1566 for the *a*same tract of land, and upon March 7th, 1905, made proof and received receiver's receipt 5045.

Page 134: H. E. 10538. Filed 1904, October 4th. Hearing 1904, November 22; line through that. December 22. Description of tract, west half of west half section 28, township forty, north of range 6 east; William Dwyer vs. John P. Harland. Date of entry, March 9th, 1904. Remarks: Notice issued October 3d, 1905. On motion of contesta*tn* the case was continued to December 22, '04· Decision of R. & R. January 19, 1905, in favor of Harland. Appeal filed July 29th, 1905, by Harland. Appeal filed ditto, ditto July 6th, 1905, by Dwyer. Sent up August 21, 1905. Decision of Hon. Commissioner December 21st, 1905, in favor of Harland. Service on contestant January 9, 1906. Appeal filed February 14th, 1906. Service of notice of appeal and s*ep*cifications of error admitted by attorney for contest*4*e, February 14th, 1906. Answer to appeal filed March 16,

(Testimon_\ of Thomas Heroditus Bartlett.)

1906, 4 P. M. All papers transmitted April 17th, 1906.

Page 190, 1905. T. & S. 1395. Filed September 19, 1904; hearing September 19th, 1904. Description of tract, north half southwest quarter, section 14, and north half southwest quarter, section 14, and north half southwest quarter, section 33, township thirty-eight north, range 5 east, William Dwyer vs. William Kincaid. Date of entry, September 9th, 1904. I. N. Smith, rem*r*aks, decision—

Mr. RUICK*P*.—(Interrupting.) I. N. Smith what? A. Nothing.

(Continuing:) Of R. & R. February 16th, 1905, favor of Dwyer. No appeal. Sent up March 31, 1905; decision of Hon. Commissioner September 5, 1905, dismissing Dwyer's protest, subject to right of appeal. No appeal filed. Re*p*rt to G. L. O., November 16th, 1905.

Page 198: Protest: H. E. and T. S. Application, H. E. 10,466. Application 1396; filed 1904, September 9th; hearing September 9th, 1905; description of tract, southeast quarter section eighteen, township thirty-eight north, range six east; William Dwyer vs. Rosco W. Saunders, and Colden V. Sanders; date of entry, H. E. February 24th, 1904; T. & S. Application June 10th, '04· Remarks: September 9th, 1904, T. & S. Applica*t*nt, submitted proof. Case continued to September 10th and claimant's witnesses were cross-examined by protestant. Decision of register May 25, 1905, in favor of entryman and protest dis-

(Testimony of Thomas Heroditus Bartlett.)

missed. Decision of receiver May 25th, 1905; dismisses p*rt*est and rejects proof of Saunders. Appeal of Saunders filed June 21, 1905; appeal of Dwyer filed June 24, 1905; sent up August 21, 1905. That completes the Dwyer contests in this book.

Q. Now kindly refer to your cash entry book.

The WITNESS.—This is the *register* monthly abstracts cash.

Q. Cash entry No. 4042?

A. In order to identify the book this is the register's monthly abstracts cash 2861 to 5457. What is the number, Mr. Ruick?

Q. 5042?

A. Page 206. Abstract of lands sold at the land office at Lewiston, Idaho, from the 1st day of March, 1905, to the 31st day of the same month inclusive? I will read the subdivisions of the column: When sold, 1905, March 6th; No. *or fe* receipts and certificates 5042. By whom purchased, name, Mary E. Sherman, residence, Lewiston, Idaho; tract purchased, section number of section southeast quarter of section 30, number of township 38 north, number of range 6 east; number of acres, 160; pro*c*e per acre dollars and cents, dollars 2.50 per; purchase money, dollars and cents four hundred; amount re*c*ived in land scrip, dollars and. cents, no entry. General land office tract being column and folio. Under this is the entry T. & S.

Q. Examine this contest record which you previ-ous*oy* testified from, and state to the jury whether or

(Testimony of Thomas Heroditus Bartlett.)

not the lands included in cash entry 5042 are identical with the land included in the homestead entry of Albert Anderson, 10493?

Mr. TANNAHILL.—It is understood that our same objection goes to all of this?

The COURT.—Yes, sir.

Mr. RUICK.—That is the understanding.

Q. 10,493, Hoestead entry?

A. I have the—

Mr. TANNAHILL.—And the further objection that the records are the best evidence, and they are in court.

The COURT.—Well, I suppose this is for the benefit of the court and the jury as you go along?

Mr. RUICK.—It is for the benefit of the jury.

Q. (The COURT.) Isn't the same matter covered by the witness as he went along. He has stated in certain cases I know—

Mr. RUICK.—Not in these particular cases. There are three exceptions to the rule, your Honor.

The WITNESS.—The land embraced in cash entry No. 5042 Mary E. Sherman is the same land as that embraced in homestead entry 10,493, made February 24th, 1904, by Albert Anderson, of Pierce, Idaho, cancelled by relinquishment December 12th, 1904, at 10:20 A. M.

Q. Now look at cash entry 5226?    A. 5226?

Q. And state whether or not the land included in that cash entry is identical with the land included in the homestead entry of Charles D. Thornberg, No. 10,496?    A. You said *cah* entry 5226?

(Testimony of Thomas Heroditus Bartlett.)

Q.   5226?

A.   No, it is not; not in the same township.

Q.   Well, the cash entry of Charles S. Myers, is that 5226?

A.   No, sir.   Charles F. Miller, 5226.

Q.   Well, pass that for the time being.   It may require a little time to search that out.   Have you the books here showing cash entry 5462?   Does it go as far as that?

A.   I think so; no, the last entry in this book is 5457.

Q.   And you haven't that late book?

A.   No, sir.

Q.   Now, turn to timber and stone application book.   I will ask you first to identify the plat to thirty-eight north five east; you can stand right where you are and state on what date that township was opened to actual filing settlers?

A.   The filing mark on the plat indicates that it was officially filed on February 24th, 1904, at which time it was open for settlement for actual settlers.

Q.   At what time was this township opened for filing by timber and stone applicatns?

A.   I presume upon the same day, subject to preferred rights of actual settlers.

Q.   Well, how relative to the pr3ferred rights of the State of Idaho?

A.   It refers to the State of Idaho also.   It is subject to that also.

Q.   Well then, when was it actually opened to filing by timber and stone applicatns?

(Testimony of Thomas Heroditus Bartlett.)

A. As I say, I think it was actually open on that day, subject to those rights.

Q. However, timb*e* and stone applica*tn*s would not be permitted to file until the period of sixty days had lapsed?

A. I think that if they might offer their filing on that day and t*hi*r filings have been received on that day their filings would be good. I don't understand that the township is reserved until a certain day until timber and stone might be filed upon it.

Q. On what day was plat thirty-nine north, five east, Boise Meridian officially filed?

A. February 24, 1904.

Q. Township forty north, five east?

A. Filed February 24th, 1904.

Q. Township thirty-eight north, six east?

A. February 24th, 1904.

Q. Township th*ri*ty-nine north, six east?

A. February 24th, 1904.

Q. Township forty north, six east?

A. February 24th, 1904.

Q. Township thirty-nine north, three east? You haven't that, thirty-nine—three east?

A. I haven't seen it yet. No, I haven't that plat here.

Q. That is all on that line, Mr. Bartlett. I will ask you, however, if these plats, the day of filing of which you have just stated, to wit, 38-5, 39-5, 40-5, 38-6, 39-6, 40-6, are all the official plats of the United States Land Office at Lewiston, Idaho?

(Testimony of Thomas Heroditus Bartlett.)

A.   These are the official plats on file in the Unitee Stztes Land Office at Lewiston, Idaho.

Q.   You may now take timber and stone application book; now give the name of the timber and stone applica*tn*s and the number of the application and the description of the land as applied for on the twenty-fifth of April, 1904, at the United States Land Office at Lewiston, Idaho. I wish the names, and numbers of the application, the description of the lands and the order in which they filed.

Be it remembered that then and there the following proceeding was had:

WITNESS.—A.   All the following filings—

Mr. TANNAHILL.—If your Honor, please, we wish to add to our general objection to this testimony the additional ground that a great many of these applications have no application to the case at bar, do not tend *t* prove or disprove any of the issues in the case, and do not tend in any way to connect the defendants or either of them with the offenses charged in the indictment.

The COURT.—Mr. Ruick, are those a*p*lications made by parties who held these relinquishments?

Mr. RUICK.—Yes, it is the line-up that was engineered at the land office by the defendants. We propose to connect the defe*e*ndants directly with it through their agents.

Mr. FORNEY.—We want in addition to that objection to object *t* it on the further ground that it is incompetent, irrelevant and immaterial, not prov-

(Testimony of Thomas Heroditus Bartlett.)

ing or tending to prove any of the material allegations of the indictment.

Mr. RUICK.—Also that the land filed on by these people in the line-up will be connected with the defendants.

The COURT.—The particular question that I had in mind is whether or not the lands that you are now referring to are the same land secured by these contestants.

Mr. RUICK.—No, they are not, your Honor. That is different. It is in the same locality, but not the same identical lands. Those other lands we have already established the filing by the record; the filing of the timber and stone in those instances. Now then, we are introducing the evidence of the filing in the land office at that time of the parties in what is known as the line-up of April 25th, 1904, in which the lands were filed upon by parties who subsequently conveyed to these defendants, and we propose to folow it up by showing by whom the line-up was conducted; we did so in the case of the land of Mrs. Frances Justice, Guy L. Wilson and numerous other parties who have already testified, several other parties who have testified, and we propose your Honor to connect this directly with the various defendants, directly with the defendants; it is a circumstance.

The COURT.—Very well; on that statement the objecton will be overruled.

(Testimony of Thomas Heroditus Bartlett.)

To which ruling of the Court the defendants then and there excepted, which exception was allowed by the Court.

And the witness answered:

A. The following entries taken from Vollmer Timber and Stone Applications, beginning at page 77, all upon April 25th, 1904, are as follows:

Number 1313, Jackson O'Keefe; residence, Cloverland, Washington; west half of the southeast quarter; east half of the southwest quarter, section twenty-three, township 38 north, range five east, 160 acres; July 8th, 1904, which latter date indicates the date of proof.

Q. Can you give the amount that was paid for it?

A. It does not show whether proof was actually made or not.

(Continuing:)  No. 1314, Charles W. Taylor, Cloverland, Washington, lots 1 and 2 and east half of northwest quarter section thirty, township thirty-eight north, range six east, 158 and eight-tenth acres; July 11th, 1904.

No. 1315, Joseph H. Prentice, Cloverland, Washington; lots 1 and 2 and the east half of the northeast quarter, section eighteen, township thirty-eight north, range six; 156.6 acres; date of proof, July 11th, 1904.

No. 1316, Edgar J. Taylor, Cloverland, Washington; lots three and 4, east half southwest quarter, section 18; townhipd 38 north, range six east; 157 acres; date of proof July 11th, 1904.

(Testimony of Thomas Heroditus Bartlett.)

No. 1317, Edgar H. Dammarel, Cloverland, Washington; northeast quarter section 19*k* township 38 north, range six east, 160 acres; July 12th, 1904; meaning the date of proof.

No. 1318, George H. Kester, Lewiston, Idaho; north half northeast quarter, southwest *a*uarter southeast quarter, southeast quarter southwest quarter—wait a minute, I will read that again, north half northeast quarter section thirty; southwest *w*quarter southeast quarter and the southeast quarter of the southwest quarter of section nineteen, township thirty-nine, north range five east, 160 acres; proof made July 12th, 1904.

No. 1319, Eugene H. Hopper, Clarkston, Washington; west half of west half section 13; township th*r*ity-eight north, range five east; 160 acres; proof made July 12th, 1904.

No. 1320, E*id*th A. *H*pper, Clarkston Washington; east half of west half section 13, township thirty-eight north, range five east; 160 acres; proof made July 12th, 1904.

No. 1321, Guy L. Wilson, Clarkston, Washington; lots 3 and 4 and northeast quarter of the southwest quarter and the northwest quarter of the southeast quarter, section 19, township 39 north, range 5 east; 158.5 acres; proof made July 13th, 1904.

No. 1322, Edna T. Kester, Lewiston, Idaho; north half of north half section fourteen, township thirty-eight north, range 5 east; 160 acres; July 13th, 1904.

No. 1323, Frances A. Justice, Clarkston, Washington; lots 3 and 4 and east half of the southwest quar-

(Testimony of Thomas Heroditus Bartlett.)

ter section nineteen, township thirty-eight north, range 6 east; 157.8 acres; July 13th, 1904; date of proof.

No. 1324, Fred E. Justice, Clarkston, Washington; east half of east half section 20, township thirty-eight north, range 6 east; 160 acres; proof made July 13th, 1904.

No. 1325, Elizabeth Kettenbach, Lewiston, Idaho; west half of east half of section 13; to township 38 north, range 5 east; 160 acres; proof made July 14th, 1904.

No. 1326, Elizabeth White, Lewiston, Idaho; south half of north half section twenty-three, township thirty-eight north, range five east; 160 acres; proof made July 14th, 1904.

No. 1327, William J. White, Lewiston, Idaho; south half of the north half section fourteen, township thirty-eight north, range five east; 160 acres; proof made July 14th, 1904.

No. 1328, Mamie P. White, Lewiston, Idaho; north half of south half section 14, township thirty-eight north, range fice east; 160 acres; proof made July 14th, 1904.

No. 1329, Martha E. Hallett, Lewiston, Idaho; lots 1 and 2, and east half of nothwest quarter section 19, township thirty-eight north, range six east; 157.4 acres; proof made July 15th, 1904.

No. 1330, Daniel W. Greenburg, Lewiston, Idaho; southwest quarter section 17, twoship 39 north, range five east; 160 acres; proof made July 15th, 1904.

(Testimony of Thomas Heroditus Bartlett.)

No. 1331, Davis S. Bingham, Cloverland, Washington; southeast quarter of section 17, township thirty-nine north, range five east; 160 ae*rs*; July 15th, 1904.

No. 1332, Albert Anderson, Pierce, Idaho; southwest quarter section 29, township thirty-eight north, range six east; 160 acres, July 15th; there is a line through that entire entry with the remark; failed to make proof.

1333, Walter S. Daggett, Southwick, Idaho.

Mr. RUICK.—Just a moment, Mr. Bartlett. You need not go into that. The Daggetts, we are not informed as to whether or not we can connect the defendants with that.

Mr. TANNAHILL.—We *w*ought to have the line-up that counsel has referred to as a line-up.

Mr. RUICK.—We have not the slightest objection to it, but it is excessive caution on our part not to get in any entries we cannot possibly connect the defendants with; we would like to have the whole thing. If there is no objection on the part of the defense, we ask the witness to proceed.

The COURT.—If they had objected the Court would have sustained the objection. I understand the purpose of the counsel in the matter of the line-up, as he calls it, is to show that all these parties were there at the instigation of the defendants.

Mr. RUICK.—The order in which the applications were tendered at the office. Your Honor remembers this was admitted under my statement that we proposed to connect the defendants with these. Now,

(Testimony of Thomas Heroditus Bartlett.)

it was true that I told the witness to stop because we were not aware we could connect the defendants with some of them. If there is no objection on the part of the defendants, they may go in. We will not assume responsibility of connecting the parties hereafter named by the witness with the defendants; he may proceed.

Mr. FORNEY.—Did we understand the counsel that he would prove we had formed the line-up there, and not that we were responsible for various parties in the line-up? He was going to connect us with the entire line-up. We object to the relevancy and competency of this evidence and we do not wish to withdraw our objection.

The COURT.—I think the Court understands the matter. Now, if it should turn out that the prosecution connects these defendants with only two or three persons in the line-up, the effect on the jury may be very different from what it would be if the defendants were connected with everyone in the line. I assume that counsel both see the bearing of this matter. However, if counsel wanted it to go in and the prosecution has no objection to it going in, I do not see that there is anything to rule on and we will proceed.

(Witness continuing:) 1333, Walter E. Daggett, Southwick; lots 2, 3, 7, 8 and 9, section 5, township 40 north, range 5 east; 149.16 acres; proof made July 15th.

1334, John R. McConnell, Moscow, Idaho; east half of the southwest quarter, section 21, north half of the

(Testimony of Thomas Heroditus Bartlett.)

northwest quarter, section 28, township 38 north, range six east; 160 acres; proof made July 15th.

Number 1335, Warren Lawrence, Nez Perce, Idaho; east half of the southwest quarter, and the southwest quarter of the southeast quarter of section 11, towhsip 38 north, range 6 east; 120 acres-proof made July 18th.

No. 1336, Hattie Rowland, Orofino, Idaho; the southeast quarter of the northwest quarter *nd* the south half of the northeast quarter, and the northeast quarter *lf* the southwest quarter, section 15, township thirty-eight north, range five east; 160 acres; proof made July 18th.

No. 1337, William McMillan, Orofino, Idaho; southeast quarter section 21, township thirty-nine north, range 5 east; 160 acres; Juy 18th, 1904.

1338, James E. Hood, Spokane, Wahingto; lots 1 and 2, the south half of the northeast quarter of section 2, townsip 37 north, range 4 east; 160.16 acres; July 19th, 1904. A mark agains that, relinquished July 19th, 1904, and a pen scratched through it.

Number 1339, John M. McClelland, Cutbank, Montana; the southwest quarter of section 1, township thirty-seven north, range four east; 160 acres; July 19th, 1904; relinquished July 19th, 1904.

No. 1340, Frank W. Cadwell, Spokane, Washington; the northeast quarter of section thirty-four, township thirty-eight north, range 6 east; 160 acres; July 19th, 1904.

(Testimony of Thomas Heroditus Bartlett.)

No. 1341, Charles V. Craig, Spokane, Washington; the northwst quarter of section 12, township 37 north, range 5 east; 160 acres; July 19th, 1904.

No. 1342, Nathan A. Egbert, Springfield, Massachusetts; the southwest quarter of section 34, township thirtt-eight north, range six east; 160 acres; July 19th, 1904.

1343, Dudly J. Gallagher, Spokane, Washington; the southeast quarter section 35, township 38 north, range six east; 160 acres; July 19th, 1904.

1344, Ernest J. LaBoutillier, Minneapolis, Minnesota; the northwest quarter of section 34, townshi thirty-eight nort, range siz east; 120 acres; July *2th.*

1345, George W. Reed, Mount Vernon, Washington; lot 3 and 4, the south half of the northwest quarter of section 5, township 37 north, range five east; 159.65 acres; July 20th, a pen line through the whole of that entry with the remark, relinquished July 20th, 1904.

1346, Dennis J. Grant, Seattle, Washington; lots 3 and 4 and the east half of the southwest quarter section thirty, township thirty-eight north; range five east; 153.2 acres; July 20th.

1347, Otto Green, Leavenworth, Washington; lots 1 and 2, and the east half of the northwest quarter of section 31, township thirty-eight north, range five east; 152.8 acres; July 20th.

1348, Frank F. Finch, Waco, Texas; the southeast quarter of section 34, township 38 north, range six east; 160 acres; July 20th.

(Testimony of Thomas Heroditus Bartlett.)

*Q.* 1349, Edward J. Broadwick, Seattle, Washington; the north half of the southeast quarter, the southwest quarter of the southeast quarter of section five, township thirty-seven north, range five east; 120 acres; July 20th, 1904.

1350, Fred W. Crane, Spokane, Washington; the northwest quarter of the southeast quarter, and the north half of the southwest quarter and the southeast quarter of the southwest quarte; section 12, township thirty-seven north, range five east; 160 acres; July 20th.

1351, William W. Felter, Brawley, California; the southeast quarter of the southwest quarter of section twenty-six, townshi; thirty-nine north, range 5 east; forty acres; July 21st. A line is drawn through that entry, relinquished June 27th, 1904.

1352, Sidney, Eberle; Moscow, Idaho; northwest quarter of section 32, township 38 north, range 6 east; 160 acres; proof made July 21st, 1904.

1353, Edward Kitts, Moscow, Idaho; the west half of the southeast quarter and the south half of the southwest quarter, section 25, township 40 north, range 1 west; 160 acres; July 21st, 1904.

That is all.

Q. Kindly refer to the tract book—I will withdraw that question. Kindly refer to the state selection book. State on what date the state selection of the state of Idaho were made and filed in the Unitee States Land Office at Lewiston, Idaho, in township thirty-eight north, range fcve east; also township 39 north, range 5 east?

(Testimony of Thomas Heroditus Bartlett.)

A. This book is not indexed by township and range. Can you give me any further data there which wi*l* enable me to find it?

Q. Scientific school: Is it indexed under that?

A. It is very poorly indexed, anywhere; scientific school, what list is it?

Q. List No. 6. Now, what was the township and range—39 north, range 5 east?

A. On page 164 of the State selection book, the following entry: For scientific school, list No. 6, filed April 21st, 1904, and the list comprises—

The COURT.—The list of what?

A. For scientific schools—list No. 6, filed April 21st, 1904. The list comprises lands in township 39 north, range 5 east, and 38 north 5 east.

Q. Does it give the number of acres th*ee* in that list?

A. Yes, sir; there is a footing at the end of the column here, 10,924.23 acres. The accuracy of that addition I ca*n*ot answer for.

Q. What was the date of the filing of those se*c*lections? A. April 21st, 1904.

Q. (Paper shown witness.) Do you identify this paper as part of the rec*o*rs and archives of the United States Land Office at Lewiston, Idaho?

A. Yes, sir; those *ar* a part of them.

Q. Did you bring them here to court with you in respon*s* to a subpoena? A. I did.

Q. What is that paper? What does it purport to be? I will ask you the question directly inasmuch as it is documentary evidence? Is that list No. 6

(Testimony of Thomas Heroditus Bartlett.)

of State lands selections to which you have just referred, which was filed on April 21st?

A. It appears to be, yes, sir. List No. 6, Scientific Schools.

Q. And the aggregate is the same as you have just given it; you will notice that on the second sheet?

A. The aggregate is the same as indicated in the book.

Q. What is it, 10,924.23 acres, meaning the amount of land selected under that list?

A. That's it.

Q. That is list No. 6 to which you have just referred?

A. *Ye,* sir; list 6 for scientific school purposes.

Be it remembered that then and there the following proceeding *ws* had:

Mr. RUICK.—I ask that this be marked for identification Plaintiff's Exhibit 53.

Mr. FORNEY.—We submit our general objection, if the Court please.

The COURT.—Objection overruled.

To which ruling of the Court the defendants then and there excepted, which exception was allowed by the Court, and the document was so marked.

Q. Now, refer to the same record book. What record book is that containing state selections. How do you designate that book?

A. It is called the State selection book.

Q. Now, calling your attention to the University selection in List No. 6. A. Yes, sir.

(Testimony of Thomas Heroditus Bartlett.)

Q.   On what day did the State make its selections in townships 40 north, range 6 east for the State University list 6?

A.   Records on page 166 of State Land selection book indicates that *th* State made the selection under list No. 6, State University, filed April 21st, 1904, for lands in township 40 north, 5 east, and 40 north, 6 east.

Q.   Aggregate it?

A.   Aggregating a total of 11,973.6 acres.

Q.   I will now show you a paper purporting to be list No. 6 of selections by the State of Idaho for the benefit of the State University of lands in township 40 north, range 5 east, and 40 north, range 6 east, aggregating 11,973.6 acres, and *ak* you if that is the application to which you have just previously referred?

A.   That appears to be the list so filed.

Q.   You say appears to be?      A.   And it is.

Mr. RUICK.—We ask that this be marked Plaintiff's Exhibit 54 for identification.   (So marked.)

Q.   Referring now to list No. 9, State University of selections made by the State of Idaho in township 38 north, range 6 east.   State what the record shows as to the date on which such selection was made?

A.   Is that No. 9, the University?

Q.   Yes.

A.   There is no such number in the index; maybe I can find it.

Q.   6911, and .56 acres on the same date?

A.   Give me the township and range again.

(Testimony of Thomas Heroditus Bartlett.)

Q. 38 north, range 6 E*at*.

A. University.

Q. University selection of land.

Mr. TANNAHILL.—When was it filed?

WITNESS.—I have not found the list yet.

The COURT.—Does the paper you have in your hand give the date of filing?

Mr. RUICK.—Yes, but I wanted it from the record; it is April 21st, 1904.

The COURT.—The same date, Mr. Bartlett?

WITNESS.—On page 165, State selection book is the filing entry—no, this is State normal list No. 9. Is that right, not University.

Q. Yes, it is State Normal; I misread it, it is my mistake.

A. State Normal List No. 9, filed April 21st, 1904, embracing land in 38, 6 east, giving the total acreage 6, 911.56 acres.

Q. When was that filed?

A. April 21st, 1904.

.Q. Look at this paper now I am showing you and state whether or not that is the original list to which you have just previously referred, filed in the land office at Lewiston, on the date referred to?

A. That is the original list to which I refer.

Mr. RUICK.—We ask that this be marked Plaintiff's Exhibit 55 for identification.

(And the same is so marked.)

Q. Turn now to the scrip selection record. What book have you now in your hands, Mr. Bartlett?

(Testimony of Thomas Heroditus Bartlett.)

A.   The record of what is known as scrip selection. Scrip filings.

Q.   Turn to selection No. 166.    A.   166.

Q.   By whom was *te* selection made?

The record indicates Goorge H. Kester, Lewiston, Idaho.

Q.   To what land?

A.   On October 20th, 1903, for the southeast quarter of the northeast quarter of section 30, township 36 north, range four east.

Q.   How many acres?    A.   I beg pardon.

Q.   How many acres?

A.   That is not the number of acres.

Q.   The record does not show?

A.   It indicates it was forty acres.   Do you wish the land in lieu of which was selected?

Q.   No, that is not necessary.   Now list 167.

A.   167, November 6th, 1903, William F. Kettenbach, Lewiston, Idaho; the northeast quarter of the northwest quarter, section 35, township 36 north, range 4 east.

Q.   List 168?

Mr. TANNAHILL.—The number of acres?

A.   Forty acres.   The northeast of the northwest.

Q.   168.

A.   168, November 6th, 1903, ditto, indicating William F. Kettenbach, of Lewiston, Idaho, the southwest quarter of the southeast quarter of sec-tion 27, township 37 north, range 4 east.

Q.   That will be how many acres?

A.   Forty acres.

(Testimony of Thomas Heroditus Bartlett.)

Q. 175?

Mr. FORNEY.—If the Court please, it is understood this all goes in under our general objection as irrelevant, incomptent and immaterial, as not connecting the defendants or being connected with any issue in this case, and not tending to prove any *issue* in this case.

The COURT.—I will ask Mr. Ruick to state the purpose.

*O.* I do not see the relevancy of it.

Mr. RUICK.—It was part of the general scheme to acquire timber lands in this particular section, if your Honor please, by showing the different methods adopted by the defendants to acquire large tracts of timber in this section; the same proposition was gone over in the Van Gesner case; the intent, motive and purpose of the parties. They were operating in different ways to acquire lands in this particular locality—lands, contiguous lands. The scrip being used to take up what might be called isolation tracts, small tracts; scrip being used for that purpose.

The COURT.—I think inasmuch as it has been partly gone into I will let counsel for the prosecution finish his proof, but under the objection I would like to have counsel *cal* my attention to those facts in the Van Gesner case at the noon hour, its relevancy is not clear to the Court at the present time.

Mr. RUICK.—I will state in addition a reason, if your Honor will pardon me.

The COURT.—Yes.

(Testimony of Thomas Heroditus Bartlett.)

Mr. RUICK.—Showing that the scrip was laid prior to the making of final proof by the stone and timber entrymen, on many of the claims on the land in the same or immediate locality, as the lands where the scrip is laid, going to show an intention, the purpose and the plan pursued by the defendants, to acquire land in this locality.

The COURT.—A plan to acquire lands legitimately, carried out of course would be—I don't see how it would be—

Mr. RUICK.—If your Honor please, the acts standing by itself might be ever so innocent, as many acts going to show a conspiracy are, but these acts are a part of the general plan or scheme to acquire timber in a particular locality, and the fact of filing scrip in this immediate locality where these entrymen are makng the entries, which entries it is alleged, and which we are seeking to show, were encouraged and procured to be made by the defendants for their own benefit, with the ulterior objects of acquiring title to them, if your Honor please, then the laying of scrip in the immediate locality, becomes significant, because forty acres of timber land, entirely separate, as your Honor can readily see from other considerable bodies of land of the same ownership, would not be worth that forty acres of land standing with others.

Mr. MOORE.—That is merely a guess.

Mr. RUICK.—That is the proposition; anybody knows forty acres of land standing entirely away

(Testimony of Thomas Heroditus Bartlett.)

from other bodies of land would not be worth anything.

The COURT.—That is perhaps true, but one might scrip land—

Mr. RUICK.—(Interrupting.) Your Honor gets the idea that the very theory is the parties starting in to acquire bodies of considerable timber land in one locality for the purpose of giving it a commercial value.

Mr. MOORE.—Van Gessner got it for sheep operations; that has no commercial value.

Mr. RUICK.—I will introduce the Van Gessner case, if you like.

Mr. TANNAHILL.—You have it nearly all before the jury now.

Mr. RUICK.—It is a pretty good case to follow, because the Circuit Court of Appeals, the highest court to go to, says it is the law.

The COURT.—If there is such a question passed upon in the Van Gessner case, the Court will follow it in that regard.

Mr. RUICK.—It is along the same lines, the same question is discussed.

The COURT.—It would be a very good case, and would be binding on this Court, and the Court will gladly follow the ruling of the Circuit Court of Appeals in that case.

Mr. MOORE.—Your Honor will note that this scrip is nearly twenty-four miles from any land they have in the record.

(Testimony of Thomas Heroditus Bartlett.)

Mr. RUICK.—Twenty miles don't mean much in Idaho. We will get some right in closer than the twenty miles in a little while.

The COURT.—Well, proceed; and at the noon hour the Court not being familiar with the whole record in the Van Gessner case, desires this part called to its attention, because if this question was passed on it would be binding on this Court, but I do not quite see the connection of the proof offered. If it is not shown, I shall strike it out.

Mr. RUICK.—Unless its relation is shown.

Mr. FORNEY.—I will ask your Honor to look at this phase of it: Under the allegations in the indictment, it is charged that the defendants did attempt to defraud the United States Government by a certain means, and those means are set out in the indictment at length and in detail, and I cannot see the relevancy of these scrip selections, and we take the position that they are immaterial and do not tend to prove any issue embraced in the indictment.

The COURT.—I am quite positive in my recollection that Judge Beatty excluded testimony in the last two trials of such a nature, but I realize those trials were upon different charges, and it may be by reason of the difference in *th* charge in this case, which is conspiracy rather than subornation of perjury, that this testimony becomes material, but you may proceed at the present time.

Mr. RUICK.—Won't your Honor let me make a statement because of my familiarity with that case lest the jury get a wrong impression from that.

(Testimony of Thomas Heroditus Bartlett.)

The COURT.—Yes.

Mr. RUICK.—Those cases were merely charges of subornation of perjury, pure and simple, of having procured parties to swear falsely in the United States Land Office in connection with their making of timber and stone entries. The Court, Judge Beatty, admitted evidence of similar transactions under the rule, but when it came to these scrip filings, the Court said as to the proposition of perjury, laid in the indictment, he did not see the application of the scrip filings, and hence it was excluded under that rule, but this being a case of conspiracy the evidence must of necessity take a different tact. Under the rule a very wide range for the purpose of showing the motives, the purpose and the plan which the parties had in view, and the concern of action between the several parties, and it is part of our plan to show the purpose of these defendants to acquire large tracts of timber land in the same locality, as I say, for the pur*p*se of giving it a commercial value, and which it will be shown here, as we believe, and as we propose to show, has a very great commercial value, in the estimate of the defendants themselves, because we propose to show the value which the defendants put upon these lands themselves, that is the purpose of it, and that is the distinction between this case and the case that Judge Beatty ruled in, an entirely different case.

The COURT.—I will ask you or your assistant to point out that matter in the Van Gessner case; I would like to see the ruling on that.

(Testimony of Thomas Heroditus Bartlett.)

Mr. RUICK.—I don't say the identical question
was ruled on, but the general proposition as showing the intention and purpose to acquire large tracts
of land, in the same locality, and it was expressly
ruled upon by Judge Hunt in that case, and is referred to, I think, in his instructions to the jury.

Mr. JOHNSON.—(*Assistant Prosecutor.*) Your
Honor will see, as soon as the plats come in, the purpose.

Mr. RUICK.—The Court permitted it to be shown
that Van Gessner endeavored to procure title to
State lands in the same locality, as part of the same
scheme. It was permitted to be shown.

The COURT.—I am quite familiar with the records in the case. The Court will be very glad to
follow the ruling if it is so. Proceed.

To which ruling of the Court, the defendants then
and there excepted, which exception was allowed by
the Court.

And the witness answered:

A. No. 175, January 14th, 1904; August Ferrier
and Marie Ferrier, by Geo. H. Kester, Lewiston;
the southwest quarter of the southeast quarter and
the south half of the southwest quarter and the northwest quarter of the southwest quarter of section 27,
township thirty-six, north range 5 east. That would
contain 160 acres.

Q. List 190, to 199, or rather scrip selection Nos.
190 to 199 inclusive.

A. 190, July 20th; W. F. Kettenbach, Lewiston,
the south half of the northeast quarter and the south-

(Testimony of Thomas Heroditus Bartlett.)
west quarter of the southeast quarter, and the southwest quarter of the northwest quarter, section 9,
township thirty-nine north, range 4 east.

No. 191, July 20th, W. F. Kettenbach, Lewiston;
the northeast quarter of the northeast quarter of
section twent township thirty-nine north, range four
east.

192, July 20th, William F. Kettenbach, Lewiston,
the northwest quarter of the southwest quarter of
section 20, township thirty-nine north, range four
east.

193, July 20th; W. F. Kettenbach, Lewiston, the
south half of the north half and the south half of the
southwest quarter section 21, township thirty-nine
north, range four east.

194, July 20; W. F. Kettenbach, Lewiston, the
northeast quarter of the northwest quarter of section
21, township thirty-nine north, range four east.

195, May 27th; W. F. Kettenbach; the west half of
southwest quarter of the northeast quarter of the
southwest quarter of section 5 and the northwest
quarter of the northwest quarter of section 8, township thirty-nine north, range five east.

196, September 26th; W. F. Kettenbach, Lewiton.
the southwest quarter of the northwest quarter of
section twenty-seven and the northeast quarter of the
southeast quarter of section 19, township thirty-nine
north, range five east and the south half of the sowth-
west quarter of section fifteen, township thirty-eight
north, range five east.

(Testimony of Thomas Heroditus Bartlett.)

179, September 26th; Patrick Lavelle by W. F. Kettenbach,—

Mr. RUICK.—What number is that?

A. 197; did you call for that?

Mr. RUICK—197? A. Yes, Patrick Lavelle by W. F. Kettenbach, of Lewiston, the northeast quarter of the southwest quarter section 28, township thirty-nine north, of range five east.

198, August Ferrier, and Marie Ferrier, by W. F. Kettenbach, under date of October 12th, the southeast quarter of the southeast quarter of section 19 and the northwest quarter of section 27, township thirty-nine north, range five east.

199, September 26th, W. F. Kettenbach, the northeast quarter of section twenty-eight, township thirty-nine north, range five east. I think that completes the list you mentioned.

Q. Now selections 261 to 266 inclusive.

A. 261, January 5th. 1906, S. P. Rolander, by George H. Kester, assignee, Lewiston, Idaho, the northwest quarter of the northwest quarter section 32 north, range thirty-nine, township thirty-nine Noth, range four east.

262, January 5th, 1906, George H. Kester, Assignee of Matilda C. Young, and Wilbur Young, the north half of the southeast quarter of section fie, township thirty-eight north, range 5 East.

263, January 15th, 1906; George H. Kester, Assignee of Burdette A. Clifton; Lot 11, section 30, and Lot 1, section 31, township thirty-nine, range four east.

(Testimony of Thomas Heroditus Bartlett.)

264, Seven-one-'05.   George H. Kester, assignee of Eli Haines.   The west half of the southeast quarter of section six, township thirt*t*-eight north, range five east.

265, Date 7-1-05.   George H. Kester, assignee of Thomas A. Boles; the no*t*h half of the northe*w*est quarter of section seventeen, township thirt*t*-eight north, range six east.

266, 8-26-'05.   George H. Kester, assignee of Will*im* F. Cavanass, the west half of the northwest quarter of sec*t*o*n* eight, township thirty-eight north, range 5 east.

Whereupon an adjournment was taken till Monday, May 27th, 1907, at 2 o'clock P. M.

Direct Examination of THOS. H. BARTLETT
(Resumed).

(By Mr. RUICK.)

Q.   Have you the patent record of the United State*z* Land Office at Lewiston, Idaho, in your custody?      A.   Yes, sir; I have it here.

Q.   Kindly turn to your rec*od* and I will ask you as a preliminary question have you checked up that record for the purpose of ascertaining what patents were delivered to Kester, Kettenbach, Dwyer, or C. W. Robnett prior to 1904.

The COURT.—Do you understand the question.

A.   Yes, sir; I have scanned the record to see what patents had been delivered to the persons you speak of, with the exception of Mr. Dwyer.   I don't think I bore that in mind as I went down the list.

(Testimony of Thomas Heroditus Bartlett.)

Be it rememberrd that then and there the following proceeding was had:

Q. Well, you may state the others.

Mr. FORNEY.—Our same objection goes to all of this?

The COURT.—What is the last question.

(Question cojtinued:) And relating—I will withdraw the propositon as to 1904, and merely state patents as to lands which patents have been delivered to any of these par*t*es referred to and then we will connect them with the lands under consideration.

Mr. FORNEY.—We object to that as incompetent, irrelevant and immaterial, not tending to prove or proving *ay* of the issues in this case, and on the further ground that it is calling for matters and things not embra*n*ced in any of the issues set forth in the indictment, and post-dating the cul*i*mination of the alleged conspiracy, and post-dating any of the acts set forth in the indictment, no time having been fixed, and let this objection run to each and all of the questions in this connection.

The COURT.—Yes.

Mr. RUICK.—These are all to lands within the tw*o*nships referred to your Honor, and also state what we propose to show, the connection of Mr. Robnett with these defendants.

The COURT.—Objection overruled; to which ruling of the Court the defendants then and there excepted, which exception was allowed by the Court and the witness answered:

(Testimony of Thomas Heroditus Bartlett.)

A. On page —————— I read from the record of patents delivered page 23.

No. 4054, William B. Benton; do you wish the date of the patent.

Q. The date of the delivery of the patent you may—yes, for the purpose of identifying it we will have the date of the patent.

A. Date of patent, February 25, 1904; delivered to C. W. Robnett, Marfh 22nd, '04·

No. 4055, Joel H. Benton; date of patent, February 25th, 1904; delivered to C. W. Robnett, March 22d, 1904.

Page 25.

No. 4199, Mattie W. Benton; date of patent, July 2d, 1904; delivered to C. W. Robnett, September 22, '04·

No. 4392, Lewis E. Bishop; date of patent, August 3d, 1904; delivered to  C. W. Robnett, September 22d, '04·

No. 4390, Benjamin H. Bashor; date of patent August 3d, 1904; delivered to C. W. Robnett, September 17th, 1904.

Page 47.

No. 4508, Ivan R. Cornell; date of patent, September 9th, 1904; delivered to C. W. Robnett, 12-6-04.

No. 4074, Henderson S. Disney, February 25, 1905; delivered to Mr. Robnett 3-31-04.

Page 89.

(Testimony of Thomas Heroditus Bartlett.)

No. 4404, Charles Dent; date of patent, August 3d, 1904; delivered to C. W. Robnett, September 22, '04·

Page 112.

No. 4291, Jame C. Evans, August 3d, '04; delivered to C. W. Robnett, Sepember 22d, '04·

Page 127.

No. 4414, Bertsell H. Ferris, August 3d, '04, is the date of the patent; delivered to C. W. Robnett, September 17, 1904.

Page 141.

No. 4351, Emery F. Gordon, August 3, 1904; delivered to C. W. Robnett, September 17th, 1904.

No. 4477, Drury M. Gammon; date of patent, September 9th, 1904; delivered to C. W. Robnett, 10-24-04.

Page 167.

Number 4412, Edward W. Hyde, August 3, 1904, date of the patent; delivered to C. W. Robnett, September 22, '04·

Number 4384, Ellsworth M. Harrington, date of patent, August 3d, 1904; delivered to C. W. Robnett, September 17, 1904.

Page 215.

Number 4357, John W. Killinger; date of patent August 3d, 1904; delivered to C. W. Robnett, September 17th, 1904.

Page 247.

Number 4049, Carrie D. Maris; date of  patent, February 25, 1904; delivered to C.  W.  Robnett, March 2, '04·

Page 268.

(Testimony of Thomas Heroditus Bartlett.)

Number 4394, Frederick W. Newman, August 3, 1904, date of patent; delivered to C. W. Robnett, September 22d, '04·

Page 298.

Number 4389, Wren Pierce; date of patent, August 3, 1904; delivered to C. W. Robnett, 9-22-'04.

Page 225.

Number 4339, Arthur W. Rainwater, August 3, 1904; delivered to C. W. Robnett, September 17, 1904.

Number 4352, Van V. Robertson, August 3d, 1904. Patent delivered to C. W. Robnett September 17, '04·

No. 4415, George Ray Robertson, August 3, 1904; delivered to C. W. Robnett, September 17th, 1904.

Number 4454, Walter S. Roberts, date of patent, August 3, 1904; delivered to George H. Kester, November 12th, 1904.

Page 364.

Number 4405, Charles Smith; date of patent, August 3, 1904; delivered to C. W. Robnett, September 27th, 1904.

Page 418.

No. 4043, C. Arthur Varney; date of patent, March 14, 1904; delivered to C. W. Robnett, 4-6-04.

Page 438.

Number 4249, Robert N. Wright; date of patent, August 3, 1904; delivered to C. W. Robnett, September 17, '04·

Number 4251, Maud B. Wright; August 3, 1904; delivered to C. W. Robnett, September 17th, 1904.

(Testimony of Thomas Heroditus Bartlett.)

Number 4365, Robert O. Waldman; date of patent, August 3, 1904; delivered to C. W. Robnett, September 17, '04· That is all.

Q. Do you know which one was delivered to Mr. Kester?

A. That was Number 4454, Walter S. Roberts.

Q. Mr. Bart'ett, there has been no patents issued this last year filed upon in 1904, have there?

A. I cannot say.

Q. Are not all patents under suspension in the office?

A. Not all patents, no, sir. There is a general order of suspension there relating to certain townshiops which I cannot tell you from memory, embracing a great deal of the lands covered.

Q. Covered?   A. Covered by the—

Q. Your testimony this morning?

A. The testimony of this morning; yes, sir.

Q. You have not the order with you?

A. No, sir.

Cross-examination by Mr. TANNAHILL.

Q. Mr. Bartlett, you *dd* not deliver those patents personally, did you?   A. No, sir.

Q. You simply testify as to what your recors show?   A. Yes, sir.

Be it remembered that then and there the following proceeding was had:

Q. It is not unsusual for you to deliver patents to persons who are not the owners of the land, if they happen to call for them, is it?

(Testimony of Thomas Heroditus Bartlett.)

Mr. RUICK.—He only testified in regard to the record, and consequently even if he had a custom that might be otherwise competent, it would not be competent for him to testify as to his custom because the patents were delivered long before he came into the office.

The COURT*F*.—I think I shall have to su*atin* this objection; but with the explanation that if there be some rule of the department, or if there is some law or rule of the department governing the action of the *of*cers of the local land office in that regard, then I think it is entirely proper to show that; but I doubt whether the presu*mt*ion can be indulged in that the registers or receivers follow the same custom in that manner where there is no rule prescribing what their conduct should be. One set of officers might follow one custom and another another.

To which ruling of the Court the defendants then and t*eh*re excepted, which exception was allowed by the C*o*rt.

Q. Mr. Bartlett, is there any rule issued by the General Land Office, or by the Register and Receiver relative to the delivery of patents?

A. I know of no rule issued from the general land office.

Q. Is there any rule issued by the Register and Receiver? A. We have no such rule.

Q. Do you know what the custom has been in the land office at Lewiston relative to the delivery of patents, say since 1904? A. I think I do.

(Testimony of Thomas Heroditus Bartlett.)

Be it *rm*embered that then and there the following proceeding was had:

Q. Well, what is the gènéral rule?

A. The custom I have adopted and prior to the time I took the office, patents had been delivered and it has been the custom to deliver them—

Mr. RUICK.—We object to that.

The COURT.—I ruled that if he stated that he knew what the custom was prior there*ot,* he could state.

Mr. RUICK.—Regarding that period, during which these patents were delivered.

The COURT.—That is*l,* if he knows what the custom was and he has so stated.

(Witness continued:) I cannot say with definiteness that I know what the custom was at the period of the delivery of these patents. I know what the custom was when I took the office.

Q. What was the custom at that time? When did you take the office, and when did you assume the duties of the office?    A. January 5, 1906.

Q. What was the custom at that time?

Mr. RUICK.—I object to it for the sake of getting the ruling of the Court on it. It is incompetent, irrelevant and immaterial for two reasons: one is it is not competent to prove custom, and in the second place, this witness has shown that he does not know wh*z*t the custom was at the time the patents were issued.

*Te* COURT.—I think you can inquire a little further as to his knowledge.

(Testimony of Thomas Heroditus Bartlett.)

Q. What knowledge have you, Mr. Bartlett, as to the custom which was in vogue prior to the time you took office?

A. Knowledge derived by conversation with my associates, Mr. Garby, who was my receiver when I came in there.

Q. Do you know how long he was receiver?

A. Some eight years; he—

Q. He was receiver at the time these patents were issued? A. He was.

Q. Now, you may state what the custom was when you assumed the duties of register?

Mr. RUICK.—If the Court pleae, we object. We put ourselves on record as objecting to it on account of it having been a long time subsequent to the delivery of these patents, annd anotehr is that it would be hearsay, and another is that these officers that Mr. Garby is himself in this city, and so is J. B. West, and so is Mr. Malloy, a former clerk of the land office, who controlled the land office prior to Mr. Bartlett's connection with the office, are here in this city. I say it is hearsay, let them prove it by the parties who know it, and we have no objection to it. But I object to it ecause Mr. Bartlett does not presume to know it except by hearsay or something somebody else told him and not from knowledge of his own of a custom which he became acquainted with.

The COURT.—Unless Mr. Bartlett knows from something other than he has stated, the Court will sustain the objection.

(Testimony of Thomas Heroditus Bartlett.)

To which ruling of the Court the defendants then and there excepted, which exception was allowed by the Court.

Q.  You referred to some persons who filed timber and stone entries on the 25th of April, I believe, 1904, which was designated as a line-up at the land office, and a large number of people filed homesteads, stone and timber entries, and there were also some scrip filings at that time, as you have ascertained from your records, were there not?

A.  I don't remember the record, Mr. Tannahill. You will have to rely upon the testimony that I have already given from the record. I know nothing else *w*but what the records indicate. I was not register in the land office then at that time.

Q.  Mr. Bartlett, it is not an unusual thing is it, for a line-up to be formed at the land office door sometimes for several days prior to the time land in certain townships are thrown open, is it?

A.  No; if your Honor please, as I understand the questio directed to me, it is as to whether a line-up has taken place during my term of office there.

Q.  Yes, sir; during your term of office, since you have been in office?    A.  Any objection to that?

Mr. RUICK.—No; no objection.

A.  Certainly there has been a line-up since I have been in the office.

Q.  How many line-ups has there been since you have been in office, Mr. Bartlett?

A.  I don't remember but one or two.

(Testimony of Thomas Heroditus Bartlett.)

Q. D*l* you remember anything about the number of persons there to file, and who did file in any of those line-ups?

A. I think upon March 18*t,* 1906, if I remember the date right, a pr*ety* fairly heavy line-up of about 20 or 25 people or maybe more.

Q. How many upon the other occasion?

A. I don't remember; somewhat less.

Q. How many tracts of land have been surveyed, and opened for settlement during your incumbency in the office or since you assumed the duties of register?

A. About what has been surveyed since I have been in office?

Q. I mean platted and thrown open to entry? Do you understand?

A. Oh, the number of plats filed in my office which were subsequently officially filed by me as Register, I believe; my recollection there is only two days.

Q. Only two days? A. Yes, sir.

Q. And at each of those times there was a line-up at the office door? A. Yes.

Mr. TANNAHILL.—Mr. Ruick I suppose we can agree that the price paid for this land, all this land under the stone and timber law, was $2.50 an acre, so I will not have to have Mr. Bartlett refer to his record.

Mr. RUICK.—Yes.

The COURT.—Yes.

Q. Mr. Bartlett, I will ask *yo* to state whether or not $2.50 is the minimum or maximum price to be

(Testimony of Thomas Heroditus Bartlett.)

paid for land acquired by virtue of or under the timber and stone act?      A.   The minmum price.

Q.   And is there a maximum price?

A.   Under certain condition.

Q.   Under the timber and stone law?

A.   Yes, sir.

Q.   What is it?

A.   Within the reservation, when land is filed on under the act within the reservation there is a maximum price of $5, just double.

Q.   Within what reservation?

A.   The Nez Perce Indian Reservation.

Q.   That is also where they have to pay the price for the land under the law, declaring or throwing the reservation open for settlement?

A.   Five dollars is the entire price.   There is no additional after that for the taking of the land.

Be it remembered that then and there the following proceeding was had:

Q.   Mr. Bartlett, I will ask you if your record discloses anything irregular in regard to those entries?

Mr. RUICK.—Objected to as incompetent, irrelevant and immaterial, and the record is the best evidence.

The COURT.—Objection sustained; to which ruling of the Court the defendants then and there excepted, and the exception was allowed by the Court.

Be it remembered that then and there the following proceeding was had:

(Testimony of Thomas Heroditus Bartlett.)

Q. I will ask you, Mr. Bartlett, if your record discloses anything irregular in regard to these contests of which you have testified?

Mr. RUICK.—Same objection.

The COURT.—Objection sustained.

To which ruling of the Court the defendants then and *tthree* excepted, which exception was allo*wd* by the Court.

Be it remembered that then and there the following proceeding was had:

Q. I will a*s*lso ask you, Mr. Bartlett, if it is not also a fact that any person can file as many contests as he sees fit under the rules of the department?

Mr. RUICK.—I object on the same ground and calling for the conclusion of the witness, based upon the law.

The COURT.—Yes, objection sustained; to which ruling of the Court the*n* defendants then and there excepted, which exception was allowed.

Be it remembered that then and there the following proceeding was had:

I will ask you, Mr. Bartlett, if it is not a fact that the local office and the general land office encouraged the filing of contests.

Mr. RUICK.—Objected to as incompetent, irrelevant and immaterial, and calling for a conclusion of the witness.

Objection sustained.

To which ruling of the Court the defendants then and *tehere* excepted, which exception was allowed by the Court.

(Testimony of Thomas Heroditus Bartlett.)

Be it remembered that then and there the foolowing proceeding was had:

I will ask you, Mr. Bartlett, if you can ascertain from your records and tell us how many homestead entries there were filed on the 25th day of April, 1904, covering land in the townships and the vicinity of this land of which you have testified, as being filed on by different timber and stone entrymen?

Mr. RUICK.—That is wholly irrelevant, incompetent and immaterial, and not proper cross-examination; purely a matter for them to bring out. We made no reference or allusion to it at all.

The COURT.—I think in the form that it is in, I will sustain the objection to that question. It is possible that some of the testimony ought to be elicited, or will be proper when the defendants make their case. The question is so general and so sweeping that it is difficult for the Court to rule upon it intelligently, and I think, Mr. Tannahill, the Court will require you to confine your attention to that particular transaction of which the witness testified when interrogated by the prosecution. *I* other words, proceed with the cross-examination if you desire, and cross-examine him as to the particular transactions he has testified about. To which ruling of the Court the defendants then and there excepted, which exception was allowed by the Court.

Q. Mr. Bartlett, can you give us the date that a homestead entry was filed upon which the contests were filed by Mr. Dwyer, referred to by you in your direct examination?

(Testimony of Thomas Heroditus Bartlett.)

A. That is all contained in the record.

Q. We want it now?

A. I can go over it again.

The COURT.—Have you got the record?

A. I think it is all contained in the contest docket.

The COURT.—Get the contest docket and see. If it has been read into the record, then it will not be read again.

Mr. TANNAHILL.—I understand these were all on the same day, and I want to get the date.

The COURT.—That is what I understood counsel desired to do.

A. I have the date entered on page 72 in the matter of William Dwyer against George James. It is February 24th, 1904. All these dates of entry are marked in each case, and it has been entered in the record.

Q. Are they on the same day?

A. Pretty much.

Mr. RUICK.—Is this the date of the filing of the contest?

Mr. TANNAHILL.—No, the date of the filing of the homestead.

A. No, they are not all on the same day; suppose I give you the exceptions not filed February 24th?

Q. Yes.

Mr. RUICK.—State the rule.

A. The rule most of them those which I do not read, were filed on February 24th, 1904. Most of the homestead entries were made upon February 24th,

ρ it remembered tht then and there the foolow-
)roceeding was hac:

vill ask you, Mr. }artlett, if you can ascertain
ι: your records andtell us how many homestead
,·s there were file' on the 25th day of April,
| covering land in te townships and the vicinity
     land of which ya have testified, as being filed
)· different timber ad stone entrymen?
[ι RUICK.—That s wholly irrelevant, incom-
     and immaterial, and not proper cross-exam-
·  ·ι; purely a matteifor them to bring out.  We
|  no reference or alusion to it at all.
         ^OURT.—I thin: in the form that it is in, I
     ·stain the objectìn to that question.  It is
     ·: that some of ιe testimony ought to be
     , or will be prope when the defendants make
     ;ise.  The questioι is so general and so sweep-
     ιt it is difficult fo the Court to rule upon it
     ·ently, and I thinļ Mr. Tannahill, the Court
     ιuire you to confin your attention to that par-
         transaction of viich the witness testified
         interrogated by he prosecution.  *I* other
         proceed with the coss-examination if you de-
     ,  1 cross-examine hiɪ as to the particular trans-
     oı  he has testified aout.  To which ruling of
     C'  rt the defendant then and there excepted,
     ch  ·ception was alloved by the Court.
).     ·. Bartlett, can ɔu give us the date that a
nest  ɪ entry was file upon which the contests
ɪe fil'  bɣ Mr. Dwɣer, 'eferred to by you in .your
     ex  .ination?

(Testimony of Thomas _ .eroditu Bartlett.)

A. That is all contai ed in te record.

Q. We want it now?

A. I can go over it a .in.

The COURT.—Have )u got he record?

A. I think it is all cc ained n the contest docket.

The COURT.—Get tl contes docket and see. If it has been read into th record then it will not be read again.

Mr. TANNAHILL.- unde tand these were all on the same day, and I ant to et the date.

The COURT.—That what understood counsel desired to do.

A. I have the date ered a page 72 in the matter of William Dwyer ainst corge James. It is February 24th, 1904. ll the dates of entry are marked in each case, a l it ha been entered in the record.

Q. Are they on the me da?

A. Pretty much.

Mr. RUICK.—Is tl the de of the filing of the contest?

Mr. TANNAHILL -No, th date of the filing of the homestead.

A. No, they are n all on e same day; suppose I give you the excepti s not fed February 24th?

Q. Yes.

Mr. RUICK.—Stat the rul.

A. The rule most f then those which I do not read, were filed on Feb lary 2th, 1904. Most of the homestaed entries we mad upon February 24th,

(Testimony of Thomas Heroditus Bartlett.)

1904. Those which were not made on that day I will so designate:

Homestead entry No. 10,638, by John McHardie was on April 18th, 1904.

That of William B. Walker, No. 10,579, is indicated in *ths* docket as made April *6h,* 1904.

My pencil memorandum says April 1st. In order to verify it *recouse* will have to be had to the Register's record of Homestead entries which I have here.

Q. Well, it is about the time; that is what I wanted, Mr. Bartlett? A. Yes, either of them.

That of John B. Harlan 10,638, was made upon March 9th, 1904;

That of Mr. Kincaid, that is a timber and stone, however, No. 1395; it has nothing to do with the homestead.

Q. I will ask you, Mr. Bartlett, if Mr. Kincaid did not change his entry to a homestead?

A. I could probably see by looking at the other register.

Q. We will just conclude and I will ask you a question about that afterwards.

A. The homestead of either Roscoe W. Sanders or of Colon B. Saunders, No. 10,466, appears here to have been made February 24th, 1904; you can strike that out; that is no exception; that is all.

Q. Now, when was that changed to a timber and stone? A. Which one?

Q. This Saunders entry?

A. September 9th, 1905.

(Testimony of Thomas Heroditus Bartlett.)

Q.   Was that one of the contests in which Register West decided in favor of Sanders and Receiver Garby decided in favor of Dwyer?

A.   Decision of Register in favor of entryman, and that of the receiver in favor of Saunders.

Q.   You say that was changed to a stone and timber September 9th, 1905?

A.   It so appears here; I can verify that by reference to the timber and stone book.

Q.   Now, Mr. Bartlett, were any of these entries proved up on under the homestead law as a homestead, these entries involved in these contests by Dwyer?     A.   In all the Dwyer contests?

Q.   Yes?

A.   I should have to make a longer inspection of the records to answer that intelligently.   I cannot do that very well in a few minutes.   I can tell you what my impression is but I cannot tell you as a matter of fact.

Q.   Give us your impression then; if you wish to verify it you may do so.

Mr. RUICK.—I object to that; it is not fair to the witness.   We know of one that was not; we know of one that was; that is the Harland case; we know that one.

Mr. MOORE.—That has not been proven up; that contest has not been decided; it is on appeal now to the Secretary of the Interior.

The WITNESS.—I think the Harland case is still before the Department, if I remember rightly.

Mr. RUICK.—The Department of the Interior?

(Testimony of Thomas Heroditus Bartlett.)

A.  Yes.

Mr. RUICK.—We have no objection to his stating that fact; he can state it, but he stated he wanted to inspect the record?

A.  No, I cannot state it without the record.

Q.  You can check up on that if you think you have not sufficient information to give us an answer now.  I think you can give us your best recollection of it from the examination you have made.

Mr. RUICK.—We object to that; let Mr. Bartlett have time to check up the book and see.

The WITNESS.—I can't answer that at the present moment.

Be it remembered that then and there the following proceeding was had:

Q.  Now, Mr. Bartlett, how many other homestead entries were filed at the same time with these homesteads which were contested by William Dwyer? That is, on February 24th, 1904, covering lands in these same townships as involved in these contested entries by Mr. Dwyer.

Mr. RUICK.—Objected to as incompetent, irrelevant and immaterial, going entirely outside, and not proper cross-examination.

The COURT.—Objection sustained.

To which ruling of the Court the defendants then and there excepted, which exception was allowed by the Court.

Q.  Now, we will ask, Mr. Bartlett, to examine his record and ascertain whether or not any of these homesteads involved in the contests of William

(Testimony of Thomas Heroditus Bartlett.)

Dwyer were ever proved up on under the homestead law?

The COURT.—That is these fifteen or sixteen contests referred to?

Mr. TANNAHILL.—Yes, your Honor.

The COURT.—I though that the record already showed that there eas either a relinquishment or the contest allowed. Don't the record alread show that?

Mr. RUICK.—Yes. In other words, he is asked to refresh his memory or make an inspection and check up that which he read this morning, and was already in the record, and which can be checked up by anybody, just as well as by this witness.

Mr. TANNAHILL.—There are some of those entries about which Mr. Bartlett testified that stopped before final proof was made.

A. Concerning those I cannot tell you what the final disposition was.

Q. Isn't your homestead record here?

A. Yes, sir.

Q. Can't you tell from that?.

A. I can tell you what the record shows but I have read that and it is all in the record at the present time.

Q. Haven't you sufficient information here to tell us whether any of these were proved upon under the homestead law?

A. No. The final disposition of some of them if they are not already indicated in the record, I can give you nothing more with the data at hand here.

The COURT.—I don't think you understand the question.

(Testimony of Thomas Heroditus Bartlett.)

Mr. RUICK.—Mr. Bartlett, can you give any information on that subject other than the information that you gave this morning?

A.  I cannot.

Q.  That you read into the record?

A.  I cannot.

### Cross-examination Resumed.

Q.  Mr. Bartlett, how many of those entries were proved up on under the stone and timber law or scrip location?    A.  I can read them over.

The COURT.—I think both sides have asked some questions from the witness that he is unable to answer.   And if Mr. Bartlett had those facts in hand, I should perhaps let you ask him to state them, but I don't like to take up the time now to allow him to make an inspection of the record.   He may be excused and you *ay* call him for that.   It will take too much time to go*v* over that in detail.

Mr. TANNAHILL.—That is all I want from Mr. Bartlett.   That is all of the cross-examination.

The COURT.—If you will state to him what you want, and let him run over the books and collate these facts, the Court will permit you to recall him, that is, these two matters; you understand it; one is as to what became of the original homestead entries and the other is what became of the timber and stone filings that were made after May.

Mr. TANNAHILL.—Yes, your Honor.   I will also ask Mr. Bartlett to especially look up the entry of *r*. Kincaid, the homestead *antr*ч of Mr. Kincaid.

(Testimony of Thomas Heroditus Bartlett.)

The contest appears on page 190, also the Sounders entry.

Mr. BARTLETT.—(The Witness.) You mean what has become of the result?

Mr. TANNAHILL.—Yes, sir.

(Excused.)

Be it remembered that then and there the following proceding was had:

Mr. RUICK.—We now offer in evidence the copy duly certified of the record of Receiver's receipts No. 3896, issued at the United States Land Office, Lewiton, Idaho, to Joel R. Benton, on the 25th day of September, 1902. It is offered for the purpose of showing the transfer of title to this land by Joel R. Benton to C. W. Robnett and a preliminary to the introduction of the deed.

Mr. FORNEY.—We object to it as incompetent, irrelevant and immaterial, not properly authenticated, no proper foundation having been laid, and on the further ground that it does not tend to prove any of the issues embraced within the pleadings in this case; that it does not further any transaction embraced within the period described within the indictment; that it is too remote, having been made long prior to the time set for any count in the indictment, viz., September 25th, 1902.

Mr. RUICK.—We will not press this offer at this time, your Honor, to save time. It would be admissible under the ruling of your Honor under the promise to connect it. I would say, however, for certain reasons, we would prefer to introduce it at this time, and

(Testimony of Thomas Heroditus Bartlett.)

I would say that we propose to connect it with the defendants Kester and Kettenbach, and also with the defendant Dwyer by the admissions of the latter before we conclude our evidence in the case. This is one of the series, if your Honor please.

The COURT.—I think I will permit you to introduce it. Is that similar to a number *tat* you are going to offer?

Mr. RUICK.—Yes, sir.

To which ruling of the Court the defendants then and there excepted, which exception was allowed by the Court.

T. H. BARTLETT recalled.

Cross-examination by Mr. TANNAHILL.

Q. Mr. Bartlett, are you able to give us any further information as to how many of the homestaed claimants or entrymen involved in the contests filed by Mr. Dwyer proved up under the homestaed law?

A. Yes, sir; none of them.

Q. How many of them proved up under the stone and timber law?

A. I find that Colon B. Saunders and Kincaid have received final receipts.

Q. How many of them relinquished before proof was made and scrip selections were filed, if any?

A. None, that I noticed.

Redirect Examination by Mr. RUICK.

(At the request of the District Attorney, the whole of the examination of this witness since 4 o'clock P. M. was read and re-read.)

(Testimony of Thomas Heroditus Bartlett.)

Mr. RUICK.—I will have to ask some questions; that is not clear to me. I desire to ask another question.

Q. Are there any of these homestead entrymen now holding their land intact except Harland under the original homestead location, homestead entry?

A. The records appear to indicate that Antone Wohlen's case is not disposed of.

Q. What is that?

A. The case of Antone Wohlen, William Dwyer vs. Antone Wohlen, H. E. 10512, that appears intact upon the plat, and has not been cancelled, either by relinquishment or direction from the Commissioner.

Q. And the Harlands?

A. The Harlen H. E. entry, 10538 appears intact.

Q. Is that all, Mr. Bartlett?

A. That is all I have to say.

Q. To clear the matter up, Mr. Bartlett, what homestead entries are still intact?

A. The Harlan entry and the Wohlen entry.

Q. What homesteaders changed their filings from homestead to timber and stone?

A. Kincaid and Saunders.

Q. In each of the other instances rcred to, in this matter of these contests, then the parties who were placed upon this land, or who filed a timber and stone on these contested homesteads made final proof under their timber and stone entries. I am not speaking now of the homesteaders, but the timber and stone claimants. A. I understand.

(Testimony of Thomas Heroditus Bartlett.)

Q. You finally proved—they made final proof and payment for the lands these other lands?

A. Yes, sir. The record so indicates.

Q. The other lands with the exception of these three which you have mentioned?

The COURT.—Four.

Q. Did you include Wohlen as one?

A. I stated Wohlen as one.

Q. Harlan and Wohlen are still original entry-men?    A. And Saunders and Kincaid.·

Q. And Saunders and Kincaid changed theirs to stone and timber?    A. Yes, sir.

Q. And proved up?    A. Yes, sir.

Q. And the balance were proved up on by the parties who filed timber and stone on them after the relinquishment had been obtained?

A. Yes, sir. Each of the parties other than those of the entrymen.

Q. Those are the ones you have already testified to this morning?    A. Yes, sir.

Recross-examination by Mr. TANNAHILL.

Q. Did you examine to see whether or not there were none of the others who changed ther homestacds to timber and stone?    A. Yes, sir.

Q. You arr sure of that?

A. We all are fallible but I think so; I examined it closely intending to find whether that was the case or not.

Be it remembered that then and there the following proceeding was had

(Testimony of Thomas Heroditus Bartlett.)

Mr. RUICK.—(To the Stenographer.) Kindly read my offer and the objection of counsel in connection with the final receipt I last offered.

(Offer read by the stenographer.)

Mr. RUICK.—What was the objection made to that?

(Stenographer reads the objection made by Mr. Forney.)

Mr. RUICK.—What is the ruling?

Mr. FORNEY.—Let me change the objection. It is still objected to as incompetent, irrelevant and immaterial in that it is not properly authenticated, etc., the same as was read by the stenographer.

The COURT.—I overruled the objection. Go on, Mr. Ruick. To much time is being wasted.

To which ruling of the Court the defendants then and there excepted, which exception was by the Court allowed, and said document is admitted in evidence, and is marked 1-x, and is as follows:

"No. 3896. Receiver's office at Lewiston, Idaho, September, 25th, 1902.

Received of Joel R. Benton of Leiston, Nez Perce County, Idaho, the sum of four hundred dollars and blank cents, being in full for the north half of the northwest quarter, and the southwest quarter of the northwest quarter and the northwest quarter of the southwest quarter of Section 35, in Township thirty-seven north, range No. 5, East B. M., containing 160

(Testimony of Thomas Heroditus Bartlett.)
acres, and blank one hundredths acres at $2.50 per acre.   C

       (Signed)   CHARLES H. GARBY,
                            Receiver.

$400.00.

Application fee,   $10.00.

Testimony fee recd., 1.25.

Number of written words, 555.

Rate per hundred words, 22½cents.

(Endorsed)  Recorded at the request of C. W. Robnett, October 1st, 1903 at 2 o'clock P. M.

       HORACE M. DAVENPORT,
               County Recorder,
          By A. H. Conner, Deputy.

And duly certified by the Recorder of Shoshone County, Idaho.

Be it remembered that then and there the following proceeding was had:

Mr. RUICK.—We now offer at this time other and similar final receipts in the following cases, which I will identify:

Mr. FORNEY.—We ask that our objection to all these documents may go as they come in.

Mr. RUICK.—That is understood.

The COURT.—Yes.

Mr. RUICK.—We offer a similar receipt Number 3898, issued to Maud L. Stowe, dated September 26, 1902, and ask that it be marked Plaintiff's Exbibit. 2X.

(Testimony of Thomas Heroditus Bartlett.)

Mr. RUICK.—We offer a smiliar receipt number 4249, of date March 11th, 1903, to Robert N. Wright, and ask that it be marked 3X.

We offer in evidence a similar receipt number 4251, issued March 11th, 1903, to Maude V. Wright, of Lewiston, Idaho, and ask that the same be marked 4X.

We offer a smilar receipt numbered 4291, issued to Orville E. Norberg of Lewiston, Idaho, dated April 10th, 1903, and ask that the same be marked Plaintiff's Exhibit 5X.

We offer a similar receipt Number 4306, dated April 16th, 1903, issued to Pearl Washburn of Lewiston, Idaho, and ask that the same be marked Plaintiff's Exhibit 6X.

We offer a similar receipt 4384, dated June 15th, 1903, issued to Ellsworth M. Herrington, of Lewiston, Idaho, and ask that the same be marked Plaintiff's Exhibit 7X.

We offer a similar receipt 4383, dated June 15th, 1903, issued to John H. Little of Lewiton, Idaho, and ask that the same be marked Plaintiff's Exhibit 8X.

We offer a similar receipt 4390, dated June 17th, 1903, issued to Benjamin F. Balshor of Lewiston, Idaho, and ask that the same be marked Plaintiff's Exhibit 9X.

We offer a similar receipt to 4389, June 17th, 1903, issued to Wren Pierce of Lewiston, Idaho, and ask that the same be marked Plaintiff's Exhibit 10X.

We offer a similar receipt, 4395, dated June 18th, 1903, issued to Francis M. Long, of Lewiston, Idaho,

(Testimony of Thomas Heroditus Bartlett.)

and ask that the same be marked Plaintiff's Exhibit 11X.

We offer a similar receipt issued to John H. Long, No. 4396, dated June 18th, 1903, and ask that the same be marked Plaintiff's Exhibit 12X.

We offer a similar receipt, 4397, dated June 18th, 1903, issued to Benjamin F. Long of Lewiston, Idaho, and ask that the same be marked Plaintiff's Exhibit 13X.

We off*e* a similar receipt 4314 of date June 26th, 1903, issued to Bertsell H. Ferris, of Lewiston, Idaho, and ask that the same be marked Plaintiff's Exhibit 14X.

We offer a similar receipt number 4415, dated June 26th, 1903, issued to George Ray Robinson, of Lewiston, Idaho, and ask that the same be marked Plaintiff's Exhibit 15X.

We offer in evidence a similar receipt, 4454, issued July 30th, 1903, to Walter S. Roberts, of Gifford, Idaho, and ask that the same be marked Plaintiff's Exhibit 16X.

We offer a similar*e* receipt number 4460, of date August 7th, 1903, issued to Harry S. Brown, of Troy, Idaho, *ad* ask that the same be marked Plaintiff's Exhibit 17X.

We offer in evidence a similar receipt number 4411, dated June 26th, 1903, issued to George Morrison of Lewiston, Idaho, and ask that the same be marked Plaintiff's Exhibit 18X.

We offer a similar receipt 4412, dated June 26th, 1903, issued to Edward M. Hyde, of Lewiston, Idaho,

(Testimony of Thomas Heroditus Bartlett.)

and ask that the same be marked Plaintiff's Exbibit 19X.

We offer a similar receipt Number 4294, of date June 17th, 1903, issued to Frederick W. Newman, of Lewiston, Idaho, and ask that the same be marked Plaintiff's Exhibit 20X.

We offer a similar receipt 4391, dated June 17th, 1903, issued to James C. Evans, of Dent, Shoshone County, Idaho, and ask that the *sae* be marked Plaintiff's Exhibit 21X.

We offer in evidence a similar receipt 4392, dated June 17th, 1903, issued to L. E. Bishop, of Dent, Idaho, and ask that the same be marked Plaintiff's Exhibit 22X.

We offer in evidence similar receipts 4393, dated June 17th, issued to Joseph B. Clute, of Dent, Idaho, and ask that the same be marked Plaintiff's Exhibit 23X.

We offer in evidence a similar receipt number 4405, dated June 23d, 1903, is*ue*d to Charles Dent of Dent, Idaho, and ask that the same be marked Plaintiff's Exhibit 25X.

We offer in evidence a similar receipt 4352, of date May 20th, 1903 is*ue*d to Van V. Robertson, of Lewiston, Idaho, and ask that the same be marked Plaintiff's Exhibit 26X.

Mr. FORNEY.—The defendants object to each and every of the foregoing instruments offered as irrelevant, incompetent and immaterial, and not properly authenticated, no foundation having been

(Testimony of Thomas Heroditus Bartlett.)

laid, and on the further ground that they do not tend
to prove any of the issues embraced within this case,
that they do not refer to any transaction embraced
within the period described in the indictment, that
the facts established thereby are too remote, having
been long prior to the time set forth in any caount
in said indictment. And that they do not tend to
prove any overt act allleged in the indictment or connect the defendants or either of them with any of the
alleged overt acts as set forth in the indictment.

The COURT.—Objection overruled.

To which ruling of the Court the defendants then
and there excepted, which exception was allowed
by the Court, and said documents were admitted in
evidence, and marked as requested, and each of which
are identical with Plaintiff's Exhibit 1X, except as
to names, dates and the lands described.

Mr. RUICK.—(Continuing:) In not reading
these into the record, I will say that they are here
for the inspection of counsel. I will say that they
show by the certificates of the recorder that the receipt of M. L. Stowe, Robert N. Wright, Maude D.
Wright, Orville Norberg, Pearl Wshburne, Ellsworth Harrington, John .H. Little, Benjamin F.
Bashor, Wren Pierce, Frances M. Long, John H.
Long, and Benjamin F. Long, were each and all recorded at the request of W. F. Kettenbach.

The Stowe certificate being recorded October 3d,
1902; Joel R. Benton, October 1st, 1902; Wright
and Wright, March 16*h*, 1903; Norburg and Wash-
burne, April 18th, 1903; Little, Bashor and Pierce

(Testimony of Thomas Heroditus Bartlett.)

June 20th, 1903; and the Longs June 22d, 1903; Ferris and Robertson July 1st, 1903; recorded at Kettenbach's request. (The Joel R. Benton certificate was recorded at the request of C. W. Robnett.)

The following were recorded at the request of Geo. H. Kester: Walter S. Roberts, 1903—they are all of the same date, so I need not repeat—Harry S. Brown, George Morrison, Edward M. Hyde, Frederick W. Newman, James C. Evans, L. E. Bishop, Joseph B. Clute, Charles Smith, Charles Dent, while that of Van V. Robertson was filed January 15th, 1904, at the request of C. W. Robnett, as was also the certificate of Joel R. Benton, on October 1st, 1902.

Be it remembered that then and there the following proceeding was had:

Mr. RUICK.—We now offer in evidence certified copies, or copies duly certified, of deeds from the following named persons, to William F. Kettenbach.

Mr. FORNEY.—The same general objection will run to these also.

Mr. RUICK.—Yes, the same general objection will run. The first is the deed of John H. Little. This deed is an instrument No. 2814, and is of date Octoer 25th, 1904, between John H. Little, and Edna Fife Little, his wife, of Lewiston, Idaho, and William F. Kettenbach of Lewiston, Idaho, consideration one dollar, conveying lands in township 39 north, Range 3 east, being the same lands mentioned in his final receipt heretofore introduced in evidence. This instrument was recorded at the request of

(Testimony of Thomas Heroditus Bartlett.)

William F. Kettenbach on October 22d, 1904, and I ask that it be marked Plaintiff's Exhibit 1-Y.

We offer a similar deed by Francis M. Long, and Anna E. Long, his wife, to William F. Kettnbach, of date August 9th, 1904, consideration one dollar, conveying land in township 39 North, Range 3 East, recorded at the request of W. F. Kettenbach on August 12th, 1904, as plaintiff's Exhibit 2-Y.

We offer instrument No. 1820, of July 25th, 1904, by Benjamin F. Long, to William F. Kettenbach, consideration $1.00, conveying lands in Township 39 north, Range 3 East, described in Long's final receipt, and ask that this be marked Plaintiff's Exhibit 3-Y.

We next offer in evidence a similar deed, being instrument number 1793, of date July 21st, 1904, from John H. Long to William F. Kettenbach, consideration one dollar, conveying lands described in his final receipt, situated *ij* Township 39 North, Range 3 cast, and recorded at the request of W. F. Kettenbach, on July 23d, 1904, and ask *tat* the same be marked Plaintiff's Exhibit 4-Y.

We offer a similar deed, number 1324, dated May 31st, 1904, from Wren Pierce and Emma Pierce, his wife, to William F. Kettenbach, consideration one dollar, being the lands described in Pierce's final receipt, in township 39 North, Range 3 East, recorded at the request of Kettenbach on June 3d, 1904, and ask that the same be marked Plaintiff's Exhibit 5-Y.

We offer in evidence a deed, being instrument No. 2173, dated June 23d, 1903, from Charles Dent to

(Testimony of Thomas Heroditus Bartlett.)

William F. Kettenbach, and George H. Kester, consideration $1,000, conveying lands described in his final receipt, in township 39 North, Range 3 East, recorded at the request of George H. Kester, on August 10th, 1903, and ask that the same be marked Plaintiff's Exhibit 6-Y.

I will say that the deeds which I shall now offer until I otherwise state will be all to William F. Kettenbach, and George H. Kester, of Lewiston, in the County of Nez Perce, State of Idaho, and the consideration will be $1,000 in each deed, except as I otherwise state.

This is instrument 2171, *o* date June 23d, executed by Charles Smith, conveying lands described in a final receipt, *i* sect*k*on 15, Township 39 North, Range 3 East, recorded at the request of Kester on August 10th, 1903, and ask that *te* same be marked Plaintiff's Exhibit 7-Y.

We now offer deed instrument Number 2169, from Jos. B. *Clute,* I ask—I would better name the consideration, the same parties, date June 17th, 1903, consideration $1,000 conveying lands described in Cluet's final receipt in section 26, Township 39 North, range 3 East, recorded at the request of Kester on August 10th, 1903, and ask that the same be marked Plaintiff's Exhibit 8-Y.

We offer deed instrument numbered 2167, dated June 17th, 1903, by Lon E. Bishop to parties named, the same consideration, and conveying lands described in his final receipt in section 23, Township 39 North, Range 3 East, recorded at the request of

(Testimony of Thomas Heroditus Bartlett.)
Mr. Kester on August 10th, 1903, as *Plaintiff* Exhibit 9-Y.

We offer deed, being instrument number 2165, of date June 17th, 1903, by James C. Evans to the parties named, the same consideration, being lands described in his final receipt, in section 25, Township 39 North, Range 3 East, *an* recorded at the request of Kester on August 10th, 1903, and ask that the same be marked Plaintiff's Exhibit 10-Y.

I now offer in evidence deed Number 2163, dated June 17th, 1903, by Frederick W. Newman and wife to the parties named, the consideration in the same, conveying lands described in Mr. Newan's final receipt in section 23, township 39 North, Range 3 East; recorded at the request of Kester, on August 10th, 1903, and ask that the same be marked Plaintiff's Exhibit 11-Y.

We now offer in evidence deeds instrument No. 2161, of date June 26th, 1903, by Edward M. *Hide,* and wife, to the same parties, consideration $1, being the lands describee in Hyde's final receipt in section 22, township 39 North, range 3 East, recorded at the request of Mr. Kester, August 10th, 1903, same to be marked Plaintiff's Exhibit 12-Y.

We next offer in evidence deed instrument number 2159, of date June 26th, 1903, by George Morrison and wife, to the same parties, consideration $1, being lands described in Morrison's final receipt*l* Section 22. Township 39 North, Range 3 East, recorded at

(Testimony of Thomas Heroditus Bartlett.)

the request of Kester in August 10th, 1903, and ask that the same be marked Plaintiff's Exhibit 13-Y.

We now offer deed, instrument number 3076, of date Octo*br* 9th, 1903, by Drury M. Gammon to Clarence W. Robnett, consideration $1, conveying lands in section 25 and 35 in township 40 North, range 3 east. This deed and the subsequent deeds which I shall rea*e* until otherwise stated will ea*c*h and all run to *Clarence Robnett.* This deed was recorded at the request of the Lewiston National Bank, on November 16th, 1904, and ask *tht* the same be marked Plaintiff's Exhibit 14-Y. We next offer deed No. 830 of date March 15th, 1904, from Nettie Knight and Edward L. Knight, her husband, of Lewiston, to Clarence W. Robnett, consideration $1500, conveying lands in section 35, township 34 North, Range 5 e*s*st. This deed is recorded at the request of Shoshone Abstract Company, on March 21st, 1904, and we ask th*a* the same be marked Plaintiff's Exhibit 15-Y.

We next offer a deed dated March 15th, 19*0*, between Edw*rd* L. Knight and Nettie Knight, his wife, to Clarence W. Robnett, consideration $1,500, conveying lands in section 35, Township 34 Nor*t.* Range 5 East, recorded at the request of Shoshone Abstr*ua*ct Comp*n*y on the 21st day of Mar*c*h, 1904, and ask that it be marked Plaintiff's Exhibit 16-Y.

We now offer deed number 834, dated March 14th, 1904, between Nellie Harri*gn*ton, a single woman of Lewiston, and Clarence W. Robnett*t* of the same place, consideration $1,500, conveying lands in section 35, Township 34 North, Range 5 East, recorded at the

(Testimony of Thomas Heroditus Bartlett.)

request of Shoshone Abstract Company on March 21st, 1904, and ask that it be marked Plaintiff's Exbibit 17-Y.

We offer deed instrument number 832, dated March 14th, 1904, between Minnie Harington, a single woman of Lewiston, Idaho, and Clarence W. Robnett of the same place, consideration being $1,500 conveying lands in section 35, township 34 North, range 5 East, recorded at the request of the Shoshone Abstract Company, on March 21st, 1904, and ask that the same be marked Plaintiff's Exhibit 18-Y.

We next offer deed number 463, of date May 20th, 1903, between Emery F. Gordon, of Lewiston and Clarence W. Robnett of the same place, consideraton $1,500, conveying land in section 30, Township 38 Nrth, Range 2 east, recorded at the request of the Shoshone Abstract Company February 8th, 1904, and ask that the same be marked Plaintiff's Exhibit 19-X.

We next offer deeed, instrument number 2727 dated May 25th, 1903, between Robert O. Waldman and wife, to Clarence W. Robnett, consideration $1,500, conveying lands in section 30, township 38 North, Range 2 East, recorded at the request of the Shoshone Absctract Compny on October 2d, 1908, and ask that the same be marked Plaintiff's Exhibit 20-Y.

We offe deed instrument number 1711, bearing date June 2d, 1903, between Carrie D. Maris, of Lewiston, Idaho, to Clarence W. Robnett of the same place. Consideration $1500, ebeing lands in sections 12 and 13, township 36 North, Range 5 east, nd ask that the same be marked Plaintiff's Exhibit 21-Y.

(Testimony of Thomas Heroditus Bartlett.)

We next offer deed number 1140, dated December 29th, 1902, between Joel H. Benton and wife of Lewiston, Idaho, to C. W. Robnett of the same place, consideration $1600, conveying lands in section 15, Township 39 North, range 3 east. This was recorded at the request of the Shoshone Abstract Company, April 27th, 1903, and I ask that the same be marked Plaintiff's Exhibit 22-Y.

We next offer in evidence deed number 1142, bearing date January 30th, 1903, by Mattie W. Benton and Joel R. Benton, her husband, of Lewiston, Idaho, to Clarence W. Robnett, consideration $1600, conveying lands in section 20, Township 40 north, range 4 east, recorded at the request of Shoshone Abstract Company on April 27th, 1903, and ask that the same be marked Plaintiff's Exhibit 23-Y.

We next offer in evidence deed No. 1138 dated in the month of January, 1902, with the day blank, executed by W. B. Benton, of Lewiston, Idah, to C. W. Robnett of the same place, consideration $1,600; lands being in section 15, Township 39 North, Range 3 East, recorded at the request of the Shoshone Abstract Company, April 27th, 1903, and ask that the same be marked Plaintiff's Exhibit 24-Y.

To each and all of which offers the defendants objected, on the ground that the same was irrelevant, incompetent and immaterial, not properly authenticated, no foundation having been laid, and on the further ground that it does not tend to prove any of the material issues embraced in this case, that it does not refer to any transaction embraced within the

(Testimony of Thomas Heroditus Bartlett.)

period described in the indictment, that it is too remote, having been made long prior to the time set
forth in any count in said indictement; *th* it does not
connect or tend to connect any of the defendants with
any of the alleged offenses set *fort* in the indictment.

Which objection was by the Court overruled, to
which ruling of the Court the defendants the*a*n and
there excepted which exception was allowed b\ the
Court, and said instrument*x* and each of them were
admitted in evidence, and marked as requested.

By agreement of counsel the statement of the pros-
ecuting attorney of the contents of each instrument
offered is a sufficient copy of the exhibits for this
record.

Be it remembered that then and there the following proceeding was had:

Mr. JOHNSON.—We will now offer in evidence
certified copies of the deed from the following named
persons to the following named persons: certified to
be true copies by the recorder of Shoshone County,
State of Idaho:

(And the said following instruments were offered
separately for the purpose of identification.)

This is instrument 1082, dated the 16th da\ of
April, 1903, from Pearl Washburn and Charles O.
Washburn to W. F. Kettenbach, amount of mortgage
$400, covering lands in section 27, township 40 north,
Range 4 East, given to secure a note of even date for
$400, due one year after date, and recorded at the re-
quest of  W. F. Ket*e*nbach,  by  the  recorder  of

(Testimony of Thomas Heroditus Bartlett.)

Shsohone County, on the 8th day of *Q*pril, 1903. We will start this as Plaintiff's Exhibit 1-Z.

We now offer in evidence instrument 1080, being a mortgage given by Orville E. Norberg, a single man, to W. F. Kettenbach, dated the 11th day of April 1903, securing a no*t* of the same day for $550 due one ye*q*r after date and recorded by the recorder of Shoshone County at the request of W. F. Kette*n*ach, on the 18th day of April, 1903, and ask that the same be marked Plaintiff's Exhibit 2-Z.

We offer in evidence instrument No. 834, being a mortgage from Maud D. Wright and Robe*ry*t N. Wright, husband and wife, to W. F. Kettenbach, dated the 12th day of March, 1903, to secure a note of the same date in the sum of five hundred dollars, an*d* recorded in the Shoshone County Records at the request of Mr. Kettenbach, on the *16h* day of March 1903, and ask that the same be marked Plainti*f*'s Exhibit 3-Z.

We offer in evidence instrument number 832, being a mortgage given by Robert N. Wright and Maud B. Wright, his wife, to W. F. Kettenbach, on the 12th day of March, 1903, to secure a note of the same date in the amount of $500, the note being signed b*y* R*p*bert N. Wright and re*c*orded by the recorder of Shoshone County at the request of W. F. Kettenbach, on the 16th day of Mar*c*h, 1903, and ask that the same be marked Plaintiff's Exhibit 4-Z.

We not offer in eviden*c*e a mortgage given b*y*—it does not seem to have any number mark, but is given by M. L. Stowe, an unmar*r*ied woman, to *W.* F.

(Testimony of Thomas Heroditus Bartlett.)

Kettenbach, on the 26*6*h day of September, 1902, to secure a note of the same date, in the sum of four hundred dollars, one year after date payable to said Kettenbach, and recorded in the records of Shoshone County, at the request of W. F. Kettenbach, on the 3d day of October, 1902, and ask that the same be marked Plaintiff's Exhibit 5-Z.

We now offer in evidence instrument Number 498 being a mortgage given by Van V. Robertson, and Nettie V. Robertson, his wife, to Clarence W. Robnett, dated the 20th day of May, 1903, to secure a note of the same date in the sum of five hundred dollars, the note being due one year after date and signed by Van D. Robertson. This is recorded in the records of Shoshone County, at the request of C. W. Robnett on the 15th day of February, 1904.

We ask the same be marked Plaintiff's Exhibit 6-Z.

We offer in evidence instrument 3583, being a mortgage given by Emma N. Foster, and unmarried woman, to Clarence W. Robnett, on the 11th day of November, 1902, to secure a note of the same date in the amount of $10, due 60 days after date, the note being signed by said Foster and running to Clarence W. Robnett and recorded at the request of George H. Kester, on the 11th day of December, 1903, in the records of Shoshone County.

We ask that the same be marked Plaintiff's Exhibit 7-Z.

I offer in evidence instrument number 3584, being a mortgage from Minnie E. Wagner, and E. C. Wagner,

(Testimony of Thomas Heroditus Bartlett.)

her husband, to Clarence W. Robnett, bearing date the 11th day of November, 1902, to secure a note of the same date in the sum of $510.00 due sixty days after date in favor of C. W. Robnett, the note being signed by Minnie E. Wagner, and recorded in the records of Shoshone County at the reqeest of George H. Kester on the 11th day of December, 1903, and ask that the same be marked Plaintiff's Exhibit 8-Z.

We offer in evidence instrument number 3583, I think it is, being a mortgage given by Harry S. Parker, and his wife of Clarkston, to C. W. Robnett, bearing date the 24th day of January, 1903, and given to secure a note signed by the same parties in favor of C. W. Robnett, in the sum of $625, due 12 months after date. This instrument was recorded at the request of George H. Kester, on the 11th day of December, 1903, by the recorder of Shohone County. That will be marked as Plaintiff's Exhibit 9-Z.

QWe offer in evidence instrument 1748, being a mortgge given by George Ray Robinson to Clarence W. Robnett, bearing date the 266h day of June, to secure a note of the same date, in favor of Clarence W. Robnett, in the sum of $728.75, note being due one year after date and signed by George Raw Robinson. This instrument was recorded at the request of W. F. Kettenbach, on the 1st day of July, 1903, in the recorder's office, Shoshone County, and ask that same be marked Plaintiff's Exhibit 10-Z.

We offer in evidence instrument number 1746, being mortgage given by Bertsell H. Ferris to Clarence W. Robnett, bearing date the 17th day of June, 1903,

(Testimony of Thomas Heroditus Bartlett.)

to secure a note bearing same date in favor of Clarence W. Robnett, and signed by Bertsell H. Ferris for $728.75, due one year afte date. This instrument was recorded at the request of W. F. Kettenbach, on the first day of July, 1903, in the recorder's office of Shoshone County, and ask that the same be marked Plaintiff's Exhibit 11-Z.

We offer in evidence instrument 1657, being a mortgage given by Benjamin F. Long, in favor of Clarence W. Robnett, on the 18th day of June, 1903, to secure a note bearing the same date in favor of Clarence W. Robnett, and signed by Benjamin F. Long, in the amount of $728.75, due one year after date, and recorded at the request of W. F. Kettenbach on the 22d day of June, 1903, in the recorder's office of Shoshone County, and ask that the same be marked Plaintiff's Exhibit 12-Z.

We offer in evidence instrument number 1665, being a mortgage given by John H. Long, to Clarence W. Robnett, bearing date the 18th day of June, 1903, given to secure a note of the same date, in favor of Clarence W. Robnett, signed by J. H. Long, in the sum of $710, due one year after date and recorded at the request of W. F. Kettenbach on the 22d day of June, 1903, in the recorder's office of Shoshone County, and ask that the same be marked Plaintiff' Exhibit 13-Z.

We offer in evidence instrument 1653, being a mortgage given by Francis M. Long and Anna E. Long, his wife, to Clarence W. Robnett, bearing date the 18th day of June, 1903, to secure a note bearing

(Testimony of Thomas Heroditus Bartlett.)

the same date and signed by the same parties in favor of Clarence W. Robnett in the sum of $728.75, due one year after date and this instrument was recorded at the request of said Kettenbach on the 22d day of June, 1903, in Shoshone County. We ask that the same be marked as Plaintiff's Exhibit 14-Z.

We ofer in evidence document 1640, being a mortgage given by Wren Pierce and his wife, in favor of Clarence W. Robnett, and the same being dated the 17th day of June, 1903, to secure a note bearing the same date, and signed by the same parties in favor of Clarence W. Robnett in the sum of $728.75, being due one year after date and recorded at the request of W. F. Kettenbach on the 20th day of June, 1903, and ask that the same be marked Plaintiff's Exhibit 15-Z.

We offer in evidence instrument 1638, being a mortgage given by B. F. Bashor and his wife in favor of Clarence W. Robnett, dated the 17th day of June, 1903, bearing the same date, signed by said B. F. Bashor in favor of Clarence W. Robnett in the sum of $550, due one year after date. This instrument ws recorded at the request of W. F. Kettenbach, on the 20th day of June, 1903, in the recorder's office of Shoshone County and ask that the same be marked Plaintiff's Exhibit 16-Z.

We ofer in evidence instrument nuber 1636, being a mortgage given by John H. Little and his wife in favor of Clarence W. Robnett, dated the 15th day of June, 1903, and given to secure a note bearing date

(Testimony of Thomas Heroditus Bartlett.)

the same day and signed by John H. Little in favor of said Robnett in the amount of $760; said note being due one year after date. This instrument was recorded at the request of W. F. Kettenbach on the 20th day of June, 1903, and we ask that the same be marked Plaintiff's Exhibit 17-Z.

We now offer in evidence instrument number 1634, being a mortgage given by Ellsworth N. Harrington and Anna E. Harrington, his wife, on the 16th day of June, 1903, to secure a note bearing the same date, signed by the same parties in favor of Clarence W. Robnett, in the amount $728.75, said note being due one year after date. This instrument was recorded at the request of W. F. Kettenbach, on the 20th day of June, 1903, in the recorder's office of Shoshone County. We ask that the same be marked Plaintiff's Exhibit 18-Z.

Mr. FORNEY.—The defendants object to each and all of the documents offered on the ground that the same are irrelevant, immaterail not properly authenticated, no foundation having been laid, and on the further ground that they do not prove or tend to prove any of the issues within this case, that they do not refer to any transaction embraced within the period described in the indictment, and that the facts proved or too remote, having taken place long prior to the time set forth in any account in said indictment, and that they do not connect or tend to connect any of the defendants with any of the alleged offenses set forth in the indictment.

(Testimony of Thomas Heroditus Bartlett.)

Which objection was by the Court overruled, to which ruling of the Court the defendants then and there excepted, which exception was allowed, and said instruments and each of them were admitted in evidence and marked as requested.

(And it is stipulated by counsel that the statement of the contents of each instrument made when o*f*ered is sufficient as a copy of the instrument for this record.)

May 28th, 1907, 9:30 A. M.

F. M. GOODWIN, a witness recalled on behalf of the Prosecution, testified further as follows, on

Direct Examination by Mr. RUICK.

Q. Mr. Goodwin, you have now in your custody what record of the—

A. The cash entry record of the Lewiston Land Office.

Q. You identif*y* that book a*s* such do you?

A. Yes, sir; inclu*dng* cash entries 2861 to 5457.

Q. You are familiar with the book and know that this is the book that it purports to be?

A. Yes, sir; I am. I have frequently examined it in that office.

Q. Give the data contained in the book relative to the timber and stone entries in the townships, Mr. Goodwin. You know the townships *y*ourself.

A. Well, I know township 35—36 North, 5 East; 34 North, 5 East; 39 North, 3 East; 39 North, 4 East; 40 North, 4 East; 40 North, 5 east; 38—5 and 38-6 and 39-5 and 6.

(Testimony of F. M. Goodwin.)

Q. Have you got a duplicate list in your hand there?

A. I have. I have preparrd a detailed list, but I have to have this to get the numbers.

Q. Is this in duplicate?

A. I haven't got the duplicate of it. The duplicate is in the office.

Q. Are there more than one carbon?

A. I don't know whether he prepared more than one.

Q. *Gie* the data contained in that book relative to timber and stone entries in the township, Mr. Goodwin. You know the townships yourself. What I want you to give, Mr. Goodwin, is the facts as shown by that record relative to the timber and stone entries in the townships you have referred to. (To reporter.) Read his answer of the townships.

(Same is read by reporter.)

Be it remembered that then and there the following proceeding was had:

Mr. RUICK.—Now we offer this.

Mr. FORNEY.—We object to it as incompetent, irrelevant and immaterial, in that it does not tend to prove or prove any allegations of the indictment, and that it does not connect the defendants or either of them with any of the transactions mentioned, nor with any of the overt acts mentioned in the indictment, and further that no proper foundation has been laid for the same.

(The question of incompetency does not go to the extent that the witness upon the stand is not the

(Testimony of F. M. Goodwin.)
custodian of the record from which he is testifying.)

The COURT.—What period does this cover Mr. Ruick? How far back does it go?

The WITNESS.—It goes back to November 12th, 1902.

Mr. RUICK.—Back to those entries that your Honor has already admitted proof on.

The WITNESS.—And it runs up to March 1905.

The COURT.—Well, the Court will permit you to go into it to that extent.

To which ruling of the Court the defendants then and there excepted, which exception was allowed by the Court. And the witness answered as follows:

Mr. RUICK.—I am confining you, Mr. Goodwin, to the particular entries which you have investigated, and which are contained in your list there. I do not call for everything that the book contains, but only what you have checked off as being in some way related to the defendants or some of them.

Mr. FORNEY.—We understand, if the Court please, that you conditionally admit this, with the understanding that it be connected later?

The COURT.—Yes.

Mr. RUICK.—That is correct. It was my remark.

The COURT.—The Court desires that counsel for the defendants call the Court's attention later if it is contended that it is not connected.

(Question read to the witness.)

A. November 21st, 1902. Cash entry, 4090, Carrie D. Marris, Lewiston, Idaho, for the south-

(Testimony of F. M. Goodwin.)

east quarter of the southwest *wuater* of Section 12, and the east half of the northwest quarter and the northeast quarter of the southwest quarter of section thirteen, Township 36 North, Range 5 East, 160 acres, $2.50 per acre, purchase money $400, and a memorandum on the margin T. & S. which stands for timber and stone application or entry.

Q. What does that November 21, indicate, the date of filing or the date of—

A. The date of the cash receipt. The date of the final proof, in other words.

Q. The date of the receiver's final receipt?

A. Yes, sir, that is the only date I am giving.

Q. Is the number also the number of the receiver's final receipt?    A. Yes, sir.

Q. The number which you give.

A. The number of the receiver's final receipt, and the date.

Q. And that applies to the number and dates on each one below?

A. Yes, sir; in every instance.

Q. November 21, 1902, cash entry 4054, William B. Benton, Lewiston, Idaho; south half *lf* northwest quarter and the north half of the southwest quarter Section 15, township 39 North, range 3 east, 160 acres, $2.50 per acre. Purchase price $400. Marginal note T. & S.

Mr. RUICK.—Of course that is an exact repetition in every instance; it ma.\ appear, Mr. Goodwin, we will ask that it may appear that except as otherwise *staed* by the *witless* the purchase price will be

(Testimony of F._M. Goodwin.)

$2.50 per acre and will in each instance, excepts as otherwise stated, be $400 in the aggregate.

Mr. TANNAHILL.—Did you identify that statement? the witness holds in his hand as a statement?

The WITNESS.—I have verified this statement.

Q. You had a statement in your hand there which you have compared with the original entries?

A. Yes, sir.

Q. In the book? A. Yes, sir.

Q. *Ad* you are therefore able to state, are you, under oath, that it is a true transcript?

A. Yes, sir.

Q. If the original entries is correct?

A. Yes, sir; I give you the names and number of the entry if you want to verify it.

Mr. FORNEY.—We make no objection to this statement other than our general objection.

Mr. RUICK.—I would like to have the name, the number and the date of the entry appear in the record for identification, but the other may go in the form of this list if there be no objection to it.

Mr. FORNEY.—Other than our general objection.

Mr. RUICK.—Other than your general objection to its competency and relevancy.

The COURT.—I think that will be the best way to put it in; the jury will get it better that way, and it will not be so wearisome.

Be it remembered that then and there the following proceeding was had:

If the Court please, it is understood that all of this of course will go under our general objection,

(Testimony of F. M. Goodwin.)

and we desire to supplement that by the further ground that the matters and things referred to by the witness are not embraced within the period set forth in the indictment, and are long prior to any dates set forth in said indictment, and are further barred by the statute of limitation, to supplement our original objection, and all the testimony of this witness goes in under our objection.

The COURT.—Yes, sir.

To which ruling of the Court the defendants then and there excepted, which exception was allowed.

And the witness answered as follows:

Entry 4055, November 21, 1902, Joel H. Benton.

Entry 4074, November 20, 1902, Henderson T. Dizney.

Entry 4192, January 23, 1903, Harry S. Parmer.

Entry 4199, January 28th, 1903; Mattie W. Benton.

Entry 1403, Jannary 28th, 1903, Henry Wohlers.

Entry 4213, February 11th, 1903, George W. Harrington.

Enty 4216, Edward L. Knight, February 12th, 1902.

Entry 4217, February 12th, 1903, Nettie Knight.

Entry 4218, February 12th, 1903, Nellie Harrington.

Entry 4219, Fcruary 12th, 1903, Minnie Harrington.

Entry 4249, March 11th, 1903, Robert N. Wright.

Entry 4251, March 11th, 1903, Maude V. Wright.

(Testimony of. F. M. Goodwin.)

Entry 4276, March 24th, 1903, Frederick E. Hogrelius.

Q. The entry of Maude F. Wright, the total consideration was slightly different, Mr. Goodwin, what was it? A. $400.70.

The COURT.—Is this important, gentlemen, that is the difference in the consderation?

Mr. RUICK.—Just simply to show there was not the 160 acres.

Mr. JOHNSON.—Only to signify whether or not it was a full claim.

The COURT.—Of course, if counsel thinks it is, you may go on.

A. Entry 4336, Pearl Washburn, April 16, 1903.

Q. Consideration?

A. Consideration, $300.00.

(Continuing:)

Entry 4350, May 19, 1903, Jerry Herrington, consideration $341.50.

Q. How about 4319? Is that cut out?

A. We cut that out.

Entry 4352, May 19th, 1903, Van W. Robertson.

Entry 4357, May 22d, 1903, John W. Killinger.

Entry 4359, May 22d, 1903, Johnnie Nelson.

Entry 4375, June 3d, 1903, James A. Storer, *entr*

Entry 4377, June 5*h*, 1903, Soren Hanson.

Entry 4383, June 15th, 1903, John H. Little, consideration $393.12.

Entry 4384, June 15, 1903, Ellsworth M. Harrington, consideration $385.97.

(Testimony of F. M. Goodwin.)

Entry 4389, June 17*tk,* 1903, Wren Pierce.

Entry 4390, June 17, 1903, Benjamin S. Bashor, consideration $360.47.

Entry 4391, June 17, 1903, James C. Evans.

Entry 4392, June 17th, 1903, Lon E. Bishop.

Entry 4393, June 17th, 1903, Jos. B. Clute.

Entry 4394, June 17, 1903, Frederick W. Newman.

Entry 4395, June 17, 1903, Frances M. Long.

Entry 4396, June 17, 1903, John H. Long, consideration $375.35.

Entry 4397, June 18, 1903, Benjamin F. Long.

Entry 4404, June 23d, 1903, Charles Dent.

Entry 4405, June 23, 1903, Charles Smith.

Entry 4411, June 26, 1903, Goerge Morrison.

Entry 4412, June 26th, 1903, Edward M. Hyde.

Entr 4414, June 26, 1903, Bertsell H. Ferris, consideration $370.25.

Entry 4415, June 26, 1903, George Ray Robinson.

Entry 4477, August 19, 1903, Drury M. Gammon.

Entry 4762, July 11th 1904, Charles W. Taylor, consideration $394.50.

Entry 4764, Jackson O'Keefe, July 11, 1904.

Entry 4765, July 11, 1904, Edgar J. Taylor, consideration $392.05.

Entry 4766, Joseph H. Pretnice, consideration $391.50, July 11th, 1904.

Entry 4767, July 12, 1904, Eugene H. Hopper.

Entry 4768, July 12, 1904, Edith A. Hopper.

Entry 4769, July 12, 1904, George H. Kester.

(Testimony of_F. M. Goodwin.)

Entry 4770, July 13, 1904, Guy L. Wilson, consideration $395.12.

Entry 4771, July 13th, 1904, Frances A. Justice, consideration $394.50.

Entry 4774, July 13, 1904, Fred E. Justice.

Entry 4773, July 13, 1904, Edna P. Kester.

Entry 4774, July 14, 1904, Elizabeth Kettenbach.

Entry 4775, July 14, 1904, William J. White.

Entry 4776, July 14, 1904, Elizabeth White.

Entry 4777, July 14, 1904, Mamie P. White.

Entry 4778, July 15, 1904, Walter E. Daggett.

Entry 4779, July 15, 1904, Martha E. Hallett.

Entry 4780, July 15, 1904, Daniel W. Greenburg.

Entry 4781, July 15, 1904, Davis S. Bingham.

Entry 4784, July 18, 1904, William McMillan.

Entry 4785, July 18, 1904, Hattie Rowland.

Entry 4799, July 25th, 1904, Edgar H. Dammarell.

Entry 4878, September 23, 1904, Benjamin F. Rowland.

Entry 4879, September 23, 1904, Albert G. Kester.

Entry 4919, October 21st, 1904, Melvern C. Scott.

Entry 4934, November 11, 1904, Lottie B. Stephens.

Entry 4943, November 18th, 1904, Charles Carey.

Entry 4950, November 23d, 1904, Edwin Bliss.

Entry 4984, December 14, 1904, George C. Davenport.

Q. How about the one just above that?

A. I don't think we want that one; I am not sure about that.

(Testimony of F. M. Goodwin.)

Q.  You cut it out, did you?     A.  Yes.

Entry 4984, December 14, George C. Davenport.

Entry 5015, January 20, 1905, William E. Helkenberg.

If you want that entry, I will put it in.

Q.  You might as well put it in under the rule, with the understanding that it will be cut out if not connected.

Entry 4970, December 1, 1905, Charles E. Knapp, consideration $203.30.

Entry, 5016, December 20, 1905, Edward M. Lewis. Consideration 392.37.

Entry 5042, March 6h, 1905, Mary E. Sherman.

Entry 4045, March 7, 1905, Margurite A. Miller.

Entry 5046, March 8th, 1905, Hiram F. Lewis.

Entry 4635, Jauary 6th, 1904, William Havernick.

Entry 4641, January 11th, 1904, Geary Van Artsdale.

Entry 5010, January 16, 1904, Mabel K. Atkinson.

Q.  That list, Mr. Goodwin, may be handed to the repprter?     A.  Yes.

List admitted in evidence and marked Plaintiff's Exhibit 57.

Cross-examination by Mr. TANNAHILL.

Q.  Mr. Goodwin, these entries comprise the same lands included in those final receipts and exhibits which were introduced yesterday, do they not?

A.  In part there arr some additional ones.

Q.  About how many additional ones?

A.  Well, I should judge maybe thirty.

Q.  About thirth additional ones?     A.  Yes.

(Testimony of F. M. Goodwin.)

Q. The others are simply repetitions of entries contained in those final receipts?

A. Final receipts, mortgages and deeds.

Q. Mortgages and deeds? A. Yes.

Q. You do not wish to be understood as saying these to be additional lists, in addition to those mortgages, deeds and final receipts? A. No.

Q. What was your business before you became connected with the land department, or the general land office? A. Attorney.

Q. How long have you been practicing?

A. Let's see; I think I was admitted twelve years ago.

Q. Where have you practiced?

A. Baltimore City, Maryland.

Q. What was your line of practice?

A. Commercial, exclusively.

Q. Commercial? And you had had considerable experience in real estate?

A. Well, I had some, yes.

Q. And that was a part of your line there, was it not? A. Yes, sir.

Q. Did you have any dealings in timber?

A. No.

Q. Taking up timber lands? A. No.

Q. That is not a timber country? A. No.

(Witness excused.)

J. M. MALLOY, a witness called and sworn on behalf of the prosecution, testified as follows on

Direct Examination by Mr. RUICK.

Q. Where do you reside, Mr. Malloy?

A. Lewiston, Idaho.

(Witness continuing):

I have resided there thirty years; I grew up there. I have known the defendants William Kettenbach and George H. Kes*tr* twenty years or more at Lewiston.

I have known the defendant William Dwyer for five or six years. I was chief clerk of the United States Land Office at Le*i*ston at one time. My employment began some time in February, 1901, and ended about December 2*5h,* 1905. During the time of my employment there in the land office, J. B. West was register and C. H. Garby receiver, during all the time I was there.

Q. As such clerk what were your duties generally in and about the office? What duties did you perform?

A. Taking proof, attending to correspondence, and many other things too numerous to mention.

Q. In that position as clerk did you become familiar with the business of the office and the records of the office?      A. I did.

Q. Have you, at the request of the United States Attorney pr*rp*ared a map in this case giving certain data which you were requested to give and place upon the map?      A. I have.

(Testimony of J. M. Malloy.)

Q. Kindly produce that map, Mr. Malloy.

(Big map produced by witness.)

Q. Have you had any experience in the United States Land Office, Mr. Malloy, in preparing plats for customers? A. I have.

Q. Making copies of plats and maps?

A. Yes, sir.

Be it remembered that then and there the following proceedig was had:

Q. Now fro what sources is the information contained on that map derived, speaking generally?

Mr. FORNEY.—If the Court please, we object to the testimony of this witness along this line on the ground that it is incompetent, irrelevant and immaterial—

Mr. RUICK.—We have not offered the map yet. It is for the purpose of laying the foundation to offer it.

Mr. FORNEYP (Continuing).—that it does not tend to connect the defendants or either of them with any of the overt acts set forth in the indictment or in the offenses charged therein, neither does it tend to prove any of the allegations contained therein, or any of the issues in this case.

The COURT.—The testimony may go in under the same objections and with the same limitations that has been prescribed with regard to the other testimony covering te same subject. I suppose it is for the purpose of illustrating the testimon.\ which has gone in under the same objection here

(Testimony of J. M. Malloy.)

Mr. RUICK.—As well as that which is to follow.

To which ruling of the Court the defendants then and there excepted, which exception was allowed by the Court, and the witness andswe*rd* as follows:

A.   From the land office records; do you wish it in detail?

Q.   Yes, I would like to have you go a little more in detail.

A.   The land marked in red—

Mr. FORNEY.—Wait a moment.   The map is not yet in.

Mr. RUICK.—No, that was not what I asked you; the information you stated we would show first is from the records in the records and papers in the land office at Lewiston.

Q.   *No* what other basis of information had you, that is what I am asking, one, two, three and four, if you had more than one source of information.

A.   From the land office records, as I stated, and from data given by Kester and Kettenbach to Don Cameron, Secretary of the Fire Association.

Q.   What do you mean, "Fire Association," for what purpose?

A.   Protecting, the association formed for the protection of timber owned by different companies in this section.

Q.   In what section?

A.   The Clearwater country, and from data obtained from Mr. Fralick, representing A. L. Fleweling, in Spokane.

Q.   Well, any other records?

(Testimony of J. M. Malloy.)

A.   I believe that covers it.

Q.   Well, how about the country records?

A.   Oh, yes, and from the county records of Nez Perce County.

Q.   And what other county?    A.   Latah.

Q.   And what other county?

A.   Shoshone County.

Q.   Three counties?    A.   Yes, sir.

Q.   Shoshone, Latah and Nez Perce?

A.   Yes, sir.

Q.   These certify these copies of deeds and mortgages that were introduced here yesterday and marked Plaintiff's Exhibits X, Y and Z, or rather Y and Z, they also appear in the information contained in those, also appear on the map?    A.   Yes.

Be it remembered that then and there the following proceeding was had:

Mr. RUICK.—We now offer this map in evidence.

Mr. FORNEY.—We object to it as last above and on the further ground that the witness has not shown himself competent. The map is not pr/perly identified to be admissable.

Mr. RUICK.—We do not offer this map, if your Honor please, as importing absolute verity as the result of actual surveys and actual exact data and official information. We introduce it for the purpose, as we have heretofore stated, as your Honor has observed, of illustrating the testimony of the witness —illustrating the testimony that has gone before, as well as that which is to follow, and the correctness

(Testimony of J. M. Malloy.)

of the map is a matter for demonstration as we go along. For that purpose we deem it competent.

The COURT.—I will permit the witness to go this far at the present time, Mr. Ruick, to state here what he intends to indicate by the different colorings there, and I think we will stop there for the present, until you call the other witnesses.

To which rulings of the Court the defendants then and there excepted, *hich* exception was by the Court allowed.

Mr. RUICK.—That is what we want.

Q. Mr. Malloy, where did you get, or how did you procure the information there from the land office that appears upon this map?

A. From the land office plat.

Q. You prepared this map where?

A. Prepared it in Lewiston, and partly prepared it in Lewiston, and finished it up here.

Q. The information that appears thereon as purporting to be based upon land office records and papers is it or is it not within your knowledge correct? A. It is correct.

Q. You are able to swear to *h*that?

A. I am *st*isfied, yes, sir.

Q. You had in your possession, did you not, blue prints of the several townships which appear upon this map? A. I did.

Be it remembered that then and there the following proceeding was had:

Mr. TANNAHILL.—We object to that as leading and suggestive.

(Testimony of J. M. Malloy.)

The COURT.—He objected to it as leading. He has answered, however; go on.

Q. And you also checked off the deeds and mortgages that were introduced in evidence on yesterday.

Mr. TANNAHILL.—I object to that as leading and suggestive.

The COURT.—Objection overruled.

To which ruling of the Court defendants excepted, which exception of the Court was allowed.

And the witness answered: A. I have.

Q. Now under the ruling of the Court, point out, in the first place point out the townships on the map, and explain the general idea of the map.

A. This is 38-1 East, and this territory is covered here from 38—

Q. Point out the townships in Range 38 North as they appear upon that map.

A. 38 North includes 38-1 East. Here is 1 East (indicating), this covers several 38-1 East and 38-2 East and 38-3 East and 38-5 East and 38-6 East.

Q. Now, Mr. Malloy, the lower tier of twonships then on the map is 38 North? A. 38 North.

Q. And what townships?

A. 1 to 6 East, inclusive.

Q. Now, then, the upper land there?

A. Townships 39 North, 1 to 6 inclusive, 1 to 6 East, inclusive.

Q. Now point out the different colored markings there and state what they are intended to indicate?

(Testimony of J. M. Malloy.)

A.   The red represents N. P. and Schofield Scrip, filed in October and November, 1900, on unsurveyed land.   The blue represents State locations.

Q.   That pale blue?      A.   All this blue here.

Q.   The pale blue?

A.   Yes, sir; the yellow represents Kester & Kettenbach scrip, the green with the names of the entrymen written in red represents Kester & Kettenbach land, to which they have deeds on record; the green with the entryman's name wrtitten in black represents lands, which they claim, or *whch* they turned a list over to the Fire Association for the protection of that timber.   The green with the entryman's name in black, also indicated by a circle, also indicated land on which Kester and Kettenbach and Robnett have given options on that land.   I believe that covers all.   This east of 38-3 East in black represents unsurveyed land, or land which cannot be taken at the present time.

Q.   That is the light black lines running across it?

A.   That in here (indicating).

Q.   With the shading on it?

A.   Yes, sir; this land here in the southwest corner of 38-1 East.

The COURT.—How colored?

A.   Blue with diagonal stripes.

Q.   With diagonal stripes?

A.   Yes, sir; that represents lands in Nez Perce County, belonging to the State of which Kester and Kettenbach claim a large portion of it by purchase.

Q.   What are the white, the square white places up in the red shading?      A.   Up in here?

(Testimony of J. M. Malloy.)

Q. Yes, what do some of them represent?

A. These red marks across the section, the whole section represents school sections wherever they occur; the other white places there represent other vacant lands, or lands taken by individuals which have no connection that I know of with these cases.

Q. Then section 16 and 36, being school sections, appear there as diagonally bounded by red lines with diagonal lines across them? A. Yes, sir.

Q. What stream appears there?

A. The North Fork of the Clearwater River.

Q. And w*h*ch part of the map is north, whi*c*h is intended to represent no*t*th, the top of the map?

A. Yes, sir; the top of the map.

Q. Now point out on that map the timber and stone entry of John H. Little? A. Right there.

Q. Frances M. Long?

A. There (indicating).

*Q.* (And witness indicates all the land of all of the following named persons.)

Q. B. F. Long? A. There.

*A.* John H. Long? A. There.

Q. Now Wren Pierce? A. There.

Q. Havernick? A. Don't show that.

Q. Charles Dent? A. Right there.

Q. Charles Smith? Λ. Right there.

Q. Joseph B. Clute? A. Right there.

Q. Lon E. Bishop? Λ. Right there.

Q. Now this—well I will read a little further—James C. Evans? Λ. Right there.

Q. Those are all in what township?

(Testimony of J. M. Malloy.)

A.   39-3 East.

Q.   39-3 East.   Which side of the North Fork of the Clearwater?        A.   West.

Q.   Now point out Frederick Newman?

A.   Right there.

Q.   Daniel Hyde?        A.   Right there.

Q.   George Morrison?        A.   Right there.

Q.   And Iver Hansett?

A.   I think that is not included within this territory.

Q.   Not included within that territory?   Is McFarland, Samuel L. McFarland, included?

A.   No.

Q.   That is in other townships which do not appear on this map?        A.   Yes, sir.

Q.   Does D. M. Gammon appear on this map?

A.   No.

Q.   Edward and Nettie Knight?

A.   That is about twenty or thirty miles southward of that territory.

Q.   That will be several townships below?

A.   Yes, sir.

Q.   The same is true of the Harringtons?

A.   Yes, sir.

Q.   Have you got Robert O. Waldman on there?

A.   Right here.

Q.   Gordon, Henry F. Gordon?

A.   Right here.

Q.   Joel H. Benton?        A.   Right there.

Q.   William B. Benton?        A.   There.

(Testimony of J. M. Malloy.)

Q. Now point out the claim, point out H. F. Lewis' claim.　　A. Right there.

Q. E. M. Lewis claim?

A. (Witness points for answer.)

Q. Francis A. Justice?

A. There is F. E. Justice.

Mr. JOHNSON.—Section 19?

A. Wh*z* township?

Mr. JOHNSON.—Township 38, Section 19—16.

A. That is right there.

Q. Let the jury see where it is located, and then where is Fred Justice?　　A. Right there.

Q. Fred E.

The COURT.—I wish you would have him point out the particular tracts of land described in the indictment for the Court's information, if the jury has already seen te*h*m.

Q. You pointed out Edward M. Lewis. Point it out to the Court?　　A. Right there.

Q. Hiram F. Lewis?　　A. Right there.

Q. And Charles Carey?　　A. Right there.

Q. You have shown Guy L. Wilson?

A. Right there.

Q. And you have shown Mrs. Francis A. Justice?

A. There.

Q. Now point out Jackson O'Keefe. Stand on this side so as not to be in the way of the jury.

A. Right here.

Q. Now Charles W. Taylor?

A. Right there.

Q. And E. J. Taylor?

(Testimony of J. M. Malloy.)

A.   There.   All in 35, I think, Section 18, Edgar J.   Is in Section 18.

Q.   38-5?      A.   38-5.

Q.   It is marked here section 18?

A.   I don't see it.

Q.   Perhaps you haven't it marked on the map?

A.   Here it is, 39-5.

Q.   Did I say 38-5?

A.   Yes, here it is right here.

The COURT.—No, that is 38-5.

A.   36-6 I should say.

Q.   It is 38-6 that is right.   We have it at last. You found Edgar J. Taylor, did you?

A.   Yes, sir.

Q.   Did you find Prentiss, too, in the same township exactly; it is the east half of the northwest quarter of section 18?      A.   Right there.

Q.   Edgar H. Dammarel?      A.   There.

Q.   Where is George H. Kester?

A.   Right there.

Q.   Where was the Hoppers connected?

A.   Those two in White.

Q.   You pointed out Guy L. Wilson?

A.   Yes, sir.

Q.   Now Edna Kester?      A.   Right there.

Q.   And you pointed out, point out again, as we go along, Fred Justice and Mrs. Justice?

A.   F. E. Justice right there, and F. A. Justice right there.

Q.   Elizabeth Kettenbach?      A.   Right there.

Q.   And Elizabeth White?      A.   Right there.

(Testimony of J. M. Malloy.)

Q. And William J. White?

A. Right there.

Q. And Mamie P. White?     A. Rigt there.

Q. And Martha E. Hallett, Lots 1 and 2 and the Northwest quarter of 19-38-6?     A. Right there.

Q. Where is that, I didn't notice?

A. Right here.

Q. Where is David, or Daniel W. Greenburg?

A. Right here.

Q. And Bingham—David?     A. Right there.

Q. And Hattie Rowland? *Rowlan* is in 15-38-5, Section 15.     A. Right there.

Q. And McFarland? Thirty-nine-5- section 21?

A. Right there.

Q. That is all on that line. Now Mr. Malloy, are you acquainted with the relationship of some of these parties to the defendants, some of them?

A. Yes, sir; some of them.

Q. What relation is Edna Kester, if any, to George Kester, the defendant, if any?

A. Wife.

Q. What relation is Elizabeth Kettenbach to either of the defendants?

A. I believe she is an aunt of W. F. Kettenbach.

Q. What relation is Elizabeth White?

Mr. FORNEY.—The Court understands that this all goes in under our general objection.

The COURT.—Yes.

Q. Elizabeth White and W. J. White and Mamie P. White?

(Testimony of J. M. Malloy.)

A. W. J. White is a brother in law of Mr. Kettenbach, the defendant; Mamie P. White, I don't know the given names of some of the ladies, I could not say which one it is.

Q. Was Mrs. W. F. Kettenbach a White before marriage?

A. Yes, sir; she was White, Mary White.

Q. What position, if any, do you remember Mrs. Hallett holding at the time of this line-up, in whose employ was she?    A. Mr. Kester's.

Q. George H. Kester?    A. Yes, sir.

Q. Do you recall the circumstances of this line-up, Mr. Malloy?    A. I do.

Q. Do you recollect the circumstances?

A. Yes, sir.

Q. Now just describe the conduct of that line-up, will you, Mr. Malloy, how they arranged it and numbered it? Just relate what you know about it?

A. When they appeared at the land office about I should judge ten days before the land was to be opened up, they numbered each one; each one had a number from one up according to how many in the line, according to the number in the line.

The COURT.—Was the one nearest the land office door No. 1?    A. Yes, sir.

Q. And when did they begin? I am referring now to the line-up of April 25, when there were so many timber and stone claims filed in these townships? That is what I refer to?    A. Yes, sir.

Q. What has been testified to as the date on which the townships were open to entry?    A. Yes, sir.

(Testimony of J. M. Malloy.)

Q.  Who do you recall was the first one in the line?    A.  I cannot say now.

Q.  You cannot state that from memory?

A.  No.

Q.  How long before this did they commence lining up there?

A.  About ten days I should judge.

Q.  After they got their numbers were they permitted to go away, or did they have to  hold  their places in line?

A.  They seemed to be permitted to go away, but there were a few who stayed there as a crowd, you know.

Q.  And they were lined up in the hall of the building?

A.  Yes, sir; in front of the land office door.

Q.  Did you have anything to do with the receiving of these applications, the sworn statements, Mr. Malloy?

A.  I marked the lands off on the plat, as they were received by the register and receiver; they were turned over to us clerks to mark them off.

Q.  State whether or not there were any conflicts in the applications of these different  parties  here whom I will now name as they presented to the land office.  Do you know whether there was or not, are you able to testify?

A.  There were no conflicts except possibly there might have been one or so in the line-up.

Q.  Between those parties in that line-up,  these parties named, you say, there was no conflict in that line-up in their entries?

(Testimony of J. M. Malloy.)

A.   No, with one possible exception.

Q.   With one possible exception? And which exception was that?

A.   I *ca* not say; I don't say there *wa* an exception, but it occurs to me now there may have been.

Q.   Not more than one?

A.   Not more than one.

Q.   Have the defendants George H. Kester and W. F. Kettenbach exercised their timber and stone right prior to this line-up?      A.   No.

Q.   Did they exercise it lately?

A.   They exercised it later, as lands were opened up for settlement.

Q.   How is that?

A.   Either at that time or later, I don't remember the date they exercised their right.

Q.   Do you know anything of your own knowledge, Mr. Malloy as to where these sworn statements were prepared? which were brought into the land office? Did you observe anything with reference to their being made up?

Mr. MOORE.—Do you mean the whole line?

Q.   The members of this line-up, all of them—well members of it, we will find out how many of them?

A.   Some of them.